MAN IN ADAPTATION

The Institutional Framework

MAN IN ADAPTATION

The Institutional Framework

EDITED BY Yehudi A. Cohen LIVINGSTON COLLEGE, RUTGERS UNIVERSITY

 ALDINE PUBLISHING COMPANY/Chicago

Copyright © 1971 by Yehudi A. Cohen

All rights reserved. No part of this publication may be
reproduced or transmitted in any form or by any means,
electronic or mechanical, including photocopy, recording,
or any information storage and retrieval system, without
permission in writing from the publisher.

Aldine Publishing Company
529 South Wabash Avenue
Chicago, Illinois 60605

Library of Congress Catalog Card Number 71-141425
ISBN 202-0195-3, cloth; 202-01096-1, paper

Printed in the United States of America

Second Printing 1973

To Lisa
who loves books and diversity
though not always of the anthropological kind

PREFACE

THIS BOOK is intended to serve as an introduction to the institutional, psychological, and ideological dimensions of the strategies of adaptation that have characterized human societies from the earliest known forms of social life to the present. In two earlier books, *Man in Adaptation: The Biosocial Background* and *Man in Adaptation: The Cultural Present*, I brought together similar collections of readings that sought to provide coherence for the study of man's physical and cultural evolution. One purpose of these volumes was to show that the study of adaptation can provide a consistent point of view for organizing and understanding man's search for increasingly viable relationships with his milieus and the implications of this search for his relationships with his fellows.

I have undertaken this third volume because the organization that was necessary for the second volume had two unavoidable results. First, several topics that are of principal anthropological concern—notably marriage, law and social control, religion and magic, value systems, personality, and art—were slighted. Second, I slighted what I consider an important methodological point: The study of cultural adaptation and evolution must focus on specific institutional spheres of activity as well as on total cultures, just as the study of physical adaptation and evolution must focus on specific organs and systems as well as on total organisms. This book is an attempt to correct these lacunae.

Although a man cannot be his own critic, nor should he try, there is a moment, just before the onset of the postpartum depression that comes with a book's completion, when one has to ask himself whether he is satisfied with his own work. I am uncertain whether I have reached my present objectives. To the best of my knowledge, this project constitutes the first attempt to discuss the variety of special topics central to conventional anthropological work in a systematic and consistently evolutionary framework. This has had both desirable and undesirable consequences. On the one hand, it has left me free of the traditions that come in the wake of others' work and that are inevitably restraining influences, so that I could proceed as I wished. On the other hand, since there is little or no literature of this kind on which to rely, I am without a basis for comparison and consequently I must leave judgment of this work to others.

But whether or not I have succeeded in my own attempt, I believe that the future of productive anthropology (and of social science generally) rests on the concepts of cultural evolution and of adaptive strategies. The fully effective application of this framework must await a great deal more research, theorizing, and argument. If these books on man in adaptation will guide students to this point of view, I will have achieved my present objective.

In organizing this third volume, I have been guided by a single question: How do the specific activities and institutions in which people are involved—family systems, religion, art, and the like—fit into the overall adaptive strategy of their society and what are the particular pressures leading to change in each of these spheres when the group's strategy of adaptation changes? More specifically: What are the human demands made by a hunting-gathering (or horticultural or peasant or industrial) strategy that lead to the development of particular family systems, modes of social control, religious beliefs and practices, values and ideologies, and personality structures, and what are the new human demands that lead to the reorganization of these aspects of life as the group moves from one level of development to another?

Against this background, two goals were uppermost. First, wherever possible I have made selections from which the reader can infer what it takes for an individual to be a hunter-gatherer, a horticulturist, a pastoralist, an agriculturist, or a person in an industrial society. Individuals in all societies learn the strategies that enable them to manipulate cultural means to personal ends, whether or not these ends are in conformity with the group's norms. Unfortunately, little anthropological effort has been devoted to the problem of individual choice and manipulation within a system and these actions can only and at best be inferred from the alternatives provided by the culture. Some of the selections are explicit; for others, I have tried to make the necessary inferences in my introductory essays.

Second, I have selected materials that I hope will increase our understanding of our own ways of life and of the changes that seem to be taking place in our own institutions and ideologies. Each section of this book begins with a discussion of hunter-gatherers in a particular sphere of activity—either in my introductory essay or in an ethnographic account—and concludes with one or two selections that deal with the same sphere of activity in a contemporary industrial society. Thus I have tried not only to illustrate the evolution of particular social institutions as accompaniments of successive levels of development but also to offer a framework for possible extrapolations that are applicable to current developments in modern societies. We have come from somewhere in history; we are now at a particular point in the evolutionary development of our species; and we are headed somewhere else. It is one aspect of anthropology's uniqueness that it can investigate the development of humanity with a consistent set of assumptions and conceptual tools. With these tools, anthropology now must not only join the 20th century—a development that has already begun— but it must also face the prospect of a 21st.

For these reasons, with a few exceptions I have included only case studies of particular societies; these are the most sharply focused products of anthropological field research. Just as the organization of the first two volumes of *Man in Adaptation* obliged me to omit from them many of the materials that are included here, so the goals that I have set for myself here have led me to exclude many good comparative studies. I have also excluded several excellent theoretical papers for this reason, but I have referred to and summarized the most important in my introductory essays.

While I have tried to follow a more or less evolutionary sequence in each section, beginning with hunter-gatherers and concluding with contemporary industrial society, I have not been unyielding in using this framework, for several reasons. First, there are not equally suitable descriptions of each sphere of activity for societies at all stages of development. Second and more substantively, there is an increasing amount of diversity at each successive stage of sociotechnological development, and once one gets beyond the advanced stages of horticulture (and possibly even earlier), the amount of intersocietal variability becomes staggering. Thus, for example, a volume of this length could be entirely devoted to studies of agricultural families alone, to say nothing of industrial families, and the same is true of every other sphere of activity. As a result, the reader may find that one or another level of social and technological development has been slighted in each part because sometimes the inclusion of material from only one or two societies might suggest an erroneous picture.

There are no studies that deal with culture change as such in this book. Instead, where possible, I have included articles that deal with changes in particular spheres of activity, such as family organization, law, religion, and value systems. Change is not a special situation. Instead, culture *is* change and change *is* culture, and it is unrealistic to study change outside the specific social and technological organization of a given society.

Although this book is in a sense a supplement to the first two volumes of *Man in Adaptation*, it can be used independently as well as in conjunction with either or both of the preceding volumes. References to selections that appear in the first two books are treated in the same way as references to articles and excerpts from other books. Hence, people using this volume together with either of the first two will sometimes find a measure of repetition, but I have tried to keep this to a minimum.

■ The Editorial introductions appear in sans serif type (as here) and are set off from the text of the selections themselves by squares like those preceding and ending this paragraph. To assist the reader who wishes to explore more thoroughly the topics that are covered in this book, I have included suggestions for further reading at the end of each introduction to each section and selection. Whenever possible, I have included books published in inexpensive paperbound editions. ■

Also, as in the first two volumes of *Man in Adaptation*, I am following the customary usage of other collections of introductory readings in anthropology by omitting all reference footnotes and bibliographies; the reader who wishes to consult the sources used by the authors of these selections can refer to the original publications. These omissions also reflect certain economic realities with which I have been confronted by my publisher, and have helped to keep the price of the book within the reach of many readers. With few exceptions, the selections are otherwise reprinted without abridgement; where there are omissions, they have been marked with ellipses in the usual way.

Once again, as in all my work, whether at my desk or in the field, I must note my obligation for the milieu created and sustained by my wife, Rhoda Cohen, which has made this book possible. Our daughter, Lisa Cohen, contributed immeasurably to this atmosphere by her patience and tolerance as she graciously allowed her rights and privileges to take second place to the demands of my work. I also wish to thank my wife for her help in handling some of the administrative details that were involved in the preparation of the book and for helping me choose among alternative selections.

Harumi Befu was among the first to encourage me to deal with many of the problems that are taken up in this volume and that were neglected in *The Cultural Present*; his suggestions and encouragement were exceptionally helpful. I also want to note my appreciation to Roy G. D'Andrade, William P. Mangin, and Jay Ruby for bringing to my attention several items which would otherwise have escaped my attention. Richard B. Lee saved me from some embarrassing errors in his usually kind way.

I must finally note my gratitude to the anonymous readers of Aldine Publishing Company for their criticism and helpful suggestions, and to Aldine's Publisher, Alexander J. Morin, for his patience, encouragement, and help; in his inimitable way, he is as much responsible for this book as I am.

CONTENTS

xi

MAN IN ADAPTATION

The Institutional Framework

THE NAKED APE

JOHN UPDIKE

(Following, Perhaps All Too Closely, Desmond Morris's
Anthropological Revelations)

The dinosaur died, and small
  Insectivores (how gruesome!) crawled
From bush to tree, from bug to bud,
  From spider-diet to forest fruit and nut,
Developing bioptic vision and
  The grasping hand.

These perfect monkeys then were faced
  With shrinking groves; the challenged race,
De-Edenized by glacial whim,
  Sent forth from its arboreal cradle him
Who engineered himself to run
  With deer and lion—

The "naked ape." Why naked? Well,
  Upon those meaty plains, that *veldt*
Of prey, as pellmell they competed
  With cheetahs, hairy primates overheated;
Selection pressure, just though cruel,
  Favored the cool.

Unlikeliest of hunters, nude
  And weak and tardy to mature,
This ill-cast carnivore attacked,
  With weapons he invented, *in a pack*.
The tribe was born. To set men free,
  The family

Evolved; monogamy occurred.
  The female—sexually alert
Throughout the month, equipped to have
  Pronounced orgasms—perpetrated love.
The married state decreed its *lex*
  Privata: sex.

And Nature, pandering, bestowed
  On virgin ears erotic lobes
And hung on women hemispheres
  That imitate their once-attractive rears:
A social animal disarms
  With frontal charms.

All too erogenous, the ape
  To give his lusts a decent shape
Conceived the cocktail party where
  Unmates refuse to touch each other's hair
And make small "grooming" talk instead
  Of going to bed.

He drowns his body scents in baths
  And if, in some conflux of paths,
He bumps another, says, "Excuse
  Me, *please*." He suffers rashes and subdues
Aggressiveness by making fists
  And laundry lists,

Suspension bridges, aeroplanes,
  And charts that show biweekly gains
And losses. Noble animal!
  To try to lead on this terrestrial ball,
With grasping hand and saucy wife,
    The upright life.

ADAPTATION AND EVOLUTION: AN INTRODUCTION

A FRIEND OF MINE, an entomologist, often comes to tell me about his most recent findings in his studies of termite and other insect colonies; he spares me the details, and instead phrases his data in terms of their evolutionary implications. Invariably he concludes his exposition with the question, "Can *you* do anything with this?" By this he means, do his laboratory findings have significance for the study of human culture? One evening I said, "Why don't you get away from your bugs and study people? Maybe then you'd be able to answer your own question." "They're too damned complicated," he answered, "I wouldn't know *how* to go about studying them."

Many people, confronting the remarkable variety exhibited in human behavior, quickly conclude that it is a staggering hodge-podge from which it is not possible to make sense or infer order or regularity. Like my friend, they are overwhelmed by an apparent infinity of curious and unrelated customs which suggest little more than that some people do things in one way and others in another.

The purpose of this book is to present an overview of man and his works from the earliest known human societies to the present, based on the concept of the adaptive evolution of man's social institutions. Adaptation and evolution—or, more concretely, the evolution of man's adaptations, as embodied in his culture—are themes that, in combination with the concept of institutions, lend coherence and continuity to human historical development and to the styles of human life at every stage of this development. Without denying that man is complicated, these unifying concepts enable us to compare different cultures, from the earliest known tribal groups to the huge metropolitan areas of modern industrial nations; they provide a framework that makes it possible to bridge the seemingly disparate interests of anthropologists as well as the apparently unconnected activities and goals of people in different societies.

I do not contend that these are the only unifying themes in anthropology or that the interpretations that I will offer are either original with me or shared by all

1

anthropologists, but only that they provide one way of making sense out of the major sociocultural events in man's history. I include in this history the changes that now seem to be taking place in our own institutions and ideologies, and I occasionally crawl out on a limb—some may say that I teeter recklessly on a crag over a bottomless pit—in an attempt to learn whether these unifying concepts can tell us anything about the significance and direction of these changes.

Culture is man's most important instrument of adaptation.[1] A culture is made up of the energy systems, the objective and specific artifacts, the organization of social relations, the modes of thought, the ideologies, and the total range of customary behavior in a social group that enable it to maintain life in a particular habitat. It is man's culture that has enabled him to free himself from the restrictions imposed by his genetic constitution and his natural milieus.

Everything that man does takes place in a context of institutions. By institution I mean here an organization of social relations—a stable grouping of persons whose activities are designed to meet specific challenges or problems, whose behavior is governed by implicit or explicit rules and expectations of each other, and who regularly use special paraphernalia and symbols in these activities. Social institutions are among the principal foci of modern anthropology because they are the frames within which man spends every living moment. From his birth to his death, man does nothing outside the institutions of his society.

This Introduction is divided into two major parts. The first deals with the concept of adaptation; the second considers the concept of evolution as it applies to the adaptation of human society and its institutions.

THE CONCEPT OF ADAPTATION

Adaptation in man is the process by which he makes effective use for productive ends of the energy potential in his habitat. The most elementary source of energy, at least as far as man is concerned, is muscular. Reliance on this source—in the use of bows, spears, bludgeons, hoes and digging sticks—is basic to the food quest in many human societies and has immediate consequences for the organization of social relations. We may contrast muscular energy with such sources of extrapersonal energy as draft animals (used for drawing plows), water (for irrigation or transportation), chemicals, steam, and electricity. Whenever people introduce a new energy system into their habitat their organizations of social relations—that is, their institutions—also change, so that the latter will be appropriate to the exploitation and efficient use of the energy source on which they rely.

An important factor in the organization of social relations of different societies is the extent to which extrapersonal energy replaces muscular energy. Thus far in cultural evolution, this replacement has not been complete. The use of a plow requires muscular energy, though less than a hoe or digging stick. Similarly, the control of production by electronic means in contemporary industrial society has not eliminated all muscular energy. Thus, a culture includes both the technology and the institutions appropriate to that technology.

---

1. Parts of this Introduction parallel, and to some degree repeat, the Introduction to *Man in Adaptation: The Cultural Present*; I also draw on several editorial and interpretative essays in that volume. Nevertheless, I suggest that the reader of both volumes also read both Introductions because they differ in emphasis, and sometimes in content.

Every culture is a special case of the adaptive process, of the complex ways in which people make effective use of their energy potentials. Thus a culture must first be defined in terms of specific sources of energy and their social correlates. Every culture can be conceptualized as a strategy of adaptation, and each represents a unique social design for extracting energy from the habitat. Every energy system requires appropriate organizations of social relations; no energy system can be effective in human society without groups that are designed for using it. A very simple example will illustrate the point.

Factory work, in which exclusive reliance is placed on, say, electrical energy, and which is devoted to the manufacture of a product that is to be sold for a profit, requires a very special type of personnel. The people recruited for the factory's tasks should be evaluated in terms of their abilities to do their respective jobs, not in terms of their relationship by blood or marriage to each other or to the factory manager. The labor force of the factory should, ideally, be composed only of the number of people necessary to produce the product, maintain the plant, acquire raw materials, and ship and sell the finished product. Such an organization could not function effectively or for very long if the people in it were recruited only because they were relatives of the owner—but that, in fact, is precisely the basis of work organization in most pre-industrial societies.

The concept of adaptation—the key mechanism in the evolutionary process—was originally developed in the study of biological evolution. In discussions of the relationship of organisms to their habitats, the term "adaptation" refers to success, measured by the ability of populations to survive and reproduce. Thus a population of organisms is considered to have achieved an effective relationship with a habitat—to be adapted to that habitat—if it has been able to perpetuate its form of life. Evolution occurs because no adaptation is permanent, because no habitat remains unchanged. New adaptations must be developed if effective relationships with altered habitational conditions are to be maintained.

Similarly, adaptation in man refers to fitness for reproduction and survival. However, adaptation in man does not take place significantly through genetic change but, rather, through his ability to make use of energy potentials in his physical habitat. In the record of successive strategies of cultural evolution each level of adaptation denotes a quantitative increase in the ability to sustain and perpetuate life. At each successive stage of cultural evolution man is better adapted for the survival of his group—that is, the survival of his adaptive unit—and, in turn, of the species as a whole.

The record of human evolution also suggests that man's cultural adaptations have increasingly freed him from the limitations of his habitats. He has accomplished this by harnessing more effective sources of energy and by shaping his institutions to meet the demands of each energy system so that he can make maximal use of it. Hence we are going to speak of levels of technological development, each successive level representing a strategy of cultural adaptation in which there are more efficient means of exploiting the energy resources available to a group. The concept of levels of technological development and adaptation refers not only to techniques but also to the configurations of institutions and social relations that are appropriate to the effective use of each particular energy system.

When we study adaptation in anthropology we are concerned with populations, not with individual organisms or persons. More specifically, we study institutions as instruments of adaptation because without institutions there can be no human adaptation, and the study of man's cultural evolution is inseparable from the study of the evolution of his institutions. The study of individual adaptation involves very different concepts.

A population's adaptation is its *relationship* to its habitat. The concept of adaptation is historical: when we say that a population is adapting we mean that it is altering its relationship to its habitat in order to make that habitat a more fit place in which to live, or to make itself more fit to live in that habitat. To take an analogy from biology, the growth of a coat of fur by a population of mammals in a cold climate is adaptive because it alters the animals' relationship to the habitat. Similarly, the historical process in which the Eskimos' unique clothing developed, enabling each man to live in a private quasi-tropical climate, is adaptive because it altered the group's relationship to the habitat. A change that does not affect the population's relationship to its milieu, such as embroidery on a parka or a moccasin, is not an adaptation. (Some anthropologists maintain that embroidery is adaptive because it provides visual variety and thus alters the milieu, but I think this is an overextension of the concept because it loses sight of the fact that such decorative activity does not facilitate the reproductive and survival capacity of the group, which is the essence of adaptation. If, on the other hand, such embroidery were used as insignia to distinguish specialized groups in the organization of labor or some other phase of social relations, it might then be an important aspect of the adaptive process. In the last section of this book we will consider the possible roles played by art, music, and literature in human adaptation.

The adaptation achieved by a population of mammals (for example, the growth of coats of fur) is the result of genetic change. In man, on the other hand, adaptation is achieved by means of culture and its institutions. The point of view taken in this book is that human adaptation is the result of the energy systems that are harnessed by a group and the organizations of social relations in the group that make it possible to use its energy systems effectively. Among nonhumans, adaptations are achieved by the breeding populations; we focus on this group in the study of biological adaptation because it is the vehicle for the gene pool, and we analyze the gene pool because it is the mechanism of biological evolution. Among humans, cultural adaptations are achieved by the social group and its institutions; this group carries the culture, and it is culture that is the mechanism of evolutionary change in man.

Thus, when we say that a human group is adapted to its habitat, we mean that it has achieved and maintains a viable relationship with its habitat. This adaptation assures the group's survival, reproduction, and efficient functioning, in the sense of doing-its-job-in-nature. The achievement of this type of viable relationship always results from reciprocal modifications in the culture and in the habitat through changes in the group's energy systems and its organization of social relations over a long period of time; it is never achieved in one generation. The historical aspect of the process of adaptation is what we call cultural evolution, by which we mean the process of sequential change that we see in culture. The fact of evolution demonstrates that adaptation has taken place; if adaptation had not characterized man, cultural evolution could not have occurred.

But the study of adaptation and evolution does not refer exclusively to static social systems, those that have achieved and maintain viable relationships with their habitats. It also includes study of periods of transition; these are no less important—

and, indeed, are much more common in evolutionary history—than periods of relative stability. This is especially significant today, when most societies in the world seem to be in rapid and radical change; these changes are accompanied by strains and conflicts among groups within the societies. Hence, wherever possible, I have included in this book case studies that illustrate transitional stages in social evolution as well as descriptions of more or less integrated and stable systems. I will return to this question in the concluding part of this Introduction.

As noted, when we speak of adaptation in anthropology we are concerned (as in other aspects of anthropological inquiry) with social groups, not with individual persons. These groups (organizations or institutions) are not directly observable; they are abstractions from the observed behavior of individuals. More specifically—and to place this in realistic perspective—we speak about the institutions of a society, but we study individuals. There are two principal reasons for this, and they are closely related to each other. The first is a practical consideration; the second is theoretical.

On the practical side, it is difficult if not impossible to study *all* the members of a tribe or community, to say nothing of a nation, in order to learn about their economic activities, kinship relations and family behavior, religious beliefs and practices, legal involvements, political activities, and the like. Hence the investigator chooses a sample he considers representative of the entire group; then, after studying it, he tries to present a picture of the group as a whole with respect to the problem he is trying to understand and the way of life he is trying to portray. Sometimes an anthropologist, although living with a group for a considerable period of time, may not have an opportunity to observe a birth, a marriage, or a funeral, and in such cases he has to rely on the verbal accounts of a few individuals ("informants," as they are usually called). So anthropologists have to adapt to the realities of the world in which they work, abstracting or generalizing from a relatively small number of informants to understand the entire group about which they speak.

The theoretical reason is also tied closely to practical expediency. Adaptation is a process, a relationship between an item of behavior and its source; it is also an abstract principle that refers to the sweep of institutions that are changing in a particular direction. No single institution—not even a single society—can give direct evidence of the evolution of man's cultural adaptations. The family organizations of nomadic bands cannot tell us about the pressures and potentials in the habitats of the hunter-gatherers who produced those systems; the development of specialized legal personnel (such as lawyers and mediators) cannot tell us about the increasing impersonality and complexity of nation-states that underlie the changes in their institutions for the maintenance of order and conformity. The organization of ancient Sumer, or of peasant communities in Latin America, cannot tell us directly about the evolution of community structure, even though each is a special case of sociocultural evolution.

In studying a particular group, the anthropologist seeks to abstract from the information gathered from representatives of that group and to portray a system, a set of principles that help explain the phenomena he has found: the relationships among factors that led to the emergence and perpetuation of a particular type of community or national organization, a pattern of kinship relationships and family organization, a system of social stratification, a legal organization, or a political structure.

The adaptations that man has achieved are perhaps the most advanced of all forms of life because in culture he has a specialized tool of adaptation that is unparalleled in other forms. Man's culture is an adjunct to the human architecture, superimposed on his genetically determined organ systems. Thus culture has made man's instruments of adaptation—his energy systems and their appropriate institutions—even more specialized than his physiological tools. Viewed in this context, man's culture is a revolutionary addition to his architecture and his most powerful instrument for adaptation. Man is now able to adapt himself—through his cultures—to different habitats long before genetic mutations can do this for him; he does not have to await genetic modification in his constitution.

THE CONCEPT OF EVOLUTION

The concept of evolution is also an abstraction; it is inferred from observations made under a variety of conditions and is used to explain relationships among observed phenomena. No one has ever observed cultural evolution directly, any more than culture itself, mutation, biological inheritance, democracy, or a patrilineal kinship system have been observed directly. All of these concepts are intellectual constructs and are intended to explain the relationships that are assumed to exist among a series of phenomena. When we speak of cultural evolution we refer to its manifestations, just as we do when we speak of physical gravity.

The concept of evolution is a theoretical framework, a convenient tool with which we try to understand how man arrived at advanced agricultural and industrial stages of cultural development from a past that began with nomadic hunting and food-gathering. It may seem gratuitous but it is nevertheless essential to point out that the first men did not plow, sail across oceans, live in metropolises, or plan the colonization of other planets and the ocean floors. Many millennia were required to achieve the mastery over the habitat that is represented by these achievements; and each achievement was accompanied by significant changes in the ways in which people organized their social life—familial, legal and political, religious, ideological, and esthetic.

The selections in this book are organized to illustrate several dimensions of social and cultural evolution. These dimensions are reflected in particular institutions which change as accompaniments of successive kinds of mastery over man's habitat. This evolutionary perspective enables us to read order into what might otherwise be a hopeless jumble of unique cultures. Among the major dimensions that are observable in the evolution of human institutions are differentiation and increasing complexity; these will be discussed below.

At the heart of an evolutionary perspective is the notion of stages or levels of development. It will be recalled that I defined culture as the artifacts, institutions, ideologies, and total range of customary behaviors with which a society is equipped for the exploitation of the energy potentials of its particular habitat. To read order into the variety of these cultural manifestations, it is first necessary to arrange them in a taxonomy of levels. But such a classification denotes more than strategies of mastery over the habitat. Every culture is also a unique environment.

I am using the terms "habitat" and "environment" differently. An environment is made up of several parts, and it is necessary to distinguish among them. By environment I mean the total system of components that interact with each other and that characterize a group or population. (I am using "environment" in much the same way that many people use "ecosystem" but I prefer the former term because it is more inclusive.) The physical or natural habitat is only one component of an environment, although it is of primary importance. In the study of biological adaptation, the species that occupies a habitat must be regarded as a distinct component of the environment because it alters the habitat by the use that it makes of it; each species places its unique stamp on the habitat that it seeks to exploit by affecting the "balance of nature" in it. The same considerations apply to man, but in a still more complex way, since human organizations of social relations—especially political institutions—constitute still another component in the human environment.

When students of evolution disagree among each other (in contrast with their disputes with those who entirely reject an evolutionary perspective) their arguments usually center around the nature of evolutionary sequences. Unless one is careful, the concept of sequences in time—the postulate of stages of cultural development—can be seriously misleading. Cultural stages are not arranged in a neat procession; nor has each culture gone through the same pattern of change. The relevant imagery for cultural evolution is a branching tree, not a straight line. All known stages of cultural development could be and in fact are represented simultaneously in the panoply of human diversity. Africa, for example, contains nomadic hunter-gatherers (such as the Mbuti Pygmies of the Congo), cultivators who use a hoe or digging stick (including neighbors of the Pygmies), plow cultivators (in Ethiopia and elsewhere), long-distance traders (in the Sudan), and industrial societies (in South Africa and elsewhere). Each of these societies may be adapted to its own habitat, exhibiting appropriate institutions for its level of development, and none may have grown from any of the others in any systematic way.

As these examples suggest, not every culture has participated fully in the sweep of evolution. In the terminology of Marshall Sahlins and Elman Service in *Evolution and Culture* (Ann Arbor: University of Michigan Press, 1960), it is useful to distinguish between "general evolution" and "specific evolution." General evolution refers to the changes that have taken place in human culture as a whole; specific evolution denotes the transformation of a particular culture from one stage of mastery over the habitat to another, each with its characteristic technology, essential institutions, ideologies, and customary behavior. This process of specific change is adaptive in the sense that it provides the group with a greater degree of mastery over its habitat than it enjoyed before, thus improving its chances of survival. A change can result from accretions in knowledge and techniques within the society itself or from the introduction of new technological procedures from other societies. The focus of this book is on general rather than specific cultural evolution, with special reference to the institutional changes that have accompanied this evolution; each of the general stages of development will be referred to as a strategy of adaptation for which specific changes in particular cultures serve as illustrations.

In what follows, I present a brief taxonomy of the major stages of human cultural development, beginning with nomadic hunter-gatherers and concluding with industrialization. In each of the sections of the book, the case studies are organized to reflect the succession of sociotechnological adaptations implicit in this taxonomy. These case studies illustrate the idea that every culture presents the individual with a particular kind of world, not merely with a set of tools with which to exploit a habitat.

The taxonomy that I now present is very schematic and is intended only to introduce the reader to one aspect of the book's organization. A fuller picture of each of these stages will be provided as needed in the context of each of the institutional spheres and in the case studies that will be considered.

Hunting-gathering refers to a particular energy system that represents, as far as we know, the first level of cultural adaptation achieved by man. In its simplest form, it is a technique of extracting a livelihood from the habitat by an almost exclusive reliance on muscular energy; collecting wild growing foods and hunting and fishing with bows and arrows, spears, bludgeons, nets, weirs, and the like. Hunter-gatherers are generally nomadic. Nomadic foragers usually live in small camps of several families, almost all of whom have other kinsmen in the group. When seasonal conditions permit, several camps will congregate. It is not always the same families that come together every summer; these groups are very fluid throughout the year and there is an important element of unpredictability in their composition. Larger encampments are places for acquiring spouses, gossiping, visiting with distant relatives, and conducting ceremonials.

Horticulture, a second strategy of adaptation, also has several varieties. It is a technique in which people plant seeds, roots, or tubers and harvest the product, using a hoe or digging stick as their principal means of production. Horticulturists, like hunter-gatherers, rely primarily on muscular energy in their exploitative activities, but with an important difference: they are responsible for the presence of much of the food on which they subsist. But the horticulturist does not turn the top-soil over, which generally sets a limit on his productivity.

The development of horticulture in the course of cultural evolution used to be called the "Neolithic Revolution" by anthropologists. It is now known from archeological research that horticulture evolved slowly and gradually; it did not burst forth in a "revolutionary" eruption. There is no single horticultural pattern; instead, there are different patterns, each representing a successive stage of development, that can be distinguished in terms of the different proportions of domesticated foods in the diet. All the horticultural societies whose institutions and ideological patterns we will consider in this book represent the most advanced stage of horticulture, in which domesticates and cultigens make up approximately 85 per cent of the diet. Villages at this stage of development are sedentary and often quite compact. Political organization is often well developed at this level and headmen may have a considerable amount of power. However, political organization in societies having this high proportion of domesticated food is varied, ranging from relatively weak institutions of authority to complex state systems.

Pastoralism is a technological system devoted to gaining a livelihood from the care of large herds of animals; like all other levels of technological development, it is a particular kind of social organization as well as a particular system of production. The essential social element of pastoralism is transhumance, a settlement pattern in which herders seasonally drive their animals from lowland areas to highland pastures to further the welfare of their flocks. Transhumance differs from nomadism in that the pattern of movement in the former is from fixed lowland settlements to highland pastures and back again, whereas nomads usually move not between fixed points but over a wide territory in search of food. After transhumant people make a move, they remain relatively stationary until the next season, unless they are faced with serious shortages of food and water; nomads generally remain stationary only for very brief periods. These different patterns of movement result in different organizations of social relations.

The several varieties of pastoralism are strategies of adaptation; they depend largely on habitational circumstance, as can be seen in the differences among East African, North American, and Asian pastoralists. In a technology devoted to the care of large herds of animals, sustenance may be derived from the herds themselves (milk, meat, blood) or from the use of the domesticated animals as instruments of production, as among North American Indians who used horses to hunt bison or among Mongols who used them to raid other human settlements.

Pastoralism is based on the mutual dependence of man and domesticated animals. Its basic requirement is that the animals be pastured, grazed, and protected; but— although pastoralists can control the migration of their animals—the availability of water is entirely beyond their control. Cattle herders usually subsist on dairy products; they rarely eat meat, except under very special circumstances, because their herds are their capital.

Agriculture, a fourth strategy of adaptation, differs from horticulture in technology as well as in social organization. Agriculture is a system of cultivation that is based on one or more of the following: plows and draft animals, large-scale and centrally controlled irrigation networks, and terracing. Each of these techniques, singly or in combination, requires a specific organization of labor to maintain and protect its sources of energy, and each involves its own modes of distributing resources and products. (Some anthropologists distinguish among these variations in the strategy of agriculture, treating them as separate levels of adaptation.)

In agriculture, the use of a plow depends entirely on the use of draft animals. (Mechanical tractors, sowers, and reapers are tools of industrialism, to be discussed below.) But the use of draft animals involves more than their domestication; there must be an adequate supply of such beasts for the entire community. The importance of this consideration can be seen in medieval English records, in which most disputes and manorial regulations seemed to have involved the allocation of draft animals to the members of the village. Similarly, social relationships that center on the ownership and use of draft animals are pivotal in such diverse agricultural societies as contemporary Mexico and India. In all such societies the maintenance of dependable supplies of livestock for draft purposes requires specialized groups of persons to care, protect, breed, and oversee the distribution of the animals.

Thus the change from hoe to plow in the course of cultural evolution involves a change in social organization as well as in technology. Many pastoralist societies— for example, those in East Africa—have great numbers of domesticated animals, practice limited horticulture and sometimes know about plows, but have not converted their domesticates into draft animals. Similarly, many grain-growers, such as the Pueblo Indians of the American South-west, have domesticated animals but have not developed livestock that can be used for draft. Here, as always, changes in social organization lag behind the possibilities of technological innovation. A further complication in the development of agriculture is that it requires drastic changes in the political organization of society, especially in the development of clearly defined social classes. I will return to this process.

Terracing and large-scale irrigation networks also are particular kinds of social systems as well as feats of engineering. Each requires the organization of labor for construction and demands appropriate institutions for regulation, protection, and repair. Agricultural technology also and inevitably involves specialization in production (including crafts), the development of markets or other means of trade, urbanization, the bifurcation of rural and urban values, and the like.

Industrialism is the fifth and last strategy of adaptation I will discuss; other strategies may intervene between agriculture and industrialism—such as mercantilism —but they will not be dealt with here. Industrialism, like other adaptations, involves a unique social organization as much as it does a technology. The use of extrapersonal energy in complex forms requires its own organization of social relations, centering on man's relationship to the machine.

For example, one of the outstanding differences between agriculture and industrialism is that machines are movable but land is not. Correspondingly, man in industrial society follows the machine; if he can better survive and better support his family by moving to a different machine in a different locality he does so, largely without regard to other people. But unlike the situation in nomadic societies, his movement does not affect the nature of the adaptive unit and the decision-making and implementing organization of the society. Industrial man holds his position in relation to his source of subsistence through an impersonal system that pays for the use of his labor power, rather than through a group of kinsmen and by inheritance. The intellectualized goal of an industrial society is to run itself like the machine on which it is based. The organization of a factory is supposed to rest entirely on rational considerations of profit, efficiency, and production—not, as in the working unit in a preindustrial society, on considerations of consumption.

This, then, in brief, is the outline of the taxonomy according to which we will organize our data. As noted, it is in part an expedient device. Details for each of the classes in the taxonomy will be added, in the context of the specific institutions that will be considered.

DIFFERENTIATION AND COMPLEXITY: DIMENSIONS OF EVOLUTION

As with most other processes, the concept of evolution can be made more understandable by knowing what it is not. Whether we are dealing with biological or social life, evolution refers to the successive emergence of new forms as a result of nonrepetitive change. In human society, this refers to sequences of harnessed energy systems and institutions. Evolution does not deal with changes in modes of thought, ideologies and values, features of personality, taste, artistic styles, and the like; changes in these aspects of human behavior cannot be considered in evolutionary terms because—at least at our present stage of knowledge—we cannot discern nonrepetitive sequences of form in them. Thus, for example, we can speak of the evolution of modes of acquiring a livelihood (or of maintaining a relationship with the habitat) but not of attitudes toward work; of kinship and family systems but not of kinsmen's and spouses' feelings toward each other; of religious organization but not of dogma; of political and legal systems but not of values with respect to authority and harmony, and so forth. The ideological superstructures of the institutions in which people are organized are essentially mental and cognitive phenomena and do not meet the criteria for change that we call evolutionary. However, as we will see, each of the changes that we refer to as evolutionary is accompanied by changes in the ideological sphere.

The sequence of adaptive strategies that we designate as evolutionary—and the entire evolutionary process itself—are characterized by two important dimensions: increasing "differentiation" and "complexity." Though they are intertwined, they must be considered separately.

Differentiation refers to the degree to which institutions or roles are separated from each other. The obverse of differentiation is *commingling*. The separation of church and state or of community (residence) and economic production are examples of institutional differentiation. A very recent example of institutional differentiation was represented in the decision of the United States Supreme Court (on June 15, 1970) that men who object to military service for purely moral and ethical reasons—rather than religious reasons alone, as previously—are entitled to exemption from conscription as conscientious objectors. The evolutionary significance of this ruling lay in the separation of military conscription from a religious test. Continued reliance on the custom of using the Bible in the ceremonial oath of office of an American president is an example of the commingling of church and state, even though it is only symbolic. The daily exodus of workers from an inner city to suburbs is an aspect of the differentiation of community organization and productive activities, as is choice of residence independent of the location of kinsmen (or settling in a particular place *because* there are no kinsmen nearby).

Role differentiation is closely related to institutional differentiation; it refers to the degree to which an individual's performance of one role—or participation in one institution—is independent of others. Economic specialization is an example of role differentiation; another is the relatively recent separation of religious and civil officials and their jobs. When the performance of political, religious, kinship, and educational roles (for example) are dependent on each other—for instance, when a man holds both political and religious office because he is an excellent provider and the oldest member of his kin group—we say these roles are commingled.

Complexity refers to the degree to which a society is composed of different groups —socioeconomic classes, estates (in Max Weber's sense of the term), ethnic or linguistic enclaves, economically and politically specialized groups, regional associations, and the like. Anthropologists often speak of societies that are further along the evolutionary scale than others as "more complex." An easily applied and measurable criterion of social complexity is the amount of occupational choice available to people in a society. Occupational choice is closely tied to role differentiation and both accompany advances in adaptation. For example, there are more than 150 roles defined in the census analysis of the occupational structure of the United States; the people in these roles are at the same time members of a large number of social, ideological, racial or ethnic, regional, and other groups. Compare this diversity to a hunting-gathering, horticultural, or pastoralist society in which a person has only one role open to him (hunter, cultivator, herder) and in which there are no economic or social subgroups, and it is readily apparent that a modern American youth in turmoil over his choice of occupation is experiencing one aspect of life in a society at the highest level of adaptation achieved thus far by man.

The further back one looks along the course of human evolution the more one can observe the commingling of institutions and roles. Thus, for example, we will see that one of the most important features of family and household organization at the levels of hunting-gathering and horticulture, as well as in pastoralism, is the submergence of the nuclear family (the unit of a conjugal pair and their offspring) in a wider kinship network; the maintenance of order and conformity and the practice of religion and magic are strongly commingled and these are undifferentiated from kinship and household organization. We will also see that art is strongly commingled with religion in many of these societies, leading in turn to its commingling with the other institutional spheres with which religious practice is itself commingled.

Also, the further back one looks along the evolutionary course the more one can observe the absence of occupational, religious, or other affiliational choices. In societies at the simplest levels of adaptation, almost every socially relevant task is (or can be) performed by almost every person; chieftainship, which is largely devoid of power and authority among the least complex societies, is the only noteworthy exception. In a hunting-gathering society, every man is a hunter and every woman is a gatherer; no real alternatives are open to an individual. In a fishing society every man is a fisherman; this is true even of chiefs or shamans and their families.

There are anticipations of role specialization in the most advanced levels of horticulture, but the first major and significant institutional differentiations occur in agricultural nation-states. Agriculture almost always is associated with an elaborate division of labor and with social specializations that proliferate with repercussions that are felt at almost every point in the society's institutional chains. In preagricultural societies the division of labor is based primarily on fixed (or ascribed) criteria, such as sex, age, and kinship; agriculturists more often emphasize criteria of achievement, such as social class. Agriculture entails specialization in food production to a greater extent; regional specializations are important, and these often are the basis of subcultural differences within a society. Craft specializations are also important; farmers become dependent on craftsmen for farming implements and craftsmen depend on farmers for food. State bureaucracies appear, and the people who fill these political roles also are specialists who have to be provided with food. Hence an important feature of a fully-developed agricultural adaptation is a centrally regulated system of distribution by which non-food-producing specialists can purchase food and regionally specialized farmers can buy from and sell to each other.

The most important evolutionary steps in the differentiation of institutional spheres accompanied the establishment of nation-states. A nation is a society occupying a limited territory, made up of many subgroups—communities and regions, classes and sometimes castes, ethnic and sometimes linguistic groups, economic and other specialized groups, a diversity of daily cycles and life styles—all of which are centrally controlled in some measure by a set of interlocking agencies or bureaucracies which are themselves more or less differentiated. These agencies constitute the state, and in turn, they are unified into a political and administrative entity under "a single person, by whatsoever name he may be distinguished" (in the words of Edward Gibbon in *The Decline and Fall of the Roman Empire*). The office of this person is central among the state's agencies and he is the key symbolic actor in the administrative and ceremonial life of the society, though he is not necessarily the person with greatest individual power. In these terms, "nation" is the territorial representation of the society and "state" is its political representation. Thus nation-states are always more complex than stateless societies.

Many adaptive advantages accrue to a centralized and politically integrated society, through specialization and economic diversification. The possibilities of gluts and shortages are reduced; the production of materials necessary for export and stockpiling can be planned; different regions of a country that are limited in particular resources or by other habitational factors can be supplied by other regions. There also are political advantages, primarily in terms of the maintenance of power and authority, that accrue from the stimulation of economic specialization.

Political power is often its own reward, and the holders of political power generally worry a great deal about being overthrown, sometimes with good reason. "Divide and conquer" is a useful strategy of domestic rulers as well as invading powers; when different groups in a centrally controlled society are stimulated to have different vested interests it is difficult for them to unite to overthrow the establishment. Alexander Hamilton (writing about an agricultural society in *The Federalist* papers) recognized this clearly when he said that political stability can be assured in a federal republic because an uprising in one petty state would fail for lack of support in another: however fierce a particular local economic interest, it was not likely to be embraced by the entire society. An excellent contemporary example of this can be seen in the divisions between students and manual workers in the United States and in France. As history demonstrates, however, it is not impossible for an entire nation, no matter how diversified, to embrace a single interest and overthrow its government. Nor is the policy of "divide and conquer" without disadvantages, especially when a society is invaded (as were the Aztecs and Incas in the premodern world and the French in 1940) and cooperation among groups with different vested interests is found to be extremely difficult. Impediments to communication as a result of the diversity of local interests are among the serious vulnerabilities of totalitarian societies.

Cutting across regional and other differences in agricultural societies are the social classes and castes into which they are usually organized. One consequence of the development of social classes and castes is that each group within the system of stratification (which crosscuts the entire society, viewed as an adaptive unit) has its own vested interests and values, and these are usually in competition. Thus one of the important sources of complexity and heterogeneity in an agricultural society is the congruence within the society of occupational and regional specializations with the values and self-serving interests of different groups in the stratification system. The values of people of high status legitimate their occupations, privileges, positions of power, and control over production and distribution; correlatively, people of lower status hold to values that are appropriate to their own positions.

Which comes first, social stratification or the centrally controlling political institutions of the nation-state? There are passionate advocates of both positions, but much more research is needed before this question can be answered. It is clear, however, that control of sources of energy, rather than control of instruments of production as such, underlies the stimulation, control, and redistribution of surpluses as well as the maintenance of political control by the ruling groups of a society. In an industrial society, for example, political control is based on the centralized control of electricity, fuels, transportation routes, and the like, and not necessarily by centralized control over machines, factories, transportation vehicles, or other tools. And it is control of the sources of energy that enables the ruling groups to maintain and extend their wealth and high standards of living. It is significant that we use the same word— power—to refer to energy systems and political control.

In all contemporary industrial nations, regardless of their political and economic ideologies, there is a consistent relationship between centralized political institutions and the society's major sources of energy. The greater the number of people who draw on a single source of energy, the greater the tendency to centralize and concentrate its control in the hands of the society's ruling groups. For example, control of steam to drive machines has almost always been localized, each factory maintaining and controlling its own power plant. In contrast, there is greater centralization of control of electricity produced by water power, and even greater centralization of control of electricity produced by nuclear energy is taking place. As we will see, this has repercussions in, for example, the extension of the "long arm of the law" in national societies.

It was at the agricultural level of cultural development that the principles for the centralized control of sources of energy were first and firmly established. The specific modes and policies of this control of course are different in industrial and agricultural adaptations because (among other reasons) they rely on different sources of energy. Industrial societies seldom maintain the same kind of concern over the allocation of draft animals that we find in plow-agricultural societies; these animals, as sources of energy, have been superseded by other forms of energy that govern the group's relationship to the habitat.

The relationship of the individual to the sources of energy on which he relies is important in establishing political states. In horticulture, each man controls and allocates his own muscular energy. Only when land is in limited supply (as in circumscribed regions, such as valleys) or water available only in limited quantities is it possible for rulers to gain control of these resources and exchange access to them for allegiance and conformity. Only when a group can withhold resources can it establish itself in political control. Only when an individual has exclusive power over the sources of energy on which he relies can he be free of centralized political control.

As we have seen, there is a direct correlation between the level of sociotechnological development of a society and the degree of internal heterogeneity and complexity that characterizes it. Thus, agricultural nation-states manifest more inner diversity than horticultural societies (whether state or stateless) and industrial nations exhibit still more intra- as well as inter-societal heterogeneity. There are no known societies in which there is perfect or complete homogeneity; nor are there any known societies in which there is so much diversity that every community or other local group lives by a unique strategy.

Another aspect of the complexity of agricultural and industrial nations is the wide range of social relations in which every individual engages. As Robert McC. Adams observes in *The Evolution of Urban Society* (Chicago: Aldine, 1966), every advance in adaptation is accompanied by an increase in the number and types of groups with which each social group interacts. Generally, nomadic hunting-gathering groups interact primarily with other such groups, and less with horticultural and other more advanced groups that may be nearby; furthermore, the number of groups with which a band associates and on which it is dependent is limited. This also tends to be the case among horticulturists, though in the most advanced horticultural societies there may be an expansion and elaboration of trade relationships and an increasing mutual dependency between cultivators and noncultivators. In agriculture, this dependency is not only between societies, as between agriculturists and pastoralists, but also between cultivators and artisans and other specialists within the society.

Urban centers depend on cultivators not only for food but also for personnel; until very recently in history, cities have not been able to sustain population growth without recruitment from rural areas. Political bureaucrats, who are generally urban, interact with a wide variety of groups—other political functionaries, priests, pastoralists, and often members of other societies as well. Reciprocally, each group looks—and is forced to subscribe—to the legal and administrative rules of the state bureaucracy. (There are instances, however, in which peasant communities are almost completely cut off from these urban influences.) Indeed, one of the usual accompaniments of cultural evolution is that at each successive stage the individual must learn to cope with an increasing variety of social categories. The most recent development of this aspect of evolution is to be seen in the range of social relations that characterizes the modern metropolis.

Thus, although it is possible within limits to speak of *the* family or *the* legal and religious systems or *the* arts in societies at lower levels of sociotechnological development, this becomes increasingly difficult in societies that are more technologically and politically complex. Specifically, this means that when we speak about modern nations we have to consider their *varieties* of family systems, ways of maintaining order and conformity, religious and value systems, personality types, arts, and the like.

To this end, the materials presented here are organized not only to describe the variations among different stages of sociotechnological development in each of the major institutional spheres (as represented by particular societies), but also to illustrate the cross-cutting aspects of growing evolutionary complexity: increasing differentiation and intrasocietal heterogeneity.

CAUSE AND EFFECT IN CULTURAL EVOLUTION

This raises the question of cause and effect in the evolution of culture. While it is not possible to do full justice to this question here, I want to point to the directions that I have taken that provide the framework for my subsequent discussion of the evolution of particular institutions. The evolutionary dimensions of differentiation and complexity are central to my point of view.

The adoption of an evolutionary perspective requires a clearcut set of hypotheses about priorities in change. Do some aspects of culture necessarily depend on other aspects? Are there changes that automatically set others into motion? Anthropologists who reject an evolutionary point of view tend to give negative answers to these questions; similarly, a denial of priorities in cultural change necessarily leads to the abandonment of an evolutionary point of view. The difficulties of "chicken and egg" propositions of this kind have plagued students of history and society in their attempts to untangle the skein of political and technological change. Is change in the institutional structure of society always the result of technological change, as Marx suggests? Or is it possible for institutional change itself to give rise to technological change? These are among the central questions in modern anthropology, which we are far from having answered definitively. It nevertheless is possible to provide some tentative answers and lines of inquiry.

Once we accept the axiom that there are necessary priorities in cultural change, our attempts to organize the record of human evolution lead to a consideration of the relationship between political organization and technological development. The two are inseparable. From the evidence, it appears to me that technological change underlies institutional change in stateless societies; conversely, changes in nontechnological (especially political) institutions underlie technological change in nation-states. In the latter case, institutional changes stimulate technological developments, and the latter in turn lead to accommodations in family and kinship systems, in many aspects of law and social control, in religion and values and ideologies. Thus the direction and sequence of events in evolutionary adaptation undergoes a reversal in societies that are integrated into nation-states from the sequence that is observable in stateless societies. In this connection, it must be remembered that most cultural evolution has occurred during less than one per cent of human history. Its source and acceleration during the last two or three millennia can be attributed directly to the increasing differentiation and complexity of society.

A stateless society is one in which the checks, balances, and controls over behavior that are prerequisite to all social life are exercised through local institutions at the community level, without the intervention of higher levels of authority. Local autonomy prevails in the maintenance of order and conformity and in the resolution of disputes; the locus of this autonomy may be in the corporate kin group where emphasis is on the rules of kinship relationships, in the community territorially conceived, or in other associations (sodalities) that crosscut the two. Local autonomy is expressed in many ways in a stateless society: in economic self-sufficiency, self-protection (including the right to feud and to wage war), the administration of land tenure, and the application of juridical controls.

Technology is the fulcrum of adaptation in stateless societies, where the quest for food is the overriding force in social organization, and almost all institutions are geared to the demands of their technology. This is made evident by the ethnographic data for hunters and gatherers, stateless horticulturists and pastoralists, and the few stateless agriculturists. Each local group is autonomous in decision-making and implementation in all spheres of production and consumption. Limitations on the amount of food produced are established by considerations of personal energy, technology, ecology (for example, rainfall, fertility of the soil, migrations of fish), and need; a family in a stateless society will produce as much food as it needs within the limits imposed by the amount of manpower, the nature of available exploitative energy, and the physical habitat. Such a group may well seek to produce a surplus, but only against an increase in the numbers of persons who have to be fed or the loss or incapacitation of productive members of the group. People in such societies do not provide a surplus for a distant political authority—a superordinate king, nobility, or temple.

Even in relatively complex stateless societies like chiefdoms, the source of economic and political authority is local, and there is no superordinate or centralizing organization. A chiefdom can be characterized as a society in which many centers independently coordinate their own social, political, and religious life; it has centralized leadership, but integration takes place within each separate nucleus, not within the society as a whole. Each nucleus splits recurrently, usually every generation, and the people strongly resist attempts to unify the entire society under a single leader. Similarly, economic activity is coordinated in each nucleus and there is socioeconomic specialization, but chiefdoms lack institutions that bind the entire society into a permanent socioeconomic entity. Each neighboring chiefdom is autonomous and refuses to recognize the political and economic authority of any larger organization. Nor do chiefdoms have legalized force to back up the demands of local rulers for tribute, a large proportion of which is redistributed to the populace at large. Chiefdoms probably represent a transitional stage between stateless and state societies.

Distribution, like production, is locally regulated in stateless societies. The flow of goods is controlled exclusively by local institutions: kinship, friendship, neighborliness, and the like. No distant political or controlling economic authority requires regular payments of taxes or other forms of tribute. Nor does any distant authority regulate the distribution of seed to a local cultivator, or implements, draft animals, and other sources of exploitative energy. There is no central agency to regulate exchange within the society as a whole or with other societies; instead, exchanges are made in face-to-face relationships.

In societies such as these, adaptive institutional changes are almost always the result of technological change. Every advance in the harnessing of extrapersonal energy leads to increasing sedentism and sociopolitical complexity, as well as to changes in family organization, religious patterns, and trade relationships. Note, however, that there are several types of states and of stateless societies, and I do not want to suggest that a simple dichotomy between the two reflects political realities; the different types have to be carefully distinguished in empirical research. I am adopting this artificial polarization for heuristic purposes, to illustrate various processes in the technological and economic spheres of society. If I wished to analyze processes of political organization, such a dichotomy would be meaningless.

The sequence of priorities in adaptation is reversed in societies that are integrated into nation-states. A state organization creates a new environment, one that is unknown in stateless societies, and its development is a watershed in cultural evolution. It is one of the achievements that has increased man's freedom from the restrictions of his habitat, because it makes possible the harnessing of more efficient sources of energy. The goals of a state organization are not only to centralize decision-making and implementation but also to exploit physical energy potentials in the service of the society as a whole. One of the characteristics of states is that they employ rational and future-oriented planning in almost all spheres of social organization—the harnessing of energy systems, economic and social policies, and the rest. This can be seen most clearly in state-sponsored construction of large-scale irrigation networks, in long-range trade, and in economic advance in the face of a lack of natural resources (as in modern Japan and Israel).

But states cannot develop in any society or under all conditions; they appear only where relatively advanced levels of technological adaptation have been attained and, apparently, in particular types of habitats. It appears from the evolutionary record that states develop principally in societies in which agriculture or advanced horticulture has become the basis of social organization; they are not unknown among pastoralists, but they are rare. We do not know of any societies at the foraging or rudimentary horticultural levels in which nation-states have been formed. Statelessness constitutes a set of limiting conditions for technological advance because there is no stimulus for the production of gross deployable surpluses in such societies. States, on the other hand, encourage the harnessing of more efficient extrapersonal sources of energy in the interest of the production of surpluses, largely for the benefit of the ruling classes. The political institutions of a state embody only the potentials for technological advance and do not guarantee that it will occur, but technological advance is always severely limited in the absence of a unifying state.

The history of irrigation perhaps provides the clearest and best-known example. Although cultivators use irrigation ditches in many stateless societies, their ditches are usually small, each cultivator digs and maintains his own, and the ditches are not part of a system of political control. In contrast, large-scale irrigation networks or centrally regulated viaducts provide a measure of freedom from ecological pressures (such as localized droughts or flooding) that is not afforded by local or private ditches. They make it possible for people to divert water from one region to another, to regulate the volume of water that is supplied to an individual farmer or to a region, and to store water. As a result, it is possible for the farmer to increase the yield of his soil, assure the appearance of his crops, and thus increase the certainty of his survival —the essence of adaptation.

Almost all students of social evolution agree that the development of large-scale irrigation networks is one of the greatest of human achievements. Recent evidence indicates that the construction of these networks has always followed the integration of a society into a nation-state by centrally unifying political institutions; they do not seem to have preceded the formation of states. (The clearest statement of this point of view is by Robert McC. Adams in *The Evolution of Urban Society*.) Although the reasons for the stimulation of irrigation networks by states are not yet clear (and not all states accomplished this), we can speculate that one aspect of the genius of the men who established nation-states and caused these networks to be built was their awareness that large populations can be more easily controlled if they must depend for water on the agencies that build, maintain, and regulate the irrigation systems. There are many gaps in our knowledge of how rulers gained such power (other than by conquest) but it can be surmised that once this dependence is established—and it is a simple matter to secure conformity and obedience if the threat of withholding water is easily carried out—it is a short step to regulating the supply of seed and draft animals, controlling trade and exchange, and centralizing monetary control. Once developments in knowledge and technology reach the point at which man can create new fuel systems or other new sources of energy, there is only a quantitative difference between a state that stimulates the construction of large-scale irrigation networks and one that subsidizes the development of rocket fuels, supersonic aircraft, artificial foods, and other materials that facilitate the perpetuation of life—and that also underwrite the growing wealth of the ruling classes.

State organizations do not give rise to identical cultural patterns in all societies or even in a single society at different historical periods. For example, ancient Egypt was characterized by very different cultural patterns during the Middle and the New Kingdoms even though both were based on large-scale irrigation networks, trade, military activities, and elaborate systems of social stratification. Among the many factors that underlay the reorganization of cultural elements between the New Kingdom and the Middle Kingdom were changes in values among the nobility and the greater concentration of wealth in their hands. Changes in foreign policy and fluctuations of fortune in international affairs also played an important part in changing patterns of life within the level of adaptation achieved by ancient Egypt.

Let us take an example that is closer to home. American society had certainly achieved an industrial level of adaptation by the first decades of the twentieth century, but American culture of the 1970s is very different from that of the 1900s or even the 1930s. Without trying to understand all the reasons for these differences within the basic adaptation, we need only consider the impact on the culture of changes in the media of mass communication, in transportation, and in the diffusion of formal education to larger segments of the population. The similarities between the two periods can be attributed largely to the constancy of the level of adaptation; the differences can be understood, in part, in terms of new relationships among the elements of the culture.

In societies that have been unified into nation-states, production as well as consumption tends to be strongly influenced, if not dominated, by the central political institutions. Centralized authorites in agricultural societies often stimulate production by decreeing how much land will be cultivated, which crops will be planted, and who will get water and seed. The principles that underlie these activities also are found in industrial societies, as in decisions about who will receive electricity, natural gas, or atomic energy, or in government control of access to waterways and air space. Centralized political institutions frequently control distribution directly through marketing systems, or, in their absence, by establishing standards of exchange and equivalences. The classes that control these institutions are inseparable from the economic apparatuses (whether state agencies or "private" corporations) in which it is decided which products will be consumed domestically and which will be used in intersocietal trade. These groups stimulate production of the surpluses they control to underwrite their standard of living, and they redistribute the surpluses to welfare-program recipients and to others who do not directly produce wealth, such as members of their bureaucracies.

Not all states control local economies in these ways but the important fact is that such centralized direction is found only in nation-states. An important feature of this process is that the strategies adopted by different groups in a national society are reflected in the political movements they initiate to protect their interests and to reduce economic uncertainty. More broadly stated, different groups in a nation maintain different kinds of relationships with the state's central agencies in exchange for access to resources; when there are no existing political groups to secure this access for them, new groups are formed. If the state's policies assure economic certainty to some groups, their political strategies are understandably conservative. Other groups, equally understandably, rock the political boat when they regard the state's policies and the established values and ideologies as inimical to their interests in the adaptive strategy. In any event, distinctive national strategies develop in a nation principally in response to politically stimulated factors in the habitat rather than to natural elements as in stateless societies. As will be seen, values and ideologies are among the most important tools in the different substrategies in a national society, and this is an important aspect of its complexity.

Do hypotheses of cause and effect in cultural evolution necessarily mean that everything in human culture must be understood within such an evolutionary and adaptive framework? My point of view leads me to answer in the negative. We have seen that the concept of evolution does not encompass all cultural change. Now, if evolution is the historical record of adaptive change, and if there are some manifestations of culture that cannot be incorporated into that record, then we must conclude that these aspects of culture are "neutral" (for want of a better term) in the evolutionary sense and must be understood outside the framework of adaptation.

But even this general statement must be qualified. Changes that are non-evolutionary—in values, ideologies, and personality processes—may be considered adaptive (or viewed as accompaniments of adaptation) if it can be shown that they are part of or contribute to institutional changes that are necessary for the effective use of harnessed energy. Family systems and particular relationships among people for the maintenance of order and conformity are as much aspects of an adaptive strategy as the organization of labor; so are the values and ideologies that reflect these social relationships because they too contribute to the effectiveness of the institutions in which they are embedded.

But there may be aspects of culture that in no way contribute to the society's perpetuation. The length of skirts or of men's suit jackets and sideburns, the change in musical styles from Mozart to the Beatles, monochrome as against decorated dinner dishes, different ballet traditions, while important from other points of view are not part of the adaptive process as far as we can determine at present. Nor—to bring this discussion closer to traditional anthropological concerns—are variations in kinship terminology, differences in wedding ceremonies (like exchanges of rings or cups of wine), or cremation versus burial.

Future research may uncover adaptive significance in some of these examples of "neutral" cultural elements. But to say that everything is adaptive is to make the term so all-inclusive as to render it meaningless as a tool for understanding change. Nor can we assume that there is a one-to-one correspondence between a particular strategy of adaptation and particular varieties of social institutions. There are variations in family and kin-group organization, legal systems, religious practice and belief at each level of adaptation and within each adaptive strategy. While much research remains to be done to explain these variations, it seems they are largely due to variations in habitational conditions in stateless societies and to political factors in nation-states. See, for example, the differences in family organization among stateless pastoralists like the Fulani of the Sudan (Selection 3) and the Jie and Turkana of Uganda (Selections 21 and 22 in *The Cultural Present*); all three exhibit the basic pastoralist organization of a patrilocal extended family, but with different degrees of solidarity and cohesiveness depending, it seems, on the beneficence and harshness of the habitat.

THE 1970s IN EVOLUTIONARY PERSPECTIVE

As we enter the 1970s, it is not possible to discuss further social evolution without taking cognizance of the conflicts among different groups in modern industrial nations. In the polarizations of the young and not-so-young, ethnic and racial groups, estates with different economic and political interests, the educated and not-so-educated, rural and urban populations, not everyone is on the same side in each of the divisions. These intertwined conflicts are aspects of social change; it is unlikely that there has ever been a transition from one stage of sociotechnological development to another that has not been marked by ideological schisms and violence. Such conflicts may have been less intense and less noticeable when it took 2,000 years to move from one stage of development to another, as was the case in the transition from hunting-gathering to horticulture. Now, however, we are experiencing a rate of change never before known in human history, not necessarily because we value change as such but rather because this rate seems to be characteristic of our stage of sociotechnological development. One of the concomitants of human evolution has been an increase in the rate of change, and this seems to be accompanied by an intensification of the antagonisms among the component groups in complex societies. Thus, if change *is* culture and culture *is* change, if the often painful conflicts we are now experiencing are adjuncts of change, and if the rate of change that characterizes us is "normal" for our stage in evolutionary history, then the intensity of our conflicts should not surprise us. To say that modern societies "have problems" is merely another way of saying that they are seeking to adapt—and that they are on this side of cemeteries, which is the only place that complete social stability is to be found.

From time to time in this book I will allude to the hypothesis that industrial man is beginning to move into a new stage of sociotechnological development—a post-industrial stage. I think this will be an adaptation based on the replacement of human labor by electronically controlled production (including education); space and under-sea exploration and colonization will be important accompaniments. Among the many consequences of this replacement of human labor is that there will be very few available jobs but many people—millions—who are willing and able to work. This will have repercussions at every point in the society's organization of social relations. It is my impression that many aspects of the conflicts that we are currently experiencing reflect the fact that university-educated young people have been trained for—and are already anticipating—this future adaptation and are impatient for the implementation of its values and ideologies. As these people often say, "The future is now." An anthropologist would add only that our understanding of the present and future—and the transition between the two—can be enhanced by a careful study of the experiments-in-nature in the laboratories of our past and our cross-cultural variability.

The reader who wishes to get a more detailed picture of the point of view taken here with respect to adaptation and evolution should consult my paper on "Culture as Adaptation," in *The Cultural Present*, pp. 40-60, as well as the editorial and inter-pretative essays in that volume. An excellent brief introduction to the study of socio-cultural evolution is to be found in Joseph H. Greenberg, "Language and Evolution," in *Evolution and Anthropology: A Centennial Appraisal*, edited by Betty J. Meggers (Washington, D.C.: Anthropological Society of Washington, 1959; reprinted as Selection 3 in *The Cultural Present*).

Among the classic works that have contributed to the concept of cultural adapta-tion are Karl Marx's *Capital* (New York: E. P. Dutton, 1951-57); Friedrich Engel's *The Origin of the Family, Private Property, and the State* (New York: International Publishers, 1942); Herbert Spencer's *Principles of Sociology* (New York: Appleton, 1923-25) and *The Evolution of Society: Selections from Herbert Spencer's Principles of Sociology*, edited by Robert L. Carneiro (Chicago: University of Chicago Press, 1967).

Among more recent general works are: *Theory of Culture Change: The Methodology of Multilinear Evolution*, by Julian H. Steward (Urbana: University of Illinois Press, 1955); *The Evolution of Culture: The Development of Civilization to the Fall of Rome*, by Leslie A. White (New York: McGraw-Hill, 1959); *Evolution and Culture*, edited by Marshall D. Sahlins and Elman R. Service (Ann Arbor: University of Michigan Press, 1960); *Primitive Social Organization*, by Elman R. Service (New York: Random House, 1962); *The Evolution of Urban Society: Early Mesopotamia and Prehispanic Mexico*, by Robert McC. Adams (Chicago: Aldine, 1966); *The Evolution of Political Society: An Essay in Political Anthropology*, by Morton H. Fried (New York: Random House, 1967); "The Origins of New World Civilization," by Robert S. MacNeish (*Scientific American* [November 1964], 211 [5]: 29-37); *Oriental Despotism*, by Karl Wittfogel (New Haven: Yale University Press, 1957) (in my opinion effectively rebutted by Adams); and *Courses toward Urban Life*, edited by Gordon R. Willey and Robert J. Braidwood (Chicago: Aldine, 1962).

In *The Dynamics of Modernization* (New York and Evanston: Harper and Row, 1966), C. E. Black seeks to show that accretions in knowledge, science, and technology have been among the most important factors in the modernization of contemporary nations. Although I believe his argument is slightly overdrawn, his book should be consulted by those who are interested in contemporary sociopolitical developments. One of the most important papers in recent years in the study of social evolution is "A Theory of the Origin of the State," by Robert L. Carneiro (*Science* [August 1970], 169 [3947]: 733-38). Also of significance is Carneiro's "Cultural Adaptation" (*International Encyclopedia of the Social Sciences* (2nd edition), 3: 551-54). An important paper combining considerations of political complexity and adaptation is "Microcosm-Macrocosm Relationships in North American Agrarian Society," by John W. Bennett (*American Anthropologist*, 69 [1967]: 441-54).

I. MARRIAGE AND THE FAMILY

WE BEGIN with marriage and family relationships because the social arrangements made for mating, the care and development of children, and the division of labor between spouses are generally regarded as the basis of all social relationships that contribute to the survival of the species. Despite the many forms taken by the human family in different societies and throughout all of man's history, all of these different arrangements provide a central core around which other social relationships are organized.

To understand particular marriage and family relationships in adaptive terms, we must distinguish between the rules governing the selection of mates and the relationships among spouses after their families have been established. Marriage refers to socially ordered mating and sanctioned parenthood; it generally leads to alliances between the mates' kinsmen and to more or less elaborate economic relationships within and between families. The family has other functions as well, such as providing a stable background for the care and rearing of children, and regulating inheritance. But our concern here is with marriage and the family as modes of acquiring a livelihood and maintaining a viable relationship with the habitat, and therefore we are oing to focus principally on the relationships among and within families and family groups. We are going to see that relationships within the family are inseparable from relationships between families, and these in turn are tied to the overall strategy of adaptation of each society. The successive changes in family organization that we refer to as evolutionary—including changes now taking place in our own family systems—can be understood as the result of changes in sociotechnological systems.

Most families include, at a minimum, a married couple and their offspring, but there are societies in which the family—however it is defined—does not include a husband of the mother or a father (or fathers) of her children. All societies have rules or standards about whom one should marry; in some, there are even prescriptions about whom one *must* marry. There are also rules in every society about whom one is forbidden to marry or to engage in sexual relations; the two sets of rules are not always the same. These are called rules of exogamy and incest, respectively. It seems from our knowledge of behavior among primates and hunter-gatherers that the rules of incest were probably the first taboos governing the selection of mates in the earliest known human societies. The reasons for the development of incest taboos appear to be inseparable from the sources of marriage and the family themselves:

> When males hunt and females gather, the results are shared and given to the young, and the habitual sharing between a male, a female, and their offspring becomes the basis for the human family. According to this view, the human family is the result of the reciprocity of hunting, the addition of a male to the mother-plus-young social group of the monkeys and apes.
>
> A clue to the adaptive advantage and evolution of our psychological taboo on incest is provided by this view of the family. Incest prohibitions are reported universally among humans and these always operate to limit sexual activity involving sub-adults within the nuclear family. Taking the nuclear family as the unit of account, incest prohibitions tend to keep the birth rate in line with economic productivity. If in creating what we call the family the addition of a male is important in economic terms, then the male who is added must be able to fulfill the role of a socially responsible provider. In the case of the hunter, this necessitates a degree of skill in hunting and a social maturity that is attained some years after puberty. As a young man grows up, this necessary delay in his assumption of the role of provider for a female and her young is paralleled by a taboo which prevents him from effective social maturity. Father-daughter incest could also produce a baby without adding a productive male to the family. This would be quite different from the taking of a second wife which, if permitted, occurs only when the male has shown he is already able to provide for and maintain more than one female. . . . A mother-son sexual avoidance may be present in some species of monkeys and this extremely strong taboo among humans requires a different explanation from the one we have offered for brother-sister and father-daughter incest prohibitions. In this case, the role conflict argument may be paramount. ("The Evolution of Hunting," by Sherwood L. Washburn and C. S. Lancaster, in *Man the Hunter*, edited by Richard B. Lee and Irven De Vore [Chicago : Aldine, 1968, p. 301].)

Although there is probably more uniformity of family organization among hunter-gatherers than at subsequent stages of development, there is nevertheless considerable diversity in the ways in which marriage partners are selected among them. One of the world's most complicated systems of marriage rules is found among Australian aborigines, and the interpretation of these rules has been the subject of one of the longest and most volatile controversies known to any science; the matter is still far from settled.

One of the reasons for the intensity of this debate is that there is considerable uncertainty about the nature and composition of social groups among Australian aborigines prior to their contact with Europeans. Some anthropologists feel that local groups among the aborigines were formless and transitory; others interpret them as having been tightly organized and identifiable. Similarly, there is considerable debate about the relationships of these groups to their territories and water holes. Though some anthropologists maintain that local groups "owned" the sites with which they were associated, the nature of this ownership remains uncertain. In any event, regardless of the size of hunter-gatherer groups, their internal organization, and the nature of their claimed relationship to their territories, there is no debate over the fact that visiting among groups was very frequent—especially during the dry season—and that even when permission was required to visit this was easily given. Moreover, even when local groups had mythologically sanctioned boundaries, they were not in fact exclusive.

Another reason for the debate is that there is often a wide discrepancy between the rules according to which marriages should be contracted and actual practice among these people. Often, it appears, the rules cannot be followed because of a lack of women in appropriate kin positions, so that men are obliged to take inappropriate wives. Some anthropologists—notably Claude Lévi-Strauss—contend that what is important is not people's actual behavior but the meaning of the rules themselves, independent of their application; others are uncomfortable with this degree of abstraction from specific and observed human behavior.

We need not stop here to consider the logic or grammar of marriage rules—references to the relevant literature are given at the end of this Introduction—except to observe that one of the outstanding features of marriage arrangements among hunter-gatherers, notably in Australia, is a system of marital exchange and "alliance." The specific rules of these exchanges regulate marriage and ceremonial life; they are not obviously related to economic and other relationships in the society. What concerns us here is the long-term adaptive utility of these systems as systems.

A system of marital exchange is based primarily on the rule of exogamy: the men of any group may not marry women from that group. Most anthropologists agree that in one way or another this rule was designed—not necessarily consciously—to maintain peace within the group. But this does not explain why some hunter-gatherers (like the Australians) went the additional length of establishing elaborate and often complex arrangements in which particular groups actually exchanged women in regulated ways. To appreciate this, we must remember that hunter-gatherers move around a lot, and more important, that local groups do not have exclusive rights to particular territories or resources (with possible exceptions in Australia). The abundance of food in their habitats varies from year to year, and flexible organization enables people to move from area to area and to join with other groups in coping with this variability. Thus one of the salient features of life at this level of sociotechnological development is that different groups take turns visiting and playing host to each other during different seasons. As a result, there develops a system of mutual and reciprocal access to resources incorporating many groups.

But men have weapons and can easily kill each other, and to survive they must restrain their dangerous capacities. People at each stage of sociotechnological development do so in ways that are appropriate to the realities of their condition of life. Later (in Selection 6 and in the Introduction to Part V) we will consider other sets of controls among hunter-gatherers that contribute to the maintenance of law and order in their groups, and we will see that these also contribute to group fluidity. Here we are concerned with the systems of marital exchange that have developed among hunter-gatherers as a result of their unique territorial relationships. One consequence of exchanging women is that each hunting-gathering camp becomes dependent on others for a supply of wives and is allied with others through the bonds that result from marriage. This contributes to the maintenance of peaceful relations among the groups that move around, camp with each other, and exploit overlapping territories. Such arrangements do not entirely eliminate aggression, but they probably help keep it down to a manageable level.

The family systems of hunter-gatherers exhibit less diversity than their systems of mate selection and less than the family systems found at subsequent stages of development. Within limits, the Hadza family system described by Woodburn in Selection 1 is representative. The focal point of this system is the individual hunter's need to have hunting partners on whom he can rely for assistance and support; the sentiments and obligations of kinship provide the basis of these alliances within the group, which are indispensable in the hazardous occupation of hunting by means of such rudimentary tools as spears and bows and arrows. In addition, kinship provides the basic lines along which food is distributed in a hunting-gathering camp; this too is important, especially in times of scarcity. As a result of these requirements, and almost without exception, a married pair in a hunting-gathering group settle in a camp in which at least one spouse has a parent, sibling, or (later in life) a married child.

With the technological advance into a horticultural strategy of adaptation, man's relationship to his habitat changed, and a most important change was the development of the notion of exclusive rights to territory claimed by a group. This exclusive territoriality was probably designed, in large measure, to protect investments of time and effort in particular plots. Hunter-gatherers sometimes practice a little crop cultivation (an example is found in Selection 6), and they too develop notions of exclusivity about their cultivated plots, but in ways that are different from those horticulturists who are entirely sedentary. One of these differences is that when a hunter-gatherer stakes out a claim to a cultivated plot of land, any of his kinsmen has a right to collect wild-growing food on it; among sedentary horticulturists, permission for this must first be secured. Second, a hunter-gatherer who claims exclusive rights to a cultivated plot does so by virtue of his own investment of time and effort; in sedentary horticultural societies, ownership is often exercised by the kin group, and individuals and families have the right to use part of that land by virtue of membership in the group. Thus a comparison of man's relationship to land in societies at these stages of development suggests that it is the investment of energy in activities intended to produce future returns that underlies the development of notions of exclusive territoriality, but these concepts have different consequences when they refer to the kin group as a whole rather than to the individual alone.

The shift from hunting and gathering to completely sedentary horticulture does not occur in one leap; the evolutionary record demonstrates that the process has been slow. At each step along the way, cultivated foods make up a larger proportion of the diet. Similarly, at each of these steps kin group organization becomes progressively stronger, with commensurate consequences for marriage and family systems. As a result of these social and technological changes, relationships among groups changed, and marriage arrangements with them. While marital exchange is not unknown among horticulturists, other types of exchange more frequently characterize this stage of development, such as the exchange of wealth that symbolizes the bonds between groups joined through the marriage of two of their members.

From an evolutionary point of view, an important influence on marriage and family organization among horticulturists is their sedentary way of life, in contrast to the mobility of hunter-gatherers. Economic cooperation among households is no less necessary, since even though horticulture represents an advance in man's mastery over his habitat, crops are variable and life remains precarious. It is difficult for a single household to clear land and plant, tend, and harvest crops without assistance. The physical and emotional investments these people make in their cultivated lands contribute to the development of the notion of exclusive rights over land, and the necessary reliance on communal subsistence activity places ownership in the basic communal organization, the kin group. This is illustrated in Selection 2.

The rules governing where a couple settle after they are married are important in the overall system of kinship. Obviously, social relationships in groups in which a married pair resides with or near the groom's family will differ considerably from those that ensue if the pair resides matrilocally, that is, with or near the bride's family. The varying consequences of these rules of residence in different strategies of adaptation are illustrated in all the selections in part I.

These considerations require a pause to consider a few of the technical terms of kinship analysis. Kin groups are based on ties of blood or marriage. Groups in which all the members claim descent from a common ancestor are called "descent groups," and one of the most important of such groups is the "lineage"—a descent group in which the members can actually demonstrate (and not merely assume) their relationship. Matrilineal (or matri-) lineages are composed of men and women who can actually trace their descent from a common female ancestor; patrilineal (or patri-) lineages trace their descent from a common male ancestor. Several lineages whose members claim (but cannot necessarily demonstrate) common descent are generally referred to collectively as a "clan."

A landowning group of kinsmen that is autonomous politically and maintains its own system of social controls is often called a "corporate kin group." Such a group exists in perpetuity, and serves as a ceremonial group and a primary or face-to-face group, in which each individual is responsible to and for other members and they are responsible to and for him. Corporate kin groups are almost always exogamous; that is, the members of the group are forbidden to marry each other.

The groups that people develop are among the instruments by which they make use of the energy potentials in their habitat. Thus, it is neither necessary nor possible for hunter-gatherers to form corporate kin groups because their relationship with the habitat involves little investment of energy in land and because their groups must split up recurrently. But horticulturists plant seeds and must wait for crops to grow and to be harvested, and because of these different relationships with the land and other resources, they develop different kinds of groups, more suitable for coping with their habitat.

Consider a lineage, for instance. This is a corporate kin group designed to deal with the allocation of land and other resources, to maintain legal and social control, to engage in short-term political relations with other groups, and to undertake religious and ceremonial activities. Hunter-gatherers do not face the horticultural problem of allocating land and other resources; hence, lineage organization is never found among the former but is widespread among the latter in one form or another (as is clearly illustrated in Selection 2, which describes the horticultural Fijians). In subsequent selections, we will see that the organization of society implicit in a lineage system does not "fit" the religious systems of hunter-gatherers, nor their modes of maintaining order and conformity, but there are close correspondence among all these aspects of life in horticultural societies.

The solidarity implicit in a lineage organization is inseparable from kin-group ownership of the land and the individual's reliance on inter-household cooperation in his productive activities. It appears that maintenance of such an organization weakens the more intense and intimate relationships of family life. Thus the corporate group organization of horticultural societies (and others in which lineages are present) is accomplished by a tendency for family and household relationships to be eclipsed by the bonds of wider kinship. Corporate kin groups must command a strong sense of allegiance and loyalty to be effective, and these qualities are often in competition with similar sentiments toward the members of the nuclear family. As the distinguished British anthropologist Max Gluckman observes, referring to the extraordinary variety of customs and taboos affecting the relations between spouses and between parents and children in many African societies:

> I think the taboos are also important because they introduce divisions—estrangements—into the family and prevent it absorbing the wholehearted emotional allegiance of its members. Husbands

are forced apart from their wives to continued association with their own kin, and children turn to more distant kin and away from their parents. The estrangements in the family are associated with the extension of ties to wider kinship groupings. These groupings support the family, but they are also inimical to the family. And they are important in building the cohesion of the larger society. . . . Wider kinship links establish interwoven webs of kinship which unite men in allegiances, often backed by mystical sanctions, over a large area. This is their political importance. The links are economically important in that they provide aid in productive tasks and safeguards against natural disasters which always threaten groups living not much above subsistence (*Custom and Conflict in Africa*, p. 57; New York: Free Press, 1955.)

Lineages are also important among pastoralists, but the basic requirement of this technology—to further the welfare of flocks and herds—requires several fundamental adjustments in household organization. Among the most important (as illustrated in Selection 3) are seasonal changes in family organization in response to climatic change. For example, during the rainy season, when all the animals in a herd are able to drink at pools close to the homestead, it is possible for all the members of the household to live together. But when the dry season occurs, grazing has to take place over wide tracts in which the grass cover is uneven; as a result, members of the household have to disperse into the surrounding territory, often for long periods, to take advantage of available grass wherever it may be found.

There is considerable variability in family organization among horticulturists and pastoralists but much more still in agricultural and industrial societies. The reasons are both habitational and political. Agriculturists are able to exploit a greater variety of habitats than people at earlier stages of technological development, and each habitat may require a different social strategy, including different marriage and kinship systems. Politically, agriculture is almost always associated with centralized state organizations, each of which will have distinctive policies with respect to taxation, the organization of labor, law, religion, and the family. Still another source of variability in the family systems of agricultural societies is in their stratification into different groups—peasants, artisans, tradesmen, priests, political elites—living different styles of life.

The agricultural family may be quite large and include several generations, usually as a result of particular local patterns of land ownership and labor relations (as illustrated for Central Italy by Sydel Silverman in Selection 23), but more usually it is small, as in Guatemala (Selection 4). Agricultural families are almost always patrilocal. Central state organizations may try to subvert local sources of solidarity, especially those based on kinship, but such ties are tenacious and difficult to eliminate. When lineage systems atrophy under national political pressures, ceremonial or ritual kinship systems are often substituted; a case in point is *compadrazgo* described in Selection 4. This is understandable in terms of the need of cultivators—even at advanced agricultural levels—to have groups of people on whom they can rely for assistance when needed.

In industrial society, where every person barters or sells his labor individually and in which the household ceases to be a productive unit, the cooperative labor of kinsmen is no longer required; hence traditional kin groups and ceremonial kinship systems tend to dissolve. In their place is a new emphasis on "neolocal" residence, in which the married pair live separately from the parents of either spouse. This involves not only separate physical placement but also different relationships with the parental households and with the world at large. Thus adaptation to an industrial stage of development involves deep strains in the entire fabric of kinship.

And thus the evolutionary record shows how changes in a society's strategy of adaptation will result in changes in all social relationships, including family and household organization. This is especially important in understanding the connection between the styles of family life and socioeconomic status in an industrial society like England (Selection 5). The heterogeneity of contemporary industrial societies is such that it is no longer possible to speak of *the* family organization as we did for tribal societies. Instead, we must consider the several types of families in a complex society in terms of people's specific places in the socioeconomic scheme of things.

The human family has always changed as man's strategies of adaptation have changed. If we assume—as I think we must—that our present stage of development is not our last, we must also assume that further changes will occur in our family organization. But these alterations will not be uniform; they will not affect everyone in every society in the same way, because different groups will start in different socioeconomic statuses—that is, in different relationships to the society's sources of energy —and will have to adjust their family and interhousehold relationships accordingly.

Will our contemporary family organizations soon become obsolete? We may have been treated to a glimpse into the future by an incident I observed recently. Early in 1970, a faculty position was open in a major United States university, and among the people competing for this one job were a husband and wife, both with the necessary certifications and equally qualified. If an industrial strategy of adaptation required that a conjugal pair maintain only weak relations with their kinsmen, what will be the imperatives of a postindustrial adaptation for the partners in marriage themselves?

My favorite general introduction to the study of the family is William J. Goode's *World Revolution and Family Patterns* (New York: The Free Press, 1963), because it effectively captures and presents a rare sense of evolutionary history in this institutional sphere. For a more detailed study of the evolution of the Western household, a delightful book is *Centuries of Childhood*, by Philippe Ariès (New York: Vintage Books, 1967). In a similar vein is *The Image of Childhood*, by Peter Coveney (Baltimore: Penguin Books, 1967), and *Parents and Children in History*, by David Hunt (New York: Basic Books, 1970).

Two introductions to marriage and family systems in tribal societies are generally regarded as classics: *African Systems of Kinship and Marriage*, edited by A. R. Radcliffe-Brown and Daryll Forde (New York and London: Oxford University Press, 1950) and *Matrilineal Kinship*, edited by David M. Schneider and Kathleen Gough (Berkeley and Los Angeles: University of California Press, 1961). Twelve brief sketches of family systems covering almost the entire range of cultural development are presented in *The Family in Various Cultures*, by Stuart A. Queen, Robert W. Habenstein and John B. Adams (New York and Philadelphia: Lippincott, 1961). Also very useful, and more historically oriented, is *Comparative Family Systems*, edited by M. F. Nimkoff (Boston: Houghton Mifflin Company, 1965). In *Kinship and Culture*, edited by Francis L. K. Hsu (Chicago: Aldine, 1969), there are 18 essays exploring the relationship between kinship and other aspects of culture.

For a very good recent example of the debate over the social organization of Australian aboriginal groups, see "Local Group Composition among the Australian Aborigines: A Critique of the Evidence from Fieldwork Conducted since 1930," by Joseph B. Birdsell (*Current Anthropology*, 11 [1970]: 115-42). Claude Lévi-Strauss presents his point of view on marriage and kinship rules in *The Elementary Structures of Kinship* (Boston: Beacon Press paperback, 1969). The logic and grammar of these rules are discussed clearly and wittily by Robin Fox in *Kinship and Marriage: An Anthropological Perspective* (Baltimore: Penguin Books, 1967). I have explored some aspects of the effects of centralized political systems on marriage in "Ends and Means in Political Control: State Organization and the Punishment of Adultery, Incest, and Violation of Celibacy" (*American Anthropologist*, 71 [1969]: 658-87). To supplement this paper, see "The Theoretical Importance of Love," by William J. Goode (*American Sociological Review*, 24 [1959]: 38-47).

1. STABILITY AND FLEXIBILITY IN HADZA RESIDENTIAL GROUPINGS

JAMES WOODBURN

Reprinted from Richard B. Lee and Irven DeVore, editors, Man the Hunter (*Chicago: Aldine Publishing Company, 1968). Copyright © 1968 by the Wenner-Gren Foundation for Anthropological Research, Inc. James Woodburn is Lecturer in Anthropology, the London School of Economics and Political Science. His major interests include family and kinship organization and ethnographic films.*

■ We can only speculate about the families of hunter-gatherers prior to their contact with the more complex societies that provided records of their ways. Hunter-gatherers have probably been in contact with societies at other levels of adaptation for thousands of years, though their influence at each level of adaptation must have been different from the others. The Hadza described in the following selection have been encroached upon by horticulturists and pastoralists, and it is difficult to tell which elements of their family system are "purely" theirs and which have resulted from contact with expanding societies at more advanced stages. But the Hadza system described by Woodburn seems to be close to the hunting-gathering norm that is suggested by a comparison with other such groups in other parts of Africa, in North and South America, and in Asia.

Unlike groups in more barren territories, such as the Shoshoneans of Nevada and the Eskimos, the Hadza have an abundance of vegetable and animal foods. Nevertheless, they display the hunter-gatherer pattern of moving around a great deal, fluid relationships, an absence of exclusive rights over resources and of institutions of authority. Woodburn makes clear that the territorial instability of Hadza groups is greater than ecological considerations would seem to require. But the Hadza way of life is itself quite stable, and family and wider kin relations are important aspects of this stability.

Woodburn focuses primarily on Hadza kinship and marriage relations ; they typify those of hunter-gatherers generally. Here we see an accommodation to the hunter-gatherer strategy in which couples and their young children are not members of a camp because of their attachment to a set of resources or to a leader who commands allegiance. Instead, family units move among camps in which they have kinsmen, and we see how a family's shifting relations with other family units—wider kin ties providing a center of gravity—hold down the population pressure on available resources.

In concluding this essay, Woodburn points to the need for standards by which group organization can be compared in different societies. Note the quantitative procedures he uses as a basis for arriving at his generalized picture of Hadza marriage, family, and kinship relations. The beginning student will find that he can readily apply these criteria in trying to understand how the same social relationships are organized in our own society and as a frame of reference for the materials about different societies in subsequent selections.

One of the best studies of family adaptations among hunter-gatherers—and a model for such research—is "The Great Basin Shoshonean Indians : An Example of a Family Level of Sociocultural Integration," which is Chapter 6 of *Theory of Culture Change : The Methodology of Multilinear Evolution*, by Julian H. Steward (Urbana : University of Illinois Press, 1955 ; reprinted as Selection 5 of *The Cultural Present*). An excellent short monograph describing marriage and family relationships among a group of hunter-gatherers is *The Tiwi of North Australia*, by C. W. M. Hart and Arnold R. Pilling (New York : Holt, Rinehart and Winston, 1960). Another good short monograph is *The Eskimo of North Alaska*, by Norman A. Chance (New York : Holt, Rinehart and Winston, 1966). A more extensive report of kinship and marriage, as well as other spheres of activity, is in *A Black Civilization : A Study of an Australian Tribe*, by W. Lloyd Warner (New York, Evanston, and London : Harper Torchbooks, 1964). ■

IN ANOTHER PAPER, "An Introduction to Hadza Ecology," also published in the volume *Man the Hunter*, I describe how the Eastern Hadza obtain their food relatively easily by hunting and gathering. Their nutritional needs are met quickly, and without much effort, coordination, or cooperation. In this paper the characteristics of Hadza residential groupings are briefly described. This account is only an introduction. A full description with the necessary supporting numerical data will be given in my forthcoming monograph on the Hadza.

Hadza residential groupings are open, flexible, and highly variable in composition. They have no institutionalized leadership and, indeed, no corporate identity. They do not own territory and clear-cut jurally defined modes of affiliation of individuals to residential groupings do not exist. The use of the term "band," with its connotations of territorial ownership, leadership, corporateness, and fixed membership is inappropriate for Hadza residential entities and I prefer to use the term "camp," meaning simply the set of persons who happen to be living together at one place at one time.

I consider first the area in which the Hadza live and the geographical regions into which they divide it. The nature of the camps, their composition and their flexibility are then examined. Synchronic and diachronic census material is presented to show the way in which groupings change through time and to demonstrate that in spite of their flexibility and variability, important underlying regularities persist.

The principal purpose of the paper is simply descriptive, but my intention is also to stress that we cannot hope to understand the residential arrangements of hunters and gatherers, especially those with flexible residential arrangements, unless we make use of numerical data, in particular diachronic numerical data.

THE GEOGRAPHICAL DIVISIONS OF THE COUNTRY OF THE EASTERN HADZA

The area the Eastern Hadza occupy consisted in the recent past of well over 1,000 square miles of land. Until the 1930s the Hadza had this country to themselves, but then two villages of outsiders were founded at fertile places right inside Hadza country and within a few years their population far outnumbered that of the Hadza. At the same time there has been constant loss of land on the edge of their country to neighboring tribes and more especially to the Iraqw. But the serious incursions are all relatively recent and had not had any effect on the Hadza system of land tenure until the Hadza were settled in 1964 and 1965.

The Hadza commonly use certain terms to refer to regions of their country and for the people associated with these regions. For example, *Mangola* is used for an area around the Mangola River. This area cannot be precisely defined, for the use of the term depends partly on context. If one asks a Hadza living far from Mangola about the whereabouts of some person and is told that he lives at Mangola, this means that he is living somewhere within an area of some hundreds of square miles around the Mangola River. On the other hand, if one is told by a man living only five miles away from the Mangola River that some person is living at Mangola, this normally means that the person is living within a mile or two of the lower reaches of the river.

The word *Sipunga*, meaning the region around Sipunga Mountain, has similar variations in meaning according to context. A third term *Tli'ika* (literally "the west") is commonly used to refer to a stretch of high ground running northeast from Isanzu between the Yaida Valley and Lake Eyasi to about half way above the lake where the fourth and final region, *Han!abi* (literally "the rocks"), begins. Han!abi, which is, as its name suggests, a mountainous, rocky area, extends along the same ridge between Lake Eyasi and the Yaida plains up to the mountains overlooking the Mangola River which are generally considered to be part of the Mangola region. Unlike Mangola and Sipunga, neither Tli'ika nor Han!abi have a focal point in a single geographical feature, but all four regions resemble each other in having no clear-cut boundary. To draw boundaries would be quite artificial; the regions grade into each other.

On the other hand, no part of the country in which the Hadza live to the east of Lake Eyasi lies outside the areas to which these terms may be applied when used with their widest connotations. We cannot separate them off from each other, but between them they cover the whole country. Only the extensive open Yaida plains are outside the classification, but this is not country in which people live. Hadza never live in the open plain, but only in the bordering thickets and hills which fall within the named areas.

The division of Hadza country into four named, roughly defined localities bears some relation to Hadza social arrangements. At any one time each of these areas is likely to contain between 50 and 150 Hadza. One commonly talks of the *Sipunganebe* (people of Sipunga), *Mangolanebe* (people of Mangola), *Tli'ikanebe* (people of the west) and *Han!abicebe* (people of the rocks). These names do not refer to a fixed body of people in each area but simply to the aggregate of individuals who at any particular time or in any particular context are associated with one locality rather than another.

Each of these areas contains sufficient sources of food and water to maintain its inhabitants throughout the year and many people, especially the elderly, restrict their nomadic movements for years at a stretch largely to a single one of these four areas. At the peak of the dry season, when water is scarce and when the berries of *Cordia gharaf*. Ehrenb. and *Salvadora persica* L. ripen in huge quantities near to these few sources of water, the majority of the inhabitants in each of these areas may be found concentrated in a few large camps within perhaps two or three miles or less of each other and close to the berries and water supplies of their area. I have never heard of any occasion on which all the inhabitants of one of these areas joined together to form a single camp, although their mode of subsistence would not of itself make this impossible.

In one of the four areas, Sipunga, there is a marked cleavage into two divisions, one lying close to the Sipunga mountains and the other centering on Yaida River. For much of the year the camps of the Yaida division are far from those of the Sipunga division, but at the peak of the dry season most of the people living near Yaida usually come to live in camps in close association with the camps of the Sipunga division among the berry trees under Sipunga Mountain. The division of the country into four areas is conspicuously linked with the fact that, wherever they may be in the wet season, camps are reasonably clearly grouped into four widely separated clusters at the peak of the dry season.

People, singly and in groups, move freely from region to region. Any individual Hadza may live, hunt, and gather anywhere he or she

likes without any sort of restriction and without asking permission from anyone. Neither individuals nor groups hold exclusive rights over natural resources, over land and its ungarnered produce, and there is never any question of people who have long been associated with a particular area having exclusive or even prior rights there. Even the expansion of neighboring agricultural and pastoral tribes into Hadza country is not opposed, and each year much land is lost.

The inhabitants at any particular time of each of these regions do not share a joint estate; nor do they unite to perform any activity; nor do they acknowledge any bond uniting them in opposition to other areas. They cannot be described as constituting a group and to use the term "band" or "horde" to describe them would be completely inappropriate.

CAMP SIZE, COMPOSITION AND NOMADIC MOVEMENT

At any time, the 400 or so Hadza who lead a nomadic hunting and gathering life to the east of Lake Eyasi are living in camps containing very varied numbers of people—from a single person to almost a hundred people. The average camp contains about eighteen adults. But the members of a camp do not constitute a stable unit, either in place, in numbers, or in composition. People do not camp continuously at a particular site for more than a few weeks and they usually move much more often. At the time members of a camp all move, they may go together to a new site; they may split up and form camps at two or more new sites; they may go as a body to join some existing camp, or they may divide, some joining an existing camp and others building a camp at a new site. Even while people are living together in a camp at a particular site, the composition of the camp changes: some people move in and some move out. In spite of this flexibility, there are interesting consistencies in the composition of camps which will be described later.

The individual members of a camp at a particular time are not present on account of their common attachment to a body of resources; nor does a camp have an acknowledged leader to whom common allegiance is owed. A camp at any particular time is often known by the name of a well-known man living in it at that time (for example, /ets'a ma Durugida—Durugida's camp). But this indicates only that the man is well enough known for his name to be a useful label, and not that he acts either as a leader or as a representative of the camp. At any particular time a camp is an agglomeration of individual members tied to each other by a variety of kinship and affinal ties.

In my doctoral thesis I use data derived from two censuses, which I describe as my synchronic and diachronic censuses, to establish which relationships of kinship and affinity are important in residential arrangements. For the synchronic census, I took down particulars of the membership of ten camps in the Sipunga and Mangola regions in June and July, 1960. These camps contained approximately 60 per cent of the Eastern Hadza. The diachronic census consists of a record of the changes and consistencies in the composition of a series of camps. Taking one particular old widow named Bunga, the mother of two married sons and two married daughters, I recorded, on 25 separate occasions spread over more than three years, the people who were living in the same camp as she was.

Bunga was, in the estimation of the Hadza, a respectable and conventional woman who lived regularly, by Hadza standards, with her close kin and affines and who moved camp less frequently than many other people, especially younger people. On all 25 occasions, the camps were in the Sipunga region. The particulars of the members of these camps tend therefore to stress the continuities rather than the discontinuities in Hadza residential groups. Yet even with this emphasis on continuity, there were radical differences in the size and composition of these camps. The minimum number of adults present was 3 and the maximum was 37. There were fewer than 10 adults present on four occasions, between 10 and 19 adults present on twelve occasions, between 20 and 29 adults present on seven occasions and between 30 and 39 adults present on the remaining two occasions. A total of 67 adults, more than a quarter of the entire Eastern Hadza adult population, lived with Bunga in at least one of these camps. The Hadza apply the word huyeti (visitor) freely to anyone living in an area in which he does not normally live or living with people with whom he does not normally associate. But the use of the term differs according to the speaker and to the context, and it is quite impossible to divide up the members of a camp into those that are residents and those that are huyeti. However, an examination of the diachronic census does permit the isolation of a set of people who were regularly associated through time, and the nature of the bonds linking these persons will be mentioned later.

With the rich food resources of their country and their knowledge of how to exploit these resources, it may seem hard to understand why the Hadza live in small, unstable nomadic groups which move at frequent intervals and constantly change in size and composition. In my monograph on the Hadza I shall discuss the way in which individuals and groups move from place to place far more frequently than is strictly necessary if movement is seen simply as a means of providing the best possible access to supplies of food and water. We ourselves are so tied down by, among other things, the sheer quantity of our possessions, that we with justification regard the movement of a household from one place to another as difficult and not to be attempted without substantial reason. But we must be careful not to allow our ethnocentrism to creep into our ethnography. The Hadza, like many other nomadic people, value movement highly and individuals and groups move to satisfy the slightest whim. Their possessions are so few and are so easily carried that movement is no problem. Indeed people often find it easier to move to the place where a game animal has been killed than to carry the meat back to their camp. The Hadza may move camp to get away from a site where illness has broken out, to obtain raw materials—stone for smoking pipes, wood for arrow shafts, poison for arrows, herbal medicines and so on, to trade, to gamble, to allow the realignment of the huts in a camp after changes in camp composition, to segregate themselves from those with whom they are in conflict, and for many other reasons. People do often move primarily because food and water are less readily available than they would like; and even where some other motive is present, they will of course at the same time try to improve their access to food and water. However, movement normally takes place long before it is essential, long before shortages have become in any way serious.

The variations in the size and in the composition of camps again cannot be interpreted in simple ecological terms. There are no grounds for suggesting that the constant and considerable changes in camp size and composition neatly parallel similarly frequent and substantial fluctuations in the available sources of food or in the arrangements used to procure food. At any season a wide variety of sizes of camp is ecologically viable. During the wet season, camps are, on average, smaller than in the dry season, but not, I think, because of any important difference in the rigor of the environmental pressures in the two seasons. Perhaps the most important single factor creating the larger camps of the dry season is that at this time of the year more large game is being killed. The meat of a large animal is by custom widely distributed through the camp and people tend to congregate in camps where there are skilled and successful hunters. The optimum size, considering this factor alone, will be the largest number of persons who can share an average-sized game animal and feel that they have had an acceptable quantity of meat. In the wet season, when few large animals are killed, there is less incentive for people to congregate in large camps and the divisive effects of quarrels tend to keep the size of the camps small. The general emphasis on seasonal polarity mentioned briefly in "An Introduction to Hadza Ecology" is also relevant. Many other factors, some ecological, some not, affect camp size, but cannot be discussed here. The limits on camp size set by the availability of food and water and the techniques used to obtain them are very broad and permit wide fluctuations; wide fluctuations in fact occur.

We must beware of any tendency to treat fixed, permanent ties linking together aggregates of people as normal, and loose, impermanent bonds as abnormal and requiring special explanation. Because the Hadza do not join in groups to assert exclusive rights over portions of land or other property, because they do not unite to defend either resources or their own persons, because they cooperate very little with each other in their subsistence tasks, there is little to bind individuals to specific other individuals. People do depend on obtaining meat from other people, but they are entitled to a share of meat simply by being in a particular camp at a time when a large animal is killed there and do not have to rely on specific categories of kin or other specific individuals to supply them. With a few important exceptions, which will be described below, people depend simply on living with *any* other Hadza and not on living with a particular set of people standing in specific relationships towards them. They range widely, associating themselves now with one collection of people, now with another, according to their desires and whims of the moment.

REGULARITIES IN CAMP COMPOSITION

I cannot here give much of the detail which is set out at length in my doctoral thesis and which will be published in my forthcoming monograph about the regularities that occur in camp composition. But the more important regularities are as follows:

MARRIED COUPLES

The Hadza refer to any man and woman who cohabit and who publicly acknowledge their cohabitation as being husband and wife, whether or not any ceremony of marriage had taken place, and whether or not the man and the woman accept the obligations which husbands and wives normally accept towards each other and each other's kin. This is not to say that these obligations are of little consequence; they are, in fact, exceedingly important and a marriage is most unlikely to last unless they are accepted.

Ceasing to live together, even for a matter of a few weeks, puts a marriage in jeopardy. A husband goes away on a visit to some other part of the country without his wife at his peril. He may well find that when he returns she has either married someone else or that she has repudiated him by putting on the dress of an unmarried girl to indicate her availability for marriage. People who are stated by informants to be married are therefore almost always co-resident with their spouses. In the synchronic census I encountered 115 spouses of monogamous marriages and of these 112 were living with their spouses. The remaining three were married according to Hadza informants; that is, informants believed that the separations were temporary and that the couples would resume cohabitation. All three of the marriages were, however, demonstrably unstable. Separation, even for short periods, may be both an indication that the marriage is not entirely successful and a contributory factor to its eventual breakdown. At the same time, not all separations are necessarily either symptomatic or damaging; spouses of successful marriages do occasionally live apart for a while, but they risk their marriages by doing so.

Compared with many other societies, marriage is relatively unstable. The calculated divorce rate is 49 per 1,000 years of marriage, though this is only a very rough approximation. Few figures for other East African societies are available in this form. The Amba have a rate of 31.5 but no figures are available for tribes near to the Hadza. The rate for England and Wales, 1950-52 was 2.8 and for the United States, 1949-51, it was 10.4.

In comparison with other Hadza relationships, the noteworthy aspect of the marital relationship is not its instability, but on the contrary its stability and strength. A marriage is broken by divorce on average only about once in twenty years of married life. In general, most Hadza men settle down and live for many years with a particular wife; to sustain the marriage they do not leave her for long on her own and they fulfill onerous obligations, described below, to her and also to her mother.

Once they marry for the first time, usually by their early twenties, very few men live for long unmarried. After the death of a wife or permanent separation from her, the husband will soon remarry. In the ten camps of the synchronic census, there was only one man who had previously been married who then lacked a wife. On the other hand there were thirteen previously married women who at the time of the synchronic census were unmarried. Of these, eight were past the menopause.

A few men have more than one wife. This complicates their residential arrangements and their position cannot be discussed here.

PARENTS AND CHILDREN

My census data shows that children whose parents are separated almost invariably live with their mother. In adult life both men and women often live with their parents, but the emphasis is on residence with the mother. If the parents are separated or the mother is dead, it is unusual to find a man or a woman living in the same camp as the father.

Both husband and wife value co-residence with their mothers. However, residence with the wife's mother is considerably more frequent. Considering only monogamous marriages in which the spouses were living together, there were in the synchronic census 28 husbands and 34 wives with mothers alive. Twelve (that is, 43 per cent) of these husbands and 23 (68 per cent) of the wives were living with their mothers. But the emphasis on residence with the wife's mother is greater than might appear from these figures.

Let us examine the residence of those monogamous individuals who are co-resident with their spouses and who have *both* a living mother and a living mother-in-law. In the synchronic census there were 42 such people (that is, 21 couples):

15 couples were living with the wife's mother
7 couples were living with the husband's mother
4 couples were not living with either mother

But five of these couples were living in camps containing both mother and mother-in-law. From these five cases, no indication can be gained of any difference between the attraction of living with the wife's mother and the attraction of living with the husband's mother. If these cases are omitted, the figures are as follows:

10 couples were living with the wife's mother alone
2 couples were living with the husband's mother alone
4 couples were not living with either mother

In other words the monogamous couples of the synchronic census who were faced with a choice between living with the husband's mother and living with the wife's mother, had exercised their choice in favor of the wife's mother five times as often as in favor of the husband's mother. Taken alone, these figures are so small as to be worth very little. I quote them here because they are consistent with observations and figures collected at other times and because they illustrate, I think, the sort of data on residence which we need (in a more detailed form) if we are to compare the residential arrangements of hunters and gatherers.

A high valuation is placed on residence with the mothers of husband and wife, yet four couples were found living in camps in which neither mother was present. As it happens, in each of these four cases, there are unusual circumstances and in quite a high proportion of cases observed at other times in which a couple is living away from both mothers, there is an obvious reason to account for their behavior.

The diachronic census data support the findings from the synchronic census and allow the matter to be taken an important step further. It enables us to see whether decisions about which mother to live with are lasting. In my diachronic census, only one couple among those with both mothers alive who lived for a time with the husband's mother did not at some other period live with the wife's mother. In this one case the wife's mother was living not among the Hadza but with a neighboring tribe.

Marriage involves an obligation, and one which is observed, to live with the wife's mother and, except in special circumstances, the only time a couple with both mothers alive will live for long away from the wife's mother is when they are living with the husband's mother. For a marriage to survive, a husband must live regularly not merely with his wife but also in the same camp as her mother. If his own mother is alive he and his wife will usually (but not always) visit her from time to time. There is no question of any obligation to live with her.

A man has important property obligations toward his wife and his mother-in-law. Long strings of bridewealth beads should be, and usually are, given by the bridegroom to his parents-in-law. They are taken and worn by the mother-in-law around her waist. Thereafter, throughout the life of the marriage, the husband should keep his wife and mother-in-law supplied with meat and with trade goods. Almost all trade is carried on by men; women rely mainly for access to these goods not on their own kin but on their husbands and sons-in-law. Beads,

tobacco, and cloth are especially keenly desired and demanded. Husbands cannot afford to fail too often if they wish to preserve their marriages.

The pattern of dyadic ties that I have described links persons into a grouping which has the same genealogical composition as a matrilineal or matrilocal extended family, that is a woman and her married daughter (or daughters), together with their husbands, and their unmarried offspring of both sexes. In a few cases in which women have survived to a great age, the grouping will contain three generations of married women: the apical woman will have both married daughter(s) and married granddaughter(s) in her grouping. These groupings are not joint or extended families since they are not corporate groups and do not have a recognized head. I prefer to use a neutral term and to refer to them as "simple residential units."

By stating that a simple residential unit has no recognized head, I mean that there is no institutionalized position of head of the unit, no person who exercises authority over other members of the unit whether by virtue of his or her genealogical position or by any other qualification. In some units one or more individuals may stand out as influential persons, but in other units this is not the case. However, the unit does have a genealogical focus in the person of the apical woman. We might, therefore, describe the units as matrifocal, but even this is, in some cases and contexts, misleading. Sometimes, especially if the wife's mother is old or of weak character, has no husband, and has only one married daughter, it can be seen that the mother is aligning herself residentially with her married daughter and her son-in-law, rather than they with her. But usually it is the mother who, more than any other person, serves as the genealogical focus around which a simple residential unit clusters. At any particular time a camp will usually contain one or more simple residential units together with a very few people who are not members of these units. When two or more units are present in a single camp, they may be linked by kinship and affinal ties or they may not. If no tie links them, they are most unlikely to stay together long. Units which are regularly residentially associated are usually bound together by a number of close kinship or affinal ties. Not even the more important ties linking together units—such as the tie between a woman and her married son or the tie between a pair of siblings—are very highly valued or involve significant property obligations. The kinship and affinal ties of the apical woman are temporally prior to those of the junior members of the unit and they tend to be more often used in establishing links between the component units of the camp.

CONCLUSION

The flexibility and variability of Hadza residential arrangements are fundamental; the regularities within the flux that is Hadza society emerge clearly only from an examination of residential arrangements through time. Such regularities as do exist are linked with the continuing property obligations of certain pairs of persons to each other, above all husband and wife, and mother-in-law and son-in-law. In Hadza society, individuals are bound to each other by dyadic property ties between relatively few categories of persons, and the type of unit that is a simple product of these ties must be distinguished from the corporate domestic and other groups, whose members cooperate, possess important joint interests, and accept authority within the group, which are characteristic of most small-scale societies.

The highly flexible social arrangements of the Hadza are by no means unique among hunters and gatherers. At this symposium, data has been presented on a number of peoples whose residential arrangements show some striking similarities to the Hadza. For instance, the !Kung Bushmen, the Mbuti, the Ik, the Dogrib, the Netsilik Eskimos, and even the Gidjingali of northern Australia all live in groupings that change frequently in size and composition.

The widespread occurrence of this flexibility brings us back to the problem of field method. The analysis of group structure is a crucial area of research, and, if comparative studies are to be of any value, it is essential that the field workers concerned develop a common body of techniques. One of the most important results to come out of the symposium on Man the Hunter may be the development of measures of general use for describing and analyzing the open and fluid social groups of hunting and gathering peoples.

2. LAND USE AND THE EXTENDED FAMILY IN MOALA, FIJI

MARSHALL D. SAHLINS

Reproduced by permission of the American Anthropological Association from American Anthropologist, *Vol. 59, No. 2, 1957. Marshall D. Sahlins is Professor of Anthropology, University of Michigan. His principal research interests are cultural ecology, primitive economics, and peoples of the Pacific. He is the author of* Social Stratification in Polynesia, Evolution and Culture (*with Elman R. Service and others*), Moala: Culture and Nature on a Fijian Island, *and* Tribesmen.

■ A particular mode of acquiring a livelihood involves more than the mere extraction of food from the habitat; it also sets into motion a complex set of rules concerning the division of labor, problems of ownership and production, the allocation and control of resources, and legal relationships. In the next selection, we encounter an example of this intricacy in Fiji. A horticultural strategy leads to different forms of family organization when people maintain different relationships to the land that they cultivate, as when they live far or near to their plots of land. In the next selection we consider two groups on a Fijian island; members of one group live distant from their lands while the others live close by them. Extended family organization predominates in the first group; nuclear family organization characterizes the second. Examining the two patterns in an adaptational framework,

Marshall Sahlins cogently shows how extended family organization in the group that lives far from its cultivated plots is excellently suited to its spatial circumstances.

An extended family constitutes a labor pool whose members, among other activities, produce and consume jointly. Land is owned by larger social units; families and individuals only have rights to use portions of the land. Although cultivated plots are not far from their villages as the crow flies, Fiji's terrain makes them difficult to reach. As a result, cultivators erect huts near their fields where they remain while clearing, planting, weeding, and harvesting, and they are away from their settlements during these work periods. Because of its size, the extended family can release some of its members for cultivating activities and allow others to remain in the village to care for local gardens, oversee the children, and the like. In contrast, the group that lives near its garden plots has no reason to maintain the traditional extended family system, and here we find nuclear family groups.

Sahlins also shows that Fijian extended families split up every few generations when they become too large. Although the lands owned by larger social units are not subdivided, control over them is decentralized when the extended family segments and each unit cultivates its own plots as a team. Sahlins also shows that the acculturative influence of British colonization cannot account for nuclear family organization in the group whose members live close to their lands because these influences are also found among those who maintain extended family organization. The principal factor' that distinguishes the two groups is the distance between their homes and the land they cultivate; in this light, as Sahlins shows, family organization must be regarded as an adaptive instrument of land utilization and exploitation.

"The Changing Family among the Bantu Kavirondo," by Gunter Wagner (Supplement to *Africa*, 12, No. 1, 1939 [Memorandum 18, International Institute of African Languages and Culture]) provides an excellent analysis of horticultural family organization from an adaptational point of view. An illuminating study of horticultural household and kinship relationships is provided in *We, the Tikopia*, by Raymond Firth (London: Allen & Unwin, 1936). For information about tradition and change among a Southern Bantu tribe (the Kgatla), the interested reader can profitably consult *Married Life in an African Tribe*, by Isaac Schapera (Evanston: Ill.: Northwestern University Press, 1966). Good studies along the same lines are *Kinship and Marriage in a New Guinea Village*, by H. Ian Hogbin (London: The Athlone Press, 1963), and two books by Monica Wilson, *Good Company: A Study of Nyakyusa Age-Villages* (Boston: Beacon Press, 1963) and *Rituals of Kinship among the Nyakyusa* (London: Oxford University Press, 1957). ■

THE HYPOTHESIS of this paper is that the traditional extended family organization of Moala Island, Fiji, depends for its continued existence on particular customs of land tenure and land use; that when these customs change, the familial form tends to change. An analysis of the family in two contemporary villages will show that in one, Keteira, the traditional family structure has been largely maintained, while in the second, Naroi, it barely survives. It is submitted that exploitation of scattered land resources in Keteira is responsible for the continuance of the extended family there, while dependence on land only in the environs of the village has contributed to the emergence of the independent nuclear family in Naroi. It is concluded that the patterns of land use are necessary determining conditions of familial structure in Moala.

To demonstrate the proposition, I will first describe the composition and operation of the traditional Moalan extended family. The familial forms present in Keteira and Naroi will then be analyzed. Finally, the relationship between family types and land usage will be described, and conclusions drawn.

Moala is an island of volcanic origin, some 24 square miles in area. It is quite hilly; the highest peak is 1,535 feet. The hills descend sharply to rocky or mangrove-bordered coasts, leaving relatively little flat land on the island. The population, numbering approximately 1,200 (all Fijian with the exception of three Chinese shop-keepers), is settled in eight coastal villages. Basic subsistence activities are the growing of root crops, taro, yams, sweet potato, and sweet manioc, by slash-and-burn techniques. Some wet taro is also grown. Copra and money have become increasingly important in the local economy, especially since the beginning of World War II. The two villages considered here, Naroi and Keteira, are located at the extreme northeastern end and on the eastern side of the island, respectively (see map). Naroi is the largest Moalan village and the home of the paramount chief of the island, Roko Tui

Moala. Keteira is about one-third as large and boasts no important chief. However, neither differences in population nor the relative political standing of the two villages has any particular bearing on the present analysis.

THE TRADITIONAL MOALAN FAMILY

This description of the traditional Moalan family is built from observation and from

will reside with his wife's family after marriage. This arrangement, which can continue for life, most often occurs when the wife has no brother to carry on her family. If a man comes from another island or is orphaned, he might also live with his wife's family.

The extended family occupies a compound of closely grouped living houses sharing a single cook house. Each living house holds one of the nuclear family constituents of the extended family. Informants state that in the "old times" more than one married pair often lived in a

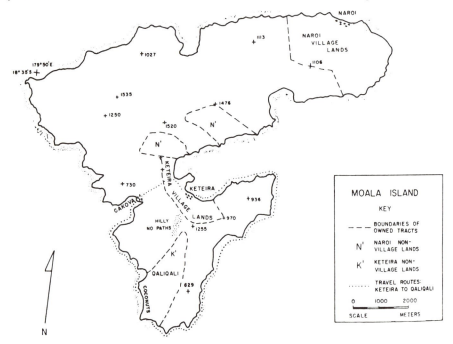

informants' opinions, ideas, and ideals. The term "traditional" does not necessarily denote "aboriginal." Moala has been subject to European influences for over a century, and to Tongan influences for an even longer period. In its essentials, the family pattern described here is almost certainly of great antiquity, but there have been minor changes in house and hearth arrangements over the past two or three centuries.

In the local dialect the traditional family may be designated *vuvale* or *vale* ("house"). It is of the patrilocal extended variety, usually composed of a man, his wife, his unmarried daughters and sons, and married sons with their wives and children. Occasionally a man

house, but this practice was made illegal by an early (1877) British regulation. While there is no evidence that the regulation was ever rigorously enforced—and it was later rescinded —nowadays each married pair and their offspring almost invariably occupy a separate living house. A single, common hearth has always been a feature of the extended family, although in pre-British times it may have been located in one of the living houses rather than in a distinct cook house. The Government also legislated that each living house should have a separate cook house, but despite prosecutions under the regulation, this has never become a customary practice in Moala. Not only does an entire extended family share a common cook house, but the group takes its meals in common, either in the cook house or in one of the living houses.

The extended family is firmly organized by a system of internal ranking based on generation and birth order. The father is leader of the family, followed by his children in order of birth. In pre-Christian times, polygyny was practiced (especially by chiefs), in which case children took precedence first by the order of marriage of their mothers and then, between

the kin terminologies of reference and address among males of the extended family. This is true everywhere in Moala, despite the fact that the words used for kin designations may vary from village to village. Status titles such as *Roko* or *Ratu*, qualifying terms such as *levu* and *lailai* ("big" and "little"), and the use of teknonomy as a sign of respect all help to express the relative rank of any pair of males in the family. I should stress that the older-younger terminological distinctions which indicate relative rank

TABLE 1

KIN TERMS FOR MALES IN THE EXTENDED FAMILY; MAN SPEAKING

Relation to Ego	Terms of Address		Terms of Reference	
	Naroi	*Keteira*	*Naroi*	*Keteira*
Father	Ratu*	Tata	Tamaqu	Tamaqu
Father's older brother	Ratu levu ("Big father") or Roko† *name*	Ratu	Tamaqu levu ("Big father")	Tamaqu levu ("Big father")
Father's younger brother	as father	as father	Tamaqu lailai ("Little father")	Tamaqu lailai ("Little father")
Older brother and father's older brothers' sons	Roko *name*	teknonomy,‡ "Father of so and so"	Tuakaqu	Tuakaqu or teknonomy, "Father of so and so"
Younger brother and father's younger brothers' sons	by name	by name	Taciqu	Taciqu

* "Ratu" is also a title used in addressing people of high rank, especially in the Bauan dialect of Fijian.
† "Roko" is another status term, reputedly ancient in the Moalan dialect.
‡ It is improper to address a superior by name only, hence teknonomy is used here as an indication of respect. Note the distinction thereby made between older and younger brothers and between father's older brothers' sons and father's younger brother's sons.

full siblings, by birth order. The principles of ranking regulate succession to family headship. Here we can focus our attention on the males of the family, since females rarely become family heads and moreover, daughters can be expected to leave the group upon marriage. The oldest son will accede to family leadership at his father's death, and indeed gradually usurps the prerogatives of headship during his father's old age. Should the oldest son die or be disqualified from succession by personality defects, his younger brothers become eligible in the order of their birth. This ranking system and succession pattern is reflected in the kin terminology appropriate between males of an extended family as described in Table 1.

As the table indicates, distinctions of seniority (based on birth order) are consistently made in

do not as consistently apply to more distant classificatory brothers and fathers than are listed in the table.

The wives of brothers of the extended family should address each other as sisters, but they usually make no rank distinctions in terminology since they are almost invariably of different natal groups. The relations among women married into a family reflect their husbands' rank, but aside from the wife of the family head, who leads the women's affairs, this ranking is not of great significance. A father treats his daughters-in-law as of approximately equal status. A man considers both older and younger brothers' wives as "secondary" wives, able to perform all the household duties of his own wife in her absence. However, sexual intercourse with brothers' wives is expressly forbidden, nor is there any leviritic marriage. If a man dies, his widow and children may simply remain with his extended family, but she may also return to her natal group or remarry. If she leaves, she takes her immature children with her, the father's family keeping older children and later reclaiming the children taken by their mother.

Ranking within the extended family is not simply a matter of kin terminology. Also involved is a complex system of etiquette which governs behavior of people of different status in the system. The behavior of senior and junior members of the family toward each other parallels in specific detail that appropriate between chiefs and people of inferior status. Chiefly etiquette is in many respects an elaborate version of familial etiquette. In fact, the genealogical position of the chief, as scion of the main line of a common descent which embraces his people, is identical in principle to the genealogical position of the head of the family relative to the junior members. The similarity goes further: a younger brother may be described as the *kaisi* of an older brother, and the older is *turaga* to him—the more common referents of the terms "kaisi" and "turaga" being "people of low status" and "chiefs" respectively. Relative status in the family is symbolized by many customary rules of every-day behavior. For example, in their common meals, father and sons are seated at the "upper" end of the eating mat according to rank; the higher the rank, the closer to the position of high status toward the rear of the house. They are served in rank order by the women, who, with the immature children, eat afterwards. So also in any gathering of men of a family under one roof, the higher one's status, the nearer he may sit toward the rear of the house. Like the relationships between Fijian chiefs and commoners, there is a distinct atmosphere of reserve between a man and his younger brothers (although less so between fathers and sons). In a family gathering, especially one involving a serious discussion, a younger brother or young son will not venture an opinion until he is asked; he generally speaks only when spoken to. This is not to say that family gatherings are drab affairs, but they are not often very gay. It is common for the reserve between brothers to amount to what is practically an avoidance relationship. The Moalans say, and

I have observed it to be true, that it is "easier" to be with cross-cousins (terminologically and behaviorially distinct from brothers) or distant brothers than with full siblings.

Nevertheless, the traditional extended family is a unit of considerable solidarity. In village affairs it frequently acts as a collectivity. Before the firm establishment of British law, the family as a whole bore the responsibility of making amends if one of its members committed a wrong against another person of the community. By the same token, a man's extended family was his first line of retaliation if a wrong were committed against him. Until quite recently, it was difficult to limit a fist fight to just two opponents.

The fundamental activities of the extended family are economic: the members form a labor pool; property and produce are pooled in providing for the common hearth; and the internal ranking scheme is primarily a means of organizing production and distribution. The women contribute a great deal to extended family living. They care for the children, keep the houses in order, prepare meals (which sometimes involves gathering firewood and vegetable greens), make mats, do most of the fishing, and collect shellfish, sea slugs, and the like. The women are organized as a cooperating labor unit, each contributing her part to the day's work. It is the role of the wife of the senior male to decide the daily work, and to delegate and apportion the labor accordingly. The most strenuous jobs, such as net fishing, generally go to the younger women, but the particular activities of any woman may vary from day to day.

The men also form a labor pool. The men's primary tasks are gardening, housebuilding, and some fishing. In earlier times, the men of an extended family often formed a work unit for house-building, clearing land, and firing it, digging irrigated taro patches, and planting and weeding gardens of yams, sweet potato, taro, and other crops. Nowadays, some of these tasks are done by suprafamilial organizations such as the village, although it is still common for members of an extended family to work together as a single labor group. When working as a unit the men are directed by the family head—father or eldest brother. But even when not working together, they act as members of a single production group since all their economic activities are directed toward providing for the entire family. On a given day any number of tasks might be apportioned among the men, such as planting, weeding, or harvesting certain gardens, bringing in food for the next day's meals or for a feast contribution, attending to business in the village or in another village, and so forth. The regulation and coordination of the men's daily activities is the most important function of the family head. At the morning meal, or perhaps the night before, he divides the day's work. Again, the heaviest burdens usually fall to the youngest. The younger sons and brothers are conceived of as the strong arms of the family; their primary duties are to serve and provide for their elders. The working sphere of the elders is generally confined to the village and its environs. Ideally, the head of a large extended family should do little other than supervise the division of labor, drink kava, and sleep. Actually he will often work in the gardens, since a knowledge of familial resources is required of him in order to coordinate the men's work properly and efficiently. When the family head is too enfeebled by age to work in the "bush," he must abdicate his position of leadership in favor of his oldest son.

The traditional extended family pools its property resources as well as its labor resources. Each mature man has a yam garden, taro patches, and plots of other plants which he calls his own, but the products are not his to dispose of. All gardens of family members are subject to the control (*lewa*) of the family head. He determines where and (formerly) when gardens are to be planted, when they are to be weeded, and when crops are to be harvested. Since the food produced is for a common hearth, and since control of the plots is centralized, the various gardens are in effect joint property. As one informant puts it, "We are planting for one pot. The gardens are separate, but they are as one garden. Any one of us can and does take without permission from any of these gardens." Very often the gardens of the extended family are quite close to each other. Extended families tend to plant gardens of each of the major crops in distinct areas, with no other family's gardens intervening in these areas.

The houses that make up the family com-

pound are similarly owned. The husband of the married pair occupying each house is considered the house owner, but all houses in the compound are subject to the decisions of the family head as to who is to live in them, the rearrangement of occupants, and the like. Household animals, pigs and chickens, are today owned in the same way; they are considered the property of a man and his wife, but control over them can be exercised by the leader of the extended family. Nowadays, the extended family head and his wife occasionally have full possession and control of all domestic animals, and other married pairs in the group have none. I cannot say with certainty which of these usages is older. Productive property such as canoes or fishing nets may be considered personal goods, but use is shared throughout the family.

While simple pooling of goods is the major form of distribution within the family, there is also a type of distribution which operates specifically between individuals. Here rank considerations are important. Any goods or services needed by seniors may be demanded from juniors or, in the case of goods, taken from juniors without permission. By the same token, the great responsibility of seniority is to give aid to younger relatives when they are in need. However, such aid cannot be taken by a junior without permission, but must be humbly requested (*kerekere*). Goods and services thus flow both up and down the hierarchy. But the milieu in which goods are given by an elder to a junior is one which emphasizes the "weakness" and inferiority of the younger, whereas the transfer of goods from younger to elder emphasizes the latter's inherent rights of control. In neither case, however, is any return of goods expected.

As a solid social and economic unit, the extended family does not go on forever. When a man's sons start to raise families of their own, the extended family gradually begins to segment. When the family head becomes too old to visit the gardens, control over them passes to his eldest son, or in the immaturity of the son, to the head's younger brother. The old man and his wife will usually move out of their large house into a smaller one, and his successor takes over his house. By slow process, the family head is thus divested of former status and power. "His time is up," Moalans say, and he is literally waiting to die. By modern, missionary-influenced ethics, an old father or family head should be properly fed and cared for by his brothers and sons. Actually he sinks into a pitiable position; aboriginally, his family might have killed him. Today he is barely kept alive; his counsel is never sought, and he is more often considered silly (even when not senile) than wise. He has no place or contribution to make in the family or in the community. When the head of a large family dies, the segmentation of the group is imminent. If the family is small, the division will be delayed until some of the men have grown children, preferably married sons, so that the new families will have the necessary labor forces. The break-up of an extended family is signalled by the division of control over houses, division of coconuts (only a recent practice), and division of control over productive property. When the family splits, each married male comes into full possession of the house which he and his family have been occupying. The successor of the former leader, usually the eldest surviving son, will divide among the mature males the coconuts formerly used by the family as a whole. The principle governing the allotment of coconuts is that an equitable division be made according to need. The older brother is here still guided by the ethic that senior members of the group are responsible for the well-being of juniors. Occasionally, however, the prerogative of coconut allotment is abused by an older brother in his own favor, and hostility breaks out among the segmenting groups. Land as such is not divided, for the traditional extended family does not hold land privately. (Rather, land is held communally by larger social units of which families are constituent elements. Families and individuals hold usufructory rights in any land which they have cleared. Such rights cease when cultivation ceases, and the land is left to regain its fertility.) But while lands are not divided, the leader's unified control of family gardens is divided. Each of the heads of the segmenting components of the family takes over full control of the gardens which any member of his household cultivates. This decentralization of control produces the ultimate sign of segmentation, the building of new cook houses for each house group—the division of the common hearth. Each house group is now an independent unit.

In each, the formation of an extended family begins anew. The various extended families so formed become bound in a larger social unit, *tokatoka*, united by common descent and led by the genealogically senior male. Eventually a tokatoka grows large, segments, and thus gives rise to a still larger descent group, *mataqali*. Tokatoka and mataqali are landowning groups, and are of great social and political significance in the local community. However, a precise description of the nature and functioning of these groups would be outside the scope of this paper.

It should be kept in mind that this description of the traditional extended family is a generalized one. Exigencies of death, different ratios of daughters and sons, residence of a man in his wife's father's family, and other circumstances may produce differences in the composition of family groups. But wherever the extended family occurs, it operates in the manner I have described.

FAMILY ORGANIZATION IN KETEIRA AND NAROI

Family organization has undergone considerable modification during the past century in Moala. However, the traditional extended family still predominates in one village in particular, Keteira. In other villages, such as Naroi, it is in the minority, having been largely replaced by independent nuclear forms of family. In this section, family composition in these two villages, Keteira and Naroi, is described in detail.

In analyzing Moalan family types, I shall use the term *nuclear family* to denote a group consisting of a married pair, with or without offspring, living in one house and exclusively using a nearby cook house. The exclusive use of a cook house is indicative of the economic and social independence of the nuclear family. *Nuclear core family* will be used for groups composed of a married pair, with or without offspring, and additional single relatives (of any kin category) of either spouse, exclusively occupying one living house and one cook house. *Extended family* will stand for the traditional extended family described in the last section. Extended families have nuclear constituents, but these share a common cook house and hence are not economically and socially independent. Table 2 summarizes the pertinent data on family composition in Naroi and Keteira.

The data indicate clearly that the traditional extended family remains dominant in Keteira, while in Naroi it has been superseded by nuclear and nuclear core families. The distribution of each type of family and the percent-

burdens of food preparation are common. These quarrels are quickly communicated to the men, who are often hard pressed to smooth things over.

The differential survival of the traditional extended family in these two villages gives an excellent opportunity to study not only the causes of its decay but also the factors which are necessary to its continued existence. I will undertake to do this in the following section.

TABLE 2

A COMPARISON OF FAMILY FORMS IN NAROI AND KETEIRA
(1954-1955)

	Naroi	*Keteira*
1. Number of People	340	115
2. Number of Independent Nuclear Families	11	1
3. Number of Independent Nuclear Core Families	18	2
4. Number of Extended Families	6	6
5. Total Number of Families	35	9
6. Average Number of People per Family	9.7	12.8
7. Percentage of People in Independent Nuclear and Nuclear Core Families	71.2	19.1
8. Percentage of People in Extended Families	28.8	80.9

ages of people living in extended families in the two villages offer the most striking evidence of this fact. Six of the nine Keteira families are extended, compared to six extended families of the 35 in Naroi. Over 80 per cent of the Keteira population lives in extended families, compared to less than 30 per cent so residing in Naroi. The extended family is the major form in Keteira and the minor form in Naroi.

Moreover, some of the extended families in Naroi are markedly unstable, which is not true of any in Keteira. For example, the large family of the paramount chief of Moala, composed of six nuclear families, has several times broken into small house groups for eating purposes. There has been considerable reshuffling of the nuclear components of these eating groups. Although food is still cooked in the cook house which serves the entire extended family, fish and other additions (*i coi*) to the basic vegetable diet are usually cooked separately by the women of each eating house group. Segmentation of this family into independent nuclear families has been discussed several times and seems imminent. In general, extended family life in Naroi is less serene than in Keteira. In Naroi, quarrels between women over proprietorship of cooking utensils and over the

LAND USE AND THE FAMILY IN KETEIRA AND NAROI

It is frequently noted that primitive forms of extended family do not survive the process of acculturation to civilization. In many cases the emergence of independent nuclear families is a result of contact with European culture. Entrance into a money economy in particular has the effect of breaking down extended family customs of pooling goods and services. But this is not a sufficient explanation of what has occurred in Moala.

Naroi and Keteira are both subject to heavy influences from European culture, and are both becoming involved in the money economy of the Colony to a substantial extent. Naroi has two Chinese storekeepers and it is the main port of Moala, connecting by boat to European centers in Suva, Viti Levu, and Levuka, Ovalau. Keteira uses a Chinese-operated store in the village of Cakova, twenty minutes walk from Keteira. In some ways, Keteira has felt more European influence than Naroi. At any given time a greater proportion of Keteira people are visiting or working in Suva or Levuka than are Naroians. (The figures run roughly 20 to 30 per cent of the married males of Keteira absent from the village as compared to five to 15 per cent married Naroi men absent.) The Keteira school is better staffed than that of Naroi; more people of Keteira learn at least a smattering of English, as well as more of other tidbits of European culture. As copra is the main source of money for Moalans, an indication of the degree to which participation in a money economy has influenced production can be had by comparing the average number of coconuts planted per man per year in each village. In Naroi the average number of coconuts planted among 29 of the approximately 75 able-bodied men in 1954 was 114; in Keteira, the average among 17 of the approximately 25 able-bodied men was 181 coconuts. To the degree that these figures represent involvement with things monetary, Keteira cannot be said to be backward. Keteira is no less aculturated than Naroi and perhaps is more so, yet the traditional extended family has survived in Keteira. It can be concluded at this point that culture contact with Europeans per se does not cause the breakdown of the old family form.

Why has Keteira maintained the traditional extended family? The answer appears to be that Keteira continues to follow an old practice of exploiting land resources both near and at some distance from the village, and that the extended family is adapted to such a pattern of land use. In recent years, Naroi and most other Moalan villages have abandoned the practice of using distant lands and have confined agricultural activities to the village environs. It is in these villages that independent nuclear families have developed at the expense of extended families. (Quantitative evaluation of this trend can only be given for Naroi, but I have noted the same phenomenon in other villages which use only nearby land.)

To support this hypothesis, it is necessary to examine the traditional patterns of land use. Since prehistoric times the lands held by Mcalan villages have not merely been concentrated around the settlement sites. Until quite recently, every village laid claim to and worked land so far away that farming necessitated the periodic and sometimes prolonged absence of the cultivators. Yam gardens, wet and dry taro gardens, and plots of other food plants were made in these distant lands. Huts were erected near the fields for shelter during the periods of clearing, planting, weeding, and harvest. Meanwhile, similar occupations were taking place in gardens near the village.

Villages obtained lands far from the settlement site by various means. The most common method was the retention of claims to land near former habitation sites. Moalan villages did not move frequently, but within a few centuries a village might occupy several sites. In time, it would come to be situated far from its old location, perhaps on another coast or side of the island. If, as was usually the custom, claims to land used in ancient times were maintained by periodic cultivation, a village came to hold widely dispersed areas of land. Traditions sometimes assign defeats in war as the cause of village shifts, but even in this case a defeated village maintained land rights around the old settlement. Very rarely, victorious villages appropriated some land of conquered villages, giving them lands in distant areas.

Although Moala is small, land more than a mile or two from any village is apt to be relatively inaccessible. The interior of the island is hilly, the gradients are often quite steep, and the "bush" cover is thick; hence, a journey of even two miles inland is quite arduous and time consuming. Travel along the coast is also limited, for the rocky shore permits walking only at low tide, and only at high tide can a boat be poled along the fringing reef. Nor are the winds favorable for daily round trips from a village to distant points by sailing canoe. Due to these difficulties, land more than one or two miles from a village can be most effectively exploited if the producers remain near it overnight.

There are a number of reasons why Moalans frequently found it worthwhile to continue to exercise claims to land far from their villages. In some cases where villages have remained in situ for long periods, slash-and-burn agriculture resulted in deforestation of surrounding lands and replacement by a thick cover of reed (gasau), which lowers the soil fertility. The forest has a better chance of regaining its former density—and the soil has a better chance of being replenished with organic materials—around abandoned habitation sites. Claims to old village lands, therefore, are valuable.

A second reason for retaining distant lands is that they may be suitable for growing types of crops that cannot be as successfully cultivated in the vicinity of the village. As a result of differences in soils, topography, and rainfall, given parts of the island have variable potentials for the growth of different plants. For example, some villages today produce more than twice the poundage per capita of taro than do others because of superior facilities (water and topography) for irrigation. Yam yields vary in different villages because of differences of rainfall. Food gathering possibilities are different in various parts of the island. The lowly mussel, *Arca culcullaea concomerata* (*kai koso*, Fijian) is so abundant in the bay off Keteira that it is daily food in almost all seasons, whereas it is extremely rare in other villages. Fish, edible sea slugs, crabs, and prawns are abundant only in particular locales. It is to the advantage of a village to hold lands in different areas of the island, thereby gaining access to soils of high potential for a number of crops and to a number of natural food resources.

The traditional Moalan extended family is well constituted for the tasks of production in different areas and for the uniform distribution of the diverse produce. The size of the family made it possible to release some members for work on distant fields without hardship for those left in the village. A man might take his wife with him to a distant garden, leaving his children to be cared for by others in the group. A common cook house and common meals, and centralized supervision of gardens ensure that the different foods will be shared among all members, regardless of their particular contribution to production. The family authority system permits the division and coordination of labor which is necessary for its multifarious and spatially separated activities. Even the usual provision that the hardest work goes to the younger members of the family is adaptive. Cultivation of distant gardens is thus undertaken by the youngest and strongest, while those older and weaker may carry out lighter tasks near the settlement—the elder men perhaps do no more than pull up crops for the daily meals. This type of family group is an ideal unit for working scattered resources without sacrificing any of the usual familial functions of child care, socialization, and the production of capable, mature members of the society. Proof of this contention is the fact that the traditional extended family has been maintained

in Keteira, where the pattern of using distant lands still obtains, whereas it has broken down in Naroi, where only land around the village is used.

Naroi also continues to hold tenure to land far from its present site, not because cultivation is maintained there, but because the Government-sponsored Lands Commission in the 1930s confirmed Naroian ownership in conformity with traditional custom. But only Keteira, in contrast to Naroi and most other Moalan villages, still uses its distant lands. A large tract in the southeast of the island, called Qaliqali (area K′, map), is extensively worked by all Keteira families. The area is claimed because of its proximity to an ancient village site of the major patrilineal descent group (*mataqali*) of Keteira. However, the use to which the land is presently put and the reasons for its continued exploitation are not traditional. Keteira retains an interest in Qaliqali because of the abundance of coconuts there, in contrast to the scarcity of these "money trees" around the village proper. The area in which Keteira is located has been a center of population concentration since prehistoric times, and as a result the environs of the village have been largely deforested by slash-and-burn agriculture. Although food plants can be grown with moderate success in this reed-covered area, coconuts do not thrive. For the all-important copra trade, Keteira continues to use Qaliqali. Due to excessive rainfall in Keteira Bay, many men (about one-third) also make their yam gardens in Qaliqali, and several have manioc plots there as well. The men of Keteira frequently go to Qaliqali for days or even weeks on end (especially during the customary May-June period of intensive copra preparation) to plant coconuts, make copra, or cultivate their gardens.

Naroi is situated in an area which has not been extensively occupied for a long period of time and which has not been so heavily deforested. The Naroi region, both near the coast and extending far upland, is planted with sufficient coconuts to take care of the villagers' needs. Because of this local supply, the Naroi people only infrequently visit their old village sites (areas N′ on map). In fact, Naroians have not extensively cultivated the old sites for at least 30 to 40 years, despite coconuts growing there. Time which would otherwise be available for work in the vicinity of the ancient villages is nowadays largely consumed by copra production in Naroi. And food purchased from stores with copra money substitutes for any advantage that could be gained by growing certain crops, such as taro, in the old sites. Rarely do Naroians exercise their ancient land claims, and then only to augment the supply of copra in an emergency. Conditions in most other Moalan villages (beside Keteira) approximate those in Naroi, and hence there has been a general abandonment of the traditional land use pattern.

A calendar of the activities of the Keteira population during several weeks in May and June, 1955, will give some indication of their dependence on Qaliqali. These were weeks of intensive copra production. A tabu placed on the nuts had been lifted so that the men could earn money to pay the head tax required of all Fijians. The calendar may also indicate some of the advantages of extended family life in light of this pattern of land use.

1. Week beginning Monday, May 16, 1955.
Monday was the first exodus to Qaliqali for copra preparation. Most of those leaving traveled overland to Cakova and along the western shore (see map). Others poled around the southern part of the island. By Monday night, about one-half of the married men and their mature sons were at Qaliqali. A few women accompanied their husbands, but most remained in the village to care for their children and to make mats in preparation for an interisland trade scheduled for August. By Wednesday the village was even more deserted, as more of the men, after bringing in several days' food supply for the women, joined their fellows in Qaliqali. On Thursday night, only seven men remained in the village, one a school teacher and two who were too old for extensive travel. On Saturday most of the men returned from Qaliqali to provide food for the weekend and to attend Sunday church.

2. Week of Monday, May 23.
The pattern of movements this week was the same. Most of the able-bodied men left for Qaliqali Monday morning. Some were accompanied by their wives, but most of the women and children remained behind. A few married couples stayed at Qaliqali into the next week, but the rest of the people returned to Keteira on Saturday.

3. Week of Monday, May 30.
The same pattern as the previous two weeks.

4. Week of Monday, June 6.
This week most of the men delayed their departure in order to clean up the village in preparation for inspection by the Government chief (*Buli*) of the island. (These inspections are supposed to take place monthly, but they are frequently neglected.) Only a few men and boys could be spared for copra

making during the early part of the week. The inspection was completed Thursday morning and most of the workers left immediately for the coconut area, returning on Saturday.

5. Week of Monday, June 13.
The same as weeks 1 and 2. By the end of this week the period of intensive copra preparation was over.

No movement of this type occurs in Naroi during these weeks. A few families (nuclear and nuclear core), whose coconuts are a mile or so from the village, do stay on their lands during this period. However, most remain in the village.

CONCLUSIONS

Comparison of family organization and patterns of land utilization in Keteira and Naroi reveals that the maintenance of the traditional extended family is dependent on strategic exploitation of productive lands distant from the village site. The Keteira extended family is adjusted to working spatially separated resources. The large size of the group, the internal ranking system and authority hierarchy, the centralized control of resources, the provisions for distribution of work on the basis of capability, and the sharing of property and food, all make it possible for the group to extend its productive operations over a large area and to distribute equitably the fruits of such production. Considered in this light, the fragmentation of the extended family after three or four generations is also understandable. Given sufficient time and patrilocal residence, each nuclear constituent of an extended family would normally expand to the point where the full complement of members necessary for carrying out extended family activities is present. By this time also, the burdens of food preparation and administration of the resources of an extended family composed of such large segments have become unwieldy. Thus there is no reason for an extended family to continue beyond three or four generations of common descent, and there is good reason for segmentation into a number of discrete families.

In Naroi, where only land in the environs of the village is productively utilized, the traditional extended family has no longer any raison d'être. Nuclear families can effectively undertake all necessary exploitative and distributive activities. With a land use pattern of this type, the influences of acculturation, especially involvement in a money economy, can be expected to hasten the disappearance of the extended family. Such indeed is the most plausible explanation of the demise of the traditional family system in Naroi. In Keteira the extended family maintains itself in the face of the encroaching money economy because the traditional land use customs have not been changed. On the contrary, the greater dependence upon money in the economy has confirmed adherence to the old practices of land tenure, since land near the village cannot support sufficient coconut growth.

That the Moalan extended family is adapted to the exploitation of scattered resources is a conclusion of great interest and possibly of more widespread application. The extended family does not characterize primitive society in every ecological situation or at every level of development. Differences in family forms are not only of themselves significant, but in view of their importance as determinants of kinship structure the study of differences in family type assumes critical proportions in the field of social organization. It is hoped that this examination of the Moalan data provides an hypothesis that can be more generally applied in explanation of crucial variations in the family systems of the primitive world.

3. HOUSEHOLD VIABILITY AMONG THE PASTORAL FULANI

DERRICK J. STENNING

Reprinted from The Developmental Cycle in Domestic Groups, *edited by Jack Goody, pp. 92-119. Copyright 1958, Cambridge University Press. At the time of his death in 1964, Derrick J. Stenning was Director of Research at the East African Institute of Social Research in Uganda. He had previously been a professor of Anthropology at University College in London and a Lecturer in the Faculty of Archeology and Anthropology at Cambridge University and had done field work with the Ankole.*

■ We should not think of a particular society's "family system" as unchanging from the time of its inception to its eventual dissolution. If we think of a family in terms of the people who compose the group, their expectations of each other and their relationships with wider networks, it is apparent that a married couple have a quite different relationship to each other after they have children than before.

In the next selection Derrick Stenning illustrates these changes over time in family relationships as an aspect of response to technological and habitational factors among the pastoralist Fulani of the western Sudan. The Fulani are characterized by patrilocal extended families, but unique adjustments in their form are required to meet the demands of the cattle herds whose welfare is their primary economic consideration.

Stenning shows how the family and its herds support each other and how domestication requires

a highly particular organization of family relationships. For example, the size of family and herd must be commensurate if both are to be viable. The composition of the family and the labor of its members depend on seasonal factors (the availability of water and grass) as well as unpredictable hazards. The status of the father in the household depends on his herding skills, so that when he is no longer able to participate in the care of the herds he is displaced by his sons and assumes an inferior social position. Whereas we often think of divorce as the end of the household, among the Fulani divorce must be regarded as part of the developmental cycle of the family. Thus we see how the structure of the family, its activities, and its very fate are tied to its method of subsistence, in this case to a pastoral strategy of adaptation.

An excellent study of habitational variability and social responses among two pastoralist groups is provided in *The Family Herds : A Study of Two Pastoral Peoples in East Africa, the Jie and Turkana*, by P. H. Gulliver (New York : Humanities Press, 1955) ; materials from this book are presented as Selections 21 and 22 in *The Cultural Present*. The reader who wants to explore further the family systems of pastoralists can consult *Nomads of South Persia*, by Fredrik Barth (Boston : Little, Brown, 1968) ; *Cattle and Kinship among the Gogo: A Semipastoral Society of Central Tanzania*, by Peter J. Rigby (Ithaca : Cornell University Press, 1968) ; *The Nuer: A Description of the Modes of Livelihood and Political Institutions of a Nilotic People*, by E. E. Evans-Pritchard (New York and London : Oxford University Press, 1940) ; and *Tribes of the Sahara*, by L. C. Briggs (Cambridge, Mass. : Harvard University Press, 1960). ■

IN THIS PAPER, family development refers to cyclical changes in the size and composition of viable domestic groupings based upon the family. These are changes brought about by the birth, marriage, and death of family members. They involve not merely changes in family constitution, but affect, and are affected by, the relation between the family and its means of subsistence, which, as a domestic unit, it manages, exploits, and consumes in close co-residence, continuous cooperation, and commensality. Such a domestic unit is viable when the labour it can provide is suitable for the exploitation of its means of subsistence, while the latter is adequate for the support of the members of the domestic unit.

The principles of these relations are explored in the context of the social organization of the Pastoral Fulani, who are the principal cattle-owning nomads of the western Sudan. Particular reference is made to the tribe . . . who inhabit the Fune, Damaturu, and Gujba Districts in the west of Bornu Emirate in north-eastern Nigeria.

In Pastoral Fulani society, the domestic unit is based upon the simple family (a man, his wife and their offspring) and its extension in the compound family (a man, his several wives and their offspring). Ownership of herds is vested in the male heads of such families, whose members carry out the essential tasks connected with cattle husbandry, forming the nucleus of a household living in a distinct homestead.

Changes occur in the size and composition of simple and compound families. A simple family commences as a legal union of husband and wife in marriage. This union is devoted to the procreation of legitimate children, their care during infancy, their socialization, and their material support until sexually mature. This unequivocal process of expansion comes to an end when the first child, particularly the first male child, marries and reproduces, setting up a similar simple family. From now on, the original family is in a state of dissolution. This may be concealed, however, by the birth of further children to it when the full reproductive span of spouses, particularly the male spouse, is utilized in polygynous unions. Complete dissolution—excluding the eventuality of death or divorce of spouses—occurs when all their offspring have married.

The relationship between transfers of cattle, first marriage, and the inauguration of distinct households and homesteads suggests that the simple or compound family is the optimum viable domestic unit in Pastoral Fulani society. However, viability of the simple or compound family is adversely affected by a number of factors. These are of three types: regular seasonal variations in the demands of the pastoral economy; irregular natural hazards; and the formal properties of the simple or compound family itself in relation to its means of subsistence throughout the period of its growth and dissolution.

In response to certain aspects of these adverse factors, domestic groupings based upon the agnatic joint family[1] emerge. However, these are of short duration, breaking up again into their constituent simple or compound families. Other aspects of the non-viability of the simple or compound family are met by forms of cooperation which do not involve the formation of wider domestic units. Most of these, like the formation of agnatic joint family domestic units, are based upon the agnatic relationship of household heads. The functions of the agnatic lineage, and to a lesser extent the clan, are thus mainly those concerned with promoting the viability of their constituent simple or compound family households as domestic units.

The formal development of the simple family begins by definition when children are born to the spouses. But in Pastoral Fulani society this must be regarded as only one stage—although a crucial one—in the formation of a domestic

1. Organized around male links [ed.].

unit based upon the family. Anterior events must be considered, and it is convenient to describe the whole formal development of the family in terms of a male who is to be a family head, a householder, and a herdowner.

In these terms, the process begins when an infant boy is given a name, seven days after birth. He now becomes a person as this is understood for males by Pastoral Fulani; he has cattle. In the presence of his male agnates, his father sets aside for him a calf or two which are the nucleus of his future herd.

The next important occasion is at his circumcision, at between seven and ten years of age. He now becomes a herdboy, competent to take cattle to daily grazing. He is given some useful token of this service—a leather apron, a gourd water bottle, or a set of Koranic charms. He is taken into his father's cattle corral and shown his beasts, and further calves are again allocated to him, again in the presence of witnesses who are his male agnates. He has the nucleus of a herd, and every herd must have its dairywoman, the wife of its owner. He is therefore betrothed to an infant girl.

The next stage, still a preliminary to the formation of a family, household and homestead, is the induction of the betrothed girl into the homestead of her future husband's father. This takes place when she is known by the latter to have begun menstruation, and is therefore believed capable of childbirth. The couple sleep together in the open at the boy's post on the perimeter of the cattle corral. In other respects—participation in ceremonial and in work—the couple have the status of unmarried youth and maiden. The youth still carries out his duties of herdsman to his father's herd, including those cattle set aside for him. The girl becomes, as it were, a daughter of her husband's father's household, and works under the supervision of one of his wives, properly the mother of her husband. The youth and girl continue to participate in ceremonials proper to those who are not herdowners or wives, and act mainly as instructors of song and dance to younger participants.

This ambiguous period ends with the conception of the couple's first child. When the girl's pregnancy is evident to her husband's father's wife, she is removed to her own father's household. There she undergoes a period of seclusion during her pregnancy, and remains for three wet seasons—two to two-and-a-half years—after which she returns to her husband.

On this occasion it is not a pair of spouses taking up residence, but a family, and all the appurtenances of family life—a distinct homestead and a distinct herd—are to be provided.

Compared with the clusters of circular, thatched mud huts which constitute in some form or other the hamlets and villages of most of the sedentary populations of the western Sudan, the homesteads, and camps, of the Pastoral Fulani seem haphazard and rudimentary. In the wet season even a large camp blends with the bush, and in the dry season it is possible to pass within a few yards of a homestead without realizing it is there, unless its herd is present. Household equipment is limited to the amount which may be carried on the head or on pack animals, and shelter must be made of whatever tree foliage the district has to offer.

In spite of the rudimentary and impermanent nature of the homestead, it exhibits an important degree of formality and uniformity.

Pastoral Fulani homesteads always face west. In all but overnight camps a curved back fence of branches cut from nearby trees is put up to ensure a measure of privacy, keep out hyena, and deflect the course of stampeding cattle frightened by their nightly visits in the wet season.

Immediately in front of the back fence are set the beds of the homestead, the essential poles, slats, and coverlets of which are transported when camp is moved. Over the bed is erected a structure similar to it which forms a platform on which are placed the household utensils. In the wet season this platform is elaborated to form a shelter. Its components are, again, transportable. Alongside, behind, or in front of the bed-shelters there may be other ancillary shelters put up for specific purposes. These are low, beehive huts of springy boughs covered with bark matting, or tall shelters of heavier leafy boughs. These shelters do not contain beds made with poles, but a rough couch made of bundled grass and bark mats.

In front of the bed shelters there is a domestic hearth, consisting of three stones or parts of white-ant nests as a support for a cooking pot, supplemented perhaps by an iron tripod.

Near these shelters and in front of them is

kept household stock other than the herd of cattle—a horse or donkey hobbled and tethered to a forked stake, and a small flock of sheep or goats sheltered in a fold made of stout branches.

In front of this group of shelters is staked down a long two-stranded leather rope, to which the calves of the household herd are tethered whenever the herd is present, to prevent their suckling except when their dams are to be milked. In front again of the calf-rope is the cattle corral. This is usually just a circular patch of earth trampled by the beasts' hooves, but where wood is plentiful a corral fence may be put up. Round the corral under convenient bushes or trees there may be rough beds of the type to be found in the ancillary shelters. In the centre of the cattle corral there is a smudge fire round which the cattle gather in the early morning and in the evening when they return from pasture. The fire is always lit, even in the

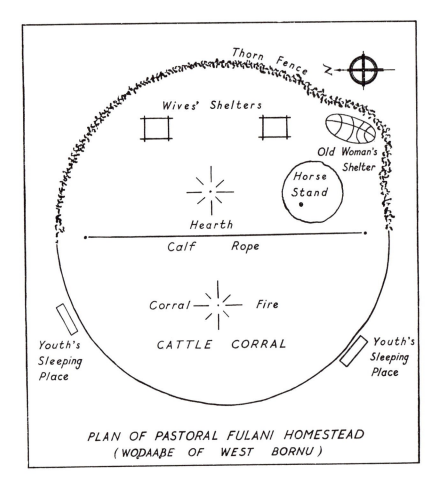

PLAN OF PASTORAL FULANI HOMESTEAD
(WOḌAAßE OF WEST BORNU)

rain, on the return of the cattle, and extinguished after they have gone out to pasture the next morning. The ritual importance of the corral fire is attested in the myths recounting the circumstances under which the first Fulani obtained cattle.

The whole homestead, consisting of one or more bed-shelters, ancillary shelters on occasion, calf-rope and cattle corral, is the basic residential unit of which all Pastoral Fulani local units, in the form of camps, are built up. The general shape of a camp is that of a rank of homesteads facing west, with their calf-ropes and bed-shelters in the same straight line from north to south. Larger camps are formed with the addition of other such ranks of homesteads pitched to the east and west, but never due east and west, of the first rank. There is no exact term for such camps in their residential aspect; the most general term for a camp is merely the plural of homestead.

The essentials of the homestead—the bed, the domestic utensils, the calf-rope and the herd—are ceremonially brought together when the wife returns to her husband with their first-born child. There is a striking symmetry in the homestead plan, which canalizes the day-to-day life of family members, and the sources from which household property accrue to the new family.

The wife's natal family provide her with the objects of a wife and dairymaid. First among these is her bed. The bed poles are cut and trimmed by her brothers, and stained red by her sisters. The grass mats and bark coverlets are made or bought by her mother. The latter is also responsible for providing the ceremonial domestic equipment of a dairymaid—calabashes, dippers, churns, spoons and so on, lashed together with leather thonging in a traditional way. The site of the wife's domestic quarters lies alongside and to the north of her husband's father's homestead; it is cleared and fenced by the latter's sons. The husband's father also provides the pack-ox, with its harness, on which the new wife's bed and domestic equipment are transported when camp is moved. That part of the homestead which is predominantly the wife's, and which is essentially feminine in character, is thus complete.

The masculine component of the new homestead is the cattle corral, and this comes into being when the husband lights his corral fire in front of his wife's shelter.

One component of the new homestead remains—the calf-rope. This is made by the husband's father and brothers, who peg it in position when the new homestead is being set up. The calf-rope divides and yet unites the two halves of the homestead.

The wife's side of the homestead is to be given over exclusively to the day-to-day execution of women's tasks. A wife will maintain her own property. She will prepare milk and butter for sale, and milk and cereal foods for home consumption. Infants of both sexes and unmarried daughters will eat with her; they may be joined by the household head's son's childless wife, his daughter home for her first pregnancy, or his widowed mother. No female will eat outside this domestic area, and no male, other than infants, will eat inside it.

On the husband's side of the calf-rope are the cattle, the main interest and preoccupation of the men, in their corral. Here, at dawn and dusk before milking time, the male household head will be joined, for an appraisal of the herd's condition, by his herdboy sons. The latter will sleep at the corral perimeter. The household head and his sons will eat in order of age seniority at a point on the western side of the corral. Here those males who are in camp during the day will work, mostly at making the many varieties of rope required in connection with livestock. Here they will also spend the evening round a fire, their circle often augmented by a ring of cattle who have "come to be admired."

As the family grows, the everyday activity of its members will be canalized by the division of the homestead into its male and female sections. In a general sense, entry into the corral is forbidden to females, entry into the wife's section is forbidden to males.

There are two important exceptions to this rule. A husband will cross the calf-rope to enter his wife's shelter, to lie with her, to beget children. A wife will cross the calf-rope to milk cattle whose calves have been released to them by her husband. The congress of husband and wife in the wife's shelter will concern children; the congress of husband and wife in the corral will concern calves.

Calves are identified with children, particularly male children, in many overt ways. A first-born son at his mother's back wears a ceremonial collar which is a replica of the halter which tethers calves to the calf-rope. Boys below herding age are expected to take care of calves close to the homestead during the day while the herd is at pasture. A group of boys or youths in a dance who are age mates are called by the term for a calf-rope.

But the calves at their calf-rope play an important part in the ceremony at which the homestead is inaugurated. The homestead is prepared, the corral fire lit, but the new herd can be constituted in only one way. While the herd of the father of the new household head is away at pasture, the calves of his son are tethered to the calf-rope of the new homestead. When the herd returns, cows allocated to the son find their calves elsewhere, and it is to the new homestead they go. The attachment, to the new herd, of cows which have no calves at the time of its constitution, must await calving, for which they are tethered in the corral of the new homestead. Bulls are separated by being tethered there for a few days and are then loosed in the evening when the herd returns from pasture, until finally they run exclusively with the new herd. But it is the transfer of calves which makes possible the orderly formation of the new herd. If the first-born is a son, there is a calf or two in the newly constituted herd whose progeny will form the nucleus of a new herd at the third human generation.

The subsequent development of the simple family is in effect the marital history of the male household head, which takes place against the background of the expansion of the herd which he owns. Normally, sons and daughters are added to the simple family. It may be expanded into a compound family by the addition of wives up to the legal Muslim maximum of four, and, again, children may be added to these matricentral components. Divorce may take place, but normally the children born to a man stay with him, or are claimed by him when they are no longer infants, at the age of seven to ten. All these developments are crucial in considerations of the viability of the simple or compound family household.

But for the moment it is convenient to turn to the usages surrounding the dissolution of a family in the period of decline in the marital history of its head. Sons have been born to him

and allocated cattle, which, in the normal course of events, have had their increase. His sons have shared the duties of herding and watering the whole herd, and, as their power and skill as herdsmen have increased, the cattle allocated to them have also increased. At the point at which, in addition, they have demonstrated their own powers of procreation, their allocations of cattle have been turned over to them on the formation of their homesteads and households. The herdsmen's skill has now been devoted to their own cattle, which in turn provide their dependents with subsistence. They have ceased to be sons, but have themselves become husbands and fathers.

But while these developments have been taking place, the father's personal power and skill as a herdsman and as a begetter have been waning. Although polygynous marriages and the children resulting from them may temporarily conceal the fact, he is steadily losing dependents as they get married. Allocations of cattle have depleted his herd. A man's last unmarried son herds his father's cattle, but on his marriage they all become his own.

Although distorted by the incidence of divorce and paternal rights to children, the case of a mother is parallel in Pastoral Fulani eyes. When her homestead was set up she was given decorated calabashes, which were never used but proudly displayed on ceremonial occasions, symbolizing her milking rights in virtue of her status as a mother. On the birth of daughters, decorated calabashes were given her by her mother and sisters. But as her children married her responsibilities for feeding them ended, while her reproductive faculties declined. She gave her own decorated calabashes to her daughters until finally, on the marriage of her last daughter, her stock of decorated calabashes and her responsibilities as a mother, housewife and dairywoman came to an end.

Sons and daughters married, the couple no longer constitute a family. The wife has no calabashes, because she has no milking rights; her husband has no herd in which she might milk. They no longer live in a homestead of their own. The shelter and the calf-rope are abandoned. The couple take up residence as dependents, each with his or her eldest son, even where this involves living in the same homestead. The old woman lives in one of the ancillary beehive shelters behind her sons' wives' shelters. The old man sleeps in the open in front of his eldest son's corral. The old woman may be of use in caring for her son's infants, who may sleep in her shelter. But an old man is regarded as of little use. He may help in making rope, but he has no voice in planning the movements of the cattle of the household. Old people in this situation spend their last days on the periphery of the homestead, on the male and female sides respectively. This is where men and women are buried. They sleep, as it were, over their own graves, for they are already socially dead.

This description has for the moment gone rough-shod over many palpable demographic, ecological, and economic factors. But it permits the salient ideal feature of family development among the Pastoral Fulani to be presented. This is that the social interpretation of the passage of the generations in a domestic context is one which provides for the formation of viable simple or compound families constituting the basis of households, living in separate homesteads and subsisting upon distinct herds. This interpretation includes the important notion that this process should take place without prejudicing the viability of the parental household. It may be summarily concluded that the optimum viable domestic unit is the simple or compound family.

Given this identification of the simple or compound family with its herd, the limiting conditions of viability may be outlined. The Fulani described here as "Pastoral" are part of that section of the Fulani population who are not farmers, fishers or traders as well as cattle owners, but whose subsistence and wealth derive solely from the herds they possess.

A herd is a distinct group of cattle consisting of at least one stock bull, and a complement of cows, heifers and calves, together with pack oxen. It is distinct in that it normally reproduces itself by in-breeding and line-breeding, spends the daytime period of grazing apart from other similar herds, is watered separately, and spends the night in a corral reserved or constructed for it and marked by its special smudge fire. As already stated, the corral is part of the homestead of the male herdowner, who is responsible for its day-to-day management and who directs the necessary activities of the simple or compound family subsisting on it.

Given circumstances in which cattle are the sole basis of subsistence for such a household, meat does not form a regular or staple diet and animals are not sold frequently, since this represents a draw on the capital stock of the herd. Killings are confined to male beasts, or where possible, sick, maimed or barren animals. Such killings occur only on important ceremonial occasions. Sellings take place only when an overriding need for cash occurs; for example, to buy corn in the dry season, or to raise tax. The family then, lives on milk; unlike some of the pastoralists to be found in East Africa, Fulani do not drink cattle blood or make blood foods. Either milk or milk products must be drunk and eaten *ad nauseam*, or milk must be sold or exchanged in favour of other foods. Thus the limiting factor in the subsistence of a given family upon its herd lies in the milk output of the latter. There is a minimum size, composition and (since lactation is a condition of reproduction) fertility of a herd in relation to the subsistence requirements of the family associated with it.

The herd has here been considered as supporting the family dependent upon it. But there is a sense in which the family supports the herd. Fulani cattle are not natural groups of wild animals followed and exploited intermittently by human groups. Fulani herds are in a particular way domesticated, and this domestication entails a degree of special organization in the families dependent upon them. The diverse pastoral skills of herdowners and their sons are directed towards the achievement or maintenance of a state in which the family can subsist on the herd's milk and the cereal foods for which it is exchanged. Desirable pastures have to be sought and cattle led to them. Water supplies have to be arranged and cattle watered regularly. Diseases and accidents of many kinds have to be avoided, or their results treated. Cattle have to be protected from the attacks of wild beasts, and thefts must be prevented. Pack oxen must be trained, and the birth of calves assisted.

The preoccupation of the wives of herdowners, helped by their daughters, is the control, by careful milking, of the supply of milk available to calves and humans, and the sale of buttermilk, butter and sour milk on as favourable terms as possible in such markets in cereal producing areas as are made available to them. The Pastoral Fulani family is a herd-owning and milk selling enterprise.

Given this strict division of labour and a herd of a given size, a family must attain a certain size commensurate with its responsibilities towards its herd, and a composition which ensures that these are efficiently carried out by appropriate members of the family.

When the size and increase of the herd is adequate for the subsistence of the family, and the size and composition of the family are suitable for the control and deployment of the herd, then family and herd may be said to be in equilibrium, and the unit as a whole is viable. But both the human social unit and the means of subsistence associated with it are breeding concurrently, each within well-defined though different limits of fertility; the fertility of each affecting, indirectly, the fertility of the other. Thus in the life-history of a family and its herd, expressed as the lifetime of a male household head, the state of equilibrium and viability is not constantly fulfilled. There arises a whole range of temporary, partial, or potential disequilibria which require resolution.

However complicated the incidence of nonviability, it can be seen to have two main aspects. In one range of cases, nonviability is a condition in which there are not enough humans to cope with the cattle assigned to them. In another there are not enough reproductive cattle to feed the humans associated with them. Finally, and more rarely, junctures in the history of family and herd arise in which both these conditions occur simultaneously.

Loss of viability occurs in three main contexts. First, it may be due to regular seasonal variations in the demands of the pastoral economy. Secondly, it may be due to irregular natural hazards. Thirdly, it may be due to the formal properties of the simple or compound family itself in relation to its means of subsistence, throughout the period of its growth and dissolution. The last context is the main concern of this paper, but it would not be doing justice to crucial conditions in the social life of Pastoral Fulani if the first and second were not discussed. Indeed, a discussion of the regular seasonal changes and irregular natural hazards does much to justify, in ecological and

economic terms, the assertion that the simple or domestic family is the optimum domestic unit.

The Pastoral Fulani inhabit the savannah zone of the western and part of the eastern Sudan. The savannah zone of the western Sudan constitutes a transition area between the Guinea zone to the south, and the Sahara desert to the north. From south to north it is characterized by a diminution of the mean annual rainfall, and progressive deterioration of the vegetation from tall tropical forest to sparse thorn scrub. Perennial tsetse fly infestation in the Guinea zone, and continuous shortage of pasture and water in the desert, preclude cattle-keeping in those zones, while the dominant characteristics of the savannah render it, in general, favourable for this form of exploitation.

But the savannah zone is not immutable as a cattle-keeping zone, and with the seasonal interplay of the wet southwest monsoon from the Atlantic and the dry northeast monsoon from the Sahara, its characteristics change. In the wet season the southerly part of the savannah zone tends to take on the characteristics of the neighboring Guinea zone and becomes fly-infested. In the dry season, the northern part of the zone becomes practically desert as standing water is evaporated and herbage dried by the sun.

These conditions enjoin upon the Pastoral Fulani of the savannah zone a movement north in the wet season and south in the dry season. This transhumance has much variation in impetus depending upon local conditions of pastoral and sedentary population density and yearly variations in the onset, intensity and duration of the rains. In west Bornu, where low sedentary population density means that movement of pastoralists is practically unimpeded by farmland, the Fulani move uniformly, every two or three days, in accordance with the phases of the moon.

But it is not merely movement which is imposed by the changing seasons upon Pastoral Fulani if their herds are to be maintained. The wet season is marked by a congregation of family households to form camps, while at the height of the dry season much smaller groups of family households, single households, and even matricentral components of compound families camp on their own. In the wet season greater concentrations of cattle are possible since there is adequate pasture and water; and greater concentrations of humans dependent upon them follow. In the dry season, the grazing area of a herd must be much larger, and households are consequently dispersed. But this is not the complete answer to the general problem of seasonal dispersal and congregation. It is likely that the total area of savannah zone land denied to Pastoral Fulani in the dry season by pasture and water shortages is considerably less than that denied them in the wet by tsetse flies and growing crops.

As these seasonal changes unfold, the family labour devoted to the herd and the sustenance obtained from it undergo significant changes. In the cool wet season, herding is at its easiest, although made disagreeable by the rain. Cattle drink at pools close to the homesteads, pasture close at hand, and may return replete to the vicinity of the camp in the early afternoon. A woman regards her wet season work as easy compared with that of the dry. Markets are probably equally available in both seasons, and for the arduous work of obtaining domestic water in the dry season is substituted the enjoyable task of preparing for wet season feasts. Milk yields are higher in the wet season, partly because of the increased number of lactations, partly because of good fodder; there is a considerable surplus for use in feasts.

These conditions deteriorate steadily till the height of the dry season. Now, daily grazing takes place over wider tracts in which grass cover is far from uniform, and in which herdboys are expected to move into surrounding bush to find stands of more profitable herbage. Meanwhile, standing water may be nonexistent, and improvement of existing water-holes, as well as the backbreaking task of watering cattle, has to be carried out. In addition, reconnaissance of potential pasture farther afield, across tracts of burnt-out country on horseback, is the task of a good husbandman. The principal addition to the work of women and girls is the task of obtaining domestic water. All these tasks place a strain on the labour resources of the family, and are of a kind which not only require men, women, boys and girls to work harder, but also demand the labour of more hands, particularly so far as herding and watering are concerned.

Complementary to these changes in the contribution of the family to the herd are the changes in the contribution of the cattle to the family. The natural breeding cycle of herds is such that calving takes place mainly in the early wet season or wet season proper. However, serving of heifers and cows is not controlled by herdowners as stock bulls run with the herd at all seasons. Milk supply is curtailed by the lower proportions of lactations occurring in the dry season, and also by the lower yield of such lactations as do occur as a result of poor fodder and high temperature.

Changes from wet to dry season are thus likely to affect the viability of a family household and its herd, both by a relative shortage of humans due to the amount and type of labour required and by a relative shortage of cattle due to the decrease in the number and yield of lactations. It is dry season conditions which bring these changes about, and no family remaining viable in the dry season is likely to find itself non-viable in the wet season.

The second context in which changes in viability occur is that of the irregular natural hazards, of accident or disease resulting in the death of cattle. The death of single beasts in the herd rarely affects the household viability, except for the death of the stock bull, which temporarily renders all the cows and heifers worthless. But bovine disease has striking effects. Noninfectious diseases, the most important of which is trypanosomiasis, may cause severe shortages of cattle in individual herds, but since in the normal course of events the location and duration of tsetse infestation are well known to Fulani, widespread incidence of trypanosomiasis is not common. Infectious or contagious diseases present a different picture. Formerly rinderpest was the most important of these, but has been largely eradicated by European veterinary measures. Nowadays, bovine pleuropneumonia, the Fulani treatment of which is normally prohibited by the Administration without any offer of an alternative, is the most deadly. Here, isolation at as great a distance as possible of small groups of cattle, with the early slaughter of infected beasts, is a measure accepted by Pastoral Fulani and encouraged by the Administration. The disease runs its course in whichever herd is affected, and few beasts recover. Where isolation is impracticable, or where the disease breaks out at a period of maximum concentration or close movement, as in the wet or early wet seasons, contagious or infectious diseases may strip of their cattle whole local communities of Pastoral Fulani.

It may be said that these extreme eventualities have little to do with the normal process of Pastoral Fulani grouping in relation to the means of subsistence. Nevertheless the eagerness with which Pastoral Fulani concur with at least the spirit of the Administration's policies regarding bovine diseases, and the horror with which the details of (for example) the great rinderpest epidemic of 1897 are recounted, are evidence to the contrary. Bovine disease is a possibility of which the herdowner has constantly to be aware. Together with the seasonal variations in amount and quality of pasture and water, the possibility of disease is a factor conditioning the salient features of human and herd organization—mobility, and ability to disperse into the smallest possible units consistent with subsistence. Finally, a consideration of seasonal variations and irregular hazards serves to show that viability is not merely an automatic aspect of the development of families and herds in the course of the lifetime of the household head.

It remains to consider the loss or lack of viability in the family household engendered by its own formal properties throughout the period of its growth and dissolution.

It is necessary first to establish the minimum viable unit, in terms of the minimum herd which will support the minimum number of persons whose labour is necessary to it. It was found that . . . informants had a clear idea of these minimums. First, they stated that there should be one prime stock bull to every twenty-five head of cattle. (Although informants did not suggest this, herd output surveys for Bornu red longhorn herds lead to the supposition that not less than half such a herd should consist of bearing cows and heifers.)

Such a herd requires the services of one dairywoman and one herdsman; and by dint of unremitting labour, a man and his wife might, and have been known to, support such a herd all the year round. However, this entails their removal from many fields of social and economic activity.

This minimum herd can, however, support more than two humans, and it is on this supposition that Fulani base a more realistic assessment of the minimum labour force required. To fill his position in society effectively, and also to exploit his means of subsistence to the full, no herdowner can devote every day to herding cattle. Other tasks have to be carried out, and other relationships maintained, if a herd of any size is to be deployed to the greatest advantage. The principal ancillary task is the making of the many types of rope continuously used, and worn out, as fetters, halters, harness and so on. The principle set of relationships are those in which intelligence concerning the natural and political conditions in the tracts of land over which herds are continuously moved, is obtained. A man herding cattle sees only the pasture to which he has been committed; a vaster range of potential grazing land and water resources is open to him, the value of which he must continually assess in conference with those who currently know it. It is in the market places, where Pastoral Fulani from the surrounding country, and sedentary non-Fulani from distant villages, foregather, that informed opinions are amassed and sifted in endless discussion for the herdowners' future advantage. Thus for the proper care of even the minimum herd its owner requires the services of a herdboy. A boy can herd cattle and carry out the tactics of herd deployment; but the decisions of strategy, which to Pastoral Fulani are more important, lie with the herdowner.

A wife, too, is only partially fulfilling her responsibilities when she is concerned solely with work, such as milking and marketing, which is directly concerned with the herd. Her responsibilities include those of childbearing and the care of infants, and these are inimical to her other duties. Thus unmarried daughters market milk when their mothers are pregnant, or take care of infants while their mothers go to market. The wider duties of both husband and wife are concerned with the future independence of the family unit, in the assurance of conditions in which the herd will flourish, or in the provision of future herdboys and milkmaids. Thus the more realistic estimate of the size and composition of the family in relation to the minimum herd is a man and his wife, and their son and daughter.

In the ideal situation, these conditions are already partially fulfilled at the inception of the family. A husband and wife acquire their separate homestead and their herd on the condition of having a child. However, at the outset of its history, a family is bound to be non-viable in one, if not both senses. It may commence with an effective minimum herd, but even if the first-born were twins—a rare and, in Pastoral Fulani eyes, most happy circumstance—it could not commence with an effective minimum family. The achievement of this condition takes at least five or six years from the installation of the family in its homestead. This is the period in which a boy will grow to the herding age of seven to nine years. Thus in spite of the creation of a separate homestead and the establishment of a herd over which its owner has full rights of deployment and disposal the family undergoes at its inception a period of non-viability, in respect of shortage of humans, and perhaps of cattle as well.

Subsequent developments in the internal constitution of the family are connected with its viability as a domestic unit. Additional children may accrue to the simple family; new matri-central components may be added by polygynous marriage. Wives leave the family by divorce; they may take their infant children with them for good, or these children may return to their father when they are no longer infants. Both wives and children may be lost to the family through death.

The social institutions regulating these fluctuations—in so far as they are able to do so—are those connected with polygyny, divorce and the affiliation of children. These are to be reviewed against the marital contract implicit in the procedure and symbolism of the establishment of the homestead and herd by first marriage. This is one in which the expectations of a husband in his wife are that she should bear him children, particularly boys, the labour force and inheritors of his herd; while the expectations of a wife are that the husband should maintain sufficient cattle for herself and her children. The principal result of the unrestricted application of such a rule would be that men with the most cattle, and therefore the most fertile herds, would be able to take to wife the most fertile women, and more of them. Similarly, men might be expected to divorce their wives when they did not bear children, women to divorce their husbands when they were provided with insufficient cattle to milk.

It may be claimed that to a large extent the data (of which only a summary can be given here) support such an interpretation. The institutional evidence with regard to women's reproductive performance in relation to marital history must first be outlined. The tensions inherent in the period of first residence of a betrothed girl with her husband, which is dominated by the interest of the husband's father in an early conception, must first be recalled. Unless brought to an end by early pregnancy, this unstable period is concluded by a breakdown of the betrothal. The establishment of a homestead and herd is traditionally contingent upon the birth of a wife's first child, and the procedure of first marriage includes this event by definition.

Although miscarriages and premature deaths of her children are not *prima facie* grounds for divorce of a woman by her husband, there is evidence to show that during the course of her marital history unduly lengthy intervals between births of her children may bring divorce upon her. This is difficult to substantiate from women's childbearing histories, but it has the support of institutional evidence. Male sterility, which may, in fact, be the cause of such intervals, is not recognized by Pastoral Fulani men and may result in the divorce of a woman by her husband. More important here are the rules concerning the custody of children after the divorce of their parents. The custody of boys who have reached herding age and thus have acquired a firm interest in the paternal herd, and of girls for whom betrothal arrangements have been made, is vested in the husband of their mother. But the custody of infants still in the care of their mother is dependent upon the circumstances of the suit of divorce. In brief, either spouse may repudiate the other, and divorce is permitted, easy and frequent, although there are important variations caused by the uneven acceptance of the jurisdiction of Muslim tribunals. Unless the spouse who is repudiated acquiesces, the spouse making the repudiation forfeits rights to infants in the care of their mother at the time of the conjugal separation which precedes divorce; and in theory at least to any child born during the wife's *edda* [period of continence or mourning prescribed by Islamic Law] which concludes it. These rules favour the maintenance of marriages in which there are infants, for the spouse initiating divorce must be prepared to lose either the present custody or the future services of such infants when grown up. For a man they also maintain the firm attachment of herdboys to the paternal herd. For a woman they may secure her old age, for however many marriages she enters, she has a right to be supported by her eldest son when she has passed childbearing age.

The conditions which render unstable a woman's marriage before she has borne children, and during gaps in her childbearing history, also make the onset of menopause a crucial period in her marital career. Whether the onset of menopause in a wife is itself grounds for divorce by her husband depends upon whether she has infants still dependent upon her, whether her husband is polygamously married, and whether her co-wives have infants dependent on them. In the absence of other grounds for divorce, a woman keeps her bed and domestic belongings, and thus her rights to milk, while she has infants to support. When this is no longer the case, and all her sons and daughters have respectively received their patrimonies or are betrothed, she is eligible for conjugal separation or divorce. Where the matricentral component of which she is the head represented the last responsibility of her husband, his family, household, homestead and herd are dissolved in the way described above. In such a case divorce proceedings do not have to be instituted, the process merely consisting of conjugal separation. It should be noted in passing that, just as it is most fitting that a man's first-born should be a boy, so should his last child. Where this is not the case, a son's marriage is delayed until his elder sister marries.

Where the husband of a woman who has reached the menopause has other wives, conjugal separation may occur and she may become dependent on her eldest son. But she may as an alternative be divorced, particularly where her husband wishes to undertake another marriage within the Muslim legal maximum. Finally it should be noted that the sanctions applicable to widow inheritance marriage (which will be discussed below) operate most effectively in the case of young widows, not those who are nearing the end of their childbearing period.

These practices are associated with others which confirm the interpretation of the marital contract set forward here. If the likelihood of divorce of a woman by her husband is greatest at the beginning and end of the menarche and in intervals in which she does not bear children, the fate of a barren woman is one of continual insecurity, unless she can marry where her domestic virtues are of more importance than her reproductive capabilities. A barren wife's best hope is in the fertility of her co-wives, for a woman who is childless but of equable disposition and a hard worker may, in certain circumstances, be a good foil to a co-wife whose main role is that of mother. There are alternative courses for barren women. Some, unable to find a domestic situation of the type just described, enter a succession of marriages which take them further from the preferred endogamous loci of marriage into "strange" clans of Pastoral Fulani; into the ranks of semi-sedentary Fulani, or sedentary non-Fulani villagers. Others move, more quickly, into prostitution in the towns.

A second consistent feature of marital histories which is associated with the foregoing conditions is that there is a growing disparity in age between a man and his successive wives.

These conditions demonstrate the institutional factors supporting the contention that the principal expectation of a Pastoral Fulani man in his wife is that she bear him children. The complementary expectation, of a wife in her husband, which is now examined, is that he maintain a herd sufficient for the support of herself and her children.

A herd may prove or promise to be insufficient for a wife's needs in two ways, each of which may occasion the recrimination of a wife and make divorce on these grounds more likely. First, the herd itself, or its milk output, may be reduced, and secondly, the household dependent upon it may be increased by a further matricentral component, so that a wife has at her disposal relatively less milk.

Actual reduction of herds by disease, loss or sale, is regarded by Pastoral Fulani women with varying degrees of contempt for the cattle owners. There are ceremonial occasions on which oblique references in extempore songs may be made by girls and women to the shame brought upon them by disease in the herds. This contrasts strongly with men's attitudes which are usually expressed in a way which suggests that a herdowner takes all reasonable precautions to avoid disease. The only true cattle medicine is good husbandry and disease is the work of Allah.

Reduction of herds by sale is not normally contemplated without pressing need for cash, and a good husband consults at least his senior wife when cash has to be raised. Women, rather than men, encourage side ventures in small stock such as sheep and goats, which can be sold when cash is needed without depletion of the herd from which their main subsistence is derived.

Conversely, women do not approve efforts of their husbands to better themselves politically when this involves presents to chiefs not in the pastoral community in whose gift a certain title may lie. Nor do they support sales of stock to purchase a horse, saddlery, a sword and gowns, which are necessary if a man is to make his mark in this way, unless the reproductive part of the herd remains untouched.

Women will also disapprove of the sudden migrations which are usually made for political motives, and the occurrence of such a migration is accompanied in marital histories and genealogies by a number of divorces of men by their wives. But normally, so long as they have access to markets and domestic water supplies, Pastoral Fulani wives support the seasonal movements of cattle.

A corollary of the opposition of women to courses of action which decrease the herd, and therefore, actually of potentially, its milk output, is that in the dry season, when milk output is unavoidably low, the conjugal separation which constitutes or leads to divorce is more likely to take place. At the height of the dry season, when temperatures are at their highest, food at its scarcest, watering and herding of cattle at its most arduous, and family units most dispersed, there is little doubt that the possibility of internal friction in the family is more pronounced than in the wet season. Fortunately, the tasks of this time of the year disperse even more than usual the personnel of the family, so that friction is automatically minimized. Nevertheless it is well recognized by Fulani that the difficulties of the dry season exacerbate any latent friction between husband and wife, and that wives are more likely to run away at this

season. It is also easier to do so without detection, owing to the dispersal of kinsfolk and the pastoral preoccupations of the season. In the wet season, when kinsfolk are congregated, an absconding wife will be quickly discovered. Moreover, this is a time when domestic friction is lost in the sense of more general unity which the ceremonies then carried out engender, and in the air of plenty and well-being fostered by easy pasturage and ample food.

The second way in which the herd upon which a wife depends for her supply of milk is decreased is a relative one, caused by the increase of the total household dependent upon it. The principal way in which this occurs is by an addition to the household head's establishment of a further wife, and, immediately or subsequently, of her children. In contrast to the reasons for divorce arising from absolute reductions in the herd, in which the interests of the husband and wife are at issue, those springing from relative reduction of the herd are based upon the antipathy of co-wives.

A wife for whom a herd was constituted, that is, a first wife by betrothal marriage, always has superior rights to milk in it over her husband's wives of inferior categories. It is said that this wife apportions rights to milk to junior wives. Although the wife for whom the herd is set up is normally a man's only wife at that time, it may happen that a husband takes another while she is away at her father's home for the birth of her first child. If such a wife remains in the household when the first wife returns, the latter's superior status is asserted in a custom in which the junior wife hides her face in her headcloth, and suffers a mock beating at the hands of the senior wife. The junior wife does not set up her bed until the senior wife is installed, and she does so to the south, or right-hand side, of the female domestic area.

This brief ceremony expresses the rivalry which is a consistent feature of the relation between co-wives. The divergence of interests of co-wives is demonstrated in three interconnected ways—in rivalry for the sexual attentions of the household head, in the achievement of greater influence in the household through the birth of children, and in the outward signs of this, the number of cattle allotted for milking. The rivalry of co-wives thus extends in some measure to their male children, the half-siblings who acquire cattle by allotment and inheritance on the basis of the differential rights of their mothers to milk specific cattle in the total paternal herd.

Rivalry for the sexual attentions of the household head is kept at a minimum by a strict rota which by its association with obligations of feeding the household head is uninterrupted during menstruation and extends well into pregnancy. Nevertheless quarrels leading to divorce do occur ostensibly on this score.

The rivalry of co-wives concerning the birth of children is seen primarily in the rules connected with parturition, conspicuous amongst which is that enjoining the mother to deliver all children but her first herself, without the assistance of her co-wives, who are normally the women nearest at hand. The operation of the rules concerning the custody of infants in divorce does not fail to produce anxiety in wives whose childbearing has temporarily or permanently ceased and the resultant tension lies between co-wives rather than between husband and wife.

Finally, a monogamous wife is loth to welcome a second wife to the household unless her domestic duties in milking and handling calves as well as taking care of children grow too great for her and any unmarried daughters she may have, owing to the size of the herd. In seeking divorce, Pastoral Fulani women may not merely be escaping from a domestic situation they regard as intolerable, but seeking one which represents an advancement for them in terms of the number of cattle they may have at their disposal for milking.

It can be seen from this brief description of the institutions of divorce and polygyny that in Pastoral Fulani society women's marital histories are highly variable. They are liable to be divorced if they bear insufficient or no children. They may initiate divorce if, when they have borne children, their husband's herd proves inadequate for their needs. They are liable either to initiate divorce or be divorced if they are living in a compound family, and the herd proves inadequate for the maintenance of the whole unit. The full extent of this instability of her marriage bond is found at the beginning and end of a woman's childbearing period, but one or all of these circumstances may recur during her marital history.

It follows that the matricentral group of genetrix and children or mater and children in Pastoral Fulani society is also unstable. It is true that a mother cannot be separated from her infant children, who go with her in conjugal separation, and it is also true that the conjugal tie is firmest when there are infant children in the family. But as children reach the age of betrothal, they may be claimed by a former husband. Only at the end of a woman's reproductive life does the maternal tie reassert itself and then only between mother and son, when she claims her right to his support. A female's life may thus be spent in a number of domestic families headed by different herdowning males. As an infant she may live in the homestead of her pater cum genitor; or of her genitor only. As a girl who has been betrothed she lives in the homestead of her pater, who may also be her genitor. She then takes up residence for the first part of her marital life in her husband's father's homestead, returning to the homestead of her own father, not of her mother, for the birth of her first child. Her subsequent marital history during her reproductive life may be spent in one, often a succession, of husband's homesteads. Her declining years are spent with a son, or close agnatic kinsman of junior generation. One point deserves special recognition here. At stages or intervals when a female is a potential wife—that is to say, when she is a betrothed girl, or a divorced or widowed woman in her *edda*—she remains with her pater or close agnatic kinsman until marriage or remarriage.

The resultant picture of a Pastoral Fulani woman's career is one of continual dependence, in some sense or other, upon males, whether pater or genitor, husband, male agnatic kinsman, or son. During the reproductive period, and indeed when it is over, the marital stability of this career is contingent upon her reproductive performance. The birth and survival of one son will secure a woman in her old age, but not necessarily keep her in one homestead all her married life. But a full and evenly spaced family is likely on the evidence to do so; and it is in these conditions that a woman transcends the status of dependent, wields considerable influence with her husband, and may even, as Pastoral Fulani say, "be greater than a husband" and seek a more prosperous herdowner as a spouse.

Consider by contrast the career of a male. Endowed almost at birth with the means of his future subsistence; incorporated at an early age into a tightly organized partnership with father or brothers and trained by constant precept and practice in the tasks of the pastoral regime until he emerges as an independent householder, the Pastoral Fulani male stands, it appears, in a more secure position. He lives in principle in two homesteads during his life—that of his father, or guardian, and his own.

This apparent security is not wholly the case, for a man's household suffers changes in composition as a result of factors for which he bears responsibility. For just as a woman's marital stability depends upon her own fertility, so does that of a man depend upon the fertility of his herd. A man's own fertility is, characteristically, not believed to enter into the question. Male sterility is not recognized; there must be a woman, somewhere, by whom a man can have children. Social institutions support this; a man may acquire a family through the clandestine adulterous relations of his wife, or a wife may bring children from a former marriage.

The fertility of the herd depends, first, upon the skill and diligence of the herdowner in securing for it the optimum conditions of reproduction within the limits of the habitat. A number of maxims and ceremonies, and much of Fulani notions of prestige, support this interpretation of the direct responsibility borne by the herdowner for the fertility of his herd. To this extent the responsibility of a Pastoral Fulani woman for her own fertility, and that of a man for the fertility of his herd, are comparable. Where a woman's fertility is inadequate she moves on, in divorce, to another man, and perhaps right outside the Pastoral Fulani community. But much can be done to prevent a herd's numbers sinking below the effective minimum, or, when they have done, to regain it, and to adjust the amount of labour available to the herd. Herdowners are members of agnatic descent groups whose members combine for greater or longer periods or in different ways to initiate, maintain, or reinstate families and herds in a state of viability. The part played by agnatic kinsmen in the various contexts and states of nonviability will now be discussed.

The first of these is in the seasonal variations. In the wet season, the congregation of house-

holds is based upon the agnatic kinship of male household heads. These gatherings have little to do with economic cooperation as such, since at this time of the year the constituent households are experiencing the least difficulty in either the amount of labour required for the herds, or the provision of subsistence from them. The wet season gatherings constitute rather a demonstration of the solidarity of the agnatic descent group in which actual economic cooperation may be expected by its members; and the wet season rituals and ceremonies express this. In addition, relationships are entered into which tend to guarantee the viability of the constituent families in the future.

It has been seen that with the advent of the dry season, the wet season congregations disperse under the pressure of natural conditions. But the dry season conditions may make a given family household nonviable in respect of shortage of labour or of shortage of cattle. Thus as the dry season wears on the demands of pastoral cooperation grow, against a more general need for dispersal.

Where the shortage is one of cattle, the necessary dispersal of families is allowed to go unhindered, and households are not merged. This shortage is met by a series of loans of cattle, including both trained and untrained oxen for transport work, and stock bulls. The principle reason for such loans in the dry season is, however, the maintenance of the milk supply of a given household. Cows or heifers with calf at foot are used for this, and transferred readily between the herds of agnatic kinsmen. Cows in calf are not transferred, for it is the task of the herdowner, who bears direct responsibility for the fertility of his herd to assist in the delivery of its calves. It should be noted that among the Fulani calves born in bush without the assistance of the herdowner are sold after weaning. Similarly cows and heifers are not placed in an agnatic kinsmen's herd to be served and eventually calve. This takes place, but it belongs to a different series, not of loans but of exchanges, between herdowners of different clans. The genetic function of such exchanges is to break the train of line-breeding and inbreeding in the herd. The social function is to secure extra clan ties. Loans between agnatic kinsmen, however, are made with no consideration of cash or kind. The obligation both to loan animals to a needy kinsman, and to return them, rests on moral sanctions, applicable to the clan, which among the Fulani are only recently challenged by the Muslim courts. Loans of this kind for milk supply do not extend beyond the weaning of the calf in question; loans of pack animals seldom extend into a second dry season.

Shortage of labor in the dry season can be met in various ways, only some of which involve merging of households. The shortages of labor apparent in the context of the seasonal variations are those of dairymaids and herdboys. Shortages of girls usually arise where a wife is in an advanced stage of pregnancy, or has an unweaned child; and the difficulties of such a situation become most obvious in the dry season. In compound families a measure of cooperation is expected of co-wives, so that when a wife is prohibited from milking in virtue of her pregnancy, her co-wife milks and markets for both. Daughters, too, are interchangeable between the matricentral components of compound family households, assisting in marketing and, in particular, sharing the task of getting water for the whole household.

In the simple family household the shortage of female labor is met by the wife's "borrowing" an unmarried sister, or sister's daughter, to help in her domestic work.

Where in the dry season the tasks of herding and watering become too arduous or various for the herdboys of a family household, the difficulty is met in two ways. Daughters and even wives may be required to help with herding or more usually with watering. But this is an extreme solution and one which appears most usually to be brought about by conditions necessitating extreme dispersal at the height of the dry season.

Normally, where through dry season conditions there are not enough herdboys, two family households merge for the purpose of herding cattle. The homesteads are pitched side by side, and each herd spends the night in its own corral in which a corral fire is lit. But the herdboys of the two households are put on a common rota for herding, and look after both herds at once in the bush, for the herds do not merge when such temporary cooperation is carried out. The herds are watered separately, girls or women perhaps being brought in to help. The herds are milked separately by their respective dairywomen, and it should be noted that there may be milch cows borrowed from agnatic kinsmen in either herd. The herds are merged only for surveillance while grazing, and one form of cooperation does not rule out another.

The loss of viability due to irregular natural hazards is met again by the cooperation of herdowners of the same agnatic descent group. Where noncontagious diseases affect only parts of herds, deficiencies are met by loans of stock on the pattern described above. Where a whole herd is stricken, and the herdowner cannot recoup by loans, he may do so by outright gifts from agnatic kinsmen and clansmen. Nowadays when slaughtering is enforced in outbreaks of infectious and contagious diseases, cash compensation is paid by the Administration. Among the Fulani the head of a herdowner's agnatic lineage group acts as his agent for the receipt of compensation. But although compensated, herdowners in many groups . . . are still reluctant to build up their herds again by purchases of stock in the open market. Indeed such purchases of unknown cattle are rightly believed to further the spread of virulent and lethal diseases like bovine pleuropneumonia. The agnatic kinsmen of such herdowners supply them with cattle in the traditional way, in return for a share in the compensation money, agreed between the giver of the stock, its recipient and the head of the agnatic lineage group. Such a persistence of the reciprocal rights and duties of agnatic kinsmen in emergencies of this kind is advantageous to all parties. The herd of the unfortunate cattle owner is reestablished with cattle of the most desirable breed, whose history is known. The givers of cattle acquire a cash return which can be set against future expenses such as cattle tax. Both parties are saved the inconvenience of buying or selling in the open market and avoid cash losses involved in the services of middlemen. The sole intermediary is the head of the agnatic descent group, and the proportion of the compensation which he receives is spent on objects such as a gown or a turban, a sword or horse trappings, which confirm his status and ultimately redound to the prestige of his followers.

When the dispersal of households is not enough to alleviate the worst effects of an epidemic, this reciprocity perforce breaks down. It is now that a herdowner may recoup on the basis of extra-clan ties arising from cattle exchanges, or on extra-clan affinal relations. But these are weaker both in number and in the material relief they bring than the cooperation of agnatic kinsmen. Although widespread epidemics thus involve the dispersal of agnatic descent groups, and their incorporation, by families or individuals, into other such groups they may also mean the removal of families from the pastoral community either temporarily or permanently.

In the context of the seasonal variations and irregular natural hazards, the agnatic descent group and the clan are agencies for the reestablishment of the viability of their constituent families. This function emerges primarily when nonviability is caused by shortages of cattle. Indeed the ability of an agnatic descent group to act in this way is contingent upon the dispersal of its constituent families. Only by endowing household heads with full responsibility for the fertility of their herds and full authority for their deployment is it possible to succour any member of the agnatic lineage group whose family cannot maintain its viability.

It remains to consider the part played by agnatic kinship of household heads in the formal process of development of the family from its foundation to its dissolution. In the case of regular seasonal changes and irregular natural hazards, the agnatic lineage group has been seen to further the maintenance or reestablishment of viability of simple or compound family households. In the present case its function lies primarily in effecting the inception of family households, and secondarily in promoting their early viability.

It has been shown that it is at the inception of a family that both its requirements in cattle and in humans are most likely to be unsatisfied. It has also been mentioned that marriage is virilocal, male residence patrilocal and inheritance patrilineal. Thus on the formation of a man's domestic unit, his new establishment lies, typically, alongside that of his father. The relation of father and son at this period is one in which the son is independent of his father in some respects, dependent upon him in others.

The degree of dependence will be seen to lie with the state of viability of the father's family.

On the formation of his domestic unit, a newly married son has, in theory, a certain independence. His wife may prepare food for him, which he may eat, if he chooses, in his own homestead. He may now sell cattle and may provide beasts for slaughter at ceremonies, the first of which is likely to be the name-giving of his second child. He may now be responsible for raising his own share of cattle tax. He has a voice in camp councils, as a herdowner, and may give not only evidence, like a herdboy, but express opinions concerning it. He may move away from his father, and other agnatic kinsmen if he so desires, in the dry season.

In practice it is found that newly married sons stay with their fathers, often all the year round, eating in their father's homestead, being assisted by him in raising tax or ceremonial obligations, and siding firmly with him in camp councils. That this is so, in spite of a degree of theoretical independence, is due to two factors. First, the control of cattle loans and gifts remains with a man's father until his social or physical death. Secondly, the state of nonviability in the sense of shortage of both humans and cattle experienced almost inevitably by a herdowner's domestic unit on its inception, in relation to the viability of the parental domestic unit, keeps the two households together, for at least the period it takes to train a herdboy in the filial family.

Although a newly married man might decrease his herd, by sale or slaughter, as soon as it is established, and is bound to ensure its increase by careful deployment, the right to maintain it in adversity by loan or gift does not lie with him while his father is alive and in control of a herd of his own. For a son in this situation to ask for loans of cattle among his agnatic kinsmen of the same or senior generations is to repudiate all the efforts of his father as herdsman and begetter. This may take place, but in repudiating his father a man repudiates his agnatic descent group; the outward sign of such disaffection is not to return to the common wet-season camp. It should be noted that a young married man, who may have ranged farther afield than his father in seasonal movements, is still at liberty to arrange exchanges of cattle with herdowners of other clans.

Given this proviso, that a father controls accession of cattle by loan or gift to his son's herd, there is considerable variation in the degree of independence of the paternal and filial family households. This variation depends upon the state of viability of the parental family— that is to say, the extent to which it is unnecessary for a father to call into action the resources of the agnatic descent group for the benefit of his son. A few examples will make this clear.

Immediate separation for all except the period of the wet-season ceremonies, and maximum independence of the two households, is found to occur at the upper end of the scale of prosperity in cattle, and in the parental household best endowed with sons. A rich herdowner has been able, at the time of the inception of his eldest son's household, to support a number or succession of wives, and to exercise rights of residence over their children. At the same time his allocation of cattle to his son has been such that the latter's herd emerges immediately as an effective herd. In a case of this sort, the eldest son of each matricentral component, except the last, of the parental household, might well acquire the services of his younger full-brother or brothers, and be able to move freely in part if not all of the dry season.

A more normal case is one in which a newly married son withdraws from herding, while the herds of father and son are herded on a rota common to the newly married man's younger brothers. Here the parental and filial households remain together until the son's herd is effective, and he has a herdboy son to look after it.

A further case at the opposite extreme is where the father has only two sons. In this case the newly married son is unable to assume completely the status of herdowner since he is occasionally required to herd cattle. Here it is not so clear which of the two households is dependent upon the other. In a final case, that of a last son, dependence is passed over to the father, who, as described above, takes up residence with his son, his herd, family and homestead having been dissolved.

In all cases there is no question of postponement of marriage of a son by his father. This contingency is eliminated on the one hand by the prolongation of the life of the father as pater or genitor, or both, in successive or simultaneous polygynous marriages. On the other it is obviated by the fact that the men who are concerned to marry off their daughters to each others' sons are precisely that group in which cooperation in loaning cattle is enjoined. Household heads of an agnatic lineage group or set of agnatic descent groups dispose of their daughters in marriage to men with whose fathers they enter into reciprocal rights of pastoral cooperation in lending cattle.

But given marriage of both men and women at the earliest possible time consistent with notions of reproductive capacity, it is certain that from the beginning a newly married son partakes of his father's status as a herdowner. At one end of the scale he becomes head of a unit consisting of himself, his family and his unmarried brothers, which is pastorally, though neither ceremonially nor in emergency, independent. At the other end of the scale, lack of cattle gives his theoretical independence little meaning, while his father's shortage of labor restricts both father and son in those activities associated with herd ownership.

Thus, in summary, the inevitable period of nonviability which falls upon a newly established household is met by merging for certain purposes the households of father and son. This association is one of dependence of the son upon the father, due to the latter's control of loans and gifts, and of the greater possibility of cooperation between agnatic kinsmen of the father's own generation than between those of the generation of his son. The minimum period of this association is five or six years, although in certain circumstances which are rare in west Bornu today an immediate separation of father and son is possible. During the dry season the separation of parental and filial families is the criterion of their mutual viability. Their camping together in the wet season is an expression of the importance of this close agnatic tie.

The management of the inevitable period of nonviability in a newly formed household has been discussed on the assumption that a father sees all his son's marriages. But the formation of all a man's sons' homesteads and herds, much less their attainment of viability, is rare among the Fulani. It is more likely that physical death of the latter precedes the point of his social death, so that he leaves behind him unmarried children, fertile wives, and unallocated cattle. A man dies in two conditions relevant to the present issue: leaving sons none of whom has married and established a family and herd, or leaving some sons married and some unmarried.

In the case where none of the sons has married, it is a principle that the dead man's brother or patrilateral parallel cousin, usually a junior, shall act as the guardian of the dead man's children and supervise their betrothals. Under the witness of the family heads of the agnatic descent group, and with the mediation of its leader, he becomes the custodian of the dead man's herd, and turns over their portions to the dead man's sons as they marry. He should inherit at least one of the dead man's widows, particularly when of childbearing age. He should devote the increase of the unallocated balance of the dead man's herd to the support and provision at marriage of any of the children he may beget by her. The inherited widow's milking rights extend over this unallocated balance. In a case of this kind, the dead man's brother or close agnatic kinsman of the same generation is as nearly as possible his substitute.

But where a family head dies leaving some sons married with families, homesteads, and herds, and others without, this substitution in the collateral lines is not practiced. Although the dead man's brothers or patrilateral parallel cousins may now act as adjudicators or witnesses in the settlement of his affairs, the guardianship of minors and the custody of the herd falls to the dead man's eldest son. A brother or cousin may marry the dead man's widow, and it is thought proper that this should happen, but in this case she and her offspring must be provided for out of his own herd, unaugmented by any of the dead man's cattle.

Thus although . . . households may come into being and be nurtured through their period of inevitable nonviability through the agency of the household heads' fathers, this is not invariably the case, and a brother or father's brother's family may act as a quasi-paternal household. In these cases the conditions governing the nonviability of the newly formed household are the same. But there are significant differences in the control exercised by the quasi-parent over loans of cattle. This control applies solely to father and son; a brother's son or brother is able to

solicit loans in his own right as soon as his homestead and herd is established. Thus a household formed under the aegis of a brother or father's brother is more readily independent when shortage of cattle is in question.

In considering the causes of nonviability of families it has been shown that this is adjusted in various ways. At the inception of a family its inevitable nonviability is met by coresidence and cooperation with a household head who stands in a parental or quasi-parental relation to the head of the newly formed domestic unit. Subsequently, nonviability due to shortages of cattle are met by appeal to agnatic kinsmen. Potential shortages of humans are met by the processes of divorce and remarriage. Actual shortages of humans in the family is a matter of herdboys or dairymaids. Temporary help of girls is obtained by a woman among the unmarried girls of her agnatic lineage group. That of herdboys is obtained by temporary coresidence of households whose heads are agnatic kin. All these arrangements are designed to correct nonviability at the earliest opportunity, so that the simple or compound family may develop and exploit its means of subsistence in conditions which permit its greatest possible independence. This independence of economic action is secured for both men and women, and hence for the families to which they belong, by the help they can receive from agnatic kinsfolk.

In Fulani society, family development, in the sense of cyclical changes in the size and composition of viable domestic groupings based upon the family, must be regarded primarily as simple or compound family development. To the field observer this is readily obvious since dwelling units of a uniform pattern are referable to a simple or compound family as a household. More striking still is the association of herds with such family homesteads. Homesteads are grouped together, but this grouping is by no means indicative that they form joint domestic units. Where joint domestic units are formed, they are joint only in the limited sense of combining for the surveillance of cattle. Combinations of this sort are transitory and depend upon factors outside the formal development of the family. Only at the inception of a family are its formal properties likely to promote its incorporation into a wider domestic unit, that of father and son, father's brother and brother's son, or of brothers. The duration and degree of dependence exhibited in these joint households varies with the state of development of the parental or quasi-parental family; indeed where the parental family is well endowed, the initial nonviability of a filial household may be completely nullified.

This fragmentation into domestic units based upon the simple or compound family is made possible primarily by an inheritance system which, in the main, throughout a man's life matches the means of subsistence to which he has title, or which he actively controls, to his own skill and strength as a herdsman or begetter of herdsmen.

This family system may be regarded as an adaptation to a set of particular natural conditions in which seasonal variations and irregular natural hazards, as well as the social environment, encourage a high degree of autonomy in the smallest social units.

4. THE INDIVIDUAL AND FAMILY RELATIONSHIPS IN GUATEMALA

RUBEN E. REINA

From The Law of the Saints: A Pokoman Pueblo and its Community Culture *by Ruben E. Reina. Copyright © 1966, by the Bobbs-Merrill Company, Inc. Reprinted by permission of the publisher. Ruben E. Reina is Professor of Anthropology and Curator of Latin American Ethnology of the University Museum at the University of Pennsylvania. He has done field work in Guatemala, Argentina, and Spain and is currently engaged in research on Guatemala in the 16th century.*

■ In agricultural as in horticultural and pastoralist societies, the family is a unit of production. But the agricultural family is generally smaller, and peasant landholdings are typically quite small. In some societies (such as Japan) it is thus not feasible for all of a man's sons to live with him, since on his death his land would have to be divided among too many descendants in tiny and uneconomical parcels; hence only eldest sons inherit, the others going to live elsewhere. In other such societies, where all children inherit equally (as among the Guatemalan peasants described in the following selection), inheritance is a source of friction resulting in a loosening of the ties of the extended family. When an extended family can hold together, the family's land is generally under the management of the head of the group, but often, as in Chinautla, the trend is toward individually owned land. Thus, as Ruben Reina observes, extended family organization is the ideal, but is adhered to only in a minority of cases.

Like every other work group, the agricultural family is organized to use its labor efficiently within the limits of the available technology. In this selection we see how the various statuses and roles in the agricultural family are defined in terms of its productive and land-owning goals.

These relationships involve not only individuals but also the nuclear family as a whole when it is part of an extended family organization. Each of these relationships is not only economic but social as well.

Whether or not the agricultural household is part of an extended family, it must rely on cooperative relationships with others, as in a horticultural strategy. However, as a result of political pressures and the vesting of exclusive rights to land in individuals rather than in corporate kin groups, lineage organizations wither away. Different substitutes for the cohesive kin groups have evolved in varying agricultural societies as accommodations to local conditions. Here Reina describes the system of *compadrazgo* (ceremonial or ritual kinship), which is one of an individual's most important lines of defense outside the household and throughout his life. It (or a comparable system) is an important feature of agricultural adaptations, especially where life is precarious.

In addition to describing social and economic relationships in this peasant household system, and the ways in which they are colored by the problem of inheritance, Reina also points to some of the important sources of change in the peasant family. Significantly, his first illustration of family relationships in this town concerns a man who is a factory employee. This kind of productive activity entails different kinds of social and economic relationships, and with a quick stroke Reina paints a picture of how nonagricultural employment leads to the breakdown of the extended family system.

The best general introduction to the institution of *compadrazgo* is "An Analysis of Ritual Co-Parenthood (Compadrazgo)," by Sidney W. Mintz and Eric R. Wolf (*Southwestern Journal of Anthropology*, 6 [1953] : 341-68) ; also see *The People of the Sierra*, by J. A. Pitt-Rivers (New York : Criterion Books, 1954). For an analogous system in Japan, see "The Oyabun-Kobun : A Japanese Ritual Kinship Institution," by Iwao Ishino (*American Anthropologist*, 55 [1953] : 695-704). For other good accounts of peasant family systems in many parts of the world, see *Tzintzuntzan : Mexican Peasants in a Changing World*, by George M. Foster (Boston : Little, Brown, 1967) ; *English Villagers of the Thirteenth Century*, by George C. Homans (Cambridge, Mass. : Harvard University Press, 1941) ; *Proper Peasants : Traditional Life in a Hungarian Village*, by Edit Fel and Tamas Hofer (Chicago : Aldine, 1969) ; and *The House of Lim : A Study of a Chinese Farm Family*, by Margery Wolf (New York : Appleton-Century-Crofts, 1968). Two comparative studies by Francis L. K. Hsu will be especially interesting to American readers : *Americans and Chinese : Two Ways of Life* (New York : Schuman, 1953) and *Clan, Caste, and Club* (Princeton, N.J. : D. Van Nostrand, 1963). A recent and interesting study of change in a peasant society is *Black Carib Household Structure : A Study of Migration and Modernization*, by Nancie L. Solien Gonzalez (Seattle and London : University of Washington Press, 1969). ■

ALTHOUGH THE NUCLEAR FAMILY is the basic unit in the marriage institution and constitutes the socially approved condition for sexual relations, the extended family, living in a compound with each nuclear family in its own hut, is considered the ideal pattern of residence. Nonetheless, only 35 per cent of the 210 Indian households are composed of an extended family. Family individualization, socioeconomic independence at an earlier stage of adulthood, and the decreasing size of properties are factors related to the 65 per cent residing as nuclear families. It is still possible, however, to observe the leading role of the head of the extended

family, a role maintained in a mixed atmosphere of respect and cooperation, friction, and confusion.

The changes taking place in status and roles for members of the family have been pointed out by informants on various occasions. One man, for example, was married twenty years ago, taking his wife to live with his parents. At that time, he was working regularly in the nearby electric plant. He said:

Before I was married I religiously brought my earnings to my parents, who disposed of the money as they chose. Each time I needed money, I had to ask them for it and satisfy them as to my purpose in requesting funds. My purchases were then submitted for their approval. After my marriage, this practice was continued, it being the normal way of conducting my financial affairs, though I was advised by my friends in the electric plant to put by a little money for my wife and myself. When I received my first raise in pay, my wife and I decided to keep it a secret from my parents, retaining the difference each payday in our own hut. It soon became obvious to my parents that they were being cheated, for they began to see us in new clothes that they had not authorized us to buy. This was the cause of a long fight, ending with the separation of the families. My wife and I left my father's compound and built our own little hut on a small piece of property that I was finally able to buy.

From a practical viewpoint, the pattern of the extended family is associated with individual dependency and subjugation, only desirable when there are other fringe benefits such as an eventual inheritance in exchange for the care of aged parents or simply a good life. It appears that the arrangements for residence relate to economic variables.

But to live as an extended family does not imply common rights to family land, fruit trees, or gardens. Those families living in an extended family pattern observe strict private property rules and have little feeling of cooperation among themselves. Each nuclear family within the extended group functions as an independent unit, and this independence extends to the subdivision of property within each family itself. Friction and discord result when property rights are not respected regardless of the age or status of the offender.

My oldest sister wants everything she owns on her side of the compound, near her house. She has *huisquiles* and looks at them very carefully every morning, even counting them to be sure that none of us [three other nuclear families] has touched them.

Often I am not on speaking terms with her because she is very self-centered and accuses me of stealing her things. She fights me even when my child goes near her place or plays with her children's things. I even have to buy eggs from her at the same price as in the store. We work separately. I make pottery with my mother, but my sister has her own place, and it is not customary for us to use each other's clay or to borrow clay or tools for work. Sometimes we borrow money, but only when there is real need for it.

Nostalgically, an old man spoke of the extended family as it used to be:

In the past, the head of the extended family had more power over his children's actions and whereabouts, regardless of their age or status. Nowadays, children without experience want to leave the household and run their own affairs as soon as they can. Parents do not mix in or advise their children, as used to be the case. Even in questions of religion, the young people choose what they want. One of my own children became a Protestant, breaking the *costumbres* that I had taught him. He also went to live with his wife separately, away from my compound.

Although this quotation could represent a theme common in most societies, that "old times were different and better," some specific factors seem to have prevented the ideal running of the extended family pattern: the fact that a new wife feels inferior in the household of her in-laws; the same feeling, though more intense, for the young husband who lives with his in-laws as son-in-law; the increasing economic independence of the Chinautla women, who can make a living if they become fast and skillful potters; and the recent loss of the men's economic solvency.

HUSBAND-WIFE RELATIONS

The husband-wife relationship seems to have been defined in terms similar to those of the traditional contract marriage, as an old conservative lady of Chinautla explained:

We were as a piece of property, bought to perform a duty within the home and to remain at the will of the husband. We made our pottery, but our husbands took it to the capital. Sometimes we accompanied them, but most often they went alone to sell the product for us. Many husbands were *muy malos* and ignorant and mistreated us. My husband was no different from most others. He drank a great deal,

and in that state he became angry, and then I was to blame for everything; besides that, he was always jealous. I could not leave him because my parents could not return to him the money he had spent to acquire me, and anyway, having failed with one man I would have had a hard time getting another. My husband died twenty-five years ago, and I was left with the children and without resources for our support.

Although women have more economic independence these days, some of the same attitudes persist. One must keep in mind that many couples seem to adjust to each other very well; nonetheless, I was impressed by the frequent tension between husband and wife. A husband who attempts to keep his wife at home all the time, who accompanies her to Guatemala City and the market with a load of pottery, and who refuses to take the bus because he thinks it is not part of the old *costumbres* is considered a very "boring" man (*aburrido*), and his wife will complain about his ways when there is an opportunity. Middle-aged women are aggressive and want to move about freely.

There seems to be much quarreling over trivialities, and middle-aged wives in particular claim that they have frequent bilious attacks (*attaques biliosos*) due to fits of anger with their husbands. On such occasions, the insult most commonly used by the husband is "Go find your lover (*casero*)." The quarrels are very intense if food is not ready on time for the husband; the husband often asks concerning his wife's recent whereabouts in order to explain the delay in the preparation of the food. If she defends herself, he says, "You're pretty courageous to talk so much" (*tenés cara de hablar mucho*) to remind her of her status and put her to shame. Middle-aged wives—active potters— seldom remain passive during quarrels. Many have been known to take their cases to the mayor or to take matters into their own hands.

In one case, a jealous husband, not finding his wife in the house at mealtime, went to look for her in the Guatemala City market. When he found her, he insulted her, shouting that she must have had an assignation (*compromiso*) with someone else. The woman, incensed on hearing this accusation, threw her recently purchased load of corn on the ground and informed her husband that if he wanted *tortillas* he could carry the corn home himself. The husband carried the corn home, but upon arrival the wife had an *ataque bilioso.*

A middle-aged wife (of 30) explained that she and her husband came to the following arrangement in order to have peace in the house:

My husband and I do what we want. If he wants to go out and stay out at night, he does it and I don't say anything [*no lo regaño*]. I can do the same thing without his nagging me all the time. Now [during December] I go to *las posadas* every night accompanying Saint Joseph and Mary, and he goes to church every night to meet with the Saint Francis order. I told him that I am *persona honrada* and that he can put me through an examination any time he wants to if he thinks I am not a good woman. Of course, I am always careful to have things ready to eat when he comes from the woods with the charcoal. I serve him well.

There is strong indication that the role of the wife is more than just that of mother and housekeeper; she tends to share economic, religious, and political matters with her husband. Her economic independence is displayed when a women sells her own pottery in the market without consulting her husband, even on the rare occasions when he is present, having helped her to take her jars to the city. After selling her work, a woman disposes of the earnings as she chooses, buying staples, clothes, or other items for her family. The making of pottery is a means of assuring a steady income in the family in case of the husband's illness or death, or in case of a separation. The independence of marriage partners is intensified in those cases in which the husband commutes daily to the city, observes schedules, works on night shifts, travels to other areas with trucking enterprises, or engages still in the newly developed pattern of growing *milpa* in the coastal area. During the periods of seeding, weeding, and harvesting the *milpa*, the wives are left alone with the children and are busy with the pottery business. The men will make no attempt to transplant their families; this cannot be attributed to their independence, however, but rather to the fact that to leave Chinautla behind is still inconceivable to Chinautlecos.

PARENT-CHILD RELATIONS

A considerable difference exists between the attitude of mothers toward their children and that of fathers. Women tend to regard children as a burden and the beginning of martydom, and to take little of the joy in them that their fathers do when they are small. Children are punished very little and allowed to play with friends throughout their leisure hours. In any trouble that may arise, fathers tend to protect their sons, mothers their daughters. Moreover, if need be, fathers protect both sons and daughters from their mother. As one informant put it, "I will beat my wife if she beats my children." In the apprenticeship of growing up and learning the skills and attitudes of the adult, men train their sons in masculine roles and women train their daughters in feminine ones. In peaceful association, the child learns by imitation and constant example.

But a great change takes place in the parent-child relationship when the children grow up. The pleasantness of childhood changes into strife between father, son, and siblings during disagreements over inheritance of land. The everlasting *pleitos* (disputes), which often lead to the use of sorcery against members of one's own family, are due to jealousy arising from "unfair" land division. The economic pressures are many nowadays, and heirs feel cheated and do not hesitate to make their feelings known if they believe that land rightfully theirs was left to someone else in reward for preferential treatment given to the old man by some other member of the family seeking a piece of property. Antagonized children are often brought to the point of seeking legal assistance in defiance of their father's will.

In an inheritance dispute between a father and his two sons, the arguments grew so bitter that the old man, in a state of exhaustion, became very ill. One son always came to them drunk and quarrelsome; the other had walked out angrily, saying he would not return to see them anymore. This led the parents to say:

Our son who is always drunk came to us today and wanted to quarrel and attempted to fight his father. We are not respected any more, and they want to forget us and our needs. We are old and can work no longer, and they seem to think that they were born under a stone. They don't want to recognize their *nana* and *tata*. They want what we own, and they want us to keep out!

Discord arises when a young man is ready to substitute for an old one. A father's authority over his children is opposed to the son's desire, on establishing his own family, to take on this role himself, and a situation of obvious and open conflict is created. The old man wishes to maintain his power, while the son is eager publicly to establish his own identity, his own adult status, and his own manhood. Considering the limited amount of land, the conditions imposed on them by the "law of the saints," and the unpredictability of the inheritance rules, many young Chinautlecos are willing to take a certain amount of risk by contradicting the ideals of the culture. There is the rationale that eventually something could be done to cover wrongdoing.

KIN RELATIONS

While the inhabitants of Chinautla recognize the fact that they all have the same ancestors and that everyone in the pueblo could be related if they go far enough in tracing their kinship, this is not considered of practical importance or significance. They do not talk about their obligations to or sentimental ties with members of the kin group. Kinship relations do not dominate the economic or political spheres, and Chinautlecos have the right to dispose of their property as they wish by drawing up a legal will through the mayor. Although kinship does become important in discussions of prospective marriage and inheritance, it does not appear to be crucial in prescribing behavior, uniting large numbers of people, or bringing about cooperation.

Marriage is avoided by those of the same surname, for the obvious historical connection turns it into an issue of incest. And to marry a cousin is not in good taste, although sexual relations among them take place. A *unión de hecho* may occur between cousins who do not consider themselves siblings (*como hermanos*)— that is, raised in the same household—and are not related ceremonially through the godparent-hood system. After some years in union and the birth of children, the union can be legalized, and the *tatahpish* will perform the ritual. Although the church does not approve, it is permitted by Guatemalan law, and the church is not consulted in such cases.

Kinsmen who are distant both socially and emotionally may activate the relationship when the possibility of inheritance, or other economic gain, exists. Claims based on "great love" or favors rendered are put forth in order to ensure qualification as a potential heir. Old people may feel that someone who deeply cares for their welfare, attends them sincerely, and, most of all, loves them should be rewarded; and nearer kin, perhaps even children, may then be passed over. In contrast, when property is not available for inheritance, distant—as well as close—relationships and obligations are disregarded.

The individual seems to stand alone among a potential web of relatives. Remarks like "because he is my blood relative, we cooperate" are the rare exception. The basic kinship structure is recognized in the very practical situations of marriage, death and inheritance, and emergency —for during family crises, relatives will give aid, but only when it is requested. Under ordinary conditions, indifference, apathy, and antagonism toward relatives of any age frequently appear.

CEREMONIAL KIN RELATIONS

The relationships among ceremonial kinfolk stands in strong contrast to that among blood relatives. From time to time, one hears co-parents speak about aiding each other, liking each other, or merely having fun together; here there is recognition of each other and much mutual assistance. The institution of *compadrazgo* has been described or mentioned in most studies of Latin America and has lately been well discussed by J. A. Pitt-Rivers in a study of Spain. This is an important institution in Chinautla, for it binds people in unique ways. The state, intensity, and variability of this ceremonial institution will therefore be described as it exists in Chinautla.

A person becomes involved in the ceremonial kinship relationship through various church rituals. In Chinautla, most common are the godparents (*padrinos*) of baptism (*de bautismo*); of marriage (*de casamiento*); of confirmation (*de confirmación*); of blessing (*de evangelios*); and of the saint (*del santo*).

Two families that enter into the *padrinos de bautismo* relationship renew the bonds with all the children born of the same parents. When a woman is pregnant, it is well known that the god-mother of her other children becomes respon-sible for the coming child. On one such occasion, the godmother was called to the mother's house early in the morning because the latter had given birth to a dead child. The godmother hurried to the home to make the sign of the cross over the face of the dead child, baptizing him in the name of Father, Son, and Holy Spirit, and to place a grain of salt on his lips, making the child Christian and thus converted into an angel. She then proceeded to find crepe paper of some bright color from which to make the shroud; she returned to the house to clean and dress the body; she fired the rockets, both at the house and in the cemetery; and she headed the pro-cession to the cemetery, burning incense along the way. She also brought one and one half quarts of *guaro*, one dollar's worth of bread, *frijoles*, and a chicken.

The link between the two families remains strong, for ideally the godparents of baptism are selected as godparents of marriage. If age permits, the godchildren (*ahijados*) request the same persons to become godparents of baptism for *their* children; if age does not allow it, a son or daughter of the old godparents is next in line. The complications that arose in the case of one of the informants indicate the role and importance of the godparents of baptism at the time of marriage:

The go-between talked to the bride about the groom's godmother. The bride had heard that this godmother had been gossiping in Chinautla about her reputation, and therefore she refused to have her as godmother of marriage. Another person who was economically able was suggested, but this person, when contacted, did not accept because she did not want to take the place of the baptismal godmother. The groom's mother went to the house of the god-mother to explain the situation and request from her permission for the other woman, selected by the girl, to become *madrina*. The godmother responded, "I was happy to learn that my *wak'un* [son] is to be married, and I was looking forward to being his *madrina* of marriage, but since the girl does not like me, you can ask the other person to be his *madrina* in my place." "*Tiosh* [thank you], *comadre*," responded the mother.

The other woman accepted the request to become godmother and fixed the date for the marriage. Simultaneously, however, the godson of this latter woman came to her, requesting her to become his godmother of marriage that same week. A serious conflict arose because she would be unable to afford the expenses of serving in both marriages during the

same week. Since she had to give preference to her own godson, the informant's wedding was postponed for three months.

Godparents are also selected for confirmation, one of the seven Catholic sacraments. A child at the age of "discretion" is given the right to have a supplementary baptism. The godparents for confirmation may often be the same as those for baptism, or if there is need for more sec-urity for the child owing to the age of the first set of godparents and parents, a new set of godparents for confirmation is selected.

When there is evidence that the child has had a serious fright, requiring blessing by the priest (*evangelios son hechados*), godparents are needed to present the child to the priest.

Finally, a godparent is appointed during the celebration of a household saint (*apadrinar el santo*); in this case, a man is chosen. The Christ of Esquipulas is taken to the owner's home by the godfather. Thus, the owner of the saint and the godfather to the saint enter into the relation-ship of co-fathers (*compadres*).

The *compadrazgo* is meaningful in the life of both child and parents. The parents do not let sentimentality or ties of friendship rule the selection of *compadres*. Theirs is a very practical viewpoint. They look for someone who can offer continuity of the ceremonial relationship to the child, who is ready to help the family in case of the child's death, and who can transmit his success to the godchild. For there is a *creencia* that *compadres* with good luck can influence the course of events in the child's life. When one looks for a godfather for one's child, according to an informant:

One must give careful consideration to the degree of success achieved in life by the *padrino*-to-be. If the *padrino*-to-be has done very well and if his future looks bright, if his family has been reared with few or no losses of children, and if very little illness has touched the family, this person will be highly sought after by those parents who have been facing difficul-ties and have not been able to rear children to adulthood.

The selection of godparents for baptism may be made across "ethnic" lines, primarily by Indians choosing Ladinos and Mengalas. It can be safely stated that the Indians cultivating a Ladinoized "self" see this as a means of building up bonds of relationship beneficial for the future of the child. However, currently there is also a strong economic factor involved in the selection of a Ladino godfather, and this is admitted by the Indians. It is relatively inexpensive to request a Ladino to be a godparent; the Ladino accepts, as a gift, a chicken or a dozen eggs. It is embarrassing, however, for an Indian asking another Indian to enter into the *compadrazgo* relationship to offer no more than a chicken; the usual gift accompanying such a request is a basket containing at least two dollars' worth of bread, three dollars' worth of meat, two dollars' worth of *guaro*, and chocolate.

One result of the *compadrazgos* established between Indians and Ladinos is that it becomes necessary for them to address each other on equal terms. They apply the same terminology used among themselves: in Spanish, *madrina* for the godmother, *padrino* for the godfather, *hijo* (the frequently used *mijo* is derived from *mi hijo*) for the godson, and *hija* or *mija* for the goddaughter. Within the relationship, Ladinos and Indians greet and refer to each other with the term *compadre*, and the child's parents (Indians) and the godparents (Ladinos) enter into the ceremonial relationship indicated by that term, which indicates a sharing of the parental prerogatives. This stands in contrast to the behavior observed in San Luis Jilotepeque (inhabited by Pokoman-speaking people), where the term *compadre* "is not much used between Indians and Ladinos, because it implies an equality which the Ladinos will not admit."

The theoretical implications here are of interest because of the paradoxical social situation. In terms of the "ethnic" factor, the social distance is considerable, but it has become economically profitable to both groups to overlook, in a sense, the distance and to enter instead into a relationship that formally implies closeness, confidence, and cooperation. However, this relationship does not seem to affect the image each group holds of the other or of themselves. It becomes just another of the many contractual arrangements characteristic of Chinautla social organization.

An outsider finds it difficult to enter into the ceremonial kinship relation for baptisms and weddings. I was asked to become a *padrino* of confirmation, but this relationship is of secondary importance. Others said, "It would be nice to have you as *padrino* for the wedding of my son, but you are leaving us, aren't you?"

Chinautlecos may turn to the city for their selection of persons for the minor *padrinazgo* of confirmation. The merchants from the markets, the *regatonas* who have traded with the Chinautlecos for several years and have developed a bond of trust with them, make themselves available. Informants state that the pattern received impetus when the women began their frequent visits to the city market, but so far it remains no more than "a nice thing to do."

Three features of the institution of *compadrazgo* merit some discussion. First, although the idea is present in the relationship that godparents can claim the godchild if his parents die, in reality this is seldom done or talked of. There is an economic interest in keeping the child in the family; in case of the parents' death, a grandmother is first in line to care for him, and then anyone in the extended family. There are only a few cases of *compadres* rearing orphans as their own children. Two of these children are Indians in the home of a Ladino *comadre*. The girls were reared from infancy in the Ladino household; they are now valued domestic helpers and also enjoy the affection of their ceremonial siblings. The two girls are aware that they had Indian parents, but they have not learned the Indian language. They dress in a poor Ladino style, wear no shoes, and have long braids. "When the time comes," says the godmother, "they will be able to marry Ladinos, Indians, or boys of the Mengala type, but we would prefer them to marry Ladinos in order to separate themselves still further from the uncivilized *costumbres* of the Indians." The Ladino "mother" is anxious for praise of her accomplishments in training her godchildren.

Second, *all* the members of the two families linked by the social act of godparenthood are involved in the ceremonial relationship, and the terminology by which they are referred to is identical to that used for relatives of the nuclear family. To illustrate, Juan was standing on a street corner one evening when his *madrina* of baptism passed by. He greeted her and ran to her to receive her blessing; she touched his forehead, saying, "God bless you, *wak'un* [son]." I asked Juan if this woman's children were related to him, and he replied without hesitation that they were his brother and his sister. On another occasion, a child received a blessing from an old lady. She was asked if this child were her godson. "No, he is the godson of my son, and I am his godgrandmother." The informants all state, furthermore, that *was imas* (brother) or *was ishak* (sister) in the ceremonial kinship constitutes a category of siblings, and that marriage among them is an act of incest. In this, the Chinautlecos extend the limits of marriage prohibition within the godparenthood relationship far beyond those maintained by the Catholic church.

Given the rules for selecting marriage partners, this strictly endogamous pueblo of about 1,500 inhabitants could develop serious conflicts if the selection of godparents was made at random, for they could enter into ceremonial relationships that would considerably reduce the number of potential marriage partners. At this point in their history, ceremonial kinship relationships are functioning for the benefit of all concerned, and so far godparenthood has not been deliberately used to block persons from marriages. There is, however, much order and predictability in the selection of *compadres*. Conflicts do not arise because of the preference for strengthening established ceremonial links rather than seeking new ones among other families, and because there is agreement to select as godparents blood relatives, persons of an older generation, childless couples, or couples across the "ethnic" lines. Interestingly enough, the people with nearly one hundred godchildren meet three of these latter qualifications. There was an old Mengala couple who, the Indians agreed, made good godparents and who were agreeable to the honor; that their daughters married outsiders is not mere coincidence. Despite all the careful consideration they give to the selection of godparents, Chinautlecos do not seem consciously aware of the consequences for marriage were the traditional bases for selection to be modified.

A third interesting aspect of the system is that changes take place in ceremonial kinship status, correlating with the rites of passage in a Chinautleco's life. I shall follow a case through time, not for its typicality but because it is considered ideal.

Juan requested Don Jesus (an Indian 30 years of age) and his wife to become the godparents of his first son, Pedro. While the child was growing up, the relationship between Juan and Don Jesus was warm although not intimate; they were co-parents of the same child. The child learned to be courteous when meeting his godfather and observed his obligation of running toward him for the ceremonial blessing. Pedro grew older, and now he greeted his godfather with a "good day, *padrino*," from the distance. The co-parents appeared distant for several years.

Eventually, Pedro arrived at a marriageable age, and a *padrino* was needed. Juan and his son approached Don Jesus again, who agreed to become godparent for Pedro's wedding. There seemed to be a renewal of emotions as they became double co-parents by baptism and marriage. Now Pedro did not identify Don Jesus as "my *padrino* of baptism"; instead he was "my *padrino* of marriage." However, the direct use of the word *padrino* was usually avoided.

A year later Pedro had a male child. Don Jesus was asked by Pedro to become the godfather of baptism for his child. Don Jesus and his wife accepted and entered in the double role of godfather of and co-parent with Pedro. At this point, Don Jesus and Pedro called each other *compadre*. In twenty years, Pedro had achieved an equal ceremonial status, regardless of age differences. Pedro appeared to enjoy the fulfillment of his manhood.

From other cases, it is possible to illustrate what would have happened if Don Jesus had died during Pedro's early childhood. Juan, Pedro, and Pedro's son would have made the following adjustments: Pedro's godmother would have played an important social role, and she would have been asked, at Pedro's marriage, to be godmother for the wedding. She could then have chosen, from any of her well-liked relatives, a person to represent her deceased husband. But the on-going relationship would have terminated here—and with it the possibility for change in ceremonial status—since at the birth of Pedro's first child a new set of godparents would have been selected and a new set of relationships established. Pedro would have decided on the godparents if he had taken residence with his father. It would have been different had he taken residence with his wife's parents; then, the choice of godparents might have been influenced by her family.

This case, which is regarded as ideal, implies that the male child tends to place the godfather in a stronger position than the godmother (the female child is more attached to the godmother); that continuity through the male line (patrilineal rule) is reinforced when residence is patrilocal; and that rites of passage are reinforced by the changing of ceremonial kinship status.

A careful planning of the ceremonial relation-ship is far more important to the individual than I had at first suspected. In looking at the extreme contrast in the quality of interaction among blood relatives and ceremonial relatives, my impression is that the greater interest in and warmth of the latter relationship could spring from the possibilities it holds for the manipula-tion of associations and benefits. Moreover, the parental blessing given at the home altar on the wedding day both frees a young couple as adults and leaves them alone; an important link between parent and child is suddenly broken. It must be gratifying to the Chinautleco to be able—by adding godparents to his social and emotional network—somewhat to counter-balance the social forces that tend to push him into a lonely and isolated life.

5. URBAN FAMILIES: CONJUGAL ROLES AND SOCIAL NETWORKS

ELIZABETH BOTT

Reprinted from Human Relations, *Vol. 8, pp. 345-384. Copyright 1955, Tavistock Publications. (Footnotes have been renumbered.) Elizabeth Bott Spillius is a social anthropologist and psychoanalyst; she lives in London. Her professional experience includes field research among the Ojibwa Indians, in Chicago and in Tonga, and in a mental hospital in England. Her principal anthropological interests concern the relationships of groups to the environment and of rank and environment in Polynesia. Her publications include* Family and Social Network: Roles, Norms, and External Relationships in Ordinary Urban Families.

■ It has been a very long time since formal or ceremonial kinship organization played much part in the structure of social relationships in England and other societies that are now industrialized. But kinship relations do not atrophy when formal kinship groups disappear. England did not develop a *compadrazgo* system, but this does not mean that wider kinship relations were unimportant there during that country's predominantly agri-cultural stage of development and that they did not exert a strong influence on family organization and relationships.

One of the accompaniments of industrialization is the differentiation of productive activities from the household, physically as well as socially, with each member of the household selling his labor as an individual rather than in conjunction with other members of the family group. But people do not devote all their time to earning a livelihood nor do all of them gain a livelihood in the same way. As a result, there is considerable variability in the noneconomic relationships in which people engage in a heterogeneous industrial nation. This is an aspect of the axiom that it is not possible to speak of *the* family system in a complex national society. Such variability probably could not occur in a stateless kin-based society.

In the next selection, Elizabeth Bott provides us with an excellent example of this variability. She shows us some of the familial consequences when married couples maintain very close relationships with wider kin and other networks in contrast to couples who live without such involvements. The first situation is accompanied by what Bott calls "segregated role relationships," in which husband and wife maintain separate circles of friendship and a very sharp division of labor within the family. The second is accompanied by "joint conjugal role-relationships," in which the couple share the same friends and often substitute for each other in household tasks. There are intermediate situations, of course, which one can interpret in terms of the complementarity of extra- and intra-household relations or as people in transition from the first to the second mode of living, though the two views are not mutually exclusive.

By the usual standards of anthologies, this selection is quite lengthy. It has been included here because of its importance in illustrating the idea of familial diversity in a modern industrial society, and because of its clarity and its signific-ance for many new hypotheses and further research. Every reader should be able to find himself some-where along the continuum described by Bott. To benefit from the full methodological and substantive importance of Bott's work, it is necessary to consult her book, *Family and Social Network*, a revised edition of which will be published in 1971.

The following suggested readings for Great Britain are highly selective and are not intended to be exhaustive. *Family and Community in Ireland;* by Conrad M. Arensberg and Solon T. Kimball, (2nd edition, Cambridge, Mass.: Harvard University Press, 1968); *Two Studies of Kinship in London*, edited by Raymond Firth (London: The Athlone Press, 1956); *Family and Kinship in East London*, by Michael Young and Peter Willmott (Glencoe: The Free Press, 1957); and *The Family and Marriage in Britain* (Baltimore: Penguin Books, 1966). For the United States, see *American Kinship: A Cultural Account*, by David M. Schneider (Englewood Cliffs, N.J.: Prentice Hall, 1968), which is based on interviews with 53 white middle class families in Chicago. A very insightful paper with considerable significance for the study of the family in the context of kinship in modern society is "The Social Structure of Grandparenthood," by Dorian Apple (*American Anthropologist*, 58 [1956]: 656-63). ■

IN THIS PAPER I should like to report some of the results of an intensive study of twenty London families. The study was exploratory, the aim being to develop hypotheses that would further the sociological and psychological understanding of families rather than to describe facts about a random or representative sample of families. Ideally, research of this sort might best be divided into two phases: a first, exploratory phase in which the aim would be to develop hypotheses by studying the interrelation of various factors within each family considered as a social system, and a second phase consisting of a more extensive inquiry designed to test the hypotheses on a larger scale. In view of the time and resources at our disposal, the present research was restricted to the first phase.

The paper will be confined to one problem: how to interpret the variations that were found to occur in the way husbands and wives performed their conjugal roles. These variations were considerable. At one extreme was a family in which the husband and wife carried out as many tasks as possible separately and independently of each other. There was a strict division of labor in the household, in which she had her tasks and he had his. He gave her a set amount of housekeeping money, and she had

little idea of how much he earned or how he spent the money he kept for himself. In their leisure time, he went to football matches with his friends, whereas she visited her relatives or went to a cinema with a neighbor. With the exception of festivities with relatives, this husband and wife spent very little of their leisure time together. They did not consider that they were unusual in this respect. On the contrary, they felt that their behavior was typical of their social circle. At the other extreme was a family in which husband and wife shared as many activities and spent as much time together as possible. They stressed that husband and wife should be equals: all major decisions should be made together, and even in minor household matters they should help one another as much as possible. This norm was carried out in practice. In their division of labor, many tasks were shared or interchangeable. The husband often did the cooking and sometimes the washing and ironing. The wife did the gardening and often the household repairs as well. Much of their leisure time was spent together, and they shared similar interests in politics, music, literature, and in entertaining friends. Like the first couple, this husband and wife felt that their behavior was typical of their social circle, except that they felt they carried the interchangeability of household tasks a little further than most people.

One may sum up the differences between these two extremes by saying that the first family showed considerable segregation between husband and wife in their role-relationship, whereas in the second family the conjugal role-relationship was as joint as possible. In between these two extremes there were many degrees of variation. These differences in degree of segregation of conjugal roles will form the central theme of this paper.

A *joint conjugal role-relationship* is one in which husband and wife carry out many activities together, with a minimum of task differentiation and separation of interests; in such cases husband and wife not only plan the affairs of the family together, but also exchange many household tasks and spend much of their leisure time together. A *segregated conjugal role-relationship* is one in which husband and wife have a clear differentiation of tasks and a considerable number of separate interests and activities; in such cases, husband and wife have a clearly defined division of labor into male tasks and female tasks; they expect to have different leisure pursuits; the husband has his friends outside the home and the wife has hers. It should be stressed, however, that these are only differences of degree. All families must have some division of labor between husband and wife; all families must have some joint activities.

Early in the research, it seemed likely that these differences in degree of segregation of conjugal roles were related somehow to forces in the social environment of the families. In first attempts to explore these forces, an effort was made to explain such segregation in terms of social class. This attempt was not very successful. The husbands who had the most segregated role-relationships with their wives had manual occupations, and the husbands who had the most joint role-relationships with their wives were professionals, but there were several working-class families that had relatively little segregation and there were several professional families in which segregation was considerable. An attempt was also made to relate degree of segregation to the type of local area in which the family lived, since the data suggested that the families with most segregation lived in homogeneous areas of low population turnover, whereas the families with predominantly joint role-relationships lived in heterogeneous areas of high population turnover. Once again, however, there were several exceptions. But there was a more important difficulty in these attempts to correlate segregation of conjugal roles with class position and type of local area. The research was not designed to produce valid statistical correlations, for which a very different method would have been necessary. Our aim was to make a study of the interrelation of various social and psychological factors within each family considered as a social system. Attempts at rudimentary statistical correlation did not make clear how one factor affected another; it seemed impossible to explain exactly how the criteria for class position or the criteria for different types of local area were actually producing an effect on the internal role structure of the family.

It therefore appeared that attempts to correlate segregation of conjugal roles with factors selected from the generalized social environment

of the family would not yield a meaningful interpretation. Leaving social class and neighborhood composition to one side for the time being, I turned to look more closely at the immediate environment of the families, that is, at their actual external relationships with friends, neighbors, relatives, clubs, shops, places of work, and so forth. This approach proved to be more fruitful.

First, it appeared that the external social relationships of all families assumed the form of a *network* rather than the form of an organized group.[1] In an organized group, the component individuals make up a larger social whole with common aims, interdependent roles, and a distinctive subculture. In network formation, on the other hand, only some but not all of the component individuals have social relationships with one another. For example, supposing that a family, X, maintains relationships with friends, neighbors, and relatives who may be designated as A, B, C, D, E, F . . . N, one will find that some but not all of these external persons know one another. They do not form an organized group in the sense defined above. B might know A and C but none of the others; D might know F without knowing A, B, C, or E. Furthermore, all of these persons will have friends, neighbors, and relatives of their own who are not known by family X. In a network, the component external units do not make up a larger social whole; they are not surrounded by a common boundary.[2]

1. In sociological and anthropological literature, the term "group" is commonly used in at least two senses. In the first sense it is a very broad term used to describe any collectivity whose members are alike in some way; this definition would include categories, logical classes, and aggregates as well as more cohesive social units. The second usage is much more restricted; in this sense, the units must have some distinctive interdependent social relationships with one another; categories, logical classes, and aggregates are excluded. To avoid confusion I use the term "organized group" when it becomes necessary to distinguish this usage from the first.
2. The term "network" is usually employed in a very broad and metaphorical sense, for example, in Radcliffe-Brown's definition of social structure as "a complex network of social relations". Although he does not define the term, Moreno uses it in roughly the sense employed in the present paper: In giving the term a precise and restricted meaning, I follow the recent usage of John Barnes: "Each person is, as it were, in touch with a number of people, some of whom are directly in touch with each other and some of whom are not . . . I find it convenient to talk of a social field of this kind as a *network*. The image I have is of a set of points some of which are joined by lines. The points of the image are people, or sometimes groups, and the lines indicate which people interact with each other."

Secondly, although all the research families belonged to networks rather than to groups, there was considerable variation in the *connectedness* of their networks. By connectedness I mean the extent to which the people known by a family know and meet one another independently of the family. I use the term *dispersed network* to describe a network in which there are few relationships amongst the component units, and the term *highly connected network* to describe a network in which there are many

reveals that the degree of segregation of conjugal roles is related to the degree of network connectedness. Those families that had a high degree of segregation in the role-relationship of husband and wife had a highly connected network; many of their friends, neighbors, and relatives knew one another. Families that had a relatively joint role-relationship between husband and wife had a dispersed network; few of their relatives, neighbors, and friends knew one another. There were many degrees of

FIGURE 1

SCHEMATIC COMPARISON OF THE NETWORKS OF TWO FAMILIES

FAMILY X:
HIGHLY CONNECTED NETWORK

FAMILY Y:
DISPERSED NETWORK

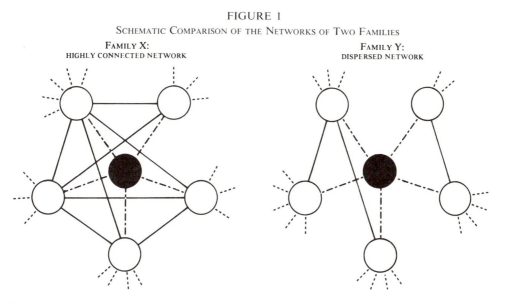

The black circles represent the family, the white circles represent the units of the family's network. The broken lines represent the relationships of the family with the external units; the solid lines represent the relationships of the members of the network with one another. The dotted lines leading off from the white circles indicate that each member of a family's network maintains relationships with other people who are not included in the family's network. This representation is of course highly schematic; a real family would have many more than five external units in its network.

such relationships.[3] The difference is represented very schematically in *Figure 1*. Each family has a network containing five external units, but the network of Family X is more connected than that of Y. There are nine relationships amongst the people of X's network whereas there are only three amongst the people of Y's network. X's network is highly connected, Y's is dispersed.

A detailed examination of the research data

3. Barnes uses the term "mesh" to denote network connectedness. In a network with a small mesh, many of the individuals in X's network know and meet one another independently of X; in a network with a large mesh, few of the individuals in X's network know and meet one another independently of X.

variation in between these two extremes. On the basis of our data, I should therefore like to put forward the following hypothesis: *The degree of segregation in the role-relationship of husband and wife varies directly with the connectedness of the family's social network.* The more connected the network, the more segregation between the roles of husband and, wife. The more dispersed the network, the less segregation between the roles of husband and wife. This relationship between network connectedness and segregation of conjugal roles will be more fully illustrated and discussed below.

No claim is made here that network connectedness is the only factor affecting segregation of conjugal roles. Among the other variables affecting the way conjugal roles are performed, the personalities of husband and wife are of crucial importance. Most of this paper will be devoted to a discussion of the effect of network connectedness, however, because the importance of this variable has been insufficiently stressed in previous studies of family role structure.

It thus appears that if one is to understand segregation of conjugal roles, one should examine the effect of the family's immediate social environment of friends, neighbors, relatives, and institutions. The question remains, however, as to why some families should have highly connected networks whereas others have dispersed networks. In part, network connectedness depends on the family themselves. One family may choose to introduce their friends, neighbors, and relatives to one another, whereas another may not. One family may move around a great deal so that its network becomes dispersed, whereas another family may stay put. But these choices are limited and shaped by a number of forces over which the family does not have direct control. It is at this point that the total social environment becomes relevant. The economic and occupational system, the structure of formal institutions, the ecology of cities, and many other factors affect the connectedness of networks, and limit and shape the decisions that families make. Among others, factors associated with social class and neighborhood composition affect segregation of conjugal roles, not solely and not primarily through direct action on the internal structure of the family, but indirectly through their effect on its network. Conceptually, the network stands between the family and the total social environment. The connectedness of a family's network depends on the one hand on certain forces in the total environment and on the other hand on the personalities of the members of the family and on the way they react to these forces.

In this paper a first attempt will be made to carry out an analysis in terms of these concepts. Part I will be devoted to a discussion of conjugal role-segregation in relation to network connectedness. In Part II the relation of networks to the total environment will be discussed.

Whether my central hypothesis, the direct relationships between network connectedness and segregation of conjugal roles, is valid for other families I do not know. At this stage I am not attempting to make generalizations about all families, and I am not concerned with whether or not the families we have studied are typical of others. What I am trying to do is to make a comparative study of the relationship between conjugal role-segregation and network connectedness for each of the twenty families considered as a social system. In so doing I have developed a hypothesis that, with further refinement of definition, preferably in quantifiable terms, might be tested on other families and might facilitate further and more systematic comparisons.

PART I. CONJUGAL ROLE-SEGREGATION AND NETWORK CONNECTEDNESS

METHODS OF COLLECTING DATA

Although this paper will be devoted primarily to discussion of the effect of external social relationships on the role-relationship of husband and wife, the research as a whole was designed to investigate families not only sociologically but also psychologically. The research techniques accordingly consisted of a combination of the field-work method of the social anthropologist, in which the group under investigation is studied as a working whole in its natural habitat in so far as this is possible, and the case-study method in which individuals are studied by clinical interviews. No attempt was made to use statistical procedures.

The families studied were "ordinary," in the sense that they did not come to us for help with personal or familial problems, and they were usually able to cope themselves with such difficulties as they had. We sought them out, they did not come to us. In order to simplify the task of comparison, only families with young children were selected; the discussion of conjugal role-segregation and network formation will accordingly be restricted to families in this phase of development. In order further to restrict the number of variables that had to be taken into account, only English families who were Protestant or of mainly Protestant background were selected. All twenty families lived in London or Greater London, but they were scattered all over the area and did not form an organized group. Although the families thus resembled one another in phase of marriage and in national and religious background, they varied considerably in occupation and in socio-economic status; the net annual incomes of the husbands after tax ranged from £325 to £1,500 [$780 to $3600].

Much difficulty was encountered in contacting suitable families, although the effort to find them taught us a good deal about the way families are related to other social groups. The twenty families were eventually contacted through the officials of various service institutions, such as doctors, hospitals, schools, local political parties, and the like, and through friends of the family. Introductions were most successful when the contact person was well known and trusted by both husband and wife, and the most satisfactory channel of contact was through friends of the family.

After the contact person had told a prospective family about the research and had got their agreement to an explanatory interview by one of the research staff, one of the field workers visited the family at their home to describe what the research was about and what it would involve for the family. The field worker explained the background of the research, the content of the interviews, and the time they would take. He (or she) made it clear that the family could withdraw at any time, that the material would be treated with professional discretion, and that if we wished to publish any confidential material that might reveal the couple's identity, we should consult them beforehand. The research staff also undertook to pay any expenses that the couple might incur as a result of the investigation. Although the provisional and explanatory nature of the first interview was always emphasized, we found that most of the couples who got as far as this interview had usually decided to take part in the research before they met the field worker, chiefly on the basis of what the contact person had told them. We have no systematic information about couples who were consulted but decided not to participate.

After a family had agreed to take part, the field worker paid several visits to them at home in the evening for joint interviews with the husband and wife. He also went at least once during the day at the weekend when he could meet the children and observe the whole family together. There were thirteen home interviews on the average, the range being from eight to nineteen. Each home interview began with half an hour of casual chatting followed by more focused discussions on particular topics during which notes were taken. The topics discussed were: kinship, family background, and personal history until marriage; the first phase of the family from marriage until the birth of the first child; an account of family life at the time of interviewing, including a daily, weekly, and yearly diary, a description of external social relationships with service institutions such as schools, church, clinic doctor, and so forth, with voluntary associations and recreational institutions, and more informal relationships with friends, neighbors, and relatives; an account of the division of labor between husband and wife in overall planning, in the economic support of the family, in domestic tasks, and in child care; and finally, questions were asked about values and ideology concerning family life, social class, money and financial management, and general political, social, and religious questions. These topics were used as a general guide by the field worker; the order of topics and the form of questioning were left to his discretion. Usually he raised a topic, and the couple carried on the discussion themselves with occasional additional questions by the field worker. The discussion frequently wandered away from the assigned topic, but little attempt was made to restrict such digressions, since all the behavior of husband and wife towards one another and towards the field worker was held to be significant data.

When the home interviews had been completed, the field worker explained the second part of the research, which had been briefly mentioned in the first interview. This consisted of a clinical investigation in which the husband and wife were interviewed at the Tavistock Institute of Human Relations. Fifteen of the twenty families came for clinical interviews. The first such interview consisted of a brief joint meeting of the couple, the field worker, and the psychoanalyst, followed by the individual administration of the Thematic Apperception Tests by two psychologists from the Tavistock Clinic. The husbands and wives then returned separately on future occasions for two or three clinical interviews with the psychoanalyst. The topics covered were health; personal development, and relationships with parents, siblings, and friends; sexual development; the personal relationship between husband and wife, and the effect of the children on the individual and on the family as a whole. Here again the topics were used only as a general guide. The informants were allowed to express their ideas and feelings as freely as possible.

After the clinical interviews were over, the sociological field worker paid a final home visit to bring the investigation to a close. Frequent supplementary visits have been made, however, partly to fill in gaps in the information and partly to work material through with the families prior to publication. All the families know that a book is to be written about them and most of them intend to read it. We plan to publish detailed sociological and psychological accounts of two families; this material has been disguised so that even people who knew the families would have difficulty in recognizing them; in these very detailed, exhaustive accounts, however, it was impossible to work out a disguise so complete that the couple would not recognize themselves, because many of the things that would have had to be altered for such a disguise were essential to the analysis. We have therefore discussed the material with the two families concerned. This process is somewhat upsetting, but the families found it much more acceptable than the prospect of suddenly recognizing themselves laid bare in print without any prior consultation. We took it for granted that the process of digesting an analysis of themselves in sociological and psychological terms would be disturbing, and we accepted the responsibility of helping them with it in so far as they felt the need of assistance. We did not force therapy on them, and we chose families whom we felt could stand the stress with comparative ease. Working the material through with the families was also important for the analysis itself; the reactions of the couples to our interpretations of the facts which they had told us helped us to evaluate and revise our analysis.

In addition to the interviews with the twenty families, discussions about families in general were held with various persons, particularly doctors, who had considerable knowledge of family life. Discussions were also held with various organized groups such as Community Centres and Townswomen's Guilds. These groups had no direct connection with the families we interviewed, and in most cases they were composed of people, usually women, who were considerably older than the research husbands and wives. These discussions were therefore not directly relevant to the analysis of the research families, but they provided useful information on the norms of family life. In a public, group situation, especially one which lasts for only one session, people seem much more willing to talk about norms than to discuss their actual behavior.

DESCRIPTION OF THE DATA

If families are classified according to the extremes of the two dimensions of conjugal role-segregation and network connectedness, four patterns are logically possible: 1. segregated conjugal role-relationship associated with a highly connected network, 2. segregated conjugal role-relationship associated with a dispersed network, 3. joint conjugal role-relationship associated with a highly connected network, and 4. joint conjugal role-relationship associated with a dispersed network. Empirically, two of these patterns, the second and third, did not occur. There were no families in which a highly segregated conjugal role-relationship was associated with a dispersed network; there were no families in which a joint conjugal role-relationship was associated with a highly connected network.

Six of the research families were clustered in the first and fourth patterns. There was one family that conformed to the first pattern, a high degree of conjugal role-segregation being combined with a highly connected network. There were five families that conformed to the fourth pattern, a joint conjugal role-relationship being associated with a dispersed network. These six families represent the extremes of the research set. There were nine families that were intermediate in degree of conjugal role-segregation and similarly intermediate in degree of network connectedness. Finally there were five families that appeared to be in a state of transition both with respect to their network formation and with respect to their conjugal role-relationship.

Among the twenty families, there was thus some clustering at certain points along a possible continuum from a highly segregated to a very joint conjugal role-relationship, and along a second continuum from a highly connected to a dispersed network. The families did not fall into sharply separated types, however, so that divisions are somewhat arbitrary, but for convenience of description, I shall divide the families into four groups: 1. highly segregated conjugal role-relationship associated with highly connected network, 2. joint conjugal role-relationship associated with dispersed network, 3. intermediate degrees of conjugal role-segregation and network connectedness, and 4. transitional families. No claim is made here that these are the only patterns that can occur; further research would probably reveal others. In the following discussion I shall be chiefly concerned not with these divisions, but rather with the fact that the order according to degree of conjugal role-segregation follows the order according to degree of network connectedness, and I shall attempt to show the mechanisms by which this relationship operates.

Highly Segregated Conjugal Role-relationship Associated with Highly Connected Network

The research set contained only one family of this type.[4] For convenience I shall call them Mr. and Mrs. N. They had been married four years when the interviewing began and had two small children. In the following discussion, I shall describe their actual behavior, indicating the points at which they depart from their norms.[5]

External social relationship. Mr. N had a semi-skilled manual job at a factory in an East End area adjacent to the one in which he and Mrs. N lived. He said that many other men in the local area had jobs at the same place, or were doing the same sort of work at similar factories and workshops nearby. Mrs. N did not work, but she felt that she was unusual in this respect. Most of the neighboring women and many of her female relatives had jobs; she did not think there was anything morally wrong with such work, but she said that she had never liked working and preferred to stay at home with the children. Mr. N said that he thought it was best for her and the children if she stayed at home, and added that he felt it was a bit of a reflection on a man if his wife had to go out to work.

The Ns used the services of a local hospital and a maternity and child welfare clinic. They expected to send their children to the local elementary school. They were also in touch with the local housing authority because they were trying to find a new flat. These various service institutions were not felt to have any particular relationship to one another, except in the sense that they were all felt to be foreign bodies, not really part of the local life. Mrs. N was a little bit afraid of them, particularly of the hospital and of doctors. On one occasion, while waiting with her baby and the field worker in an otherwise empty hospital room for a doctor to attend to the baby, she said in a whisper, "My husband says that we pay for it [the hospital services, through National Health subscriptions] and we should use it, but I don't like coming here. I don't like hospitals and doctors, do you?"

To the Ns, the local area was definitely a community in the social sense, a place with an identity of its own and a distinctive way of life. They spoke of it with great pride and contrasted it favorably with other areas. "It has a bad name, they say we are rough, but I think it's the

---

4. As stated above, I am not primarily concerned in this paper with whether the research families are typical of others, but it is perhaps of some interest that families with highly connected networks and pronounced conjugal role-segregation are by no means rare, and that they appear to occur primarily in long-established working-class areas. Supplementary data about such families was collected in group discussions. In Part II of the present paper I shall discuss some of the factors involved in living in long-established working-class areas, and how these factors affect network connectedness.

5. Problems concerning norms will be taken up in a subsequent paper. I use the term "norm" to mean those items of behavior which are felt by the members of a family to be prescribed and/or

typical in their social circle. Ideal norms are those prescribed rules of behavior which it is felt that people ought to follow; norms of expectation are those behaviors which are felt to be typical or usual. In my view, norms are partly internalized through experiences with other people and through reading, listening to the radio, and so forth; in part norms are a construction of the members of the family, who re-interpret and re-order the received norms, within limits, in accordance with their own needs. It follows that families vary considerably in their norms, although families with similar social experiences will tend to have broadly similar norms.

best place there is. Everyone is friendly . . . there is no life in the West End compared with the East End. They drink champagne and we drink beer. When things are la-di-da you feel out of place." They took it for granted that the other inhabitants had similar feelings of local pride and loyalty. Both the Ns had grown up in the same area, as had most of their relatives and friends. Trips outside the area were like adventures into a foreign land, especially for Mrs. N, and very few informal social relationships were kept up with people outside the area. Physical distance was felt to be an almost insuperable barrier to social contact.

Physically, the area was far from ideal as a place to live, for the houses were old-fashioned, inconvenient, and crowded. The Ns were faced with a difficult choice of whether to move out of London to a modern flat on a new housing estate, or to stay put in cramped quarters, in the old familiar local area with their friends and relatives. They knew of several other young couples who were faced with a similar dilemma. Group discussions at a local community center and the research of the Institute of Community Studies indicated that many local residents feel this to be an important social and personal problem.

The Ns felt that their neighbors were socially similar to themselves, meaning that they had the same sort of jobs, the same sort of background, the same sort of outlook on life.[6] Because the Ns had grown up in the area, as had many of their relatives and neighbors, they knew a very considerable number of local people, and many of the people they knew were acquainted with one another. In other words, their social network was highly connected. In fact there was considerable overlap of social roles; instead of there being people in three or four separate categories—friend, neighbor, relative, and colleague—the same person frequently filled two or three or even four of these roles simultaneously.

The Ns took it for granted that Mr. N, like other husbands in their social circle, would have some form of recreation that he carried on with men away from home. In his case it was

football, although the most common form of recreation was felt to be drinking and visiting in the local pub, where many husbands spent an evening or two a week with their friends; quite frequently some of these men were friends of old standing, men who had belonged to the same childhood gang, and others were colleagues at work. Mr. N had kept in touch with one or two friends of his childhood; he also played football and went to matches with some of his colleagues at work; he mentioned that several of his friends knew one another. Mrs. N knew a bit about these men, but she did not expect to join in their activities with her husband. She had a nodding acquaintance with the wives of two or three of these men, and occasionally talked to them when she was out shopping.

Mrs. N also had her own separate relationships in which her husband did not expect to join. She knew many of her female neighbors, just as they knew one another; she took it for granted that a friendly relationship with a neighbor would be dropped if the woman moved away. Neighbors saw one another on the landings, in the street, in shops, occasionally over a cup of tea inside the flat or house. They talked over their own affairs and those of other neighbors. Neighbors frequently accused one another of something—of betraying a confidence, of taking the wrong side in a children's quarrel, of failing to return borrowed articles, of gossip. One has little privacy in such a situation. But if one wants to reap the rewards of companionship and small acts of mutual aid, one has to conform to local standards, and one has to put up with being included in the gossip. Indeed, being gossiped about is as much a sign that one belongs to the neighborly network as being gossiped with. If one refuses to have anything to do with one's neighbors one is thought odd, but eventually one will be left alone; no gossip, no companionship.

With the exception of visiting relatives and an occasional Sunday outing with the children, the Ns spent very little of their leisure time in joint recreation with each other; even though they could have got their relatives to mind the children for them, they rarely went out together. In particular, there was no joint entertaining of friends at home. From time to time Mr. N brought a friend home and Mrs. N made tea and talked a bit to the friend; female neighbors

6. Unless otherwise noted, the phrase "socially similar" will be used throughout this paper to describe people who are felt by a husband and wife to belong to the same social class as themselves.

often dropped in during the evening to borrow something, but they did not stay long if Mr. N was there. There was no planned joint entertaining in which Mr. and Mrs. N asked another husband and wife to spend an evening with them. Such joint entertaining as existed was carried on with relatives, not with friends. Poverty does not explain the absence of joint entertaining, for the Ns considered themselves to be relatively well off. It did not seem to occur to them that they might spend their surplus money on entertainment of friends; they felt that such money should be spent on furniture, new things for the children, or on large gatherings of relatives at weddings, funerals, and christenings.[7]

There was much visiting and mutual aid between relatives, particularly by the women. The Ns had far more active social relationship with relatives than any other research family, and there was also a great deal of independent contact by their relatives with one another in addition to their contacts with the Ns themselves. In brief, the network of kin was highly connected, more highly connected than those of neighbors or friends. The women were more active than the men in keeping up contacts with relatives, with the result that the networks of wives were more highly connected than the networks of their husbands. Although husbands were recognized to be less active in kinship affairs than their wives, Mr. N paid occasional visits to his mother, both by himself and with Mrs. N. Furthermore, there were some activities for which joint participation by husband and wife was felt to be desirable. At weddings, funerals, and christenings, there were large assemblages of relatives, and on such occasions

7. The absence of the pattern of joint entertainment of friends made our technique of joint interviews with husband and wife somewhat inappropriate for the Ns. Mrs. N was more relaxed and talked much more freely when she and I were alone or when we were together with other women. This was not because of bad relations with her husband; in fact she felt that they had a very successful conjugal relationship and that she was fortunate in having an unusually generous and thoughtful husband. But in spite of this, she felt she could not talk as freely when he was there, and in all probability he had similar feelings. Because of the difficulty in conducting joint interviews, we considered the possibility of interviewing them separately, Mrs. N by the female field worker and Mr. N by the male field worker. But there were two difficulties: first, we wanted to use the same technique with all families so as to simplify the task of comparison, and secondly we felt that separate home as well as clinical interviews would make each partner too suspicious and anxious about what the other was saying.

it was felt to be important that both husband and wife should attend. Recent and prospective weddings, twenty-first birthday parties, and christenings formed an important topic of discussion throughout the interviews with the Ns.

In a group discussion, a man living in the same local area as the Ns and having a similar sort of family life and kinship network summed up the situation by saying, "Men have friends. Women have relatives." Very succinctly he had described the overlapping of roles mentioned above. For Mrs. N, there was no independent category of "friend;" friends were either neighbors or relatives. She had had a succession of girl friends in her adolescence, but she said that she did not see so much of them since they had all got married and had had children. She always described them as "girl friends," not as "friends." Both Mr. and Mrs. N used the term "friend" as if it applied only to men; the term "neighbor," on the other hand, seemed to refer only to women. Mr. N looked rather shocked when I asked him if he saw much of the neighbors.

Later on in the group discussion, the same man observed, "Women don't have friends. They have Mum." In Mrs. N's case the relationship between herself and her mother was indeed very close. Her mother lived nearby in the same local area, and Mrs. N went to visit her nearly every day, taking her children along with her. She and her mother and her mother's sisters also went to visit Mrs. N's maternal grandmother. Together these women and their children formed an important group, helping one another in household tasks and child care, and providing aid for one another in crises. Within the network of relatives, in other words, there was a nucleus composed of the grandmother, her daughters, and her daughters' daughters; the relationships of these women with one another were sufficiently intense and distinctive to warrant the term "organized group" in the sense defined above. Mrs. N's female relatives provided some of the domestic help and emotional support that, in other research families, a wife expected to get from her husband. Mrs. N felt tremendously attached to her mother emotionally. She felt that a bad relationship between mother and daughter was unnatural, a complete catastrophe. She would, I feel sure, have been deeply shocked by the seemingly cold and objective terms in which many of the women in the other research families analysed their mothers' characters. The close tie with the mother is not only a source of help, however, but may also be a potential source of friction, for if her husband and her mother do not get along well together, a young wife is likely to feel torn by conflicting loyalties. Mrs. N felt that she was particularly fortunate in that her husband and her mother liked each other.

In brief, there was considerable segregation between Mr. and Mrs. N in their external relationships. In effect, Mrs. N had her network and Mr. N had his. The number of joint external relationships was comparatively small. At the same time, there were many links between their networks: the husbands of some of Mrs. N's neighbors were men who were colleagues of Mr. N, some of Mrs. N's relatives also worked at the same place as Mr. N, and in a general way, his family was known to hers even before Mr. and Mrs. N got married. In other words, the connectedness of the combined networks of Mr. and Mrs. N was high compared to that of the families to be discussed below. But the N's total network was sharply divided into the husband's network and the wife's network. Furthermore, her network was more highly connected than his: many of the relatives and neighbors with whom she was in contact saw one another independently of her, whereas there were fewer independent links between Mr. N's colleagues, his football associates, and his friends from childhood.

Conjugal role-segregation. The previous description reveals considerable segregation between Mr. and Mrs. N in their external relationships. There was a similar segregation in the way they carried out their internal domestic tasks. They took it for granted that there should be a clear-cut division of labor between them, and that all husbands and wives in their social circle would organize their households in a similar way. One man said in a group discussion: "A lot of men wouldn't mind helping their wives if the curtains were drawn so people couldn't see." Although the Ns felt that major decisions should be made jointly, in the day-to-day running of the household he had his jobs and she had hers. He had control of the money and gave her a house-keeping allowance of £5 [$12] a week. Mrs. N did not know how much money he earned, and it did not seem to occur to her that a wife would want or need to know this. Although the Ns said that £5 [$12] was the amount most wives were given for housekeeping, Mrs. N had great difficulty in making it cover all the expenses of food, rent, utilities, and five shillings' saving for Christmas. She told Mr. N whenever she ran short, and he left a pound or two under the clock when he went out the next morning. She said that he was very generous with his money and she felt that she was unusually fortunate in being spared financial quarrels.

Mrs. N was responsible for most of the housework and child care, although Mr. N did household repairs and helped to entertain the children at weekends. Mrs. N expected that he would do some of the housework if she became ill, but this was usually unnecessary because her mother or her sister or one of her cousins would come to her aid. Indeed, these female relatives helped her a great deal even with the everyday tasks of housework and child care.

Attitudes towards the role-relationship of husband and wife. Mr. and Mrs. N took it for granted that men had male interests and women had female interests and that there were few leisure activities that they would naturally share. In their view, a good husband was one who was generous with the housekeeping allowance, did not waste money on extravagant personal recreation, helped his wife with the housework if she got ill, and took an interest in the children. A good wife was a good manager and an affectionate mother, a woman who kept out of serious rows with neighbors and got along well with her own and her husband's relatives. A good marital relationship was one with a harmonious division of labor, but the Ns placed little stress on the importance of joint activities and shared interests. It is difficult to make any definite statement on the Ns' attitudes towards sexual relations, for they did not come to the Institute for clinical interviews. Judging from Mrs. N's references to such matters when Mr. N was absent, it seems likely that she felt that physical sexuality was an intrusion on a peaceful domestic relationship rather than an expression of such a relationship; it was as if sexuality were felt to be basically violent and disruptive.

The findings of clinical workers and of other research workers suggest that among families like the Ns, there is little stress on the importance of physical sexuality for a happy marriage.

Families Having a Joint Conjugal Role-relationship Associated with a Dispersed Network

Among the research set there were five families of this type. All the husbands had professional or semi-professional occupations. Two of the husbands had been upwardly mobile in occupation relative to the occupations of their fathers. All five families, however, had a well-established pattern of external relationships; they might make new relationships, but the basic pattern was likely to remain the same. Similarly, all had worked out a fairly stable division of labor in domestic tasks.

External social relationships. The husbands' occupations had little intrinsic connection with the local areas in which they lived. All five husbands carried on their work at some distance from the area in which their homes were located, although two husbands did some additional work at home. But in no case was there any feeling that the occupation was locally rooted.

Whether or not wives should work was considered to be a very controversial question by these families. Unless they were very well off financially—and none of these five families considered themselves to be so—both husband and wife welcomed the idea of a double income, even though much of the additional money had to be spent on caring for the children. But money was not the only consideration; women also wanted to work for the sake of the work itself. It was felt that is she desired it, a woman should have a career or some sort of special interest and skill comparable in seriousness to her husband's occupation; on the other hand, it was felt that young children needed their mother's care and that ideally she should drop her career at least until the youngest child was old enough to go to school. But most careers cannot easily be dropped and picked up again several years later. Two of the wives had solved the problem by continuing to work; they had made careful (and expensive) provision for the care of their children. One wife worked at home. One planned to take up her special interest again as soon as her youngest child went to

nursery school, and the fifth wife was already doing so.

These husbands and wives maintained contact with schools, general practitioners, hospitals, and in some cases local maternity and child welfare clinics. Most of them also used the services of a solicitor, an insurance agent, and other similar professional people as required. Unlike the first type of family, they did not feel that service institutions were strange and alien; it did not bother them when they had to go out of their local area to find such services, and they were usually well informed about service institutions and could exploit them efficiently. They were not afraid of doctors. There was no strict division of labor between husband and wife in dealing with service institutions. The wife usually dealt with those institutions that catered for children, and the husband dealt with the legal and financial ones, but either could take over the other's duties if necessary.

These husbands and wives did not regard the neighborhood as a source of friends. In most cases husbands and wives had moved around a good deal both before and after marriage, and in no case were they living in the neighborhood in which they grew up. Four were living in areas of such a kind that only a few of the neighbors were felt to be socially similar to the family themselves. The fifth family was living in a suburb that the husband and wife felt to be composed of people socially similar to one another, but quite different from themselves. In all cases these husbands and wives were polite but somewhat distant to neighbors. In order to have become proper friends, the neighbors would have had to be not only socially similar to the family themselves, but would also have had to share a large number of tastes and interests. Establishing such a relationship takes a long exploratory testing, and the feeling seems to have been that it was dangerous to make the test with neighbors since one ran the risk of being pestered by friendly attentions that one might not want to return. Since many of the neighbors probably had similar feelings, particularly when the neighborhood was socially heterogeneous, it is not surprising that intimate social relationships were not rapidly established. Since these families had so little social intercourse with their neighbors, they were very much less worried than the first type of family about gossip and conformity to local norms. Indeed, in the circumstances one can hardly say that there were any specifically local norms; certainly there was not the body of shared attitudes and values built up through personal interaction since childhood that was characteristic of the local area inhabited by the Ns.

The children were less discriminating than their parents. Unless restricted by their parents, they played with anyone in the street. This caused some of the parents a certain amount of anxiety, particularly when they felt that the area was very heterogeneous. Other parents adopted the view that mixing with children of other social classes was a good thing. In any case, all parents relied on their own influence and on the education of the children to erase any possibly bad effects of such contact.

It seemed very difficult for these families to find the sort of house and local area in which they wanted to live. They wanted to own a reasonably cheap house with a garden in central London, a house within easy reach of their friends, of plays, concerts, galleries, and so forth. Ideally they wanted a cheap, reliable cleaning-woman-cum-baby-sitter to live nearby, possibly even with the family if they could afford it. Only one family had achieved something approaching this aim. The others were making do with various compromises, impeded by lack of money as well as by the scarcity of suitable houses.

For these families, friends were felt to provide the most important type of external relationship. Not all of each family's friends knew one another; it was not usual for a large number of a family's friends to be in intimate contact with one another independently of their contact with the family. In brief, the network of friends was typically dispersed (unconnected). Husband and wife had usually established friendships over a period of years in many different social contexts —at school, during the course of their professional training, in the Services, at various jobs, very occasionally even because of living in the same neighborhood. Their friends were scattered all over London, sometimes even all over Britain. Because the network of friends was so dispersed, their social control over the family was dispersed and fragmented. The husband and wife were very sensitive to what their friends thought of them, but since the

friends had so little contact with one another, they were not likely to present a unified body of public opinion. Amongst all the different bits of advice they might receive, husband and wife had to make up their own minds about what they should do. They were less persecuted by gossip than the first type of family, but they were also less sustained by it. Their friends did not form a solid body of helpers.

In marked contrast to the Ns, nearly all of the husband's and wife's friends were joint friends; it was felt to be important that both husband and wife should like a family friend, and if a friend was married, then it was hoped that all four partners to the relationship would like one another. Exceptions were tolerated, especially in the case of very old friends, but both husband and wife were uncomfortable if there was real disagreement between them over a friend. Friendship, like marriage, required shared interests and similar tastes, although there was some specialization of interests among different friends. For example, one couple might be golfing friends whereas others might be pub and drinking friends; still others were all-round friends, and it was these who were felt to be the most intimate.

Joint entertainment of friends was a major form of recreation. Even when poverty made invitations to dinner or parties impracticable, friends were still asked over jointly even if only for coffee or tea in the evening. It was considered provincial for husbands to cluster at one end of the room and wives at the other; everyone should be able to talk to everyone else. These husbands and wives usually had enough shared interests to make this possible. Many of them were highly educated, so that they had a common background of general topics, but even those who lacked such education usually make an attempt to talk about matters of general interest.

After these couples had had children, it had become increasingly difficult for them to visit their friends. Since their friends often lived at a considerable distance, and since most of them were also tied down by young children, mutual visiting had become more and more difficult to arrange. Considerable expense and trouble were taken to make such visiting possible. It was obvious that friends were of primary importance to these families.

There were usually other forms of joint recreation besides visiting friends, such as eating in foreign restaurants, going to plays, the cinema, concerts, and so forth. After children were born, there had been a marked drop in external joint recreation in preference for things that could be done at home. Going out had become a special occasion with all the paraphernalia of a babysitter and arrangements made in advance.

These five families had far less contact with their relatives than the Ns. Their relatives were not concentrated in the same local area as themselves, and in most cases they were scattered all over the country, and did not keep in close touch with one another. They formed a dispersed network. It was felt that friendly relations should be kept up with parents, and in several cases the birth of the children had led to a sort of reunion with parents. It seems likely that becoming a parent facilitates a resolution of some of the emotional tensions between adult children and their own parents, particularly between women and their mothers. It is possible that in some cases the arrival of children may exacerbate such tensions, but none of these five families had had such an experience. There are of course some obvious practical advantages in increased contact with parents; they are usually very fond of their grandchildren, so that they make affectionate and reliable babysitters; if they live close enough to take on this task their services are greatly appreciated.

Among the families with dispersed networks, there was not the tremendous stress on the mother-daughter relationship that was described for Mrs. N, although women were usually rather more active than men in keeping up kinship ties. There were also fewer conflicts of loyalty; it was felt that if conflicts arose between one's parents and one's spouse, one owed one's first loyalty to one's spouse. Unless special interests, particularly financial interests, were operating among relatives, there was no very strong obligation towards relatives outside the parental families of husband and wife. Even towards siblings there was often very little feeling of social obligation. These families were very much less subject to social control by their relatives than the Ns, partly because they saw less of them, but also because the network of kin was dispersed so that its various members

were less likely to share the same opinions and values.

In brief, the networks of these families were less highly connected than that of the Ns: many of their friends did not know one another, it was unusual for friends to know relatives, only a few relatives kept in touch with one another, and husband and wife had very little contact with neighbours. Furthermore, there was no sharp segregation between the wife's network and the husband's network. With the exception of a few old friends and some colleagues, husband and wife maintained joint external relationships.

Conjugal role-segregation. As described above, these families had as little segregation as possible in their external relationships. There was a similar tendency towards joint organization in their carrying out of domestic tasks and child care. It was felt that efficient management demanded some division of labor, particularly after the children had been born; there had to be a basic differentiation between the husband's role as primary breadwinner and the wife's role as mother of young children. But in other respects such division of labor as existed was felt to be more a matter of convenience than of inherent differences between the sexes. The division of labor was flexible, and there was considerable helping and interchanging of tasks. Husbands were expected to take a very active part in child care. Financial affairs were managed jointly, and joint consultation was expected on all major decisions.

Husbands were expected to provide much of the help that Mrs. N was able to get from her female relatives. The wives of these families with dispersed networks were carrying a tremendous load of housework and child care, but they expected to carry it for a shorter time than Mrs. N. Relatives sometimes helped these wives, but only occasionally; they usually lived at some distance so that it was difficult for them to provide continuous assistance. Cleaning women were employed by four families and a children's nurse by one; all families would have hired more domestic help if they could have afforded it. In spite of their affection for their children, all five couples were looking forward to the time when their children were older and the burden of work would decrease. Insofar as they could look so far ahead into the future, they did not expect to provide continuous assistance to their own married children.

It seems likely that in the cases of Mrs. N and other wives with highly connected networks, the burden of housework and child care is more evenly distributed throughout the lifetime of the wife; when she is a girl she helps her mother with the younger children; when she herself has children, her mother and other female relatives help her; when she is a grandmother she helps her daughters.

Attitudes towards the role-relationship of husband and wife. Among the families with dispersed networks, there were frequent discussions of whether there really were any psychological or temperamental differences between the sexes. These differences were not simply taken for granted as they were by the Ns. In some cases, so much stress was placed on shared interests and sexual equality (which was sometimes confused with identity, the notion of equality of complementary opposites being apparently a difficult idea to maintain consistently) that one sometimes felt that the possibility of the existence of social and temperamental differences between the sexes was being denied. In other cases, temperamental differences between the sexes were exaggerated to a point that belied the couple's actual joint activities and the whole pattern of shared interests that they felt to be so fundamental to their way of life. Quite frequently the same couple would minimize differences between the sexes on one occasion and exaggerate them on another. Sometimes these discussions about sexual differences were very serious; sometimes they were witty and facetious; but they were never neutral—they were felt to be an important problem. Such discussions may be interpreted as an attempt to air and to resolve the contradiction between the necessity for joint organization with its ethic of equality on the one hand, and the necessity for differentiation and recognition of sexual differences on the other. "After all," as one husband said, to conclude the discussion, "*vive la différence*, or where would we all be?"

It was felt that, in a good marriage, husband and wife should achieve a high degree of compatibility, based on their own particular combination of shared interests and complementary differences. Their relationship with each other should be more important than any separate relationship with outsiders. The conjugal relationship should be kept private, and revelations to outsiders, or letting down one's spouse in public, were felt to be serious offenses. A successful sexual relationship was felt by these couples to be very important for a happy marriage; it was as if successful sexual relations were felt to prove that all was well with the joint relationship, whereas unsatisfactory relations were indicative of a failure in the total relationship. In some cases one almost got the feeling that these husbands and wives felt a moral obligation to enjoy sexual relations, a feeling not expressed or suggested by the Ns.

The wives of these families seemed to feel that their position was rather difficult. They had certainly wanted children, and in all five cases they were getting a great deal of satisfaction from their maternal role. But at the same time, they felt tied down by their children and they did not like the inevitable drudgery associated with child care. Some were more affected than others, but most of them complained of isolation, boredom, and fatigue. "You must excuse me if I sound half-witted. I've been talking to the children all day," was a not uncommon remark. These women wanted a career or some special interest that would make them feel that they were something more than children's nurses and housemaids. They wanted more joint entertainment with their husbands, and more contact with friends. These complaints were not levelled specifically at their husbands— indeed in most cases they felt that their husbands were doing their best to make the situation easier—but against the social situation in which they found themselves and at the difficulty of satisfying contradictory desires at the same time. One wife summed it up by saying, "Society seems to be against married women. I don't know, it's all very difficult."

It may be felt that the problem could be solved if such a family moved to an area that was felt to be homogeneous and composed of people similar to themselves, for then the wife might be able to find friends among her neighbors and would feel less isolated and bored. It is difficult to imagine, however, that these families could feel that any local area, however homogeneous by objective criteria, could be full of potential friends, for their experience of moving about in the past and their varied social contacts make them very discriminating in their choice of friends. Further, their dislike of having their privacy broken into by neighbors is very deeply rooted; it diminishes after the children start playing with children in the neighborhood, but it never disappears entirely.

Intermediate Degrees of Conjugal Role-segregation and Network Connectedness

There were nine families of this type in the research set. There was considerable variety of occupation amongst them. Four husbands had professional or semi-professional occupations very similar to the occupations of the second type of family described above. It was in recognition of the fact that these four families were similar in occupation but different in conjugal role-segregation from the second set of families that I concluded that conjugal role-segregation could not be attributed to occupational level alone. Of the five remaining husbands, one was a clerical worker, three had manual occupations similar in general level to that of Mr. N, and one changed from a highly skilled manual job to an office job after the interviewing was completed.

There was considerable variations among these nine families in conjugal role-segregation. Some tended to have a fairly marked degree of segregation, approaching that of the Ns described above, whereas others were closer to the second set of families in having a relatively joint role-relationship. These variations in degree of segregation of conjugal roles within the nine intermediate families did not follow exactly the order according to occupational level. If the occupations of the husbands are arranged in order from the most joint to the most segregated conjugal role-relationship, the order is as follows: manual worker, professional, professional, clerical worker, professional, manual worker, professional, manual worker, manual worker. The variations in degree of segregation follow more closely the variations in degree of network connectedness. The families with the most dispersed networks had the most joint role-relationships, and the families with the most connected networks had the most conjugal role-segregation. The families with the most dispersed networks were those who had

moved around a great deal so that they had established relationships with many people who did not know one another.

For brevity of description, I shall treat these nine intermediate families collectively, but it should be remembered that there were variations in degree amongst them, and that both network connectedness and conjugal role-segregation form continua so that it is somewhat arbitrary to divide families into separate types.

External social relationships. The data suggest two possible reasons for the intermediate degree in the connectedness of the networks of these families. First, most of them had been brought up in families whose networks had been less connected than that of the Ns, but more connected than that of the second set of families. Furthermore, with one exception these couples had moved around less than the second type of family both before and after marriage, so that more of their friends knew one another; several of these families had had considerable continuity of relationships since childhood, and they had not developed the pattern of ignoring neighbors and relying chiefly on friends and colleagues that was described as typical of families with very dispersed networks.

Secondly, these families were living in areas where they felt that many of the neighbors were socially similar to themselves. In four cases these were "suburban" areas; in five case they were mixed working-class areas in which the inhabitants were felt to be similar to one another in general occupational level although they worked at different jobs. Five families were living in or near the area where one or both of the partners had lived since childhood. In two of the remaining four cases, the area was similar to the one in which husband and wife had been brought up. In two cases, the present area differed considerably from the childhood area of one or other partner, but the couple had acclimatized themselves to the new situation.

If the husband and wife were living in the area in which they had been brought up, each was able to keep up some of the relationships that had been formed before their marriage. This was also true of the Ns. The intermediate families differed from the Ns chiefly in that their jobs, and in some cases their education, had led them to make relationships with people who were not neighbors. Many neighbors were friends, but not all friends were neighbors. Even in the case of families in which one or both partners had moved to the area after marriage, each partner was able to form friendly relationships with at least some of the neighbors, who were in most cases felt to be socially similar to the couple themselves. Husband and wife were able to form independent, segregated relationships with neighbors. In particular, many of the wives spent a good deal of their leisure time during the day with neighboring women. Husband and wife also joined local clubs, most of these clubs being unisexual. (Voluntary associations appear to thrive best in areas where people are similar in social status but do not know one another well; the common activity gives people an opportunity to get to know one another better.)

In local areas inhabited by the intermediate families, many of the neighbors knew one another. There was not the very great familiarity built up over a long period of continuous residence such as was described for the area inhabited by the Ns, but there was not the standoffishness described as typical of the families with very dispersed networks. The intermediate families had networks of neighbors that were midway in degree of connectedness, and the husbands and wives were midway in sensitivity to the opinions of neighbors—more susceptible than the second set of families, but better able to maintain their privacy than the Ns.

Husbands and wives had some segregated relationships with neighbors, but they could also make joint relationships with them if all four partners to the relationship liked one another. Some relationships were usually kept up with friends who had been made outside the area. Couples usually tried to arrange joint visits with these friends. These friends usually did not become intimate with the neighbors, however, so that the network remained fairly dispersed.

Relations with relatives were much like those described above for the second set of families. But if the relatives were living in the same local area as the family, there was considerable visiting and exchange of services, and if the relatives lived close to one another, the kinship network was fairly well connected.

The networks of these families were thus less highly connected than that of the Ns, but more highly connected than that of the second set of families. There was some overlapping of roles. Neighbors were sometimes friends; some relatives were both neighbors and friends. The overlapping was not as complete as it was with the Ns, but there was not the complete division into separate categories—friend, neighbor, relative—that was characteristic of the second set of families. The networks of husband and wife were less segregated than those of the Ns, but more segregated than those of the second set of families.

Conjugal role-segregation. In external relationships, husband and wife thus had some joint relationships, particularly with relatives and with friends, and some segregated relationships, particularly with neighbors and local clubs.

In carrying out household tasks and child care, there was a fairly well-defined division of labor, a little more clearly marked than in the second type of family, more flexible than in the case of the Ns. Husbands helped, but there was a greater expectation of help from neighbors and relatives (if they lived close enough) than among the second set of families.

Attitudes towards the role-relationship of husband and wife. Although there were variations of degree, considerable stress was placed on the importance of shared interests and joint activities for a happy marriage. In general, the greater the stress that was placed on joint organization and shared interests, the greater was the importance attached to sexual relations. Like the families with dispersed networks, the intermediate families stressed the necessity for conjugal privacy and the precedence of the conjugal relationship over all external relationships, but there was a greater tolerance of social and temperamental differences between the sexes, and there was an easier acceptance of segregation in the activities of husband and wife. Wives often wanted some special interest of their own other than housework and children, but they were able to find activities such as attending evening classes or local clubs that could be carried on without interfering with their housework and child care. And because, in most cases, they felt that at least some of the neighboring women were similar to themselves, they found it relatively easy to make friends among them, and they had people to talk to during the day. They complained less frequently of isolation and boredom than did the wives in families with very dispersed networks.

Transitional Families

There were five families in varying states of transition from one type of network to another. Two phases of transition can be distinguished among these five families. (*a*) Families who were in the process of deciding to move from one local area to another, a decision that was requiring considerable restructuring of their networks, and (*b*) somewhat "de-socialized" families (2), that is, families who had radically changed their pattern of external relationships and had not yet got used to their new situation. There were other families who had gone through the process of transition and had more or less settled down to the pattern typical of families with dispersed or intermediate networks.

Families in the process of deciding to move. There were two such families. Both had relatively highly connected networks, and both had been socially mobile and were contemplating moving to suburban areas, which would be more compatible with their new social status. In both cases this meant cutting off old social ties with relatives and neighbors and building up new ones. One couple seemed to feel too bound to the old network to make the break; they also said they did not want to lower their current standard of living by spending a lot of money on a house. The second family moved after the interviewing was completed, and a brief return visit suggested that they would in time build up the intermediate type of network and conjugal role-segregation.

Somewhat de-socialized families. There were three families of this type. All three had been brought up in highly connected networks similar to that described for the Ns, and all had moved away from their old areas and the people of their networks. For such a family, any move outside the area is a drastic step. This contrasts with the intermediate families who are not too

upset by moving, provided that they move to an area of people who are felt to be socially similar to themselves.

One family had been very mobile occupationally, although they had moved primarily because of the requirements of the husband's occupation rather than to find a neighborhood compatible with their achieved status. They were living in relative isolation, with very few friends, almost no contacts with neighbors, and very little contact with relatives, most of whom were living at a considerable distance. They seemed to be a bit stunned by the change in their immediate environment. They had some segregated interests, but they felt that joint organization and shared interests were the best basis of a conjugal relationship.

The other two families were working-class and had not been occupationally mobile. These two families were particularly important to the conceptual analysis of conjugal role-segregation, for although they were similar to the Ns in occupational level and in general cultural background, their conjugal role-relationship was more joint. It was their relatively dispersed networks that distinguished them from the Ns.

These two families had moved to a different local area because they could not find suitable accommodation in their old neighborhoods. They also wanted the amenities of a modern flat, and since their parents had died and many of their relatives had moved away, they felt that their main ties to the old local area were gone. Both these couples seemed to feel that they were strangers in a land full of people who were all strangers to one another, and at first they did not know how to cope with the situation. They did not react to their new situation in exactly the same way. In both cases, husband and wife had turned to one another for help, especially at first, but for various personal reasons, one husband and wife were making a concerted effort to develop joint activities and shared interests, whereas the other couple did not take to the idea of a joint role-relationship with any enthusiasm.

In the first case, husband and wife tried to develop more joint relationships with friends, but this was difficult for them because they had had so little practice; they did not know the culture of a joint role-relationship, and their new acquaintances were in a similar predicament so that they got little external support for their efforts. The husband tried to get his wife to join in his club activities, but the structure of the club was such that her activities remained somewhat segregated from his. The husband helped his wife extensively with household tasks and child care, although he continued to plan the family finances. In the second case, the husband busied himself with his work and friends and spent a great deal of time on various committees with other men; his wife was becoming isolated and withdrawn into the home. They had more joint organization of domestic tasks than they had had before; she urged him to help her because her female relatives lived too far away to be of much assistance.

In both cases, however, nothing could really take the place of the old networks built up from childhood, and both couples felt a good deal of personal dissatisfaction. The husbands were perhaps less drastically affected, since they continued to work at their old jobs and their relationships with colleagues gave them considerable continuity. Both husband and wife often blamed their physical surroundings for their malaise, and they idealized their old local areas. They remembered only the friendliness and forget the physical inconvenience and the unpleasant part of the gossip. On the whole, although one family had carried the process further than the other, both seemed to be developing a more joint division of labor than that which they had had before, and it seemed likely that they would eventually settle down in some intermediate form of network connectedness and conjugal role-segregation.

The research set did not contain any families who had moved in the other direction, that is, from a dispersed to a more connected network. But personal knowledge of families who had been accustomed to a dispersed network and were having to come to grips with a fairly highly connected one suggests that this type of change is also felt to be somewhat unpleasant. The privacy of husband and wife is encroached upon, and each is expected to take part in segregated activities, a state of affairs that they regard as provincial. These families could have refused to enter into the local network of social relationships, but in most cases they felt that the husband's career required it.

THE NATURE OF THE RELATIONSHIP BETWEEN CONJUGAL ROLE-SEGREGATION AND NETWORK CONNECTEDNESS

The data having been described, the nature of the relationship between conjugal role-segregation and network connectedness may now be examined in more detail.

Connected networks are most likely to develop when husband and wife, together with their friends, neighbors, and relatives, have all grown up in the same local area and have continued to live there after marriage. Husband and wife come to the marriage each with his own highly connected network. It is very likely that there will be some overlap of their networks; judging by the Ns' account of their genealogy, one of the common ways for husband and wife to meet each other is to be introduced by a person who is simultaneously a friend of one and a relative of the other.

Each partner makes a considerable emotional investment in relationships with the people in his network; each is engaged in reciprocal exchanges of material and emotional support with them; each is very sensitive to their opinions and values, not only because the relationships are intimate, but also because the people in his network know one another and share the same values so that they are able to apply consistent informal sanctions to one another.

The marriage is superimposed on these preexisting relationships. As long as the couple continue to live in the same area, and as long as their friends, neighbors, and relatives also continue to live within easy reach of the family and of one another, the segregated networks of husband and wife can be carried on after marriage. Some rearrangement is necessary; the husband is likely to stop seeing some of the friends of his youth, particularly those who work at a different place and go to different pubs and clubs; after children are born, the wife is likely to see less of her former girl friends and more of her mother and other female relatives. But apart from these readjustments, husband and wife can carry on their old external relationships, and they continue to be very sensitive to external social controls. In spite of the conjugal segregation in external relationships, the overlapping of the networks of husband and wife tends to ensure that each partner finds out about the other's activities. Although a wife may not know directly what a husband does with his friends away from home, one of the other men is likely to tell his wife or some other female relative who eventually passes the information on, either directly or through other women, to the wife of the man in question. Similarly any defection on the part of the wife is likely to be made known to her husband.

Because old relationships can be continued after marriage, both husband and wife can satisfy some of their personal needs outside the marriage, so that their emotional investment in the conjugal relationship need not be as intense as in other types of family. Both husband and wife, but particularly the wife, can get outside help with domestic tasks and with child care. A rigid division of labor between husband and wife is therefore possible, since each can get outside help. In other words, the segregation in external relationships can be carried over to activities within the family.

Networks become dispersed when people move around from one place to another, or when they make new relationships that have no connection with their old ones. If both husband and wife have moved around a good deal before marriage, each will bring an already dispersed network to the marriage; many of the husband's friends will not know one another; many of the wife's friends will not know one another. After the marriage they will meet new people as well as some of the old ones, and these people will not necessarily know one another. In other words, their external relationships are relatively discontinuous both in space and in time. Such continuity as they possess lies in their relationship with each other rather than in their external relationships. In facing the external world, they draw on each other, for their strongest emotional investment is made where there is continuity. Hence their high standards of conjugal compatibility, their stress on shared interests, on joint organization, on equality between husband and wife. They must get along well together, they must help one another as much as possible in carrying out familial tasks, for there is no sure external source of material and emotional help. Since their friends and relatives are physically scattered and few of them know one another, the husband and wife are not stringently controlled by a solid body of public opinion, but they are also unable to rely on consistent external support. Through their joint external relationships they present a united front to the world and they reaffirm their joint relationship with each other. No external person must seriously menace the conjugal relationship; joint relationships with friends give both husband and wife a source of emotional satisfaction outside the family without threatening their own relationship with each other.

In between these two extremes are the intermediate and transitional families. In the intermediate type, husband and wife have moved around a certain amount so that they seek continuity with each other and make their strongest emotional investment in the conjugal relationship. At the same time, they are able to make some segregated relationships outside the family and they are able to rely on considerable casual help from people outside the family, so that a fairly clearly defined division of labor into male tasks and female tasks can be made.

The transitional families illustrate some of the factors involved in changing from one type of network to another. Husbands and wives who change from a connected to a dispersed network find themselves suddenly thrust into a more joint relationship without the experience or the attitudes appropriate to it. The eventual outcome depends partly on the family and partly on the extent to which their new neighbors build up relationships with one another. An intermediate form of network connectedness seems to be the most likely outcome. Similarly, in the case of families who change from a dispersed to a more highly connected network, their first reaction is one of mild indignation at losing their privacy, but in time it seems likely that they will tend to develop an intermediate degree of network connectedness and conjugal role-segregation.

PART II. NETWORKS IN RELATION TO THE TOTAL ENVIRONMENT

Having discussed the relation of the family to its network, I should like now to consider the factors affecting the form of the network itself.

First the general features characteristic of all familial networks in an urban industrialized society will be examined, then I shall turn to consider some of the factors affecting variations from one urban familial network to another.

FACTORS AFFECTING THE GENERAL FEATURES
OF URBAN FAMILIAL NETWORKS

As described above, all the research families maintained relationships with external people and institutions—with a place of work, with service institutions such as schools, church, doctor, clinic, shops, and so forth, with voluntary associations such as clubs, evening classes, and recreational institutions; they also maintained more informal relationships with colleagues, friends, neighbors, and relatives. It is therefore incorrect to describe urban families as "isolated"; indeed, no urban family could survive without its network of external relationships.

It is correct, however, to say that urban families are not contained within organized groups, for although they have many external relationships, the institutions and persons with which they are related are not linked up with one another to form an organized group. Furthermore, although individual members of a family frequently belong to groups, the family as a whole does not. There are marginal cases, such as the situation arising when all the members of the family belong to the same church or go to the same general practitioner, but in these cases the external institution or person controls only one aspect of the family's life, and can hardly be said to "contain" the family in all its aspects.

In the literature on family sociology, there are frequent references to "the family in the community," with the implication that the community is an organized group within which the family is contained. Our data suggest that the usage is misleading. Of course every family must live in some sort of local area, but very few urban local areas can be called communities in the sense that they form cohesive social groups. The immediate social environment of urban families is best considered not as the local area in which they live, but rather as the network of actual social relationships they

maintain, regardless of whether these are confined to the local area or run beyond its boundaries.

Small-scale, more isolated, relatively "closed" local groups provide a marked contrast. This type of community is frequently encountered in primitive societies, as well as in certain rural areas of industrialized societies. A family in such a local group knows no privacy; everyone knows everyone else. The situation of the urban family with a highly connected network is carried one step further in the relatively closed local group. The networks of the component families are so highly connected and the relationships within the local group are so clearly marked off from external relationships that the local population can properly be called an organized group. Families are encapsulated within this group; their activities are known to all, they cannot escape from the informal sanctions of gossip and public opinion, their external affairs are governed by the group to which they belong.

In many small-scale primitive societies, the elementary family is encapsulated not only within a local group, but also within a corporate kin group. In such cases, the conjugal role-segregation between husband and wife becomes even more marked than that described above for urban families with highly connected networks. Marriage becomes a linking of kin groups rather than preponderantly a union between individuals acting on their own initiative.

These differences between the immediate social environment of families in urban industrialized societies and that of families in some small-scale primitive and rural communities exist, ultimately, because of differences in the total economic and social structure. The division of labor in a small-scale society is relatively simple; the division of labor in an industrial society is exceedingly complex. In a small-scale, relatively closed society, most of the services required by a family can be provided by the other families in the local group and in the kin group. In an urban industrialized society, such tasks and services are divided up and assigned to specialized institutions. Whereas a family in a small-scale, relatively closed society belongs to a small number of groups each with many functions, an urban family exists in a network of many separate, unconnected institutions each with a specialized function. In a small-scale, relatively closed society the local group and the kin group mediate between the family and the total society; in an urban industrialized society there is no single encapsulating group or institution that mediates between the family and the total society.

One of the results of this difference in the form of external relationships is that urban families have more freedom to govern their own affairs. In a small-scale, relatively closed society, the encapsulating groups have a great deal of control over the family. In an urban industrialized society, the doctor looks after the health of individual members of the family, the clinic looks after the health of the mother and child, the school educates children, the boss cares about the individual as an employee rather than as a husband, and even friends, neighbors, and relatives may disagree amongst themselves as to how the affairs of the family should be conducted. In brief, social control of the family is split up amongst so many agencies that no one of them has continuous, complete governing power, and within broad limits, a family can make its own decisions and regulate its own affairs.

The situation may be summed up by saying that urban families are *more highly individuated* than families in relatively closed communities. I feel that this term describes the situation of urban families more accurately than the more commonly used term "isolated." By "individuation" I mean that the elementary family is separated, differentiated out as a distinct, and to some extent autonomous, social group. Of course, in most societies the elementary family is individuated to some extent; one could not say that it existed as a distinct group if it were not. The difference in individuation between an urban family and a family in a relatively closed community is one of degree. It should be remembered, however, that urban families differ among themselves in degree of individuation; families with highly connected networks are less individuated than those with dispersed networks.

The individuation of urban families provides one source of variation in role performance. Because families are not encapsulated within governing and controlling groups, other than the nation as a whole, husband and wife are able, within broad limits, to perform their roles in accordance with their own personal needs. These broad limits are laid down by the ideal norms of the nation as a whole, many of which exist as laws and are enforced by the courts. But informal social control by relatives and neighbors is much less stringent and less consistent than in many small-scale societies, and much variation is possible.

FACTORS AFFECTING VARIATION IN URBAN FAMILIES' NETWORKS

Although the immediate social environments of all urban families resemble one another in assuming network form, there are important differences from one urban family's network to another. As has been demonstrated in Part I above, these differences lie in the degree of connectedness of families' networks. Such differences are most clearly marked in the area of informal relationships, that is, in relationships with friends, neighbors, and relatives. These relationships are felt to be of much greater personal and emotional importance than the more specialized and formal relationships that are maintained with doctors, clinics, schools, and so forth, and they are usually maintained with people who are felt to be socially similar to the family themselves.

In the introduction to this paper it was suggested that network connectedness is a function on the one hand of certain forces in the total environment and on the other hand of the family themselves. It now becomes appropriate to discuss this statement in greater detail.

The highly developed division of labor in an industrial society produces not only complexity but also variability. Sometimes conditions are created that favour the development of relatively highly connected networks, sometimes conditions are created that favour relatively dispersed networks. To examine these conditions in detail would take the discussion far away from families and their networks into a study of the ecology of cities and the economic structure of industries and occupations, a task obviously beyond the scope of this paper. I should like, however, to suggest tentatively several factors that appear likely to affect network connectedness.

Economic Ties among the Members of the Network

Economic ties operate more forcibly between relatives than between friends and neighbors, but there is a wide range of variation in the operation of such cohesive forces even among relatives. The connectedness of the kinship network is enhanced if relatives hold property rights in common enterprises, or if they expect to inherit property from one another.

The connectedness of kinship networks is also enhanced if relatives can help one another to get jobs. Only certain types of occupations allow such help; in occupations requiring examinations or other objective selection procedures—and most professional and semi-professional occupations fall into this category—relatives cannot give one another much help in this respect, whereas in some less skilled occupations and in certain businesses, particularly family businesses, relatives are able to help one another more directly.

The important point here is that neither the occupational system nor the distribution of property is uniform. Different families are affected in different ways. This means that although families' networks in general and their kinship networks in particular do not play a very large part in the economic and occupational structure, there is a great deal of variation in the way in which economic forces affect families' networks.

Type of Neighborhood

Type of neighborhood is important not so much in and of itself, but because it is one of the factors affecting the "localization" of networks. If a family's network is localized, that is, if most of the members live in the same local area so that they are accessible to one another, they are more likely to know one another than if they are scattered all over the country.

Since the members of the informal network are usually felt by the family to have the same social status as themselves, localized networks are most likely to develop in areas where the local inhabitants feel that they are socially similar to one another, that they belong to the same social class, whatever their definition of class may be. Such feelings of social similarity appear to be strongest in long-established working-class areas in which there is a dominant local industry or a small number of traditional occupations. As described above, the Ns, the family with the most highly connected network, were living in such an area. It was also an area of low population turnover, at least until the recent war. Formerly people were born, brought up, and died there. Highly connected networks could develop not only because the local area was homogeneous but also because people stayed put. Now, as some of the inhabitants move away, the networks of even those people who remain in the area are becoming more dispersed.

There were no comparable homogeneous neighborhoods of people belonging to one of the full professions.[1] Neighborhoods were found, however, in which the inhabitants were relatively homogeneous with regard to income, although they had different occupations. The type and cost of the dwelling was probably an important factor contributing to this type of homogeneity. Such neighborhoods were found in suburbs; they were also found in certain mixed working-class areas in which there was no dominant local industry. Most of the families with intermediate and transitional networks were living in such areas; one family with a dispersed network was living in such an area, but they ignored their neighbors, whom they felt were socially similar to one another but not to themselves. Finally, there were some areas that were extremely heterogeneous with regard to occupational level, income, educational background of the inhabitants, and so forth; most of the families with very dispersed networks were living in such areas.

---

[1] University towns are perhaps the closest approximation to a homogeneous area of a single profession. Study of networks and conjugal role-segregation in such areas should be of considerable interest, for certain factors in the situation would be likely to foster a high degree of network connectedness whereas others would discourage it. A homogeneous local area, if perceived as such by the local inhabitants, encourages a high degree of network connectedness. The sexual segregation in the social structure of the colleges may also tend to increase connectedness among men and to reinforce segregation between husband and wife. But most professional men move around during their education and early occupational training, and have professional contacts with people outside their local area, which would discourage network connectedness. As described below, continuity of residence by all members of the network is also an important factor; it seems likely that the population turnover of university towns is relatively high, and that there are few families in which husband and wife are born, brought up, and die in the same university town. Such lack of continuity would tend to prevent a high degree of connectedness.

In a very complex way, neighborhood composition is related to occupation and social class. It is possible to have fairly homogeneous areas of, say, dockworkers or furniture workers, although not all manual occupations are heavily localized, but the structure of the professions is such that it would be most unusual to find a homogeneous area of, say, doctors or lawyers or chartered accountants. On the basis of our data on families, no attempt can be made to analyse the many factors contributing to the formation of local neighborhoods. The most one can say is that the industrial and occupational system is so complex that it gives rise to many different types of urban neighborhood. Some are more homogeneous and stable than others. If one were making a detailed study of network connectedness in relation to neighborhood composition, it would be necessary to work out detailed criteria of homogeneity so that neighborhoods could be systematically compared; one could then study the relation of different degrees and types of objective homogeneity to the attitudes of local inhabitants towards one another; one could also compare the formation of the networks of families in different types of area. My guess would be that one would not find families with highly connected networks in heterogeneous areas of high population turnover, but that one might find both families with highly connected networks and families with dispersed networks in relatively homogeneous, stable areas.

It is most unlikely that one would be able to predict degree of network connectedness from knowledge of the local area alone. Too many other factors are involved—type of occupation, where the husband works, how long the family has lived in the area, perception of the area, and so forth. The family's perception of the people in the area is particularly important. Objective measures of social homogeneity give only a rough indication of how families will feel about their neighbors. Furthermore, it is always necessary to remember that a neighborhood does not simply impose itself on a family. Within certain limits families can choose where they will live, and even if they feel that their neighbors are similar to themselves they are not compelled to be friendly with them; other criteria besides felt social similarity enter into the selection of friends.

Opportunities to Make Relationships outside the Local Area

Networks are more likely to be highly connected if members do not have many opportunities to form new relationships with persons unknown to the other members of the network. Thus, in the case of the family with a highly connected network described above, the husband's work, the relatives of husband and wife, and their friends were all concentrated in the local area. There are no strong sanctions preventing such families from making relationships with outsiders, but there is no unavoidable circumstance that forces them to do so. In the case of the professional families in the research set, their education and professional training had led them to make many relationships with colleagues and friends who did not know one another. Even if such families keep on living in the same area throughout their lives, which is unusual though possible, the husband's pursuit of an occupational career leads him to make relationships with people who do not belong to the family's neighborhood network, so that the network tends to become dispersed.

In brief, network connectedness does depend, in part, on the husband's occupation. If he practices an occupation in which his colleagues are also his neighbors, his network will tend to be localized and its connectedness will tend to be high. If he practices an occupation in which his colleagues are not his neighbors, his network will tend to become dispersed. One cannot predict this solely from knowledge of occupational level. Most professional occupations require a man to get his training and do his work in different areas from the one he lives in. Some manual occupations require or permit this too; others do not.

Physical and Social Mobility

Network connectedness depends on the stability and continuity of the relationships; a family's network will become more dispersed if either the family or the other members of the network move away physically or socially so that contact is decreased and new relationships are established.

Among the research set, there were clear indications that networks became more dispersed when physical mobility had been great. When the number of local areas lived in by both husband and wife before and after marriage is added up, the averages according to network formation are as follows: Families with dispersed networks, 19; families with intermediate networks, 8.2; families with transitional networks, 9.6, and the Ns, the family with the most highly connected network, 2. (In all cases, Service career was counted as one "area".)

Many factors affect physical mobility. Here again the occupational system is a relevant factor. Some occupations permit or encourage social and physical mobility so that networks become dispersed; other occupations encourage stability of residence and social relationships. Social mobility is often accompanied by physical mobility. In the research set, seven families had been occupationally mobile and three had moved or were contemplating moving to an area appropriate to their achieved status. The other four had moved too, but not primarily for status reasons. In general, the networks of socially mobile families tend to become less connected not only because they move physically but also because they are likely to drop old social ties and form new ones. Among the mobile families of the research set, most of the rearranging had been done in adolescence and in the early years of the marriage, and it involved chiefly friends and distant relatives. However mobile the family, husband and wife felt an obligation to maintain contact with their parents; occupational and social achievements were usually felt to be a positive accomplishment for parents as well as for the husband and wife themselves.

Occupation may affect physical mobility even when there is no social mobility. Among the research families many of the professional couples had moved frequently from one local area to another and even from one city to another, and they tended to treat the requirements of the husband's career as the most important factor in deciding whether to move or not; this applied as much to families who were not socially mobile as to those who were. The manual and clerical workers were less likely to give the demands of the husband's career as a chief reason for moving, and only one such family had moved very frequently. The relations between occupation and physical and social mobility are obviously very complex. The important fact is that the occupational system is not uniform; it permits much variation in physical and social mobility and hence much variation in network connectedness.

But decisions to move depend not only on occupational considerations but also on the housing shortage, the type and cost of the house or flat, the family's views on the welfare of their children, relations with relatives, neighbors, and friends in the old area, and on potential relations in the new area, and doubtless many other factors as well. All these considerations must be weighed together when the decision to move is made, although one or other factor may be dominant. Sometimes all considerations point in the same direction; more frequently they have to be balanced against one another. But whatever the reasons, once the move has been made the family's network becomes more dispersed. Even if the family itself does not move, its network will become dispersed if friends and relatives move away.

Network connectedness thus depends on a very complex combination of economic and social forces. Instead of the relatively homogeneous environment of a small-scale, relatively closed society, the total environment of an urban family is exceedingly complex and variable. Many forces affect a family's network, so that there is considerable latitude for the family to choose among several courses of action, and a wide range of variation is possible.

Individual Decision and Choice

The connectedness of a family's network depends not only on external social forces, but also on the family itself. Although the members of a family cannot control the forces of the total environment, they can select from among the various courses of action to which these forces give rise. It is the variability of the total environment that makes choice possible, but it is the family that makes the actual decisions. Decisions are shaped by situational factors but they also depend on the personalities of the members of the family, on the way they react to the situational factors.

Through acts of personal decision and choice husband and wife may affect the connectedness of their network, often without any deliberate intention of doing so; by changing the connectedness of their network they affect in turn their conjugal role-segregation. Thus, if a family with a highly connected network moves out of their old area to a new housing estate, their network will rapidly become more dispersed, and for a time at least they will develop a more joint relationship with each other. If a professional family with a dispersed network moves to a university town because of the husband's career, their network is likely to become slightly more connected even though they may not plan to make it so. If a family with a dispersed network decides to move to a distant suburb because that is the only place where they can find a house that they can afford to buy, they may find themselves extremely isolated—cut off from their friends, unable to make relationships easily with their neighbors, and even more dependent on each other than usual.

Among the research set there were several couples who, for various personal reasons, had almost no informal network at all. Thus two families were living in a state of voluntary isolation or near isolation; they kept up necessary contacts with service institutions and paid a few duty visits to relatives, but that was all. Or again, a husband and wife of the second set of families, for various personal reasons, had almost no friends, although they saw a good deal of their relatives and rather more of their neighbors than the other families of this set. In so far as they had an informal network it was dispersed, but there were far fewer members in it than usual. One of the intermediate families could, if they had wished, have had a network almost as highly connected as that of the Ns, but for various personal reasons they had cut themselves off and had adopted a more home-centered outlook and a more joint role-relationship. Slightly deviant families of this type are aware that their behavior does not coincide exactly with their own norms, although they usually do not like to discuss their deviance unless they feel that they are above their norm rather than below it.

Personality characteristics may thus affect conjugal role-segregation indirectly because they are a factor in shaping choices that affect the form of the family's network. But personal needs and attitudes, both conscious and unconscious, also affect performance of conjugal roles directly. Two families may have similar networks but slightly different degrees of conjugal role-

segregation. Thus the two transitional families discussed above (pp. 93-95) were living in approximately the same social situation, but in one case the husband and wife were trying to develop as joint a conjugal relationship as possible whereas in the second case they were not. Personality factors are of necessity involved in performance of familial roles—and of any role for that matter—but it is only where there is a lack of fit between the personal needs of husband and wife, the social situation in which they find themselves, and the expectations of the members of their networks, that such needs stand out as a separate factor.

Social Class, Network Connectedness, and Segregation of Conjugal Roles

Because of the complexity of the situation it is not surprising that we could not find a simple correlation between class position and segregation of conjugal roles. In my view such segregation is more directly related to network connectedness than to class status as such, although there are probably some aspects of class position that affect conjugal role-segregation directly. For example, if both husband and wife are highly educated, they are likely to have a common background of shared interests and tastes, which makes a joint relationship easy to conduct. Although it is unlikely that teachers deliberately plan to teach children about joint conjugal relationships, higher education is probably a chief means of passing on the ethic appropriate to a joint relationship from one generation to another, and of teaching it to socially mobile individuals whose parents have had a more segregated relationship. It is doubtful, however, whether such education alone could produce joint conjugal relationships; it works in conjunction with other factors.

But for the most part factors associated with class—however one defines that complex construct—affect segregation of conjugal roles indirectly through having an effect on the connectedness of the family's network. To sum up the empirical resultant: Families with highly connected networks are likely to be working-class. But not all working-class families will have highly connected networks.

It is only in the working-class that one is likely to find a combination of factors all working together to produce a high degree of network connectedness concentration of people of the same or similar occupations in the same local area; jobs and homes in the same local area; low population turnover and continuity of relationships; at least occasional opportunities for relatives and friends to help one another to get jobs; little demand for physical mobility; little opportunity for social mobility.

In contrast, the structure of professions is such that this pattern of forces almost never occurs. Homogeneous local areas of a single profession are very rare; a man's place of work and his home are usually in different local areas; professional training leads him to make relationships with people who do not know his family, school friends, and neighbors; in most cases getting a job depends on skill and training rather than on the influence of friends and relatives; many professional careers require physical mobility. Almost the only factor associated with high-class status that tends to foster network connectedness is ownership of shares in common enterprises by relatives—and this is less likely to occur among professional people than among wealthy industrialists and commercial families.

But because a man has a manual occupation he will not automatically have a highly connected network. He may be living in a relatively heterogeneous area, for not all manual occupations are localized. He may live in one place and work in another. He may move from one area to another. Similarly his friends and relatives may move or make new relationships with people he does not know. A high degree of network connectedness *may* be found in association with manual occupations, but the association is not necessary and inevitable.

In brief, one cannot explain network connectedness as the result of the husband's occupational or class status considered as single determinants. Network connectedness depends on a whole complex of forces—economic ties among members of the network, type of local area, opportunities to make new social contacts, physical and social mobility, etc.—generated by the occupational and economic systems, but these forces do not always work in the same direction and they may affect different families in different ways.

Finally, network connectedness cannot be predicted from a knowledge of situational factors alone. It also depends on the family's personal response to the situations of choice with which they are confronted.

In a situation of such complexity, little is to be gained by trying to explain conjugal role-segregation in terms of single factors. In the approach to this problem, the most useful conceptual model has proved to be that of field theory: "behavior is a function of a person (in this case a family) in a situation." Performance of conjugal roles is a function of the family in its social network. The form of the social network depends, in turn, partly on the members of the family and partly on a very complex combination of forces in the total social environment.

SUMMARY

1. The conjugal role-relationship of all twenty urban families studied in this research contained both segregated and joint components. There were differences of degree, however. Some couples had considerable *segregation* in their conjugal role-relationships; in such families, husband and wife expected to have a clear differentiation of tasks and a considerable number of separate interests and activities. At the other extreme there were couples who had as much *joint organization* as possible in the role-relationship of husband and wife; in such families husband and wife expected to carry out many activities together with a minimum of task differentiation and separation of interests. There were many degrees of variation between these two extremes.

2. The immediate social environment of an urban family consists of a network rather than an organized group. A *network* is a social configuration in which some, but not all, of the component external units maintain relationships with one another. The external units do not make up a larger social whole. They are not surrounded by a common boundary.

The network formation of the immediate environment of an urban family is brought about by the complexity of the division of labor in the total society. Whereas a family in a relatively closed community belongs to a small number of groups each with many functions, an urban family exists in a network of many separate institutions each with a specialized function. Urban families are not isolated, but they are *more highly individuated* than families in relatively closed communities; urban families are not encapsulated within external governing groups other than the nation as a whole, and they have a relatively large measure of privacy, of autonomy, and of opportunity to regulate their own affairs.

3. The networks of urban families vary in degree of *connectedness*, namely in the extent to which the people with whom the family maintains relationships carry on relationships with one another. These variations in network connectedness are particularly evident in informal relationships between friends, neighbors, and relatives.

These differences in network connectedness are associated with differences in degree of conjugal role-segregation. *The degree of segregation in the role-relationship of husband and wife varies directly with the connectedness of the family's social network.* Four sets of families have been described, and the relationship between the connectedness of their networks and the degree of their conjugal role-segregation has been discussed.

4. Conceptually, the network stands between the family and the total social environment. Variations in network connectedness cannot be explained in terms of any single factor. Such variations are made possible by the complexity and variability of the economic, occupational and other institutional systems that create a complex of forces affecting families in different ways and permitting selection and choice by the family. It is suggested that the connectedness of a family's network is a function on the one hand of a complex set of forces in the total environment, and on the other hand of the family themselves and their reaction to these forces. Several situational factors possibly relevant to the connectedness of families' networks have been suggested, including: the extent to which members of the network are bound to one another by economic ties; the type of neighborhood; opportunities to make new relationships even while continuing to live in the same area; opportunities for physical and social mobility.

II. LAW AND SOCIAL CONTROL

IT IS A TRUISM that no social group can long survive without procedures for the maintenance of order and conformity. Formal and informal rules by which disputes are resolved and by which people are kept more or less in bounds are among the means by which orderly group life is maintained.

During the past few years, the phrase "law and order" has become a slogan around which many groups in the United States are organized, sometimes divisively. Hardly anyone believes that legal forms and the maintenance of order are unnecessary; instead, dissent centers around the means by which order will be maintained and the types of action to which legal and administrative controls will be applied. These issues have become sharply focused as a result of the fundamental reorganizations of social and technological relations that are taking place in our society and in anticipation of new changes that are just beginning to take place in our strategy of adaptation. Those who advocate "law and order" usually seem to mean that they advocate the retention of traditional laws and customary means of maintaining order, whether in connection with capital punishment, premarital sexual standards, relations among ethnic and racial groups, or means of registering political dissent. On the other side are people who seem to feel that traditional standards are inappropriate to current and emerging conditions of life.

There are many definitions of law, none of which are entirely adequate, but there is nearly universal agreement that law is only one aspect—though a very important one—of the maintenance of order in society. For our present purposes, a law can be defined as a statement which specifies that an action will incur penalty, in threat or in fact, by a human agency—as distinct from a supernatural agency—and that involves a predetermined, specified penalty (loss of life, limb, freedom of movement, privileges, rights, or possessions) that is commensurate with the infraction. Whether a penalty is commensurate with an action is, of course, culturally defined; in some societies adultery is penalized by capital punishment, in others by a fine. (This definition of law will be modified in my discussion of Selection 11.)

It is well known that people are not liable for the same acts nor punished in the same degree in all societies. For example, predetermined homicide is not considered criminal in some societies, and even where this act is regarded as criminal, it sets different kinds of liability and responsibility into motion in different societies. In some, an individual has to answer to some corporate political body (such as a clan or the state) for his act, while in others punishment can be exacted not only from the murderer himself but also—if he cannot be apprehended—from his kinsmen.

One of the most important aspects of every strategy of adaptation is its mode of distributing resources and goods, which is always reflected in the legal system in one way or another. Every society has rules concerning property—that is, people's relationships to things—that are appropriate to its level of development; when the strategy of adaptation changes, property laws also change. And again, the concepts of responsibility implicit in a legal system cannot exist for long in contradiction to the *feelings* of responsibility which people hold; there has to be a "fit" between notions of the "self" and notions of legal liability and responsibility.

There are four major themes in the anthropological study of law that will be explored in this essay and exemplified further in the case studies in this section: (1) The differences between customary and formal law; (2) the relationship between different strategies of adaptation and their legal systems; (3) law as an illustration of the processes of commingling and differentiation; and (4) the diversity of systems of social control in societies at advanced stages of social and technological development and the implications of this diversity for the application of laws to members of disenfranchised groups. As will be seen, these aspects of law overlap considerably.

Let us begin with the distinction between customary and formal law, which is one of the basic concepts in the anthropology of law. Customary law is made up of established rules and procedures that are not codified, that remain informal and personal in application. In a system of customary law, the resolution of disputes takes place in the course of face-to-face relationships within the community. Justice—to the extent that it is ever done—emerges from the collective judgment of the community, often tacit rather than explicit. The force of law is in consensus, and the personalities and backgrounds of the disputants play an important part in the outcome.

How can laws be enforced when there are no formal procedures, like courts, lawyers, judges, and sheriffs? In his discussion of the legal system of the Yurok Indians of the Northwest Coast of California, A. L. Kroeber (one of the major figures of American anthropology) noted:

"It may be asked how the Yurok executed their law without political authority being in existence. The question is legitimate; but a [more profound] one is why we insist on thinking of law only as a function of the state when the example of the Yurok, and of many other [societies], proves that there is no inherent connection between legal and political institutions. The Yurok procedure is simplicity itself. Each side to an issue presses and resists vigorously, exacts all it can, yields when it has to, continues the controversy when continuance promises to be profitable or settlement is clearly suicidal, and usually ends in compromising more or less. Power, resolution, and wealth give great advantages; justice is not always done; but what people can say otherwise of its practices? The Yurok, like all of us, accept the conditions of their world, physical and social; the individual lives along as best he may; and the institutions go on" ("Principles of Yurok Law," in *Handbook of the Indians of California*, Bureau of American Ethnology, Bulletin 78, 1925, p. 22).

Formal law is administered through formal and often ritualized legal procedures. In such systems, lawyers and judges emerge as specialized technicians who study the law and rely on precedent and stereotyped actions in determining what it is and how it is to be applied. The specialized roles of lawyers and judges are part of the more elaborate division of labor that is generally found in national social organizations, and especially in urban centers. A concern with precedent and ritualized procedure is intimately related to the use of impersonal criteria as *ideal* standards in the administration of law.

One of the reasons for the development of impersonal standards in the application of laws is that in an urban situation it is impossible for a judge to know much about the disputants in an argument. In the nation as a whole, it is impossible for the paramount ruler—who is often the court of last appeal—to know the parties to a case. Thus the difficulty of applying the customary law of stateless societies (in which personal relationships play a significant role) in centralized nations becomes mandatory in their legal systems. Not only is it difficult for a judge to know the disputants in a case but he must now be disqualified if he does know them. This change is closely related to the development of rules against nepotism in industrial nations and it is an aspect of the consistent attempt by a nation's rulers to undermine the solidarity of local corporate kin and other groups.

In hunting-gathering societies, the means that are used for maintaining order and conformity have to be viewed against the background of their strategy of adaptation: the necessity for groups to split up recurrently to keep down pressure on available resources, the fact that neither groups nor individuals have exclusive rights to resources, the related fact that there are no chiefs with the power or authority to enforce decisions, and the strong emphasis on kinship in daily social relationships.

As illustrated in Selection 6, when disputes break into the open among nomadic hunter-gatherers, one or both partners to an argument pack up and go to join another camp, and this technique fits well with their ecological realities. Owning few articles and having no deep attachment to any territory, they are able to split off from each other with considerable ease when necessary. Because of extensive intermarriage with other groups, they rarely have any difficulty in finding a camp in which there are kinsmen. Also (as will be seen in the Introduction to Part V) there are very strong emotional bases among hunter-gatherers for this pattern of coping with overt aggressiveness within the group.

But splitting off from the camp is generally a last resort. All hunting-gathering societies have a variety of techniques, usually symbolic in form, for trying to keep tensions within reasonable bounds. These techniques may include witchcraft and sorcery, joking and ribaldry, and competitive singing in which the parties to a dispute defend their positions and the assembled members of the community judge who is the victor (as among many Eskimo groups). It is only when these techniques fail, when feelings get out of hand and violence breaks out, that people will leave for another camp, perhaps for several hours or months or permanently.

Because local groups among hunter-gatherers do not have exclusive rights over resources, and because every member of a local group has an equal right to hunt and gather over a territory, there are no chiefs or other authorities who can enforce decisions by threatening to withhold access to resources. Individuals may try to settle quarrels, but whether they succeed depends entirely on their prestige and the willingness of the disputants to abide by their recommendations. Authority of this kind develops only at more advanced levels of adaptation, when it becomes possible for the head or representative of a group to deprive people of resources or access to them.

Among hunter-gatherers, then, every man has to settle his own disputes and each seeks to enforce resolutions as best he can. Each person is his own lawyer and judge, abiding by the customary standards of the group in determining whether it is sensible to continue a quarrel or a claim. He holds these positions because he is an adult, an economically productive person, and also because he has kinsmen in the group on whom he can count for support; but so does everyone else. Such groups are almost always characterized by an extreme degree of egalitarianism, each adult male occupying (or having the right to occupy) the same statuses and perform the same roles as all other men in the group; a parallel organization exists among the women. There is thus in such societies an extreme degree of commingling of roles and an almost complete lack of differentiation among institutions, legal and other.

The legal systems of horticultural societies are quite different from those of hunter-gatherers, because cultivation makes different demands on people and because the institutional requirements by which people live are changed by this technological development. This is admirably exemplified in Selection 7, in which Walter Goldschmidt analyzes the law of the Sebei of East Africa as an adaptive system. The most important difference between hunter-gatherers and horticulturists is in their relationship to land; in horticultural societies, groups acquire exclusive rights to land and individuals are given rights to use portions of this territory. These rights are secured through membership in the group—usually based on considerations of kinship—and both rights (to land and to membership in the group) are inherited. This is inevitably reflected in the legal system.

Sedentism, the investment of personal energy in tracts of land, and the commingling and inheritance of group membership and rights in land lead to the development of rules of property in horticultural legal systems to an extent never found among hunter-gatherers. At the same time, the fact that cultivable land is generally in limited supply means that ultimate control over its distribution to individuals and households must be vested in the groups—such as lineages and clans—which have exclusive rights to it. This is one of the most important factors in the development of chieftainship or headmanship in horticultural societies; and whether or not the head of a kin group ever exercises his right to deprive members of access to land, this theoretical power is basic to his authority in resolving disputes or punishing transgressions. Very often, this power is cast in magical or religious terms, as when a chief threatens a disobedient member of his group with a curse, and this reflects the still considerable commingling of legal, religious, kin, and economic institutions in horticultural societies.

This can be put in more general terms. When we look at law as one means among others for maintaining order and conformity, and when we view these processes in a comparative and evolutionary perspective, it becomes apparent that not all societies have legal institutions in the sense of formally defined groupings. As Richard Schwartz and James Miller have shown in their study of "Legal Evolution and Societal Complexity," the institutionalization of legal relations is a progressive accompaniment of sociotechnological development (*American Journal of Sociology*, 70 [1964]: 159-69; reprinted as Selection 33 in *The Cultural Present*). There are many societies in which there are no administrators of law—no councils, mediators, courts, judges, or police, no lawyers, legislators or other codifiers, no prisons or executioners.

One of the conclusions that can be drawn from such studies is that as cultural evolution occurs—that is, as a society harnesses increasingly efficient extra-personal sources of energy—the institutional structure as a whole and the legal system in particular is characterized by a greater degree of differentiation. Thus, for example, a lineage chief in a horticultural society is simultaneously the organizer of economic activities, the main religious functionary of the group, its political head, the eldest male member of his kin group, and the legal arbiter of disputes within the group. Even so, his roles reflect a greater degree of institutional differentiation than can be observed in hunting-gathering societies, where every man is his own legal arbiter and no one has the authority to enforce decisions.

Thus it is in horticultural societies that the first embryonic differentiation of the legal sphere occurs. Although there is more commingling than differentiation in these societies, we begin to observe here the use of the office or council of the chief to arbitrate disputes; often these offices are more honorific than possessed of real power, but they are important as evolutionary beginnings. But legal roles—whether honorific or authoritative—are still directly dependent on kinship status, military exploits, age, sex, and the like.

The single most important evolutionary step taken in the differentiation of the legal sphere, like others, was the establishment of states and the formation of nations. The state represents a great social advance, and one of its effects is to replace customary with formal law. In almost all cases, this substitution first began to occur in agricultural societies that were organized into nation-states. Why do I believe that it was the political variable that was responsible for these developments, and not the economic and technological imperatives of an agricultural strategy? Because when we compare agricultural societies organized into nation-states with those that are not, we see that it is the political factor that is of overriding importance. This is illustrated by the Ifugao of the Philippines, whose legal system is the subject of Selection 8 (by Roy Barton). The Ifugao are stateless agriculturists who cultivate on elaborate terraces, and their legal system, as will be seen, more closely resembles that of the horticultural Sebei (Selection 7) than it does that of the Babylonians (Selection 10). This comparison is further underscored by the Kuba (Selection 9), who are horticulturists organized into a nation-state and whose legal system reflects the differentiation that is characteristic of agricultural nations more than it reflects stateless horticulturists.

The replacement of customary by formal law does not occur overnight or automatically, any more than does the equal application of the law to all groups in the society, and the two are closely related in the evolutionary process. When states are first established and nations formed, a bifurcation usually develops in the legal sphere. Informal law is often allowed to continue in matters relating exclusively to personal or village relationships, such as interhousehold cooperation and reciprocity, parent-child relations, and care of the indigent. Formal law, on the other hand, is made to apply in matters involving the central government—such as treason, taxation, military service, and land tenure—and to people who do not live in face-to-face interaction, such as those who meet only in the marketplace.

A comparison of stateless and state societies at different stages of technological development suggests that the political institutions that make up a state system constitute one of the most important elements in the milieu of local groups in the nation. The state is the only group in a national society that is in constant touch with all the other groups in the nation; it is thus part of the habitat to which these local groups must adapt. States are constantly issuing orders, formulating new policies, embarking on and stimulating new economic ventures, exploiting and harnessing new sources of energy, entering into different kinds of relations with different nations, and so forth. Each of these has consequences at every level of society, and these consequences increase geometrically because the state has to respond in turn to the changes that it has produced at local levels and, then, produce still other changes.

An important element in this politically stimulated habitat is one of the paradoxes in the social organization of a national society. On the one hand, those who speak in the name of the state seek to achieve the uniform implementation of laws as a means of achieving political control. At the same time, however, for reasons to be spelled out in a moment, they underwrite a system of social stratification in which different groups have unequal access to the energy systems on which the society relies. Stratification does not necessarily entail unequal administrations of the society's laws, although so far in history this has usually been the case.

These cross-cutting themes are clearly expressed, for example, in the Code of Hammurabi (Selection 10). On the other hand, as in the epilogue of the code, repeated reference is made to the law of "the land," outweighing the laws of the various groups that had been conquered and out of which the Babylonian kingdom was formed. On the other hand, reflecting the social stratification and inequality that is an accompaniment of all nation-states, the code prescribes penalties that vary with the status of the parties concerned. For example:

If a man strikes the cheek of a (free) man who is superior (in rank) to him(self), he shall be beaten with sixty stripes with a whip of ox-hide in the assembly.

If the man strikes the cheek of a free man equal to him(self) in rank, he shall pay 1 maneh of silver. . . .

If a man strikes the daughter of a (free) man (and) . . . that woman dies, they shall put his daughter to death.

If he causes the daughter of a villein to . . .[die], he shall pay $\frac{1}{2}$ maneh of silver" (*The Babylonian Laws*, edited with translation by G. R. Driver and John C. Miles [London: Oxford University Press, 1955, Vol. 2, pp. 77-79]).

A major characteristic of social evolution is that at each successive stage of technological development in which more and more people rely on a single source of energy—a few draft animals that serve an entire community or region, water for irrigation, steam, electricity, atomic power—control over the energy system is in the hands of fewer and fewer people. There are several ways of explaining this development. It can be argued that centralized control is more efficient than a system in which every local group or person exercises control over its own energy systems. This is obviously true, but does not provide a causal explanation. I hypothesize that centralized political control is achieved when a small group—which only later becomes a social and economic class—gains control (usually by force) of the sources of energy on which people rely (such as seed and draft animals) or on which they can be maneuvered into relying (such as irrigation water). Once a group gains economic control, it becomes a ruling class and is able to press its subordinates into producing economic surpluses; it does this not only to underwrite its own standard of living, to provide food for its bureaucrats and functionaries, and to support those people in the population who are not productive, but also as a demonstration of its power and authority.

A good example is provided by societies that rely on plow agriculture (see Selection 10). Plows are inextricably tied to the use of draft animals; hence plows are inseparable from people organized into particular social relationships that provide assurance for the care and provision of those animals. These livestock generally come to be under the monopolistic control of one or a few individuals, and this is one of the major bases of social stratification in plow-agricultural societies; draft animals have to be borrowed, rented, or exchanged for other services or for food or money. But regardless of the medium of exchange, access to these resources (and to comparable resources at other levels) is always predicated on political conformity and obedience.

In principle, conformity is best achieved by uniform laws and regulations, but it is clearly discernible from the study of the evolution of legal and political systems that unequal administration of law persists, largely as a result of local vested interests. The Mississippi and Louisiana planters and their equivalents throughout human history have never been champions of uniform and equal application of the law. It is in the interest of those who control a nation's central political apparatus, however, to achieve legal uniformity. The principles that give rise to the conflict between the nuclear family and the corporate kin group—discussed in the Introduction to the previous section—are also evident throughout the course of political evolution in the relationship between the central state and local groups which seek to retain their autonomy; the relationships between the states and the federal government in the United States is a good example.

Does this mean, then, that social stratification and the unequal application of the law are inevitable? The evolutionary record suggests that stratification is an inevitable accompaniment of national social organization, but it is not inevitable that systematized inequality will continue to be based on the disenfranchisement of whole ethnic, racial, or religious groups. Instead, stratification in a future stage of technological development may be based on achievement.

To clarify, let us retrace some of the major features of the evolution of strategies of adaptation. In hunting-gathering societies, in which each man controls his own muscular energy and where no groups or individuals control limited resources, there are no political controls and no institutionalization of legal relations. In advanced horticultural societies, each man also controls his own muscular energy and his own hoe or digging stick, but here we see the beginnings of political control and institutionalized legal relations accompanying the controlled allocation of limited land. In agricultural nations, where land is in limited supply or water and seed are available in limited quantities, rulers are able to gain control of these resources and provide access to them in exchange for allegiance and conformity. But such resources are then in the hands of very few people who tend to aggrandize legal as well as political privilege.

Current political rhetoric notwithstanding, there is probably much less—and less painful—inequality in most industrial nations than in agricultural states. Without denying that even a little inequality is too much, the evolutionary record is clear on this, and it also points to a probable further reduction in inequality in future stages of development. In contemporary industrial nations, regardless of their political and economic ideologies, there is a pattern in the relationship between centralized political institutions and the society's major sources of energy. The greater the number of people who draw on a single source of energy, the greater the tendency to concentrate its control in the hands of the society's ruling groups, and this is always achieved at the expense of the autonomy of local groups and the people who control them, like local planters in Mississippi. For example, the control of steam to drive machines has almost always been localized, each factory maintaining and controlling its own power plant, and generally, the worst legal horrors in an industrial society are committed in communities that are based on such localized energy systems. In contrast, there has been greater centralization of control of electricity produced by waterpower, and even more for electricity produced by nuclear energy. Each of these technological developments is accompanied by increased equality in the administration of law. If we are beginning to move into a postindustrial stage of development in which the control of nonmuscular sources of energy will be still more centralized, we can expect that the application of law will become still more uniform throughout society, even if a system of stratification remains. We will return to other aspects of this problem in Part IV, in connection with current ideological conflicts in the United States.

The reader who wants a deeper acquaintance with the evolution of legal institutions as an aspect of the overall evolution of social organization has a vast literature from which to choose. The basic work that has influenced almost all thought on this subject is *Ancient Law: Its Connection with the Early History of Society and its Relation to Modern Ideas*, by Sir Henry Sumner Maine, first published in 1861, and of which there are many reprints. *The Division of Labor in Society*, by Emile Durkheim, has also played a major role in anthropological and sociological theories of legal evolution, but it has not withstood the test of time and empirical research like that by Schwartz and Miller (cited in the text). The basic anthropological introduction to this area of research has been *The Law of Primitive Man*, by E. Adamson Hoebel (Cambridge, Mass.: Harvard University Press, 1954); I have taken issue with many of Hoebel's formulations, especially in regard to clan law, in *The Transition from Childhood to Adolescence: Cross-Cultural Studies of Initiation Ceremonies, Legal Systems and Incest Taboos* (Chicago: Aldine, 1964). An excellent legal-historical survey of legal evolution is *Cases and Readings on Law and Society*, by Sidney Post Simpson and Julius Stone, editors, with the collaboration of M. Magdalena Schoch (St. Paul, Minn.: West, 1949; three volumes).

In 1966 there began appearing a quarterly journal, *Law and Society Review*, containing articles and reviews covering the entire range of the anthropology and sociology of law. There have also recently appeared several collections of largely nonhistorical studies that can profitably be consulted by the interested reader: *Law and Warfare: Studies in the Anthropology of Conflict*, Paul Bohannan, editor (Garden City, N.Y.: The Natural History Press, 1967); *War: The Anthropology of Armed Conflict and Aggression*, Morton Fried, Marvin Harris, and Robert Murphy, editors (Garden City, N.Y.: The Natural History Press, 1969); *Law in Culture and Society*, Laura Nader, editor (Chicago: Aldine, 1969); *The Sociology of Law: Interdisciplinary Readings*, Rita James Simon, editor (San Francisco: Chandler Publishing Company, 1968); and *Law and the Behavioral Sciences*, Lawrence M. Friedman and Stewart Macaulay, editors (Indianapolis: Bobbs-Merrill, 1969). Also useful is an anthology dealing with *Anthropology and Early Law: Selected from the Writings of Paul Vinogradoff, Fredric Maitland, Frederick Pollock, Maxime Kovalevsky, Rudolf Huebner, Frederic Seebohm*, Lawrence Krader, editor (New York and London: Basic Books, 1967); Krader often assumes considerable prior historical knowledge on the reader's part, but such information is indispensable for the student of the evolution of law.

6. THE IMPORTANCE OF FLUX
IN TWO HUNTING SOCIETIES

COLIN M. TURNBULL

Reprinted from Richard B. Lee and Irven DeVore, editors, Man the Hunter *(Chicago: Aldine, 1968). Copyright © 1968 by the Wenner-Gren Foundation for Anthropological Research, Inc. Colin Turnbull is Professor of Anthropology, Hofstra College. Prior to assuming that post, he was a Curator of Ethnology at the American Museum of Natural History. He has done extensive field research in Africa; his publications include* The Forest People: A Study of the Pygmies of the Congo; The Lonely African; *and* Wayward Servants: The Two Worlds of the African Pygmies.

■ Not all disputes are settled by resort to law. If a man and his neighbor in even a small city in the United States have a serious disagreement—say, because one's pet dog pulls up the other's flowers —they can easily evade the issue by scurrying behind their locked front doors after exchanging words or they can evade it by turning the matter over to the impersonal agencies of their lawyers. It is unlikely that their dispute will affect their respective networks of social relationships, because urban people do not "neighbor" very much (except sometimes when they have young children who are playmates) and because they are not likely to be economically interdependent.

But the conditions in a hunting-gathering camp are very different. There the effective social unit is small, personal relationships are close and continuous, almost all activities are conducted in the open, and all the members of the group are economically interdependent; additionally, hunter-gatherers have close kinship ties, which themselves often produce emotional tension. Although hunter-gatherers usually seem to have strong ethical standards that require everyone to mind his own business, it is hard to live by these rules under the conditions just described. As in all societies, people in hunting-gathering camps occasionally become violent, often as a result of marital disputes; quarrels in such a setting have a way of spreading and involving many—and sometimes most—members of the group.

At the same time, hunting-gathering groups have no one with the power or authority to settle disputes, and they must cope with the feelings they arouse and resolve their quarrels by consensus. One such technique, described by Colin Turnbull in the following selection, is for the group to split up, different family units attaching themselves to different camps. This fits neatly with another imperative of a hunting-gathering way of

life: the need for groups to divide periodically, in order to hold down the population pressure on the available resources. Whether dispute resolution or the limitations of habitational resources is the more frequent cause of fission, it is clear that these ruptures serve adaptive purposes.

What Turnbull describes is not law in the formal sense. But the processes involved here suggest that the modes by which people resolve disputes— whether in a foraging camp or in an industrial city— must always conform to the kinds of relationships they maintain with their fellows, which are themselves an aspect of a particular strategy of adaptation.

There is an excellent description of hunter-gatherer law and social control in *The North Alaskan Eskimo: A Study in Ecology and Society,* by Robert F. Spencer (Washington, D.C.: Smithsonian Institution, Bureau of American Ethnology, Bulletin 171, 1959). Another very good description of hunter-gatherer techniques for maintaining law and order is to be found in *The Andaman Islanders,* by A. R. Radcliffe-Brown (New York: The Free Press, 1964, pp. 22-87); this monograph is generally regarded as one of the classic studies of hunter-gatherers. ■

THIS PAPER EXAMINES the flexibility of social organization characteristic of two East African small-scale societies, the Mbuti Pygmies of the tropical rain forest of the northeast Congo and the Ik of the dry, open mountains near the borders of Uganda, Kenya, and Sudan. Both the Ik and Mbuti, as hunters and gatherers, work within their respective environments rather than attempting to alter them. Because neither is under the rigid control a truly marginal economy might impose, each is able to maintain a fluid band composition, a loose form of social structure, and to utilize flux as a highly effective social mechanism.

By flux I mean the constant changeover of personnel between local groups and the frequent shifts of campsites through the seasons. This apparent instability is, in fact, the very mechanism that gives these societies their cohesion. Both the Mbuti and the Ik are composed of many constantly shifting elements forming established patterns. Flux is expressed as recurrent fission and fusion which affects the composition of local bands. A similar state of flux is found in a number of hunting and gathering societies, such as the Hadza and Bushmen, and may be characteristic of the majority of peoples described at the symposium. Before undertaking a comparison of flux in Mbuti and Ik society, a brief ethnographic sketch of each will be given.

MBUTI

The Mbuti Pygmies have been previously described by Schebesta, Putnam, and Turnbull. They live by hunting and gathering in the interior of the Ituri forest. There are two economic divisions: the net-hunters who live in large camps of seven to thirty families, based on communal or cooperative hunting, and the archers, who live in much smaller groups, and who hunt individually with bow and arrow. The residential units of both net-hunters and archers constantly change in composition as individuals and families circulate between the territorially based bands.

The total population of Mbuti appears to stand at about 40,000 and all of these are more or less closely associated with their Sudanic and Bantu neighbours, the Lese Mangbetu, and Bira. This association has existed for at least several hundred years and as a consequence all pygmies speak only the languages of the village cultivators adjacent to them. What makes the continuation of their hunting life possible is the existence of the forest itself, which their neighbors fear to penetrate and to which the pygmies have become closely adapted. Their adaptation to the forest is conspicuously expressed in their technology and subsistence but is also deeply rooted in their ideology.

The Mbuti of the Epulu area, with whom I did field work in 1954 and 1957–58, practiced no agriculture, although they did engage in trade with the villagers, and spent brief periods living with these neighbors and eating their foods.

The villagers regard the Pygmies as their vassals, but, as I have argued elsewhere, the Pygmies manipulate this relationship to their advantage and maintain their primary orientation to the forest.

IK

Very little is known about the Ik, and to all outward appearances, they are predominantly cultivators. Yet, because one year out of every four or five brings a drought which destroys all crops, the Ik periodically abandon cultivation and revert to hunting. Thus, although they are cultivators for 75 per cent of the time, for the remaining 25 per cent they are 100 per cent hunters and gatherers.

The Ik, who number somewhat over 1,500 have previously been known as Teuso or Teuth, a name they reject as being applied to them only by the Dodos. They distinguish themselves from all pastoral tribes, such as Dodos, Turkana, and Karimojong, and they associate themselves with nearby hunting tribes, such as the Niangea and Napore, and even the more distant Tepes. They do so, despite a mutual unintelligibility of languages, by describing themselves and their fellow hunters as *kwarikik*, meaning "mountain people"; but they claim no closer connection with the other "kwarikik" than the common mountain environment. There is no thought of common origin. Nevertheless, though separated by hundreds of miles, the environmental factor seems important enough to all kwarikik for them to recognize and feel a unity, against all others who are not mountain people.

The Ik live during the agricultural cycle in small, isolated, heavily stockaded villages that are almost as discrete as their hunting bands. Even within each village there are numerous divisions that prevent any solidification into effective corporate units much larger than the nuclear family. The divisions and subdivisions do not necessarily follow any lines of kinship, nor are they permanent. The groups may not even last the maximum duration of any one village site, namely, two years. Clan membership is only significant as a convenience for a rough reckoning of whether or not a proposed marriage is allowable. Marriage within the clan, however, does occasionally take place, and then the clan is said to have divided. One side of the dividing line is called "big," and the other "small." These features are all directly comparable to the Mbuti band, and when the Ik village converts itself into a hunting and gathering band, the same principles of organization operate with equal effectiveness, and equal fluidity.

COMPARISONS

ENVIRONMENT

The environments of the Mbuti and Ik contrast sharply. The forest of the Mbuti, for the most part is flat with occasional hilly regions. Its climate varies scarcely at all throughout the year. The maximum annual temperature range is 20°, and the normal daily variation is usually far less, perhaps 5° (between 75° and 80°F.). Rain falls evenly over the entire area, and is evenly spread throughout the year. Game and vegetable supplies are similarly uniform in distribution, and are abundant throughout the area. There is nothing that makes one part of the forest more or less desirable than any other part at any time of the year.

On the other hand, the mountain territory of the Ik is for the most part arid, though studded with richly wooded valleys and gorges. Some areas are much more wooded while others may verge on desert. Far from the absence of seasons characteristic of the Ituri forest, the Ik habitat is one of violent climatic extremes. During the summer, the sun scorches the ground dry with its fierce intensity, while in the winter, the clouds obscure the sun, making the air cold and damp. Violent gales blow up and down the valleys, sweeping the torrential rains with them. Dry gorges become swollen rivers in minutes and, as quickly, become dry again. Small, tightly localized areas can become devastated by wind and flood, while all around these areas,

it may be calm and dry. A region that fares well one year may fare badly the next. The game population is seasonally nomadic and edible vegetable supplies are tighly localized rather than evenly distributed.

In the light of this contrast between the Mbuti and the Ik environments, a curious feature emerges. The Mbuti treat their stable environment as though it were unstable, creating imaginary seasons of plenty and scarcity, while the Ik treat their highly unstable environment as though it were stable, and consequently bring upon themselves alternating periods of real plenty and scarcity.

However, it should be stressed that the usual notion that hunters live a marginal existence does not apply in either case. The economies, at first glance, may give the impression of being precarious, but in fact this is not the case. Famine or anything approaching it is utterly unknown to the Mbuti who have an axiom that "the only hungry Mbuti is a lazy Mbuti."

The same axiom would have applied to the Ik, up to the drastic encroachments of both the central administration and the neighboring pastoral tribes in recent years which have hemmed them in, confined them, and hampered their traditional economy in every possible way. Yet even now it would be true to say that the only hungry Ik is one who is unable or unwilling to run the gauntlet of the various armed forces that forbid them access to major portions of their former subsistence range.

LAND USE AND GROUP SIZE

Naturally, the methods of exploitation of the resources vary according to the environment, as does the hunting organization and the gathering pattern. Both Mbuti and Ik hunting bands fluctuate in size from seven to thirty nuclear families, but whereas an Mbuti band is territorially circumscribed, and is so defined, it is much less so with the Ik. An Mbuti band can comfortably confine its movements from one year to the next within 100 square miles, due to the uniform distribution of the game in the forest. An Ik band is forced by climatic fluctuations to undertake seasonal movements over large areas, up to about 10,000 square miles.

Differences due to migration patterns of game and to seasonal differences in the availability of vegetable foods have social consequences as well. The Mbuti band, as a territorial unit, retains independence for most of the year and rarely needs to share its territory with another band, while the Ik bands often come together in larger concentrations in order to exploit the localized resources.

table foods is fully as important a factor in diet as is hunting. Although hunting is a more prestigious activity, gathering strategies play a large part in determining the band's daily and seasonal movements. Even in the direction of their all-male spear hunt, the Ik take the distribution of vegetable foods into consideration and women are called on for advice. Thus a common basis of abundant vegetable food sources may make possible alternate and equally felicitous styles of hunting.

SUBSISTENCE TECHNIQUES

What is more remarkable than the differences between these two areas is the range of subsistence organization *within* each area. Among both the Mbuti and the Ik, two styles of hunting organization are in use. The Mbuti are divided into net-hunters and archers, and the Ik into net-hunters and spear-hunters.

Regarding the Mbuti, there is no environmental reason why half of them should be net-hunters and the other half archers, although there may be some historical explanation. Nonetheless, the forest is so divided and each division regards the other as somewhat quaint and wonders how the other can survive. Yet on investigation it became clear that each half is well versed in the other's hunting technique; visitors from one division to the other have no difficulty at all in adapting to the different hunting methods. And it is strange indeed that in the same environment and with equally adequate technologies, the net-hunters regard the brief honey season as a time of plenty, while the archers see it as a time of scarcity. Each group takes appropriate measures to meet the perceived situation, the net-hunters splitting into small units, and the archers congregating into larger ones!

Among the Ik, it is equally difficult to discern why some should hold to the net-hunt (of the Acholi type) while others say that hunting with spears is more effective. Again, there appears to be no discernible differences in habitat which would explain the different styles of hunting.

Part of the explanation may lie in the fact that in both cases, the environment is generous enough to allow alternative hunting techniques. In common with other tropical hunter-gatherers discussed at the symposium, gathering of vege-

THE IMPORTANCE OF FLUX

Among the Mbuti, the constant process of fission and fusion that characterizes every band, is more predictable than among the Ik. The flux appears as a systematic pattern which I have analyzed elsewhere. The focal point of the process is the honey season, during which the net-hunters spread out into fragmented sub-bands, sometimes uniting siblings, sometimes dividing them, but always separating antagonistic elements. At the end of the honey season, the band begins to re-form, carefully avoiding any lines of fracture that remain unhealed. The net-hunters normally form bands larger than those of the archers, for a net-hunt demands cooperation between a minimum of six or seven nuclear families, and allows a maximum of thirty. The honey season, they say, is a time of such plenty that the game can easily be caught by hand, and so there is no need for the large cooperative net-hunt. During the previous ten months, the necessity of constant cooperation, and the proximity and intimacy in which all band members must live with one another, invariably gives rise to numerous latent antagonisms and even a few open hostilities. If hostilities were to go unchecked, it would destroy the essential unity of the band and consequently ruin the success of the hunt. Thus the honey season is an important safety-valve, allowing for the radical reconstitution of face-to-face groups.

The archers, in exactly the same environment, do precisely the reverse. They hunt in maximal bands *only* during the honey season, and for the rest of the year split up into minor and ultimately minimal segments. Their stated rationale is that the honey season is a time of poor hunting, and thus, maximum cooperation is demanded. The reality is that whereas the net-hunting band is of necessity united throughout the bulk of the year, the archer band is splintered into tiny segments, sometimes only two or three families, each independent of others. The ideal number of archers for either tracking or ambushing game is three; five would already be felt as unwieldy. The composition of these small segments does not remain constant throughout the year, anymore than does the composition of the net-hunting band, but the net-hunters must endure close association with much greater numbers of people than do the archers.

When hostilities come into the open, the solution is for one or the other disputant to pack up and leave. But the very size of the minimal archer segments means that the healing of internal disputes is of much less concern to them during the honey season than it is to the net-hunters. The problem for the archers is how to maintain any semblance of band unity under such conditions, and band unity must be expressed, for territory is defined by bands, just as bands are defined by territory. It is essential that territorial boundaries should be known so as to avoid any conflicts that might arise due to allegations of trespass or poaching. The need, then, is for each band to draw together all its scattered segments and to act as a band, within its territory, for at least some part of the annual cycle. On the excuse that hunting is poor at the honey season (I could find no justification for the excuse, though I prefer to leave it an open issue), the archers of each band gather together and participate in the *begbe*, or communal beat, which in technique is similar to the net-hunt.

The Ik band is similarly in a constant state of flux, and again, its composition is determined primarily by noneconomic factors. The process, though less predictable than that of the Mbuti, clearly does not follow any unilinear descent pattern in fission. Age and territoriality are prime factors in the regulation and definition of the band, and the conflict-resolving aspects of its shifting composition are predominant. The Ik also have a honey season, which comes at a time of general abundance. Communal activity breaks down, even during the agricultural cycle, and major changes in band composition are

likely to take place in adjustment to political factors by separating antagonistic segments. The honey season is followed by a termite season which breaks the band into its minimal segments and takes these far afield—during the hunting year. At the end of this season, the bands gradually re-form into agricultural units, if rain promises well, and cooperate in the building of new villages and the hoeing of new fields. However, each village retains the internal divisions of the hunting bands, though, as with the Mbuti, the Ik seldom revert to previous groupings.

POLITICAL AUTHORITY

There is no form of centralized authority in either society, apart from the nominal authority vested by the European administrations in their appointed headmen. This lack is perhaps at first surprising, considering that both Mbuti and Ik are divided into virtually autonomous bands with no formal system of interrelationship, and that each band is constituted in such a way as to create the minimum of cohesion within itself. Even nuclear families are not the solid social entities we might expect them to be. It is difficult to see what are the threads that hold each society together as such, for despite the apparent lack of cohesion, both the Ik and Mbuti are strongly united, as peoples, in oppostion to their neighbors.

On the contrary, in each case there is a strong hostility felt towards any individual who aspires to a position of authority or leadership. Hostility is even shown towards those who, without any such aspirations, are plainly better fitted to lead than others by virtue of sheer ability.

Part of the answer lies again in the environment, for while it determines certain aspects of the mode of economic exploitation, within that general framework it leaves a large margin of latitude and always allows the certainty of, at the very least, a sufficiency of food, if not a surplus. This assurance of food is clearly seen in the unpredictability of the daily hunt. Even when game is known to be close, a band (in either soiety) may well at the last moment decide not to go hunting at all. It may find an excuse, such as a trivial dispute, or it may not bother to find any. The result may even be hunger on that day. Yet when already sated with successive days of good hunting and feasting, a band may decide to set off in the most unlikely direction and return, at the end of a long and arduous day, with nothing to show for it. Sometimes rain will make hunting impractical and again hunger might ensue since neither society (the Ik considered in their hunting cycle, here) will store or keep anything for the morrow. After two or three consecutive rainy days, which is about the maximum that can be expected, a fine day may dawn and find the band still determined to stay in camp and attend to unimportant chores.

A band may hunt as a single unit, or it can split up and hunt as several independent units. There is no predicting which it will do among the Ik, where seasonal variations are strongly marked, yet among the Mbuti where there are virtually no seasons (except for the two months of the years during which honey is available in addition to all the usual food supplies) the process of fission and fusion is clearly predictable.

It all seems to be a rather topsy-turvy world for both Mbuti and Ik, where the things that happen are those that could least reasonably be expected. I am perhaps somewhat over-emphasizing the lack of organization, but here that seems important, for all too often hunters and gatherers are expected to set a shining example of social organization at its simplest and its clearest, and illustrate with crystalline lucidity the fundamental principles upon which all respectable social systems are based.

The fact is that both the Mbuti and the Ik work within their permissive environments rather than attempting to control them. They are unencumbered by the rigid imperatives that would be imposed by a truly harsh environment. Thus they are able to maintain a fluid band composition and a loose social structure; and are able to utilize this flux as a highly effective social mechanism, providing scope for action in all aspects of social life.

CONCLUSIONS

In summing up, I want to stress three points. First it seems clear that it is environmental permissiveness and not environmental rigor that makes possible the system of flux. Second, the major function of flux is not ecological adaptation but what could be called political adaptation. And third, the fission and fusion of individuals and groups does not follow lines of kinship.

The relative abundance of food that obtains in both traditional situations permits the system of flux. It allows for the fluidity of composition that affords a simple means of averting disruption without imposing a legal mechanism that would in itself be even more disruptive to the total society. The predictability of food supplies allows for neighboring bands to plan their movements so as to avoid conflict.

It is plain that in each case the process of fission and fusion follows lines of dissent rather than those of descent, and that the major function is conflict-resolving. At no time during the process can any trace of the concept of unilinear descent or affiliation be found. The band can only be defined as that group of individuals living and hunting within recognized territorial boundaries at a given time. A cross-cutting loyalty is formed by attachment and cooperation between age-mates, age being the vital bond that takes clear precedence over kinship, among both the Mbuti and the Ik.

Another function of flux might be said to be religious, for, by deemphasizing stability in interpersonal relations, the process throws the people into closer recognition of the one constant in their lives, the environment and its life-giving qualities, Under such conditions of flux where band and even family relations are often brittle and fragmentary, the environment, in general, and one's own hunting territory in particular, become for each individual the one reliable and rewarding focus of his attention, his loyalty, and his devotion.

7. THE DYNAMIC ADAPTATION OF SEBEI LAW

WALTER GOLDSCHMIDT

Originally published by the University of California Press; reprinted by permission of The Regents of the University of California. From Sebei Law *by Walter Goldschmidt, pp. 245-260. Walter Goldschmidt is Professor in the Department of Anthropology of the University of California at Los Angeles and is the holder of a Senior Scientist Award from the National Institutes of Mental Health. In addition to his work on Africa, a portion of which is reported here, he has engaged in research on California Indians and on the modern American community. He was editor of the* American Anthropologist *from 1956 through 1969. He is the author of* Man's Way *and* Comparative Functionalism, *both theoretical treatises, and of a number of other works, including* Sebei Law, *from which this exerpt is taken, and* Kambuya's Cattle: The Legacy of an African Herdsman, *which also deals with the Sebei.*

■ The major theme of this book is that changes in social institutions can be understood as the result of evolutionary changes in sociotechnological systems. We have seen an example of this in the variations of family life in contemporary England (Selection 5). In the next selection we observe the same process taking place in the legal system of the Sebei of western Kenya, in East Africa.

As described by Goldschmidt, the Sebei arrived in their present habitat as pastoralists. The legal system that they developed fits the demands made by the economic activities of that strategy of adaptation, especially the need for pasture, water, and salt that is basic to the welfare of herds. One of these legal adaptations is to be found in pastoralist property systems : land and water must be freely accessible to all.

Sebei economy underwent an important change when they adopted a horticultural system, and their law was changed adaptively. In horticulture, people invest time and effort in particular plots of land with a view to future returns, and this investment requires the development of exclusive territorial rights. The Sebei illustrate the process by which ownership is vested in corporate kin groups, leaving individuals and households only with rights of use in the group lands.

But the Sebei did not give up herding completely ; pastoralism merely shifted to secondary importance. Furthermore, laws are not changed like piston rings in an automobile ; the history of a group and the deep-seated attitudes of its members are brought to the new situation and impose limitations on legal and other changes. Thus, the present law of the Sebei reflects a combination of two sets of elements. It consists of an admixture of the demands of horticulture with the remnants of a pastoralist background, reflecting not only tradition but also the continuing (though secondary) importance of cattle along with cultivation in their economy. Goldschmidt describes this adaptation, showing how the shift from a pastoralist to a predominantly horticultural mode of existence affected contracts and sales, age and military organizations, and the entire legal sphere.

In the concluding part of this selection, Goldschmidt provides an excellent example of the commingling of religion and magic with law at this stage of social and technological development. The theory and method of this investigation is described in "Theory and Strategy in the Study of Cultural Adaptability," by Walter Goldschmidt (*American Anthropologist*, 67 [1965] : 402-407 ; reprinted as Selection 19 in *The Cultural Present*). Goldschmidt's research along these lines includes not only the book from which this chapter is taken but also a detailed record and analysis of a legal case among the Sebei in *Kambuya's Cattle : The Legacy of an African Herdsman* (Berkeley : University of California Press, 1968).

A very significant—and delightfully written—paper dealing with social control is "Gossip and Scandal," by Max Gluckman (*Current Anthropology*, 4 [1963] : 307-16). Another paper that may be consulted at this point is "Two Concepts of Authority," by Walter B. Miller (*American Anthropologist*, 57 [1955] : 271-89). The interested student can explore further in the following three volumes : *Political Systems and the Distribution of Power* (A.S.A. Monographs 2, London :

Tavistock; New York: Praeger, 1965); *Political Anthropology*, Marc J. Swartz, Victor W. Turner, and Arthur Tuden, editors (Chicago: Aldine, 1966); and *Local-Level Politics: Social and Cultural Perspectives*, Marc J. Swartz, editor (Chicago: Aldine, 1968). ∎

THE LEGAL INSTITUTIONS of the Sebei have their roots in the past; they are fundamentally attuned to the social demands of a cattle-keeping economy, and the attitudes and orientations thus implied. But the Sebei had acquired, in the century or so prior to European contact, an increasing dependence upon hoe-farming, and particularly the intensive use of land associated with the cultivation of plantains. It is the burden of this chapter to demonstrate that important institutional adjustments in the realm of law accompanied this economic shift; that is to say, the legal institutions of the Sebei underwent a process of adaptation to meet the new needs and circumstances that arose as a consequence of the new economy. It is therefore an example of institutional adaptation.

ECONOMIC CHANGE AND ITS SOCIOLOGICAL INVOLVEMENTS

In the historical summary I pointed out that the Sebei arrived on Mount Elgon as a primarily pastoral people, cultivating only small plots of millet and sorghum on a shifting basis. Their population was sparse; land was freely available to stock except for the cultivated plots. They subsequently learned the cultivation of plantains from their Bantu neighbors to the west, and brought this new mode of economy onto the northern escarpment in the mid-nineteenth century. They also acquired maize. As a result, the population density increased, arable land was increasingly brought under cultivation, good land became scarce, and permanent land use became possible. Cattle never lost their economic usefulness (though cattle-keeping declined in importance), and the social and psychological meaning of the livestock continued. These changes did not occur with the same intensity in different parts of Sebeiland, farming being more intensive in the west and less so in the central, more arid part of the escarpment and on the plains.

The research program of which the general study of Sebei culture was a part (and of which the present book is an ancillary product) was directed to the understanding of ecological adaptation. In the broader investigation, a team of scholars analyzed four separate tribes, each characterized by spatial differentiation in economic activities between pastoral and farming emphases. The details of the theoretical assumption, the methods and techniques employed, and some of the data have been set forth elsewhere. Most simply stated, it is an effort to examine the spatial variation in institutions and attitudes in order to determine whether a common process of adaptation took place among them, in accord with a general ecological theory of culture. In this chapter I am concerned with the theoretical problems, but am dealing directly with temporal change rather than spatial variation.

The theory may be briefly stated: Institutions are instrumentalities for the maintenance and coordination of group activities; the nature of such group actions is significantly related to the means by which a people gets its livelihood; when the form of economic exploitation changes the institutional requirements also change; hence, with a shift in economy, certain institutions become dysfunctional and tend to disappear while other functions become requisite, and institutional machinery will develop to meet these needs.

Cattle-keeping and hoe-farming are economic activities that make very different demands upon man, and offer different circumstances; indeed, they represent as wide a differential as any that can readily be found in preindustrial societies. These differences relate to matters of annual and daily life cycle, to the kinds of work activities, to the needs for movement, to the character of social rewards, to the density and permanence of settlement. When the differences are very nearly absolute as, say, between the Masai and the Chagga, the differential in life modes is sharp. When, as often happens—and did happen with the Sebei—the difference is one of emphasis rather than being absolute, the evidence of social differential is less obvious, but it is nevertheless there.

Let us briefly review some of the areas where we may reasonably expect differences that will have relevance to law, on the basis of our general knowledge of the problem, and taking the extreme contrasts as our first point of approach.

1. The most obvious differential between the two economies lies in their relationships to land. Cattle-keeping people almost universally recognize the right of any stockowner to pasture, water, and salt; they make no restrictions other than a broad territoriality because anything else would quickly destroy the herds. One might make the proposition: if cattle-herding is to remain the paramount economic activity, then land and water will be freely accessible to all animals (and their owners). Conversely, a farming people (where land is permanently usable) must protect the farmer's right to continuous use; therefore private rights to land will be found.

2. Pastoral people must be free to move around to meet the requirements of water and pasturage; they cannot be tied to a locus. Farmers, on the other hand, must be tied to the land, which is their sustenance; they cannot freely move about, however much they might want to.

3. As a direct corollary, social units must develop around spatially defined areas in a farming society, while narrowly defined spatial units are dysfunctional for pastoralists.

4. Farmers must therefore develop institutions for the preservation of spatially defined communities, both those necessary to protect them against the predations of other peoples, and those required to maintain internal harmony.

5. The reward system of a cattle-keeping people is more closely tied to the individual fortunes of a person, is dependent upon the efficacy of his personal decisions, and assigns greater importance to individual action. It is also more given to wide changes of individual fortunes, as raids, diseases, famines, and good husbandry decimate or multiply a man's herds. By contrast, a farmer's rewards are steadier, if not surer; his circumstance is less closely tied to his personal decisions and achievements than to the circumstances of his birth. He is more dependent.

Such contrasts as these, which can be substantiated in the comparative literature but have been put forward here in terms of general observations, apply to the broad spectrum of social institutions and cultural attitudes. For purposes of this study of law, however, it is sufficient to deal with those in which a demonstrable adjustment in legal institutions has been made. We will deal (1) with matters pertaining to land, (2) with matters pertaining to military organization as a control system, and (3) with the development of a kind of community law under ntarastit.[1]

THE DEVELOPMENT OF LANDOWNERSHIP AND CONTRACTS

The distinction the Sebei make between things that may be privately owned and things that are a public good is so consistent and far-reaching that there is no reason to assume it is not an ancient Sebei tradition. Furthermore, there is every reason to believe that this distinction was operative with respect to cultivated lands, that is, plots that were sown to millet and sorghum. Even though, according to ethnographic description, women went down in work groups to prepare land on the plains as a matter of mutual protection, each women, it was said, had her own plot, and if they returned to the same area each reclaimed the same parcel. The rights to individual cultivated parcels, therefore, goes as far back as ethnographic memory can reach. But when the Sebei were predominantly pastoralists there was no dearth of land, and it is unlikely that severe disputes arose over this resource, or that any legal machinery was needed to attend to such rights as did exist. As farming supplants cattle-keeping, however, and land fills up, the need to delineate ownership (both physically on the ground and legally as a set of rights) develops, and the provision for transfers of such rights becomes requisite.

Fee-simple private property ownership is not necessarily the solution of choice for a society engaged in hoe-farming, especially where there is a long-fallowing rotation or constant movement to new land. More frequently we find some kind of kin-based corporate group either with basic ownership or with some kind of administrative prerogative over the land. There apparently was some tendency among the Sebei, after they had adopted intensive farming in the west and then pushed (with their plantains) into the

1. Ceremonial affirmation of Community Law.

central sector, to settle into clan-communities and exert some influence over clan holdings. But, as the discussion of landownership shows, this tendency never developed into corporate property control. The reason seems clear to me: Sebei property concepts applicable to livestock were precise; they were based upon deep psychological orientations, and they were reinforced by many social situations. Rather than adopt some communal solution to land, the Sebei adapted their notions of livestock ownership. It would seem that the individuation in Sebei behavior and the close identification between the individual and what he owned were attitudes too deep-seated to change, and it was easier ultimately to adapt landholding to the attitudes than to change the attitudes themselves.

The system of legal rights which was operative with respect to livestock came to be applied to land, though the social uses of cattle were not so applied. Ownership is universally in the hands of the men, despite the fact that most of the cultivation is actually done by women. The man allocates land to his wives in a manner similar to the allocation of cattle, even keeping some back "for his own use" if he wishes. There seems to be more freedom for the man to retrieve these allocated rights when he remarries (and this is a subject of no little dispute between co-wives and between a father and his sons), but the pattern is essentially the same. The land is inherited by sons, so that it remains within the clan; and like anointed cattle, it is inherited by the son whose mother cultivated that particular plot. A man has an obligation to supply his wife with land and to provide his sons with land.

On the other hand, the social uses and meaning of cattle were not, as already stated, applied to landholdings. Land does not figure either in bride-price or in wergild. We have the occasional instance of a matrilocal residence and of land given by a father to his daughter, but none of these were expressed in terms of marital regulations and seem rather to be but instances where an atypical behavior suited mutual convenience; nowhere is there a case of a man giving to his father-in-law a piece of land in lieu of cattle as part of the bride-price. And while we do have instances where land was taken over in lieu of wergild, these seem to be deficiency adjustments. They reiterate the value placed upon land in

these agricultural sectors, but do not suggest even the beginnings of an institutionalized change, or a psychological identification. There is no land equivalent of cattle praise songs, nor is there any ceremonial expression of the allocation of land to a wife, as there is with cattle.

It does not follow, however, that land is disregarded as a mark of social status, or that Sebei do not jealously regard their holdings. The Sebei have boundary markers and fear land encroachment, and even in areas of relatively sparse settlement they dispute over land rights. Some Sebei have built up large personal holdings. In the farming village subjected to intensive study, one old man was busily engaged in increasing his holdings by purchasing plots from more impecunious neighbors. The modern practice is in part an acceptance of Western legal patterns, but it also has its roots in old Sebei custom.

In the discussion of contracts regarding land it was pointed out that the Sebei apply the namanyantet[2] exchange in the purchase of field crops. There is no reason to believe that this is not an old practice in Sebeiland, for it would fit well a pattern of exchange under a system of pastoralism with secondary cultivation. Yet it is difficult to escape the feeling that even namanyantet exchange was an adaptation of the standard cattle contract to the uses of agriculture. Everything the Sebei said supports such a notion, though they did not specifically say that it was an adaptation. The evidence for such a thesis is that (1) the Sebei etymologized the word namut[3] as "catch stomach," with the implication that it refers to the pregnancy of the heifer, and though the etymology is doutful, the attitude implicit in the folk-etymologizing is itself suggestive; (2) the Sebei regularly and frequently use the contract in animal exchanges, but instances of its use for crops is rare; (3) the exchange creates a quasi-kinship, associated with strong psychological identification with the cattle, which does not fit attitudes respecting the land, let alone the food crops of the land; (4) this kin term was glossed by interpreters as

2. Contract in which a bullock, or other consideration, is given in exchange for a heifer, which is returned after she has produced a heifer, which is kept.
3. Cows held in another person's kraal under namanyantet exchange contract which will return to owner when contract is fulfilled.

"kin of the cow"; (5) there is a close delineation of contractual obligations under diverse contingencies when the contract is related to cattle, but no such clear detailing of obligations was found in exchanges involving crops; indeed, in one or two of the instances there was a suggestion of freedom to maneuver for advantage; (6) the pattern of cattle exchanges has been reported widely among cattle-keeping peoples in East Africa, but no similar report of exchange for crops is to be found; and finally, (7) there are animal-for-animal exchanges and animal-for-land/crop exchanges, but none solely within the agricultural realm. None of these reasons is compelling alone, but taken together (and with the known increase in the importance of agriculture) they form a syndrome of circumstances that make it a reasonable assumption that the namanyantet contractual arrangement was an adaptation of a pastoral legal institution to the uses of farming.

A second adaptation appears also to have taken place, more in keeping with the sale of land than with the sale of crops or with limited use to the land. In obtaining clan histories in the area of intensive cultivation I learned that a number of clans had moved from the area now belonging to the Bagisu. Some had merely expropriated the land, but others, according to their grandsons who were my elderly informants, had "purchased" the land for one or a few animals. These events took place in the nineteenth century. But as we have seen in the discussion of pororyet[4] affiliation, at a still earlier date there was the custom of slaughtering an animal and giving a feast to establish membership in one's adopted homeland. By the turn of the century, outright land purchases were made with livestock, and for the period when the rupee was currency in Uganda (*ca.* 1910) I have an instance of cash sale. Nowadays, there is a fairly active market in real estate.

This sale of land, which would have been entirely meaningless in an earlier epoch of Sebei economy, I view as a syncretic development, first out of diverse Sebei customs and later with European land practices. The Sebei practices that went into this develoment are (1) the furnishing of animals as a means of affiliating with the new area of residence, (2) the custom of namanyantet exchange, and (3) the

4. Basic etrtriorial unit; subdivision of tribe.

practice of outright purchase of crops for livestock.

There is one further adaptation of the legal system of the past to the uses of commercial transaction in land: the use of options. Sebei told me that this was an old practice in marriage arrangements; a man might want to marry a young girl after she matured and would make a payment "to hold her down." Such a payment was an earnest of intent, and while under prevailing regulations it did not—and does not now—force ultimate performance, it was an effective instrument in a closed community. This practice has been adapted to the acquisition of land.

All in all, it seems entirely reasonable to assume that the institutional apparatus for ownership and exchange which had applied to the control of livestock came to relate to matters of land, and the assumption is supported by a good deal of internal evidence. At the same time, it is worthwhile noting that not all the elements of stock ownership transferred. The people in the densely farmed area today are quite absorbed in landholdings, as the prevalence of land cases testifies, and individuals gain status through their control of land; yet the strong psychological identification—or at least the institutional expression of such identification—is not found. There is no equivalent to praise songs, "bull of the herd," wergild, or bride-price which makes it possible to say that the individual and his land are psychologically one, or that social relations are translatable into land relations. If the shift to farming had reached so far into the substratum of Sebei culture, so deep into the psychological attitudes as that, it had still not been given any social expression.

The individuated attitudes, the personal independence of each adult male, had, I think, the effect of preventing the development of cooperative or communal holding of land, despite the fact that territories were taken over by clans, and despite the patterns of collaborative work parties. The contractual work arrangement may be seen as an institutional mode of circumventing the need for communal activity, and it fits the individuated basis of Sebei life.

In sum, the adaptation of ownership and contractual patterns from livestock to land represents a shift in the rules, the formal level of culture . . .; it does not represent a shift on the ideational level to any significant, or at least visible, degree.

THE AGE-SET IN SEBEI LEGAL STRUCTURE

Early in this analysis of Sebei legal institutions it is stated categorically that the age-set[5] system had no role to play in Sebei juridical procedures or (with a minor exception) in the substantive aspects of Sebei law. This is most surprising, for the initiation by which a man enters his age-set is a focal element in ritual life, and furthermore, age-set membership is an important dimension of the social system in its nonlegal aspects. Every man and most women know their age-set; they greet in special ways their fellow age-set members; they are under obligation to entertain them specially; they utilize this bond in asking favors, and the like.

The age-set system in Sebeiland is a local variant of a widespread institutional pattern in East Africa, and in most instances these units play a major role in tribal governance. This role may have either or both of two aspects: (1) there is an internal control system within the age-set which coordinates its activities and gives the unit some aspects of a corporate group, and (2) the several age-sets play explicit social roles in the community at large—warriors, elders, and the like. When these operate together, they actually form an institutional structure for governance and hence for matters of law. There is every reason to believe that the Sebei, who share this institutional system (even sharing age-set names with some tribes), must once have utilized it in legal action. If my informants were correct in saying that the Sebei once lived in age-graded manyattas,[6] then certainly they would have had to have an important governing role.

Of such a role, the only aspects touching upon authority which remain are the regular recognition of seniority, the generic pattern of age deference, and the control of initiates over the behavior of preinitiated children. None of these is a matter reaching into the realm of law.

5. An organized association including everyone of a given age and sex.
6. Masai term for an enclosed village, usually all men of the same age-set.

It is fair to ask why so radical a change has taken place.

The age-set organization is functionally relevant to its two major and closely interrelated pastoral roles: herding cattle and military activity. Among such peoples as the Masai, who are perhaps the world's most devoted pastoralists, the cattle were in the charge of a junior age-set, young men in the full vigor of their youth. They were thus charged not because their livestock required such strength and agility—East African cattle are generally very docile and can normally be handled by a child—but because they were under constant threat of an enemy raid, and less importantly, of quadrupedal predators. Thus the age-set was prepared to fight, and inevitably also to retaliate. The age-set was the corporate structure that took over the military role and therefore had to have systematic internal control. The ceremonial and social supports for internal harmony were far-reaching. Under the inexorable pressure of time, the members of such a unity lose their youthful vigor while a later generation reaches it, and the role of warrior must be transferred. The older generation, however, does not lose its long-established sense of identity, nor would its members readily relinquish power. The corporate group remains a unity of elders and preserves a power derivative of seniority, thus performing functions of governance.

As cattle decline in importance, the economic and military roles of youth wane. It is true that some herding continues, but now it is near houses. Furthermore, the caves and escarpments of Mount Elgon make it possible to endeavor to hide from the raiders. While as a matter of fact the Sebei were repeatedly subject to attack and frequently lost both cattle and lives, they did utilize hiding as a regular tactic. The age-set was largely deprived of its useful role through the diminution of cattle, and to have preserved their strong unity would have created a potential for disruption—youthful gangs are not notoriously constructive social groups—while depriving the economy of their services to agriculture, slight as these were.

In addition to this negative influence, a positive force was at work making for a change of behavior. A sedentary farming people must be organized to defend a territory; hearth and property must be protected. Sebei military activity was organized on a territorial basis, each pororyet being responsible for its own defense. Military pressures were so severe that it made no sense to have a separate cadre of warriors; all able-bodied men were expected to help defend their territory. Military organization, therefore, appears to have been restructured from an age-set warrior band enterprise to a vertically integrated, spatially delimited operation. At the same time, military prowess lost much of its cachet (youths in the farming area today view it as simply foolishness) as well as many of its rewards. The Sebei did (and in the pastoral area still do) mount raids, but they tend to be retaliatory rather than initiatory, and not very profitable.

A contributory factor to this development may have been internecine strife among the Sebei. Bagisu pressure, as already indicated, pushed Sebei of the populous western region onto the north escarpment, where they in turn used their superior force against their fellow Sebei in a manner hardly calculated to preserve the lateral sense of harmony that would have made age-set military organization effective.

In this account there is perforce a good deal of conjecture over the causes for and the course of events with respect to the declining importance of the age-set. But comparisons with close neighbors of the Sebei and statements made by Sebei render it virtually certain that the pinta was once an important institution for social control; manifestly it is not so now. This basic change must certainly have deprived the Sebei of an orderly means of social control.

NTARASTIT AS A TRANSFER OF AUTHORITY TO THE COMMUNITY

The sedentarization of Sebei life in response to the development of agriculture, the concentration of population, and the consequent formation of permanent geographically based communities created a condition that required social restraints of a new kind. This need arose at the very period when (for the same basic ecologic reason) the juridical authority that we must assume once resided in the age-sets disappeared. I believe it is entirely reasonable to assume that the development of the unusual, not to say

peculiar, custom of ntarastit was the Sebei means of seeking a sanction for community control of individual behavior, and in this section I want to examine it in that light.

It will be recalled that ntarastit was a Sebei-wide ceremony, initiated by the prophet and performed sequentially by the men of each pororyet, starting from the east and progressing to the west. Informants were in disagreement as to the frequency with which the ntarastit ceremony was held, but the general import of their statements indicates that it was at no regular interval, but was undertaken when the prophet felt the level of its moral force had so reduced itself as to require reaffirmation. Thus: "The time we punish in this manner is when we insist that the laws be obeyed and the time that we don't do this is when the law is not in effect. . . . In the third year, laws become weak and are forgotten and if the pororyet tries to take this kind of action, there will be a war."

The ntarastit ceremony consisted chiefly of an oath by all adult men of the pororyet, who swore a kind of fealty of acceptance on the pain of supernatural death. All circumcised men gather naked at the specified location, and before an altar of implanted branches of certain specified plants of ceremonial significance, swear as follows: "Anybody who kills anybody passing by (or who takes things belonging to others, etc.), may the earth eat him." They thrust their spears at the altar in unison each time they recite this formula, naming a different kind of offence.

This oath has the same basic form as the oath of accusation normally performed between clans when an accusation was made. There, too, the men gathered naked around an altar of specified plants and thrust their spears toward it in unison, the clansmen of the injured party and of the accused party expressing their accusation or their innocence respectively in turn. Such a ceremonial oath was a means by which the supernatural forces of retribution would ultimately being reprisal against the clan of the wrongdoer.

Ntarastit in its formal aspects is so like the sorcery that serves as underlying sanction for legal clan law that it is difficult to doubt that the two are related, that the one derived from the other. Ntarastit is, in effect, an invocation of supernatural authority for the maintenance of peace in the community. It differs from the sorcery underlying clan law on four counts:

1. Unlike the curse that follows a delict and seeks out the doer of an evil act, ntarastit precedes the act and stands in readiness as a retaliation against some future misdeed. It is thus a public affirmation of the law.

2. The oath is a community affair; it involves all the men of a pororyet and thus unites a geographic entity into a bond, without respect to age-set or clan, without respect to economic status—a bond that asserts a public right in the behavior of each individual and the personal obligation of each individual to maintain peace in the community.

3. Its sanction does not rest upon mystical forces, but in the action of the community; it asserts the right of the community to try, convict, and punish the offender, and to engage in such punishment free of either personal or supernatural retaliation.

4. It may also be viewed as significant that the oath refers to the fact that the *earth* will "eat" the person guilty of the delict. I believe oaths generally refer to the specific things involved. I do not mean to emphasize the use of earth here as being relevant to its agricultural productivity, but rather in its implication of locality or place—though both aspects may well be relevant.

I have already presented cases involving, and described the nature of community action under, ntarastit rule, but will summarize its operation here. The ritual brings any delict into the jurisdiction of the pororyet, which can then punish the responsible party. The punishment takes the form of destruction of his property— killing his livestock, slashing his plantains, destroying his crops, seizing his stored grain, and even burning down his house.

Before action is taken, apparently there is an informal hearing to decide that the punishment is proper. Once embarked upon, however, such retaliation appears to have been more a wild mob scene. While the ntarastit justifies the action of the community, it is always possible that the man they seek (and his clansmen) will resist the action. As one informant said, "Women and children don't go—it is a little like a war." Presumably the similarity to war varies to the degree that the moral imperative of the ceremonial act has been dissipated by the passage of

time. Punishment does not legally eliminate the demand for compensation by the injured clan, .though in none of the cases I collected was compensation obtained. One participant said: "You can punish the murderer's clan by taking property because they broke the law—still, the murder is not forgotten. The clan of the deceased must take revenge by killing a member of the murderer's clan or can accept compensation paid by that clan."

Ntarastit punishment is meted out both for murder and for theft. The punishment is the same, except that (appropriately enough) retaliation against a murder involves the destruction of property of the whole clan—or significantly that segment that resides in the pororyet—while in cases of theft the action is directed only at the household of the thief. This practice is in accord with the basic principle of Sebei law that violence is a matter of clan law and action is always against the clan, while the law of property is individual law and is always directed at the individual. The punishment in cases of theft, however, is severe in the extreme: one man was literally ruined by the destruction, during a famine, of his resources in retaliation for the theft of a bushel or two of millet. Another person suffered heavily for the theft of a single stem of plantains. One case indicates that several pororisyek took concerted action, which in view of general attitudes is surprising.

Some informants believed that ntarastit was an invention of the prophet Matui, others that he reinstituted it. It is not possible to reconstruct the history of the development of the institution. In addition to the above suggestion that ntarastit was a recent innovation, however, two important relevant facts must be borne in mind. First, it is nowhere reported among other Kalenjin or neighboring tribes, so far as I can discover, and thus must be a Sebei development. Second, it is clearly associated with the prophet Matui, who operated in the western, heavily cultivated region of Sebeiland.

The ntarastit, then, creates a kind of loose citizenship. This citizenship has two levels of applicability. It is quite explicitly pororyet-oriented, which is to say it reinforces the very social unity that is the military protective unit: it holds together the very people who have to stay together for protection against the constant marauding of neighbors. Secondarily, by co-ordination of the several pororyet ceremonies under the guidance of a single prophet, it also reinforces a sense of commonality and harmony among the Sebei as a whole. One case cited suggests that the ntarastit sanctions the punishment of individuals across pororyet lines, and informants spoke of the amity among all Sebei developed under the influence of the prophet Matui.

From this examination of ntarastit it is difficult not to think of it as an effort on the part of Sebei leadership, and particularly on the part of the prophet, to reorder the basic character of interpersonal relationships. Though even among pastoralists no man is an island unto himself alone, the need for community action is far less compelling. It is not merely because the population is more sparsely scattered over the land, but rather because of the freedom of movement that cattle-keeping permits. As Spencer writes regarding the Samburu, "In theory any stock owner has the right to live . . . where he pleases," and ". . . if two people quarrelled then they generally moved apart and kept apart." This privilege is not, as I have already stated, readily available to a farmer.

As a solution, the ntarastit left much to be desired. Indeed, its very crudity—one might almost say it was only semi-institutionalized—suggests the recency of its development. It did not offer precise procedures, it did not adjust the level of punishment to the seriousness of the offense, and above all it did not demonstrate those staying powers that would make it a reliable instrument for the maintenance of order. Yet one cannot help but feel that at about the time Sir Henry Maine was analyzing ancient law and discussing its evolutionary develop-ment, Sebei leaders were taking a first tentative step away from the law of status to the law of contract.

ADAPTATION OF LAW AND CULTURAL EVOLUTION

The evolution of culture is not the progressive rise to higher levels of social existence; it is the adaptation of instrumental institutions to novel circumstances. It is in the detailed changes of explicit situations, changes made possible or requisite by shifts in technology, environment, or exploitative opportunities, that an understanding of the evolutionary process is to be found. The Sebei had made a major economic shift in their productive techniques not long before their mode of life was overwhelmed by the impact of Europeanization, and this economic development had important consequences for demography, settlement pattern, military needs and potentials, and the meaning of natural resources. It is not surprising that these changes should, in turn, render old institutions obsolete and new ones desirable. In short, they had an influence on the character of Sebei law.

I have shown in this chapter that in at least three areas the Sebei legal system did make adaptations to the new situation. As should be expected, the changes that were made involved the adaptation of existing institutions to new needs and the elimination of useless functions from continuing institutions. In cultural evolution, as in biological evolution, the essential process does not pose an opposition between adaptation and continuity; rather it sees continuity in adaptation.

8. IFUGAO LAW

ROY F. BARTON

Originally published by the University of California Press; reprinted by permission of The Regents of the University of California. From Ifugao Law *by Roy F. Barton, pp. 85-88. Roy Franklin Barton lived from 1883 to 1947. Wholly self-taught in anthropology—he was originally a dentist—he produced some of the best ethnography of the Philippines. Beginning there as a supervising teacher in the civil service in 1906, he soon shifted to full-time study of Ifugao culture, returning to the United States in 1916. In 1930 he visited the Doukhobors and other cooperative colonies and, in that year, migrated to the Soviet Union where he continued his ethnological work until 1940. He returned to the Philippines in 1941 and soon thereafter was captured by the invading Japanese armies and spent three years in an internment camp. Among his other works are* The Religion of the Ifugaos, The Kalingas: Their Institutions and Custom Laws, The Half Way Sun, *and* Philippine Pagans: The Autobiographies of Three Ifugaos.

■ The legal system of the Sebei, as we saw in the last selection, is an adaptation to the requirements of their economy and their stateless political organization. I suggested in the Introduction to this section that customary law is characteristic of stateless societies and that it is the establishment of statehood that underlies the development of formal law. I based this hypothesis on a comparison of stateless horticulturists and agriculturists with horticultural and agricultural kingdoms. The Ifugao of the island of Luzon in the northern Philippines, described in the following selection, are stateless agriculturists; they number about 120,000 people. As will be seen, their legal system bears closer resemblance to the customary law of the Sebei than to the formal law of the agricultural Babylonians to be described in Selection 10. The book from which this selection is taken is widely regarded as one of the classics in the anthropology of law.

As described by the late Roy Barton, Ifugao agriculture is conducted in elaborate mountain terraces. Social and political controls are completely decentralized, and there are correlative variations in the legal system among the several Ifugao groups, but these are minor, as we would expect from the uniformity of their social and technological organization. The enforcement of law is exclusively in the hands of the family; there are no corporate political groups in whose name laws are enforced. Thus, for example, a man who commits an offense (like incest) that affects only his family cannot be punished, unlike a formal system in which, ideally, the "long arm of the law" reaches all miscreants. In the following selection we are able to see some of the basic principles and procedures of an agricultural system of customary law and its commingling with religion and kinship.

There are several good studies of customary law that the reader may consult: "Extra-Processual Events in Tiv Political Institutions," by Paul Bohannan (*American Anthropologist*, 60 [1958]: 1-12), and "Structural Change and Primitive Law: Consequences of a Papuan Legal Case," by Leopold Pospisil (in *Law in Culture and Society*, Laura Nader, editor; Chicago: Aldine, [1969], pp. 208-29, which also has references to Pospisil's other works in Kapauku law). Indispensable for an understanding of customary legal relationships is Robert Gardner's remarkable film "Dead Birds," (distributed by Contemporary Films, Inc. and the University of California). ■

THE HABITAT OF the Ifugaos is situated in about the center of the area inhabited by the non-Christian tribes. In point of travel-time, as we say in the Philippines, for one equipped with the usual amount of baggage, Ifugao-land is about as far from Manila as New York from Constantinople. To the northeast are the Wild Gaddan, to the north the Bontoc Igorot, to the northwest, west, and southwest the Lepanto and Benguet Igorots; to the east, across the wide uninhabited river basin of the Cagayan, are the Ilongots. This geographic isolation has tended to keep the Ifugao culture relatively pure and uninfluenced by contact with the outside world. Two or three military posts were fitfully maintained in Ifugao by the Spaniards during the last half century of their sovereignty; but the lives of the natives were little affected thereby.

Ifugao men wear clouts and Ifugao women loin cloths, or short skirts, reaching from the waist to the knees. Wherever they go the men carry spears. Both sexes ornament their persons with gold ornaments, beads, agates, mother of pearl, brass ornaments, and so forth. Ifugao houses, while small, are substantially built, of excellent materials, and endure through many generations.

It may safely be said that the Ifugaos have constructed the most extensive and the most admirable terraces for rice culture to be found anywhere in the world. The Japanese terraces, which excite the admiration of tens of thousands of tourists every year, are not to be compared with them. On these steep mountains that rise from sea-level to heights of six to eight thousand feet—mountains as steep probably as any in the world—there have been carved out, with wooden spades and wooden crowbars, terraces that run like the crude but picturesque "stairsteps" of a race of giants, from the bases almost to the summits. Some of these terrace walls are fifty feet high. More than half are walled with stone. Water to flood these terraces is retained by a little rim of earth at the outer margin. The soil is turned in preparation for planting with a wooden spade. No mountain is too steep to be terraced, if it affords an unfailing supply of water for irrigation. The Ifugao, too, makes clearings on his mountains in which he plants sweet potatoes, and numerous less important vegetables. Without his knowing it, he bases his agriculture on scientific principles (to an extent that astounds the white man) and he tends his crops so skillfully and artistically that he probably has no peer as a mountain husbandman.

Of political organization the Ifugao has nothing—not even a suggestion. Notwithstanding, he has a well-developed system of laws. This absolute lack of political government has brought it about that the Ifugao is a consummate diplomat. After an eight years' residence among them, I am convinced that the Ifugaos got along very well in the days before a foreign government was established among them. Through countless generations the Ifugao who has survived and prospered has been the one who has carried his point, indeed, but has carried it without involving himself in serious trouble with his fellows.

The Ifugao's religion is a mixture of an exceedingly complex polytheism, ancestor worship, and a mythology that is used as an instrument of magic. His religion seems to be far more highly developed than that of the other non-Christian tribes.

Attempts made by Spain to colonize the Ifugao in the lowlands invariably met with failure. The Ifugao is a hillman, and loves his hills. He is of an independent nature and cannot stand confinement. A great many prisoners jailed by American officials have courted death rather than endure incarceration.

While there are well defined tribal divisions that mark off the various mountain-Malay populations of northern Luzon, the cultures of all of the tribes are basically similar. Numerous parallelisms, too, are found with the lowland Filipinos, even now, in features of daily life, religion, taboo, law, and marital relation. The dialects of all the tribes inhabiting the islands are branches of the great family of Malay languages—languages spoken over more than half the circumference of the globe. The linguistic differences that exist between the mountain and the lowland tribes seem to be not much greater than the linguistic differences between the various mountain tribes themselves.

Many things lead us to believe that the culture of the Ifugaos is very old. We have to do with a people who possess both as individuals and collectively a most remarkable memory. Ifugao rich men lend to considerable numbers of clients and others every year during the "hungry time"—to these, varying numbers of bundles of rice, to this one a skein of yarn, to that one a pig, and to another again a chicken. All these bargains and their amounts and their varying terms, our wealthy Ifugao remembers, unaided by any system of writing or other artificial means. Many Ifugaos know their ancestors back to the tenth or even the fourteenth generation, and, in addition, the brothers and sisters of these ancestors. If we consider the racial or tribal memory of these people, we find a mythology fully as voluminous as that of the Greeks. But the Ifugaos have no recollections of having ever migrated. Unless they have lived for many centuries in their present habitat, it seems certain that they would have retained at least in mythical form the memory of their migration.

Another consideration that is significant lies in a comparison of the rate of rice-field building in these peaceful times, when such work is not hindered but instead vigorously stimulated by the government, with the amount of such work accomplished by past generations. One who stands on some jutting spur of the mountain-side in Asin, Sapao, or Benaue can scarcely help being impressed with the feeling that he is looking upon a work of tens of centuries. Any calculation must be based on vague and hazardous figures of course, but, without having any theories to prove, and making due allowance for increased rate of building during peaceful times and for the pressure of the needs of increased population, from a comparison of the estimated area of voluntary rice-field building with the areas already constructed, I come to the conclusion that the Ifugaos must have lived in their present habitat for at least two thousand years, and I believe that these figures are too small.

SOURCES OF IFUGAO LAW AND ITS PRESENT STATUS OF DEVELOPMENT

The Ifugaos have no form of writing: there is, consequently, no written law. They have no form of political government: there is, therefore, no constitutional or statuory law. Inasmuch as they have no courts or judges, there is no law based on judicial decisions.

Ifugao law has two sources of origin: taboo (which is essentially religious) and custom. The customary law is the more important from the greater frequency of its application.

Relation of taboo to law.

The Ifugao word for taboo is *paniyu*. The root, which appears under the varying forms *iyu*, *iho*, *iyao*, and *ihao*, means in general "evil" or "bad." The prefix *pan* denotes instrumentality or manner. The word *paniyu* means both by derivation and in use, "bad way of doing," or "evil way." By far the greater number of taboos have their origin in magic. A very large number of them concern the individual, or those closely related to him by blood ties, and for this reason have no place in a discussion of law. Thus a pregnant woman may not wear a string of beads, since the beads form a closed circle and so have a magic tendency to close her body and cause difficult childbirth. This, however, is not a matter that concerns anybody else, and so could be of no interest at law. It is taboo for brothers to defecate near each other, but only they are harmed thereby, and the matter is consequently not of legal interest.

The breaking of a taboo that concerns the person or possessions of an individual of another family is a crime. The following instances will illustrate:

In nearly all districts of Ifugao it is taboo for persons of other districts to pass through a rice field when it is being harvested. It is also taboo for foreigners to enter a village when that village is observing its ceremonial idleness, *tungul*, at the close of harvest time. One who broke this taboo would be subject to fine. In case it were believed that the fine could not be collected, he would be in danger of the lance.

It is taboo to blackguard, to use certain language, and to do certain things in the presence of one's own kin of the opposite sex that are of the degrees of kinship within which marriage is forbidden or in the presence of another and such kindred of his, or to

make any except the most delicately concealed references to matters connected with sex, sexual intercourse, and reproduction. Even these delicately concealed references are permissible only in cases of real necessity. The breaking of this taboo is a serious offense. One who broke the taboo in the presence of his own female kin would not be punished except in so far as the contempt of his fellows is a punishment. In Kiangan, before the establishment of foreign government, breaking the taboo in the presence of another and his female kin of the forbidden degrees is said to have been sometimes punished by the lance.

It is taboo for one who knows of a man's death to ask a relative of the dead man if the man is dead. The breaking of this taboo is punishable by fine.

If asked, Ifugaos say that it is taboo to steal; to burn or destroy the property of another; to insult, or ruin the good name of another; to cause the death or injury of another by sorcery or witchcraft; in short, to commit any of those acts which among most peoples constitute a crime.

The word *taboo* as understood among ourselves, and as most often used among the Ifugaos, denotes a thing rather *arbitrarily* forbidden. It seems likely that moral laws—from which most criminal laws are an outgrowth—originate thus: the social conscience, learning that some act is antisocial, prohibits it (often in conjunction with religion) or some feature of it, or some *semblance* of it, arbitrarily, harshly, and sometimes unreasonably. Thus the first taboo set forth above has the semblance of being aimed against interruption in the business or serious occupation of another, or against his worship. The mere passing near a rice field when it is being harvested or the mere entrance into a village during the period of ceremonial idleness are arbitrarily seized upon as acts constituting such interruptions. The second taboo arose from the purpose of the social consciousness to prevent marriage or sexual intercourse between near kin. It is most sweeping and unreasonable in its prohibitions. A third person may make no remark in the presence of kin of the opposite sex as to the fit of the girl's clothing; as to her beauty; nor may he refer to her lover, nor play the lover's harp. Many ordinary things must be called by other than their ordinary names. Even the aged priests who officiate at a birth feast must refer in their prayers to the foetus about to be born as "the friend" and to the placenta as "his blanket." A great number of things are forbidden in the presence of kindred of opposite sex that would not shock even the most prudish of our own people. The third taboo seems to be aimed against the bandying or the taking in vain of the name of the dead.

It would seem that a primitive society, once it has decided a thing to be wrong, swings like a pendulum to the very opposite extreme, adds taboo upon taboo, and hedges with taboo most illogically. With the ardor of the neophyte, it goes to the other limit, becoming squeamish in the extreme of all that can in the remotest conception be connected with the forbidden thing.

Ultimately reason and logic tend to triumph and eliminate the illogical, impertinent, and immaterial taboos, remove the prohibitions contained in the useful taboos from their pedestal of magic, and set them upon a firmer base of intelligence, or at least practical empiricism.

A small part of Ifugao law consists even yet of taboos that are arbitrary and, except in essence, unreasonable. But the greater part has advanced far beyond this stage and is on a firm and reasonable basis of justice. Much of it originated from taboo—even yet the taboos are remembered and frequently applied to acts that constitute crimes among ourselves—but the immaterial and arbitrary taboos have been eliminated. Although the Ifugaos say that adultery and theft and arson are tabooed, nevertheless their attitude of mind is not the same as that toward things that are *merely* tabooed. It is the attitude of the human mind toward things that are prohibited by law and by conscience.

Scope of customary law.

The customary law embraces that which pertains to property, inheritance, water rights, and to a great extent, family law and procedure. There is a certain amount of variation in customs and taboos throughout Ifugao land. This accounts to a certain extent, perhaps, for the reserved behavior of visitors to a district distant from their own. Visitors are afraid of unwittingly breaking some taboo. In general, however, it may be said that laws are very nearly uniform throughout the Ifugao country.

Connection of law and religion.

Religion and law appear conjointly in (*a*)

transferals of family property; (*b*) ordeals; (*c*) certain taboos; (*d*) payments of the larger fines; (*e*) peace-making. The ifugaos state that a large part of their customary law and procedure was given them by Lidum, their great teacher, a deity of the Skyworld, and an uncle of their hero-ancestor, Balitok.

General principles of the Ifugao legal system. Its personal character.

Society does not punish injuries to itself except as the censure of public opinion is a punishment. This follows naturally from the fact that there is no organized society. It is only when an injury committed by a person or family falls on another person or family that the injury is punished formally.

Collective responsibility. Not only the individual who commits an act but his kin, in proportion to the nearness of their kinship, are responsible for the act. Their responsibility is slightly less than his. This applies not only to crimes but to debts and civil injuries.

Collective procedure. Legal procedure is by and between families; therefore a family should be "strong to demand and strong to resist demands." *A member of an Ifugao family assists in the punishment of offenders against any other member of his family, and resists the punishment of members of his family by other families.* A number of circumstances affect the ardor with which he enters into procedures in which a relative is concerned and the extent to which he will go into them. Among these are: (*a*) the nearness or remoteness of his relationship to the relative concerned in the action; (*b*) relationship to the other principal in the action; (*c*) the loyalty to the family group of the relative principally concerned in the procedure and the extent to which this relative discharges his duty to it; (*d*) evidence in the case bearing on the correctness of the relative's position in the controversy.

A corollary of the above principle. Since legal procedure is between families, and never between individuals, nor between a family and an individual, crimes of brother or sister against brother or sister go unpunished. The family of the two individuals is identical. *A family cannot proceed against itself.* But in the case of incest between a father and a daughter the father might be punished by the girl's mother's family on the ground that he had committed a crime against a member of that family. It is true that just as great an injury would have been committed against the family of the father, since the relationship of the daughter to that family is the same as to her mother's family. But the father, the perpetrator of the crime, being a nearer relative of his own family than his daughter, his family certainly would not take active steps against him. Were the crime a less disgraceful one, the father's kin would probably contest his penalty.

The family unity must at all hazards be preserved. Clemency is shown the remoter kin in order to secure their loyalty to the family group. A large unified family group is in the ideal position of being "strong to demand and strong to resist demands." The family is the only thing of the nature of an organization that the Ifugao has, and he cherishes it accordingly.

Collective recipiency of punishment. Just as the family group is collectively responsible for the delinquencies of its members, but in less degree than the delinquent himself, so may punishment be meted out to individuals of the group other than the actual culprit, although naturally it is preferred to punish the actual culprit; and so may debts or indemnities be collected from them. But only those individuals that are of the nearest degree of kinship may be held responsible; cousins may not *legally* be punished if there be brothers or sisters.

Ifugao law is very personal in its character. For the different classes of society there are in the Mampolia-Kababuyan area five grades of fines in punishment of a given crime, four in the Hapao-Hunduan area, and three in the Kiangan area.

Might is right to a very great extent in the administration of justice. For a given crime, one family, on account of superior war footing, or superior diplomacy, or on account of being better bluffers, will be able to exact much more severe penalties than another. Especially is Ifugao administration of justice likely to be unfair when persons of different classes are parties to a controversy. I doubt very much, however, whether this characteristic of Ifugao administration of justice be more pronounced than it is in our own.

Stage of development of Ifugao law.

Reasons have already been given for believing the Ifugao's culture to be very old. His legal system must also be old. Yet it is in the first stage of the development of law. It is, however, an example of a very well developed first-stage legal system. It ranks fairly with Hebrew law, or even with the Mohammedan law of a century ago. R. R. Cherry in his lectures on the *Growth of Criminal Law in Ancient Communities* demonstrates these stages of legal development: First, a stage of simple retaliation—"an eye for an eye, a tooth for a tooth, a life for a life." Second, a stage in which vengeance may be bought off "either by the individual who has inflicted the injury or by his tribe." Third, a stage in which the tribe or its chiefs or elders intervene to fix penalty-payments and to pronounce sentence of outlawry on those who refuse to pay proper fines. Fourth, a stage in which offenses come to be clearly recognized as crimes against the peace and welfare of the king or the state.

No Ifugao would dream of taking a payment for the deliberate or intentional murder of a kinsman. He would be universally condemned if he did so. However, he would usually accept a payment for an accidental taking of life. There is still, however, an element of doubt as to whether even in such a case payment would be accepted. For nearly all other offenses payments are accepted in extenuation. Ifugao law, then, may be said to be in the latter part of the first stage of legal development.

THE FAMILY IN RELATION TO PROCEDURE

Family unity and cooperation.

The mutual duty of kinsfolk and relatives, each individual to every other of the same family, regardless of sex, is to aid, advise, assist, and support in all controversies and altercations with members of other groups or families. The degree of obligation of the various members of a family group to assist and back any particular individual of that group is in direct proportion: *first*, to the kinship or the relationship by marriage; *second*, to the loyalty the individual in question has himself manifested toward the family group, that is, the extent to which he discharges his obligations to that group.

The family is without any political organization whatever. It is a little democracy in which each member is measured for what he is worth, and has a voice accordingly in the family policy. It is a different body for every married individual of the whole Ifugao tribe. There are a great many relationships that complicate matters. An Ifugao's family is his nation. The family is an executive and a judicial body. Its councils are informal, but its decisions are none the less effective. The following rules and principles apply to the family and to individuals in the matter of procedure.

Brothers of the blood can never be arrayed against each other. They may fall out and quarrel, but they can never proceed against each other. This is for the reason that their family is identical (before marriage at least), and a family cannot proceed against itself.

Cousins and brothers of the half-blood ought never to be arrayed against each other in legal procedure. In case they should be so arrayed, the mutual kin try to arrange peace. Only in the event of serious injuries may a cousin with good grace and with the approval of public opinion collect a fine from another cousin, and even then he should not demand as much as from a non-related person. In the case of minor injuries he should forego punishing his kindred. The following is an example:

A steals some rice from his cousin B. Theft and thief become known. A takes no steps against the thief; but A's wife cannot overlook it—and the injury was an injury to her as much as to A. Her kin take the matter up. They collect half the usual indemnity for their kinswoman. A foregoes his half of the indemnity.

In cases of minor injury, procedure against more distant kin is frowned on, but sometimes occurs.

It is the duty of mutual, equally related relatives and kin to try to arrange peace between opposing kin or relatives.

In the event of procedure on the part of one kinsman against another, those who are related to both take sides with him to whom they are more closely related. Besides blood relationship, there is marriage relationship oftentimes to make it a very complex and difficult problem for a man to decide to which opponent his obligation binds him. This is most frequently the case among the remoter kin. A man who finds himself in such a position, and who knows that on whichever side he may array himself he will be severely criticized by the other, becomes a strong advocate of compromise and peaceful settlement.

In case a kinsman to whom one owes loyalty in an altercation is in the wrong and has a poor case, one may secretly advise him to compromise; one must never openly advise such a measure. One may secretly refuse him assistance and backing—one must never oppose him.

One owes no obligation in the matter of procedure to another merely because he is a co-villager or inhabitant of the same district.

The obligation to aid and assist kinsmen beyond the third or fourth degree is problematic, and a question into which elements of personal interest enter to a great extent. One of the greatest sources of the power of the principal *kadangyang*[1] lies in their ability to command the aid of their remote kin on account of their prestige and wealth and ability to dispense aid and favor.

There is also a class, small in number, corresponding somewhat to the "clients" of the chiefs of the ancient Gauls. This body is composed of servants who have grown up in the service and household of a master, and who have been well treated, and in times of need sustained and furnished with the things needful to Ifugao welfare; another division consists of those who habitually borrow or habitually rent from one who stands in the nature of an over-lord to them. This class is most numerous in districts where most of the lands are in the hands of a few men. The duty of the clients to their lord and of their lord to them seems to be about as those duties have always been in a feudal society; that is to say, the duty of rendering mutual aid and assistance.

The first step in any legal procedure is to consult with one's kin and relatives. In initiating steps to assess a fine or collect an indemnity, the next step is the selection of a *monkalun*.

1. A wealthy person.

THE MONKALUN OR GO-BETWEEN

Nature of his duties.

The office of the *monkalun* is the most important one to be found in Ifugao society. The *monkalun* is a whole court, completely equipped, in embryo. He is judge, prosecuting and defending counsel, and the court record. His duty and his interest are for a peaceful settlement. He receives a fee, called *lukba* or *liwa*. To the end of peaceful settlement he exhausts every art of Ifugao diplomacy. He wheedles, coaxes, flatters, threatens, drives, scolds, insinuates. He beats down the demands of the plaintiffs or prosecution, and bolsters up the proposals of the defendants until a point be reached at which the two parties may compromise. If the culprit or accused be not disposed to listen to reason and runs away or "shows fight" when approached, the *monkalun* waits till the former ascends into his house, follows him, and, *war-knife in hand*, sits in front of him and compels him to listen.

The *monkalun* should not be closely related to either party in a controversy. He may be a distant relative of either one of them. The *monkalun* has no authority. All that he can do is to act as a peace making go-between. His only power is in his art of persuasion, his tact and his skillful playing on human emotions and motives. Were he closely related to the plaintiff, he would have no influence with the defendant, and *mutatis mutandis* the opposite would be true.

Ultimately in any state the last appeal is to a death-dealing weapon. For example, in our own society a man owes a debt which he does not pay. Action is brought to sell his property to pay the debt. If he resists, he is in danger of death at the hands of an agent of the law. Much more is he in danger if he resists punishment for crime. The same is true in the Ifugao society.

The lance is back of every demand of importance, and sometimes it seems hungry.

An Ifugao's pride as well as his self-interest—one might almost say his self-preservation—demands that he shall collect debts that are owed him, and that he shall punish injuries or crimes against himself. Did he not do so he would become the prey of his fellows. No one would respect him. Let there be but one debt owed him which he makes no effort to collect; let there be but one insult offered him that goes unpunished, and in the drunken babbling attendant on every feast or social occasion, he will hear himself accused of cowardice and called a woman.

On the other hand, self-interest and self-respect demand that the accused shall not accept punishment too tamely or with undue haste, and that he shall not pay an exorbitant fine. If he can manage to beat the demands of the complainant down below those usually met in like cases, he even gains in prestige. But the *monkalun* never lets him forget that the lance has been scoured and sharpened for him, and that he walks and lives in daily danger of it.

The accuser is usually not over anxious to kill the accused. Should he do so, the probabilities are that the kin of the accused would avenge the death, in which case he, the slayer, would be also slain. The kin of each party are anxious for a peaceful settlement, if such can be honorably brought about. They have feuds a-plenty on their hands already. Neighbors and co-villagers do not want to see their neighborhood torn by internal dissension and thus weakened as to the conduct of warfare against enemies. All these forces make for a peaceful settlement.

It is the part of the accused to dally with danger for a time, however, and at last to accede to the best terms he can get, if they be within reason.

9. A TRADITIONAL LEGAL SYSTEM: THE KUBA

JAN VANSINA

Originally published by the University of California Press; reprinted by permission of The Regents of the University of California. From African Law: Adaptation and Development *edited by Hilda Kuper and Leo Kuper, pp. 97-119. Jan Vansina was born in 1929. He studied anthropology at University College, London, and received the Ph.D. in history at the University of Louvain, Belgium, in 1952. He spent the next eight years in Africa studying the Kuba, Rwanda, and Burundi, and in 1963-1964 studied the Tio of the Republic of the Congo-Brazzaville. Since 1960, he has taught in the Department of History at the University of Wisconsin, where he is Wisconsin African Research Professor.*

■We have seen that the legal systems of stateless agriculturists (like the Ifugao) are much like those of stateless horticulturists (like the Sebei), and we will see that both are unlike the law of agriculturists in a nation-state. On the basis of such comparisons, I believe it is the political variable, the establishment of a nation-state, that is responsible for the replacement of customary law by formal law, and not the other way around. This hypothesis is given further support by horticultural states like that of the Kuba, described here, which show many of the features of formal (though unwritten) law.

Although formal law generally emerges from national social systems, not all such systems give rise to formal law. In the following selection we consider the legal system of the Kuba, a horticultural kingdom in what is now the Republic of the Congo. Though unified to an extent by a central state organization—the kingdom and its bureaucracy—the legal system of the Kuba took a traditional form. While Vansina's intent here is primarily descriptive, it is nevertheless possible to consider the Kuba and their legal system in evolutionary perspective.

In stateless societies—the vestiges of which are clearly discernible in the Kuba—the controls over behavior that are prerequisites of social life are exercised through local institutions without the intervention of authority from outside the community. Local autonomy characterizes the maintenance of order and conformity; the locus of authority may be the corporate kin group, the community conceived territorially, sodalities that cross-cut these two, or still other social forms. Autonomy is expressed in many ways, such as economic self-sufficiency, the right to feud and to wage war, the administration of land tenure, and the application of juridical controls. Even in chief-

doms there are multiple centres of power. Chiefdoms are redistributional societies with permanent but local agencies of economic and other forms of coordination. One of their central characteristics is a notable resistance to centralization.

But centralized authority in a state society is almost always accomplished at the expense of lineage relations and other local groups that strive for autonomy and sovereignty. A state's rulers try to acquire more power at the expense of the local community; holders of local power try to retain as much autonomy, power, and privilege as they can. Sometimes the fight is waged physically, at other times it is ideological and symbolic, and often it is both. In any event, it must be understood in terms that distinguish between early and late stages in the histories of particular state organizations.

A successful state is one that has secured the transfer of loyalty and the exercise of authority from local communities to itself. Local divisions continue to exist, but they are used primarily for administrative purposes and for the distribution of the state's bureaucratic representatives. These personnel transmit and enforce the state's laws and regulations; they are loyal only to the state and automatically yield to it whenever its interests conflict with those of local groups. In a nation thus successfully integrated by a central organization, the individual's loyalties are only to the state; they are not divided with or among local groups.

The Kuba, as described by Vansina in the following selection, appear to have moved recently into statehood. This is indicated in their retention of traditional (stateless) legal procedures along with many of the inchoate features of a formal system of law. Stereotyped procedures such as the Kuba trials by ordeal are frequently found in early agricultural state societies. This article has been revised by Professor Vansina for inclusion in this volume.

The reader who wishes to explore traditional law further should consult two works by Max Gluckman that have exerted a profound influence on the anthropological study of law: *The Judicial Process among the Barotse of Northern Rhodesia* (2nd edition, New York: Free Press, 1967) and *The Ideas in Barotse Jurisprudence* (New Haven and London: Yale University Press, 1965). The reader also can consult *Law Without Precedent: Legal Ideas in Action in the Courts of Colonia Busoga,* by Lloyd Fallers (Chicago and London: University of Chicago Press, 1969). For additional background to this paper, see Vansina's "The Bushong Poison Ordeal," in *Man in Africa*, Mary Douglas and Phyllis M. Kaberry, editors (London: Tavistock, 1969).■

THE KUBA CONSIST of a group of culturally different tribes, numbering about 70,000 persons united in a single kingdom. They dwell between the rivers Kasai, Sankuru, and Lulua in the former Western Province of the Democratic Republic of Congo. They are matrilineal, organized in shallow three- or four-generation-deep matrilineages. The localized cores of these lineages consist of a few elderly men and women, for marriage is virilocal and males live with their fathers until the latter die. Then the men move to the residences of their mothers' brothers. Several lineages form a clan. The number of members belonging to a clan may vary from ten or twenty to several hundred, with a mode of less than fifty.

A village, the smallest political unit, consists of several clan sections, that is, the localized cores of the lineages and dependents. There is no dominant lineage in the village, and its headman, usually the oldest man in the community, may be drawn from any section. The headman represents the village but has little authority. The community is governed by a council made up of the heads of all the clan sections and by *mbeem* and *mbyeeng*, officials who represent the two sides of the village, for villages are built on two sides of a long street. These and other less important village officials are appointed for life by the village council, and no position is hereditary in any sense.

Villages are organized into chiefdoms. There is a special clan in every chiefdom from which chiefs may be elected. This clan may be different from one chiefdom to another. Chiefs are elected from available candidates by a council of electors. There are nine, or a multiple of nine, seats per council, and every seat is hereditary in a different electoral clan. But every elector is chosen from among the available men of such a clan by the other members of the council. This council elects chiefs, may depose ruling chiefs, and has to be consulted on the most important political decisions to be made by the chiefdom, such as questions of peace and war. Besides this council there is another council, *makaang* or *mbok ilaam*, composed of the ten or so highest titleholders and of the chief, which functions as a day-to-day administrative and legislative body. Some titleholders are nominated by the chief and some have to be chosen by the chief from one or more clans in which the title is vested, after approval of the other main titleholders. In the field of law the chiefdom is the highest political unit. Conflicts between chiefdoms are settled by war or through diplomatic arbitration, but there is no court system at a higher level than the chiefdom.

Chiefdoms may be linked informally together in clusters when they share common chiefly and common electoral clans. Clusters may be linked together informally when they belong to common tribes, that is, when there is public recognition by their neighbors and by themselves that they share a common culture, different from that of the neighbors. Above these informal levels the chiefdoms are all united in a single kingdom.

The kingdom is ruled by the Bushoong, a centrally located tribe organized in a single chiefdom. It is the largest in the country and dominates the others by military means. The Bushoong chief is automatically the king of the Kuba. He alone has the title *nyim*, king. The central institutions of the kingdom are those of the Bushoong chiefdom, whose organization is a little more elaborate than that of other chiefdoms. There are nine provinces headed by four provincial chiefs who reside in the capital, and the provinces are subdivided into districts which comprise a few villages each. The council of electors, *ibaam*, consists of two halves, each with nine members. The council, mbok ilaam, is the equivalent of the makaang in other chiefdoms. There exists, however, still another council for day-to-day affairs, the *ishyaaml.*

Mbok ilaam convenes only when there is a conflict between the ishyaaml and the king. Finally, a fourth council, *ibaanc*, holds public sessions. It meets only in the event of a national emegency. Membership in the different councils is arranged as follows: in ibaam the titleholders are drawn from the electoral clans and cannot sit on any other council, with the exception of the president of the more important half, the *mbyeemy*. The ishyaaml is composed of the four provincial chiefs whose titles are vested in a number of electoral clans: the mbeem and the mbyeeng of the capital, who must be respectively a son and a grandson of former kings; the *kikaam*, or highest-ranking titleholder, who must be at the same time a king's son and belong to an electoral clan; and, if they want to be present, the mbyeemy, the *katyeeng* and the *mbaan* of the capital (the female counterparts of mbeem and mbyeeng), and the *mwaaddy*, the oldest living son of a king. Mbok ilaam includes all the members of ishyaaml, the king, and a handful of other titleholders. Ibaanc includes all the hundred or so titleholders.

The links between the Bushoong chiefdom and the others are, from an institutional point of view, only the following. Every other chiefdom has a representative, *ibwoon*, at the capital, who serves as intermediary between the king and the chiefdom and is responsible for the annual payment of tribute by the chiefdom. Every chiefdom gives a wife to the king, and she may also act as go-between. These institutions are indicative of the true relations between the Bushoong chiefdoms and the others, which are quasi-diplomatic relations. Every chiefdom is autonomous internally and externally except for the payment of annual tribute and the rule that when it elects a new chief, he has to be acknowledged by the king, who cannot refuse to do so. Moreover, from a more descriptive point of view, it is clear that chiefdoms heeded royal commands or paid tribute only when they felt threatened by the royal army. This situation explains why it is that one has to speak about a single kingdom, but still has to regard the system, from the point of view of law, as polycentric, with interchiefdom relations regulated, not by law, but by war or arbitration. This is, of course, true if one accepts a definition of law as peaceful decision-making in a monocentric power system.

THE JUDICIAL SYSTEM

The judicial system consists of two different systems, the moots and the courts, and of three levels, the lineage or clan, the village, and the chiefdom. Cases that do not involve murder or rebellion may be settled at the lower levels, but all cases of bloodshed are likely to come to the chiefdom. The courts are located at the chiefdom level; the moots, at the other levels.

A moot is an assembly of neighbors (village) and kinsmen (lineage or clan) who decide disputes. Moots are different from courts in that they have no fixed membership. Decisions cannot be enforced, and the aim is arbitration rather than dispensation of justice. In the lineage or clan assemblies all older men, and occasionally even youngsters and women, participate in the discussions. In the village all the older men sit on the moot; in the single case that was carefully investigated, one of the younger men was the most active member of the group. A sign that this is not a village council meeting is that the proceedings are public and that all sit together on one side of the village plaza, except the accuser and the accused who face the moot. There are no spectators; there are only participants. The counterpart of the village level at the capital is the compound, *laan*. Here again disputes are settled by the members of the compound or the compounds if there is a quarrel involving two compounds. In addition, the parties invite older men, known for their wisdom, the *bangol a moot*, to help in the moot. These are men from any place in or out of the capital; many are judges on the courts but sit here in a private capacity. Moots attempt to reconcile the parties involved in a conflict and, therefore, try not to attribute all the blame to any single party. They are judiciary institutions, but, as they do not come to legal decisions, they are not here considered further.

The courts, ibaanc, have a complex structure based on the title system. The basic significance of most titles has to do with the judiciary systems, except for the highest titles which play a prominent role in the council system as well. Every case in court is heard by a panel of judges, chosen because of their particular competence to hear that case. Each title carries with it a particular field of jurisdiction. The system . . .

reveals that jurisdiction is determined by the personal status, the residential status, and professional role of the litigants, and by the type of conflict. Panels are chosen so that the largest possible number of background facts about the litigants and the case can be known to the judges. No knowledge is irrelevant in Kuba courts, and out-of-court knowledge is considered very desirable.

From the basic court, appeals (*abaan laan*, to climb a compound) to a similar court headed by the titleholder *baang* may be made. From that court, appeal may be made to a similar one presided over by the kikaam, and from there to a supreme court. The latter, consisting of the more important half of the council of electors, is presided over by the mbyeemy. The king assists but does not preside; his only supreme right is to grant a stay of execution.

The personnel of the courts is the same as the personnel of the councils, but the courts themselves are different. The distinction between the judiciary and other organs of government thus reflected is not common elsewhere.

PROCEDURAL LAW IN THE COURT

A case is introduced by one of the disputing parties. He brings his complaint to any judge in the capital, who directs him to a competent judge. The party deposits a payment of 700 cowries for the formal lodging of the complaint. Through consultation the judge then forms a panel. In cases where a public authority has been flouted, the responsible political official, a village headman, for instance, lodges the complaint. When the day of hearing is set, usually a few days after reception of the complaint, the judges send somebody to notify the defendant. The messenger may be the child of one of the judges or *nyim shapdy*, a special messenger. The messengers must be well treated in the villages, for courts can hold villages in contempt. The courts of appeal have their own means of summoning the defendant: baang sends the *iyol abaang*; kikaam and the supreme court have the summons announced on the main square of the capital by the town crier. Anybody who meets the accused is under obligation to notify him. When an accused person refuses to

answer the summons, he is fined and arrested either by his covillagers or by slaves of the king or the chief, who form the police force. He is then bound and put in the stocks at the jail in the kikaam's compound. The stocks are used only for preventive detention of this sort. Any person may arrest any other *in flagrante delicto*, a fact that often leads to fights. A wise man notifies the two village policemen who exist in every village.

Before the session of the court opens, the accused pays 700 cowries to the panel, and the 1,400 cowries of both parties is divided among the judges. This amount consititutes their salary. Both parties, one after the other, then tell the facts, the plaintiff being the first speaker. At this stage they may be interrupted only by judges or spectators who want to elucidate one or another detail. Eyewitnesses or character witnesses are then called in and are cross-examined by the judges, who also cross-examine the parties. Usually the statements of the parties and the testimony of the witnesses elicit the facts to the satisfaction of the judges. The latter, in any event, have a general knowledge of the facts, having heard about the matter through gossip at the capital or through inquiries made beforehand by the provincial chief. Sometimes, however, the facts are not clear and there are no witnesses. The accused may then propose to swear an oath (*ndokl*). He says that he is innocent, invokes the Creator God as a witness, and steps over a leopard skin, the symbol of political authority. If he lies, he should die on the spot. But the oath is rarely used, for it is believed that the Creator punishes those who swear for trifles. I believe that the judges feel that swearing an oath is taking the matter out of court. A milder oath also exists, but it is considered no more than an emphatic form of speech.

After the evidence is heard and the facts are elicited to the satisfaction of the judges, they withdraw to deliberate. They must reach a unanimous verdict. After doing so, they emerge and proceed to the announcement of the verdict, which is introduced by the following formula:

The king doesn't walk with a bow
the collecting of conflicts, the verdicts of the cases.
The black genette eats the white termites
Be not afraid of the grass the genette carries

The old animal of the councilors of the supreme
    court
when he proceeds to decide cases, he doesn't like
    protests.
Above the thieves, the leopard of the witches
the spoon of the porridge
is the instrument which proves the depths of the
    fire.
It dawns at the chasm which begets the hills
at the world which begets the living.
The river of trade bears the weak ones.
It becomes daylight at Mbeky Butwiim
at Makum maNyaang
at the king who stares intently at the verdicts
at Mboom Kol Mishumn.

The formula means:

The king is in court to
settle the conflicts.
The king destroys the criminals
the innocents must not be afraid.
The king in the supreme court
does not stand for protests against the verdicts.
Despite the thieves, the king
can find the culprits.
It dawns at the king's who creates the world
who creates all the living beings.
The king protects the weak.
It dawns at the famous capitals
at the king's capital when he holds his court.

The formula is given in full because it is
typical of Kuba thought. It emphasizes that the
court holds its authority from the king, and that
the king has authority by virtue of divine
kingship. It reminds the guilty parties that justice
will find them out, and the innocent parties that
they are protected by the king. It reminds all
that verdicts should not be questioned. It
expresses the Kuba philosophy of law, and
stresses that fundamentally the law has equity. It
is guaranteed by the powers of the king, but
the equity of the king himself is guaranteed by
the supreme court.

The verdict announced by one of the judges
designates explicitly who lost the case and
inflicts a fine on the loser, half of which goes to
the kikaam and half to the king. It sets the
amount of a payment to be made by the loser to
the winner in compensation for the harm done.
Punishment never includes terms in jail or
corporal punishment. The loser may appeal,
failing which he must carry out the sentence. If
he does not, he will be arrested by the slaves of
the king and put in the stocks. If he cannot pay,
he must leave some of his personal belongings in

pawn with the court, which will deposit them in
the house of one of the judges.

This whole description of the court is valid for
precolonial times, but since then a few changes
have been made. There are only a small number
of judges who are recognized by the judicial
authorities. The panel system still functions,
but the judges take turns and decide all cases,
irrespective of their nature, so long as they fall
within the category labeled "civil" by the
Congo Code. Cases that are labeled "criminal"
are also handled if they do not involve murder
or attempted murder. Under the colonial
regime, all cases involving Europeans were
outside the competence of the courts in Kuba
land, but all cases dealing with non-Kuba
(other than Europeans) living on Kuba land
were dealt with by the Kuba. Little or nothing
has changed in procedural law, except that
nowadays the messengers are policemen of the
regular police force. Sentencing to a term in jail,
and the practice of making the parties pay for
the administrative costs of the case, have come
into usage. But, for the rest, very little has
changed. The procedural law dealing with
injuries or death has, however, practically
disappeared, and I have had to reconstruct it
from accounts by older titleholders.

When the conflict entails injuries, the wounded party is brought to the chief policeman of
the capital, the iyol. He starts proceedings by
setting himself on an inverted mortar (a symbol
of military authority), and asks from the
defendant a small sum which he uses to buy a
meal. He eats (the symbolism of the meal
remains somewhat unclear), and then informs
the king about the case. If the small sum is
refused, the defendant is taken into preventive
custody. Then the usual court procedure is
followed, but the final penalty consists of a fine
which is not divided between kikaam and king,
but goes to the king only. The penalty includes
compensation as well as the fine. Compensation
consists of a serf woman, who must be either a
serf woman or a woman of the lineage of the
culprit.

In a case of murder the king is notified and
the responsible territorial official is ordered to
bring the culprit in without delay. If the man
resists arrest, he is killed by the slaves of the
king without further trial. Otherwise he is placed
under guard of the *nyibit*, the commander of the

army. The case is tried by the supreme court at night. When the verdict is given, the usual formula is omitted as the court gives it in the presence of the king. There is no delegation of judicial powers. The king then confirms the judgment. When he does so, the mbeem and the mbyeeng of the capital beg him to spare the life of the culprit. The king may turn down their appeal. If he does not, the condemned person becomes a royal slave, as likely as not, is put in the village from which *nkukuun* (slaves to be sacrificed at the death of the king) will be chosen. The nkukuun are always criminals condemned to death, but spared previous execution. If the appeal is turned down and stay of execution not granted, special officers among the king's slaves take the culprit home so that he can bid his farewells. They leave him there, coming back a little later to ask ceremonially for him. They address their demand to the head of the settlement in which the man lives, and use symbolic objects and gestures signifying royal power and the death sentence. The man is ceremonially given up. What happens next is unclear. It is said that the murderer is allowed to inebriate himself on palm wine and then is urged to hang himself in the forest. What happens if the criminal refuses to do so is also unclear. In all cases of murder the lineage of the criminal has to pay a person—this time not a serf woman, but a slave—to the king. The power over life and death has been taken away from the Kuba since the period 1910–1916, which explains why the recollections are vague.

The procedure in the case of murder illustrates a cardinal point in the Kuba conception of kingship and chiefship. The king and the chief are the only persons who hold rights over life and death; they hold them because kingship and chiefship exists by divine right. Kingship and chiefship are responsible for the general fertility of the country, and the king holds this right because it has been given in so many words and by symbolic ceremonial to him at his accession. One of the formulas then used stresses that "the head of the criminal belongs to the king." In practice, a murderer who resists arrest is killed, and his head has to be brought to the king.

The same procedure illustrates the concept that royal authority, although it is supreme, has to be checked. The trial is held by a court that the king does not lead, although he is present.

The only court that can hold a murder trial is the election council; that is why the more important half of the council sits as a court. The same holds true for the other chiefdoms, where that council or part of that council also acts as a court in murder trials.

Appeals may be made by any of the parties involved in a case. The party who appeals must first pay 150 cowries to the lower court so that it will desist from acting in the case. The procedure at all higher courts is similar. Appeals are discouraged, however, because sentences tend to become heavier. The usual sentence for any case coming to the supreme court is reduction into slavery of the whole lineage of the loser, or the payment of a very large amount of goods to the king or the chief. The latter penalty has the same effect, for, in order to pay the fine, the condemned person would have to sell several relatives into slavery or at least pawn his matrilineal womenfolk as serf women. At this level no compensation is ever paid to the winner. The Kuba feel, therefore, that one who does appeal to the supreme court must be motivated by hatred. Moreover, the court may turn down any appeal on the grounds that the case is too trivial and was handled correctly in the lower court.

Procedural law shows two further characteristics: first, some form of symbolic ceremonialism is used; second, the graver the offense, the more the symbolism that is attached to the ceremonial. In this way the social meaning of what is happening is made clear to all. The symbolism used always stresses in part that law is dispensed by the political system and its head, the king or the chief. Procedural law also shows that there are two types of cases: those that involve bloodshed and those that do not. These types are distinguished in the following discussion of substantive law.

SUBSTANTIVE LAW

CASES WITHOUT BLOODSHED

The Kuba court may deal with any conflict that arises in society, with the exception of particular situations to be discussed later. The composition of the court varies with the type of case, and some cases are reserved to the courts of appeal. The baang hears all matters pertaining to marriage, in the first instance, and the kikaam hears all cases of debts. The types of cases heard by a modern court and their relative frequency are best illustrated by listing the cases from the *chefferie* court that succeeded to the court of first instance in the Bushoong chiefdom. . . . First, the present so-called customary law is distorted in terms of modern Congolese law, based on the Code Napoléon. Some of the listings under both civil and criminal headings are odd, which explains why reports from scribes or collections from legal journals are often almost useless. Second, most of the cases deal with marriage problems (adultery, marriage, divorce, bridewealth), with claims on goods (debts, pledges, bridewealth, loans), and with violence in word or deed (insults, threats, assault, slander). Marriage problems total 51.5 per cent of the cases; claims on goods, 52.5 per cent; and violence, 40.5 per cent. (Overlap between categories explains the total of 144.5 per cent.) In fact, violence seems to be generally an expression of conflict, not of the grounds of conflict, and it may safely be said that most cases involve either marriage or the transfer of goods. This is even more true of the pre-colonial period, when a number of cases . . . would not have existed (for example, modern administration, drunkenness). We might expect, therefore, that most substantive law deals with these matters.

The Kuba view on substantive law is reflected in their division of cases by types and in the assignment of special judges to special types. Debts come immediately to the kikaam's court, and marriage affairs go to the baang. The number of appeals is therefore limited, and the first court tends to hand out the final judgment. in addition to these two, there are only two judges for cases not involving bloodshed: one for thefts and one for attempted murder by the use of charm. And as a transfer of goods is involved in the case of theft, the kikaam might be called in even at the first trial.

The Kuba, whether or not they are judges, have no code of substantive law, if only because they lack writing. A notion of consistency in law is certainly prevalent. If one asked a Kuba man about a specific problem he would state that such and such constitutes an offense and that the penalty would be this and that. More-

over the chances are that the man in the street and the judge would give about the same answer and would even concur to a large extent as to what rules were involved in the solution. It is, therefore, possible to build up a corpus of substantive law, by following cases brought to court and by questioning in terms of hypothetical trials. To set all these rules of substantive law forth in a brief paper is impossible. Furthermore, I believed at one time that the very notation and the order of presentation of such rules would imply a grave distortion of the legal norms held by the Kuba, because the legal norms—that is, rules explicitly stated by the Kuba—are social norms, and nothing more than the usual social norms for the regulation of behavior which are implied by the institutions concerned with the case, as illustrated by the following instances. But just as Kuba institutions and social structure can be explained in terms of the conceptions of sociology, so their legal institutions and behavior can be analyzed in the framework of the concepts of comparative law. The very cases which follow do support this. For the concept of "reasonable man" can be applied to them. The Kuba may not hold this concept explicitly but as a principle of comparative law the notion can be fully applied, just as we apply the sociological notions of status and role, which the Kuba do not hold explicitly either.

Instance no. 1. The younger brother steals a wife. X accused Y of adultery with his wife. X and Y were full paternal parallel cousins, and Y was the elder brother of X. Y answered, "Certainly X is my younger brother. Therefore I could not possibly take his wife. But he is wicked [*ipaangt*, a technical term] for his wife was first mine. X was a messenger for a European firm and lured my wife away. I had to abandon her because my younger brother had married her. Why, on top of all this, does he accuse me now?" The judges found out that X had worked for a European firm and that his wife had been Y's. They did not even deliberate, but handed a verdict of innocence to Y and had X pay the costs of the trial. One judge scowled, "You knew, X, from the villagers that the girl was the wife of your elder brother. Why have you married her in turn?"

The interest of the case lies in the fact that it arose as a case of adultery, but as soon as it became known that the younger brother took the wife of the older one, that aspect crowded out the matter of adultery. The norms involved are that elder brothers, even classificatory ones, may never have sexual intercourse with the wives of younger brothers, whereas the latter may banter with the wives of their elders and inherit them after the death of the elder brothers. To steal a wife of an elder brother puts the latter in a position where he has to divorce her. It is wicked because it is the illicit exploitation of a norm of behavior to one's unfair advantage. Once it was established that X had acted in full knowledge, he lost the case. The legal reason as written in the court's register would be that the accusation was not proven. The real reason was, of course, the behavior of X.

Other cases in which such general norms of behavior apply are legion. For instance, in one case a man accused another of slander because the latter had hinted that the plaintiff had put poison in his food. The case was dismissed because the defendant had not asked the plaintiff to settle the matter by the poison ordeal, which was the proper thing to do, even though use of the ordeal had been forbidden by the European administration thirty years before. In another case a father accused his son of having wounded him. The boy was not even allowed to speak, but was sent to jail "until the wound healed," and then only would the case be tried. In another case a father simply asked to have his son jailed because the latter did not obey him. The son was promptly jailed. The cultural norm in these cases was the expected behavior of a son toward his father. As deviance from the norm had been serious, punishment was inflicted even without full investigation.

When two norms of behavior conflict, the judgment may be more difficult.

Instance no. 2. The careless wife.

A sued his wife B. He said that he had cultivated his cornfield, but, when harvesting time came, his wife had not harvested and the corn had been destroyed by bush pigs. B explained that she had left her home to assist her pregnant daughter. One judge asked her in wonder, "Why did you, a woman, go to live elsewhere when the crops were ripe in the forest?" The woman was condemned but not fined.

The norms involved are clear: a woman shall reap the harvest planted by her husband and a woman shall assist her pregnant daughter. When the two conflicted, the judges felt that the first duty was more imperative than the second. But, realizing that there was some choice possible between the norms, they did not fine the woman, although they may have refrained from doing so in order not to endanger the marriage.

A curious aspect of these norms is that they cover the amount of compensation to be paid if a norm is breached. In cases of adultery, where the breach is very clear, the penalties are as follows. An adulterer pays 300 cowries as a fine, and a compensation of one *mapel* (man's dancing cloth, worth 20 dollars) and one *ikul* (man's knife, worth 1 dollar) to the wronged husband. If a woman introduces a complaint, the adulteress pays one *ncak* (woman's dancing cloth, worth about 10 to 15 dollars). If the plaintiff is a king's child, the amounts are doubled. If the defendant is a king's child, no compensation is paid. Three cases judged in 1954 adhered to these penalties, replacing the customary 300 cowries with 300 francs and adding a month in jail in all cases. Other instances may easily be cited. In case of theft, the stolen goods must be returned, but no other compensation is given. In cases of beating without bloodshed, the compensation is 600 cowries. In cases of attempted murder with the use of charms, it is 3,000 cowries. (In practice, this sentence would often mean that the culprit would have to pawn a woman as a serf woman in order to raise that much money.)

These tariffs do not seem to be organized in a system, yet they are. For the graver the offense, the heavier the penalty and the Kuba are well aware of it. What is curious about the tariffs is their very specificity. This may have developed during the colonial period. But it probably existed long before this. For all of Kuba society is permeated by the obsession with ranking. And specific penalties allow for a specific ranking of torts and crimes. Also the development of an elaborate court system would lead to some standardization in tariffs. For the judges were professional and would compare cases in terms of gravity, using analogy. This then resulted in a more systematic scale of penalties.

Moreover judges did take into account the rank of persons involved as is shown in the tariffs given for adultery. Again the principle of hierarchy is involved and this point makes clear why personal status is a criterion of competence for the jurisdiction of titleholders. One is entitled to judgment by one's peers . . . at least one judge should be one's peer.

CASES WITH BLOODSHED

There is a distinction between cases involving bloodshed and others, as is evident from the description of procedural law. The distinction does not overlap with Western notions of criminal and civil law, as may be illustrated by the following type of case. When orders, from a political authority other than the king have been transgressed, the complaints are lodged by the authorities involved. When the case is decided against the accused, compensation is awarded on a personal basis to the authority who introduced the matter, as if he were simply an ordinary plaintiff. Such a case does not involve bloodshed, yet it might very well be criminal in Western eyes.

The serious concern shown by the Kuba political structures about the settlement of conflicts involving violence is revealed by the special procedures and symbolic ceremonials that are used. The concern is also clear from the types of cases assigned to special types of judges. As against four specialists for cases without bloodshed, which constitute the large majority of all cases that come to the courts, five are found for five types of cases involving bloodshed. Distinctions are made among involuntary homicide, suicide—an involuntary homicide by the relatives of the deceased—simple injuries, injuries inflicted by a weapon of war, and murder. In the last three instances, where accident is excluded and intent seems clear, the offense must be reported at once to the king or to the chief of the chiefdom, and the procedure is of a special type. In all instances, compensation involves a human being and is paid, not to the wronged party, but to the head of the chiefdom.

Substantive law with regard to cases without bloodshed was said to be based on social norms of the relevant institutions. Cases of violence have in common that they are a breach of a fundamental political norm and that peace should be maintained, and also, of the norm in a case of murder, that only a king or a chief can take a life. It is because a fundamental political norm is broken that cases of bloodshed are distinguished from the others. The fact that such cases are a threat to the political system explains why the reaction is so dramatic, why the specialized judges are all military officers when intent of bloodshed can be shown, why the king or the chief has to be notified, why the procedure moves more rapidly than usual, and so on.

It is characteristic of the Kuba political system that the use of physical force is strictly limited to the political authorities, excluding selfhelp under practically any circumstances. The Kuba have gone further in this respect than many other African states, including even the interlacustrine kingdoms, where feuds are still allowed provided the kings have given their permission to the lineage of the victim. But Kuba political structure has to react vigorously, for the spirit of the feud—the principle of a life for a life—is not dead. It is still applied between clans in connection with poison ordeals, and in the institution of serf women whose transfer is usually a transfer of lives and life potentialities. The principle is present in law as well; when a murder has been executed, his group still has to hand over a person to compensate for the victim. But that person is not given to the group of the victim, but to the king or the head of the chiefdom, the representative of the whole political structure.

In recent times most instances of bloodshed have not been tried in Kuba courts, and it is not possible to obtain detailed evidence on earlier cases. But the norms still exist, and so do the tariffs for breaches of different norms. In a case of suicide, as also in involuntary homicide, the surviving relatives had to pay nine slaves. When blood was shed with or without a weapon of war, a serf woman was paid to the king along with bells, lances, swords (note the symbolism; these are weapons of war or symbols of military authority), and cloth in large amount, which probably meant that the culprit would have to pawn several girls of his lineage as serf women. If somebody wounded a person for the second time, the offense was tantamount to murder. In a case of murder, a slave was paid to the king or the chief if the murderer was executed. If not, it could happen that the murderer and his whole immediate lineage were condemned to slavery. These tariffs entail two sorts of judgment: compensation, which has to be a life; and penalty, which may be death, payment in goods or slaves, or enslavement. The fact that compensation and penalty are directed toward the same authority obscures the distinction between them at first glance, but the distinction is relevant to Kuba law as a whole.

LAW AND THE POISON ORDEAL

The legal institutions described so far cannot cope with accusations of witchcraft, which are made very frequently. Yet no moot, no court, will accept them. The proper technique is to ask for a poison ordeal. The accused drinks poison; if he dies he is guilty, and if he survives he is innocent. Normally the head of the clan of the victim—often the clan of the suspected witch as well—makes a public accusation and asks the suspect to drink poison. A village headman may do the same with regard to suspects in his village, but he may not accuse dependents (slaves, serf women, spouses married into the village) without the permission of their masters; if they drank poison, they would take it in their villages of origin. If the suspect does not belong to the clan of the victim, the head of the victim's clan asks the head of the suspect's clan to submit his man to the ordeal. The request is almost never refused, but, if the man in innocent, compensation must be given by the victim's clan, either by payment of 200–400 cowries or, as is often done, by having one of their men take the poison. This is the closest the Kuba ever come to a feud, and they recognize that such cases may create permanent hatred between some clans.

After the accusation is formally voiced, the accused person agrees to take the poison. If he should refuse, the poison would be slipped into his food or drink anyway. Many suspects themselves cheerfully ask to drink the poison so as to clear their names. The ordeal itself is a complete ritual performed by a specialist. It is supposed to be directed supernaturally by the Creator God and the nature spirits.

Why do the Kuba courts not take control over the adminstration of the ordeal? Matters of life and death are matters of kingship and chief-ship, and they are vital to the political structure. And by far the most numerous accusations of murder concern witchcraft. Yet the courts do not act. The Kuba recognize that in a way the poison ordeal is a legal instrument; in the myth that supports the institution, the ordeal is invented by a man named Justice. After his death, long ago, the courts used to administer preliminary ordeals leading to the poison ordeal, if no witnesses were available and an oath had been taken. But later the ordeal developed in its present form and became restricted to accusations of witchcraft. The courts withdrew completely from this field. It is tempting, but untenable, to hold that the courts are not concerned with witchcraft because the alleged crime is supernatural and cannot be established by natural means. The use of black magic is forbidden, and action is taken in court when accusations of this nature arise. That no material evidence can be offered in cases of witchcraft should not necessarily stop the courts, for, when there are no witnesses and there is no evidence, the defendant takes an oath which the court accepts as evidence.

In fact, alongside the moots and the courts, the poison ordeal may be considered the third major institution of the Kuba legal system. It might be argued that the poison ordeal is not adminstered by the courts partly because of the large number of cases that arise, which would have justified the creation of a special court to deal with the problem. But the nature of the ordeal is such that the whole community in which the drama of witchcraft has unfolded itself plays a part in the drama, in a way not unlike the participation of the whole village in a moot. This community encompasses all persons who are interested in the case, and none of those who are not. The latter circumstance suggests that cases of witchcraft are not seen as affecting the whole large political community, and can be dealt with by an institution like the moot at the village level. That the ordeal has to be impartial, and not a condemnation, is clear from the type of crime—it cannot be traced—and from the type of judging body—no person could condemn a fellow villager or clansman and not disrupt the fabric of social relations in the village. The condemnation is not given by the villagers; it comes from above, and nobody but the dying witch can be blamed for it.

Most witchcraft accusations involve women or, rarely, elderly men. On the other hand whispered accusations are often made against kings, chiefs, or their competitors for power. It is remarkable to see that these categories of persons appear only infrequently in courts. Further investigation discloses that the procedures by which women and elderly men bewitch are very different from the procedures attributed to mighty chiefs or their challengers. It can be stated as a rule that resolution of conflict among the Kuba usually occurs as follows: for women and elderly men by witchcraft, for men through court action, for persons with power by witchcraft (in fact sorcery with the use of black magic). The reason for this situation is that equity in court can be expected only for men. Women have become too dependent and if they conflict with men, they will usually lose the case anyway. So their only avenue of redress is to attempt witchcraft. The elderly men who are accused of witchcraft are those who are left without relatives and who have therefore lost all social importance. Or they are vying for political supremacy in a village or a chiefdom. As for kings and chiefs, it is Kuba common sense that struggles for power cannot be settled in court at all. The court would have no way of enforcing decisions, which are the emanation of the power of the very persons involved in such conflicts. Hence the three different ways in which conflict can be settled and the reason why poison ordeals have judicial aspects. If Man cannot act with equity, his God will.

For the same reason, a number of conflicts cannot be solved by law, as law has been defined. These are conflicts between the king or the head of a chiefdom and one of his subjects, and conflicts between chiefdoms. The king is outside the law. He is immune. No case is known of a king ever being brought before a court. And a king who feels he has been wronged may ignore the legal machinery completely, and act on his own. For instance, in 1921 a man was supposed to have committed adultery with one of the ruling king's wives. The king kept him chained for months, and only after long pleading did the titleholders obtain his release. Scores of instances are known in which kings have killed paramours of their wives and tortured their wives. Nobody ever interferes. Gossip has it, and it has been substantiated in some instances,

that kings who dislike certain key titleholders have them poisoned. In a well-known case the king went out at night and himself set fire to the house of a man he disliked, though the man had committed no wrong the king could complain about. Yet, even for actions like these, the king is still immune from the law, as are chiefs in their chiefdoms. If kings kill too many people, however, they themselves are killed, not through a process of law, but by the national charm. If chiefs kill too many people, they are pushed out of office and sometimes are killed by their electors or by a mob.

The Kuba say that the king is immune because the authority of king and chiefs is supreme. This authority, to be maintained, must be backed not only by the prestige derived from wealth and title but by the possibility of physical action against rebels. The king or the chief is the symbol of the kingdom or of the chiefdom. Nobody can engage in a conflict with either of them and be "right," for the conflict would be against the kingdom or the chiefdom. Also, nobody can admit that a court would find against a king or a chief, since it finds in the name of the king and its authority derives from the king. In fact, kings and chiefs are immune simply because they are at the apex of the political structure, and law is a function of that structure just as the courts are a structural part of it.

Law cannot solve conflict between chiefdoms because the Kuba kingdom is a multicentric power system. The Bushoong dominate the other chiefdoms militarily, but every chiefdom remains a power system. If its power is not very inferior to that of the Bushoong, as is true of the Ngongo, the chiefdom is practically independent; if its power is puny compared with that of the Bushoong, the chiefdom becomes almost a supplementary province, as is true of the Bulaang. But there is no machinery to unite all the chiefdoms for the purpose of the exercise of the law. The limit of the legal system and of law is set at a lower territorial level than the upper limit of the total political system, the kingdom. Therefore, conflicts between chiefdoms lead either to war or to arbitration by an outside chief, who is asked to act by the warring chiefs. The arbitrator is often the king, mainly because he has the biggest army. Arbitration does not aim at finding a guilty party, but at reconciling the factions without putting the blame on anybody. If war then does not solve conflict, a form of diplomacy does.

Besides the conflicts mentioned, another type of breach of behavior, incest, falls outside the scope of the law. A logical explanation would be that, as both parties are guilty, there could be no plaintiff and therefore no action by moot, court, or ordeal. But the Kuba say that incest falls outside judicial action because the offense is punished automatically by the Creator God, who inflicts lepra on the culprits. Very few cases of incest are actually known. The one recent case, in 1953, was involuntary incest, and the man hanged himself to escape public scorn as soon as he discovered it. So few cases seem to occur, and they are kept so secret for fear of public ostracism, that it is largely hypothetical speculation to question further why the courts do not handle these matters.

THE NATURE OF KUBA LAW

The legal system of the Kuba is part of their political structure. Titleholders have other tasks besides their legal duties. The limitations of the legal system, and the special care taken in cases involving bloodshed, make the point. If a generalization is possible, and I think it is, we might say that whatever political systems are different, legal systems are different too. Traditional societies in Africa might have centralized political systems with a monarchy, as the Kuba have, or they might have such systems without a monarchy. There might be segmentary lineage systems, age-grade organizations, simple village organizations, and all sorts of intermediate types between these major ones. Moreover, different variants of Muslim law were accepted in differing degrees in West and East Africa. In short, one might justifiably expect a wide variety of traditional legal systems; the Kuba system is only one of them.

Kuba law had no fixed corpus juris and the norms of the law were those of the institutions concerned. Kuba courts do not seem to have invoked specific precedents but legal analogy was used. The scale of penalties alone indicates that comparison between cases was made. For the more common cases, for example, matters of marriage or inheritance analogies were easy to find in the recent past and judges could

remember them. In rare cases such as an offence in relation to initiation *nkaan* there was less guidance. Here the verdict seems to have been based primarily on what the judges agreed was the sensible thing to do. The concept of the "reasonable man" was used.

It is clear that insofar as possible, Kuba law should be analyzed first on its own terms. The folk-system of law can be discovered by examining the use of legal vocabulary and formulae and by exploring the specific structural and institutional features of the system itself. Once this is done however the next logical step is to submit this body of data to analysis, using concepts derived from comparative law. Only in this way do Kuba data become truly comparable with other cases. At the first level of enquiry therefore one will stress that the division between cases without bloodshed and cases with bloodshed does not wholly correspond to the distinction between civil law and criminal law. At the comparative level one will emphasize however that the underlying Kuba notion is one of civil versus criminal. The scope of the following discussion is restricted to the folk-system of law only.

The legal formula cited states that the process of law is based on equity and vested in political authority. An examination of the most important legal terms shows even more clearly what law means to the Kuba. The terms for custom, mores *iya* includes the meaning of "law." *Look* means the ability to judge, the capacity to listen and includes the notion of justice. Justice is "the ability to hear a case and give a good judgment," for *look* is a nominal deriving from the verbal *wook*: "to listen." This nominal is used *only* in legal contexts whereas *iya* is not. The idea of justice seems closely tied to the court or the moot, where parties present cases. The process of law is itself most often referred to by the name of the court, ibaanc, and the judges are the "chiefs of ibaanc." As in the English "court," the notion "ibaanc" covers a plaza, a judicial court and sometimes the entourage of a king or chief. The Kuba word also means in addition the great council that meets on the plaza. A "case" is *matyeen*: "things looked at with care," "things scrutinized"; the connection with the court is clear. All other terms found so far deal with a case in court or with ordinances and all can be used with other meanings outside legal situations. Thus *waabwaak*: "you fell" means in court: "you lost the case." The terminology shows judges "overcoming" cases by "looking intently" at them and parties "falling" or "being elevated."

One could conclude that the whole vocabulary is nontechnical because it shows few or no exclusively legal terms. It is equally true however and more congruent with the very existence of specialized judicial institutions that the vocabulary is technical because the same precise specialized meanings are always given to the same terms in courts of law. Those specialized meanings confirm that there is a corpus of law. After all much of the Latin terminology in Roman law consists of terms which had, when they came in use, primarily meanings which were not legal. And no one will deny that Roman law had a technical vocabulary.

The sources of Kuba law are the norms of behavior existing in the society, and they change as rapidly as it does. But there are also statutes and orders, which in time become norms. *Nkyeenc* are orders given by the king, probably without consultation with his councils, and *shyaang* are statutes given after proper consultation with the councils. Instances of such statutes are legion. In 1953 the king forbade dancing and singing during the night within the borders of the capital. A recently formed witch-finding cult was flourishing, and had just started to hold nightly shows. When many people complained about the noise, the king's order was promulgated. About 1910 a new charm had made its way, and was being used to kill one's enemies. So many people died that the king had to forbid the possession of such a charm under penalty of death. The two instances cited exemplify adaptations to changes in the society. But sometimes statutes initiate changes, or favor change, in certain directions. Oral history has it that around 1680 a king proclaimed special prerogatives for royal children in matters of marriage, bridewealth, and adultery. The statute aimed at enhancing the status of such persons, and later history shows that their status was indeed improved shortly afterward. The two sources of Kuba law, social norm and statute, may be expected in all African monarchies, and indeed are fairly typical for them. For example, in Rwanda and Loziland the situation is essentially similar. But

statutes as a source of law cannot be expected outside the monarchies, for there would be no supreme authority to proclaim the edicts.

The main divisions of Kuba law, indicated above, follow logically from the absence of a written codex and the differences in laws of procedure between cases involving bloodshed and cases without bloodshed. In contrast with the moot, the legal procedure in court is not merely a process of arbitration. Courts are institutionally defined as to membership and competence, moots only vaguely so; courts can coerce, moots cannot; and, most important, a court has to designate clearly who is the loser, and has to fine him. That is, a court may blame one party for this, another for that, but it holds one party responsible for breach of the peace and the creation of conflict. Poison ordeals are like courts in all these respects except that the culprit is not designated by man; the judge, being supernatural, is in fact absent. The active part played by the spectators, however, brings the ordeal close to the moot.

In court decisions, two forms of action are clearly involved. The first is restoration of the former situation if at all possible (for example, a thief hands the stolen goods back, but pays no further compensation), or new action by the guilty party (for example, the payment of mapel and ikul to atone for adultery). What the atonement shall be is often determined by the norms of the institution involved. This type of legal action is very close to the type proposed in a moot. In fact, cases are known in which an adulterer simply paid mapel and ikul to the wronged husband, even without calling a moot. In this action of the court, its decision can be accepted by all involved because it conforms so strictly to known norms. The second action of the court has to do with the situation of conflict itself, the responsibility for conflict. Somebody is held responsible and must be penalized. The fine goes to the political structure which has been injured by the existence of conflict. The distinction between compensation and penalty is clear in cases not involving bloodshed, but it applies also to cases with bloodshed, as shown above. The difference between cases of bloodshed and others is simply that in the former instance compensation goes to the political authority, and not to a private plaintiff. The distinction between the moot and the poison ordeal in this respect is simply that the moot imposes no penalty, restoration being the only aim, whereas in the ordeal compensation is absent, the penalty being the only aim.

10. THE LAW OF ANCIENT BABYLONIA

J. B. BURY, S. A. COOK, AND F. E. ADCOCK

Reprinted from Cambridge Ancient History, *edited by J. B. Bury, S. A. Cook, and F. E. Adcock, Vol. 1. Copyright © 1928, Cambridge University Press. The three editors of this work are historians of ancient civilization and are considered to be among the leading authorities in the field.*

■ I have suggested that the evolutionary transition to formal law can be understood as an adaptation to the development of statehood. What are the demands made by a nation-state on its rulers that lead to this? It must be remembered that most states are established by the sword, and regardless of the symbols or euphemisms in which it is cloaked, it is at sword's point that most citizenries are kept in line.

One of the aims of national rulers is to achieve political control, but its establishment over a wide territory must be carried out against the background of many different groups which must be welded into a political entity; this process can be regarded as the dominant sociopolitical element in the habitat of such societies. Law is indispensable for political control, and a uniform legal code is essential for a central state's hegemony over local groups. But a legal system is not only made up of laws; an integral part of every such system— whether customary or formal—is an administrative procedure by which people are required to proceed. These procedures are described for Babylonia in the following selection; when we compare them with the legal procedures of the Ifugao (Selection 8), we see that the difference between customary and formal law is qualitative and not merely one of degree.

The diversity of groups comprising a national society makes a system of formal law beneficial to the nation's rulers in two additional respects. First, a uniform, formal legal system is much more efficient than one in which each group is dealt with in terms of its own traditions and peculiar customs. Second, such a system lessens the possibility that some groups will feel that others are favored and they are discriminated against.

Babylonia is a good example of an agricultural nation formed out of many different groups. The plethora of languages referred to in the Biblical account of the Tower of Babel probably refers to Babylonia's national heterogeneity, to its many and diverse territories, mostly conquered. Its legendary tower may refer to its monumental architecture—a frequent accompaniment of early statehood—or to the stele on which the famous Code of Hammurabi was inscribed, or possibly both. This heterogeneity is adumbrated in the preamble to Hammurabi's code of laws:

> When the exalted Anum king of the Annunaki (and) Illil [Bel] lord of heaven and earth, who allots the destinies of the land, allotted the divine lordship of the multitude of the people unto Marduk the first-born son of Ea, magnified him amongst the Igigi, called Babylon by its exalted name (and) so made it preeminent in the (four) quarters of the world, and established for him an everlasting kingdom whose foundations are firmly laid like heaven and earth, at that time Anum and Illil for the prosperity of the people called me by name Hammu-rabi, the reverent God-fearing prince, to make justice appear in the land, to destroy the evil and the wicked that the strong might not oppress the weak, to rise indeed like Shamash [the Sun] over the dark-haired [black head, in other translations] folk to give light to the land (The Babylonian Laws, edited with translation and commentary by G. R. Driver and John C. Miles, Vol. 2, p. 7; Oxford: Oxford University Press, 1955).

This portion of Hammurabi's preamble not only points to Babylonia's heterogeneity but also exemplifies the commingling of religious, political, kinship, and legal institutions that is characteristic of preindustrial societies. This commingling was expressed legally as well: "If a man has stolen property belonging to a god or a palace, that man shall be put to death." Such a law is obviously important in a society in which political legitimacy is religiously based. Another example is in the second law of the code which contains two characteristic themes of societies at this stage of development: a concern with witchcraft (see the Introduction to Part III) and the use of trial by ordeal.

Indispensable for the study of this civilization is *The Evolution of Urban Society: Early Mesopotamia and Prehispanic Mexico*, by Robert McC. Adams (Chicago: Aldine, 1966) and *Ancient Mesopotamia: Portrait of a Dead Civilization*, by A. Leo Oppenheim (Chicago: University of Chicago Press, 1964). The *Encyclopedia Britannica* (14th edition) has a fairly complete article on "Hammurabi" that can be consulted for background information on his legal code. Another valuable and well written book is *The Greatness that was Babylon*, by H. W. F. Saggs (New York: Praeger, 1969). ∎

HAMMURABI SUCCEEDED to the throne of Babylon (2123–2081), young, vigorous, and a genius full of fire, destined to be both a law-giver and a fighter, a man who would have made an admirable Governor-general of modern Irak. His reign of forty-three years marks our Fifth Section during which the Babylonian empire was consolidated.

There is a cryptic entry in the date-lists for Hammurabi's first action which is variously translated "when he put order (or righteousness) in his land" or "he and his prefects put order in the land." It may perhaps indicate reforms, but it is equally probable that it shows a state of unrest after Rim-Sin's victories. He began by building certain minor fortifications and finally, when his plans were ready, swept down on Erech and Isin and captured them both from Rim-Sin in 2117. Four years later he recaptured Rapikum, taking Shalibi in addition, and thereby stripped Rim-Sin of almost all his conquests. Rapikum was, as will be remembered, one of the allies under Erech; a variant in the date-lists attributes the capture to Ibik-Ishtar....

Such were his activities as a soldier and pious ruler. Great though his deeds may have been as they are set out above, they pale before his wonderful creation, the Code of Laws, one of the most important documents in the history of the human race. That he was not the inventor of these laws, numbering some two hundred and eighty-five, is now well known, for Sumerian originals exist . . . but it was his genius which codified them and published them abroad in his empire. Even down to the seventh century B.C. it was studied apparently under the name of The Judgments of Righteousness which Hammurabi, the great King, set up. This was the Code wherewith the land was governed, and it shows the laws of Babylonia of this period to have been in advance of those of Assyria at a much later time.

The Code, as we have it, consists of a block of black diorite found in the French excavations at Susa by De Morgan in 1901. It had been carried off from Babylonia by some Elamite conqueror in a raid, and he has erased five of its columns, doubtless with the intention of inscribing his own name there. On the obverse is a picture of Hammurabi receiving the laws from the Sun-god; and a prologue sets forth the king's exploits, and is followed by the laws themselves with the penalties attaching thereto.

Great was his pride in his empire, as shown in the summary of his life in the prologue. Even a district of Cappadocia was partly populated by Assyrian emigrants, and Assyria was so far under his control that its ruler was a mere patesi or local governor; and even fifty years later outraged inhabitants would journey from Arrapachitis to Babylon, presumably in order to lay their plaint before the king himself. Indeed, it was no new conquest of the north from Babylon, for, already, Naram-Sin appears to have set up a stele near the modern Diarbekr. Hammurabi was actively a benefactor of the temples and cities of Babylon, Borsippa, Kish, Cuthah, Sippar, Dilbat, Nippur and Duranki, Lagash, Adab, Larsa, Erech, Khallab, Isin, Ur, Eridu, Kesh and Mashgan-shabra, and even Nineveh. He carried his arms westwards far up into the Euphrates districts of Mari, where the people worshipped Dagan; and in one of the inscriptions of his period he is called King of Amurru, the west land. That his occupation of the Euphrates was no mere invention is suggested by the marriage-lines of two wedded folk in that district which still exist in the form of a clay-tablet dated in the year "when Khammurapikh, the king, opened the canal Khabur-ibal-bugash from the city Zakku-Isharlim to the city Zakku-Igitlim." The mention of the name Khabur shows the provenance of the tablet: it is one from the Khabur district on the middle Euphrates, with a local dating of its own. The final word *bugash*, the distinctive Kassite word for god, in the name of the Canal is curious, and for this reason there is a doubt about the date of this tablet; it may be remembered that a tablet dated in the reign of Kashtiliash, probably the Kassite king of 1708–1687, is extant.

GOVERNMENT AND SOCIETY

The government of the country changed greatly after the early Sumerian kings of the third millennium, as must naturally happen when the control of the land is becoming centralized. In the very early period the exact relation in meaning of the two words *lugal*, king, and *patesi*, prince-priest, is quite uncertain: Ur-nina (*c.* 3100 B.C.) calls himself king of Lagash, but Eannatum (*c.* 3000 B.C.) takes the title patesi of Lagash. As time goes on, and we reach the period of the Dynasty of Ur about the middle of the third millennium, we can be more definite; the patesi from being the chief secular and religious ruler of a city-state drops to a position of dependence on the overlord, who is now holding the reins of control of the nucleus of an empire in his hands. He has sunk to the minor position of a local governor, natural enough as the stronger states absorbed the weaker. Babylonia by now was no longer divided into just so many states as there were mounds, but had reached the time when city-states were being amalgamated into groups, each under its own king, when Ur held the hegemony of a greater part of the lower plain between the two rivers. The patesi remained in control of his township, but it was as a minor official.

The tablets from Drehem show how numerous these patesis were in the time of the Dynasty of Ur. We know of more than forty districts or townships controlled by them; and in fact almost complete lists of patesis can be made from Umma, Nippur and Lagash from the thirty-fifth year of Dungi until the third of Ibi-Sin. There were many places in Elam under the local control of patesis at this period, as was only natural, since many of the kings of Ur at

this time were overlords of Susa and Elam. Of Kazallu we know the names of four (Zarik, Kallamu, Gimilmama, Abillasha); and on a tablet from Susa we find Zarikim taking office in the presence of ten witnesses, several of whom are obviously Semites. Although the power of the patesis declines, even in the time of the Dynasty of Ur they had the right of legal decision; they were, however, compelled to pay taxes, and might be transferred from one district to another. One of their duties was to take charge of sheep sent in for the temple or for the king. They were, as a rule, appointed to the office, and did not inherit it—although there is one exception: and they found it advantageous to be mindful of the sacrifices to the gods. They might be absent from their posts for a time, probably while on official missions, their places being taken by temporary deputies; for instance, at Umma two are named for the fifty-seventh year of Dungi, and for the fifth year of Bur-Sin. Provisions, consisting usually of food, beer and oil, were supplied both for the journey out and back. From references to kings' daughters at this period it would appear that patesis married them; "the daughter of the king" marries the patesi of Zabshali, "the daughter of the king" marries the patesi of Anshan. Ni . . . midaku, another king's daughter, was actually elevated to the rule of the principality of Markhashi; but in the two former instances there is equally the possibility that they became the patesis, rather than that they married them.

With the advent of the Semitic kings of the Isin and Larsa dynasties in 2357 the office of patesi was shorn of much of its splendour, and although it continued to exist, the mayor of provincial towns (called *rabianu*) was soon to become a more powerful personality. Hammurabi was not a king with whom decentralization would be popular; he could not grant his subordinates a full measure of power, except in minor cases. Moreover, although meticulously careful of religious matters, he seems to have brooked no challenge from the priests in the matter of control, for we find the old priestly courts disappearing in his reign. Hence may have arisen the reason that the office of patesi, with its priestly reminiscences, as well as its Sumerian origin in its disfavour, fell rapidly from power. The word patesi now represents an officer who takes his orders not directly from the king, but from some official between him and the king. Thus Hammurabi says to Sin-idinnam: "I wrote to thee that Sin-ilu the patesi who was under Taribatum, whom thou didst assign to *ridūti* (officers of the levy), should be restored as a patesi to the control of Taribatum." The office is a long way from the king by now. Apparently the governor of Larsa thought he could make a patesi into a *ridū* or officer of the levy, but Sin-ilu must have appealed directly to Hammurabi, availing himself of a privilege as popular with the toadying underling as with the condescending monarch. Such an officer might beg the king to allow him to exchange his district: Apil-Martu, the son of Mini-Martu, a patesi who takes orders from Enubi-Marduk, appeals through Sin-idinnam to Hammurabi that he may serve another chief, and the king assents, providing that the new chief, by name Nabiummalik, gives a patesi to Enubi-Marduk in exchange. Elam relinquished the patesi soon after Dungi's reign, replacing the office by that of the *sukkal*, an indication of Kutur-nakhkhunte's conquest of Babylonia.

The judicial procedure in the time of the Dynasty of Ur appears to have been carried out by a *mashkim* (Semitic *rabiṣu*), who is found present in all trials. Men of this class were not, properly speaking, magistrates; according to Pélagaud they played the part of jury, expert, arbitrator, judge and notary, and there were many of them. Before them were decided all kinds of important cases, particularly of sales. Sometimes the *mashkim* appealed to the *Galu-enim-ma*, a semi-official person whose rôle is not clear. Finally, in cases which the *mashkim* was not capable of deciding, professional judges were added, called *Sa-Kud*, of whom there might be from two to four. The decisions of even these latter might be challenged and an appeal lodged against them.

In the period of the Ist Dynasty the administration of Babylon and some of the other large towns (such as Sippar-Amnanu) appears to have been in the hands of the *shakkanakku*, governor. Indeed, the *shakkanakku* of Babylon became such an institution that it is usual to find later kings such as Sargon calling themselves by this title rather than *sharru*, king. During the Dynasty of Ur at least a dozen towns or districts have such an officer, but the number appears to have been reduced as time went on. Most of the towns of Babylonia were under a *rabianu*, mayor. Both *shakkanakku* and *rabianu* could preside over courts, the one in Babylon and the other in the inferior courts of Babylon and the provincial towns.

Justice was maintained by a series of courts with a final appeal to the king. But in Hammurabi's time we have still to make the distinction between a priestly and a civil jurisdiction. Under previous kings the priests had the right of judicial decision, and it is only during the Ist Dynasty that we find civil courts with secular judges in full power. Under Hammurabi's rule both the priestly and civil jurisdiction held good, but the ecclesiastical courts were obviously being ousted, and we can see the transformation at work, the civil judges replacing the priests. The alteration was perhaps due to a change in the character of the kingdom: the king does not now represent himself as a god, like Naram-Sin and Dungi, for instance, but calls himself merely "the favourite the of gods" and their representative. The Sumerian deification of royalty, especially after death, was however continued under the Ist Dynasty, even down to the time of Ammi-zaduga.

There were at least two civil courts prepared to try cases: a lower court, under a *rabianu* in the provincial towns, which disposed of cases in which no appeal was brought, and high court of appeal at Babylon, consisting apparently of the king's judges, over which the *shakkanakku* may have presided. Our knowledge, however, does not allow us to speak of these courts with any certainty. Beginning with the lower court, we may consider it fairly certain that the mayor (*rabianu*) was the magistrate charged with the maintenance of order in provincial towns. One Nannarmanse writes about a field with which Sin-ishmeanni, the *rabianu* of Kish, and Gimil-Marduk, his successor to the office, had been concerned. Ibi-Sin addresses a letter to the *rabianum* and *shibūti* (elders) of Bulum. If robbery were committed within his town, it was the duty of the *rabianu* to arrest the malefactors; if he failed, then he and the town were liable to make good the loss of any property stolen. This is still the usual custom in the east.

The *rabianu* at the time of the Ist Dynasty was president of an assembly of old men or notables, a practice which went on into the Neo-Babylonian period. These elders, whose name is synonymous with witnesses, may have formed the assembly before whom (so the Code of Hammurabi lays down) a man was scourged or a prevaricating judge expelled. Ibi-Sin of Ur addresses a letter to the *rabianu* and *shibūti* of Bulum, which shows that the Semites inherited the court from the Dynasty of Ur. The *shibūti*, who appear in the contracts as official witnesses, are doubtless the same as those mentioned in this court. The addressee of letters addressed by name "Unto X, the Kar-Sippar, and the Judges of Sippar" by Samsu-iluna and Abeshu', was probably the *rabianu* of the town. In a record of a trial of Hammurabi's period we find judgment given by the *rabianu* of Sippar, by name Isharlim, along with the Kar-Sippar. It is uncertain whether this court of Kar-Sippar, the wall of Sippar, is to be kept distinct from the Judges of Sippar, on the grounds that the address quoted above always makes the distinction. We have probably also to reckon with a court of similar or equal powers in the provinces, consisting of the judges, with whom the *rabianu* might sit.

The court of appeal at Babylon appears to have been the next in order for a dissatisfied litigant. The difficulty arises at once in defining this or other courts, as the legal decisions are rather vague in their references to the Judges of Babylon. We know, however, that the high governor of Babylon (*shakkanakku*) could preside over a court, which consisted in one case of six persons, among whom were a judge, a prefect (*sha-tam*), and a *mashkim* (see above), a definite survival from Sumerian times. In another court the governor's council consisted of a *rabianu* and ten others. This, then, was the position of the high governor in law, though, whether he was regularly president of the court of appeal at Babylon we cannot be sure. For instance, in a re-trial of a case about an estate in which a priestess of the sun-god (at Sippar) was concerned, the phrasing used makes it impossible for us to determine much about the court; the case was tried before the judges of Babylon and Sippar, and, except that this clearly indicates a court of appeal, we cannot glean much of the details of it. It must of course be remembered that Babylon had its ordinary district court, inferior to the court of appeal. In a case which was tried at Babylon, the parties

concerned, being dissatisfied with the ordinary tribunal, consisting of four judges and two other members, appealed to the higher court, consisting of five judges of whom four had already appeared in the lower; finally, being still dissatisfied, they appealed to the king himself. This right of personal appeal was maintained to its utmost during the Ist Dynasty. It was a survival of the old personal element of Semitic nomad conditions, the summary procedure of the sheikh, and the king was active in seeing personally that justice was done.

Instances of royal interest in legal matters, appeals and re-trials, are common. The king Abeshu' writes to "Sin-idinnam, the Kar-Sippar, and the Judges of Sippar" about two men whose plaint against an elder brother had been pending for two years in the Sippar court, but they had been unable to obtain redress against him. The king directs that this elder brother should be sent to Babylon with the witnesses "in order that their case may be concluded"; he probably guessed that the real cause of the delay was that the elder brother had probably no case, and had bribed the judges. Bribery, although it can hardly have been as common as it was more recently, did, of course, occur. Hammurabi writes to Sin-idinnam about an alleged case in Dur-gurgurri. A man named Shumman-la-ilu had made a report direct to the king about a bribe; the very man who had taken it, and a witness to the act had been brought before him. The king gave orders that official cognizance should be taken of the matter: "and if bribery (really) have taken place, set there a seal upon the money or upon that which was offered as the bribe, and cause it to be brought to me. Send also the man who took the bribe, and the witness who hath knowledge of these matters, whom Shumman-la-ilu shall point out to thee."

The actual procedure in the courts appears to have been for the parties at law to settle on a day, and then appear in court, be it the local temple or the traditional Gate, where the judges first saw the pleas, the plaintiff pleading first and then his opponent, with the deeds relating to the case in front of them. Witnesses were sworn by the local god and the king, and any tampering with witnesses was penalized by the Code. Hammurabi himself was well aware of the worthlessness of evidence after the witnesses had discussed the case together, and in one of his letters gives explicit orders for the separate despatch of men concerned in a trial: "but when thou shalt send them, thou shalt not send them together, but each man thou shalt send by himself." In a criminal case a man was given six months grace by the Code in order to produce his witnesses.

The judges then pronounced their decision. They might also give orders for direct action, as in the case of the restoration of a dowry, where the judges of Babylon wrote to Mukhaddu (who appears to have been a seer in Samsu-ditana's time) thus: "Concerning the suit of Ilushu-ibishu and Mattatum, we announce (our) judgment to them, according to the law of our lord (the king): Whatever dowry there may be, which Mattatum had given her daughter and had brought into the house of Ilushu-ibishu, we have decided to restore to Mattatum. We will send down a constable . . . with her: let them hand over to Mattatum everything in good condition which they shall find there."

We do not know if judges received any remuneration, but they belonged to the highest class of officials, and if they revoked their own decisions were liable to be publicly deposed.

Records of criminal cases are rare, but one exists in which suspicion of theft has fallen on the servants of a dead man, which has already been mentioned. It appears that one Ibgatum was killed, and after his death, which was not duly notified by these servants to the son and heir, certain of his furniture was found to be missing from the house. The servants were prosecuted, but the judges of Babylon considered that there was no proof of guilt; yet at the same time they agreed to test the defendants on oath and invited them to swear in the Gate of Nungal that first they recognized their omission in not notifying death, and secondly they had stolen nothing. For obvious reasons they declined, and a new trial took place again at Babylon which again failed. The prosecutors then addressed the king direct; one affirms before a god that his father was killed and he was not informed, but he does not venture now to accuse the defendants directly of theft. Had he done so he would have incurred a risk of a breach of the first section of the Hammurabi Code: "if a man accuses another, and has not proved him guilty, the accuser is liable to death."

Unfortunately we do not know how the case ended.

Leaving the administrative and judicial heads and going to the active agents who controlled the state labour, we find two officials coming into prominence both in the Code and in the letters of the period, the *rid ṣabi* and the *ba'iru*. The former is the officer in charge of a levy, for whatever purposes it may be used, and the latter a kind of warrant officer. They obeyed the bidding of the king, to go on his errands when ordered; and they might not, on a maximum penalty of death, send a substitute. The natural inference from this is that cowardice would be the normal reason for shirking the duty in person. Even without this indication we can be certain that both were liable to military service, as the Code lays down the procedure for their ransom if they were taken prisoner; if they could not afford to pay the enemy for their release, the temple of their native town must provide, or, in the last resort, the state. This makes it clear that they received considerable benefits and perquisites from the state, and owed fealty to it. Service abroad might keep them long absent from home, and a son might act in the stead of either, and in such a case was to enjoy the benefice which appears to be their right, except that a third part was deducted for the wife of the absent husband with which she might bring up the children. This benefice or feoff was in land, garden, house, sheep, cattle, and a salary, directly ascribed to the king as benefactor, and normally, if the officer were at home and neglected it, he ran the risk of forfeiting it.

There is, in fact, a letter from Samsu-iluna in existence which appears to relate to the relinquishing of such a benefice. The king writes to Marduk-naṣir and the administrators of the (royal) domain of Imgur-Ishtar about one Ibni-Adad, who is under the authority of Belanum, who held and subsequently relinquished an estate in Imgur-Ishtar: "[Now in place of the tenure] which he has relinquished [another has been granted to him in Dur-Sumu]la-il, tenure of Ibni-Adad, which [he has relinquished]. Give them to Walī, the Elamite, who is under the authority of Belanum, the *Gal-Martu*. Furthermore, write afresh on a tablet the designation of the field, land, and boundaries of the field which you shall give: let me have the old one, send it to me: let a sealed document be delivered to him." Now we fortunately possess the sequel to this letter, the instructions from Marduk-naṣir to Sin-gamil and Ninurta-mushalim about this estate. "A letter has arrived from my lord (the king) that this field is to be given to Walī the Elamite, who is under the authority of Belanum, the *Gal-Martu*. I have sealed (it) and am sending it on to you." The estate of Ibni-Adad is to be given to Walī. "As for the designation of the field, land, and boundaries of the field which you shall give, let me have its ancient (one), and send it to me, that I may (send) it to my lord. Let a sealed document be delivered to him."

It appears that the levy might be called out for military service, or might even be taken locally for repairing temporary damage to the canals of their own city. In the press-gang or levy it was no protection in Hammurabi's time for a man to be on the staff of a patesi, for twice at least did the king write to Sin-idinnam, telling him to arrest, in one case, two men, and, in another, four men who were under the control of a patesi. But the persons of the patesis themselves, although liable to taxes, were in a measure sacrosanct as regards transference against their will to another department. The old religious side of their profession still appears as a reminiscence in one of Hammurabi's letters which mentions a priest of Anunit who is also a patesi of Anunit.

We have little knowledge of the police-system that was in vogue in Hammurabi's time, but certain inferences may be drawn from a letter sent by Etil-pi-Marduk to Shumma-Anum: "Idin-Ishtar, the Chief of Police (*pa-khat sha sab-maṣṣar-a-tim*) hath thus spoken: 'Etirum of the police of my house hath deserted and is (now) living in Dilbat with Shumma-Anum, the shepherd. I have sent to arrest this Eṭirum, but Shumma-Anum, the shepherd, hath not surrendered this Etirum to the man whom I sent to arrest him.'" We cannot say definitely whether the police were under the control of one head or whether each city had its own system, but Idin-Ishtar would hardly have arrested a deserter in Dilbat on his own initiative if there had been a different police control in that city; the correct method in such a case would have been for him to write to the chief of the Dilbat police to arrest his man. If, however, Idin-Ishtar

were supreme chief of police in Babylonia he, might reasonably send an officer direct to Shumma-Anum's house to effect his purpose.

The Code of Hammurabi allows us to speak with no little accuracy of the laws of Babylonia and the penalties attached for their breach. What strikes the reader at first sight is the severity of the punishments, as being contrary to the opinions which the thousands of contracts and letters of this period naturally induce. These, the most human documents which survive, do not necessarily breathe the ferocity involved in their quotations from the ancient laws threatening the dire penalties which will overtake either party who shall break the contracts; they quote, but they do not compel conviction that they are always in earnest.

The fact is most probable that these ancient laws, preserved by a naturally conservative race who adopted them from their Sumerian inventors, were never repealed: the antiquated and severe penalties doubtless put into force in early times, merely represented to the Ist Dynasty the *maximum* penalties which the state could inflict. The Semites of Hammurabi's period were neither modern savages nor Europeans of a couple of centuries ago. It is true that the penalty laid down in a contract of this period from the middle Euphrates (doubtless not far from the neighbourhood of Hit, the bitumen city) is that the delinquent shall have his head smeared with hot tar; it might be as cruel as the pitch-cap once used in Ireland, but it might not be more uncomfortable than tar-and-feathering. The particular penalties inflicted by the Code, which appear to be out of all proportion to the offence, are death by fire for a temple votary who opens a beer-shop or even enters one, death by drowning for a beer-seller for some malpractice in selling beer, and impalement for a wife who procures her husband's death. It must be doubted whether such penalties had not fallen into desuetude by the time Hammurabi set up his Code. Besides these penalties a tablet of the period of Shagarakti-Shuriash shows that imprisonment was a form of punishment.

The Code lays down the death-penalty, in some cases specifying the method, for the following crimes (the number in brackets refers to the section:—(Rape (CXXX). Brigandage, burglary and theft in various forms (IX *sqq.*,

XXI *sq.*; in the case of a governor XXXIV); especially of goods from palace or temple, including the receiver (VI), and (in the case of a man who is too poor to pay compensation) of animals or a boat belonging to temple or palace (in this case it may be compounded by richer folk, VIII). A thief stealing from a burning house was to be burnt (XXV). Stealing the son of a man (*amelu*, XIV). Adultery with a daughter-in-law (the man to be drowned, CLV). Incest with a mother (both to be burned, CLVII). Adultery of a married woman (CXXIX) (both to be drowned, unless the husband save his wife, or the king his servant: cf. also CXXXIII). A flagrantly careless and uneconomical wife (to be drowned, CXLIII). A wife causing her husband's death, in order to marry another (to be impaled or crucified, CLIII). A *Sal-Me*-priestess, or *Nin-An*-priestess, not living in a cloister, opening a wine-shop, or even entering one (to be burnt, CX). Harbouring (or helping to escape) runaway slaves of the palace, or of a *mushkinu* (XV *sq.*, XIX). In the old Sumerian law it is laid down that if a man harbour a slave "during a month, he shall give slave for slave, or failing that, twenty-five silver shekels." Cowardice in the face of the enemy and neglect of duty by certain officials (XXVI, XXXIII). A builder who builds a house which falls and causes the death of the owner (CCXXIX); or in the case of its killing the son of the owner, the builder's son is to be put to death (CCXXX). If the son of a *mushkinu* on whom a distraint has been levied, be taken in distraint and die from hunger or blows in the house of the distrainer, the son of the distrainer is to be put to death (CXVI). If a man strike the daughter of an *amelu* when she is pregnant, so that she die, his daughter shall be put to death (CCX). Malpractices in selling beer (the proprietress of the tavern to be drowned, CVIII). Harbouring outlaws in a tavern (the proprietress liable, CIX). Bringing a false accusation, sorcery, etc. (I *sq.*). Wrongfully accusing witnesses of perjury in a capital charge (III). Purchase, or receipt as deposit, of goods belonging to a man from either his son or his slave without witnesses or bonds (VII). Failing to bring witnesses in an accusation of theft (XI).

Trial by ordeal existed, when a man was accused of sorcery, or a woman accused of adultery without sufficient evidence (II, CXXXII). In both cases the accused were to leap into the river, their innocence being established if they came out alive. Many of the minor penalties are based on the principle of the *lex talionis*; if a man strikes his father, his hands are to be cut off (CXCV); if he knock out the eye of an *amelu* or break his limb, the same shall be done to him (CXCVI *sq.*); the tooth of an equal demands the same retaliation (CC). Cutting out the tongue putting out an eye, or cutting off a nurse's breasts come under the same head (CXCII *sq.*). A man might be scourged with sixty strokes of an ox-hide whip for striking a superior (CCII); he might be banished from the city for incest with a daughter (CLIV). False accusation of adultery against a wife or *Nin-An*-priestess was punished by marking or branding the forehead of the accuser (CXXVII).

The law laid down the fees for surgeons, veterinary surgeons, the wages of builders, brickmakers, tailors, stonemasons, carpenters, boatmen, ox-drivers, herdsmen, shepherds, or labourers, and the hire of oxen and asses (CCXXVIII *sq*). The unfortunate surgeon who made a mistake in his treatment was liable to severe penalties [loss of his hand—ed.].

Fines were a common form of penalty. Restitution threefold was exacted for cheating a principal (CVI), five-fold for loss or theft by carrier (CXII), six-fold for defrauding an agent (CVII), ten-fold for theft from temple or palace by a *mushkinu* (the lower orders), and thirty-fold by an *amelu* or gentleman (VIII).

With this mention of the social castes in Babylonia it is well to turn aside to see how sharply divided the aristocracy, the middle classes, and the slaves were.

Throughout Babylonia by Hammurabi's time the population, owing to various invasions, was a mixed one. In the earlier times the Elamites had descended on southern Babylonia, only to be subjugated by the Sumerians who were of an entirely different race. These and the Semites represent the three chief types. There must also have been some small infiltration of Kassites and possibly even of Hittites, although perhaps this is anticipating. At all events, the Code makes provision for three orders or classes of individuals—the *amelu* or noble, the *mushkinu* or plebeian, and the slave. The *amelu* formed the predominant class, and Dr Johns thought that they came from the conquering race of Semites, the word in the Tell el-Amarna letters (*c.* 1400) being still used as an official title. The *mushkinu* is more difficult; it is a word which ultimately reached Europe, the French being *mesquin*. But in southern Arabia the corresponding word means, according to Snouck Hurgronje, those who are neither descendants of the Prophet, nor nobles related to the family of the Prophet, nor secular nobles. They are labourers, workmen, merchants, school-masters, courtiers, beggars; they have not the right to carry arms; no organization; they are entirely under the dominion of the nobles. According to the Hammurabi Code the *mushkinu* is inferior to the *amelu* but better off than the slave.

In these two classes, it is curious to see that the punishments were more severe on the *amelu* "patrician" than on the *mushkinu*; difference of race or, perhaps, *noblesse oblige* may have been at the base of it. The *mushkinu* was punished in a less primitive and ferocious manner than the *amelu*, frequently being simply fined; where the noble was dealt with eye for eye and tooth for tooth, the plebeian was merely mulcted in damages. This certainly suggests that a very sharp line was drawn between the two classes, indicating a difference of race. The *mushkinu* was in no wise a slave; he might hold slaves and goods, he seems to have been liable to conscription, and in Sippar he had his own particular quarter, the *Mushkinutu*. But he differed from the *amelu* in that he was not of the governing classes. *Amelu*, in fact, came in time to be used as meaning simply a respectable person.

Among the higher professional ranks we must reckon the learned pursuits of scribe, physician, and priest, and the upper government. The son of Ur-negun, a patesi of Umma, follows the profession of letters; so does a son of Ne . . . an, patesi of Cuthah, about the end of the IIIrd Dynasty of Ur. Even the son of Gudea himself, Lugal-shi-dup, and Lugal-ushumgal, the patesi of Lagash, call themselves scribes. The office was not a priestly one; it was a profession by itself, and when a record of a contract was necessary, the scribe wrote the whole of the document himself, including witnesses' names. Doubtless the lower orders of the profession sat about the streets as they do to this day, with style and blank clay tablet or lump of moist clay, ready to write letters home for the ignorant and homesick sojourners.

Women were not debarred from carrying on professions or trades, and even that of scribe is not omitted in their various callings. They might act as witnesses to a deed or rent property. As a rule, however, we usually find women attached to the temple, and as kings' daughters certainly as early as the Ist Dynasty down to the time of Nabonidus could be priestesses, we may take it that the profession ranked very high in Babylonian society. Social custom allowed women great independence; even as early as the Ist Dynasty Babylonian law recognized in the free woman a broad capacity in legal matters. We are not certain whether marriage altered her status. The husband and wife together would make contracts, for example, in the purchase of a slave; and in eleven out of sixteen purchase-tablets from Sippar, of the Ist Dynasty (published by G. S. Duncan, 1914), women are buyers, and in six they are sellers. Particularly noticeable is the freedom with which rich priestesses conduct their own monetary affairs; their capacity for business, as will be discussed further on, appears to have been great.

The institution of slavery dates back to the earliest time. Even on the stele of Manishtusu (c. 2800 B.C.) we find a slave-girl who is worth thirteen shekels, while nine other slaves, male and female, are reckoned for one-third of a mana each. (A mina or mana weighed approximately 500 grams; it contained 60 shekels and was $\frac{1}{60}$ of a talent.) According to the Code (XVI–XVIII), it is clear that the slave was personally the property of his owner; he might not run away (which he did occasionally), it was illegal to harbour him if a fugitive, and a reward was fixed for his recapture. A slave was subject to the "levy" for forced labour (XVI); he might be sold, or pledged for debt (CXVIII), and in theory his property belonged to his owner (cf. CLXXVI), but on the other hand, it was his master's duty to pay the doctor's fees if he were sick (CCXIX, CCXXIII). There appears to have been less of the stigma attaching to a slave than we are accustomed to associate with the word, for he might marry a free woman, and in that case the children were free (CLXXV *sq.*); the slave and his free wife might acquire property, half of which would fall to the wife and children after his death (CLXXVI). In just the same way children borne by a slave-woman to her master were free after his death, and the mother after the death of her master would go free (CLXX *sq*). The slave was marked (CCXXVI *sq.*), but how we are not able to say for certain; the probability is that it was by branding or tattooing. In later times the slave wore a little clay docket attached to his person like a soldier's identification disk.

Captives taken in battle became slaves. For instance, in the time of the Kassite king Burna-Buriash, a man called "Elamite" is said to be worth ten shekels of gold; on a tablet of the time of Abeshu' a slave-girl from Subartu (north of Babylonia) is mentioned; in Ammi-ditana's time a slave-girl named Ina-Eulmashbanat, from the town of Ursum (presumably a foreign place), was worth actually fifty-one shekels of silver. There was a wide variation in the value of a slave; in Ammi-ditana's reign a man-slave reached the high price of ninety shekels, while we find a woman fetching so little as $3\frac{5}{6}$ shekels under Samsu-iluna.

A significant law enacts that any *amelu*, "patrician," who steals the babe of another *amelu* shall be put to death (XIV). Native Babylonians might be made slaves if they transgressed certain laws. A worthless wife became a slave in her own house if her husband took another wife (CXLI), or an adopted son might be sold if he repudiated his parents. Again, a maid whom a *Sal-Me* gave to her husband in order that she might bear him children, might be sold into slavery if she did not have offspring; and, if children were born by her and she arrogated to herself equal status with her mistress, she rendered herself liable to be reckoned again among the maidservants (CXLVI *sq.*).

Slaves, as ever, ran away from their masters. A certain Warad-Bunene, in the time of Ammi-ditana, whose master had sold him into the land of Ashnunnak for $1\frac{1}{2}$ manas of silver, had served there for five years, and then ran away home to Babylon. Here two officials, Sin-mushallim and Marduk-lamassashu, found him and, on the grounds that he had ceased to be a slave, made him liable for military service. But Warad-Bunene, like many another and more modern inhabitant of Babylon, declared that he would not serve as a soldier, as he was going to carry on the service of his father's house. This was allowed him; and so long as he should live, he was permitted to carry on the business of his father's house with his brothers unchallenged. Ingenuous indeed is the promise made by a slave in the presence of witnesses in the second year

of Ibi-Sin that he will not escape. On the other hand, we find gifts made to slaves by royalty: "Kukka-nasher, the mighty vizier, the vizier of Elam, lord of Shimash . . . son of the sister of Silkhakha, has shown favour to Shukshu and Makhishi of the town of Khumman, slaves," and presented them with a piece of land.

Leaving the subject of the different social castes we can now treat of the ordinary life of the individual.

PRIVATE LIFE

Marriage was for life, and a contract was an essential; the Code is explicit on the point that a woman is not a wife unless she has her bonds (*rikistu*) or marriage lines (CXXVIII). There is no proof of any ceremony other than the legal contract before witnesses: the tablet which some years ago was thought to contain a wedding-service is merely a practice tablet with quotations first from the Gilgamesh epic, where Istar proposes marriage, and afterwards from an incantation tablet against demons. Nor do we know whether love-matches were common, whether the oriental "middling-gossip" aided the lovers as a go-between, or how much the young couple saw of each other before the ceremony.

The suitor came to the father of his intended bride bearing a bridge-gift (*terkhatu*), the relic of the old purchase-money. The conventional amount, to be returned on divorce, was one mana of silver for a patrician (CXXXIX) and one-third of that amount for a plebeian (CXL); actually ten shekels was paid in one case in Hammurabi's time. The father of the bride was expected to give her a dowry, and she would bring a trousseau with her. Dr Johns thinks that men married while they were young and living at home; certainly, the Code comtemplates the bride being brought to live in the father-in-law's house. The curious passage in the Legend of Gilgamesh, where the hero taunts Ishtar with her past loves, seems to have some bearing on this:

Thou didst love Ishullanu, gardener he of thy sire,
Faithfully bringing thee blossoms (?) (and) each day
    he brightened thy platter,
So that thine eye fell upon him, and (straightway
    thus) didst address him:
"Ishullanu of mine, come, let us (now) taste of thy
    manhood."

So she goes on: and Ishullanu answers her:

> "Bethink thee, what dost thou ask me,
> Ne'er have I eaten of aught (unless) my mother hath
>   baked it,
> What I should eat would be bread of shame and
>   adultery."

There is, it must be admitted, a difficulty in translating the crabbed line, the last but one.

The law is definite in the case of breach of promise, when the suitor has already made advances to the family of his prospective bride. If he changes his mind about the lady (having looked upon another woman, as the Code says, CLIX), her father is entitled to retain the purchase-price which the suitor has already paid. If, on the other hand, the lady's father, after the negotiations are complete, refuses to give the suitor his daughter, he must pay him double the amount which he has received (CLX). Again, if everything is ready for the marriage, but the father of the bride hearkens to slander against the bridgegroom and repudiates the bargain, he is to pay back twice the amount as before, "and the slanderer shall not have his wife" (CLXI).

It was usual to have only one chief wife, but additions were frequently made to the harem. In the Epic of Gilgamesh the mourner is addressed as one who is so fearful of the dead that he dare not make himself conspicuous.

Thou darest not set shoe to thy foot, not let echo the earth (with thy footfall), Nor kiss the wife whom thou lovest, nor beat the wife whom thou hatest.

In the case of a lasting illness the man might marry another wife, but he would have to provide for the first one (CXLVIII). Such a second wife held full legal position, and her children were legitimate. But he might take a concubine or second wife (*Shu-Ge-tum*) with inferior status. A man in Sin-muballit's time took two sisters to wife at once, Taram-Saggil and Iltani, but there was no doubt about the precedence. It is laid down in the deed of marriage that Iltani is to wash the feet of her sister, and to carry her stool to the temple of her god. There is a penalty against the unfortunate Iltani if she should rebel against her inferior status, for if she say to Taram-Saggil "thou art not my sister," or if she should say to her husband "thou art not my husband," they shall throw her into the river. In another case, one Akhuni

pays a *terkhatu* to the father of a girl named Ishtar-ummi; he already has a wife Kadimatum, and if the new wife should annoy Kadimatum, the latter may sell her into slavery.

The position of the slave-girl as concubine was entirely different from that of the wife. She was not a wife, and her children were not free, unless the father declared them to be legitimate, in which case they were on the same footing as the legitimate children with right to inherit. For instance Mar-irṣitim took Atkal-ana-belti, a slave-girl, to wife. If she should ever be unfaithful, a mark was to be set on her and she was to be sold. Whatever she possessed at the time of the contract and whatever she should possess future, belonged to Mar-irṣitim. Again, in Hammurabi's time, a girl, Shamash-nuri, was bought from her father by a man Bunene-abi and a woman Belissunu to be a wife to Bunene-abi and a slave to Belissunu. If she should say to the latter "thou art not my mistress" she was to be marked and sold. In another case (in Sumu-la-ilum's time) the daughter of a woman appears to have been bound in some way to her mother. "Ana-Aya-uzni is the daughter of Salimatum. Salimatum has cleansed her, and has given her to Belshunu, son of Nemelum, in marriage. Ana-Aya-uzni is free: no one can make any claim against Ana-Aya-uzni." The rite or ceremony of "cleansing" implies apparently that all rights over the girl have been given up; it is the usual phrase for freeing a slave-girl. One Dushuptum ("honey-sweet") manumits her maid, "her forehead she has cleansed." A woman dedicates her daughter to the goddess Ishtar: "Amat-Ishtar is the daughter of Kunutum; Kunutum, her mother, has given her to Ishtar: she is clean," that is, is clear of obligations.

According to the Code divorce was a simple matter for the man, but far more serious and difficult for the wife. A man might repudiate his wife, nominally on payment of a douceur; but in a stipulated case in Hammurabi's time, if the husband repudiated his wife, he was compelled to leave her the house and go out empty-handed. The woman was in an entirely different position. Regarded as a possession and a chattel, for her to repudiate her husband, presumably by adultery, rendered her liable to death by drowning, or by being thrown from a tower. The husband, however, might divorce her for folly and carelessness in the household management; he merely said "I divorce her" and need pay nothing. Should he not do so, doubtless, of course, after the case had been legally proved, the foolish wife would, if the man took another wife, be in the position of a slave in the house (CXLI). Ill-treatment on the part of the husband resulting in dislike and hatred for him on the part of the wife, was sufficient grounds for a woman to take her dowry back and return to her father's house, always presuming that her conduct had been above reproach (CXLII). If, however, it were found that she had been indiscreet in the past and (presumably) had alleged her husband's treatment as a cause for her leaving him, she incurred the risk of drowning (CXLIII). At the same time, when Enlil-idzu, the priest, married Ama-sukkal, the penalties for divorce on her side were not heavy. "Enlil-idzu, priest of Enlil, son of Lugal-azida, has taken Ama-sukkal, daughter of Ninurta-mansi to wife. Nineteen shekels of silver Ama-sukkal has brought to Enlil-idzu, as his wife. In future, if Enlil-idzu says to Ama-sukkal, his wife, 'Thou art not my wife' he shall return the nineteen shekels of silver and in addition, pay half a mana as her divorce-money. If Ama-sukkal says to Enlil-idzu, her husband, 'Thou art not my husband' she shall forfeit the nineteen shekels of silver and in addition, pay half a mana of silver. In mutual agreement they have both sworn by the name of the king."

A side-light is thrown on the slave-raiding razzias—they are nothing more—of enemy neighbours. If a woman's husband was captured by a foe, she was bound to remain faithful to her absent husband if he had provided for her; and if she went off with another man she was treated as an adulteress and incurred death (CXXXIII). But if the maintenance left behind for her by her husband at the wars was not enough, she was allowed to marry again if he was captured, and she might bear the new husband children (CXXXIV *sq.*). If however the prisoner escaped from the hands of the enemy, and returned, the woman was obliged to return to him, although the children of her new family remained with their rightful father (CXXXV). As a concrete instance we may cite the following divorce. In the time of Sin-muballiṭ, Shamash-rabi, gives his wife a bill of divorcement: "Shamash-rabi has divorced Naramtum . . .

she has received back her dowry. If any one marries Naramtum, Shamash-rabi will raise no claim."

The Code punished adultery with drowning, but it had to be flagrant and not merely suspected (CXXIX, CXXXI). The private contracts of marriage also indicate death by drowning for adultery, but sometimes, as an alternative, declare that the woman shall be thrown from a high tower. But a husband might forgive his wife on this count, or the king himself intervene to save the adulterer who was his servant (CXXIX). Section CXXXII of the Code provides, as we have already seen, an ancient ordeal for a woman suspected of adultery.

The rights of a father, and in a less degree, of a mother over the children, appear to be despotic. A man could treat his child like a slave as a chattel to be pledged for debts, to work off the debt for three years, but in this he had the same rights even over a wife (CXVII). Daughters were at their father's disposal for marriage, and he was expected, though not bound, to provide them with a dowry: he might dedicate them to a temple, also with a dowry, which bears the vivid suggestion that they were married to the god (CLXXVIII *sqq.*). In the old Sumerian code the father had a perfect right to disinherit his son with the words "Thou art not my son." Hammurabi limited this absolute power, making a legal process necessary with good reasons for the act (CLXVIII). In the old laws a child who repudiated his father met with stern treatment, which degraded him to the status of a slave, and he might also be branded. The mother in early times held much the same rights as the father: her undutiful son was branded and expelled from house and city, although he was not sold as a slave. In the older laws she could thus disinherit her son, a right for which the Code of Hammurabi gives no authority.

Children were frequently adopted into Babylonian families, and the reason appears often to be that the parents, having married off their own children, feared to have none to look after them in their old age. The relationship was the same as that of a son born in matrimony; the deed expressly stated the responsibilities of the new son and the inheritance he might expect. For an adopted child to repudiate his new parents was regarded as unspeakably base, and he could be sold into slavery. This fear of destitution in old age is apparent in a wedding contract of the time of Zabum, where a mother, doubtless in this case a widow, gives her daughter in marriage in a marriage-deed. "Innabatum hath given Akhkhu-ayabi her daughter, in marriage to Zukaliya. If Zukaliya leaves her, he will pay her one mana of silver; if Akhkhu-ayabi takes a dislike to him, they shall throw her from a tower. So long as Innabatum lives, Akhkhu-ayabi shall support her, (but) after the death of Innabatum no one shall have any claim on Akhkhu-ayabi." Indeed when a woman grew old she would anticipate her bequests to her children in return for maintenance. In the reign of Bur-Sin (of Isin) Nin-me-dugga bequeaths a house and maid to her daughter Nin-dingir-azag-mu, in return for which, during the mother's lifetime, the daughter was to give her mother $\frac{1}{2}$ gur, 5 ka of food yearly (gur = 300 ka; later 180 ka).

After the death of a father a division of property among the children (and the widow) followed. The sons inherited equally, and there was no right of primogeniture as in Israel, although a father might bequeath a special legacy to a favourite (CLXV). The daughter who had already a dowry is excluded from a share in the inheritance; otherwise her brothers portioned her off (CLXXXIII sq.). There are special clauses about daughters who have become priestesses (CLXXVIII sqq.). The widow inherited the same share of the property as each of the children, as well as her original marriage portion; she had the right to stay on in the home until she died, being thus head of the family. If, however, she wished to marry again, she might choose for herself without having to be given in marriage, and she could take with her her original dowry; but she must leave behind any settlement from her husband. There was a lien even on her dowry, because if she bore children to her new husband, they and her former children shared it equally after her death (CLXXII sq.). The Code is elaborate in regard to the inheritance of children by different wives, concubines and maidservants.

If a man's wife died childless, the husband was bound to return to her family the dowry she had brought with her, but he could deduct the value of the terkhatu which he had paid to her father, if it had not already been returned to him as was due (CLXIII sq.).

The business of selling a piece of property was conducted on definite and traditional lines. The clay tablet of the contract was written out by the scribe on an ancient model, constantly in Sumerian or, at any rate, full of Sumerian words, which gradually dropped out in the time of the Ist Dynasty, although the usage can be traced down to the time of the Kassites. The transaction was witnessed by several people, male or female, whose names were attached by the scribe, and the sealings were made by rolling on the clay the carven stone cylinders possessed by all who could afford them. The contracting parties would swear by the local gods and the king by name, that no claim would be made either by themselves or their heirs against the new purchaser in regard to the property. For instance, at Sippar, in Sumu-abum's time, Shamash and the king are invoked, at Dilbat it is Urash and the king. After the time of the Ist Dynasty of Babylon the practice of recording a formal oath began to die out and various devices were used as a substitute, for example, the impression of finger-nails or seals, and above all the pronunciation of an additional malediction or benediction. In Kassite times at Nippur the gods invoked in addition to the king were Enlil, Ninurta and Nusku.

Babylonian law distinguished between real and personal property. If in certain circumstances an adopted child is disinherited the Code allows him a third of the share of a son in the father's goods, but no share in the fields, gardens, or house (CXCI). Pasture-land, on the other hand, as Dr Johns pointed out, was not owned, and if this applies to desert land, after the spring rains, which is the usual grazing ground for the cattle near villages, this is explicable. Grazing land represents common land probably, and Dr Johns' suggestion that to have brought it under cultivation was originally enough to establish a title to it is probably the correct one. Land was not uncommonly let out on the metayer system, the landlord providing draught cattle and seed, and the harvest obtained by someone else's labour paying his share of the profit (XLIII sq., CCLIII). But fields might also be let at a fixed rent, usually payable in kind; the tenancy was generally for three years (XLIV). Houses were commonly leased on a yearly tenancy, the average rent having been calculated to be one shekel yearly. The cost of repairs fell on the tenant; he usually paid down some part of the rent as earnest-money, and until this was done he was not allowed to make alterations.

The custom of giving a *bakshish* in addition to the arranged price was in vogue even from earlier times. In the Semitic document of Manishtusu (*c.* 2800 B.C.) not only is a price paid, but a present is given to the seller; in a contract of Abeshu's time, one-sixth of a shekel is thrown in as *sibika*, or additional *bakshish*, to the proper price of six shekels for a slave.

Loans, as is natural in a country where the population is largely agricultural and coined money does not exist, are frequently in kind to be repaid in kind. The period at which expenses were highest was of course the harvest when labour was dear and very often difficult to obtain; and adventurous spirits from neighbouring countries, like the Kassites, would come in for work on the harvest, just as well-paid excavations on ancient mounds or modern railways will draw them. It is common to find loans made, especially by the temples, in anticipation of the harvest, either for labour in sowing and particularly in reaping. The date for the return of the money is constantly given as the day of the harvest. The harvest was given as an excuse for absence or delay; Hammurabi complains to Sin-idinnam that he has already written to him about sending one Sheb-Sin, a scribe of the merchants, whose duties appear to have been those of a revenue-collector, but that he had not appeared. "Thou dost reply 'The scribes of the merchants say "Since it is now the time of harvest, we will come after the harvest is over."'' After this fashion spake they unto thee, and thou didst write (of it). Behold, the harvest is now over."

Men constantly went into partnership, especially when they were speculating in corn-sowing. For instance, six people join in renting a field near the village of Tukhamu amid *khilbi* (wood?) and *ṣiri* (desert) to sow it with corn and share the results after the harvest. When the partnership terminated it was usual to go to the temple, particularly the door of the temple, to complete the division of assets.

From this rapid survey of the government and the laws we may turn to the literature and religion.

RELIGIOUS INSTITUTIONS

It need hardly be said that every town of any eminence had a temple to its tutelary or patron deity. In Babylonia, during the Ist Dynasty of Babylon, with the rise of the city of Hammurabi the power of Marduk, his great god, was correspondingly promoted until he attained a position in the pantheon from which only Ashur thrust him. But, although Hammurabi might consider him as peculiarly his patron god, the popular view of the local powers of the different gods was far too strong to allow Marduk the hegemony over the pantheon. However devoutly Marduk might be worshipped in his temple of E-sagil in Babylon, in Larsa or Sippar it would be the sun-god Shamash in his own temple E-Babbara, and in Erech the mother-goddess Innini, or Ishtar, in her shrine E-anna. The moon-god Nannar had his temple E-gishshir-gal in Ur, Enlil his temple E-kur in Nippur, Nabū his temple E-zida in Borsippa; there was no end to them.

But although each city recognized its own patron god, it was by no means so exclusive as to eliminate the worship of other gods within its precincts. In this the Babylonians were catholic and open minded: they recognized the existcnce of an Olympus made up of many deities, the result doubtless of a growth which had been going on for hundreds of years, an amalgamation of different local tribal gods. In Lagash, the city protected by Ningirsu, long before our period Eannatum had built a temple E-anna to Innini, which was burnt in a raid by the troops of Umma in the time of Urkagina. In Babylon where Marduk was supreme, was a temple to Adad called E-namkhe; in Sippar, the city sacred to the sun, was E-ulmash to Anunit. It was open to any ruler to found temples to gods other than the special guardian gods in any city, and equally open to anyone to build a private chapel of his own. In the time of Sumu-ilum a certain Nur-ilishu, son of Enlil-nada, built a temple to his god Lugal and goddess Shullat (neither of them well known), and gave the land for that purpose. He installed Puzur-Shamash as priest, and signed a deed promising not to raise any claim against the priests in future.

The gods of the old Sumerian Olympus, such as could be easily identified by the Semites with their own deities, were retained under Semitic names: Babbar, Nannar, Innini and Enlil become Shamash, Sin, Ishtar, and Bel. The sun-god Shamash (sometimes in the form Samsu in names, as in Arabia), worshipped at Sippar and Larsa, is as much a Semitic god as Babbar was Sumerian; the moon-god Sin, worshipped at Harran and called Sahar in Syria, can easily take the place of Nannar or Enzu at Ur. Innini is the mother-goddess and as such is the same as Ishtar, whose name is repeated in the west as Astarte (the biblical Ashtōreth), and in Arabia as a male Athtar. She is to be found in various forms in the near east, frequently as a naked female figure offering her breasts; there is a large sculpture of her at Carchemish, full face in relief, and probably the broken statue of a goddess dedicated by Assur-bel-kala, which was found at Nineveh and is now in the British Museum, was the same. This last must undoubtedly have marked the position of E-mashmash, the temple of Ishtar; it was found by Hormuzd Rassam at Kuyunjik behind Sennacherib's palace, near where his inscriptions would lead us to locate it. The name of Bel, "the lord," represents the familiar ba'al of the western Semites, and the worship of this specific god in the form Bel, Bil, Bēlos, appears to have spread from Babylon into the western lands, rather than eastwards to Mesopotamia from Syria.

11. THE OFFER OF A FREE HOME: A CASE STUDY IN THE FAMILY LAW OF THE POOR

HERMA H. KAY

Reprinted from Laura Nader, editor, Law in Culture and Society (*Chicago: Aldine, 1969*). *Copyright © 1969 by the Wenner-Gren Foundation for Anthropological Research, Inc. Herma H. Kay did her undergraduate work at Southern Methodist University in Dallas, Texas, where she majored in English. She earned her J.D. degree at the University of Chicago Law School, and has been a member of the law faculty at the University of California at Berkeley since 1960. Her specialties include family law, conflict of laws, the ethnography of law, and women's rights. She is the author of many articles in legal periodicals and has contributed to the* American Anthropologist's *special issue on the ethnography of law (Volume 67, 1965).*

■ We generally think of laws as enacted by legislators or judicial bodies, or as decrees of heads of state, and as enforced directly by police or in the shadows behind the tax collector, the judge, and the signs proclaiming "No smoking" or "No trespassing." However, one of the consequences of social evolution is that modern industrial nations have become so complex that it is virtually impossible even for the law-givers themselves to keep abreast of all the society's problems. The Code of Hammurabi contained 282 laws. The laws of nations like the United States and England number in the uncounted thousands.

Part of this complexity ensues from the fact that more laws affecting a United States citizen derive from regulatory agencies than from the legislatures charged with the law-making task. *The Federal Register*, in which the regulations of national agencies are published, is larger than the book of statutes enacted by Congress. There are now more than 50 federal regulatory agencies, of which the most important are those dealing with trade, communications, interstate commerce, aviation, securities exchanges, electric and other sources of energy, and labor. The National Labor Relations Board, for instance, decides more cases each year than all Federal Courts of Appeal combined. In addition, there are the laws of the states and the actions of their regulatory agencies, though more and more of their activities are controlled by the Federal government each year.

The following selection illustrates this entire process well. Herma Kay describes in microcosm the ways in which the daily life of ordinary citizens in this country is affected by the proliferation of controls. These controls affect us from the moment we are awakened by an electric alarm clock (whose energy source is regulated by national and regional agencies) or an automatic radio (whose content is supposedly monitored by a national agency). We eat breakfast foods whose content is supervised by Federal and state agencies; we go to work by bus, car, or train, each of which operates on license from one or another agency; we use the telephone several times at rates that are agency-controlled; we buy alcoholic beverages on the way home at prices fixed by several agencies; we settle down at home to watch television (regulated by all sorts of codes) and finish our evening to the playing of the national anthem, with prayerful thanks that we are free men and not the subjects of one of "those" totalitarian countries grimly portrayed on the late evening news.

The following case study bears on several aspects of our legal adaptation to the requirements of an industrial strategy. The study deals with the circumstances under which the California State Department of Social Welfare can disburse Federally provided funds under the program known as Aid to Families with Dependent Children (AFDC). Administrative rulings in this matter do not specify illegal acts or penalties; they deal, rather, with the kind of question that in traditional societies is handled by local community and kin institutions: the care of the indigent and the support of their children. This shift, I suggest, is an adaptive response to the complexities of a modern industrial society, specifically to high rates of geographical mobility and dispersal of kinsmen. Kay's work also suggests a further problem: the allocation of resources among the people in a complex society. The establishment of nation-states is accompanied by an unequal distribution of resources, and social adjustments—of which AFDC is one example—that must also be made to this aspect of the sociotechnological habitat. The relationships between the individual and the corporate political bodies of a modern industrialized society are a far cry from the intimate local groups and relationships of hunter-gatherers and horticulturists.

Formal law involves the establishment of a judicial bureaucracy and specialized legal personnel, like lawyers. In this selection, we will see that still other specialized but nonlegal personnel, such as social workers are being added to this legal machinery. This expansion of the bureaucratic machinery is related to the proliferation of regulations that specify neither illegal acts nor penalties but deal increasingly with every aspect of everyday life.

It is interesting to note that the rules adopted by this agency were abandoned—as was the entire problem studied by Kay—because they were found to be unworkable and because the problem was eventually defined as outside the competence of the agency in question. This is an example of the process of trial and error by which every society arrives at a legal system that fits the conditions under which it lives. Here in microcosm is an example of an inegalitarian system trying with difficulty to solve some of its most basic man-made problems.

Several aspects of administrative legal change in contemporary society are discussed in "Law and Social Change," by Yehezkel Dror (*Tulane Law Review*, 33 [1959]: 787-802). An excellent and timely example of current concerns with formal law is provided by the first "state of the judiciary message" address by Supreme Court Chief Justice Warren E. Burger on August 10, 1970. A very well written account of the ways in which law is changed by judicial ruling in the United States is *Gideon's Trumpet*, by Anthony Lewis (New York: Vintage Books, 1966). An interesting discussion of the relationships among ideological, social, and legal change will be found in *Social Action and Legal Change: Revolution Within the Juvenile Court*, by Edwin M. Lemert (Chicago: Aldine, 1970). ■

ANTHROPOLOGISTS INTERESTED in the study of tribal law have thus far tended to concentrate on the "trouble case" decided by a court, moot, or other judicial group. They have used the "trouble case" both as a field-work tool for the collection of data and as an analytical instrument for probing the relationship between a people's law ways and their generalized culture. As the chief model for such studies, the Western judge may not provide an image that is flexible enough to fit the tribal pattern. The judge in Western political systems is commonly a figure in a three-part governmental structure: the judicial, the executive, and the legislative. That observation is important to this paper because Western judges typically are not charged with policy-making functions. In deciding specific cases, judges of course "make law" and occasionally even initiate sweeping new policies; but they are not given responsibility for governing in this fashion. In some tribal societies, however, and particularly at the village level, the political head of the society is also one of its judges. In the analysis of the law ways of such a society, the Western administrative agency may be more useful than the Western court as a model for anthropologists.

It is the purpose of this paper to describe the promulgation of a rule by an administrative agency, the evaluation of the workings of that rule through cases heard and settled within the agency, and the ultimate withdrawal of the rule partly as a result of the experience developed through the hearing process. The same point could have been made using any rule issued by an agency and then tested through case appeals. The particular illustration chosen for treatment here, however, has broader significance: the rule to be described was finally withdrawn, partly because the agency believed itself to be an inappropriate forum for the resolution of the problem it had raised. Ultimately the question is posed whether any conflict-resolving agency in the society, including the courts, could have satisfactorily accommodated the conflicting values found to exist in these particular cases. This question, too, may be relevant to anthropologists, for it suggests, first, that the choice among available remedy agents made by persons with grievances may depend in part on how broadly a particular remedy agent conceives its own functions and powers, and, second, that certain conflicts cannot be entirely resolved within the existing social system. It goes without saying that these indissoluble problems will probably be different for different societies and that much could perhaps be learned about a given society by asking which conflicts it has been unable to resolve.

The administrative agency discussed in this paper is the California State Department of Social Welfare, which, among its other duties, is charged with supervising the Federal Social Security programs in California. The particular program under discussion is one of the categorical aid programs administered under the Social Security Act and called Aid to Families with Dependent Children (AFDC); the nature of the rule that was promulgated by the Department as part of the AFDC program will become apparent from the material that follows.

BACKGROUND: STRUCTURE OF THE AFDC PROGRAM AND THE FAIR HEARING APPEALS

The Federal Social Security Act of 1935 authorized an appropriation of $24,750,000 to be used for payments to the states equal to one-third of the sums expended by them for Aid to Dependent Children in Their Own Homes. The program can be traced to the White House Conference of 1909 called by President Theodore Roosevelt, at which Rabbi Emil G. Hirsch suggested that public moneys be made available to mothers of dependent children so that the children could be supported at home rather than in institutions. Although the idea did not gain immediate acceptance on the federal level, the individual states took it up. In 1911 Illinois enacted the first mothers' aid law; by the end of 1913 twenty states had passed similar laws, and by 1936 only two states lacked such provisions. The statutes were in general broadly phrased; but it is reported that in practice the aid was extended mainly to widows and their children.

The federal act followed the now familiar technique of the grants in aid. The federal government provided part of the funding to states that met the approval of the Social Security Board, the federal administering agency. State plans could not be approved for matching funds unless certain conditions were met, including the provision that the state must "provide for granting to any individual, whose claim with respect to aid to a dependent child is denied, an opportunity for a fair hearing before such State agency."

In California, the AFDC program is administered through the County Departments of Public Welfare under the supervision of the State Department of Social Welfare. Applicants seeking to establish their eligibility to receive aid under the program must first apply to the county departments. If the county either declares the applicant ineligible to receive aid or discontinues aid previously granted because of a discovered fact establishing that eligibility is no longer being maintained, the applicant may ask for a "fair hearing" before the state agency. According to Dr. Jacobus tenBroek, then Chairman of the State Social Welfare Board, in testimony before a Senate investigating committee, the procedure for obtaining a hearing is quite simple: "All they [the recipients] have to do to appeal is to make this [their dissatisfaction with the county decision] known to the county or to the State department and this can be done very informally and is generally done very informally. Once we have a knowledge, then a hearing officer is assigned to set up a hearing and conduct the case." Testifying before a Senate Committee, the Department's Chief Legal Officer, Mr. Michaels, said of the hearing procedure: "The classic case is a letter we once received on a little piece of paper four inches by six inches which said, 'Dear Sir, I have been did wrong and I want to be did right.' We considered this and as far as I know always will consider this as a request for a hearing."

Despite the ease of the procedures for obtaining a fair hearing, however, some doubts has been expressed that recipients actually make wide use of their right of appeal. Thus, in reporting the results of interviews with a sample of ninety-six recipients of AFDC-U (the new program that provides aid to intact families with dependent children in which the father is unemployed, rather than absent from the home, the requirement for aid under the AFDC program), Briar discovered that 60 per cent of the families said they were not informed of their right to a fair hearing. Briar concludes that the informants were probably given the information by the social worker, but "this information probably is not particularly meaningful and useful to a person who sees himself as a suppliant and therefore it may be ignored or soon forgotten." Much the same point is made by J. M. Wedemeyer, the former Director of the California Department of Social Welfare, who reported in 1966 that "the prosecution of an appeal demands a degree of security, awareness, tenacity, and ability which few dependent people have. The same factors which compel the dependent person to avoid controversy in settling grievances make him avoid this avenue. He may create more immediate problems than he would face by accepting the initial decision."

During the period discussed here, the procedure was a follows: if an applicant from Los Angeles County, for example, had been found ineligible for aid by the county welfare worker, she could notify either the county or the state department in Sacramento that she objected to the ruling. One of several state hearing officers (called referees) would then be assigned to the case and a date would be set for a hearing at Los Angeles.

Referees are social workers, not lawyers. In Dr. tenBroek's view, the experience of the Department has been that lawyers "were at their best when they were handling problems that are of the type that lawyers frequently handle, questions involving the distinction between real and personal property, but when they came to the types of questions that involve social work, issues which are also embedded in the laws and which need to be decided in these cases for example, the suitability of a home, there they are weaker." Since "the important issues in our field and the more numerous issues in our field are social-welfare type issues," the department chose to use social workers as hearing officers under the direction of a Chief Hearing Officer who is a lawyer.

At the appointed time the applicant, representatives of the county department, and any witnesses that either desired to call appear before the referee. The applicant is entitled to representation by counsel of his choice, but such representation is extremely rare. An effort is made to be informal. The governing statute provides in part that "The hearing shall be conducted in an impartial and informal manner in order to encourage free and open discussion by participants." The applicant is encouraged to tell her own story in her own way, without the hindrance of technical rules of evidence applicable in courtroom proceedings. The aim of the proceeding is to establish the true facts bearing on eligibility. The hearings are recorded.

After the hearing, the referee prepares a proposed decision. A conclusion is reached, together with its supporting facts and reasons, on the issue of eligibility for aid. The proposed decision must be approved by the chief referee of the State Department of Social Welfare, who is a lawyer. After his approval, the proposed decision went, at the time of the cases here discussed, to the State Social Welfare Board for final action. The Board consists of seven members, who are chosen by the governor with the advice and consent of the state senate. They serve at the pleasure of the governor and are chosen "for their interest and leadership in social welfare activities without regard to political or religious affiliation or profession or occupation."

The Board's method of deciding the Fair Hearing Appeals Cases, as they were called, has been described in detail elsewhere. Briefly, the procedure was for the Board to divide the cases among its members for study. The proposed decisions were available at each meeting and could be acquired by board members, the department staff, the parties to the cases— including the county representatives—and other persons present at the meeting who had a legitimate interest in the work of the board. At the board's monthly meeting the cases were read out by number and a motion was made to adopt the proposed decision of the hearing officer. Unless a board member objected to the decision in a certain case and asked to have it considered separately, the cases were approved en masse. From time to time the director or a board member might call the board's attention to a specific case that could be precedent-setting if approved. The board's decisions were based on its own prior actions; its staff recommendations; its own notions of what the policy and fair administration of the program required in the individual case; and its understanding of California law embodied in statutes, court decisions, and the state constitution. If the Board upheld the county's decision to deny or discontinue aid, the applicant could appeal its decision to the courts.

At the time of these cases, the board was the only body empowered by statute to make the rules and regulations that implemented the state statutes in the administration of the welfare programs. The function of the appeals cases in helping the board make policy was clearly understood by the Chairman, Dr. tenBroek. He commented that "The appeals serve the board as an active and continuous test of policy . . . They indicate whether a given regulation is working well and as contemplated when adopted. They quickly bring to light the inequities of policies in operation, their harsh, undue, and unanticipated results."

THE OFFER OF A FREE HOME: PROMULGATION OF AN ADMINIS- TRATIVE RULE

Public moneys are granted only to families who can establish their need for such support. Proof of eligibility involves many elements, including the federal requirement that the state must "take into consideration any other income and resources of any child claiming aid to dependent children." The impetus for the "offer of a free home" rule came from the ambiguity of the phrase "any other . . . resources" in the federal act.

Section 11264 of the California Welfare and Institutions Code provides that

No child maintained in an institution for whom a bona fide offer of a proper home has been made is eligible for further aid; but no institution shall be required to surrender a child to any person of a religious faith different from that of the child or the parents of the child. [Added 1937.]

No appellate cases interpreting this section have been found. Its intent, however, appears to be similar to that of the earlier mother's aid laws: wherever possible, children should be kept in family homes rather than in institutions. There is a significant difference: the mother's aid laws, as we have seen, provided public funds to support the child in the mother's home. Thus, a child was not denied public support by his removal from an institution to a private home. Section 11264, however, appears to contemplate that the "proper home" will also be a "free home"—that is, the public obligation to provide aid for the child will terminate if it can be established that a private home is available where the child will be cared for and supported by private means. Section 11264 required the department to take account of an offer of a proper home as a resource affecting eligibility for continued aid only when the child was institutionalized. The rule that was ultimately adopted by the department as Regulation C–316, however, was not limited to children living in institutions, but was extended to all children receiving public support, even to those living at home with their mothers or fathers.

It should be made very clear what was involved in the offer of a home. If, for example, a child was living in its mother's home and AFDC funds were being paid to the mother for the child's support, and if the father living with his second wife, offered a free home to the child, the AFDC case worker was required to determine whether the father's offer was a financial resource available for the child's support that must be considered in establishing the child's continued eligibility for public support. If the worker decided that the father's home was proper from the point of view of the child's financial and emotional security, she might conclude that the child was not in need of public support for the reason that the father was able and willing to assume his private support obligation for the child. Once this conclusion was reached, the child was no longer eligible for aid in the mother's home. The caseworker's decision was not, of course, a legal requirement that the child go to the father's home. The welfare agency lacked authority to force a change of custody in such cases; and, indeed, the referees took great comfort in this point. Nevertheless, in practice, if the mother could not afford to keep the child without public support, the agency's decision to terminate aid forced the child to change homes. This reality appears to have haunted the case workers from the beginning.

It is not clear exactly when the State Department staff first expanded the requirement of considering an offer of a home as a resource for institutionalized children to include all children receiving public support. The departmental records on this subject begin with a letter dated May 3, 1941, from the AFDC (then ANC) supervisor to a county welfare official from Santa Clara County. The county had before it the following case: two illegitimate children, aged 11 and 13, were living with relatives who had been appointed the children's legal guardians. The natural father had been located and, although he had never before contributed to the support of his children nor had they ever lived with him, he now professed himself willing to take them into his home and support them. What should the county do? The supervisor, foreshadowing later departmental policy, replied in part that "while it is true that an offer of support must be considered in determining eligibility, it should also be ascertained whether or not it is to the best interests of the children to be placed in the home offering such support." Santa Clara was advised that the children should continue to receive aid while the father's home was being investigated.

It is significant that the close relationship between child support and child custody that embodied the conflicting values underlying these cases made its appearance in the first case raising the issue of the offer of a free home. The legal standard for deciding custody matters,

binding on courts in cases involving two parents, is "the best interests of the child." In effect Santa Clara County was being asked to decide whether these two children would be better cared for in the home of their legal guardian or of their natural father. To be sure, even if the county decided to terminate public support, the guardians would still retain their legal authority, but their legal rights to the child's physical custody might become practically unexercisable.

The next mention of the offer of a free home appears in an office memorandum from the ANC supervisor to the department head and staff, dated January 8, 1943. The memo called attention to a fair-hearing appeal case scheduled for hearing by the board later in January. The case involved the denial of aid by Los Angeles County to two illegitimate children who were living with their mother. The mother's husband, who lived in Mississippi, offered to support his wife, his own child, and the two illegitimate children provided they returned to him in Mississippi. The mother refused to return. The county thereupon ruled that she had refused to take advantage of an offer of private support available to her and the children and denied her application for public support.

Calling attention to the fact that "the major question raised is presented for the first time, therefore the decision will be important as a precedent for future guidance," the supervisor pointed out that Section 11264 was limited to children living in institutions. She continued, "Section 1503 outlines the purpose of the ANC law to keep children in ther own home wherever possible, and Section 1526 provides that a mother, who is living separate and apart from her husband, may establish residence for her children. The appeal therefore raises the question as to whether the denial by Los Angeles County is a proper one." The Board ruled that the offer by the father, since it was conditioned on the mother's return to his home, would not suffice to render the child ineligible for aid.

Questions from the counties continued to be handled informally for the next several years. Letters from the supervisor to Los Angeles County in 1944, San Luis Obispo County in 1945, and Imperial County in 1946 reiterated her understanding of the basic policy: the offer of a home would be considered as an available resource that should be explored by the county, but aid should not be terminated unless the free home was found to be "suitable" for the children.

In 1949 a new supervisor was appointed for the ANC bureau. In reply to a question regarding the offer of a free home from Butte County, he reviewed the files and cases that had accumulated since 1941. His summary of the department's working policy was sent to the area offices in Los Angeles and San Francisco, as well as to the Butte County inquirer. The memo covered the following points: if the child was living "in a foster home, institution . . . or with a relative other than a parent and the offer was made by a parent, it would be considered a potential resource that should be explored." If the offered home was entirely suitable in every way, the child would be ineligible on the basis of need. If, however, the home was not suitable, the offer would not be considered an available resource. If the child was living with a parent who had legal custody and the other parent made the offer, the county need not consider the offer unless the parent having custody was willing to let the child go. If the child was living with a nonparent and another nonparent offered to take him, the department would consider the child's desires in the matter.

Inquiries from the counties continued to appear, and it became apparent that the question could no longer be handled informally by the staff. In 1951 a declaration of working policy in the form of a handbook section, was presented to the State Social Welfare Board together with a supporting memo from the ANC staff. C–390 provided that

If a child receives an offer of a home from a relative, other person, or agency, the county shall assist in evaluating such offer and in determining whether the child would benefit thereby.

The county shall make its services available to the family for such purposes as investigating the suitability of the home and interpreting the legal, social, and emotional implications of the offer. Usually the county can request qualified agencies to investigate the suitability of distantly located homes.

If a child has adequate emotional and physical security in his present home, moving him might have a serious effect on him. If it is decided that it would be best for the child's growth and adjustment that he be moved the suitability of the home offered should be evaluated to determine whether it can provide the necessary physical and emotional security or educational, financial, and social benefits.

When the family has reached a decision and a suitable plan has been made, the county may be able to provide other related services, such as preparation of the child for the move, preparation of the new family for the child, or, if the home is rejected, interpretation of the decision to the person who made the offer. . . .

Then, in 1957, the board acted formally to promulgate its first regulation on the subject. Regulation C–316 was issued effective July 1, 1957. It read

OFFER OF A FREE HOME: Decision as to the eligibility of a child who is offered a free home by a relative, other person, or agency, is to be made on the basis of the legal, social, emotional, and financial security for the child in the home offered as compared to his present home.

The accompanying handbook material, which interpreted the regulation to the county case workers and which is suggestive rather than mandatory for the county personnel, amplified upon the point as follows:

C-316   OFFER OF A FREE HOME

Sometimes an offer of a free home is made by a parent, relative, other person, or agency for a child receiving ANC. When this happens the worker is responsible for deciding if the offer is resource to be considered in determining if the child is needy.

In general, if the child is living with a parent, and the offer is made by a person other than a parent, the offer would not be considered a resource. If, in such a case, the parent with whom the child is living requests the agency to evaluate the offer, the worker should make the agency's services available for this purpose.

In other instances where such an offer is received the worker should consider the following in determining if the offer is a resource:

1. Was the offer made in good faith, that is, is the person making the offer actually interested in giving the child a home and the necessary care, or, for example, was the offer made by a parent only for the purpose of evading his responsibility for support regardless of the child's location?

2. Can the offered home provide the necessary physical and emotional security, financial and social benefits; are there any aspects of the offer, the home, or the new family situation which would be detrimental to the child's welfare?

3. Would it be detrimental to the child's welfare to remove him from his present home? Such factors as relationships and emotional ties with the present family, health problems, length of time he has been in the present home, number of times the child has been moved in the past, his adjustment to neighborhood and school, are taken into consideration.

The study necessary to these determinations is primarily the responsibility of the worker. Assistance and consultation should be obtained as indicated by the individual situation from school authorities, psychologists, physicians, psychiatrists, etc. Where the offered home is distantly located, a qualified social agency in the locality should be requested to make the study of that home.

On completion of the study the worker makes an analysis of the total situation and decides if the offered home is a resource to be considered in determining if the child is needy. It is considered a resource only if the offer was a bone fide one, if the home can provide the child with the necessary physical and emotional security and financial and social benefits, and if it would not be detrimental to the child's welfare to move him from his present home.

The above decision is made only for the purpose of determining eligibility to ANC. The decision as to whether the offer is to be accepted belongs to the parent or relative with whom the child is living or who has custody, or the court if the child is a court ward. If the responsible person rejects an offer which the study has shown to be an acceptable resource, the worker should explain why the child is ineligible to ANC. In this event, as well as where the study indicates that the offer is not an acceptable resource, the worker should explain the reason for the decision to the person making the offer.

If the responsible person or agency decides to accept the offer, the worker offers the services of the agency in preparing the child for the move, and preparing the new family for the child.

Thus was created Regulation C–316 and its accompanying interpretive material. From July 1, 1957, when it became effective, to November 1, 1962, when it was withdrawn, the regulation accounted for a total of twenty-three fair-hearing appeals cases that were decided by the State Social Welfare Board. In addition, sixteen appeals cases had been decided by the Board under C–390, making a total of thirty-nine cases that had to do with the interpretation and enforcement of the Board's policy in this matter. To these cases we now turn.

OFFER OF A FREE HOME: THE FAIR HEARING APPEALS CASES

A sampling of the cases will provide an illustration of their range.

Case: A husband and wife had been divorced without obtaining a custody order from the court. The two children of the marriage, together with another child whose paternity the husband denied, lived with the mother. After the divorce she had established a "stable relationship" with another man and had had four children by him. The father, meanwhile, had remarried and was earning approximately $500 per month. He and his second wife offered a free home to the oldest child, a girl aged 10. The mother, then living alone with the seven children, wished to keep the girl at home although a careful evaluation of the father's home indicated that it was a "good one in terms of love, understanding and emotional and financial security," the board decided to continue the AFDC grant to support the girl in her mother's home. The decision was based on the girl's attachment to her mother, her express desire not to be separated from her brother and sisters and because "we cannot consider that the home offered is a suitable substitute for her present home or that the care reportedly available to her in the home of her father and stepmother ... might adequately replace the emotional security that a mother can give her own children and which is essential to their well-being" (*E.*, September 1957).

Case: The mother and father, who were both married to other spouses, had been living together for four years and had produced two children. The couple had separated, and the mother applied for AFDC support for the children. Los Angeles County denied her application on the ground that "appellant has been offered full support for her family if she would reconcile with her common-law husband. However, she has chosen a fatherless home in order to get public assistance, rather than a united family without dependence." The mother testified that the father had never fully supported her; that he drank to excess and that he was violent and abusive to her daughter when he drank, although "when he became sober and calmed down, he expected everybody to forget all about his behavior when he was drinking." The Social Welfare Board held that the aid should be granted despite the County's insistence that the mother be forced to reconcile with the father of her children (in whose home, it might be pointed out, it was a crime for her to live, since their adulterous cohabitation constituted a "double misdemeanor" for which both could have been fined $1,000 or imprisoned in the county jail for one year, or both.

The thirty-nine cases suggest some of the strains in the California welfare system. Of the thirty-nine cases, twenty-three arose from Los Angeles County, six more from its neighbor county, San Diego, and only six were from the San Francisco Bay Area. The impact on Los Angeles County of California's population explosion is reflected in these cases, and the cases illustrate the county's attitude that many of the AFDC mothers had left other states for the purpose of getting relief in California. In many of the cases the worker appeared convinced that the mother, having left her husband in Oklahoma, Louisiana, or Mississippi, was motivated by California's high welfare standards to come to California in order to qualify for relief. In one case the county workers seemed to believe that the size of California's monthly payment had motivated the family break-up: the mother, they claimed "forsook her spouse for a monetary advantage, looking to the high ANC standards in California." (S., September, 1961). In twenty-seven of the thirty-nine cases, the person offering the free home resided outside of California; in only twelve of the cases did the offer come from persons living within the state. Thus, the cases lend support to the suspicion that the regulations concerning the offer of a free home, with their emphasis on the child's financial security, could be used to send the child (and sometimes the mother) back to the state he or she had left.

One of the pervasive problems of Regulation C–316 was the question of establishing the good faith of the person offering the free home. In most of these cases the absent father had been located by the district attorney and reminded of his duty to support his children. All too often the offer to take the child into the home was a compromise with the alternative of paying the mother for the support of the child. As one staff member expressed it, "We will no doubt get more 'offers' as absent fathers are located and support demanded. Somehow, they always feel it would be cheaper to give the support at their home—or they're mad at momma and will punish her by offering to take the children away." The appeals cases lend support to this view: in thirty-two cases the child was living with the mother, and in all cases (not all the same cases) the offer of a free home was made by the father.

In outcome, the appeals cases were heavily in favor of the appellant. In twenty-eight cases the State Social Welfare Board reversed the county to order that the aid payments be granted, if they had been denied, or continued, if they had been suspended. In only eleven cases were the county's refusal to grant or termination of the grant upheld. The board was consistent, however, in looking at all the cases from the point of view of the AFDC program. Although the staff had at one point suggested that if the child were living with a person having legal custody, the offer of a free home would not be considered without the consent of the person

having custody, the cases do not treat the question of legal custody as decisive. At the same time, however, the point is not ignored. Thus, in several cases the mother had legal custody and the children were receiving AFDC in her home. In these cases the board tended to refuse to permit the withdrawal of funds to be used as a lever to force the mother to give up custody to the father. This decision was made in one case even in the face of an indication that the mother's home might be considered unfit. If, however, the father had legal custody and the children were being supported by AFDC in the mother's home, the decisions were in conflict. In some cases the grant was continued because the father had not "actually exercised" his right to legal custody; because his home was not immediately available for the child; or, in one case, apparently because the worker thought the child was better off in the mother's home. In other cases, including one where the mother had deserted the family prior to reclaiming the children, the father's right to custody was enforced by terminating the aid.

Other unique problems were presented by fathers who agreed to provide a free home for their children only if the mother would consent to return as well, and by grandparents who agreed to provide for their grandchildren if the minor mother-daughter would return to the family home. Without exception the board properly refused to permit the withdrawal of AFDC funds to be used to force marital reconcilations. Nor was the erring daughter required to return home, at least if she was within a year or so of attaining full majority and it was not entirely clear that her parents' offer was bona fide.

WITHDRAWAL OF REGULATION C–316

Attention has previously been directed in this paper to Dr. tenBroek's emphasis on the function of the appeals cases as a test of the policy and regulations formulated by the Social Welfare Board. The point is illustrated by these cases involving the offer of a free home. The primary impetus that led to the ultimate withdrawal of Regulation C–316 came from an appeal case heard before the Board in April 1961. The facts in the D case were as follows:

The mother and father were divorced in April 1952 in Missouri. Custody of the three children was given to the mother; the father was ordered to pay $20 per month per child as support. Following the divorce, the mother came with the children to live in Santa Clara County. Although the father made the monthly payments provided in the divorce decree for the support of the children, the mother applied for ANC in October 1952 to supplement this meager allowance. In 1955 she moved with the children to San Diego County to live with her parents and again applied for ANC. The father was notified of the application and asked if he was able to increase the payments. He had remarried and was living in Missouri with his second wife and their child. Both were schoolteachers. They lived in a small home with one bedroom (he planned to enclose a large porch for additional sleeping space), which they were purchasing. The father's annual salary was approximately $4,000 per year. When notified of his first wife's application for ANC, he replied that he was unable to increase the monthly support payments to the children but that he and his wife would be glad to take the three children into their home. The district attorney, upon being notified of the father's offer, declined to seek legal action to increase the father's support payments.

The County Welfare Department elected to consider the father's offer of a free home as a resource available for the children's support, and aid was terminated as of August 31, 1960.

The mother appealed, and the case was set for hearing in San Diego County on January 24, 1961. At the hearing it was disclosed that San Diego County had initiated proceedings through the juvenile court to test the fitness of the mother's home. The probation report alleged that the children had been observed at least once in the street without adult supervision at 1 a.m.; that they habitually allowed to roam the streets in a filthy condition, begging the neighbors for food; that on two occasions adult males had remained overnight in the home; that the children were taken away and kept away from their home for a week by the mother following an argument with her mother about a man; that the public health nurse at the school was concerned about the children because of their dirty clothing and their apparent lack of proper food; and that the children were nervous and inclined to petty theft, fighting, and other attention-getting devices at school. All allegations contained in this report were denied by the mother and her witnesses, who were present at the ANC hearing. At the time of the ANC hearing the case was pending before the juvenile court.

The State Department referee filed a proposed decision on March 17, 1961, affirming the county in deciding that the father's offer of a home was a resource available to the children. The draft opinion stressed the father's stable remarriage, the intellectual advantages his home would provide for the children, and his strong desire to have the children in his home. When the case came before the Board for hearing on April 20, 1961, the director of the state department, Mr. Wedemeyer, asked that the case be put over so that another draft opinion could be prepared. He stated before the Board that the current situation pending the appeal was that aid had been terminated, the juvenile court was involved on the question of placement, and

in the meantime because of the cessation of aid we have left the children in effect in an undesirable home situation without even the basic needs for support for several months, thus I think miscarrying the basic ideas that have been advanced around the program and for which I have felt we should stand, that is ... not penalizing the children by leaving them in a situation where they were in want unless other alternatives have been developed which would assure that their needs were being taken care of.... Now, in view of these facts, I think we should take this back and deal with the question of where these children are and their need and whether or not ... the denial of the grant is a proper way to enforce the proper placement of the children. It certainly does not appear to be one that is serving that purpose at the present time. The question of who has custody of the children should be a court decision in my opinion.

Following the board meeting, Wedemeyer sent a memorandum to the Chief Referee, in which he made the point that the *D* case illustrated a new trend in the offer-of-a-home cases in that it furnished detailed evidence of the living conditions in the home provided for the children as well as evidence of the children's eligiblity for aid. The director suggested that the department had a dual responsibility in such cases:

first of all financial help to the persons having the responsibility for the care of the children, and second, the protective service to see that the situation is constructive for the children. The latter is carried out wherever possible [within the Department] by counseling, guidance, and help to the parent or custodian of the children. When this is not adequate it is carried out by working with and referring to those agencies or sources [outside the Department] who have responsibility for determining matters of custody and developing the base on which alternative plans can be carried out. *Until such steps are taken, the children must be provided for to the extent that they lack the essentials for adequate maintenance.* We need to observe here the principle that denial of aid cannot be used in the absence of an adequate alternative, which can be achieved either through the cooperation and voluntary effort of the caretaker or through the intervention of the proper enforcement agency. [Italics added.]

The rewritten decision . . . which conforms to the director's views expressed to the Board and in his memo to the legal staff, stated in part that

The evidence presented in this matter indicates the children may well be benefitted socially and emotionally and may enjoy increased financial security if they were living in the home of their father. However, the legal aspects of the situation are such that the offer of a free home cannot be considered a resource in determining eligibility for Aid despite the apparent benefits arising from the other factors.

At the time of the hearing, the appellant had the legal custody of three minor children. The question of custody is exclusively for the courts to decide and so is the question of the fitness of the home provided by the mother. Since the question of custody is outside the jurisdiction of this Board, a finding of ineligibility based upon the present circumstances would not be proper in this case. It is necessary that Aid be rendered in order to assure the maintenance of the children, for the appellant has the legal custody and the children are living with her. The granting of such aid is necessary in the absence of a voluntary acceptance by the mother of the offer of a home so that the children's physical needs may be met while they are in her home. Any contrary finding, no matter how desirable, would by indirection be the probable cause of a change of duly authorized legal custody as denial of Aid in this case would necessarily operate as a lever to force this mother to relinquish the custody of these children to their father and thus interfere with judicially-determined custody. The solution to the problem of the unfitness of the mother's home as shown by the evidence presented is being sought by the county through the juvenile court.

Thus, dissatisfaction with the Department's policy in the offer-of-a-home cases had already been expressed by the director and concurred in by the board when a report prepared for a senate committee by a law professor on the role of the Board in the ANC program criticized, almost in passing, the Board's policy in these cases. Sweet found that the Board's actual decisions in the offer-of-a-home cases had "by and large, shown good sense." But he stressed the inappropriateness of allowing the board's decision on aid to thwart, in practice if not in theory, the court decision on custody of the child; and he pointed out that the board's action in extending the concept of an offer of a free home as a resource from institutionalized

children, as provided in Section 1524, to all children receiving public support was wholly gratuitous. He indicated that federal officials did not concur in the board's interpretation of the federal requirement of considering all resources available to the child as including the offer of a free home. He suggested that a feasible solution would be to grant aid based on physical possession of the child, but to condition such aid on the custodian's obtaining a court decree granting her custody within a specified period of time.

In a response to the . . . report prepared by the Department staff, the point was conceded that the offer-of-a-home regulation "represented an extension of W & I Code 1524 and was also promulgated to be consistent with the basic rule in ANC that all income and resources for the support of the child shall be determined and related to the total needs to establish that a child is needy." And in a memo to the ANC staff, dated July 20, 1962, the point is made that the Department's present position was based on Director Wedemeyer's decision in the *D* case of 1961:

The Director actually initiated the revision of this policy in April 1961 on the basis of the *D.* appeal. In his memo of April 25, 1961, he set forth the principles which he later confirmed in response to the Sweet report. His position that the Department's two basic responsibilities in these cases are payment of financial aid and protection of the child rules out the offer of a free home as a resource to an otherwise eligible child. This in effect requires that Regulation C–316 be repealed. The offer of a Free Home in essence would become a factor to be taken into consideration in providing services for the protection of children.

On November 1, 1962, by recommendation of the Department staff, Regulation C–316 was changed to read as follows:

OFFER OF A FREE HOME. Except as provided in Welfare and Institutions Code 1524, aid shall not be denied or discontinued for an otherwise eligible child who is offered a free home.

Section 1524, now renumbered 11264, is the section covering children who live in institutions for whom an offer of a proper home is made Appeals cases involving Regulation C–316 after 1962 appear only rarely. For all practical purposes, the books are closed on the Offer of a Free Home in California. Practical experience with the actual cases presented by the appeals process had convinced the board that its broad interpretation of the federal requirement of considering all resources was unwise in this situation. Therefore the board, acting in its role as legislator and informed by its experience as a judge, changed the law.

CONCLUSION

Public welfare exists today in the center of controversy and conflicting interests. One such conflict is long-standing; its adversaries are found chiefly among the more conservative taxpayer groups, on the one hand, and, on the other hand, the social workers who are the professionals of the welfare system. Thus, at a hearing in California before the Senate Fact Finding Committee on Labor and Welfare in 1960, District Attorney Nedjedly of Contra Costa County charged that the welfare caseload exhibited "on the one hand moral decline evidenced by the casual acceptance of illegitimacy and the abrogation of marriage or any marital or family responsibility and upon the other side the collapse of the character of the individual who finds it simpler to qualify for welfare than to seek assistance first from himself." Other witnesses expressed the similar view that AFDC mothers regularly produced illegitimate children in order to increase the size of their monthly checks and that, in any event, the money was as likely to be spent by a mother to buy the boyfriend's gin as to provide the baby's milk. Nor are such views confined to senate hearings. For a time in California it appeared likely that local judges had found an effective means of terminating illegitimacy: AFDC mothers charged with welfare fraud, or even with being in a place where narcotics were unlawfully smoked with knowledge that the activity was occurring, were to be placed on probation instead of being jailed only if they consented to "voluntary" sterilization. Happily for the administration of justice in California, this practice was brought to an abrupt end when a superior court held that such orders were beyond the power of municipal judges.

The professional social workers tend to counter such charges with the argument that the AFDC programs' chief problem is that it mis-

takenly provides only money to the recipients rather than money plus services. Miss Angell, testifying at the 1960 Senate hearing on behalf of the California Social Workers' Organization, urged that if more trained social workers could be made available to work with the AFDC families, more damaged individuals could be helped to reclaim themselves and get off the relief rolls.

A broader controversy, just beginning to be noticed by lawyers sensitive to infringements of individual liberty and to the right of privacy, concerns the vulnerability of poor persons to the regulations of the system, and to pressure from social workers. Thus, Professor Reich: "the poor are all too easily regulated. They are an irresistible temptation to moralists, who want not only to assist but to improve by imposing virtue. They are subject to social workers' urges to prescribe what is best. It is significant that 76 per cent of Briar's informants thought that when the welfare social worker suggested that a recipient see a psychiatrist, the recipient should be expected to go and 66 per cent thought the recipient must go in order to continue receiving aid.

Dr. Bernard Diamond, a psychiatrist, has concluded that deeper emotions than mere concern over the proper use of public funds produce these sweeping attacks on welfare recipients. Speculating that "society simultaneously loves and hates its poor, its dependent, and its disabled," he suggests that this ambivalence gives rise to a typically neurotic solution in the shape of welfare policy which

provides aid and nurture, but only to the degree that it ensures that they [the recipients] remain nonpersons. Nonpersons must not be allowed to suffer to the point where they might be tempted to reverse the social order. At the same time, they must be constantly reminded, through the infliction of punitive sanctions and discriminatory exclusions, that they are nonpersons.

This alleged unconscious aim of the welfare system has been recently attacked by two staff members of the Columbia University School of Social Work. In two articles, Cloward and Piven have announced a strategy they hope would create a political crisis "that could lead to legislation for a guaranteed annual income and thus an end to poverty." The strategy, proposed in 1966, was "a massive drive to recruit the poor *onto* the welfare rolls" with the result of causing "bureaucratic disruption in welfare agencies and fiscal disruption in local and state governments," which in turn would "generate severe political strains, and deepen existing divisions among elements in the big-city Democratic coalition: the remaining white middle class, the white working class ethnic groups and the growing minority poor." If this strategy were followed, the authors predict, "to avoid a further weakening of that historic coalition, a national Democratic administration would be constrained to advance a federal solution to poverty that would override local welfare failures, local class and racial conflicts and local revenue dilemmas." In a second article in 1967 the authors report substantial progress toward organization of the poor but reiterate that the movement's most potent strategy lies in continuous recruitment of eligible persons to the welfare rolls. Only then, they suggest, will the "nonpersons" described by Dr. Diamond be able to command enough numerical strength to create a crisis and thus force major reforms in the system at the national level.

Regulation C–316 and its attendant fair-hearing appeals cases must be seen within this context. The power to determine the fitness of a child's home obviously must be exercised with great restraint. As the decisions made clear, the welfare laws and regulations did not require the case workers to assess the fitness of the home as a condition for eligibility. The assumption of this power must have greatly threatened the recipients. Other agencies in the community, notably the juvenile court and its probation department, are charged with the responsibility of providing protective services for children. If the probation department has reason to believe that a home is unfit for child-rearing, it may bring an action to have the child declared a "dependent of the juvenile court." Strict standards of proof are required under the statutes to establish the unfitness of a home; even if the court takes jurisdiction, the child may be returned to the home under supervision of the probation case worker. Referrals from the AFDC caseworker to the probation department are by no means rare; although precise figures showing how many AFDC children are referred

to probation departments or other protective service agencies as "neglected" children are apparently not available, a two-months sample of neglect referrals from all sources in the Minneapolis-St. Paul area showed that, although only 3 per cent of families in the general population were on public assistance, 42 per cent of the families against whom neglect petitions had been filed were relief recipients. A California study estimated that during the twelve months ending June 30, 1964, a "substantial" number of the 21,264 children who were referred to probation departments from all sources as possible dependent and neglected children were located in the AFDC case load.

When the welfare worker was instructed by Regulation C–316 and its accompanying handbook material to evaluate the home offered the child in comparison to his present home, the worker was in effect directed to make a determination similar to that required of the probation staff, but without its attendant safeguards. Director Wedemeyer's decision to limit the function of the welfare worker to seeing that the children were protected in the sense of being provided with the necessities of life pending the investigation of the home by the probation department or other protective service agency, must be seen as a recognition of the differing functions of other local welfare and probation departments.

Thus the conflict posed by Regulation C–316's implicit requirement that the welfare case worker balance the adequacy of a child's present home against his need for public support was finally resolved by a complete separation of task and authority; the agency providing public support was forbidden to evaluate the child's home, and the agency charged with investigating the fitness of the home had no public funds to disburse. The conflict between what is best for the child and what is most economical for the taxpayer no longer arises within a single agency.

The point is not merely that the conflict could not be resolved in a fair and equitable manner, given the setting in which it arose. Possibly no other agency could have resolved the conflict posed in those terms. The narrower point of this paper is to call attention to the process by which the law-giver set himself a problem to solve, promulgated a solution in the form of a rule, discovered that the rule was not adequate in the light of case-developed experience, withdrew the rule, and abandoned the problem as one proper for him to solve. The recognition of this process, I suggest, may provide an additional tool to supplement the "trouble case" for discovering law and legal institutions in tribal settings.

III. RELIGION AND MAGIC

MAN'S PROGRESS from hunting and gathering to industrialization has been characterized by increasing mastery over the habitat. But man has not been able to eliminate uncertainty and danger entirely. Nothing colors and shapes people's images of themselves as much as the degree and kind of control they maintain over their habitat and the effectiveness of their techniques for perpetuating life. The perception of danger and uncertainty is an important element in the habitat of all societies, and it thus becomes a significant part of people's view of themselves as productive and life-sustaining beings. And the central principle in the anthropological study of religion is that man creates the deity in his own image, consistent with his view of himself.

We do not know why man tries to cope with danger and uncertainty by means of supernatural concepts. It may be asked, how else can he cope with them? A more fundamental question is, why does he feel impelled to cope with them at all, why does he not simply accept them as given? The answers to all these questions are unknown, although they are among the most important problems presented in the study of human behavior.

Our point of departure is the simple and basic observation that concepts of the supernatural—and accompanying ways of behaving—are found in all societies. In our present state of knowledge, we cannot perceive significant evolutionary regularities in concepts of the supernatural themselves, but we do observe a close "fit" between these ideas and the adaptive strategies by which people live. An evolutionary point of view can then be applied to the organization of social relations in which people use these concepts to cope with the residues of danger and uncertainty unsolved by their technologies.

It is necessary first to consider a few definitions, and especially to distinguish between religion and magic. (It is also necessary to distinguish between religion and superstition. I have forgotten the source of this adage, but the best way I know of separating the two is by the criterion that religion is what I believe and superstition is what the other fellow believes.) Religion refers to those organized social relationships, practices, and beliefs that mediate the relationship of the members of a group to the deity or deities associated with that group. A deity is considered to be a spirit (sometimes the ghost of an ancestor) which is omnipresent, a source of ultimate power

177

for the group in the sphere of activity with which it is associated, which receives offerings or prayers or both, which is individualized and named, and whose acceptance is obligatory by the members of the group.

Although both religion and magic involve supernatural phenomena, they can be distinguished by the means used to produce desired consequences. Action and thought are designated as religious when the desired goal is associated with the intervention of a deity or deities. That is, the deity is believed to be the mover in a series of events, whether he is thought to act independently or in response to such actions of individuals as prayer, sacrifice, ceremonies, or transgression. Action and thought are designated as magical when the desired goal is associated with the intervention of a human being or an object with special powers.

Both religious and magical systems of thought and action provide a view of cause and consequence in which a purposeful will and agency is believed to be involved. Both presuppose and seek a cause in terms of "who" produced a consequence in order to explain events which, it is believed, cannot be explained in terms of general laws such as the laws of probability. In religious and magical systems of thought, every event is explainable in terms of particular causative agencies.

This is the attractiveness of religion and magic for people at lower levels of technological development, who are largely without the naturalistic explanations that we are accustomed to. To illustrate (and as will be seen in Selection 27), the Hopi Indians believe that if *all* Hopi behave properly, the gods will send rain. Thus if there is neither too much nor too little rain, this is evidence that the gods are pleased with the Hopi. If there is flood or drought, this is evidence that the gods have been angered by someone's failure to perform a ceremony properly or because someone has had bad thoughts (or, in Hopi terms, has kept a bad heart).

Now it is probable that in a population of a few thousand people someone will, at some point, make a mistake in the elaborate rituals. If there is flood or drought, such an error has to be discovered and corrected, and then the people wait to see whether the gods have been appeased. If they are not, this is taken as evidence that they have been offended by something else, say, a bad heart. Now it is also unimaginable that no one in a population of a few thousand will have hostile or other negative feelings. To appease the gods, people must begin searching their hearts and confess. As long as there is too much or too little rain, the Hopi are certain that there is still at least one person remaining at large with unconfessed evil thoughts. When the rains do finally come in desirable amounts, this is evidence that the last proper confession has been made and all hearts are now good.

There is no religion without this underlying logical system of cause and effect, within the limits set by the group's level of development. As mastery over the habitat increases, it is not the chain of cause and consequence that is altered; we do not, after all, blame the deity for the failure of Apollo XIII or for our military setbacks. Instead, these activities and others (like food production) are no longer regarded as being in the province of supernatural control. Religion is a no-lose system of thought.

Magical personnel—sorcerers, magicians, and the like—sometimes perform religious acts, as when a shaman propitiates a deity with prayers in behalf of a group in the belief that because of his special supernatural powers he may be successful in other spheres of supernatural activity. Similarly, religious personnel may perform magic and religious paraphernalia may be used magically—for example, when a cross is worn to bring luck or a miniature replica of a holy book is placed on a door as a talisman to ward off evil. These actions may be regarded as magical because the desired effects are believed to be caused by the object rather than by the deity with which it was originally associated.

At the lowest levels of development, represented here by the Washo Indians of California and Nevada (Selection 12), almost all productive activities—but especially those in which there is uncertainty and danger—call into play religious and magical beliefs and practices; so do physical crises such as birth, illness, and death. This is understandable when it is remembered that hunter-gatherers have little mastery over their habitat, no matter how abundant particular sources of food may be, and are in no way responsible for the presence of the food on which they subsist. Similarly, they may have palliatives for pain and illness, but their mastery over these critical events is minimal.

We saw earlier that in such societies every person is politically and legally autonomous; each man is also his own religious functionary, propitiating the deities himself as appropriate situations arise. No one is designated to serve regularly as a religious functionary for the group or to mediate relationships with the deities associated with the group. Just as kin, political, legal, and economic roles are undifferentiated, so are religious roles commingled with all the others. There are more or less specialized magical roles in many hunting-gathering societies, but shamans, witches, and sorcerers are roles that are theoretically open to all members of the group rather than confined to (say) the elders of a kin group. Similar patterns are observable among simple horticulturists (who rely a great deal on hunting and gathering) and among pastoralists, although there is a greater degree of specialization of magical roles among the latter.

The first anticipation of differentiation in religious organization makes its evolutionary appearance in the later stages of horticultural development, as an accompaniment of the formation of solidary and sedentary kin groups (as among the Tallensi of West Africa; Selection 14). In such societies we often observe a system in which the political and jural representative of a kin group—the eldest living male—performs religious acts on behalf of and in the name of the group and in its presence. But he is not a full-time specialist, and his religious role is commingled with his economic, kin, political, jural, and age status. Another important development at this level of development is that group solidarity is almost always expressed and reinforced in communal religious activity. In many of these societies, a person's failure to participate in ritualized ceremonials is regarded as an assault on the group's integrity, a denial of its authority as well as an affront to its deities. Is this analogous to the equation in many contemporary industrial societies of "disrespectful" behavior to national symbols (such as the flag) with assault on the society itself?

Ritual, which begins to proliferate among advanced horticulturists, serves as the bridge between the institutional and ideological aspects of religion. The terms ritual and rite derive from the Latin word *ritus*, and they are akin to the Greek word *arithmos*, which means number. (Many readers will be familiar with the notion of "doing things by the numbers." The terms ritual and rite are closely related to arithmetic and rhyme.) Thus a ritual is a prescribed (numbered) manner of behaving, used under particular and repeated conditions and as established by tradition.

Religious ritual is only one kind of ritualized behavior. In secular life, there is ritualized behavior in caste and military relationships (e.g. saluting), coronations and inaugurations, the rituals of gift-giving on birthdays and at Christmas, the rites of the Freemasons, and, in societies such as the Tallensi and the Chinese, acts of obeisance between father and eldest son. All such rituals, whether in connection with religious or other spheres of activity, are accompaniments of social solidarity and exclusiveness. This can best be exemplified by considering again the contrast between hunting-gathering and horticultural societies.

As we have seen, the recurrent splits in hunter-gatherer camps are a response to the intensity of social relations in them and the need to hold down the pressure on available resources. Since no group has exclusive rights to territory, and people do not invest labor in particular plots of land, they can easily split up when hostilities erupt; there are few external anchors. But people's orientations to each other are quite different in societies at advanced stages of horticulture. Groups, like lineages, obtain exclusive rights to land, and people invest considerable energy in their holdings; hence they are reluctant to leave their territories and each other. These landholding groups are generally exclusive, which not only means that people are kept out but also has repercussions on the quality of life within the exclusive group itself.

One of the inevitable premises of life in an exclusive group is that its members think of themselves as being alike, as indeed they are by virtue of their criteria for membership. A major characteristic of such groups is that their members do not tolerate sustained and outspoken dissent from established opinions and decisions (this is exemplified in Selection 20). In such groups, there are clearly defined alternatives to unresolvable heterodoxy: an individual who refuses to yield will lose his membership by being banished, ostracized, or declared a nonperson. If a sizeable portion of the group will not yield, as in a schismatic movement, the group will split up.

This leads to an important potential degree of instability in such groups—though superficially they may give the opposite impression—and their members are concerned about eruptions of dissent; understandably, they are often preoccupied with the danger of splits, and some groups (such as the Bantu Kavirondo of Kenya and the Hopi, discussed in Selection 27), establish elaborate rituals to govern such splits in the event they do occur. In subsequent sections we will see how these horticulturally-appropriate pressures to conformity are reflected in the spheres of values and ideologies, personality processes, and art.

But under these conditions of group exclusivity, the need to remain sedentary to protect investments of time and effort in cultivated plots, and intense social and emotional relationships, "doing things by the numbers" provides an important degree of safety and certainty. It reduces unpredictable spontaneity and prevents actions and impulses from getting out of hand. While ritual rarely extends to the everyday occasions that produce tension, it is an important symbolic reinforcement of the legal and political controls, values and ideologies, and personality predispositions that are invoked daily in ordinary social relations.

In tribal and other societies in which there is a high degree of ritualization of social relations there is usually a very strong sense of traditionalism. Here rituals serve an additional purpose: In the regular repetition of collective acts, a symbolic statement is made that the social order—which is also ideologically exclusive—continues as before in the face of threatened change, unharmed by innovations and adjustments, and in equilibrium. Ritual is a communicative bond that ties the members of the group not only to each other but also to past and future generations. (I am indebted to Corinne Black for bringing this point to my attention.) As will be seen in the discussion of "Hehe Magical Justice" in Selection 13, the use of magic in maintaining social solidarity also is often ritualized.

The role of religion as a link between a horticultural group and its habitat is especially clear in the distribution of the group's resources; see, for example, Rappaport's analysis of the interplay between the religious rituals of a New Guinea group and their system of pork production and distribution (Selection 15). But such relationships are not confined to horticulturists. Max Weber, in his classic studies of Protestantism and the religions of India and China, showed the consequences of religious belief and practices in the economic and political life of very complex societies. Following Weber's mode of analysis, Bellah has examined the consequences of religious attitudes in Japan during the Tokugawa period (Selection 16). Similarly, the religious festivals of Latin American peasants—for which festival sponsors often impoverish themselves—may be looked at as a mechanism for redistributing wealth and equalizing socioeconomic status (Selections 17 and 22).

Are these practices, which appear to have begun in horticultural societies, precursors of the "charity" and philanthropy of industrialized nations, which used to be (and in some instances still are) controlled largely by religious institutions? The allocation of resources and the distribution of goods are integral aspects of every strategy of adaptation, and religious institutions have played an important part in the allocative systems of societies at various stages of development and for a very long time. Even today, if we regard the civil rights movement in the United States as in part a political process to change the lines along which wealth is distributed in our society, it is important to remember that religious institutions—including Negro fundamentalist religious groups—have played a very important role in this.

In any event, in horticultural societies the role of supernatural beliefs is clear. When life is insecure, "man lives, after all, very near the starvation level, either continually, or at certain seasons of the year. Thus the constituents of his daily diet, and his rules and habits of eating, are all linked in one emotional system with the institutions and activities by which food is produced. The bulk of his energies and imaginative effort is centered on the problem of making his supplies secure. . . . Any means, real or illusory, by which the primitive man gains power over the natural resources of the environment, are bound to give him power and authority in the group. . . . Moreover, since the savage believes that he cannot succeed in his food-getting activities without the help of supernatural forces, magic power must be reckoned, like any definitely material asset, as a means of gaining security as to the food supply" (*Hunger and Work in a Savage Tribe: A Functional Study of Nutrition among the Southern Bantu*, by Audrey Richards [Glencoe: The Free Press, 1948], p. 87).

Melford Spiro is similarly explicit in relating supernatural concepts among the people of Ifaluk (in the Caroline Islands) to their technology:

Malinowski's observation [in *Magic, Science, and Religion*] that magic is used in those areas of life in which the degree of control and predictability is slight, is borne out in Ifaluk. There is no garden ritual of any kind that we could discover. The taro grows regularly, only weeding and transplanting with fertilization being required. There has never been a crop failure, or drouth or any other unforeseen contingency that has affected the supply. Breadfruits and coconuts grow without tending. Thus in those matters there is no magic, though there are a number of taboos, the violation of which will adversely affect the food supply. In hazardous undertakings, however, as in house construction, in which there is the chance of men being crushed to death, or in ocean voyages, in which storms may sink the canoe or drive it off its course, or in canoe construction, in which a faulty job will endanger lives, magic is used. . . . These formulas assure the navigator that the canoe will be speedy, that it will not drift off its course when on a journey, and that it will not be shattered (*An Atoll Culture: Ethnography of Ifaluk in the Central Carolines*, by Edwin G. Burrows and Melford E. Spiro [New Haven: Human Relations Area Files, 1953], p. 235).

Priesthood, which implies full religious specialization, is an institution and involves roles that accompany the formation of nations and the establishment of central state organizations in agricultural societies. Differentiations of this kind are adaptive responses to the demands inherent in the establishment of complex national bureaucracies. No nation, however small, can be administered by means of the simple and direct procedures used by the headmen of lineages and hamlets. Nations are too heterogeneous and dispersed for the people who speak in the name of the state to know everyone and to keep all administrative, political, legal, and economic details in their own heads. They must delegate authority and responsibility to different people in charge of different spheres of activity, and religious specialization is part of this overall process.

One of the largest gaps in our knowledge about the establishment of the earliest nation-states is about this delegation of authority and responsibility. How were such decisions arrived at and what were their politics? We can make only the vaguest guesses, highly conjectural because of our automatic predilections to think in terms of specialization and because the rulers of these early nation-states left no records of this process. But it was an aspect of the genius of these men that, although the first rulers of nations—such as Babylonia, Aztec Mexico, Inca Peru—could not have learned from each other's experiences, they generally followed the same course. Did the first emperor of Babylonia (or of Azteca or the Inca empire) say to an underling, "Look, I don't have the time to concern myself with these religious problems; why don't you handle it for me?" Did he at some point say, "We will never get the loyalty of the local peasants until we smash their pagan cults, build our own churches, and get the people to attend them. But there are too many villages for me to officiate in; I have an army, trade treaties, weights and measures, land laws, a criminal code to worry about. Why don't you handle it for me and remind them, while you are at it, that street demonstrations are sinful?" Or did such processes occur inadvertently and without planning, before anyone realized what exactly had happened, in response to the inexorable logic of the situation—in much the same way that rulers of modern "democratic" nations have slipped into patterns of secretiveness in domestic as well as foreign policy.

In any event, differentiation begins slowly, and though it is greater in the early agricultural nation-states than in even the most advanced horticultural societies, there is still considerable commingling. The great temples and ceremonial centers of Mesopotamia, Azteca, Rome, India, and Davidic Judea were political, economic, juridical, and educational as well as religious institutions. As we have seen, the stability and effectiveness of a state system requires that the solidarity and autonomy of local groups be undermined. The integrity of these groups is almost always symbolized, legitimated, and reinforced religiously. To subvert this local power and transfer it to the state system is necessarily a slow and complex process.

Viewed in this way, state religions are not unique or more dominant in shaping the lives of people than the religions of lineage organizations or localized clan communities, or than any other organization of social relations; they are all adaptations to existing social conditions. Established religion everywhere provides legitimation of the ideologies that help to maintain order and conformity and validates the exercise of power and authority. The political sectors of states use the temples they have built and the priesthoods they have created to gain compliance with their policies. Peasants will toil for their masters more readily if they are convinced the deities have decreed they should do so, and every head of state proclaims—as did Hammurabi—that he is merely carrying out the will of the gods. The processes involved are the same as when the head of a lineage invokes the group's ancestors in validating his leadership and authority. Thus there is no basis for regarding religious institutions as the prime movers in the establishment of states; they only help to provide legitimating ideologies for the political institutions that are the significant constraining elements in the habitats of these societies.

There are no known political systems without religious legitimation, whether we consider the political empire of the medieval Roman Catholic Church or the contemporary U.S.S.R. In the Soviet Union there is a state religious cult based on the veneration of Lenin; that the rulers of the Soviet Union have replaced Yahweh with Lenin's ghost in their national cult no more warrants a denial of its religious nature than would an assertion that the polytheistic Washo Indians (Selection 12) or the ancestor-venerating Tallensi (Selection 14) are without religion at all. The cult of Lenin has all the trappings of a national religion, the Soviets' claim to the contrary notwithstanding. There is a huge portrait of Lenin in the altar of the Leningrad Cathedral; Soviet citizens make pilgrimages to Lenin's tomb, a shrine abutting the seat of power in the Kremlin; his prophets periodically reinterpret his words: and the Soviet equation of the charge of anti-Leninism with an assault on the state's integrity differs not a whit from medieval religious inquisitions in Western Europe. These are essential ingredients of a religious cult. Most good Soviet citizens have a portrait of Lenin in their sitting rooms; I do not know if they keep one over their beds.

Just as there are no political systems without religious legitimation, every group's ethical standards tend to be cast in religious terms. When national rulers imposed restrictions on sexual behavior these were often legitimated religiously, as in the Judeo-Christian tradition. The Protestant Ethic—whether referring to sexual austerity, keeping one's nose to the grindstone (and later the lathe), or capital investment—is an outstanding though far from unique example of the fusion of secular values and religious ideology. Slavery, the epitome of human degradation, was defended from almost every pulpit in every society where it was adopted (with appropriate Biblical footnotes) and then declared anathema to God after it had been abandoned (again with appeals to Biblical authority). The Union of South Africa practices the same religions as England and Holland, yet each finds validation for its treatment of its citizens in the same religious creeds and in the same Book. The civil rights movement in the United States did not receive much attention from established religions until after it had been rendered politically "hot" by President John F. Kennedy in 1962; the essential dignity of all men went undiscovered by many congregations prior to that date.

This is not to say that there are not individuals in all societies who dissent from religio-ethical standards—and who thereby are usually marked by epithets—but my principal concern here is with the established symbolic behavior of societies, not the adjustment or maladjustment of individuals. Such notions as the equality of men arise out of particular political and economic conditions and may be without religious overtones. Viewed in this way, the shift of many Jews from egalitarian ideologies in Western societies (where they held minority status) to an ideology supporting elaborate inegalitarianism in Israel (where they are in the majority) has to be examined in terms of political and economic factors rather than in religious and ethical terms.

We generally think of the adaptive process in terms of the development of an increasingly successful sociotechnological organization of society. When we examine magic in evolutionary perspective, however, we see a different kind of development. A belief in magic is observable in almost all societies, but this is not the same as saying that all individuals believe in magical modes of reasoning. It is evident from a historical examination of this aspect of human behavior that as technology advances, there is a progressive suppression or inhibition of reliance on magical thinking and on the use of magic in integrating social institutions. Instead, at more advanced levels of technological development the individual is expected to rely more and more on nonmagical (rational) processes of thought.

Belief in magic is not inherently pathological, but it may be considered so when it contaminates the rational intellectual processes appropriate to advanced technological systems. Reliance on magic in the medical practice of a horticultural population seems less inappropriate than in modern surgery, industrial production, or space flight. We cannot equate a man in contemporary society who carries a rabbit's paw or avoids the number 13 with a horticulturist or pastoralist who will not carry out productive activities without the invocation of magical formulae.

But the displacement of magical thought by rational modes of reasoning did not come until relatively late in human social and technological development. In Egypt during the Middle Kingdom, for example, great heights were reached in surgery, mathematics, architecture, and other areas, but magic was not wholly displaced.

Kings inscribed pottery bowls with the names of hostile tribes in Palestine, Libya, and Nubia; the names of their rulers; and the names of certain rebellious Egyptians. These bowls were solemnly smashed at a ritual, possibly at the funeral of the king's predecessor; and the object of this ritual was explicitly stated. It was that all these enemies, obviously out of the pharaoh's reach, should die. But if we call the ritual act of the breaking of the bowls symbolical, we miss the point. The Egyptians felt that *real* harm was done to the enemies by the destruction of their names. The occasion was even used to cast a propitious spell of wider scope. After the names of the hostile men, who were enumerated "that they should die," were added phrases such as: "all detrimental thought, all detrimental talk, all detrimental dreams, all detrimental plans, all detrimental strife," etc. Mentioning these things on the bowls to be smashed diminished their actual power to hurt the king or lessen his authority (*The Intellectual Adventure of Ancient Man*, by H. and H. A. Frankfort [Chicago: University of Chicago Press, 1946], p. 13).

At the same time, there is clear cut evidence of attempts to displace magical thought in response to the demands of the technology of Egypt's Middle Kingdom:

The Edmund Smith Surgical Papyrus concerns itself chiefly with broken bones. The surgeon describes each break, states whether he believes that he can deal with it successfully, and gives the indicated treatment. The text is full of glosses, explaining the technical or strange terms which were no longer in the language of the day. There is remarkably little magic in the treatise. With one glaring exception, the surgeon confined himself to manual treatment, rest, diet, and medicaments. Further in certain cases where the surgeon confessed himself unable to deal successfully with a serious fracture, he went on to observe the progressive stages of the ailment. This is very significant; he did not ascribe a hopeless case to the malignant activity of some divine or daemonic force; he did not resort to magico-religious hocus-pocus; with dispassionate scientific curiosity, he noted the succession of purely physical symptoms. Within the mythmaking mind of the times, this matter-of-fact attitude was rare and very creditable (*The Culture of Ancient Egypt*, by John A. Wilson [Chicago: University of Chicago Press, Phoenix Books, 1951], p 57).

Like religion, magic cannot be understood only in terms of technological imperatives; it also has a sociopolitical aspect. The rulers of agricultural nations often tried to outlaw or otherwise control the practice of witchcraft and sorcery by local practitioners, meanwhile—as in the case of Middle Egyptian kings—retaining magic as a royal prerogative. There seem to be two principal reasons for this behavior; they are closely related to each other, and can be understood as aspects of adaptation to the social and political elements in the habitat.

First, in stateless horticultural groups and other technologically less advanced societies, witchcraft and sorcery are important means of self-defense and social control, intertwined with most other aspects of daily life. The magical practitioner is thus an important figure in the social and psychological security systems of these groups. By controlling the practice of magical procedures at local levels, the rulers of nation-states seek to demonstrate that the population is dependent on the agencies of the state for protection rather than on local ties and symbols.

Second, because of the power of magical practitioners, they are capable of fomenting sedition and rebellion. This is especially important during the early stages of state formation, when state and local groups are engaged in their greatest struggles. One of the foremost tasks of those who speak in the name of the state is to protect themselves against insurrection, just as they must guard against flood, drought, and food shortages. Seditious leaders who are—or who can make use of—magical practitioners have a potentially broad social and emotional base at the local level for staging rebellion or organizing mass resistance. Hence from the point of view of a nation's rulers, they are dangerous and must be suppressed, controlled, or replaced by centrally regulated symbol systems.

It is not enough that a nation's rulers legitimate their political authority by religious and other symbolic means; their subjects must at the same time accept their rule as an adaptation to the social and political habitat. This too is done in religious ideologies and through religious practices, by which established power and authority are validated. When subjects accept political rule they come to feel that they have as much at stake in the political *status quo* as their rulers, and this includes their social status as well (though they may aspire for higher status for their children); this process is examined in Selection 18. More important, a commitment to existing political institutions and status relationships—which is also religiously expressed— embraces an equally firm espousal of the technology and organization of social relations to which the political system is tied.

Residues of danger and unpredictability have been greatly reduced by our industrial technology, and as we might expect, religion plays almost no role in the technological aspects of modern industrial adaptation. This is not to say that there is no uncertainty in our habitat, but it is perceived as coming from evil men who reject the ideology that the existing order is supernaturally foreordained. But just as established religion legitimates established authority, challenges to this authority may also be cast in religious terms. The civil rights movement in the United States cannot be understood without recognizing the role of the Negro store-front and other fundamentalist churches—usually regarded as bastions of conservatism—and the clerical status of Martin Luther King and other black leaders.

Can we then say that the Montgomery bus boycott was precipitated by religion rather than that it was a religious legitimation of changing conditions and values? Even retrospective prediction is risky, but I do not think that the beginning of the modern civil rights movement could have occurred without the desegregation decision of the United States Supreme Court in 1954, and that ruling was in response to political and economic requirements of the society. Is it any wonder that the slogan "Impeach Earl Warren" (who symbolized the decision) was most strongly voiced among economically marginal, white, religious fundamentalists who felt they had the most to lose if the status of Negroes and other disenfranchised groups was improved? It is against this background that Bryan Wilson's chapter (Selection 18) should be read, in which he discusses religion in England and the United States as aspects of our respective status systems. Religion is one of the stages on which conflicting social, economic, and political interests are acted out symbolically. Such conflicts in our time may be viewed as anticipatory aspects of adaptations to a post-industrial stage of development.

There are many varied and useful books presenting points of view on the anthropological study of religion. A good brief introduction is in the articles on "Religion" and "Ritual" in *The International Encyclopedia of the Social Sciences* (2nd edition, New York: Macmillan, 1968). One approach that has gained much popularity in recent years is in the work of Victor W. Turner; see his *The Forest of Symbols: Aspects of Ndembu Ritual* (Ithaca: Cornell University Press, 1967) and *The Ritual Process: Structure and Anti-Structure* (Chicago: Aldine, 1969). *The Peyote Religion among the Navaho*, by David F. Aberle (Chicago: Aldine, 1966) is one of the finest studies available, dealing not only with important substantive issues but also with methodological considerations in the study of religion.

An important paper illustrating the idea that the communications embodied in religion go beyond mere ritual is "Religion and Social Communication in Village North India," by John J. Gumperz (in *Religion in South Asia*, Edward B. Harper, editor [Seattle: University of Washington Press, 1964]). "Some Aspects of Ritualized Behavior in Interpersonal Relationships," by Yehudi A. Cohen (*Human Relations*, 11 [1958]: 195-215) discusses secular ritual in military and caste organizations. Also significant in this connection are two more books by Max Gluckman: *Essays on the Ritual of Social Relations* (New York: Humanities Press, 1962) and *Politics, Law, and Ritual in Tribal Society* (Chicago: Aldine, 1965). There are several very important articles in *Anthropological Approaches to the Study of Religion* (A.S.A. Monograph 3; New York: Praeger, 1966).

The major textbooks and general anthologies dealing with the anthropological study of religion are *The Heathens: Primitive Man and his Religions*, W. W. Howells, editor (Garden City, N.Y.: Doubleday, 1962); *Reader in Comparative Religion*, William A. Lessa and Evon Z. Vogt, editors (New York: Harper and Row, 1965); *An Introduction to Anthropology of Religion*, by Annemarie de Wall Malefijt (New York: Macmillan, 1968); *Gods and Rituals*, John Middleton, editor (Garden City, N.Y.: Natural History Press, 1967); *Religion in Primitive Society* by Edward Norbeck (New York: Harper, 1961); *Sociology of Religion*, by Joachim Wach (Chicago: University of Chicago Press, 1944); and *Religion: An Anthropological View*, by Anthony Wallace (New York: Random House, 1966). Important for its influence on work in this special field is *Magic, Science, and Religion*, by Bronislaw Malinowski (Glencoe: Free Press, 1948). Other important works will be cited in the introductions to the essays in this section.

12. SPIRITS, POWER, AND MAN

JAMES F. DOWNS

From The Two Worlds of the Washo: An Indian Tribe of California and Nevada, *by James F. Downs. Copyright © 1966 by Holt, Rinehart and Winston, Inc. Reprinted by permission of Holt, Rinehart and Winston, Inc. James F. Downs, before becoming an anthropologist, worked as a newsman, horseman, and farmer. His professional anthropological experience includes field research among the Washo of California and Nevada and the Navajo of Arizona, and he has done research on Tibetan culture. He has taught at the Universities of Washington, Rochester, Wyoming, and Arizona.*

■ We begin with an example of the religious and magical systems of hunter-gatherers : the Washo of California and Nevada. People at this stage of development are always polytheistic, believing in many deities ; however, polytheism is not confined to hunter-gatherers and is found at almost every level of development.

Subsistence was often precarious for the Washo. During the summer months they camped on the shores of Lake Tahoe—though without the diversions of gambling casinos and night clubs—where fish were abundant. Unlike the Indians of the Northwest Coast, however, the Washo never stumbled on techniques of preserving fish and hence were unable to develop surpluses to carry them through the winter months. When the supply of fish dwindled, they left their lakeside camps and turned to hunting and gathering. Thus they exemplify a strategy of adaptation (and its accompanying modes of thought) that characterizes people who do not control the presence of the food on which they subsist.

In the following selection, James F. Downs introduces us to the religion and magic of the Washo by posing some of the questions about the nature and problems of life for which all men seek answers. The Washo have tried to answer some of these questions by religious modes of thought and others by magic ; sometimes the two overlap, but they are inextricably parts of a total way of life. The relatively poor mastery of the Washo over their habitat forces them into a heavy reliance on religion and magic. The inability of people at this stage of development to form kinship and other solidary groups leaves each man relatively autonomous in his legal relationships ; paralleling this is a religious system in which each man is his own religious functionary, propitiating the deities with the same individualism with which he settles disputes and safeguards his own interests and those of his family.

There is a very good description of Eskimo religious and magical beliefs and practices in "The Religion of the Eskimos," by Margaret Lantis (in *Ancient Religions*, V. Ferm, editor [New York : Philosophical Library, 1950]). Another useful account of a polytheistic religion as an aspect of an overall strategy of adaptation can be found in *Naskapi*, by Frank G. Speck (Norman : University of Oklahoma Press, 1935) ; see also *Ojibwa Religion and the Midewiwin*, by Ruth Landes (Madison : University of Wisconsin Press, 1968). ■

WITHIN THE SCOPE of his limited technology, the Washo was a rational person, well aware of cause and effect and prepared to handle the exigencies of his position. However, the precarious balance of Washo society often made survival seemingly dependent on chance. Why should a well-trained hunter locate his quarry only to have it escape him at the last moment? How could a well-made and well-aimed arrow miss an easy shot? Why should one man on a raid be wounded or killed and another escape unscathed? Why should the pine nut tree be fruitful one year and not at all the next? How was it that sickness struck down one person and passed over another? Why indeed should a man, unwounded and unhurt, die at all? These questions plague all societies and in many, including our own, are more or less successfully resolved in sophisticated theologies. Among many primitives, the basis of religion is an explanation of both the how and the why of the vagaries of life. The ritual of many primitive peoples, including those of the Washo, are both expressions of the Washo view of cause and effect and an attempt to maintain an understandable order to life.

The Washo did not articulate a complete

philosophy or theology. Their religious life dealt with the practical day-to-day events: hunting, war, love, birth, health, and death. Yet we can present an organized picture of Washo religious life. We must remember, however, that a systematic presentation of Washo religion is a device which helps us understand a foreign and confusing point of view. It does not reflect the minds of the Washo as they go about their daily tasks, scarcely separating the sacred and the profane.

POWER

To many of the questions posed above the Washo's answer was "power." A successful hunter was more than skilled and careful, he was aided by a special power. A man who dreamed of rabbits or antelope was more than simply lucky, he was a possessor of a special power. The nature of this power is not clearly defined in all cases. We can see how power works most clearly if we learn how a man becomes a "doctor," or shaman, among the Washo. The shaman was expected to carry his share of the burden of living, but his special powers set him apart from his fellows and contributed to his livelihood because his services were valuable and demanded payment. The shaman's special power was the ability to diagnose and cure illness.

Illness might come from three sources. A ghost, angry because some piece of his property was being used by the living, might make the user sick. A sorcerer might cause illness by using magic to "shoot" a foreign body into his victim. Or a person might become ill because he had violated some taboo such as mistreating pine nuts or piñon trees. To affect a cure, a shaman was called to perform a ceremony over the patient. The cure was felt to be brought about not by the shaman's skill but by his "power" which was felt to be apart from the person of the shaman himself. The shaman served as a medium through which the power could be used to the benefit of the sick person. A treatment required that the shaman work for four nights. In addition to the shaman, the patient's family and a number of friends gathered. On each of the nights the shaman prayed to his power to assist him, smoked

tobacco, frequently a sacred or semi-sacred act among Indians; and sang special songs which were his alone. Accompanying his singing with a rattle made of dry cocoons, he passed into a trance and while in this state located the site of the illness and identified the cause. If a ghost was the cause, the shaman would identify the contaminating object and instruct the patient as to whether he should get rid of it or perhaps simply treat it differently. If, on the other hand, an enemy had "shot" a sickness into the patient, the shaman would remove it by sucking, employing an eagle feather and tobacco smoke to make the extraction easier. When the object was removed and shown to the patient and his guests, the shaman would lecture it and then throw it away into the night. He was able to produce an object by means of legerdemain. He did not, however, feel that this was in any way hypocritical. His ability to perform these slight-of-hand tricks was part of the exercise of his power. We might compare his use of slight-of-hand to instill confidence in his power to the bedside manner of a modern doctor attempting to instill confidence in his patients. For his services a shaman was paid in food and valuable objects. The process of becoming a doctor illustrates the nature of power as the Washo conceived it.

The power to become a shaman was not sought by the Washo, it came unsought and often unwelcomed. The first signs of receiving power were often a series of dreams. In these dreams an animal, a bear, an owl, a "ghost" or some other being would appear. The vision would offer him power and assistance in life. The Washo feared power; it was dangerous for one who had it and the greater and more clearly defined the power, the more dangerous it was. The trancelike state which was part of the curing ceremony seemed to many Washo to be akin to death, a loss of spirit. Because of this, a young man might ignore the offers of spiritual power. But a spirit being, or *wegaleyo*, frequently refused to be ignored. It would begin to inflict a series of ailments upon its chosen vehicle. Although it was not considered good social form to brag of having power or to openly seek it, some men did secretly hope for power. Men of this type today invariably complain of a long series of illnesses, seizures, and ailments. To the outsider such a person might appear to be simply a hypochondriac, but the Washo recognized this as a veiled claim to power. Under pressure from the *wegaleyo*, a man would usually succumb and accept his power. Once he had made this secret decision, his dreams would become instruction sessions. The *wegaleyo* would tell him where he could find a special spring or pool. This was "his water" to be used in ceremonies or for ritual bathing or to decontaminate sacred articles collected by the shaman in his career. The spirit also taught his pupil a special song which he would remember word for word when he awoke. In later years a shaman might learn many such songs from his spirit. He would also receive instructions as to what equipment to collect. This would always include a rattle and eagle feathers. Individuals might also possess special stones, shell jewelry, or animal skins. These objects were usually obtained under unusual or miraculous circumstances. One shaman, for instance, had a stone shaped like a human molar which attracted his attention by whistling until he located the stone. In addition to his instructions direct from his spirit, a prospective shaman would seek out an established practitioner and apprentice himself to the older man. The tutor would instruct his apprentice in the arts of legerdemain, ventriloquism, and such feats as smoking several pipefulls of tobacco without allowing the smoke to escape from his lungs. In time, after his powers were known through participation in ceremonies held by his mentor, a shaman would be asked to perform cures of his own.

Shamans were always considered to be potential sorcerers. Their power was neither good nor bad in itself and could be used for whatever ends the shaman sought. The ability to use power against others is illustrated in a traditional Washo tale, which also points out the basic suspicion held by southern Washo toward northern Washo. According to the story, a northern Washo appeared at a camp in Carson Valley and there asked for food. Because he was a stranger, he was refused by all but one old woman. She fed the stranger and allowed him to sleep in her camp. The man left the camp determined to work vengeance on the people who had been so miserly with him. Walking west from Carson Valley, the northerner rested at the hot springs near Markleville. There performing some unknown magic, he pointed his finger in the direction of the camp. The power he controlled killed all the members of the camp, save the old woman who had been generous to him. Modern Washo insist that one can see a barren line in the earth stretching from Markleville to Carson Valley. They also insist that the campsite is covered with skeletons and abandoned equipment. This winter camp may well have been struck by the plague or some other epidemic disease.

Tradition describes other uses of shamanistic power. In what might be described as advertising contests, shaman engaged in tests of power, particularly at gatherings such as the *gumsaba*.[1] The most common demonstration of power was said to be setting a number of stakes in a line. The shaman would point at the sticks and the winner of the contest was the shaman who could knock down the most sticks. Shaman are reported to have engaged in casual displays of power by offering an unsuspecting victim a pipe, or in later times, a cigarette. The shaman's power would remain in the pipe or cigarette and the smoker would be knocked flat or perhaps unconscious. To possess such power was dangerous and inconvenient. A person who received his power from the deer, for instance, could no longer eat deer meat. If he did, he would become ill and perhaps die. The possession of power also made one subject to frightening and mysterious experiences. A well-known shaman in the early part of this century staged a curing ceremony during which he fell into the fire while in a trance Burning his trousers off, he had to go home wearing his shirt as a loin cloth although he was not hurt. On his way the shaman stopped at a stream to bathe. As he bent over the water, he fell into a faint and was taken down into the water. There he was greeted by Water Baby, a spirit creature said to inhabit all bodies of water in the Washo country. The Water Baby took the shaman into a strange land to meet the king of the Water Babies who lived in a large stone house. There the shaman was entertained by five young girls who taught him a special song. The Water Baby guide then took the shaman back to the surface and left him where the frightened man awoke floating in the water.

If a shaman lost his sacred paraphernalia or it was destroyed, he would most certainly become seriously ill. Because of these dangers, many

1. "Big Time" gathering at the time of Piñon Harvest.

men tried to avoid power if it was thrust upon them and would employ a shaman to help them rid themselves of the persistent spirit. If this was successful they could resume the normal Washo life. If not, they had little choice but to quiet the spirit and accept its gift.

The nature of power is most clearly seen in the complex of Washo shamanism, but *wegelayo* often provided special powers of a less general nature. Some men with a water *wegelayo* were believed to be able to bring rain. Others who had been visited by the bear *wegelayo* might on occasion act like a bear and be particularly brave or notably short tempered. Others might have the power to handle rattlesnakes with impunity and cure rattlesnake bites. The Water Baby might act as a *wegelayo* and give a person the power to walk under water. There is said to be a broad road of white sand across the bottom of Lake Tahoe. This was the special route of men with Water Baby *wegelayo* who wished to visit the beds of wild poison parsnips on the north shore of the lake. These poison plants used to be eaten with impunity as a demonstration of power. Some specially powerful men received their power from a number of different sources all of which helped in curing or performing other miracles.

The most dangerous task for a shaman was to recover the soul of a person who had apparently died. It was believed that with the help of his *wegelayo* a shaman could go into a trance and, in spirit form, follow the soul of the dead person into the land of the dead. This was described as a place in the sky to the south of Washo country. Its approaches were guarded by a number of fierce warriors. Behind these sentries was a spring. If the shaman could overtake the soul before it had drunk from the spring he could return it to its earthly body and revive his patient. This land of the dead was said to be a happy place where people played games and gambled and danced unless they had committed a murder. Murderers were banned by the other shades and placed in a kind of heavenly coventry.

We have spoken of shaman as being males, but women could also become shaman and many did. Their experiences and training did not differ from those of men. Power was not exclusively a gift of the spirit beings to humans. In a general way, everything was viewed as having some power. Merely to live required some supernatural assistance. Successful survival was a sign of power and thus old people had demonstrated that they were powerful. There was a widespread belief that old people were dangerous and should not be offended or harmed lest they retaliate by using their power. This belief worked to assure that an ancient Washo in his final years would receive support from those who were obligated to him. Even though he might be unable to share the burdens of life, he could avenge himself on those who did not behave ethically. This general power was extended to all living things, animals, and plants and, as we have seen, was the basis of many of the behavior patterns associated with hunting, fishing, and gathering.

GHOSTS

The spirits of the dead were to be greatly feared and avoided. No Washo ever thought of his ancestors as benign figures concerned with his happiness and welfare. Instead they were angry and vengeful. If their property was used or misused, if their burial was not properly conducted, or for any one of a dozen other sins of ommission or commission, the dead might return to plague the living. Therefore Washo funerals were not ceremonies designed to honor the dead or comfort the living. They were ways of making sure the dead person's spirit would not return. It was for this reason that his home was burned or abandoned. If he returned to familiar haunts, the house and family would be gone. For the same reason his clothing and personal property were burned or buried with him. A person using some possession of a dead man was always liable to a visit from the ghost who had located his property and found the user. The brief Washo burial prayers were really exhortations to the dead person to accept his death and leave the living alone. He was told that no one had killed him and that no one was angry at him. Association with the dead was slightly contaminating and upon returning from funerals people washed themselves before handling food or touching children lest the contamination spread and attract the ghost. The Washo argue that it is the nature of things that the dead should remain dead and not bother the living. For this reason they say a rain storm always occurs after a death to wipe out the footprints of the deceased and thus remove all traces of his existence. The taboo on using the name of the dead was another such precaution. Despite all these precautions, the dead did return. Sometimes they came on specific missions of vengeance and on other occasions to simply wander in the vicinity of human beings. The twirling dust devils so common in the summer in this region were thought to be ghosts, and a sudden puff of warm air on a still summer night was most certainly a shade. The belief in ghosts and personal power was an important factor in Washo child raising practices. Parents avoided striking or spanking a child for fear of angering some dead relative. In this instance the ghost seemed to have some friendly concern for the living, but the manner of showing it was to cause the death of the child as a punishment to the parents. The fear of sorcery led the Washo to encourage their younger children to remain within their own family groups. Associating with strangers, particularly old strangers, could be dangerous. This belief is obviously related to the development of deep ties of dependence on one's close relatives and the strengthening of the all important Washo family unit. The two major concepts of Washo religion are: ghosts, to be feared, avoided, and appeased; and power, to be used to accomplish the business of living. But, these were not all the facets of Washo religion. Like most people the Washo had explanations for the natural and human environment in which they found themselves. These explanations were preserved in a body of mythology. The corpus of myth was not an elaborate and involved body of scripture. Rather, it consisted of a number of rather simple tales, many of which seem confused and inconsistent to foreigners.

there was a different set of inhabitants, the modern Indians representing the fifth inhabitation of the earth. The creation of the various cultural groups known to the Washo is attributed to "Creation Women" who made the Washo, the Paiutes, and the Diggers (a generic term for California Indians) out of the seeds of the cattail. Still another tale tells of how a different personage, "Creation Man," formed the three groups by separating his three sons so they would not quarrel. The natural features of the Washo country are usually explained by reference to a pair of weasels. These two, *Damalali* (short-tailed weasel) and *Pewetseli* (long-tailed weasel), traveled together. The wiser *Pewetseli* usually managing to save the day threatened by the impulsive behavior of the rascal *Damalali*. The general structure of these tales is reminiscent of a common theme of adventuresome twin brothers found throughout much of western North America. The many lakes in the mountain region are, for instance, said to be caused by one such misadventure of the weasels. *Damaladi*, the story says, came upon a Water Baby and took it prisoner. The water creature at first begged for his freedom and finally threatened to flood the world. When neither pleading nor threats moved the weasel, the Water Baby made good his threat and caused a flood to come which covered the mountains to their tips. *Pewetseli*, furious at his companion's irresponsibility, forced him to release the water spirit and begged the creature to lower the waters. This the Water Baby did, but in every mountain valley a lake remained. The adventures of this pair are seemingly endless, many of the incidences are virtually meaningless to the outsider, and in many cases the modern Washo appear to have forgotten the real significance of the episode. In other cases they appear to be simply humorous or sometimes salacious stories told for amusement.

CREATION

Two myths deal with creation and although they are quite different, the inconsistency seems not to trouble the Washo who use whichever set of tales seems most appropriate at the time. The world is described in one set of myths as having gone through a number of stages. In each stage

OTHER FIGURES

A number of other miraculous figures appear in Washo mythology, all of them threatening and dangerous at least in part. *Hanglwuiwui*, a great one-eyed, one-legged giant, is said to have hopped from hilltop to hilltop in search of his favorite food, Indians. Near Gardenerville,

Nevada, there is a cave called by the Washo
Hanglwuiwuiangl, the dwelling of Hanglwuiwui,
which is still avoided or approached with caution
although most Washo say that the giant has
been dead for a long time.

Another fearsome feature of Washo mythology was the *Ang*, a great bird which carried off
human victims and terrorized the world. Birds
such as this figure in many Indian myths. The
Ang is said to have died and fallen into Lake
Tahoe where its skeleton formed a reef, which
the Washo insist can be seen by anyone flying
over the lake. The failure of white airplane
pilots to report the reef is felt to be a conspiracy
to discredit Washo belief.

The coyote, a figure found almost universally
in Indian mythology, was prominent in Washo
legends. As is true in other tribes, the nature of
coyote is exceedingly difficult to define. In some
episodes he is a dangerous and threatening
force, in others quite benevolent, and in yet
others a rather stupid fellow given to jokes and
tricks and generally finding himself the laughing stock. One such tale describes the coyote
attempting to seduce a young woman who
thwarts him by inserting a seed pot between her
legs and injuring coyote in an embarrassing
and painful manner. Most coyote tales still told
emphasize his lecherous and rascally nature and
are told as salacious stories rather than moral
fables. Some persons were felt to be able to turn
themselves into coyotes and threaten their
fellow men. Stories of such occurrences are not
unknown today.

In addition to the one-legged giant, the
Washo believed that the mountains were
inhabited by another race, possibly human but
possessed of much more power than ordinary
people. These giants or wild men figure in many
stories of disappearance or mysterious occurrences while on hunting trips. Occasionally, they
directly attacked humans, trying to steal food
from them or otherwise bother them. In most
cases in stories dealing with these direct con-
frontations, the wild man was bested by the
cleverness or courage of the Washo. In 1911 an
Indian appeared in Oroville, California, attempting to steal scraps from a local slaughterhouse.
He was eventually identified as Ishi, the last
survivor of a small band of southern Yana who
had maintained a furtive and fearful freedom in
the Sierra foothills. His appearance caused a

minor sensation as the "last wild Indian" in the
United States. Modern Washo believe that he
was not an Indian but one of the wild men of
their myths.

One Washo tale tells of a great battle between
the Washo and the giants in which the giants,
who had no bows, were defeated after building
a fort and throwing stones at the Washo. It is
possible that the wild men represent some
previous culture inhabiting the region. References to them and to a great battle in which
they were exterminated are found in the mytho-
logies of many groups in the Great Basin. Many
of the Washo myths have been forgotten or have
become garbled as the Washo world changed
and the conditions that they have described and
explained disappeared. One figure has maintained its vitality and dominates the supernatural life of the modern Washo as it did that
of the aboriginal tribe. This is the Water Baby
mentioned previously. These little creatures are
described as being two or three feet tall with
long black hair that never touches the ground
but instead floats behind the Water Baby when
it walks. They are grey in color and soft and
clammy to the touch and possess immense
power. Every body of water, lake, river, stream,
pond, sink, or modern irrigation ditch is
occupied by Water Babies. There is, according
to Washo tradition, a tunnel from Lake Tahoe
to the Carson Valley used by the Water Babies
when they travel. All Washo today have heard
the high mewing call of the Water Baby luring
them toward some body of water at night.
When they hear such a summons they hide
in their houses and resist the temptation to
follow.

In aboriginal times certain springs and lakes
were considered to be favorite haunts of the
Water Babies. Persons seeking their assistance,
in curing an illness for instance, made or
purchased an especially fine basket and deposited
it in the lake or pond as a gift. Water Baby was
a frequent *wegelayo* for the most powerful
shamans. As individuals, Water Babies visited
human beings. Some Washo believed that simply
to see a Water Baby brought illness or death.
Others felt it was a good omen, a chance to
obtain power. Some others argue that a Water
Baby did not give power but instead exchanged
it for a human life. A gift of Water Baby was
repaid with the life of a relative.

While many of the figures of Washo mythology have grown vague, their stories half forgotten and their place in Washo life reduced, the Water Baby has demonstrated an amazing vitality. Stories of visitations, or hearing Water Baby calls from streams or ponds, of seeing Water Baby footprints are still told. In fact, the Water Baby has kept abreast of the times and one informant with whom I talked stubbornly insisted he could tell a female Water Baby's footprints because she wore high-heeled shoes! Almost all the Washo are somewhat fearful of the consequences of the ignorance of white men in the matter of Water Babies. Fishermen or hunters, they fear, might catch or kill a Water Baby by mistake. One such misadventure is said to have resulted in the San Francisco earthquake of 1906. A fisherman caught a Water Baby and gave it to the San Francisco aquarium. Despite the warnings of a famous Indian leader who went to San Francisco to talk to the mayor, the creature was kept in the aquarium. It remained there until the earth shook and the water came up over the city. When the water receded the Water Baby, of course, was gone.

A most important element of the Washo world was the view that animals were not really any different than human beings. That is, they had societies of their own and languages and a special place in nature and a supernatural power which in some cases was greater than man's. The large and ferocious animals like the bear were considered to be intrinsically more powerful than men and we have seen that to kill a bear was an act which conferred power. Other animals, like men, might or might not have power. But the old buck who successfully eluded the hunter and even a wily rabbit who would not be killed were considered to have special power and to be *mushege* or "wild animals." But the term was not limited to animals alone. A man of particular fierceness or power, one who hunted successfully or was a renowned fighter or who simply had an unpredictable temper, was also called *mushege*. This partial equation of men and animals and the behavior which it engendered, as we shall see, was particularly important in developing the contacts between the Washo and white invaders of their land.

SUMMARY

In this chapter we have examined some of the basic concepts and figures of Washo religious life. Washo religion was not based on a well-developed theological scheme but instead must for the most part be analyzed from the behaviour of people in day-to-day life. There were few, if any, purely religious acts. Instead, we see ritual reflecting a Washo view of the supernatural woven through nearly every act of the day. Hunting ritual, dreams of rabbits and fish and antelope, special power to obtain food, respectful treatment of the remains of animals, the minor ceremonies of childbirth and childhood were all viewed as essential parts of the actitivties with which they were associated. To go hunting without taking the proper ritual steps would be as foolish in Washo eyes as failing to take a bow or using a crooked arrow. To try and hunt with a weapon contaminated by a menstruating woman would be as hopeless as going into the field with a bow but no bowstring. Another feature of Washo religion was that its observance seldom required the participation of specialists or of special groups of people. The ritual of life was the ritual of individuals or individuals within the family group. Certain occasions when people could come together for extended periods were also times when religious rituals were performed. But they were also occasions for games and gambling and courtship and could not be considered purely religious occasions. Even in curing, when a specialist was needed, any shaman would do, if his power was great enough. There was no special caste of priests and any person, man or woman, might become a shaman. Shamans said to have Water Baby power were believed to have a secret cave which could be entered by sinking into Lake Tahoe and then rising inside a great rock. This is the nearest thing to an assocation or guild of specialists.

In short, Washo religion offered an explanation for the universe as it existed and for the accidents and misadventures of life. It also provided a system of ritual to be used in the business of life which probably allayed some of the fear and uncertainty of the hunting and gathering existence. Because each step in ritual was associated with practical matters, the sacred actions may have provided a framework within which the practical actions could be more easily learned and remembered. As simple as it might be, Washo religion played an important role in aboriginal life and has, as we shall see, a cornerstone of Washo cultural survival in the modern world.

13. HEHE MAGICAL JUSTICE

EDGAR V. WINANS AND ROBERT B. EDGERTON

Reproduced by permission of the American Anthropological Association from American Anthropologist, *Vol. 66, No. 4, 1964. Edgar V. Winans is Professor of Anthropology and Chairman of the department, University of Washington. His principal research interest is social and economic change in developing nations. He has done fieldwork in Tanzania, Kenya, and Uganda on problems of human ecology, political and economic organization, and development planning. His publications include* Shambala: The Constitution of a Traditional State. *Robert B. Edgerton is Associate Professor of Anthropology at the University of California, Los Angeles, jointly in the Department of Anthropology and the Department of Psychiatry. His major field research has included work among East African tribes, the Menomini Indians, Mexican-Americans and part-Hawaiians. His principal publications include* The Cloak of Competence, Drunken Comportment (*with C. McAndrew*), Changing Perspectives in Mental Illness (*with S. Plog*), and The Individual in Cultural Adaptation.

■ We have seen that in sedentary horticultural societies, corporate kin groups develop along with notions of exclusive territoriality; these property concepts protect the investment of time and effort in cultivated plots with a view to future returns. Since land ownership in most such societies is vested in the corporate kin group, rather than in the individual or his family, the integrity of this group is considered to be inviolate. One of the characteristics of corporate groups—whether lineages or nations—is that they are symbolized and reinforced by religious means.

All groups, including corporate groups, produce and cope with tensions, but groups at different levels of social and technological development have different ways of meeting the problem. In hunting-gathering societies, group fission is the prevalent technique, but in horticultural societies, people must stay put and therefore must develop other means of reducing tension. One of these is a reliance on particular religious and magical concepts, which are themselves reinforced by the precariousness of this mode of acquiring a livelihood.

An example of these concepts and relationships is provided by Edgar Winans and Robert Edgerton in their description of the Hehe of East Africa. As they show in the following selection, magic here is no more a matter of idiosyncratic belief and practice than religion; instead, it is an orderly and But cross-cutting all of the solutions—whether systematized mode of behavior, connoting sets of shared expectations, roles, and statuses.

We saw in the description of Kuba law in Selection 9 that magical tests play an important role there; Winans and Edgerton similarly describe the interplay of magic and the tensions of normal interpersonal relationships among the Hehe. The authors begin by describing a universal phenomenon—father-son conflict—which has always been a human problem and which every society must handle in terms of its preconceptions about kin and other social relations. (The prodigal son is a major theme in the art and literature of many kin-based societies.) Among horticulturists, the acquisition of rights to the use of land claimed by the kin group is inherited. Under such conditions, amicable relations between father and son are indispensable, since the father also represents the authority of the larger group. When tensions erupt, symbolic means—such as those of magic and religion—are used to hold them in check and thereby maintain the integrity of the group.

The following selection illustrates how in every society there is a logical base—a set of related preconceptions and assumptions—on which people act in determining how conflicts are to be resolved. The authors show us what alternatives are open to the Hehe in each type of conflict; sometimes there are none, and the solution is dictated by the nature of the particular problem.

they involve civil, religious, or magical means—are certain themes that are repeatedly invoked, such as confession of wrongdoing, apology, and the payment of compensation.

The research on which this paper is based was part of a project investigating culture and ecology in East Africa of which Walter Goldschmidt's study of Sebei law (Selection 8) was also a part. Another useful report stemming from this collaborative research is "'Cultural' vs. 'Ecological' Factors in the Expression of Values, Attitudes, and Personality Characteristics," by Robert B. Edgerton (*American Anthropologist*, 67 [1965] : 442-47 ; reprinted as Selection 24 in *The Cultural Present*).

The reader who wishes to explore further in this sphere of social activity will find the following works unusually rich in data and ideas : "Witchcraft in Four African Societies : An Essay in Comparison," by S. F. Nadel (*American Anthropologist*, 54 [1952] : 18-29) ; *Navaho Witchcraft*, by Clyde Kluckhohn (Boston : Beacon Press, 1967) ; "The Social Function of Anxiety in a Primitive Society," by A. I. Hallowell (*American Sociological Review*, 6 [1941] : 869-81 ; reprinted in Hallowell's *Culture and Experience* [Philadelphia : University of Pennsylvania Press, 1955, pp. 266-76) ; *Paiute Sorcery*, by Beatrice B. Whiting (Viking Fund Publications in Anthropology, Number 15, 1950) ; "Witch Beliefs and Social Structure," by Monica H. Wilson (*American Journal of Sociology*, 56 [1951] : 307-13) ; "Witchcraft and Co-Wife Proximity in Southwestern Kenya" (*Ethnology*, 1 [1962] : 39-45) ; and *Witchcraft, Sorcery and Social Categories among the Safwa*, by Alan Harwood (New York and London : Oxford University Press, 1969). ∎

THE EXPRESSION OF legitimate grievance and the quasi-legal rectification of wrongs appear to be very important components of many systems of magical belief. Marett's venerable position that magic is basically antisocial appears to be misleading in the light of accumulated ethnographic experience. Similarly, the distinction often drawn between religion as public and moral, and magic as private and amoral is simplistic. For example, "white" magic is almost universal and magic used for explicitly moral, or quasi-legal ends is reported from many parts of the world. The Azande, Nyakyusa, Ifugao, Trobrianders, and Cheyenne, to mention but a few well-known cases, all possess such magic. Thus Evans-Pritchard tells us, "When a man dies Azande consider that he is a victim of witchcraft or sorcery and they make vengeance-magic to slay the slayer of the dead man. It is regarded as a judge which seeks out the person who is responsible for the death, and as an executioner which slays him. Azande say of it that 'it decides cases' and that it 'settles cases as judiciously as princes.' Like all good magic it acts impartially and according to the merits of the case."

We have chosen to term magic of this sort "moral magic." This choice is based not simply on the fact that this magic does not have an immoral status, but because it is so manifestly a negative sanction against violation of moral norms. In the Hehe view, it will not work if the cause is not just. If there has been no violation of morality by the intended victim the magic not only fails to harm him, it rebounds on its maker who has used it unjustly. This positive moral character of magic is not peculiar to the Hehe; it may be found in numerous other societies, and we suggest that viewing magic as, at best, an amoral instrumentality runs against a substantial body of ethnographic fact.

Reveiwing the literature on several societies, Hoebel concludes: ". . . magic, the use of the supernatural for moral ends, long remains the handmaid of the law, mopping up where the broom of the law fails to sweep clean." In Hehe society, the handmaid wields her magical mop in a most vigorous manner, for not only is some magic moral, it is jural as well. Magic, divination, confession, apology, and compensation provide a moral-jural complex in which grievance is expressed and justice is achieved. Courts and moots also exist and are often used, but the frequency of their use is rivaled, if not exceeded, by recourse to magical-jural techniques.

A vast range of Hehe supernatural beliefs exists in addition to that which concerns us in this paper. We intend to explore here only the relationship of magic, morality, and justice through the presentation of case materials selected to illuminate this aspect of Hehe social control.

THE SETTING

The Hehe are a Bantu-speaking people who occupy the Iringa Area of the Southern Highlands Region of Tanganyika. To the north and west their country is bounded by the Great Ruaha River and to the south and east by the escarpment of the Kilombero Valley. Nearly the whole of the area is relatively high, rolling country covered by deciduous *miombo* woodland, windswept grassland, and, in the highest parts, tropical rainforest. The people, who number some 250,000 if immigrants from other parts of Tanganyika are included, practice a mixed economy based on the cultivation of maize, beans, cassava, squash, and other crops in smaller amounts, together with the herding of modest numbers of cattle, sheep, and goats.

Historically, the Hehe are a political amalgam of some 30 odd small chieftaincies, which were united about four generations ago through the aggressive warfare and diplomacy of the famous warriors of one of the clans in one of these chieftaincies. These, men, the most celebrated of whom were Muyugumba and his son Mkwawa, extended their control over an immense region of south central Tanganyika in an expansionist policy which came to an end only after the inception of German control. After initial military success against the Germans, Mkwawa was finally defeated and Hehe political hegemony was restricted to approximately its present boundaries. Great regions which had been recently conquered and which were culturally distinct regained their independence at this time. The 30 odd small chieftaincies forming the heart of the Hehe state remained under a unitary system of administration, however. The present administrative boundaries are thus approximately coincident with the most closely knit portion of the Hehe state, and they encompass a region of relatively great cultural and linguistic homogeneity. There is systematic regional variation within the area, but it is not great.

The Hehe live in dispersed homesteads which form loosely articulated neighborhoods. Each homestead, which is minimally composed of a male head of household, his wife or wives, and children is surrounded by its fields of maize, millet, and other crops. Beyond the fields of the homestead lie the fields and houses of neighbors, and it is rarely the case that more than a few of the houses that make up a neighborhood can be seen from any one house. Such neighborhoods are bound internally, however, by a network of kin and friendship ties which are constantly acted out in mourning ceremonies, marriages, co-operative work parties, and beer drinks. Such ties extend beyond the neighborhood to other nearby neighborhoods and in a gradually attenuating fashion to numerous neighborhoods at greater distances.

Certain of such ties are theoretically binding at any distance though in practice the force varies with the frequency of contact and interaction. The most important of these is kinship. The Hehe recognize patrilineages (*mulongo*) and clans (*ndanzi*), but they also regard descent from the mother as important and give recognition to a group termed the *lukolo* composed of the localized members of several patrilineages which possess matrilateral linkages. The ties of membership in the lukolo are often greatly reinforced by frequent interaction because of nearness of residence, and this group appears to emerge in more sorts of joint action than any other kin group at the present time. Representatives of the lukolo are invariably present at such important events as births, deaths, mourning, and litigation involving other members.

In nearly all circumstances, whether within the homestead or larger kin group, with friends and neighbors, or among strangers, the Hehe preserve a decorum and formal politeness marked by niceties of repeated greeting, handshake, and control of expression. Such courtesy is a powerful obligation and must be observed even under circumstances which would seem to obviate the necessity for protracted formality. For example, one of the authors and a Hehe informant were crossing the edge of the maize fields surrounding a homestead. The maize was half-grown and the house of the owner was a good 50 yards from the path being used. Suddenly we were halted by a shout and a long rebuke for bad manners. The informant was greatly distressed and we made a detour up to the house to offer greetings and apologies to an elderly woman seated in the shade along the wall of the house. That the woman had been virtually invisible in the shade and from that distance made no difference. The informant offered profuse apologies, greetings were exchanged, and our journey resumed, although the informant was agitated and worried by the encounter. In this instance, there was no kin tie

between the individuals involved, nor membership in the same neighbourhood, nor special
friendship, but simply a general expectation that
failure to observe a greeting under any circumstances is a deliberate affront and never an
oversight.

The Hehe themselves sometimes recognize
that these encounters are insincere: "You must
be polite to a man even if you don't like him,
even if you hate him. You must be careful never
to offend him and if you are not very polite, he
will be offended." The Hehe often volunteer that
they hate and fear each other and this conversation is regularly punctuated by critical gossip,
jealous accusations, and suspicion. Thus it
would appear that this heavy emphasis on the
acting out of deference and courtesy masks
pronounced fear and hostility. The informant
described in the encounter above remained
uneasy and worried about the incident for over
two weeks and was greatly relieved when an
opportunity to visit the area again presented
itself. On this occasion he found it possible to
perform a favor for the son of the woman and
obviously gained reassurance when the son
accepted the favor.

This stress on courtesy and etiquette in greeting is only one aspect of Hehe concern and
caution in interpersonal relations. The expectation of affront constantly plagues men and
women alike and makes them extraordinarily
sensitive to insult. Insult is viewed as a grave
offense and courts are not loath to exact fines
and award compensation in any cases of this
sort brought to them. The following case heard
in the court of a sub-chief illustrates this type of
litigation.

Complaint: The Defendent, Gidalika, insulted the
woman Siyagumunyamale without reason and
before many witnesses.
Defendent: I admit I insulted this woman but I
was only joking with this grandmother and I
did not intend to harm her.
Witness (Siyagumunyamale): This woman said
that I was a dirty old thing and this made me
sad to be called that before many people who
were there drinking *pombe* and enjoying. I am
not dirty and I have never harmed this woman.
Why should she abuse me so that many people
can hear and despise me.
Judgment of the Court: Although the defendent
says she was joking, she joked before many
people and caused this woman Siyagumunyamale too much pain and therefore she is guilty

as charged. The court orders a fine of Shillings
10/- or 14 days in prison. The defendent is also
ordered to pay compensation of Shillings 20/-
to Siyagumunyamale.

Although there is great emphasis on etiquette,
tempers are explosive and both verbal abuse and
physical assault occur impulsively. A male
informant explained this in the following
fashion: "When men become angry, no words
alone will stop them—you must hold them or
they will kill each other. An angry man cannot
think, he can only kill. A father can even
become angry, and badly injure his small child.
It is bad that we Hehe have such tempers and it
is bad that we lose our tempers so much, but
that is how we are." It is understood that
people do not think well of each other, and as a
female informant put it: "Everyone here fears
other people, and is jealous of other people.
And we know that other people feel this way
about us. So we must be on our guard at all
times. You can trust no one; not your husband,
or parents or even your own children."

Despite this remarkable degree of fear,
mistrust, and anger in Hehe life, open conflict
does not often occur except for occasional outbursts of impulsive violence or insult. For
instance, of the 2471 criminal cases heard in the
Iringa Area in 1961, (exclusive of Iringa Township, which is a mixed urban area) approximately 700 involved any kind of interpersonal
aggression. This means that in a population
(according to the census of 1957) of approximately 100,000 adults only about 1,400 were
involved in cases of violence or insult. To put it
another way, less than two persons per thousand
were so involved.

On the one hand, this relatively low incidence
can be partially explained by the fact that many
disputes are mediated by the *jumbe* or the
kalani, lesser chiefs who wield great influence
and have power in other matters. But, on the
other hand, Hehe magical beliefs and practices
have a constant and pervasive controlling
influence on interpersonal behavior.

The magico-religious beliefs of the Hehe are
complex and varied and are made the more so
by the wide contact with other peoples which
the Hehe have experienced through their own
history of conquest and through the penetration
of Islam and Christianity. The most important
features of their beliefs are the concept of a

high god (*Nguluvi*) who is remote and little concerned with the everyday affairs of men, ancestor worship which centers on the patrilineal ancestors of the living but which includes recognition of maternal ancestors as well, control of rain which is achieved primarily through the agency of ancestors, the use of "medicines," (that is, magic), belief in witches, and finally, divination. We are not here concerned with the description of this total complex of belief but rather with the social function of certain of these beliefs and behaviors, particularly magic and divination. These beliefs have much in common with those described for many other peoples throughout the world in providing a means by which the relation between men and misfortune is explained and conduct regulated.

The Hehe constantly resort to diviners and to omens and oracles, and, as a matter of course, they refer daily to the operation of magic, to the activities of witches and less frequently to the blessings or displeasure of their ancestors. In all of this there is a strong element of morality by which the Hehe discover the punishment of wrongdoing in the death of a cow or kinsman, in the collapse of a roof, the contracting of an illness, the failure of the crops, or any other of the countless disasters and annoyances which beset them. Of course, there are wholly evil witches and sorcerers that must be defended against and whose actions are capricious, but much magic is sanction for proper behavior and in no way capricious in its action.

Every adult Hehe, whether man or woman, can exercise moral magic. Nearly everyone possesses some personal magic and, in general, older people have more than younger people, and men have more than women. To supplement this personal moral magic. Hehe turn easily and frequently to more powerful kinsmen or neighbors. Fees for consultation are not prohibitively high nor is access secretive or dangerous. The same cannot be said for evil magic which is expensive to obtain, requires great secrecy, and is dangerous to the user as well as to his victim. This moral magic is used to defend one's proper interests by the threat or actual practice of magical retribution against others who offend or injure one's legitimate rights. The moral and jural character of these practices is most effectively illustrated through the consideration of detailed cases observed in the field by the authors.

THE FATHER'S CURSE

Conflict between father and son is both frequent and serious. Conflicts may arise over authority or for other reasons but usually they involve cattle or other wealth. A son may attempt to kill his father to inherit his property, or the conflict may involve the payment of brideprice. Regardless of the source of the ill feeling, sons have been known to attempt to poison their fathers and to perform sorcery against them. Such a son is obviously and terribly wrong, and if the father learns of the wrongdoing he has two alternative courses of action. He may curse his son or he may work retributive magic against him. The curse is the more appropriate action in such a case, and it is bad form to use magic. However, certain elements present in the curse procedure also occur in magical procedure. We first consider a curse to illuminate Hehe attitudes and actions in a situation involving a clear-cut moral violation and a clearly religious manner of absolving that violation. We shall then take up cases of magic in order to compare the attitudes, actions, and classes of person involved

A teen-age boy named Edifons had repeatedly disobeyed his father and despite warnings by the lukolo had continued to defy the father and threatened to work magic against him. The father was sad and angry, and he talked to the lukolo to decide what should be done. They decided that the boy must be cursed and sent away. Accordingly, the members of the lukolo listened while the father spoke the curse: "You refuse to obey me. You wrong me. All right, so be it. If you are truly my son, then go and wander about the world and birds will defecate upon you, everyone will chase you like a dog, everyone will hate you like a smelly thing, the world will sit upon and crush you, nothing will be yours. Let God hear this curse. I swear it and I give great offerings to my dead father and mother and my grandfather and grandmother—all these watch you. Roam about like a lost person. You will have no work, no help anywhere." As the father repeated the curse he stopped and spat water. Spitting water is a "gift" to the ancestors and it invokes their sanction upon the curse.

The boy, Edifons, was not present while the curse was uttered, but he was soon informed of this most solemn and terrible action. He was frightened, for it is known that such a curse must be effective; the son becomes "mentally confused" and wanders aimlessly until he dies, for the father's curse is just and no one will help the son. After a few days of agonized waiting, Edifons took the only sensible action. He chose to confess all his wrongs, to make a full apology, and to offer compensation.

To do this, Edifons had to enlist the aid of several old men to approach the father and entreat him to hear the apology and confession. After some reluctance, which was probably feigned, the father agreed, and it was arranged that the apology and confession would be heard. Once again, the lukolo assembled (plus a number of unrelated but very interested bystanders), this time at the junction of two paths as is necessary in such cases. The old men took Edifons to the grave of his grandfather where he scooped up some sand from the top of the grave into a large wooden spoon. They then returned to the waiting crowd at the junction of the paths. Meanwhile, the old men had arranged to get an eminent old man to oversee the meeting, and they had acquired a sheep for compensation.

When the old men ushered Edifons into the meeting, the father rose and everyone was silent. The father began to repeat all the reasons why he was angry with Edifons. When he finished, the old man who was presiding asked, "Have you said all the words?" The father said, "Yes." "Then throw the spoon," he was told. He threw the spoon containing the sand and it fell with the bowl of the spoon down. This indicated that "All the words of his anger were not out." So the father added some grievances against the son that had brought about the curse, all the while spitting water to the ancestors as he had done before. This time the spoon fell bowl up and "all the anger was out."

Now it was Edifons' turn. He confessed his wrongdoing, spitting water to the ancestors as he proceeded. The spoon fell up to indicate that the confession was complete. He then offered long and contrite apology, asking that his father forgive him, remove the curse and accept him once more as a son. This decision is not the father's alone. He answered that he wanted to forgive his son but he would of course have to consult the ancestors. He slaughtered a goat and while it was being roasted, he walked to the graves of his ancestors, threw the spoon, and found, to the pleasure of all, that the ancestors were willing. Both father and son then ate a slice of meat from the goat, signifying that the curse was ended and Edifons was once more a son.

Then Edifons' sheep was slaughtered and a celebration followed. Everyone congratulated the father and son on their success in obtaining the help of the ancestors in removing the trouble between them. Edifons returned home and the trouble was over. Except of course, that he had to pay for both the sheep and the goat and give a handsome present to the old man who had presided over the ceremony.

The father's curse is a religious sanction applicable only to the parent-child conflict. It is our intention here to point up the important features of the handling of such a curse in order to demonstrate the parallels which exist in the resolution of other conflict situations among the Hehe. That is, to underline the moral components as well as the jural components of certain forms of Hehe magic which make them resemble the explicitly moral curse as well as the actions of a secular court. In the procedure of the curse, God and the ancestors are invoked; the lukolo is consulted; a joint decision is made; a unanimous sentence is agreed upon; divination is employed to confirm the morality of the undertaking, the cursed son is required to confess his wrongdoing, to apologize, and to pay compensation; finally, the episode is observed and approved throughout by witnesses.

In the form of magic termed by the Hehe *litego*, many of these features also occur. *Litego* is a Kihehe word which means trap and which by extension is applied also to certain types of magic. Cognate terms occur in many other Bantu languages and with similar extensions of meaning. Thus in Kiswahili *mtego* means magic used primarily to catch thieves or adulterers against whom evidence is otherwise lacking. For instance, mtego may cause an adulterous couple to become stuck and to remain that way until the outraged husband returns home. In the Hehe usage, litego may be used precisely in this sense; the hand of the thief swells and he cannot remove it from the jar or the mat sticks to the back of the adulteress. That is, it provides a magical technique whereby evidence of wrongdoing can be obtained for subsequent court action, or punishment may be directed toward an unknown wrongdoer. Moral preventive and retributive magic of this sort is widely reported throughout the world.

In Hehe usage, litego is much more than "trap" magic. The cases of litego which we shall present repeat many of the moral and jural features of the father's curse yet each is an act of personal retributive magic. Such magic may be applied in an *ex post facto* situation and not simply as an anticipation of suspected wrongdoing. Indeed, it may be applied where good evidence as to the identity of the offender exists and charges might well be sustained in the courts. It requires that the offender then comes forward and make public confession and apology and offer compensation for his offense. This compensation may be punitive in that it may exceed the value of the original injury but it is subject to some discussion between the parties to the dispute. Such discussion cannot be long, however, since the magic is a powerful coercive sanction which hangs over the head of the offender.

LITEGO: MISFORTUNE TO THE OFFENDER

Retribution may take the form of exceptionally severe misfortune to the offender or to his family, or it may be more minor—sickness, loss of property, and the like. Much depends upon how quickly corrective action is taken. We shall consider two cases in which misfortune occurred and violation of moral behavior was identified as the source of the trouble. The first case has less severe results, while the second involves several deaths.

A man about 30 years old fell ill with a fever. Although he was worried about his condition and its possible cause, it was not until the second day when his fever rose that he sent his brother to fetch the *mbombwe*. The mbombwe (often called by the Swahili term, *mganga*) is a diviner who may also be a curer and magician but does not necessarily combine all of these functions. When the mbombwe arrived he immediately entered the house of the sick man without questioning anyone outside. After the customary elaborate greetings, the mbombwe sat and solemnly prayed to *Nguluvi*, the high god, to give him the power to see the cause of this sickness and to understand what ought to be done. He then took out his *lyang'ombe*, a two-by-three-inch piece of metal that appeared to be an old brass buckle, kissed it to imbue it with God's power, and began to divine. This was done with an apparatus termed *bao* which is widely used in Tanganyika. The bao consists of a paddle-shaped board about eight inches long by three inches wide with a groove running diagonally across its upper surface in which a small wooden cylinder is rubbed. The mbombwe placed the paddle on the ground, put the *lyang'ombe* on its tang, and held both objects down with his foot. He then poured water on the groove and began rubbing the counter in the groove. As he manipulated the bao, the mbombwe chanted in a low singsong voice interrupted from time to time by a question addressed to the bao. As the water in the groove dries up, the counter moves less easily and at some point it will stick. This is taken as an affirmative answer to the last question addressed to the bao. As long as the counter moves freely, the answers

to questions addressed to it are taken to be negative. In this case, as in any case of misfortune, the mbombwe asked five preliminary questions: did the patient commit adultery? did he steal? did he borrow money and refuse to repay it? did he quarrel with someone? did he actually fight someone? In some cases, the answer is no to all questions, and it has been determined that the patient has been made ill for no good reason and that therefore effective counter magic must be made against the evil person who has performed magic or witchcraft without cause. But in this case, as in many cases, the bao answered that there had been a quarrel and went on to say that the quarrel had been with an old man who lived nearby to the east.

The mbombwe then rose and announced that the patient was afflicted with litego. Litego refers to the condition caused by moral, retributive magic. It cannot be cured by the mbombwe. The person suffering from litego must confess his wrongdoing, apologize to the person he has wronged, and then offer to pay compensation. Only then will the person who caused the litego remove it. Should the mbombwe attempt to employ medicine it would fail and should he attempt counter magic he too would fall ill and die, for the litego is the result of a violation of morality and it can be cured only by voluntary confession, apology, and compensation. Anything less and the victim cannot be cured. After a short hesitation, the patient dramatically announced that the bao was correct. It was litego. He had been wrong. He had quarreled with old Elemiasi, had abused him terribly, and had even threatened to strike him. As soon as the confession was completed the tension in the room relaxed. The cause of the illness had been determined and a specific course of action, namely, apology and compensation, would bring about a cure.

That same day arrangements were made to see Elemiasi. The apology was offered and accepted, and a goat was offered in compensation. Considerable haggling over the quality of the goat followed, and demands were made for several chickens in addition, but, after a time, the offer was accepted and Elemiasi agreed to remove his magic.

In a few days the fever subsided. A breach of propriety had occurred. The offended party had taken recourse to retributive magic as he had a perfect right to do. The offender had fallen ill, had recognized and confessed his wrongdoing, and had made restitution. The affair, though ostensibly involving only the two men, had been followed throughout by the entire neighborhood. It was agreed that the incident had been handled correctly. After all, if Elemiasi had not been wronged, his magic would not have been effective; indeed, it would have rebounded and killed him. And, of course, the mbombwe with his bao had shown that it was litego and that Elemiasi had a right to inflict magical retribution. The offender had to confess, apologize and pay compensation or he would have died. Everything was clear; everything was settled. There were no hard feelings.

LITEGO: MASSIVE MISFORTUNE

The events leading to the application of retributive magic are often complex and may span long periods of time. We did not witness the early parts of the following case, but were only present during the period of its climax. Thus in this account the events leading up to the climax were described by participants whom we interviewed at the time of the settlement.

In about 1940 a man named Omari married a young girl of the Mukimbu lineage named Hawa. Hawa divorced Omari after about 18 months of marriage on the grounds that he had failed to make her pregnant. She returned to her father's house and was soon married a second time. This second marriage, to a man named Guvumingi, was more successful, lasting about eight years and resulting in the birth of two daughters. Eventually, however, Hawa divorced Guvumingi and returned to her father's house again. Here she and her daughters stayed for some time. In about 1949 she married a man of the Kigula lineage, named Wangiling'ombe, who supported her during a three year period marked by drought and food shortages. When times got better again, she left him when a man of the Kihagise lineage asked her to marry him. Wangiling'ombe returned to his home filled with bitterness towards Hawa, who had accepted his support throughout the period of famine and left him to marry another man as soon as the shortages had ended. He made very powerful magic and simply waited for it to take effect. Within a year two boys, an adult woman, and a girl, all members of the Kihagise lineage, died. In addition, Hawa's elder sister hanged herself, and her mother and mother's younger sister died. Not long after this, Hawa's younger brother died.

Other members of the two lineages had heard rumors that Wangiling'ombe had made magic against them, so they met together and decided to consult a diviner. They sent several men to consult different diviners and were told in all cases that Wangiling'ombe had made magic and that he intended that all members of both lineages should die because his wife was seduced and lured away from him, and neither the family of the woman nor the family of her seducer made any move to stop such immoral behavior. The diviner said to one of these men, "You die because Hawa, who is one of your lineage, is running away with this man and you do not advise her to stay with Wangiling'ombe, even though she is married to him by oath and even though she was preserved by him in the famine time. You were told that if she wanted to leave him then you should return all the cattle and other things that he paid and all the food that he gave her, but you refused. Now you and the people of her seducer's lineage must go to Wangiling'ombe and he will stop all these deaths."

Wangiling'ombe met a delegation from the two lineages, and he agreed to accept an apology from them. He then ordered them to bring one bull and one ram to him to be used in ending the magic he had made. On the appointed day all the members of the two lineages who could be gathered together travelled to the graves of the ancestors of Wangiling'ombe. There he killed the bull and ram and cut off their heads, which were to be used in making the antidote. The rest of the meat was cooked and eaten by all the participants. It could not be carried away or the antidote would fail. The antidote was prepared in a very large earthen pot of the type used in beer preparation which has a capacity of about 25 gallons. It consisted of the two heads, a large bundle of roots of various kinds about six to eight inches long, an old buckle, a spearhead, a knife blade, pounded leaves of three sorts, a large amount of maize kernels, several kinds of bark, and quantities of water. While this was simmering, a party under the direction of Wangiling'ombe opened the grave of Wangiling'ombe's father from which he extracted large numbers of worms. These were added to the pot and cooked for about an hour. Finally, every person present drank some of the medicine. The maize in it was then carefully divided into small gourds to be sent to all members of the two lineages who were not present at the ceremony. It was stressed that every lineage member must receive and eat some of these grains or the earlier magic would surely kill them. By the time all of this had been accomplished it was nearly night and Wangiling'ombe instructed everyone to go home and to return on the following day bringing five cows and shillings 200/- as compensation for the injury that had been done to him. The members of the two lineages departed and spent nearly the whole of the night discussing the compensation to be paid and attempting to arrive at an agreement as to who would contribute what. The following morning they had not yet agreed, for the compensation was very large, in fact more than the original bridewealth. They discussed sending an emissary to ask for a one-day delay. It was decided that this was too dangerous and it was agreed to have one lineage pay three cows and the other lineage two cows and 200 shillings. Everyone then returned to the graves where the compensation was handed over and Wangiling'ombe made a speech accepting the apologies offered and swearing that he was satisfied.

The marriage which had brought on the case was terminated, although Hawa did not return to Wangiling'ombe and he stated he did not wish her to. About two months after her divorce she married again, this time to a man who had not been involved in the previous trouble in any way. All informants stated that this was perfectly all right and felt satisfied that there would be no trouble over this marriage. Hawa herself was not punished in any way for having brought on the trouble and apparently her new husband did not feel himself in any danger for having married her. The case was discussed over a wide area, however, and most people seemed to agree that Hawa had behaved badly but that the greater wrong had been committed by her family and her lineage in their refusal to observe the return of the bridewealth. An informant put it in this way, "So Hawa caused very terrible deaths, and herself did not die, only her family suffered to hell, but that is all settled now and she cannot do what she used to do in the days when she caused death to her family."

THREAT OF MORAL MAGIC

In some instances where injury has been done to an individual, he will counter with a verbal threat of litego if conditions are not improved. Ordinarily no such warning is given before the magic is applied because it is feared that the man who has received the threat may kill his adversary on the spot to avoid the application of magic. Of course, once litego has been applied, the offender dares not kill his opponent since only he can remove the litego. We do not know what is done if the person who has applied magic should die or be killed. No cases of this could be discovered and informants would not consider the possibility except in the sense that it proves the magic to have been wrongly applied, and thus to have rebounded. In the following case the threat was made because of the kin connection between the individuals involved.

One morning while seated in the dooryard of a house with several men, we were interrupted by the arrival of Kopolo, a middle-aged man of considerable standing in the community. This man acted as an assessor in the court of one of the sub-chiefs and was known for his calm wisdom and skill in the law. On this particular morning he was agitated and obviously angry. After the usual greetings, which he gave with some brusqueness, he turned to the owner of the house before which we were seated and addressed him with great urgency. He observed that he had great respect for him and knew him to be a man of reason and good will and also a man of authority and position in his own lineage and one who did not wish his lineage to have a bad name or suffer from trouble. Old Kazialedi, to whom all of this was addressed, assented that it was all true and then lapsed into silence, clearly waiting for the heart of the matter.

After a short silence, Kopolo launched into a rapid and voluminous description of an affair between a young man named Simoni and Kopolo's wife. He claimed that they were meeting at Kopolo's own house while he was away and observed that his wife was old enough to be Simoni's mother and that Simoni was an idle and shiftless boy who did nothing but cause trouble and who had a wife and baby for whom he should be working. Kopolo then observed that Simoni was the son of Kazialedi's younger brother and went on to remark that this younger brother was not much better than his son and obviously could not control the son. He then turned to Kazialedi's virtues and concluded by observing that Kazialedi should be able to control his brother's son since he, Kazialedi, was a man of honor and power.

Kazialedi sat for some time in silence and then remarked that he had not seen Simoni and Kopolo's wife together and wondered if Kopolo had, and, if he had, why they were not in court where fines could be collected. Kopolo replied that he had evidence but not for the court. He then paused and said very quietly that everyone knew he was a great magician, that Simoni was young, and that it was too bad that he would soon be dead. He concluded by remarking that he said these things only because Kazialedi and he belonged to the same lukolo and that there should be no trouble between members of one lukolo. Otherwise Simoni would already be dead. Kazialedi quickly arose and agreed that trouble in a lukolo was bad and that he had just remembered some business he had with his younger brother. At this Kopolo shook his hand and Kazialedi walked rapidly away towards the neighborhood where his brother and his brother's son lived. Kopolo stayed and talked to us quite jovially for about 30 minutes and then took his leave.

Simoni left the area to find work in Dar es Salaam about a week after this incident, and everyone who had witnessed the exchange agreed that Kopolo was a reasonable and merciful man and that there was no doubt that he could have killed Simoni if he had wished to. Everyone agreed that Simoni had been committing adultery with Kopolo's wife and that this particular solution to the problem was very good since no one died and no compensation had to be paid, either eventuality being very undesirable within the lukolo to which all parties belonged.

Perhaps the most important point which emerges from this case is the avoidance of the use of litego within the lukolo. None of our informants doubted that it could have been used, but they were unanimous in praising Kopolo for having given warning of his intention to use litego if the offensive behavior did not stop. They also agreed that such forbearance would be unlikely where no kin-tie existed between the parties to a dispute. Indeed, a case of threat of litego between non-kin could not be found even by questioning informants over a wide area and asking them to try to recall if they had ever heard of such a case. We did, however, record a case in which litego was applied within the lukolo. In fact, it was applied within a lineage. This case is a record of remarkably bad judgment since litego was not only used within the kin group, but also used wrongly as no offense had been given.

LITEGO WRONGLY APPLIED

That magic of the type we have been discussing is strongly moral is underscored by the Hehe belief that litego wrongly applied will rebound on its author. If a man is overcome by misfortunes while his neighbors seem to prosper he may decide that they are harming him and that he must work litego against them. The Hehe claim that this is frequently simply the result of jealousy and constantly warn each other to consult a diviner before deciding that they are really suffering from misfortune caused by some enemy. Nevertheless, men will often work litego in the heat of the moment and only afterwards begin to worry about the possibility that they may have been too precipitate.

Vangemamile and Juma are brothers, both quite senior, with married sons and daughters. Vangemamile, the older of the two, has three adult sons and Juma has two. All three of Vangemamile's sons went to school up to Standard X, and two of these men are now employed as clerks while the third is a teacher, Vangemamile has two younger sons who are still in school and doing well. On the other hand, Juma's two married sons are without work and both have been involved with the police. The older of the two was sent to school when a boy, but ran away every day and finally simply refused to go any longer. The younger son went to school for only one year. Neither is literate, and both are poor. Juma, who is getting older himself, can expect no help from his sons in his old age.

Juma has brooded about this for a long time and constantly complains to Vangemamile that his sons are proud and hate him. He gossips about Vangemamile's boys continually and was successful in one instance in causing a quarrel between Vangemamile and his eldest son. The two remained estranged for several months but finally the son apologized to Vangemamile and good relations were re-established.

Not long after this reconciliation Juma went away on a visit and remained away for over a month. When he returned he constantly gossiped about the sons of Vangemamile and complained that his own sons had done poorly in school because Vangemamile's sons troubled them.

One day not long after Juma returned from his trip, his wife made beer and we were sitting with a large number of people drinking and talking when one of Juma's roosters walked to the front door of the house, crowed, and fell dead on the doorstep. Everyone sat in dismay for a moment and then began talking excitedly. Juma himself quickly disappeared

and it wasn't long before nearly the whole of the crowd had also left. Our informants agreed that the incident had a dangerous meaning, but they were unsure of what it could be. Two days later the word spread that Juma had appeared at the house of Vangemamile's eldest son, confessed working litego against the man, and begged forgiveness. The son agreed but demanded that Juma apologize in public and pay a sheep in compensation for all the damaging things he had said. About two weeks later we heard that several prominent men were to meet at a place in the neighborhood where two paths crossed to hear the confession and witness the payment of the sheep. When we arrived, a small pot was boiling over a fire built in the path and Juma was confessing that he had decided that Vangemamile's sons were working magic against him and had travelled to Malangali at the other end of the Iringa Area to have litego made by a powerful magician he knew there. The magician was present at the ceremony and corroborated Juma's account and went on to state that he had advised Juma against litego but that Juma had insisted. Juma then confessed to jealousy, spat water as a blessing to the ancestors, and begged the sons of Vangemamile to forgive him. He then threw a spoon and it landed bowl up indicating that he spoke truly. Vangemamile and his sons then accepted the apology and also threw the spoon successfully. After this, everyone congratulated all parties, the sheep was inspected and accepted, and Juma, Vangemamile, and his sons drank some of the medicine which had been cooking in the path.

The case was closed, and everyone went home. Two days later we asked about three goats being driven along the path and were told these were presents which Juma was sending to the men who had served as witnesses in the ceremony. No further mention was ever made of the incident in our hearing during the remainder of our work in this location.

At the time of the confession and compensation, however, Juma received a great deal of criticism. This was not only because he succumbed to unreasoning jealousy, but also because he had attempted to apply litego within the very close circle of kin composed of brothers and brother's sons. It was clearly wrong to have done so without attempting to settle supposed troubles by other means. Nevertheless, the litego did not fail because it was used within the kin group, but only because it was wrongly applied. It is simply bad form to use this magic towards kinsmen; it will not nullify the operation of the spell. The proscription against litego within the circle of kin is a proscription against the use of coercion in this group until all other means of settling differences have been exhausted. There is no immoral connotation to its use if other less stringent means should fail.

If we now turn from the practice of litego to the consideration of Hehe witchcraft, we find a totally different kind of supernatural power. The Hehe believe witchcraft to be evil. It is initially inherited, or at least a propensity towards the practice is inherited. To become really effective, however, it must be increased by various means. The evil nature of witchcraft is revealed by the strongly anti-social nature of the means of increasing it, which the Hehe claim the witch practices. The commission of incest, intercourse with very young children, the killing of one's own son, father, or brother are all acts which the Hehe say the witch indulges in to maintain and enhance his power.

The witch is believed to possess the power to kill and to exercise this power simply from evil intent. Once embarked on such a course, the witch cannot turn back. His power grows and he must "feed" it, to use the Hehe metaphor. If he fails to kill regularly, the power he possesses will kill him. Informants insist that the witch may kill anyone—kin, neighbors, or even strangers.

Our purpose in taking up a case of witchcraft is to consider the techniques by which such cases are settled. There is the application of magic of a moral nature which will kill the witch if the evil power is not confessed to and if the witch does not then submit to removal of the power. Compensation must be paid, and public apology is necessary. All of these elements are also present in cases of sorcery where the power is from a magical formula rather than from an inherited propensity. Indeed, these elements are present in all of the cases we here consider, whether we are talking about the settlement of a father's curse, the use of litego, or the practice of evil. The same confession, apology, and payment of compensation are also to be found in the hearing of cases by Hehe chiefs. What varies in all of these instances is the mode of hearing and the means by which the decision as to guilt is made. The settlement remains essentially similar in all of these parallel juridicial or quasi-juridicial techniques.

WITCHCRAFT

Nyawana was married twice. Her first husband died after she had borne him two sons, and while she was still young. She married again within a few years and bore five children by her second husband, Vangitosa. When Nyawana's children by her first husband were adults themselves, trouble began to plague them. Both of them lost young children through deaths of various kinds. Finally, the wife of Iddi, Nyawana's younger son by her first marriage, became sick. Iddi consulted a diviner and was informed that his step-father, Vangitosa, was a *muhavi* (witch) and was killing his wife. Iddi returned home very angry, got his spear, and started out to the house of Vangitosa with the intention of killing him. He was stopped by his elder brother, who persuaded him to go to a mbombwe instead. There he bought medicine, and his wife gradually recovered.

Not long after this, Alfan, the youngest son of Vangitosa and Nyawana, began courting the daughter of Rashidi, who lived in a nearby neighborhood. When Vangitosa sent representatives to open marriage negotiations, he was directly refused even though the girl wished to marry Alfan. Shortly thereafter, another man carried the girl away, but she ran away from him and returned home within a few days and upon her return behaved very strangely. Her father, Rashidi, immediately consulted a diviner and was told that Vangitosa was a muhavi and had caused her "mental confusion" as revenge for the refusal of marriage. Rashidi and Iddi then met together to discuss what they might do about Vangitosa who was clearly a public menace. The two men decided to go together to consult some dream diviners (vanyalisoka) who are the most powerful diviners in Hehe country, much more effective than those diviners who manipulate the bao. The lisoka, or spirit familiars of these diviners, instructed the two men to bring Vangitosa before them, and they returned home and carried Vangitosa before the vanyalisoka by force. The vanyalisoka then declared Vangitosa to be muhavi and told him that it was necessary that his powers be removed. One of the *munyalisoka* then shaved Vangitosa's head and cut off all his pubic hair. He was bathed in decoctions, which had been previously prepared, and powerful "objects" (unspecified) were removed from his body. He was then warned that, if he attempted to use his power again, he would die.

Iddi and Rashidi then took Vangitosa home, but once he was safely home he ordered his daughter, Bumalakutwa, to take certain objects which increased the power of his wuhavi (witchcraft) and hide them in her own house, for she had inherited the power from him and was muhavi herself. About two years later, Vangitosa decided he was now safe and so took back his objects and killed the daughter of Iddi because he was still angry at him. Iddi, when he saw his child dead, returned to the vanyalisoka, and they told him that Vangitosa was again to blame. When he heard this, Iddi asked the lisoka to kill Vangitosa. The lisoka agreed, and a year passed during which Iddi visited the lisoka from time to time to remind them. Finally Vangitosa became sick and in his dreams and delirium kept crying out, "Somebody is killing me, somebody is choking me; it is Iddi." He also confessed to having killed as many people as there are grains of sand in a handful. His wife was very frightened, but she told no one what she had heard. Finally, he died. When he was buried, gossip has it, a snake appeared by his grave, and when his sons tried to kill it, they could not. (This is taken as certain evidence that the deceased was a witch.) All of Vangitosa's children deny that any snake was seen, but everyone believes that the gossip is true.

After the burial, Vangitosa's sons went to a munyalisoka to discover the causes of their father's death and were told the whole story. The lisoka then informed them that they would have to go to Iddi and Rashidi and confess, apologize, and see the matter settled. So the sons of Vangitosa went to these two men and asked that the case be ended, and both men agreed that the death of Vangitosa was enough and that no more men should die. Then they all returned to the munyalisoka together and were there instructed to bring many things to end the deaths: *liteleko* (a large jar), one ram, one black bull, maize, and many roots and barks. The animals were killed and cooked together with all the other things which had been brought. They ate the meat and drank the liquid there, and some was sent to all the members of both the families, no matter how far away they lived. This brought an end to the magic which killed Vangitosa. The children of Vangitosa still had compensation to pay, however. Iddi and Rashidi were paid 2000 shillings, three cows, and one bull and the lisoka received 200 shillings and two cows. The total costs amounted to approximately $650.00. This, in a country with an annual per capita income of less than $100.00. The case was ended except that Vangitosa's sons are still quarreling among themselves because one son paid the bulk of the fines and got very little help from his brothers. This is regarded as a matter internal to the family, however, and does not effect the fact that relations among the three lineages involved have been restored to a peaceful basis.

DISCUSSION

The use of litego is a common and important means of resolving conflicts in Hehe society. Its incidence is difficult to estimate, but in one of the neighborhoods where intensive fieldwork was carried out there were four disputes which were carried to the court of a sub-chief and six handled through the use of litego in a seven month period. It seems likely that its use is at least as frequent as is resort to the courts of record in respect of those sorts of violations to which it has any relevance. Of course, this leaves to one side all those cases which are

handled by the *kalani* or the *jumbe*. Although both the jumbe and the kalani are recognized members of the administrative hierarchy, only the jumbe is a salaried officer, and neither of these positions carries any judicial powers within the governmental framework. Thus, even though both may settle cases by arbitration, neither has any power to impose sanctions nor keep records of hearings. Again an estimate must be made of the frequency of cases, and again we are not confident of the extent to which our estimate can be generalized, but in two different *jumbeates* in which we worked, the jumbe heard approximately one or two disputes a week. Here we can make no distinction between what in Western law would be called "civil" and what would be "criminal." Really serious "criminal" actions would be sent immediately to the police by any chief, however, and we can assume that most of the actions which the jumbe agrees to hear are more minor than would be appropriate to a sub-chief's court or the use of litego. Jumbes' hearings probably have a range of frequency of between four and ten cases of all types per month within a jumbeate with a population of anywhere from one to five thousand persons. Litego, then, is an important public method of dealing with injury in Hehe society. It is probably as important as any other single method, though perhaps less important than all court actions of all grades of chiefs taken together.

The whole situation is, in some ways, analogous to early English law. That is, alternative modes of juridical action are available with few guidelines favoring one over another. Thus at the time of the Norman Conquest there were possible: Pleas of the Crown, trial by battle, the ordeal of hot iron, the ordeal of boiling water, the ordeal of cold water (used primarily for the unfree), the ordeal of the cursed morsel (used only for clergy), and "wager of law" or compurgation. In certain of these procedures, that is, the ordeals, it is a supernatural force which determines guilt. Indeed, Plucknett tells us that procedure in the ordeal was such that either party to the dispute might be designated to undergo the ordeal; it was not always the accused.

This early English parallel to the Hehe situation is made more striking if we recall that in both cases we are dealing with a period of rapid change. In England, change induced by the Norman Conquest, and in Uhehe, change induced by British and German conquest. In both instances, certain new concepts of justice and procedure were introduced and new authorities to administer these were also introduced. It seems reasonable that such rapid and far-reaching change should be reflected by the law in the form of alternative procedure for obtaining justice. The choice of procedure may then be idiosyncratic. Each aggrieved person must consider many factors: the magnitude of his grievance, the nature of the wrongdoing, his relationship to the wrongdoer, how he wishes to appear to his neighbors and kinsmen, the influence of the local jumbe, and the relations between the jumbe and sub-chief. He may also consider the way in which the case will be handled in the British-influenced courts. That is, will the court give recognition to the offense? what is likely to be the scale of punishments applied? how much will the litigation cost in fees and bribes?

The Hehe individual who has suffered injury appears to have a wide range of options with respect to the securing of redress. To some extent, these options are governed by kinship considerations. That is, he may utilize the curse as a sanction against a close agnatic kinsman of a lower generation providing he feels there is sufficient moral justification. Such reassurance that the curse is justified usually comes from consultation with other members of the lineage and of the matrilineally linked lineages of mother and father's mother (the lukolo). Thus the curse is an extremely powerful sanction, but its religious nature and its narrow range of application make it pertinent only in certain highly specific circumstances. On the other hand, there is not a single example of litigation between close agnates among whom the curse is possible in our sample of cases heard in the courts of sub-chiefs. It seems at least a reasonable working hypothesis that these two modes of handling conflict are mutually exclusive in Hehe society. Of course, we are not here considering other alternatives of non-moral, extra-legal nature to which these persons may resort, (for example, beating, murder, witchcraft, sorcery).

The question of kinship also enters into the use of litego, but in a rather different way. As we have seen, litego may be used against kin with every expectation of success if the complaint is just. There is, nevertheless, a widespread feeling that one ought to exhaust every other means of redress before resorting to litego within the circle of kin. The proper mode of action here is to arrange a hearing in the presence of the older and more influential members of the lineage, or of the lukolo. Such a hearing may be quite informal, but should result in a consensus of opinion as to the use of a curse, or alternatively, if the curse is inappropriate, an attempt should be made to persuade the disputants through resort to arguments advanced by men of standing. A kinsman who utilizes litego merely demonstrates his lack of judgment and also his lack of respect for kinship.

The arena within which litego is right and proper appears to be precisely the arena within which the courts of the chiefs are also right and proper. That is, disputes between neighbors, strangers, or very distant kinsmen. Here we have no clear guide as to which choice the disputant may make. Either course of action merits public approval. That litego should assume a status equal to that of the courts is in part due to its prominently moral nature. It appeals to the ancestors for approval and assistance. It depends upon divinatory confirmation of its morality in each case. It is understood by all that it will only be effective if the cause is just, otherwise it will fail and may even bring disaster to the person who used it wrongly. Success is not so much dependent upon the power of the magical formula or spell as upon the justice of the cause. If the cause is just, no counter-magic can prevail against it, and no workings of fate can deflect it from its target.

This type of magic is an efficient instrument of justice not simply because of its appeal to morality but also because it has the force of law. Litego is used against an offending person with the full sanction of society. This in itself is not uncommon. The Azande, for example, recognize a kind of magic which takes action against thieves or adulterers with general sanction to do so, and many societies, including the Hehe, work magic over property or wives to punish any potential thief or adulterer. But this is not the same thing as a man taking magical vengeance against another man when there is good evidence of wrongdoing. For example, the

Azande insist that where such evidence against a specific person exists, that action be taken in court, not magically. There is no such restriction for the Hehe. No matter what the offense may be and regardless of how much evidence is available, a Hehe has the right to employ magical retribution or go to court. Except, of course, when the national government becomes aware that a "crime" has been committed and invokes its police powers.

The process of magical justice is marked by jural acts. In each case of magical retribution, a resolution of the conflict is begun by confession. The Hehe do not confess to discover which "sin" is causing their misfortune as do the Nyakyusa, or to effect psychic catharsis and moral reintegration into the community through the expression of shame or guilt as do the Eskimo, or Saulteaux. Hehe confessions are analogous to court confessions; they are an admission of wrong-doing and an acceptance of responsibility for making restitution. The subsequent apology and compensation further work along legal lines. The confession itself may not have been public, but the apology must take place not only before the person who has been wronged and has taken magical action, but usually before an audience as well. The apology is not so much an act of contrition as it is a public confession of responsibility for wrongdoing. Finally, the offer of compensation confirms the wrongdoing of one person and attests to the right of the other person to have taken magical action against him. The action of confession, apology, and compensation not only calls down the weight of community sanction upon an act of magical retribution; it accomplishes the useful task of making the wrongdoer himself initiate and carry through his own punishment in the form of apology and compensation (which is also, incidentally, his salvation). Consequently, grievances, feuds, or bad feelings are less likely to follow.

In Hoebel's terms, litego is both "private" and "public" law, for it extends to each aggrieved person the right not only to defend his own interests but simultaneously to defend those of the population as well.

14. PIETAS IN ANCESTOR WORSHIP

MEYER FORTES

Reprinted from the Journal of the Royal Anthropological Institute of Great Britain and Ireland, *Vol. 91, pp. 166-191, 1961. Meyer Fortes was born in South Africa and received his professional degrees from the University of Cape Town and the University of London. Originally trained as a psychologist, he turned to anthropology under the influence of C. G. Seligman and Bronislaw Malinowski. He is William Wyse Professor of Social Anthropology and a Fellow of King's College at Cambridge University. Ghana (formerly the Gold Goast) is the area of his major field work; he has also worked and traveled in Nigeria and South Africa. His books include* The Dynamics of Clanship among The Tallensi, The Web of Kinship among the Tallensi, Oedipus and Job in West African Religion, *and* Kinship and the Social Order: The Legacy of Lewis Henry Morgan.

■ Ancestral veneration, an example of which is discussed in the following selection, is a system of religious practice and belief in which the spirits or ghosts of deceased ancestors are deified; it is a religious system that is often associated with lineage and clan organization or with other kin-based social relations. It is also designed to symbolize existing social relations and to reinforce the integrity of a corporate kin group. Ancestral veneration is grounded in several fundamental assumptions. First, the kin group as a whole and each of its segments exists in perpetuity from generation to generation. Second is the ideological corollary of this presupposition: that there is an unbroken link from generation to generation within the group as a whole and in each of its segments. Third, ancestors are regarded as fully functioning members of their kin groups even though they are deceased; their status is one among the several important status distinctions in such societies, based largely on position within the personal developmental cycle. Fourth, it is assumed that the quick and the dead are in constant interaction with each other; specifically, the living are charged with the maintenance of the tradition of their ancestors and the latter oversee the actions of their descendants, rewarding and punishing as may be appropriate.

The following selection illustrates how these basic assumptions are applied in the daily lives and religious organization of the horticultural Tallensi. Here we see that Tale generations are inextricably locked into each other, in life as well as in the cult of ancestral veneration. An important point, which Fortes cogently stresses, is that the other side of the piety that is a parent's right is his obligation to his children: just as a child cannot reject a parent, the latter may not reject a child.

The Tallensi are an advanced horticultural group living in the Northern Territories of the Gold Coast of Ghana (formerly French West Africa). They are patrilineal and sons live near or with their fathers after marriage; these rules of descent and residence are at the core of their social organization. There is no political unity beyond the clans and in each clan the several autonomous lineage segments have their own unity and solidarity. As Fortes makes clear, two of the most prominent principles underlying Tale social organization are a son's submission to his father and a high degree of economic cooperation and reciprocity among kinsmen of the same generation. These are inseparable, given the group's technological and social strategy of adaptation.

Because "piety" sometimes has derogatory connotations in English, Fortes prefers to speak of "pietas." In either case, this quality always reflects and reinforces political authority, and authority in stateless societies always grows out of the organization of economic relationships. In horticultural societies like the Tallensi, the cornerstone of the social and technological system is kin-group ownership of the land in which a man has rights of use through his kinship status and succession to his father. The role of an obedient son is indivisible from good standing in the lineage. Ancestral veneration thus symbolizes and reinforces filial submission and group solidarity.

We, living according to the moral bases of an industrial society, may find it difficult to empathize with the social-ethical-religious system of the Tallensi. Moreover, psychoanalytic psychology provides us with a rational basis for our difficulty, stressing as it does the tensions and feelings of rejection in parent-child relationships. But we must bear in mind that people in an industrial society proceed from an entirely different technological base—and, hence, an entirely different ethical system, in which kinship relations are a less important part—from the Tallensi. Among the latter, a man gains access to land largely by membership in good standing in his kin group and through his kin and jural relationships with his father; the generations are interlocked precisely because it is kinship that provides a man with access to the resources of his society. He cannot sell his skills and services to an impersonal bureaucracy as we do. Occasionally Tallensi sons do pack up and leave to seek their fortunes elsewhere, but as Fortes notes, there are more instances when this is followed by tragedy rather than success, and the ethical presuppositions of the society are reinforced.

For a discussion of another system of ancestral veneration, see "Ancestor Worship: Two Facets of the Chinese Case," by Maurice Freedman, in *Social Organization: Essays Presented to Raymond Firth*, Maurice Freedman, editor, (Chicago: Aldine, 1967, pp. 85-103). The interested reader will find the following works significant: "Reflections on Durkheim and Aboriginal Religion," also in book edited by Freedman, cited above; *Aladura: A Religious Movement among the Yoruba*, by J. D. Y. Peel (New York and London: Oxford University Press, 1969); *History of an African Independent Church: Vol. I: The Church of the Lord (Aladura); Vol. II: The Life and Faith of the Church of the Lord (Aladura)*, by H. W. Turner (Oxford: Clarendon, 1967); and *The Sociological Role of the Yoruba Cult-Group*, by William R. Bascom (Memoir 63, American Anthropological Association, 1944). ■

WHEN I BEGAN my field work among the Tallensi in 1934, the controversy aroused by Malinowski's assault on the Freudian hypothesis of the Oedipus complex was still simmering. Though he himself was in the phase of behaviouristic revulsion against psychoanalysis, his earlier views remained influential both as a challenge to psychoanalytical theory and as a stimulus to anthropologists in the field. Just what sort of field investigation of the problems in dispute could feasibly be attempted by an anthropologist, was the subject of lively discussion. The main theoretical issues had been elucidated with characteristic impartiality and clarity by Seligman, in his Huxley Lecture (1932). But all that was certain was that the primary social field within which the oedipal drama might be expected to manifest itself in custom and behaviour was that of family and kinship. The tricky question of what inferences could legitimately be made from overt customary behaviour to the hidden motives and fantasies identified by psychoanalysis, was left unresolved, as indeed it still is to a great extent. However, a distinctive orientation towards both field-work and theory emerged as the ethnographic monographs and studies of the thirties and forties testify. As it shaped itself for me there were three basic rules. The first, learnt from Malinowski, was that a custom, or body of custom, whatever its historical source may have been, is meaningful in the contemporary social life of a people, and that the anthropologist's essential task is to investigate this fact. The second, learnt from Radcliffe-Brown, was that custom is embedded in social structure and is significant of social relations. The third, due to the prevailing climate of psychological thought, was that custom is the socially tolerable expression of motives, feelings and dispositions that are not always acknowledgeable and may include potentially disruptive as well as constructive elements.

Kinship and ancestor cult are so prominent in the household and neighbourhood arrangements, the economic pursuits, and the routine of social relations among the Tallensi, that I was obliged to make myself adept in these matters from the outset of my field work. I arrived in the middle of the dry season. It is the time of the year when funerals are celebrated, both because the weather permits and because there is grain for beer and leisure from farming. For the same reason, it is also the preferred season for communal ceremonies and for many major domestic rituals.

Thus far from being in a position to establish my good faith by showing an interest in such neutral topics as string figures (which have no significance except as an amusement for children), material culture, or crops and markets, I was flung straight into divination, funeral ceremonies, domestic sacrifices, and the Harvest and Sowing Festivals. And it quickly became apparent no understanding of these ritual and ceremonial activities was possible without a thorough knowledge of the kinship, family, and descent structure. For the Tallensi, like most African peoples with a highly developed system of ancestor worship, patently associated with

descent groups and institutions, fit very well the paradigm of the religious community, in what he spoke of as "early stages," sketched with such masterly insight by W. Robertson Smith in *The Religion of the Semites*. I refer to his observation that "it is not with a vague fear of unknown powers, but with a loving reverence for known gods who are knit to their worshippers by strong bonds of kinship" that religion begins. He was struck by the parental characteristics of early Semitic divinities and connected this with the composition of the congregation of worshippers as invariably a "circle of kin" whose greatest kinsman was the worshipped god. "The indissoluble bond that united men to their god," he concludes, "is the same bond of blood fellowship which . . . is the one binding link between man and man, and the one sacred principle of moral obligation." And particularly worthy of recollection, for its bearing on my theme to-day, is his comment that "the feelings called forth when the deity was conceived as a father were on the whole of a [more] austere kind" than those directed to a maternal deity because of the father's claim to be "honoured and served by his son."

Robertson Smith was not the only scholar of his generation who perceived the connection between the institutions of kinship on the one hand, and religious beliefs and practices on the other. He was indeed anticipated by a quarter of a century by that other inspired precursor of our current ideas, Fustel de Coulanges, to whom I am specially indebted. But for him the linkage was to all intents the other way round. Where Robertson Smith supposed parenthood and kinship to underly the worship of their gods by the Semites, Fustel argued that it was the ancestral cult of the Romans which imposed agnatic kinship. "The source of kinship," he says, "was not the material fact of birth; it was the religious cult" ; and he goes on to demonstrate brilliantly how succession and inheritance are interlaced with the domestic ancestor cult. I quote: "Man dies but the cult goes on. . . . While the domestic religion continues, the law of property must continue with it," and further, with regard to the law of succession, "since the domestic religion is hereditary . . . from male to male, property is so too . . . what makes the son the heir is not the personal wish of his father . . . the son inherits as of full right . . . the continuation of the property, as of the cult is an obligation for him as much as a right. Whether he desires it or not it falls to him." The essential point, by his reasoning, was that in early Greek and Roman Law descent in the male line exclusively determined the right to inherit and succeed to a father's property and status but it was primarily a religious relationship. Hence a son who had been excluded from the paternal cult by emancipation was also cut off from his inheritance, whereas a complete stranger who was made a member of the family cult by adoption thus became a son entitled to inherit both the worship and the property.

Robertson Smith was not immune from the fallacies of his day and has been justifiably criticized for this, and Fustel, 1 understand, is considered by some Classical scholars to have subordinated scholarship unduly to conjecture. Be this as it may, we cannot but admire their perspicacity in directing attention to the social matrix of the type of religious institutions they were concerned with. For at that time the orthodox approach to early religions was by way of their manifest content of belief. From their pinnacle of intellectual rectitude, most scholars saw no further than the false logic, the erroneous cosmology, and the emotionally distorted superstitions which their preconceived theories revealed in nonChristian religions. This was the school of thought whose first concern was with what Robertson Smith designated as the nature of the Gods and with which he contrasted his own procedure. This is the tradition of Tylor, Frazer, and Marett, and the host of their followers, amplifiers and expositors too numerous to list (and mostly now quite obsolete). And this, fundamentally, purified of its grosser bias, is the tradition of Malinowski and of Lévy-Bruhl, as well as such famous ethnographers of Africa as Rattray and Junod, Westermann and Edwin Smith.

I lay no claim to having been aware of the bearing of Robertson Smith's and Fustel's theories on the religious institutions of the Tallensi when I studied them in the field. That came much later. It was simply that ancestor worship was too conspicuous to be missed and that the framework of genealogical bonds and divisions was an aspect of ritual to which both participants and commentators freely drew attention. But given the general orientation 1 have described, what started me thinking about the cruciual factors of ancestor worship was the casual observation recorded in the book which originally aroused my interest in the Tallensi.

In 1932 there appeared the first systematic ethnographical survey of the tribes of Northern Ghana, R. S. Rattray's *Tribes of The Ashanti Hinterland*. It is, in fact, a somewhat disconnected compilation of Rattray's own observations and informants' texts. But with his uncanny knack for field enquiry, in following up some of the kinship customs of the Nankanse, who are neighbours of the Tallensi and differ little from them in language and culture, Rattray discovered a rule which he reports in these words:

> Among the Nankanse, as also among many other tribes, it is forbidden for the firstborn (male and female) to make use of any personal property belonging to the parents, for example, to touch a father's weapons, put on his cap or skin covering, to look into his grain store or into his *tapo*, leather bag, or in the case of the female, to pry into her mother's *kumpio*. "Parents do not like their firstborn and it is unlucky to live with them." I think [comments Rattray] the idea is that they are waiting, as we would say, "to step into the dead man's shoes."

That parents and children are often opposed and even antagonistic to one another is widely acknowledged. It is a common enough theme of European novels and plays. Anthropologists have long been familiar with the parallels in primitive society. But its cardinal importance in social life was only beginning to be understood in 1932, partly through coming into the limelight of psychoanalysis but more particularly through the kinship studies of Malinowski and Radcliffe-Brown. Radcliffe-Brown's revolutionary paper on the Mother's Brother had made us realize the significance of respect and avoidance customs as expressions of the authority held by fathers over children in a patrilineal family structure, and Malinowski had revealed the conflicts that go on under the surface of matrilineal kinship norms. The Nankanse custom seemed to betray outright hostility between parent and child of the same sex, linked to open admission of the wish for the parent's death. It was curious also in singling out the first-born. No anthropologist alert to the current controversies concerning kinship and family structure could fail to be intrigued.

The avoidances observed by first-born children towards their parent of like sex were quickly and frequently brought to my notice among the Tallensi. As I have described elsewhere they are not only a matter of common knowledge but have a critical significance for Tale social structure both within and beyond the domestic domain in which they are primarily operative. The personal avoidances of the Namoo first-born are public moral obligations in that adherence to them is a symbol of alinement by clanship. Not surprisingly, therefore, first-borns often spoke of their situation with a tone of pride, though it might seem, to the outsider, to be irrationally burdensome and fraught with the humiliation of rejection. Of course, first-borns are inured from babyhood to the disabilities of their status and these are ritual injunctions stamped with absolute inviolability from the outset. But what a first-born is inured to looks, to the outsider, more like a deprivation loaded with threat. From early childhood he must not eat from the same dish as his father lest his finger scratch his father's hand. Tallensi say that if this happened it would cause misfortune, possibly even death, to the father. But he sees his younger brothers share their father's dish with impunity. If they scratch his hand by chance no harm ensues. And it is the same with other observances—the prohibition against wearing his father's clothes, using his bow, and looking into his granary. Yet first-born sons do not speak with resentment of their situation. They accept it with equanimity, with good grace, often, as I have said, with a kind of pride. It is, quite simply, from their point of view, a rule of life, in their language, an ancestral taboo (*kyiher*); but not an arbitrary and irrational one.

This is of great importance. It is accounted for in terms of rational interpretation of the social and psychological relationships of fathers and sons—an interpretation which makes sense equally from the point of view of Tale social structure and Tale values and from that of the anthropological theory of kinship. To see how apposite it is, one has to remember that Tale fathers are devoted to their children and are not denied by custom the freedom to show affection and familiarity towards their sons. The picture given by Professor Carstairs of the attitude of fathers to their children, and especially of the relationships between fathers and sons, among

the Hindus of Rajasthan would horrify Tallensi; they would not even agree unreservedly with the maximum that a 'man must always defer unhesitatingly to his father's word," though they insist that fathers must be accorded respect and obediance. Carstairs makes much of the aloofness, the lack of spontaneous warmth and intimacy, in the relations of father and son, and connects this with the strict obligations that exist for both sides. The Tallensi are not so severe. They do not idealize the father, like these Hindus, as a feared and remote model of austerity and self-control in whose presence everything associated with pleasure, levity, and most of all sexual life is forbidden. For them, too, the ultimate disaster, beside which death itself is insignificant, is to die without a son to perform one's funeral ceremonies and continue one's descent line. But having no notion of an after life corresponding to hell and *nirvana*, they would not properly comprehend the Sanskrit maxim quoted by Carstairs that "a son is he who rescues a man from hell" and assures his attainment of *nirvana*. As we shall see, for Tallensi, to have a son is to ensure one's own ancestorhood, and that is all the immortality one aspires to. With their nebulous ideas of the mode of existence of ancestors, Tallensi do not have beliefs that it can be influenced by the conduct of offspring and descendants.

I have cited Carstair's observations in order to bring out the relatively rational attitude and amicable compromise achieved by Tale custom, at any rate in its manifest and public aspect, in handling the tensions in the relationship of father and son, as focused upon the first-born son. As I have shown elsewhere this fits in with the lineage system, the domestic organization, and the widely ramifying web of kinship that together form the basis of Tale social structure. As in all societies in which patrilineal descent is the key principle of the social structure, the relationship of fathers and sons is the nuclear element of the whole social system. Opposition and interdependence, to use rather noncommital terms, are mingled in their customary conduct to one another. But what is of particular interest for my present theme is that Tallensi recognize quite frankly and even with some irony that the opposition between fathers and sons springs from their rivalry. Moreover, they regard this rivalry as inherent in the very nature of the relationship. If they had the word they would say that it was instinctive. In particular, they perceive that the prohibitions followed by first-born not only give customary expression and legitimacy to this fact but serve as a means of canalizing and dealing with the potential dangers they see in it. They are also well aware of the economic, jural, and moral factors in the situation.

It will help to clothe this bald summary with versimilitude and to lead to the next step in my argument if I stop to give you a typical instance from my field records. Saa of Kpata'ar, a man of about forty-two, was showing me his home farm one day and explained that until five years before he had lived and farmed with his father.

"Then," he said, "my father told me to come and build a house for myself and my wives and children on this land where his grandfather had formerly lived and to farm and provide for my wives and children by myself. Now he lives in his house and my younger brother, and his own younger brother live and farm with him." [Then, with a humorous glint in his eyes and half smiling, he went on] "You see, I am my father's eldest son. In our country, for all of us, whether we are Talis or Namoos, this is our taboo; when your eldest son reaches manhood he either goes out on his own or cuts his own gateway in his father's house. If my father and I were to abide together it would not be good. It would harm us. It would harm me and would that not be injurious also to my father?"

Now I knew Saa's old father quite well and had often seen him at his father's house assisting and advising in family and lineage affairs. Their public intercourse seemed to be as friendly and their mutual loyalty as staunch as was overtly the case with most elderly fathers and their mature sons. I therefore pressed Saa further, asking how he and his father could conceivably harm each other merely by living in the same household and farming together. He relied in the same matter-of-fact manner in which he had earlier given me some details of his farm work.

"It's like this," he said, "if we abide together our Destinies wrestle with each other. My Destiny struggles that he shall not live and his Destiny strives that I do not live. Don't you see, there sits my father and he has his ancestor shrines; if he were to die to-day it would be I who would own them. Thus it is that my Destiny strives for him to die so that I can take over his shrines to add to my Destiny and his Destiny strives for me to die so that my father can keep his shrine to sacrifice to them." [He spoke as if he were describing the action of external forces that had nothing to do with his own will and desires. I remarked that this suggested a standing enmity between his father and himself. He responded in a more personal, but still philosophical tone of voice.] "Indeed," he mused, "we don't like an oldest son, we care for the youngest son. As for my father, of course I am attached to him. If he were to die to-day I would have a hard time of it. His younger brothers would take possession of the family home. I am only a minor person. It is because my father is head of the family, on his account, that I have a house of my own and possess this farm. If he were to die his next brother inherits the family property and that includes what I have. Nowadays, if a big sacrifice is performed my father gets his share and he gives some to me; his brother would not do this. Nowadays, I act on my father's behalf in public affairs; when he dies I shall become a nobody. I want him to live." [I pointed out that he seems to be contradicting himself; to which he replied:] "When my father and I dwelt together he used not to heed what I said. If there was a dispute he would listen to others, never to me. Now that he does not see my every day and I have my house and he has his, his soul at length turns towards me. True, I only left him recently. That was because I was not ready for it before. As I farmed with him I was entitled to have him pay the bride price for any wife I married. When he had provided for me to marry to my satisfaction I was ready to go out on my own. My younger brothers have remained to farm with him. They can't inherit his ancestor shrine when he dies, so their Destinies have no quarrel with his."

This revealing confession sums up the normal and conventional conception of the relations of men with their sons among the Tallensi. Many such statements, supported by observations of people's attitudes and behaviour in many situations, confirm its accuracy and sincerity. What Saa tells us is that three is a latent antagonism between a man and his eldest son all through life. In the son's youth it does not stand in the way of their daily association and their amicable cooperation in farming and other household concerns. But when the son marries, and in due course becomes a natural father in his own right, responsible for the support and care of wife and children, his further growth in social achievement and personal maturity begins to be felt as a threat to the father. Unconscious antagonism turns into potential strife.

What is at stake is clear enough. It is the status of fatherhood. This is exhibited in the possession of the rights of disposal over family property, but, more significantly, is conferred by attaining custody of the ancestral shrines.

But what matters is that it is a unique status. Given the patrilineal lineage system, there can be only one father-of-the-family, in the sense of the person vested with supreme authority in the family, at any time. And there is only one way in which this status can be attained and that is by succession. But this presupposes the death of the holder (to borrow Dr Goody's valuable concept which brings out the natural transiency of such holding). And this is the crux. To safeguard the rightful holder from the competitive aspirations of his rightful heir-apparent is the issue. It is presented as a curiously impersonal issue, as if it were a given fact of human nature. And this fits in with the way it is dealt with by means of the quasi-impersonal imperative of taboo. What is accomplished, in fact, is the segregation of the protagonists from each other in respect of the two primary spheres of paternal authority, the control over property and dependants and the monopoly of the right to officiate in the worship at ancestor shrines. As Saa claims, voicing common sentiments, relationships of goodwill and mutual affection on the personal level are not disturbed. These go back to a father's devoted care for his children during their infancy. And we can see the point of the avoidances imposed at this stage. In the patrilineal and patrilocal joint family system of the Tallensi, fathers have to support, bring up and educate their sons to follow in their footsteps and succeed them. A son cannot be socially and materially segregated in childhood.

The social structure and economy of the Tallensi rules out the possibility of sending a child away to be brought up by maternal kin, as is done among the Dagomba, for instance, nor are the age-villages exploited by the Nyakyusa to segregate successive generations feasible.

How can the son, designated by jural and ritual custom to be his father's successor, be kept submissive to paternal authority in childhood except by excluding him from activities and relationships that smack of sharing in his father's status? How can the son be equipped to perceive and feel his obligatory separation from his father; how can he dutifully make plain that he is not his father's equal and does not covet his father's position? Physical separation being ruled out, the answer is found in the symbolic avoidances described earlier. In the circumstances they have to be more explicit and

categorical than the forms of etiquette by means of which respect for parents and elders are in some African societies, even, for instance, among the Thonga where the eldest son's situation is very close to that of the Tallensi. For what is demanded is more than respect though less than the extreme spatial and politico-ritual insulation of filial from parental generation that is found among some Central African peoples. (I have instanced the Nyakyusa, but the custom is widespread in Central Africa.) What is symbolized is that an eldest son must not pretend to equality with his father as economic head of the household (hence the granary taboo), in respect to the rights he has over his wives (hence the taboo on eating with the father, since one of the main duties of a wife is to cook for her husband) in his status of mature manhood, as an independent jural and ritual person, which can, as I shall presently emphasize, only be reached upon the death of the father (hence the taboo on the father's bow and quiver), and lastly, in his capacity as a unique individual (hence the ban on wearing his father's clothes). And these observances must be kept—I can vouch that they are so kept—without destroying the personal warmth and trust that is also an essential component in the relationship of the son with his father.

This will be clearer if I hark back to note that what I said earlier about inheritance and succession was elliptical in one respect. I should have pointed out that a father of a family has two distinct elements of status. He is father of his children by right of begetting as Tallensi say, and by this token his sons are simply extensions or parts of himself during his life time. They have no jural standing in their own right, even if they are economically self-supporting and live separately. This is a basic norm of Tale social structure. I was vividly confronted with it when a young man employed by me appealed to me with mingled anger and resignation. He had married a girl by elopement and the placation gifts had been accepted. But his father had refused to complete the formalities on the grounds that he could not afford to pay the bride price cattle. Yet my young friend had saved enough to buy two cows which would be an ample first instalment on the bride price. Why, I asked, did he not, then, himself hand over the cows to his father-in-law? It would be outrageous, he replied, even if the wife's lineage kin were unscrupulous enough to accept them. You can't pay your wife's bride price yourself while your own father is alive, not even while one of your father's own brothers is alive. It would be "setting myself up as my father's equal," he explained. "We should quarrel, he would curse me and refuse to sacrifice on my behalf; does not one man surpass another in standing?"

His one hope was that I might persuade his father to give in. But note an important corollary. My informant would have been no better placed, jurally, to take a wife even if he already had one wife and children of his own; for a man does not have the jural autonomy to act independently, on his own behalf, even in regard to rights over his own children, until his father dies.

The other side of a father-of-a-family's status is his position as head of the lineage segment which constitutes the core of the family. He arrives at this status, not by having children or by succeeding his father by right of filiation, but by succeeding to it by seniority in the lineage. By this reckoning lineage brothers succeed first and then sons; and of course all brothers who survive can in time suceed. There is not the specificity of filial succession. Thus Tale fatherhood conforms to Maine's dictum that patriarchal power is not only domestic but political. Taking fatherhood as a status in the politico-jural domain, in which the relationships between holder and prospective heir are modelled on siblingship, we see that there are no avoidances between a man and his prospective lineage successor either of a ritual or of a secular nature. Brothers borrow each other's clothes and may inherit each other's widows. As lineage head a man cannot frustrate his brother or his brother's son in the matter of bride price as arbitrarily as a father can, nor can he refuse to sacrifice to a common ancestor without grave cause.

We must conclude that the first-born's avoidances are to be understood as referring to his father's strictly paternal and his own strictly filial status in the domestic domain during his father's life time. This is an inescapable nexus; and this explains why Tallensi account for the opposition of father and first-born son, prescribed by custom though it is, by means of spiritual concepts rather than in jural and economic terms. Breach of the taboos would be

an affront to the father's soul (*sii*) and Destiny (*yin*). For a man's soul is in his granary and his vitality is in his garments and weapons because they are covered with the sweat and dirt of his body. This is more vividly brought out among the Talis clans which do not impose avoidances between father and first-born as taboos, though they follow the practice for what they regard as reasons of propriety. Among them a first-born son may be sent by his father to fetch grain from his granary. But when a father dies his bow and quiver and leather pouch are hung up inside his granary by the officiating elders. From that day until the final obsequies, which may not take place for two or three years, the eldest son may not look inside the granary. If he did, he would see his dead father and himself die. A younger son can enter the granary with impunity. He would never see the dead. At the final obsequies the hidden articles are brought out and eventually taken by the eldest son to be deposited in the sacred grove of the lineage ancestors. Thereupon he legitimately succeeds to the status which gives him the ownership of the granary and all that goes with it.

I am concentrating on the first-born son, but two qualifications should be added. Firstly, Tallensi understand quite clearly that he is singled out by reason of his place in the sibling group so to speak; he is, they say, the nearest to the succession. Secondly, first-born daughters have parallel avoidances in relation to their mothers and to some extent to their fathers. This shows how critical is the position of the first-born irrespective of sex. As Tallensi point out it is the first-born whose birth transforms a married couple into parents once and for all.

But I fear that I may be conveying an impression of pervasive tension and antagonism in the relations of parents with their first-born children, the children whose fate it is to have conferred parenthood upon them and to be waiting for the succession. I do want to stress again that there are no obvious signs of anything of this sort in their normal relationships and in their every-day behaviour towards one another. Fathers speak with pride, affection and trust of their eldest sons; rather disconcertingly so when, as so often happens, a father follows a eulogy in the son's presence by adding, "of course, he is my first-born and though he is still so young he wouldn't care if I died to-day. He is only waiting to step into my place." Eldest sons, likewise, as I have already noted, are normally attached and loyal to their fathers. Tallensi are very critical of sons who leave their natal settlement to work or farm abroad for many years. They would be appalled at the idea that a son might resort to violence, or even parracide, as is reported of the Bagisu, in order to assert his claims on his father.

On the contrary Tallensi never cease to emphasize the duty of what I have elsewhere called filial piety; and that they faithfully observe it is constantly shown. It is illustrated by the attitude of the youth whose father refused to pay his wife's bride price. But similar incidents are of daily occurrence. For example, I happened to meet Toghalberigu just after a stormy argument with his father, who accused him of neglecting the family farm in order to get ahead with the weeding of his own private strip of land. Complaining to me he ended, more in sorrow than in anger, "It is right, the way he treats me? Yet how can I leave him since he is almost blind and cannot farm for himself? Would he not starve to death? Can you just abandon your father? Is it not he who begot you?"

Here lies the crux. Filial piety is a parent's unquestioned and inalienable right because he begot you—or, in the mother's case, she bore you. Character and conduct do not come into it. Bad parents are just as much entitled to filial piety as good parents. It is an absolute moral rule. Nor is it purely one-sided; for it is an equally impregnable moral rule, adhered to with great fidelity according to my observations, that a parent may not reject a child, no matter how he misconducts himself. Piety, in fact, is a reciprocal relationship, compounded of reciprocal sentiments, ties and duties. And its source (though not its *raison d'être*) is the irreducible fact of procreation, the fact that confers parenthood in the elementary sense in which a person achieves parenthood independently of lineage membership.

What I am calling piety, then, is a complex of conduct and sentiment exhibited *par excellence* in the relations of a man with his eldest son and felt to be an absolute norm of morality. It pervades all their relationships in a curiously interdependent partnership of growth and development during life. Yet when Tallensi speak of this relationship they say that the supreme act of piety required of any man is what falls to him on the death of his father. It is the duty then of the first-born son, and failing him of the oldest living son, to be responsible for his father's mortuary and funeral rites. I am translating the Tale phrase *maal u ba koor*, for in actuality the elaborate sequence of rites is supervised and largely carried out by fellow members of the dead man's lineage, aided by representatives of allied lineages and other kinsfolk. The children, widows and grandchildren undergo ritual and observe ritual taboos. They do not officiate.

Nevertheless the essential rites cannot, by right, be carried out without the presence and the lead of the eldest son. And whether or when he takes the necessary steps for this is solely his own responsibility There are no sanctions of a jural or material kind that can be brought to bear on him. He can, if he wishes, also turn a deaf ear to public opinion, which may be impatient if the deceased held an office, since no successor can be appointed until his final obsequies are performed. Nor may a younger brother take action. That would be usurpation and contrary to the rules of age and generation priority in the sibling group and the lineage. Indeed, it would be an act of impiety against the deceased, even if he had been his father's favourite son. It is wholly a matter of conscience with the responsible son, or as Tallensi put it, it lies between him and his ancestors. If he delays the funeral inordinately, the ancestors will take offence and he will suffer. Funerals are frequently delayed, often for lack of livestock and grain supplies that are required to perform them, but sometimes for motives interpreted by the Tallensi as perverse or selfish. When Nindoghat procrastinated over his father's funeral, among the motives attributed to him were arrogance and malice due to the hostility between his lineage segment and that of the prospective successor to his father's office. So it is not uncommon for diviners to reveal that sickness and deaths are due to wrath of ancestors offended by the delay of a funeral.

Tale mortuary and funeral rites are elaborate and locally varied but here I am concerned only with the most important of those in which the participation of the eldest son is ideally indispensable. (I say "ideally" because the Tallensi are a practical people and in exceptional circumstances the lineage will act without him.) These are, firstly, the rites by which the deceased is established among his ancestors and is thus transformed from a living person into an ancestor; and secondly and consequentially, those by which the son is invested with his father's status or is made eligible for this. Significantly, it is the eldest son who should make the rounds of all the ancestor shrines that were in his father's custody and, with the customary libation, apprise them of his death. Then, he must attend the divination session at which the ancestral agent of his father's death is determined; for he must concur in the verdict since the sacrifices to appease the ancestors and to reconcile them with the living are his responsibility. Finally, he (usually accompanied by his first-born sister) is the main actor in rites which free him to do those things which were forbidden to him in his father's lifetime or, in Talis clans, during the period of suspended paternal status since his father's death. No display of grief is permitted in these rites but strict silence is enjoined on the actors in the most solemn of them. This is because the dead is deemed to be participating with them and would strike down anyone who broke the ritual silence.

I want to stop for a moment to consider the implications of these rites. We must remember that among the Tallensi the ancestors constitute the ultimate tribunal, the final authority in matters of life and death. Every normal death is their doing. The deceased is said to have been slain or to have been summoned by them, and it is always in retribution for neglect of ritual service demanded by them or breach of promises made or duty owed to them. A son is a jural minor during his father's lifetime. As such he has no standing in relation to the ancestors and therefore only indirect and minor ritual liabilities towards them. Thus when he informs the ancestors of his father's death he is, in effect, presenting himself to them as the prospective successor to his father's responsibilities towards them. As heir he must accept the penalty imposed by the ancestors for the fault for which his father incurred death; but though he provides the animal to be offered he may not perform the sacrifice. His father's status has not yet devolved

on him. So one of his younger brothers acts as if deputizing for the father.

Then as to the rites of silence, these mime eating and drinking with the dead father, hitherto prohibited to the son. But he must be freed to do so in the future, if he is to be able to sacrifice to his ancestor-father, since this requires partaking of the offering. To end the funeral among the Talis, he takes his father's bow and quiver from the tabooed granary to the external *boghar*. There he hands it to the assembled lineage elders to be deposited among those of the other forbears with whom the father is now joined. Among the Namoos, he is clad in his father's tunic turned inside out, girt with his father's mimic bow and quiver and very solemnly shown the inside of the tabooed granary with gestures that symbolize compulsion from the lineage elders to submit. (It should be noted that the "bow and quiver" used are small mimic articles made for the funeral and therefore expendable.) At this point he stops being the heir and replaces his father in status. Henceforth he is his own master (within the limits of lineage obligations) jurally, economically, and above all ritually, with authority over his dependants and his family property, and with the right to officiate in sacrifices to the ancestor shrines of which he now becomes the custodian. But he will never cease to be reminded that he holds his status solely in virtue of being his father's successor; for his weal and woe, and that of his dependants hangs upon the will of the ancestors, and they can be influenced only in one way and that is by pious tendance and ritual service, which cannot be rendered except through the intermediation of his dead father.

It is pertinent to add that various offerings of animals and beer are made to the deceased in the course of the funeral rites. They are accompanied by a constant refrain. Always the officiant calls upon the deceased by name to accept the offering "in order that you may reach and join your father and forefathers and let health, peace, childbearing, fertility of fields and livestock now prevail." Thus the climax of filial piety is for the eldest son to see to the proper dispatch of his father to the community of the ancestors of which he now becomes one, and thereupon to displace him in status. It is perhaps not unreasonable or illogical that ancestors, thus dispossessed and thrust out of society by the cruel inevitability of nature, should be known to have a mystical existence, and believed to retain final authority, chiefly by virtue of the pain and misfortune they inflict on their descendants from time to time. No wonder Tallensi declare that it is harder to serve and honour the ancestors with piety than the living. No wonder, too, that they have to find consolation in the belief that the ancestors are always just.

Filial succession relates to paternal status in the domestic domain. I have never heard an heir express gratification over this. In fact his attitude, until he is invested with paternal status, is more likely to be one of resignation and submission to what must be. But a lineage successor to office may and does take pride in it. It is rash to speculate about underlying motives in customary behavior as I hinted at the beginning of this lecture. But I do not think it is going too far to see a connection between these attitudes and, on the one hand, the avoidance relationship between father and son, on the other the equality of lineage brothers. In a lineage system like that of the Tallensi, paternal status merges into lineage eldership just as and because the relations arising from filiation become relations of common descent in the next and subsequent generations. This provides the framework for the extension of filial piety from the domestic to the lineage level. It is in fact quite directly mediated by the relegation of the father, when he becomes an ancestor, to the communion of all the ancestral forebears symbolically accessible in a shrine dedicated to them collectively.

We are left with the critical question, which I have so far evaded, but which must at length be faced: why piety? or in language which may sound a bit old fashioned to-day, what is the function of piety in the context of the kinship and religious institutions I have described?

Piety is a word packed with ambiguity, for us, and not altogether free of derogatory associations. If, as the *Oxford English Dictionary* tells us, it commonly stands for habitual reverence and obedience to God (or the gods) and faithfulness to duties naturally owed to parents and relatives, etc., it also carries overtones of hypocrisy and, to quote the same dictionary, of fraud and the like practices for the sake of

religion. This is no doubt an understandable ambiguity in a culture which deems it specially meritorious for outward forms of manners and conduct to match inner states of sentiment and belief. Prevarication and hypocrisy are not, however, confined to our civilization. People of good repute among the Tallensi speak of such practices with contempt. At the same time there is little or no questioning of the sincerity of outward conduct. Morality is what is seen in a person's conduct and actions and these are deemed to be expressions of genuine intention, feeling or belief. This is assumed in Tale religious custom and ritual practices, as it seems to have been in the cultures I shall presently refer to, those of ancient Rome, and of traditional China.

To avoid the flavour of unctuous conformity carried by the English word, I venture to use its Latin ancestor, *pietas*, in this lecture, though not without hesitation. Is it not redolent for many of us of long hours of wrestling with the tedious affairs of the Pious Aeneas? "We are wearied," confesses even the great Virgilian scholar, John Conington, writing in more pious times than ours, "by being constantly reminded of his piety." Significantly though, he adds that this "may be partly owing to our misapprehension of the epithet," for Aeneas's piety "is not merely nominal; it shows itself in his whole feeling and conduct to the gods, his father and his son." What adds to our understanding of this luckless epithet, as another commentator calls it is the observation that it is never applied to Aeneas in the Fourth Book while he is Dido's lover but is restored to him when, to quote this commentator, "*pietas* has conquered self" and he leaves her to inspect his fleet. This marks what Warde Fowler describes as the "taming of his individualism" in the interests of the state; for, he continues, "*pietas* is Virgil's word for religion (not knowledge, or reason or pleasure) is the one sanction of Aeneas's conduct."

The Tallensi do not have a concept for that complex of reverent regard, moral norms, ritual observance and material duty in the relationship between parent and child, more particularly of son to father, both during the lifetime and after the death of the parent, which I am calling pietas. But they would readily understand the Roman ideal alluded to in Conington's apology for Aeneas. A modern authority contrasts pietas as concerned with the circles of family and kinship with fides which pertains to the extra-familial, that is the political, side of Roman life. Originally, we are told, it meant the conscientious fulfilment of all the duties which the *di parentes* of the kin group demand. Later it meant both the dutiful discharge of cult obligations to the divine members of the kin group and reverence and consideration towards the living human members. An apocryphal story, recorded by various writers of antiquity as an example of superlative piety, and quoted by most commentators, tells of the daughter who kept her aged father alive in prison with milk from her breasts. This story would strike Tallensi as bizarre but not fantastic. They would applaud the praise implied in the luckless epithet for Aeneas's filial love and would comprehend the definition of pietas as "dutiful conduct towards the gods, one's parents, relatives benefactors and country." And they would agree with the significant implication that it belongs to the realm of parenthood not to that of marriage and sexual life.

This need not surprise us. Considering only Fustel's account and overlooking the differences due to the more complex civilization of the Romans, we can see that their patrilineal descent and patriarchal family system, closely bound up with an ancestral cult, has close parallels with those of African peoples like the Tallensi, the Yoruba, the Thonga, and many others who also have segmentary patrilineal lineage systems and patriarchal family structures inextricably tied to ancestor cults. For the nuclear element in all these systems is one and the same phenomenon, the ambivalent interpendence of father and son in the nexus of final authority versus subordination, identification by descent versus division by filiation, transient possession of paternal status versus its inevitable and obligatory supersession by the filial successor.

However, by all acounts the *patria potestas* of the Roman father in the domestic domain was far more absolute than is that of a Tale, or any other patrilineal African father. Age made no difference, as the example of Anchises in the Aeneid shows. Fowler notes that he is the typical Roman father maintaining his authority to the end of his life, "to whom even the grown up son, himself a father, owes reverence and obedience." I do not know if Roman sons were

compelled to practise avoidances towards their father, but if Cicero's attitude in *De Officiis* is typical it suggests considerable shyness and formality in their personal relations. It is difficult to believe that there was not a good deal of latent antagonism in the relations of sons to fathers. The savage punishment traditionally prescribed for parricide and stories of fathers who sacrificed sons for the public weal lend colour to this inference and fit in with the rigorous jural sanctions that supported paternal authority. It is understandable, therefore, why the right of filial succession was not only very strictly entrenched, but was in part enforced as an inescapable obligation to the *familia* in law and to the ancestral deities in ritual. One can easily imagine the legal constraint and moral compulsion that was required to bind a son in loyalty to his father, until the time when, as Maine puts it, the paternal power was extinguished by his death. For not till then was the son jurally adult and autonomous, which meant *ipso facto* having the capacity to officiate in religious rites, as Aeneas does in *Aeneid* V, in commemoration of his father's death. Nor is it without significance that this should be his first important religious act.

In the same way, Tale norms of pietas resemble those of Confucian ethics in China, if allowance is made for the refinement and elaboration added by literary transmission through the agency of specialists and scholars. Tallensi would accept the Confucian ideal of pietas as consisting in "serving one's parents when alive according to propriety; in burying them when dead according to propriety and in sacrificing to them according to propriety," to follow Douglas's translation or according to ritual in Waley's version of the *Analects*. For propriety and ritual are overlapping categories among the Tallensi, too. We have already seen that Namoos define the avoidances of first-borns as taboos, whereas Talis say they observe them out of propriety; and this is typical of many Tale religious ideas and practices.

The common ground lies again in the basic similarities between Tale patrilineal descent group and family organization, with its religious projection in ancestor worship, and that of the Chinese. Granted the differences in range and scale due to the greater complexity of a literate, economically and socially differentiated, technologically sophisticated, culturally wealthy and historically orientated civilization, these similarities are noteworthy. Classical treatises on ethics and ceremonial are echoed in the field observations of sociologists and anthropologists of to-day. All testify to the Chinese veneration of pietas (*hsiao*) as the supreme virtue in the relationship of children to parents, especially of sons to fathers, both in life and after the elevation of the father to ancestorhood.

Filial piety, in the modern Chinese community described by Hsu; is said to be the foundation stone of its social organization and is given exactly the same sense as in my quotation from the *Analects*. But what is more to the point is the weight given by recent students, also in accord with classical treatises, to the patri-filial nexus in the Chinese family and descent system. "The basis of kinship is patriliny," states Hsu, "and the most important relationship is that of father and son. The father has authority of life and death over the son, and the son has to reverence and support his parents. Mourning and worship after the death of the parents are integral parts of the sons' responsibility." Tale fathers do not have unrestricted authority of life and death over their children, but with qualifications this formula would be acceptable to Tallensi.

Furthermore, it appears that in China, too, the first-born son has a unique place in the sequence of the generations, though it is not, apparently, marked by avoidances. Thus it seems that in former times the eldest son being the direct propagator of his father's line, had the sole right to make sacrifices to deceased parents. This was associated with preeminent rights of inheritance in regard to property and ancestors. Judging from the references to primogeniture in recent literature, this rule still prevails. We learn from Dr Lin's fascinating story of the fortunes of a Chinese lineage that the first-born has a legal right to an extra portion of the joint property as a special recognition of his primogeniture, and, incidentally, that this may give rise to serious conflicts in the family.

The general impression one forms is that fathers treat their sons with affection and indulgence during infancy, but with increasing authority and formality as they grow to manhood. The emancipation of jural majority, economic independence and the ritual autonomy demonstrated in the right to perform sacrifices to the ancestors comes (as in ancient Rome) at length only after the death of the father, as Hsu specifically states. This coincides with the dead father's establishment as an ancestor; and it is noteworthy that tablets dedicated to ancestors are so arranged that those of fathers and sons are on opposite sides of the ancestral hall, successive generations being thus kept apart after death, as they were divided by degree in life, and alternate generations being grouped together in accordance with the well-known principle of the merging of alternate generations.

I have digressed from Africa to look briefly—and I fear too superficially to satisfy the experts—at the two civilizations which are most renowned for the exalted place accorded to the rule of pietas in their schemes of moral and religious values. These are the paradigmatic cases, often discussed by scholars. They have the advantage that more or less formulated doctrines can be examined to see what is meant by the concept of pietas. But what is most instructive in comparing these paradigmatic institutions with their relatively amorphous Tale—and I believe, more generally, African—counterparts is to consider the reasons for their indubitable efficacy amongst all these peoples, irrespective of how much explicit doctrine there is. It is unnecessary to go farther afield in order to propose some hypotheses. Indeed even if I wished to explore the African data more fully there would be little profit in it. For I know of only one modern study of an African religious system in which the observance or neglect of pietas has received particular attention and that is Dr John Middleton's impressive work on Lugbara ancestor worship.

Among the Lugbara, as among the Tallensi, the Romans, the Chinese, and all other ancestor-worshipping peoples, a man becomes an ancestor when he dies not because he is dead but because he leaves a son, or more accurately, a legitimate filial successor, and he remains an ancestor only so long as his legitimate lineal successors survive. This goes with the rule that ancestors have mystical power only with respect to their descendants and not, for example, with respect to collateral kin. On the other side, a man has no jural authority in his family and lineage, whatever his standing may be in wealth or influence or prestige, if he has no ancestors and until he acquires the status which permits him to officiate in the cult of his ancestors. For, as Dr Middleton demonstrates at length, authority comes not by delegation from those over whom it is exercised but by transmission and assumed devolution from ancestors. That is why jural authority can be acquired only by succession, in these systems.

But let us consider the paradoxes in these requirements. To become an ancestor a man must have sons; hence the inordinate value attached to male offspring; Tallensi say that a man who dies sonless has wasted his life, and the Chinese, according to Hsu, compare him to a tree without roots. We might well ask what deeper motives underly this profound desire for sons, but that would be an unwarranted digression. All we have to note is that sons are desired and needed so that the apotheosis of ancestorhood may be attained; but it can be attained only by so cherishing sons that they eventually supplant one. On the other side, legitimate status in family, lineage, and community can be acquired only by being legitimately fathered; but jural autonomy, which is the source of authority and power even in the domestic domain, can be achieved only upon the death of the father and by assuming his mantle —quite literally so among the Namoos.

But that is not the end. Purely descriptively considered, as Dr Middleton acutely observes, both as father in his family and as elder in his lineage, the man who holds authority in the name of his ancesors is, by that token, subject to their authority and, in the last resort only to that authority. But it is not the same kind of authority as that of a living person over his dependants. It is imputed to account for things that happen to and amongst his descendants.

So we have the paradox that a man may desire to be allotted responsibility towards the ancestors for ills that befall himself and his family, since this is evidence for all to see that he is directly subject to ancestral authority and by that token jurally autonomous, hence entitled to exercise secular authority in family and lineage affairs as well as to officiate in ritual service of the ancestors.

I must resist the temptation to expatiate on this point, and return to the question why pietas? and I shall begin with a proposition that must here be stated dogmatically, though there is ample evidence in the literature I have cited to justify it. In the type of social system we are discussing, at any rate within the domains of kinship and descent groups, jural autonomy and authority are highly prized, indeed the most highly prized capacities a man can aspire to, since he cannot reach full adulthood without them. They are, in a sense, scarce goods, since they are attached to exclusive genealogical positions in a descent group. But jural authority is also indispensable to the organization of society; indeed it is the very heart of the social system. And this must be the reason why authority never dies—must never be allowed to die—though its holders of a given time have to, by the laws of nature. I argue that jural autonomy and authority are attributes of fatherhood. Indeed they issue solely from paternal status, in this type social system. We see this at all levels of social structure, for lineage eldership presupposes paternal status in the holder and is modelled on it. It is not an empty metaphor when Tallensi say that a clan or lineage head is the father of the whole group. And paternal status is not only the kingpin of the social structure in patrilineal systems; it is, among the Tallensi, deeply embedded in each person's life experience by upbringing and through daily cognizance of its existence.

Thus when we say that jural authority never dies and must not be allowed to die we can translate this to mean that fatherhood never dies and must not be allowed to die though fathers in the flesh have to die. There is, of course, a very tangible sense in which fatherhood never dies where patrilineal descent is the governing principle of social structure. For as long as a man's descendants last, their place in society and their social relations to one another and to the rest of society are ordered by reference to his paternal career. They are himself, replicated by social selection as well as by physical continuity. But I am here concerned with the moral and religious representations of this fact. From this position, ancestorhood is fatherhood made immortal, in despite of the death of real fathers; that is to say, it is paternal authority, above all, that is made immortal and impregnable in despite of the transience of its holders. But fatherhood which confers the capacity for authority is worthless without its antithesis of sonship; and sonship is meaningless without the right to attain the coveted status of fatherhood. So we see father and son bound to each other in ineluctable mutual dependence, one might even say in tacit collusion, to maintain this precious value, yet inescapably pitted against each other for its eventual possession, as Tallensi recognize.

In this relationship the sons are at a disadvantage, being under the authority they must support, and what is more, restrained by the premise of kinship amity which outlaws strife between kin. Nor must we forget that fathers do love and cherish their sons, and at heart most of all their first-borns, as is apparent from the grief of a father whose son pre-deceases him. Both among the Chinese and among the Tallensi, they do so openly in their sons' formative years, and still, among the Tallensi, behind the façade of the avoidances, in later years, when their own life situation, and Tale beliefs about human nature, prompt recourse to the defence of thrusting first sons out. Can sons do other than strive to reciprocate their fathers' devotion even while, perhaps only inarticulately coveting their status?

But the problem remains how to reconcile the moral imperative of kinship amity with the rivalry of interests between the generations or, to put it from the angle of the individual's life experience and motivation, how to preserve the trust and affection engendered by the life-long reciprocity of parental solicitude and filial dependence against the pull of the underlying mutual antagonism generated in this very relationship of upbringing. It is, in short, a question of resolving the ambivalence that is built into the relations of successive generations in the unilineally-organized descent systems we are considering. We should bear in mind that there is no means of total escape from the family and lineage structure other than by complete severance of all ties with kin and community and the consequential abandonment of all rights and claims to sources of livelihood, jural status, ritual insurance, and political protection. Traditionally, in a society like that of the Tallensi, one could not live in a community except as either a legitimate member of a lineage and a family, or a kinless and rightless slave attached to a lineage and a family and able to survive only by virtue of being accorded

quasi-kinship status. There are good structural reasons, therefore, for institutional devices and cultural values that will serve to regulate the potentiality of schism between successive generations.

Ancestor worship provides the medium through which this end is attained. It represents not only the apotheosis of parental authority but its immortalization by incorporation in the universal and everlasting dominion of the lineage and clan ancestors. How subtly the beliefs and ritual practices of ancestor worship lend themselves to regulating the opposition between successive generations can be appreciated from the manner in which Tallensi rationalize it by recourse to the concept of Destiny. This enables them to externalize the latent conflict in symbolic guise, and thus to acknowledge it, without destroying the relationship to which it belongs. But the inequality of power and authority is not eliminated. To accept this more is needed than symbolic cognizance of its character. And here pietas comes into play.

Pietas is rooted in the relations of living parents and children, as I have already emphasized. It enjoins obedience and respect towards parents, submission of personal will and desires to their discipline, economic service to them, and acquiescence in jural minority. The tangible reward for keeping the rules is the gratification of parents and kin, and the diffuse approval of society. There is also a moral reward in that pietas towards the living is *eo ipso* pietas towards the ancestors and is deemed to conduce to their benevolence. We might therefore regard pietas as the temporary renunciation of self-interest in order to maintain indispensable social relationship. But I would rather avoid such conjectures and merely say that conformity to these norms is an avowal of contentment with parental authority and power. The upshot is that sons who might be tempted to rebel and fathers whose patience is exhausted are both kept in check. But this does not wholly rule out the chances of acrimony or discord between them. Tallensi would say that human nature is like that. There are people who resent authority, or evade customary duties, or flout religious precepts. Sanctions are necessary but must not be expected to work unfailingly. That is how it is even with such emotionally and institutionally compelling rules as the avoidances of first-borns. Tallensi certainly perceive how these observances segregate the spheres of father and son and enable them to put an interpretation on their relationship which reduces friction and suppresses open rivalry especially in the all-important matter of rights over persons and property. But though breach of first-born taboos is unheard of, Tallensi say that faithful adherence to them is a matter of the kind of propriety, and the kind of morality which I have called pietas, not of blind fear. And where pietas is wanting sons may turn against their parents and fathers repudiate their sons, in defiance of both sentiment and religion. I have recorded instances elsewhere and, as we might anticipate, it is usually a mature first-born of an aging father who rebels and breaks away. But I have not heard of a case in which the ultimate sanction of pietas did not eventually prevail. When the father dies the son must—and in my experience always does—return to perform the funeral and assume his inheritance. Kologo's tragic fate was widely cited as an object lesson. He quarrelled with his father and departed to farm abroad. But when messengers came to tell him that his father had died he hurried home to supervise the funeral. He had barely taken possession of his patrimony when he fell ill and died. The general belief was that this was retribution for failure to make up his quarrel with his father. When he came home for the funeral he made submission to the lineage elders and they had persuaded his father's sister to revoke his father's curse. But this was not enough, as his death proved. The diviner revealed that his father, now among the ancestors, still grieved and angered by his desertion, complained to them of his impiety and so they had slain him.

It is pietas then, which makes living authority acceptable. Transposed into ritual form it becomes the pietas towards the ancestors which is the essence of their worship. This corresponds to the continuity between the living and the ancestors that is embodied in the descent group. But there is tangible foundation for this transposition from mundane custom to religious practices and belief. Among the Tallensi, as among the Chinese but perhaps more conspicuously and familiarly, the ancestors, far from being remote divinities, are part and parcel of the everyday life of their descendants. Their shrines stud the homesteads, their graves are close by, their names are constantly cited in social transactions. It is often impossible to tell, when Tallensi speak of a father or a grandfather, whether they are referring to a living person or to an ancestor. In a large expanded family not a week passes without some sacrifice or libation to the ancestors. And the attitude of the officiant in domestic rites of this kind is but a more reverent version of his relations with a living parent.

I have often taken part with the head of the family in rites that seem so informal as hardly to merit the title of religious worship. On the eve of the sowing season, for example, every family head goes round his homestead and his home farm pouring a libation of millet flour mixed in water upon each of his ancestor shrines in turn in order to inform the ancestors of the tasks that lie ahead. He addresses them with deference and pleads for their protection against accidents and for health, fertility, and well-being for all. But his matter-of-fact manner and conventional words might easily mislead an onlooker to see no religious meaning in his actions. Characteristically, when I found one of my friends supervising the sowing of his home farm he explained that he was late in starting because, as he put it, "I had to tell my father first." As his own father was still alive, I asked if he meant he had to inform him first. "Yes of course I had to tell him," he said, "one can't do anything so important without telling one's father. But I don't mean him. I mean my father who became my Destiny, my ancestor." Pietas towards the ancestors consists primarily in ritual tendance and services in the form of libations, sacrifices and observances whenever they are demanded. The parallels with pietas towards the living is seen, among the Tallensi, in their description of sacrificing as giving food and drink to the ancestors, though they make it clear that this is not meant in the material sense. In return, they say, ancestors "back up" (dol) their descendants.

However, the aspect of ancestor worship which I wish to dwell upon is its value in resolving the opposition, structural and interpersonal, of successive generations. Granted the premises of belief and value, death palpably removes fathers; but it is not assumed to extinguish fatherhood. On the contrary, it furnishes the conditions for elevating fatherhood above mundane claims and commitments. What is more, it provides the occasion for society to compel sons to accept their triumph as a moral necessity and to make up for it by undergoing the ritual exigencies that metamorphose fathers into ancestors. It is reassuring for a son to know that it is by his pious submission to ritual that his father is established among the ancestors forever. He sees it as the continuation of submission to the authority that was vested in his father before his death.

And let me interpolate that we must not be deceived into assuming that funeral rites are necessary in order to turn a dead person into an ancestor for what are vulgarly thought of as superstitious reasons. Similar rites are performed on behalf of living men in order to confer office and status. Ancestorhood is a status in a descent structure as Van Gennep showed and as such students of African religions as . . . the late Dr Edwin Smith often emphasized. The ritual establishment of ancestorhood defines the realm of events and social relations within which the power and authority of ancestors are believed to be displayed.

To go back to what I have been saying, it should be recollected that death is legitimated as the doing of the ancestors. It is they themselves, the fountain-head of authority and the final sanction of pietas, who remove fathers and open the way for sons to succeed. That they cut down fathers in just retribution for conduct which they are believed to regard as impious is consistent with their status. Is there a more effective way of asserting power and authority than by imputing and punishing disobedience?

It can be seen that in these systems a person never escapes from authority. The jural authority of the living father is metamorphosed into the mystical authority of the ancestor father, backed by the whole hierarchy of the ancestors and the more formidable for that reason. Thus a father's status is held by grace of the ancestors. For all its rewards, it is not an easy office, for it carries not only material responsibilities for dependants but the more onerous ritual responsibilities to the ancestors. But to succeed him need not be interpreted as supplanting the father, but rather as taking over and continuing the office that was temporarily

vested in him. It is submission to duty and this divests it of guilt, the more readily so since the opposition between successive generations is not ended but merely transposed to a new level. And it is in some ways more acute, for misfortunes, disease, and death are the lot of mankind and quite unforeseeable. These are interpreted, in Tale philosophy, as manifestations of dissatisfaction on the part of ancestors. The man who holds paternal status is constantly faced with unforeseen demands from the ancestors. The right to officiate in sacrifice to them gives jural and economic power and authority over living dependants. But it also imposes the burden of responsibility for the proper tendance and service of the ancestors. And one can never be sure that one is fulfilling these obligations satisfactorily, as one can be with one's duties to living parents.

The saving grace is pietas. If one conducts one's life to the best of one's lights, in accordance with the dictates of pietas, one can have faith in the justice of the ancestors. What is more one can accept what comes from them without remorse and in a spirit of submission to authority that cannot be quesioned. Hope remains; for expiation and reconciliation are always open to one. This is no more than admitting that one has failed in pietas, a very human failing, and the institutional means are there for reinstatment. To give the ancestors what they demand in sacrifice, service and observance is to submit to their discipline and so to recover pietas.

I do not think I have embroidered extravagantly on the ethnographic facts. As far as the Tallensi are concerned, a man's ancestor-father and forefathers are, as I have said, believed to be in his vicinity all the time, ritually accessible to him at the shrines dedicated to them. This is not a superstitious fiction, protective no less than disciplinary, is intimately felt to be ever present in normal life, just as living parents are. I was reminded of this on an occasion when the Tongraana was discoursing to his elders about a dispute between two clan heads at which he had been asked to give evidence as an authority on native custom. He explained how he had felt obliged to refute the claims of one of the parties, even though he was a kinsman.

"He was lying," said the Tongraana, "and lies only get you into trouble. I hate deceit. I will not tell lies, cost what it may. If a man has been properly brought up by his father he will not be a liar. When I was a small boy my father used to beat me and beat me if I deceived him or told lies, that is why I do not speak lies. My father will not permit this."

The "father" referred to was long dead but the speaker's manner, gestures and affectionate tone of voice made it sound as if he was there in the room, by his side. I have often had this experience with Tallensi.

To take another instance. Teezien was patiently trying to make me grasp the point of the last fruits rites at the external *boghar* at the end of the dry season.

"We provide for them (that is, the ancestors) he said, and beg crops. We give him (that is, the *boghar* personified as the collectivity of all the ancestors) food so that he may eat and on his part grant us something. If we deny him he will not provide for us, he will not give to us, neither wife nor child. It is he who rules over us so that we may live. Supposing you are cultivating your farm and the crops spoil, will you not say that it is your father who let this happen? If you are breeding livestock and they all die, won't you say your father permitted this? If you give him nothing will he give you anything? He is the master of everything. We brew beer for him and sacrifice fowls so that he may eat to satisfaction and then he will secure guinea corn and millet for us."
[Ancestors, I protested, are dead; how can they eat and do such material things as making crops thrive?] "It is exactly as with living people," he answered imperturbably, "If you have a son and you are bringing him up and he refuses to farm, you upbraid him. You say you fathered him with tribulation and here he is refusing to farm what then are you to eat? If he doesn't farm will he ever get himself a wife, will he achieve children? Now if someone does you a favour wouldn't you go and thank him? And if you do someone a favour and he comes to thank you with however small a token would you not do him a favour again?"

I have reproduced exactly as I recorded them at the time, these reflections on fathers and ancestors of two of the most esteemed, sagacious and well informed clan heads whom it was my privilege to converse with in Taleland. It should be added that Tallensi can, at a pinch, call upon and make offerings to ancestors, wherever they happen to be, though ideally the right place for this is at the shrines in the home settlement. You go to a cross roads, and squat facing the direction of your home settlement to make a sacrifice to your ancestors if you are away from home. For your ancestors are always available to you.

We can see that fathers are held in mind as if they had never died. And the image in which they are cast is one that accentuates the authority and discipline which they exercised. They are recalled with pious gratitude for the moral scruples they inculcated and the obedience they exacted, but also with affection for the benevolence they showed to loyal sons. This is more revealing since Tale fathers, in reality, very rarely have recourse to corporal punishment and normally have easy-going and tolerant relationships with their growing sons, as I have previously noted.

In this way the concept of ancestorhood and the religious institutions in which it is ritually and socially embodied serve as the medium that enables the individual to keep up his relationship with his father, even after his death, as if he were a part of himself. The father who controlled his conduct during life turns into an internal censor of his conduct when he becomes an ancestor. And this is effective because he is, at the same time, externally available both for the imputation of absolute power and authority, and for acts of appeasement. This provides grounds that seem rational and objective for the rituals of solicitude by means of which a man may hope to control, or at least to influence and certainly to negotiate the changing fortunes of life. Pietas is the bridge between the internal presence and the external sanctity of paternal authority and power.

To forestall inevitable and justifiable criticism, may I say that I have purposely taken a narrow view of my theme. I have tried to concentrate on the hard core of ancestor worship in one type of social system, and more particularly in a single specimen of the type. I have ignored the ramifications and substitutions by means of which the elementary principles of ancestor worship are extended throughout the entire religious system of a people like the Tallensi. I have, for instance, paid no attention to the extremely important role of maternal ancestors in patrilineal ancestor cults. I have also restricted comparative evidence to the minimum needed for my argument. I wish it had been possible to examine matrilineal descent systems with ancestor cults. I can only say that such studies as those of Dr Colson and Dr Gough seem to me to confirm my main thesis. Again Polynesian moral and religious customs and beliefs, especially those of the Tikopia on which we now have such splendid and rich material throw penetrating light on the nature of paternal authority and its apothesis. Granted the differences in religious values and beliefs, there is basically a common pattern, in this regard, among Tikopia and Tallensi. The relationships of fathers and sons in Tikopia are characteristically patrilineal and strikingly resemble those of the Tallensi.

At all events, the course I have followed was chosen in the belief that the best way to arrive at clear hypotheses is to isolate for analysis what is generally agreed to be the nuclear institution of ancestor worship. Ancestor worship is primarily the religious cult of deceased parents; but not only that. For it presupposes the recognition of ancestry and descent for jural and economic and other social purposes. It is rooted in the antithesis between the inescapable bonds of dependence, for sustenance, for protection from danger and death, in status and personal development, of sons upon their father, on the one hand, and the inherent opposition of successive generations, on the other. The ambivalence that springs from this antithesis is due to the fact that a son cannot attain jural autonomy until his father dies and he can legitimately succeed him. The ancestor cult permits this ambivalence to be resolved and succession to take place in such a way that authority itself, as a norm and principle of social order, is never overturned. But to accept the coercion of authority throughout life, first as a jural minor and then in ritual and moral submission, without loss of respect, affection and trust towards the persons and institutions that must be vested with it for the sake of social order might be difficult if not intolerable. This is where the ideal of pietas enters as a regulative and mollifying directive to conduct.

I said that I have purposely eschewed wide comparison. But I cannot refrain from adducing one striking negative instance in support of my argument, though I am well aware that its value is circumstantial rather than conclusive. Dr Stenning's brilliant analysis of the developmental cycle of the family among the Wodaabe Fulani (Selection 3) presents a picture of jural

and economic relations between successive patri-filial generations which are in radical contrast to those I have described. Fathers relinquish their control over herds and their authority over persons step by step to their sons during the course of the sons' growth and social development. The process begins when a man's first son is born and culminates when his last son marries with the final handling over to the sons of what is left of the herd and what is felt of paternal authority. The father then retires physically, economically, and jurally, becomes dependent on his sons, and is, in Dr Stenning's words, to all intents heenceforth socially dead. A parallel process takes place with women. With this is associated progressively increasing skill and responsibility in cattle husbandry for boys, parallel growth into marriage after betrothal for both sexes in early childhood, and a pattern of complementary co-operation between the sexes and the age groups that rules out coercive parental authority. Finally, Wodaabe descent groups generally have a genealogical depth of not more than three or four generations.

In this context of social structure, where there is no need for a man to wait for dead men's shoes in order to attain jural autonomy and economic emancipation, the tensions between successive generations that are characteristic of the patrilineal systems I have been concerned with, do not appear to develop. Does this account for the absence of an ancestor cult among the Wodaabe? Or is it due to their adoption of Islam? Dr Stenning does not think it is due to Islam; and I am naturally attracted to this conclusion since it supports the main thesis of this lecture.

A last question. Is pietas bound up exclusively with ancestor worship or does it reflect a general factor in the relations between successive generations that is only mobilized in a special degree and form in ancestor worship? Do the Wodaabe Fulani, for example, have this notion or not? I cannot attempt to answer this question here. But I am reminded of one of the most delicate descriptions of filial piety known to me.

It occurs in that masterpiece of period ethno-fiction, Anthony Trollope's *Barchester Towers*. You may remember the scene. The old Bishop ("who had for many years filled the chair with meek authority") is dying. His son, Archdeacon Grantly, is by his bedside, and the question that is in everybody's mind is troubling him, too. Would his father die before the out-going government fell? If he did the Archdeacon would undoubtedly, to quote the narrator, "have the reversion of the see." If not, another would as surely be elected. Clearly and compassionately, as one who is himself no stranger to such an event and to such emotions, Trollope describes the old man's last moments and the son's thoughts and feelings. "He tried to keep his mind away from the subject, but he could not," remarks the chronicler. "The race was so very close and the stakes were so very high." He lingers by the bedside for a few minutes and then continues:

But by no means easy were the emotions of him who sat there watching. He knew it must be now or never. He was already over fifty, and there was little chance that his friends who were now leaving office would soon return to it. No probable British prime minister but he who was now in, he who was soon to be put out, would think of making a bishop of Dr Grantly. Thus he thought long and sadly, in deep silence, and then gazed at that still living face, and then at last dared to ask himself whether he really longed for his father's death.

The effort was a salutory one, and the question was answered in a moment. That proud, wishful, worldly man sank on his knees by the bedside, and taking the bishop's hand within his own prayed eagerly that his sins might be forgiven him.

I need quote no more to establish that the Trollopians were deeply imbued wlth the sentiments and habits of pietas. It can hardly be an accident that so acute an observer as the narrator of this history should depict the Archdeacon's emotions in the setting of a mature son's compunction over his half-hidden ambition to succeed to his father's office. Nor is it by chance that the Archdeacon is shown to pray for his sins to be forgiven rather than for his father's recovery, improbable as that might be.

Nor is pietas unknown in our present era of unprecedented technological audacity. The other day we learnt from *The Times* (14 April 1961) how the first cosmonaut prepared himself for his spectacular venture. We are told that "Major Gagarin was brought to Moscow just before the flight and went to Lenin's tomb in the Red Square 'to gather new strength for the fulfilment of his unusual task'." And nearer home, is not the celebration of Founder's Day at institutions like my own college in Cambridge an act of pietas not too remote in spirit from some of the rites and attitudes I have been discussing?

15. RITUAL REGULATION OF ENVIRONMENTAL RELATIONS AMONG A NEW GUINEA PEOPLE

ROY A. RAPPAPORT

Reprinted by permission of the author and publisher from Ethnology, *Vol. 6, pp. 17-30. Copyright 1967, Ethnology. Roy A. Rappaport was born in New York City in 1926; he received his B.A. from Cornell University in 1949. After a career in business, he returned to school in 1959 and earned his Ph.D. in anthropology in 1966. He participated in an archeological field expedition in the Society Islands in 1960; the field work in New Guinea, on which the next selection is based, was conducted in 1962-1963. Dr. Rappaport is Associate Professor of Anthropology at the University of Michigan.*

■ We are now going to consider still another example of religious practices in a stateless horti-cultural society, to illustrate an additional aspect of the adaptive significance of this sphere of activity. Although religion mirrors and validates social and technological organization—for example, in the religious individualism of hunting-gathering groups and in its corporate kin setting in horticultural societies—its consequences do not stop there. An important feature of every strategy of adaptation is an appropriate orderliness in productive activities and in the distribution of resources. It is often the case that a group's cycle of production and distribution is marked by a religious ceremonial calendar, which is superimposed on these activities to assure the economic and nutritional stability of the group as a whole.

We see a graphic example of this in the following selection, outlining the consequences of religious ritual among the Tsembaga Marin of highland New Guinea. Rappaport focuses on the production and consumption of meat, which is their principal source of protein. The essence of adaptation is the survival of the group; hence the strategy for providing an adequate diet must take into account the requirements of the group from one season to the next, not only the needs of the individual on a day-to-day basis. In these terms, the ritual regulation of meat production and distribution must be regarded as part of the Tsembaga Marin's energy system. This relationship between religious ritual and exploitative activities is further intertwined with relationships among groups within the society, including marriage arrangements and sexual liaisons.

Rappaport's analysis is also important from a methodological point of view. The reader will note the importance here of careful measurement in the study of social behavior. Such quantification is relatively new in the anthropological study of the ways of life of tribal groups, but it is becoming increasingly important. At the same time, these techniques cannot displace the equally important elements of hunch, insight, and a subjective "feel" for a group's way of life in anthropology any more than in other scientific disciplines. There were no formulas to lead Rappaport to his understanding of the interrelationships among religious ritual, the regulation of available resources, the consumption of protein, and social relationships. Such insights can only come from a careful balance of quantitative procedures with those qualitative approaches that often seem more subjective.

The ideas in this paper are explored in greater detail in Rappaport's book, *Pigs for the Ancestors : Ritual in the Ecology of a New Guinea People* (New Haven and London : Yale University Press, 1968). Also relevant is "The Potlatch System of the Southern Kwakiutl : A New Perspective" by Stuart Piddocke (*Southwestern Journal of Anthropology*, 21 [1965] : 244-64). I consider the following two books by Raymond Firth to be among the most important in the anthropological study of religion : *Tikopia Ritual and Belief*

(Boston : Beacon Press, 1967) and *The Work of the Gods in Tikopia* (New York : Humanities Press, 1967). ■

MOST FUNCTIONAL STUDIES of religious behavior in anthropology have as an analytic goal the elucidation of events, processes, or relationships occurring within a social unit of some sort. The social unit is not always well defined, but in some cases it appears to be a church, that is, a group of people who entertain similar beliefs about the universe, or a congregation, a group of people who participate together in the performance of religious rituals. There have been exceptions. Thus Vayda, Leeds, and Smith and O. K. Moore have clearly perceived that the functions of religious ritual are not necessarily confined within the boundaries of a congregation or even a church. By and large, however, I believe that the following statement by Homans represents fairly the dominant line of anthropological thought concerning the functions of religious ritual:

Ritual actions do not produce a practical result on the external world—that is one of the reasons why we call them ritual. But to make this statement is not to say that ritual has no function. Its function is not related to the world external to the society but to the internal constitution of the society. It gives the members of the society confidence, it dispels their anxieties, it disciplines their social organization.

No argument will be raised here against the sociological and psychological functions imputed by Homans, and many others before him, to ritual. They seem to me to be plausible. Nevertheless, in some cases at least, ritual does produce, in Homans' terms, "a practical result on the world" external not only to the social unit composed of those who participate together in ritual performances but also to the larger unit composed of those who entertain similar beliefs concerning the universe. The material presented here will show that the ritual cycles of the Tsembaga, and of other local territorial groups of Maring speakers living in the New Guinea interior, play an important part in regulating the relationships of these groups with both the nonhuman components of their immediate environments and the human components of their less immediate environments, that is, with other similar territorial groups. To be more specific, this regulation helps to maintain the biotic communities existing within their territories, redistributes land among people and people over land, and limits the frequency of fighting. In the absence of authoritative political statuses or offices, the ritual cycle likewise provides a means for mobilizing allies when warfare may be undertaken. It also provides a mechanism for redistributing local pig surpluses in the form of pork throughout a large regional population while helping to assure the local population of a supply of pork when its members are most in need of high quality protein.

Religious ritual may be defined, for the purposes of this paper, as the prescribed performance of conventionalized acts manifestly directed toward the involvement of non-empirical or supernatural agencies in the affairs of the actors. While this definition relies upon the formal characteristics of the performances and upon the motives for undertaking them, attention will be focused upon the empirical effects of ritual performances and sequences of ritual performances. The religious rituals to be discussed are regarded as neither more nor less than part of the behavioral repertoire employed by an aggregate of organisms in adjusting to its environment.

The data upon which this paper is based were collected during fourteen months of field work among the Tsembaga, one of about twenty local groups of Maring speakers living in the Simbai and Jimi Valleys of the Bismarck Range in the Territory of New Guinea. The size of Maring local groups varies from a little over 100 to 900. The Tsembaga, who in 1963 numbered 204 persons, are located on the south wall of the Simbai Valley. The country in which they live differs from the true highlands in being lower, generally more rugged, and more heavily forested. Tsembaga territory rises, within a total surface area of 3.2 square miles, from an elevation of 2,200 feet at the Simbai river to 7,200 feet at the ridge crest. Gardens are cut in the secondary forests up to between 5,000 and 5,400 feet, above which the area remains in primary forest. Rainfall reaches 150 inches per year.

The Tsembaga have come into contact with the outside world only recently; the first government patrol to penetrate their territory arrived in 1954. They were considered uncontrolled by the Australian government until 1962, and they remain unmissionized to this day.

The 204 Tsembaga are distributed among five putatively patrilineal clans, which are, in turn, organized into more inclusive groupings on two hierarchical levels below that of the total local group. Internal political structure is highly egalitarian. There are no hereditary or elected chiefs, nor are there even "big men" who can regularly coerce or command the support of their clansmen or co-residents in economic or forceful enterprises.

It is convenient to regard the Tsembaga as a population in the ecological sense, that is, as one of the components of a system of trophic exchanges taking place within a bounded area. Tsembaga territory and the biotic community existing upon it may be conveniently viewed as an ecosystem. While it would be permissible arbitrarily to designate the Tsembaga as a population and their territory with its biota as an ecosystem, there are also nonarbitrary reasons for doing so. An ecosystem is a system of material exchanges, and the Tsembaga maintain against other human groups exclusive access to the resources within their territorial borders. Conversely, it is from this territory alone that the Tsembaga ordinarily derive all of their foodstuffs and most of the other materials they require for survival. Less anthropocentrically, it may be justified to regard Tsembaga territory with its biota as an ecosystem in view of the rather localized nature of cyclical material exchanges in tropical rainforests.

As they are involved with the nonhuman biotic community within their territory in a set of trophic exchanges, so do they participate in other material relationships with other human groups external to their territory. Genetic materials are exchanged with other groups, and certain crucial items, such as stone axes, were in past obtained from the outside. Furthermore, in the area occupied by the Maring speakers, more than one local group is usually involved in any process, either peaceful or warlike, through which people are redistributed over land and land redistributed among people.

The concept of the ecosystem, though it provides a convenient frame for the analysis of interspecific trophic exchanges taking place within limited geographical areas, does not comfortably accommodate intraspecific exchanges taking place over wider geographic areas. Some sort of geographic population model would be more useful for the analysis of the relationship of the local ecological population to the larger regional population of which it is a part, but we lack even a set of appropriate terms for such a model. Suffice it here to note that the relations of the Tsembaga to the total of other local human populations in their vicinity are similar to the relations of local aggregates of other animals to the totality of their species occupying broader and more or less continuous regions. This larger, more inclusive aggregate may resemble what geneticists mean by the term population, that is, an aggregate of interbreeding organisms persisting through an indefinite number of generations and either living or capable of living in isolation from similar aggregates of the same species. This is the unit which survives through long periods of time while its local ecological (*sensu stricto*) subunits, the units more or less independently involved in interspecific trophic exchanges such as the Tsembaga, are ephemeral.

Since it has been asserted that the ritual cycles of the Tsembaga regulate relationships within what may be regarded as a complex system, it is necessary, before proceeding to the ritual cycle itself, to describe briefly, and where possible in quantitative terms, some aspects of the place of the Tsembaga in this system.

The Tsembaga are bush-fallowing horticulturalists. Staples include a range of root crops, taro (*Colocasia*) and sweet potatoes being most important, yams and manioc less so. In addition, a great variety of greens are raised, some of which are rich in protein. Sugar cane and some tree crops, particularly *Pandanus conoideus*, are also important.

All gardens are mixed, many of them containing all of the major root crops and many greens. Two named garden types are, however, distinguished by the crops which predominate in them. "Taro–yam gardens" were found to produce, on the basis of daily harvest records kept on entire gardens for close to one year, about 5,300,000 calories per acre during their harvesting lives of 18 to 24 months; 85 per cent of their yield is harvested between 24 and 76 weeks after planting. "Sugar-sweet potato gardens" produce about 4,600,000 calories per acre during their harvesting lives, 91 per cent being taken between 24 and 76 weeks after planting. I estimated that approximately 310,000

calories per acre is expended on cutting, fencing, planting, maintaining, harvesting, and walking to and from taro–yam gardens. Sugar–sweet potato gardens required an expenditure of approximately 290,000 calories per acre. These energy ratios, approximately 17:1 on taro–yam gardens and 16:1 on sugar–sweet potato gardens, compare favorably with figures reported for swidden cultivation in other regions.

Intake is high in comparison with the reported dietaries of other New Guinea populations. On the basis of daily consumption records kept for ten months on four households numbering in total sixteen persons, I estimated the average daily intake of adult males to be approximately 2,600 calories, and that of adult females to be around 2,200 calories. It may be mentioned here that the Tsembaga are small and short statured. Adult males average 101 pounds in weight and approximately 58.5 inches in height; the corresponding averages for adult females are 85 pounds and 54.5 inches.

Although 99 per cent by weight of the food consumed is vegetable, the protein intake is high by New Guinea standards. The daily protein consumption of adult males from vegetable sources was estimated to be between 43 and 55 grams, of adult females 36 to 48 grams. Even with an adjustment for vegetable sources, these values are slightly in excess of the recently published WHO/FAO daily requirements. The same is true of the younger age categories, although soft and discolored hair, a symptom of protein deficiency, was noted in a few children. The WHO/FAO protein requirements do not include a large "margin for safety" or allowance for stress; and, although no clinical assessments were undertaken, it may be suggested that the Tsembaga achieve nitrogen balance at a low level. In other words, their protein intake is probably marginal.

Measurements of all gardens made during 1962 and of some gardens made during 1963 indicate that, to support the human population, between .15 and .19 acres are put into cultivation per capita per year. Fallows range from 8 to 45 years. The area in secondary forest comprises approximately 1,000 acres, only 30 to 50 of which are in cultivation at any time. Assuming calories to be the limiting factor, and assuming an unchanging population structure, the territory could support—with no reduction in lengths of fallow and without cutting into the virgin forest from which the Tsembaga extract many important items—between 290 and 397 people if the pig population remained minimal. The size of the pig herd, however, fluctuates widely. Taking Maring pig husbandry procedures into consideration, I have estimated the human carrying capacity of the Tsembaga territory at between 270 and 320 people.

Because the timing of the ritual cycle is bound up with the demography of the pig herd, the place of the pig in Tsembaga adaption must be examined.

First, being omnivorous, pigs keep residential areas free of garbage and human feces. Second, limited numbers of pigs rooting in secondary growth may help to hasten the development of that growth. The Tsembaga usually permit pigs to enter their gardens one and a half to two years after planting, by which time second-growth trees are well established there. The Tsembaga practice selective weeding; from the time the garden is planted, herbaceous species are removed, but tree species are allowed to remain. By the time cropping is discontinued and the pigs are let in, some of the trees in the garden are already ten to fifteen feet tall. These well-established trees are relatively impervious to damage by the pigs, which, in rooting for seeds and remaining tubers, eliminate many seeds and seedlings that, if allowed to develop, would provide some competition for the established trees. Moreover, in some Maring-speaking areas swiddens are planted twice, although this is not the case with the Tsembaga. After the first crop is almost exhausted, pigs are penned in the garden, where their rooting eliminates weeds and softens the ground, making the task of planting for a second time easier. The pigs, in other words, are used as cultivating machines.

Small numbers of pigs are easy to keep. They run free during the day and return home at night to receive their ration of garbage and sub-standard tubers, particularly sweet potatoes. Supplying the latter requires little extra work, for the substandard tubers are taken from the ground in the course of harvesting the daily ration for humans. Daily consumption records kept over a period of some months show that the ration of tubers received by the pigs approximates in weight that consumed by adult humans,

i.e., a little less than three pounds per day per pig.

If the pig herd grows large, however, the sub-standard tubers incidentally obtained in the course of harvesting for human needs become insufficient, and it becomes necessary to harvest especially for pigs. In other words, people must work for the pigs and perhaps even supply them with food fit for human consumption. Thus, as Vayda, Leeds and Smith have pointed out, there can be too many pigs for a given community.

This also holds true of the sanitary and culti-vating services rendered by pigs. A small number of pigs is sufficient to keep residential areas clean, to suppress superfluous seedlings in abandoned gardens, and to soften the soil in gardens scheduled for second plantings. A larger herd, on the other hand, may be trouble-some; the larger the number of pigs, the greater the possibility of their invasion of producing gardens, with concomitant damage not only to crops and young secondary growth but also to the relations between the pig owners and garden owners.

All male pigs are castrated at approximately three months of age, for boars, people say, are dangerous and do not grow as large as barrows. Pregnancies, therefore, are always the result of unions of domestic sows with feral males. Fecundity is thus only a fraction of its potential. During one twelve-month period only fourteen litters resulted out of a potential 99 or more pregnancies. Farrowing generally takes place in the forest, and mortality of the young is high. Only 32 of the offspring of the above-mentioned fourteen pregnancies were alive six months after birth. This number is barely sufficient to replace the number of adult animals which would have died or been killed during most years without pig festivals.

The Tsembaga almost never kill domestic pigs outside of ritual contexts. In ordinary times, when there is no pig festival in progress, these rituals are almost always associated with mis-fortunes or emergencies, notably warfare, illness, injury, or death. Rules state not only the con-texts in which pigs are to be ritually slaughtered but also who may partake of the flesh of the sacrificial animals. During warfare it is only the men participating in the fighting who eat the pork. In cases of illness or injury, it is only the victim and certain near relatives, particularly his co-resident agnates and spouses, who do so.

It is reasonable to assume that misfortune and emergency are likely to induce in the organisms experiencing them a complex of physiological changes known collectively as "stress." Physiological stress reactions occur not only in organisms which are infected with disease or traumatized, but also in those experiencing rage or fear, or even prolonged anxiety. One important aspect of stress is the increased catabolization of protein, with a net loss of nitrogen from the tissues. This is a serious matter for organisms with a marginal protein intake. Antibody production is low, healing is slow, and a variety of symptoms of a serious nature are likely to develop. The status of a protein-depleted animal, however, may be significantly improved in a relatively short period of time by the intake of high quality protein, and high protein diets are therefore routinely prescribed for surgical patients and those suffering from infectious diseases.

It is precisely when they are undergoing physiological stress that the Tsembaga kill and consume their pigs, and it should be noted that they limit the consumption to those likely to be experiencing stress most profoundly. The Tsembaga, of course, know nothing of physiological stress. Native theories of the etiology and treatment of disease and injury implicate various categories of spirits to whom sacrifices must be made. Nevertheless, the behavior which is appropriate in terms of native understandings is also appropriate to the actual situation confronting the actors.

We may now outline in the barest of terms the Tsembaga ritual cycle. Space does not permit a description of its ideological correlates. It must suffice to note that Tsembaga do not necessarily perceive all of the empirical effects which the anthropologist sees to flow from their ritual behavior. Such empirical conseqences as they may perceive, moreover, are not central to their rationalizations of the performances. The Tsembaga say that they perform the rituals in order to rearrange their relationships with the supernatural world. We may only reiterate here that behavior undertaken in reference to their "cognized environment"—an environment which includes as very important elements the spirits of ancestors—seems appropriate in their "operational environment," the material en-

vironment specified by the anthropologist through operations of observation, including measurement.

Since the rituals are arranged in a cycle, description may commence at any point. The operation of the cycle becomes clearest if we begin with the rituals performed during warfare. Opponents in all cases occupy adjacent territories, in almost all cases on the same valley wall. After hostilities have broken out, each side performs certain rituals which place the opposing side in the formal category of "enemy." A number of taboos prevail while hostilities continue. These include prohibitions on sexual intercourse and on the ingestion of certain things—food prepared by women, food grown on the lower portion of the territory, marsupials, eels, and, while actually on the fighting ground, any liquid whatsoever.

One ritual practice associated with fighting which may have some physiological consequence deserves mention. Immediately before proceeding to the fighting ground, the warriors eat heavily salted pig fat. The ingestion of salt, coupled with the taboo on drinking, has the effect of shortening the fighting day, particularly since the Maring prefer to fight only on bright sunny days. When everyone gets unbearably thirsty, according to informants, fighting is broken off.

There may formerly have been other effects if the native salt contained sodium (the production of salt was discontinued some years previous to the field work, and no samples were obtained). The Maring diet seems to be deficient in sodium. The ingestion of large amounts of sodium just prior to fighting would have permitted the warriors to sweat normally without a lowering of blood volume and consequent weakness during the course of the fighting. The pork belly ingested with the salt would have provided them with a new burst of energy two hours or so after the commencement of the engagement. After fighting was finished for the day, lean pork was consumed, offsetting, at least to some extent, the nitrogen loss associated with the stressful fighting.

Fighting could continue sporadically for weeks. Occasionally it terminated in the rout of one of the antagonistic groups, whose survivors would take refuge with kinsmen elsewhere. In such instances, the victors would lay waste their opponents' groves and gardens, slaughter their pigs, and burn their houses. They would not, however, immediately annex the territory of the vanquished. The Maring say that they never take over the territory of an enemy for, even if it has been abandoned, the spirits of their ancestors remain to guard it against interlopers. Most fights, however, terminated in truces between the antagonists.

With the termination of hostilities a group which has not been driven off its territory performs a ritual called "planting the *rumbim*." Every man puts his hand on the ritual plant, *rumbim*, as it is planted in the ground. The ancestors are addressed, in effect, as follows:

We thank you for helping us in the fight and permitting us to remain on our territory. We place our souls in this *rumbim* as we plant it on our ground. We ask you to care for this *rumbim*. We will kill pigs for you now, but they are few. In the future, when we have many pigs, we shall again give you pork and uproot the *rumbim* and stage a *kaiko* (pig festival). But until there are sufficient pigs to repay you the *rumbim* will remain in the ground.

This ritual is accompanied by the wholesale slaughter of pigs. Only juveniles remain alive. All adult and adolescent animals are killed, cooked, and dedicated to the ancestors. Some are consumed by the local group, but most are distributed to allies who assisted in the fight.

Some of the taboos which the group suffered during the time of fighting are abrogated by this ritual. Sexual intercourse is now permitted, liquids may be taken at any time, and food from any part of the territory may be eaten. But the group is still in debt to its allies and ancestors. People say it is still the time of the *bamp ku*, or "fighting stones," which are actual objects used in the rituals associated with warfare. Although the fighting ceases when *rumbim* is planted, the concomitant obligation, debts to allies and ancestors, remain outstanding; and the fighting stones may not be put away until these obligations are fulfilled. The time of the fighting stones is a time of debt and danger which lasts until the *rumbim* is uprooted and a pig festival (*kaiko*) is staged.

Certain taboos persist during the time of the fighting stones. Marsupials, regarded as the pigs of the ancestors of the high ground, may not be trapped until the debt to their masters has been repaid. Eels, the "pigs of the ancestors

of the low ground," may neither be caught nor consumed. Prohibitions on all intercourse with the enemy come into force. One may not touch, talk to, or even look at a member of the enemy group, nor set foot on enemy ground. Even more important, a group may not attack another group while its ritual plant remains in the ground, for it has not yet fully rewarded its ancestors and allies for their assistance in the last fight. Until the debts to them have been paid, further assistance from them will not be forthcoming. A kind of "truce of god" thus prevails until the *rumbim* is uprooted and a *kaiko* completed.

To uproot the *rumbim* requires sufficient pigs. How many pigs are sufficient, and how long does it take to acquire them? The Tsembaga say that, if a place is "good," this can take as little as five years; but if a place is "bad," it may require ten years or longer. A bad place is one in which misfortunes are frequent and where, therefore, ritual demands for the killing of pigs arise frequently. A good place is one where such demands are infrequent. In a good place, the increase of the pig herd exceeds the ongoing ritual demands, and the herd grows rapidly. Sooner or later the substandard tubers incidentally obtained while harvesting become insufficient to feed the herd, and additional acreage must be put into production specifically for the pigs.

The work involved in caring for a large pig herd can be extremely burdensome. The Tsembaga herd just prior to the pig festival of 1962–63, when it numbered 169 animals, was receiving 54 per cent of all of the sweet potatoes and 82 per cent of all of the manioc harvested. These comprised 35.9 per cent by weight of all root crops harvested. This figure is consistent with the difference between the amount of land under cultivation just previous to the pig festival, when the herd was at maximum size, and that immediately afterwards, when the pig herd was at minimum size. The former was 36.1 per cent in excess of the latter.

I have estimated, on the basis of acreage yield and energy expenditure figures, that about 45,000 calories per year are expended in caring for one pig 120–150 pounds in size. It is upon women that most of the burden of pig keeping falls. If, from a woman's daily intake of about 2,200 calories, 950 calories are allowed for basal metabolism, a woman has only 1,250 calories a day available for all her activities, which include gardening for her family, child care, and cooking, as well as tending pigs. It is clear that no woman can feed many pigs; only a few had as many as four in their care at the commencement of the festival; and it is not surprising that agitation to uproot the *rumbim* and stage the *kaiko* starts with the wives of the owners of large numbers of pigs.

A large herd is not only burdensome as far as energy expenditure is concerned; it becomes increasingly a nuisance as it expands. The more numerous pigs become, the more frequently are gardens invaded by them. Such events result in serious disturbances of local tranquility. The garden owner often shoots, or attempts to shoot, the offending pig; and the pig owner commonly retorts by shooting, or attempting to shoot, either the garden owner, his wife, or one of his pigs. As more and more such events occur, the settlement, nucleated when the herd was small, disperses as people try to put as much distance as possible between their pigs and other people's gardens and between their gardens and other people's pigs. Occasionally this reaches its logical conclusion, and people begin to leave the territory, taking up residence with kinsmen in other local populations.

The number of pigs sufficient to become intolerable to the Tsembaga was below the capacity of the territory to carry pigs. I have estimated that, if the size and structure of the human population remained constant at the 1962–63 level, a pig population of 140 to 240 animals averaging 100 to 150 pounds in size could be maintained perpetually by the Tsembaga without necessarily inducing environmental degradation. Since the size of the herd fluctuates, even higher cyclical maxima could be achieved. The level of toleration, however, is likely always to be below the carrying capacity, since the destructive capacity of the pigs is dependent upon the population density of both people and pigs, rather than upon population size. The denser the human population, the fewer pigs will be required to disrupt social life. If the carrying capacity is exceeded, it is likely to be exceeded by people and not by pigs.

The *kaiko* or pig festival, which commences with the planting of stakes at the boundary and the uprooting of the *rumbim*, is thus triggered

by either the additional work attendant upon feeding pigs or the destructive capacity of the pigs themselves. It may be said, then, that there are sufficient pigs to stage the *kaiko* when the relationship of pigs to people changes from one of mutualism to one of parasitism or competition.

A short time prior to the uprooting of the *rumbim*, stakes are planted at the boundary. If the enemy has continued to occupy its territory, the stakes are planted at the boundary which existed before the fight. If, on the other hand, the enemy has abandoned its territory, the victors may plant their stakes at a new boundary which encompasses areas previously occupied by the enemy. The Maring say, to be sure, that they never take land belonging to an enemy, but this land is regarded as vacant, since no *rumbim* was planted on it after the last fight. We may state here a rule of land redistribution in terms of the ritual cycle: *If one of a pair of antagonistic groups is able to uproot its rumbim before its opponents can plant their rumbim, it may occupy the latter's territory.*

Not only have the vanquished abandoned their territory; it is assumed that it has also been abandoned by their ancestors as well. The surviving members of the erstwhile enemy group have by this time resided with other groups for a number of years, and most if not all of them have already had occasion to sacrifice pigs to their ancestors at their new residences. In so doing they have invited these spirits to settle at the new locations of the living, where they will in the future receive sacrifices. Ancestors of vanquished groups thus relinquish their guardianship over the territory, making it available to victorious groups. Meanwhile, the *de facto* membership of the living in the groups with which they have taken refuge is converted eventually into *de jure* membership. Sooner or later the groups with which they have taken up residence will have occasion to plant *rumbim*, and the refugees, as coresidents, will participate thus ritually validating their connection to the new territory and the new group. A rule of population redistribution may thus be stated in terms of ritual cycles: *A man becomes a member of a territorial group by participating with it in the planting of rumbim.*

The uprooting of the *rumbim* follows shortly after the planting of stakes at the boundary. On this particular occasion the Tsembaga killed 32 pigs out of their herd of 169. Much of the pork was distributed to allies and affines outside of the local group.

The taboo on trapping marsupials was also terminated at this time. Information is lacking concerning the population dynamics of the local marsupials, but it may well be that the taboo which had prevailed since the last fight— that against taking them in traps—had conserved a fauna which might otherwise have become extinct.

The *kaiko* continues for about a year, during which period friendly groups are entertained from time to time. The guests receive presents of vegetable foods, and the hosts and male guests dance together throughout the night.

These events may be regarded as analogous to aspects of the social behavior of many nonhuman animals. First of all, they include massed epigamic, or courtship, displays. Young women are presented with samples of the eligible males of local groups with which they may not otherwise have had the opportunity to become familiar. The context, moreover, permits the young women to discriminate amongst this sample in terms of both endurance (signaled by how vigorously and how long a man dances) and wealth (signaled by the richness of a man's shell and feather finery).

More importantly, the massed dancing at these events may be regarded as epideictic display, communicating to the participants information concerning the size or density of the group. In many species such displays take place as a prelude to actions which adjust group size or density, and such is the case among the Maring. The massed dancing of the visitors at a *kaiko* entertainment communicates to the hosts, while the *rumbim* truce is still in force, information concerning the amount of support they may expect from the visitors in the bellicose enterprises that they are likely to embark upon soon after the termination of the pig festival.

Among the Maring there are no chiefs or other political authorities capable of commanding the support of a body of followers, and the decision to assist another group in warfare rests with each individual male. Allies are not recruited by appealing for help to other local groups as such. Rather, each member of the groups primarily involved in the hostilities appeals to his cognatic and affinal kinsmen in other local groups. These men, in turn, urge other of their co-residents and kinsmen to "help them fight." The channels through which invitations to dance are extended are precisely those through which appeals for military support are issued. The invitations go not from group to group, but from kinsman to kinsman, the recipients of invitations urging their co-residents to "help them dance."

Invitations to dance do more than exercise the channels through which allies are recruited; they provide a means for judging their effectiveness. Dancing and fighting are regarded as in some sense equivalent. This equivalence is expressed in the similarity of some pre-fight and pre-dance rituals, and the Maring say that those who come to dance come to fight. The size of a visiting dancing contingent is consequently taken as a measure of the size of the contingent of warriors whose assistance may be expected in the next round of warfare.

In the morning the dancing ground turns into a trading ground. The items most frequently exchanged include axes, bird plumes, shell ornaments, an occasional baby pig, and, in former times, native salt. The *kaiko* thus facilitates trade by providing a market-like setting in which large numbers of traders can assemble. It likewise facilitates the movement of two critical items, salt and axes, by creating a demand for the bird plumes which may be exchanged for them.

The *kaiko* concludes with major pig sacrifices. On this particular occasion the Tsembaga butchered 105 adult and adolescent pigs, leaving only 60 juveniles and neonates alive. The survival of an additional fifteen adolescents and adults was only temporary, for they were scheduled as imminent victims. The pork yielded by the Tsembaga slaughter was estimated to weigh between 7,000 and 8,500 pounds, of which between 4,500 and 6,000 pounds were distributed to members of other local groups in 163 separate presentations. An estimated 2,000 to 3,000 people in seventeen local groups were the beneficiaries of the redistribution. The presentations, it should be mentioned, were not confined to pork. Sixteen Tsembaga men presented bridewealth or child-wealth, consisting largely of axes and shells, to their affines at this time.

The *kaiko* terminates on the day of the pig slaughter with the public presentation of salted pig belly to allies of the last fight. Presentations are made through the window in a high ceremonial fence built specially for the occasion at one end of the dance ground. The name of each honored man is announced to the assembled multitude as he charges to the window to receive his hero's portion. The fence is then ritually torn down, and the fighting stones are put away. The pig festival and the ritual cycle have been completed, demonstrating, it may be suggested, the ecological and economic competence of the local population. The local population would now be free, if it were not for the presence of the government, to attack its enemy again, secure in the knowledge that the assistance of allies and ancestors would be forthcoming because they have received pork and the obligations to them have been fulfilled.

Usually fighting did break out again very soon after the completion of the ritual cycle. If peace still prevailed when the ceremonial fence had rotted completely— a process said to take about three years, a little longer than the length of time required to raise a pig to maximum size— *rumbim* was planted as if there had been a fight, and all adult and adolescent pigs were killed. When the pig herd was large enough so that the *rumbim* could be uprooted, peace could be made with former enemies if they were also able to dig out their *rumbim*. To put this in formal terms: *If a pair of antagonistic groups proceeds through two ritual cycles without resumption of hostilities their enmity may be terminated.*

The relations of the Tsembaga with their environment have been analyzed as a complex system composed of two subsystems. What may be called the "local subsystem" has been derived from the relations of the Tsembaga with the nonhuman components of their immediate or territorial environment. It corresponds to the ecosystem in which the Tsembaga participate. A second subsystem, one which corresponds to the larger regional population of which the Tsembaga are one of the constituent units and which may be designated as the "regional subsystem," has been derived from the relations of the Tsembaga with neighbouring local populations similar to themselves.

It has been argued that rituals, arranged in repetitive sequences, regulate relations both within each of the subsystems and within the larger complex system as a whole. The timing of the ritual cycle is largely dependent upon changes in the states of the components of the local subsystem. But the *kaiko*, which is the culmination of the ritual cycle, does more than reverse changes which have taken place within the local subsystem. Its occurrence also affects relations among the components of the regional subsystem. During its performance, obligations to other local populations are fulfilled, support for future military enterprises is rallied, and land from which enemies have earlier been driven is occupied. Its completion, furthermore, permits the local population to initiate warfare again. Conversely, warfare is terminated by rituals which preclude the reinitiation of warfare until the state of the local subsystem is again such that a *kaiko* may be staged and completed. Ritual among the Tsembaga and other Maring, in short, operates as both transducer, "translating" changes in the state of one subsystem into information which can effect changes in a second subsystem, and homeostat, maintaining a number of variables which in sum comprise the total system within ranges of viability. To repeat an earlier assertion, the operation of ritual among the Tsembaga and other Maring helps to maintain an undegraded environment, limits fighting to frequencies which do not endanger the existence of the regional population, adjusts man-land ratios, facilitates trade, distributes local surpluses of pig throughout the regional population in the form of pork, and assures people of high quality protein when they are most in need of it.

Religious rituals and the supernatural orders toward which they are directed cannot be assumed *a priori* to be mere epiphenomena. Ritual may, and doubtless frequently does, do nothing more than validate and intensify the relationships which integrate the social unit, or symbolize the relationships which bind the social unit to its environment. But the interpretation of such presumably *sapiens*-specific phenomena as religious ritual within a framework which will also accommodate the behavior of other species shows, I think, that religious ritual may do much more than symbolize, validate, and intensify relationships. Indeed, it would not be improper to refer to the Tsembaga and the other entities with which they share their territory as a "ritually regulated ecosystem," and to the

Tsembaga and their human neighbors as a "ritually regulated population."

16. JAPANESE RELIGION: A GENERAL VIEW

ROBERT N. BELLAH

Reprinted with permission of The Macmillan Company from Tokugawa Religion: The Values of Pre-Industrial Japan *by Robert N. Bellah. © by The Free Press, a Corporation, 1957. Robert N. Bellah was born in 1927 at Altus, Oklahoma; was educated in the public schools of Los Angeles, California; received his B.A. and Ph.D. from Harvard University; and thereafter studied for two years at the Institute for Islamic Studies at McGill University, Montreal, Canada. From 1957 to 1967 he taught in the Department of Social Relations at Harvard University. Since 1967 he has been Ford Professor of Sociology and Comparative Studies and Chairman of the Center for Japanese and Korean Studies at the University of California at Berkeley. His publications include* Apache Kinship Systems, Tokugawa Religion, Religion and Progress in Modern Asia, *and* Beyond Belief: Essays on Religion in a Post-Traditional World.

■ In the following selection we turn to an example of religion in an agricultural nation-state : the religious system of Japan during the Tokugawa period, from about 1600 to 1868. When considering this period in Japan's cultural evolution, we make more than a shift from one place to another ; we are encountering a qualitatively different way of life. We move here from a horticultural to an agriculturally-based society in precisely the period in which the process of its nation-building and the establishment of a central state system was taking place.

We saw in connection with Babylonian law (Selection 10) that among the important problems facing a new nation's rulers is how to cope with heterogeneity. To establish political control, they must not only formalize the legal system but also legitimate their rule religiously. Although central state systems often sponsor or adopt nationwide religious cults to this end, it is ordinarily difficult for them to displace local religious groups that are associated with (and symbolize) the economic, regional, and ethnic divisions in the nation. Thus, one of the challenges facing a nation during its early stages of development is to mobilize the different religious groups of the society—paralleling the canalization of economic specialties into a single system—so that they feed into and support the nation's political and economic organization.

Tokugawa Japan provides a very good example of this, with Buddhism and Confucianism functioning alongside the official Shinto cult along with

subgroups in each. As Bellah shows in the following chapter from his already classic book, each contributed in its own way to the legitimation of the social and political order. This order included not only centralizing tendencies in the national society as a whole but also, and just as important, the management of the pressures toward local autonomy and separateness that were manifested by local groups being forced to relinquish their sectarian sovereignties.

There is a vast literature on Tokugawa Japan, which is one of the best documented subjects in all pre-modern history. Chapter 2 in Bellah's book (from which this selection is taken) is a concise summary of the social system and should be consulted by the reader who wants a broader background. Another important book is *Education in Tokugawa Japan*, by R. P. Dore (Berkeley and Los Angeles : University of California Press, 1965), and there are several excellent historical surveys of the period, notably *A History of Japan : Vol. 3 : The Tokugawa Epoch 1652-1868*, by James Murdoch (London : Kegan Paul, 1926) and *A History of Japan, 1615-1867*, by George Sansom (Stanford, Calif. : Stanford University Press, 1958). Post-World War II Japanese development has been accompanied by the rise of several new religious movements ; in this connection, see, for example, *The Rush Hour of the Gods : A Study of New Religious Movements in Japan*, by H. Neill McFarland (New York : Macmillan, 1967).

Also relevant at this point in our discussion is "Religion, Politics, and Economic Development in Ceylon: An Interpretation of the Weber Thesis," by Michael M. Ames, in *Symposium on New Approaches to the Study of Religion*, Melford E. Spiro, chairman; June Helm, editor, pp. 61-76 (Seattle: University of Washington Press, 1964); there is an especially good bibliography in Ames' article. One of the best studies of religion in a national context is *The Religion of Java*, by Clifford Geertz (New York: Free Press [paperback edition], 1964); see also Geertz's articles on "Ritual and Social Change: A Javanese Example," (*American Anthropologist*, 59 [1957]: 32-54) and "Religious Belief and Economic Behavior in a Central Javanese Town," (*Economic Development and Cultural Change*, 4 [1956]: 134-58). In *Islam Observed: Religious Development in Morocco and Indonesia* (New Haven and London: Yale University Press, 1968), Geertz compares the fates of Islam in Indonesia and Morocco. A recent study by Melford E. Spiro, *Burmese Supernaturalism* (Englewood Cliffs, N.J.: Prentice-Hall, 1967), is valuable in the present connection, and another closely related and important study is *Religion in Chinese Society*, by C. K. Yang (Berkeley and Los Angeles, 1960). ■

AS THE TITLE to this chapter indicates, there is some validity in speaking of Japanese religion as an entity in spite of the variety of its manifestations. Especially by Tokugawa times so much borrowing had occurred between the various major regions that one can abstract out certain elements which are nearly universal and label these "Japanese religion." In the national and family religions all the great religious traditions were represented and almost inseparably fused. Confucianism and Shintō had borrowed Buddhist metaphysics and psychology; Buddhism and Shintō had borrowed much of Confucian ethics; and Confucianism and Buddhism had been rather thoroughly Japanized. In spite of considerable homogeneity, however, some sects stressed certain of the common tenets more than others, and in each the common tenets were formed into slightly different configurations. Consequently there will be frequent occasions to discuss the different religious strands separately.

Some further remarks concerning the theory of religion which underlies this work must perhaps be made before turning to the descriptive material. The chief social functions of religion as we see them are to supply a context of meaning for the central values of the society and to meet the threats to these values posed by the ultimate frustrations of the human situation. Both of its primary functions require orientation to a superordinate system characterized by the attribute of ultimacy. The superordinate system supplies a metaphysical context for the central values and thus some ultimate basis of meaning for them. It also supplies a source of ultimate power and meaning which can support and fulfill human motivation in the face of the ultimate frustrations. Within certain limits, threats to the social system which cannot be met on the reality level, and thus generate an unreleased reservoir of tension, can be met by the religious mechanisms of ritual, rationalization, expiation, etc. Beyond these limits, however, such threats may undermine the institutionalization of the religious system itself. The old metaphysic may be felt to be inadequate to give meaning to new conditions and the old source of power inadequate to handle new threats. Under these conditions the old conceptions of the superordinate system may be altered and new religious institutions develop which channel the flow of religious motivation in new directions. Changes may also occur in such situations which do not involve the development of new religious institutions. The old religious system may lose some of its power to maintain the value pattern and manage tension without any compensating tendency. This would result in greater *anomie* and higher levels of tension in the society with consequent impairment of the non-religious functions as well. Beyond certain limits such tendencies would lead to the destruction of the society but societies can continue to function even with rather high rates of *anomie* and tension and there is probably a considerable variation in these respects from society to society. Conversely to what we have just discussed, change without the development of new religious institutions in a situation of strain may occur as a strengthening of the old religious system. Religious efforts to maintain the pattern and manage tension may become more intense and systematic, and more motivation may be channeled into some of the non-religious subsystems, rather than less.

This last situation would seem to be that of

Japan in the Tokugawa Period. No really new religious orientation developed, but in response to strains in part due to the growing differentiation and complexity of the society itself, the existing religious system was strengthened and its effects ramified. It is [our] purpose . . . to discuss the old religious system as it existed at the beginning of the Tokugawa Period. . . .

UNDERLYING CONCEPTIONS

There seem to be two basic conceptions of the divine in Japanese religion. The first of these is that of a superordinate entity who dispenses nurturance, care and love. Examples include the Confucian Heaven and Earth, Amida and other Buddhas, the Shintō deities, as well as local tutelary deities and ancestors. This category shades off imperceptibly into political superiors and parents, both of whom are treated as in part, at least, sacred. Religious action toward these entities is characterized by respect, gratitude for blessings received, and attempts to make return for those blessings.

The second basic conception of the divine is more difficult to explain. It might be described as the ground of being or the inner essence of reality. Examples, are the Chinese *tao;* the neo-Confucian *li*, often translated as reason, and *hsin*, heart or mind, when identified with *li;* the Buddhist concept of the Buddha-nature; and the Shintō term *kami* in its most philosophical interpretation. Religious action toward these entities is the attempt on the part of the communicant to attain some form of union or identity with this ground of being or essence of reality. These types of religious action will be discussed in detail in a later section.

The two conceptions of the divine should not be thought of as competing. They are both to be found in almost every sect and they were not felt to be in any way mutually exclusive. Any potential conflict was resolved by a theory of levels of truth, the second conception of the divine being considered perhaps more profound. Only some of the more extreme forms of Zen, however, radically rejected deities of the first type. The Pure Land sects, on the other hand, stressed devotion to Amida, a deity of the first type, in rather exclusive terms, but always left the door open for metaphysical interpretations which could approach the second type of conception of the divine. Between these extremes most of the various sects and movements stressed some combination of these conceptions.

The conception of nature shares both aspects of the attitude toward the divine. Nature is both a benevolent and nurturing force toward whom man should express gratitude, and a manifestation of the ground of being. Man may attain insight into the essence of reality and union with it through the apprehension of some natural form. Nature is not alien to the divine or to man but is united with both.

Man is the humble recipient of endless blessings from divinity, nature, his superiors, and quite helpless without these blessings. At the same time he is both "natural" and "divine." He is a microcosm of which divinity and nature are the macrocosms. He is a "small heaven and earth," he contains within himself the Buddha-nature, or the *tao*, or *li*, or his true heart (*honshin, ryōshin*) is the same as *li*. Clearly from what has been said here human nature is conceived as good. Mencius' solution of the problem of human nature, then, can be considered typical of most Tokugawa religion. It should be pointed out, however, that it is only man's basic or true nature that is good. In actual life this nature may be obscured by the dirt of selfishness and personal desire.

Radical evil tends to be denied in man, nature, or divinity. Evil is explained either as relative, only seeming evil but in a larger context not really so, or as a sort of "friction" attendant on daily living or "weight" due to our having bodily substance. This friction or weight diverts us from our true natural orbit. Freeing ourselves from selfish desires will allow our natural selves to take their appropriate places without hindrance. The Buddhist conception of evil as due to the moral working out of causes in a former existence was also widespread in the Tokugawa Period.

What has been said about the unity of man, nature and divinity should not be interpreted as a static identity. Rather it is a harmony in tension. The gratitude one owes to superordinate benevolent entites is not an easy obligation but may involve the instant sacrifice of one's deepest interests or even of one's life. Union with the ground of being is not attained in a state of coma but very often as the result of some sudden shock in daily living. Something un-expected, some seeming disharmony, is more apt to reveal the Truth than any formal orderly teaching. Japanese art and aesthetic attitudes toward nature are also concerned with the unexpected with moments of tension which reveal the inner life of the object in all its particularity. Symmetry is abhorred. There is harmony, but it is a tense harmony.

All three of the main religious traditions were oriented to a historical past when things were felt to be better than in the present. For the Confucians it was the age of the sages; for the Buddhists the present age, the *mappō*, was a corrupt age during which it was hard to under-stand the Buddha's teachings. The revival Shintoists harked back to the days when the emperors ruled in pristine Japanese simplicity. The Buddhist and Confucian theories of his-torical change were essentially cyclical. Better times are followed by worse in endless succession and the contemporary period was seen as merely a temporary trough. The Shintō belief was not cyclical, however, but one-way. It alone of the major religious traditions had the concept of a creation, even if in the form of a rather primitive myth. To Shintō Japanese history could be seen as the unfolding of the will of the gods, and religious ends might be fulfilled in time and history as the destiny of the Japanese people. Nichiren adapted some such view in his own unique form of Buddhism and in the Tokugawa Period various Shintō movements made use of it.

The above very condensed exposition of the underlying conceptions of the divine, nature, man and time may serve as an introduction for the discussions which follow.

FROM MAGIC TO METAPHYSICS

In this section we must review briefly certain lines of development of Japanese religion which precede the Tokugawa Period. These develop-ments reveal a tendency toward rationalization on both philosophical and ethical levels which went far in freeing the world of primitive magic. Such a development was a precondition for the use of religious motivation in rationalizing the world in nonreligious spheres and so is of the first importance for the present study.

Early Shintō was concerned perhaps more than anything else with fertility. Ceremonies for praying for harvest and thanksgiving for harvest had a prominent place in the ritual calendar. In the villages phallic rites were employed to ensure fertility through a sympathetic magic, and even in the formal state cult the reliance was primarily on offerings and the promise of praises to the deities if good harvests were forth-coming. The *Engishiki*, a document dating from the early 10th century, gives the text of a prayer for harvest given annually on the 4th day of the second month by a member of the priestly Nakatomi family at a large ceremonial gathering in the capital. An excerpt from it will perhaps give some of the flavor of this early Shintō:

> I declare in the presence of the sovran gods of the Harvest. If the sovran gods will bestow in many-bundled ears and in luxuriant ears the late-ripening harvest which they will bestow, the late-ripening harvest which will be produced by the dripping of foam from the arms and by drawing the mud together between the opposing thighs, then I will fulfill their praises by setting-up the first fruits in a thousand ears and many hundred ears, raising high the beer-jars, filling and ranging in rows the bellies of the beer-jars. . . .

We have a number of texts of early ceremonies for the warding off of calamity from fire, storm or pestilence, and for settling spirits in their sanctuaries. Purification held a central place in early Shintō ritual. Offences, deliberate as well as inadvertent, were felt to bring contamination or pollution and required various acts of purification such as lustration, fasting, absten-tion. Leprosy, tumors and "calamity from creeping things" were given in the same list as wounding and killing, incest, and bestiality as causes of pollution requiring purification.

Fertility, purification, and similar forms of ritual continued down to recent times in more or less the same "primitive" forms as have been sketched above, but beginning at least as early as the 13th century there developed, especially around the cult center at Ise, a marked trend to philosophical and ethical rationalization. There is no doubt that this occurred under the stimulus of Buddhist influence, but it is a genuine re-working of the Shintō tradition and not merely a Buddhist overlay.

One of the earliest documents which reveals this trend is the *Shintō Gobusho* compiled by the Gekū priests of Ise probably in the 13th century, some of its materials undoubtedly being of even earlier date. With respect to offerings it says, "The gods desire not material gifts, but offerings of uprightness and sincerity," and with respect to purity, "To do good is to be pure; to commit evil is to be impure. The deities dislike evil deeds, because they are impure." The monk Musō-Kokushi (1271-1340) recounts a visit to the Ise shrine not long after the period of the presumed compilation of the *Shintō Gobusho*. His account is as follows:

At the Ise Daijingū offerings are not allowed, neither is the reading of any Buddhist sutra or incantation. When I went to Ise I stopped for a while near the Gekū and questioned a Shintō ritualist styled Negi whom I met there on this point and he said, "When anyone comes here to worship there is both an outer and an inner purity. The former consists in eating clean food and observing the ritual purification and keeping oneself from defilement, but the latter means ridding the mind of all ambitious desire." The usual thing is to make offerings at shrines and have *Kagura* performances held in order to petition the deities for some benefits that are desired, which is very far from inward purity and so is declined here.

Here we can see how the old ideas of offerings and purification are given ethical and symbolic significance. The implication of this idea of inner purity for the relation of man to the divine is brought out in the following quote from a 14th century visitor to the Ise shrine:

And particularly is it the deep-rooted custom of this shrine that we should bring no Buddhist rosary or offering or any special petition in our hearts and this is called "Inner Purity." Washing in sea water and keeping the body free from all defilements is called "Outer Purity." And when both these purities are attained there is then no barrier between our mind and that of the deity. And if we feel to become thus one with the divine, what more do we need to pray for? When I heard that this was the true way of worshipping at the shrine, I could not refrain from shedding tears of gratitude.

The earlier notion of deity, one that continues to be held down to modern times, is in the above passage tending to be replaced by the second concept of the divine which was discussed above in the section on underlying conceptions. This is clearly brought out in a statement by the 14th century Shintō theologian Imbe-no-Masami-chi in his *Shindai Kuketsu* (1367):

Kami [the native Japanese word for deity] is from *kagami* [mirror]. This is abbreviated and read *Kami*. The Divine Mind, like a clear mirror, reflects all things in nature. It operates with impartial justice and tolerates not a single spot of uncleanness. That which in Heaven is *Kami*, in nature is Spirit and in man is Sincerity. If the spirit of nature and the heart of man are pure and clear, then they are *Kami*.

To round out the discussion we may turn to a very popular Shintō work of the Tokugawa Period, the *Warongo* or *Japanese Analects*. In the following quote we can detect both of the basic conceptions of deity and the final assertion of the pre-eminence of inner over outer purity:

That the God dislikes what is unclean, is equivalent to saying that a person who is impure in heart displeases God.

He that is honest and upright in heart is not unclean, even though he be not ceremoniously so in body.

To God, inward purity is all important; mere external cleanliness avails not. This is because God is the Essential Uprightness and Honesty, and therefore, it is His Heavenly Ordinance that we should lead an honest and happy life in harmony with the Divine Will.

If a man is pure in heart, rest assured that he will ever feel the Divine Presence with him, and possess the immediate sense of the Divine within him.

Buddhism in Japan underwent a course of development very similar to that sketched above for Shintō. Though there were undoubtedly from the first a certain number of sincere Buddhist monks who understood something of the more philosophical forms of their religion, it would be hard to deny that the importance of Buddhism in the early centuries of its development in Japan was largely magical. Sutras were read often not for their intrinsic content but for the magical results such reading was thought to bring. For example, in the 7th century we have records of sutras read to bring rain, the *Maha-megha-sutra* being thought especially suitable for this purpose. Other sutras were read to stop rain when floods were feared. Ritual vegetarian feasts were given for large numbers of monks to gain various ends such as restoring the health of lengthening the life of some noble patron or for the benefit of some departed soul. Large convocations were held to read certain sutras in various special ways, that is, facing certain directions or speaking with a certain degree of loudness or softness, etc., to obtain various magical results. The *Ninnōkyō* or *Sutra of the Benevolent Kings* was often read in such convocations. Its principal aim was to ensure peace and prosperity to the empire, but it was also read to bring rain, to stop pestilences of smallpox, leprosy or other epidemics and to avert the evil consequences of bad omens such as eclipses, comets, etc. Virtuous acts, such as the granting of a general amnesty, or issuing a prohibition against the killing of animals, or having some pure person retire from the world, were also employed to obtain results like the ending of a drouth or the recovery of a sick emperor.

At the personal level, Buddhism in these early years was largely a matter of spells and charms and devotions to especially favored Bodhisattvas. Certainly a considerable amount of this sort of thing continued in general practice right down to modern times, but nevertheless the 12th and 13th centuries marked a great turning point in Japanese Buddhism during which a strong trend to free the religion from magic took hold. This is most markedly shown in the three great sects or congeries of sects which arose in those centuries, the Zen, Nichiren and Jōdo or Pure Land sects.

Eisai (1141-1215), founder of the Rinzai school of Zen in Japan, taught that knowledge of the Buddha-mind could only be gained intuitively through meditation (*dhyana*), and not by worshipping Buddhas, reciting sutras or other such religious practices. He held that no physical media could express or symbolize the Buddha-mind. It could only be found within one's own mind through meditation. "Find Buddha in your own heart, whose essential nature is the Buddha himself," he said.

Zen did not consider the older religious practices as "abominations" but merely as inefficacious, and so did not lead a drive to eliminate them. Among its own adherents, however, and these numbered among the more important intellectual and military figures of the upper classes, it did serve as a definite force in breaking the hold of the old magical religious attitudes.

Nichiren (1222-1282), founder of the sect which bears his name, taught worship to only one Buddha, the Buddha of the *Lotus Sutra*. Worship of any other Buddha he felt was not merely inefficacious but wicked and disloyal to the true Buddha. He urged the repression of all other sects on these grounds. His message was primarily ethical and he did not stress performing rituals or engaging in mystical contemplation as proper means for worshipping the Buddha. Rather he taught that faith should be reposed in

the Buddha, to be signified by the repetition of a brief phrase in praise of the *Lotus Sutra*, sacred above all other sutras and in some way identical with the Buddha himself. Faith ought to be actualized in life through ethical actions, chief of which are, he held, reverence for sovereign, teacher, and parent.

The Pure Land sects went in some ways the farthest of any of the new currents in Buddhism in the direction of freeing religion from magic, superstition, and ritual. The Jōdo Shinshū, founded by Shinran Shōnin (1173-1262), went farther than any other of the Pure Land sects in this direction and, since it is much the largest not only of the Pure Land sects but of all the sects of Japanese Buddhism, the following remarks will be confined to it.

The core of the Shinsū belief was that only faith in Amida could bring salvation. Shinran wrote:

Two things are essential to Faith. The first is to be convinced of our own sinfulness; from the bondage of evil deeds we possess no means of emancipating ourselves. The second is, therefore, to throw our helpless souls wholly upon the Divine Power of Amida Nyorai in the firm belief that His Forty-eight Vows were for the express purpose of saving all beings who should put their trust in Him without the least doubt or fear. Such souls will be born surely into His Pure Land.

Since faith in Amida alone is efficacious it follows that all ceremonies, charms, worship of other Buddhas, etc., is in vain. Shinran said:

An evidence of the increasing degeneracy of the world is visible in the religious life of both priests and laymen of the present time. They are Buddhists in outward appearance, but in reality followers of a false religion.

How sorrowful it is that they look for "lucky days," worship other gods on earth and in heaven, indulge in fortune-telling and practise "charms."

The stress on "faith alone" made many of the older Buddhist practices seem to be outmoded supersititions. The prohibition on clerical marriage was dropped, as was the prohibition on eating meat. Consequently occupations which were formerly held in disrepute were now exonerated. Shinran said:

There is no difference among those who are living upon fishing with a line or net from ocean or river, those who are dragging out an existence with hunting game or fowling on field and mountain, and those who are getting along in trade or tilling the soil. Man may do anything (whatever), if moved by his karma.

Rennyo Shōnin (1415-1499), often called the second founder of the Shinshū because of his great influence on its development, extended the work of Shinran. He opposed the practice of austerities and meditation as merely giving the mind an opportunity for evil thoughts. He insisted on the practice of the Confucian virtues in daily life and on obedience to state authorities, while at the same time one's inner life was to be wholly given up to Amida. Rennyo opposed any worship of Shintō deities and it is due to him that there are no *kamidana* (household Shintō shrines found in most Japanese homes) in Shinshū homes to this day.

Confucianism needs only a mention at this point. It had gone through a process of rationalization comparable to that discussed above for Shintō and Buddhism many centuries earlier in China. Arthur Waley sees this as a transition from an "auguristic-sacrificial" stage to a "moralistic" stage, a transition which began about 400 B.C. or perhaps earlier and was essentially completed by the time of Hsün Tzu (c. 298-c. 238 B.C.). Thus Confucianism in Japan was from the first a rationalizing influence in the sphere of ethics. Later when the neo-Confucian philosophy of Chu Hsi (1130-1200) and others began to be imported (beginning in the 13th century) largely by Zen priests, Confucianism had some rationalizing influence in philosophy and psychology as well. This reached its greatest extent during the Tokugawa Period when philosophical Confucianism had its most prosperous days. Needless to say the importations of popular Taoism and other folk belief from China had an effect in the opposite direction.

The importance of the rationalizing processes we have been describing is that they create the possibility of religious action based on a rather small number of premises and applied systematically in a wide number of contexts. The earlier magical stage tended to have few ethical cr metaphysical generalizations with relation to which behavior could be ordered but rather contained a vast number of discrete and often contradictory prescriptions and prohibitions almost all of which had compulsive moral legitimacy in their own right rather than with reference to some more general obligation. It is our next task to examine this relatively highly rationalized religious action in some detail. Having done that we will be in a position to determine the relation between this religious action and action in other spheres.

MAIN TYPES OF RELIGIOUS ACTION

As we have indicated above, traditionalistic religious action of a generally magical type has remained important throughout Japanese history. No religious movement has been able to break through it as decisively as Protestantism has done in some Western countries, though Jōdo Shinshū went fairly far in this direction. Though never utterly broken, this type of religious action was often overridden by religious action of a more rationalized type. For our purposes the magical variety needs no further discussion, though its prevalence should not be forgotten in the following discussions. Attention will be focused here on the type of religious action with respect to the two main categories of the divine as previously analyzed.

Action with respect to deity as a benevolent superordinate gets us at once into the theory of *on*. Deity in some form dispenses blessings (*on*) and it is the obligation of the recipient to make return for these blessings (*hōon*). Religious action, then, is the various forms this *hōon* may take.

The term *hōon* is probably of Buddhist origin. It does not appear, apparently, in Chinese literature earlier than the Six Dynasties Period, when Buddhism had already become popular. The term *on* does appear in the *Mencius* and in the *Li Chi* several times, and a term somewhat similar to *hōon*—*hōtoku*—appears in the *Analects* and the *Li Chi*, etc. But *hōon* seems to be of Buddhist origin and reflects an important aspect of early Buddhist ethics, the stress on indebtedness or return for kindness. The *Anguttara Nikaya*, an early Buddhist work, quotes the Buddha as saying, "The wicked person is one who is not grateful and who does not bear in mind any good rendered to him." Another quote from the *Anguttara* is interesting because it shows the early connection of the theory of *on* with filial piety and because it maintains that *on* can never be fully requited:

We may carry our mothers on one shoulder, and our fathers on the other, and attend on them even for a hundred years, doing them bodily services in every possible way, and establishing them in the position of universal sovereignty: still the favour we have received from our parents will be far from requited.

In the *Mahayana-mulajata-hridayabhumi-dhyana-sutra* (Nanjo 955) the Buddha is described as having preached on four sorts of debt which the Buddhists owe: to parents, fellow-beings, sovereign, and the three holy treasures of Buddhism (the law, the church, and the Buddha).

The theory of *on* and *hōon* is found prominently in Japanese Buddhism, especially in the great "reform" sects of the 12th and 13th centuries. To start with Zen, the 13th century founder of the Sōtō branch of that sect wrote in a manual for his students:

That we can now see Wisdom and hear the law, is a mercy that comes to us from laying hold of the actions of former founders of religion. If the founders of our religion had not handed it down, how would it have reached to our day? We must be thankful for the kindness that gives us one maxim or one law. Much more therefore must we return thanks for the great mercy of the unsurpassed Great Law. The sick sparrow never forgets a kindness: the rings of the three Great Ministers are no surer token. The distressed tortoise forgets not a kindness: the seal of Yofu is no surer token. Beasts even show their gratitude. How shall men not feel it?

Nichiren in his work "Recompense of Indebtedness" held that "the most significant aspect of ethics, namely, the signfication of life, consists in the recompense of indebtedness or grace, and he firmly believed that the true orders of human society will be born from it." In his great work *Kaimokushō* Nichiren quotes with great approval the following passage from the *Saddharmapundarika-sutra*:

We are greatly indebted to Sakyamuni. He loved us and taught us and bestowed on us grace. We cannot repay his great benefits to us even if we endeavoured to do so for countless aeons. Even if we offer to him with hand and foot and worship him with bowed heads, we cannot repay his favors toward us. Even if we take his feet on our upturned palms and carry him on our shoulders through aeons countless as the sands of the Ganges, or honor him with all our hearts, or offer ambrosia or innumerable robes or richly worked cloth of gold, or costly bedding, or offer precious medicines or build for him great monasteries with wood of sandal and adorned with precious jewels, or if we spread the floors of the monasteries with rich carpets, yet shall our debt remain unpaid.

This sentiment is echoed in a common exhortation of the Jōdo Shin sect, "One returns thanks to the source of the Buddha's benevolence by pulverizing one's body and breaking one's bones for countless kalpas." The Pure Land sects, indeed, are among the most fervent in insisting that men owe everything to a single deity, Amida, and that ". . . our whole life must be one long expression of gratitude: we must regard life as a service which Amida demands of us."

Many Confucians stress the importance of *hōon* often in connection with the duty of filial piety but also often with a more general metaphysical underpinning. For example, Kaibara Ekiken (1630-1714) says,

Man is greater than all other beings, and owes the universe an extremely great debt of gratitude; for this reason, what men should do is, needless to say, to serve their parents with all their power and at the same time to revere the universe all their life, in order that they may repay their great debt.

And in a similar vein Nakae Tōju (1600-1648) wrote,

All men acknowledge the duty of gratitude, and filial obedience is merely showing the edge of gratitude. Even crows feed their parents, and lambs show their respect by stooping as they eat. It is the beginning of all the virtues, and when we forget it we cloud the soul with lust, dim the illustrious virtue, and are astray in the night.

It would be possible to continue to marshal evidence from various periods and various religious sects and movements as to the great importance of *on* and *hōon* in Japanese religious thinking, but in order to avoid needless repetition we may close this discussion with a rather long quote from Ninomiya Sontoku (1787-1856), founder of the Hōtoku movement which will be discussed later, as this quote admirably sums up the very broad application of this theory.

My teaching is that we should reward grace and virtue. If asked for an explanation I would say this means that we make return to heaven, man and earth for gracious benefits we have received from them. Heaven's blessing is given in the light of the sun and moon. The sun rises and sets. The four seasons come and go. In every living creature there is both development and decay. In these and other ways heaven's blessing is manifested toward us. Earth manifests her favor in the growth of grasses, trees, and grain; in the fact that birds, animals and fish live. Man's grace is manifested in the fact that sages teach the truth; emperors govern their subjects; high officials protect the country and people;

farmers distribute commodities. We all live by the grace of heaven, earth and man, and so we must make it our first principle of conduct to make return to them for their gracious contributions to our welfare. From the Emperor on down to the humblest peasant, this spirit must prevail.

Religious action conceived as a return for blessings from a benevolent superordinate, then, is based on a view of man as weak and helpless by himself. Only with the help of benevolent beings can he live, and the blessings he receives are so much greater than his ability to return them that actually he can only return an infinitesimal amount. By devoting himself utterly to returning these blessings he assures to himself the continuation of them, and in some sense he is thereby saved from his weakness. But he can never repay; he always stands in debt. This theory, it would seem, has some of the dynamic potentialities of the idea of original sin. It presents a fundamental "flaw" in human nature which cannot be overcome by man alone but only by some intervention from above. It is only in this sense that they are similar; in other respects they are quite different. It is interesting to note that the theory of *on* holds for superordinates within the social system, such as parents or political superiors, in exactly the same terms as it holds for entities above the social system, gods or Buddhas, etc. The significance of this will be commented on at a later point.

The second major type of religious action is that which seeks to attain unity with the divine conceived as the "Great Ultimate," or the *Tao*, or whatever the term may be. We can distinguish within this second major type two main divisions. The first attempts to attain this unity through private religious exercises or experiences, through withdrawal from the world. Elaborate techniques of breath control or meditation may be devised to attain this end or it may be considered that only giving oneself up to a life of "pure experience" and waiting for enlightenment to burst forth at some unexpected moment can attain it. Stated theoretically, this approach seems to be an attempt to destroy the self as an ontological entity, to destroy the dichotomy between subject and object. The second main division attempts to attain unity with the divine through the accumulation of ethical acts or "works of love," through partici-

pation in the world rather than withdrawal from it. The ethical acts may be relatively specific "acts of charity" or they may merely be those acts which make up a "good life." Stated theoretically this approach seems to be an attempt to attain unity through the destruction of the self as an ethical entity, by destroying the division between self and other, mine and thine, in a word by destroying selfishness.

Fung Yu-lan makes this distinction with respect to early Chinese philosophy. He gives the Taoism of Chuang Tzu as an example of the first type and the Confucianism of Mencius as an example of the second. Sir Charles Eliot seems to be making the same distinction between the two main branches of the Zen sect in the following quote. He says the Sōtō sect

". . . lays greater stress on the need of good conduct and morality in spiritual life, whereas the Rinzai, without being in the least open to the charge of immorality, emphasizes the importance of a sudden spiritual enlightenment without insisting so strongly that a good life is the best training for such an enlightenment and a sure result of it."

Both of the divisions of the second type of religious action are to be found in Japan. The first, unity through cognitive experience, we are probably safe in saying, had only a limited influence among the upper classes, whereas the second, unity through moral action, has had a fairly broad and general influence and is, in fact, closely linked with the first type of religious action, that based on the theory of *on*.

Mencius is undoubtedly the major source of the idea that mystical unity can be attained through moral action or acts of love. It would be difficult to overemphasize the influence of Mencius on the thought of the Far East, at least since the Sung Period. He was, of course, extremely familiar to all educated Japanese of the Tokugawa Period, so that he must be considered not only as the beginning of a long line of influences but as a continuing contemporary influence throughout the Tokugawa Period, and indeed even up to the present.

Following Fung's tentative interpretation that Mencius' famous "moving force" (*huo jan chih ch'i*) is the spiritual quality of those persons who have attained the state of mystical unity, let us note what Mencius has to say about this force:

Such is the force (*ch'i*): it is most great and most strong. Being nourished by uprightness (*chih*), and sustaining no injury, it fills up all between heaven and earth.

And on how to develop it, he says:

Such is the force: it is the correlate of righteousness (*i*) and morality (*tao*). Without it, [man] is in a state of starvation. It is produced by the accumulation of righteous deeds, and not to be obtained by incidental acts of righteousness.

The whole Confucian practice of moral self-cultivation, then, is to be seen as religious action of this second subtype, the attempt to attain unity with the universe through moral action. Already with Mencius we get the idea that the mind (*hsin*) within man is in its true form identical with essential nature, and needs but to be cultivated in order for this identity to be fully attained:

He who has exercised his mind to the utmost, knows his nature (*hsing*). Knowing his nature, he knows heaven. To keep one's mind preserved and nourish one's nature is the way to serve Heaven. To be without doubleness of mind whether one is to have untimely death or long life; and having cultivated one's personal character, to wait with this for whatever there may be: this is to stand in accord with Fate (*ming*).

It was the neo-Confucians of the Sung Period that developed this idea, incorporated aspects of Buddhism and Taoism in it, and made it one of the most important religious influences in the Far East ever since. Fung Yu-lan summarizes the views of one of the greatest of the neo-Confucians, Che'en Hao (1032-85), as follows:

According to Ch'eng Hao, man's original state is that of union with the universe which, however, becomes lost through the assertion of the individual ego. Hence the aim of spiritual cultivation is to destroy the barriers created by the ego, and return to the state of universal oneness.

Spiritual cultivation consists precisely in the cultivation of the classic Confucian virtues. Oneness with the universe can be achieved by the following means, says Ch'eng Hao:

The student must first comprehend love (or humanity, *jen*). The man of love is undifferentiably one with other things. Righteousness (*yi*), propriety (*li*), wisdom (*chih*), and good faith (*hsin*): all these are love. Get to comprehend this truth and cultivate it with sincerity (*ch'eng*) and earnestness (*ching*); that is all.

Japanese Confucians of the Chu Hsi and the Wang Yang Ming (1472-1529) schools both held views of spiritual self-cultivation which were variations on what has already been said. The differences between them are considerable and the controversies not uninteresting, but for our purposes these can safely be ignored. Here what we wish to stress is that which they had in common, the notion of a process of moral self-cultivation with the religious aim of some sort of identification with the universe.

This basic type of religious action was not confined to the Confucians. Rather it permeated a great deal of Japanese religious thinking. Many of the quotes above, especially of the Shintō rationalizers, show a similar notion. The following is from a popular Shintō work of the 17th century:

The heart of man is the abode of God (*kami*); think not that God is something distant. He that is honest, is himself a God (*kami*), and if merciful, he is himself a Buddha (*hotoke*). Know that man in his essential nature is one and the same with God and Buddha.

An even more vulgarized version of the same basic idea is to be found in the *kakun* or family instructions of a Tokugawa *samurai*, Ise Teijo (1714-1784):

If the heart is honest and in the right way, even though you pay them no worship the gods will vouchsafe their protection. Hence the saying that a god makes its abode in an honest man's head. If a man's heart be not honest, and he loses his grip of the five moral constants and the rules of the five social relationships, then, even though he pays them worship, the gods will not grant him their protection. On the contrary, retribution will overtake him.

It is selfishness which obscures the true self and keeps us from attaining the state of oneness. Consequently moral self-cultivation is a constant effort to combat selfish desires. Only the sage is finally successful in this effort. For others, the eradication of selfish desire is approached but not absolutely attained. The obligation to make the effort, however, like the obligation to return *on*, is unrelenting, and not dependent on the feasibility of the task. Here is another dynamic factor in Japanese religious action.

It is interesting, I think, to view the two main types of religious action to which we have given considerable attention not merely as two parallel types but as reciprocals, as two sides of the same coin. The first type, that concerned with the return of *on*, focusses primarily on the relation of the individual to objects outside himself. The second, that concerned with self-cultivation, focusses more on the integration of the individual's personality within itself. For both, selfishness is the great sin. It disrupts the proper repayment of obligations without, and it disrupts the true harmony of one's nature within. Selfless devotion, on the other hand, establishes a "perfect" relation with the benevolent superordinate and at the same time allows the individual to identify with him, lose himself in the divine. Through this identification he finds his own inner nature fulfilled, because his own inner nature in its essence is identical with the divine.

We must remember that both the main types of religious action call for vigorous activity in this world. If the Chinese neo-Confucians at times leaned in the direction of contemplation and quietism and a rather static sort of harmony, this is not true of the Japanese—Confucian or otherwise. Japanese Confucians were vigorous in praising activism and attacking quietism in all its forms. The next stage in the argument, then, is to discuss exactly what sort of activity in the world was implied in the Japanese theories of religious action.

RELIGION AND THE WORLD

It might be well to begin this section with a few concrete examples of *hōon*. What follows is a continuation of the remarks of the Japanese founder of the Sōtō branch of the Zen sect which were quoted above on page 244:

In showing this gratitude, men need not go to extraneous or superabundant laws; the performance of daily duty is the path of justifying (proving) one's gratitude. That which is called reason is the not neglecting of one's daily life, not wasting it in selfishness.

As an amplification of this we may quote a Shinshū tract:

The will of the Buddha is manifest everywhere and in everything, it is present in the person of our teacher, parents, brother, wife, children, friends and also in the state or community to which we may belong; the Buddha is protecting, nourishing, consoling, and instructing us in every possible way. What we owe to the Buddha is not only when we

are carried into his Pure Land, but even when we are living our daily life on earth, for which latter fact we must also be deeply grateful. Let us not forget how much we are owing to our present surroundings, and to regard them with reverence and love. We must endeavor as much as we can to execute our duties faithfully, to work for the growth of Buddhism, for the good of family, state, and society, and thus to requite a thousandth part of what we owe to Amida. To work thus for the world with a sense of gratitude is the true life of the Buddhist.

The method of attaining "true knowledge," the aim of the second type of religious action, turns out to be not far from what is enjoined above. Muro Kyūsō (1658-1734), one of the more famous Tokugawa Confucians, says,

Read, learn the "laws" and then search them out in conduct and affairs; this is the true knowledge, the knowledge that is the beginning of right conduct. The "Way" of the Sages is not apart from the things of every day. Loyalty, obedience, friendship, all the relations are in this "learning" and not a movement, not even our resting, is without its duty.

The above quotes may serve to give an indication of a view which had become quite common in the Tokugawa Period. Religious action, whether it be *hōon* or the quest for personal enlightenment, took primarily the form of fulfilling one's obligations in the world. Ritual prayer or meditation all took second place to the primary ethical obligations. What concretely tended to be most stressed was obligation to political superiors and obligation to family. In the above quotes such obligation might be considered as the temporal fulfillment of more ultimate obligations. A further example of this would be Nichiren's injunction to a *samurai* disciple: "Consider your daily works in your Lord's service as being the practice of the *Hokkekyō* (*Lotus Sutra*)." But there was also a tendency to make these moral obligations ends in themselves, that is to endow them with ultimacy and make them "religious" in their own right. Such a tendency is strikingly illustrated in a quotation from the *Warongo*:

All ye, my people, high and low, rich and poor! Before you pray to Heaven and Earth as well as to the myriad other deities, it is essential that you should first show filial piety by being obedient to your parents, for in them you can find all the gods of "Within" and "Without." It is useless to pray to the gods who are "Without," if you do not serve your parents Within (at home) with filial piety.

We may cite one interesting and rather extreme example of the tendency to fuse what we would separate into the categories of religious and ethical. This is Nakai Tōju's cosmic interpretation of *kō* (filial piety):

Before the heavens and the earth were conceived *kō* was the divine way of heaven. The Heavens, earth and man, yea, all creation were conceived by *kō*. Spring and summer, autumn and winter, thunder and rain and dew had not been except for *kō*. Benevolence, righteousness, propriety and understanding are the principles of *kō*.

Kō dwells in the universe as the spirit dwells in man. It has neither beginning nor end: without it is not time or any being; there is nothing in all the universe unendowed with *kō*. As man is the head of the universe, its image in miniature, *kō* endows his body and soul, and obedience to the way is the very pivot of existence.

The true understanding of *kō* leads to a perception of man's identity with the universe:

If we seek for the origin of things we find that, as our bodies are divided from our parents but still are one with them, so are their bodies divided from the spirit of heaven and earth, and the spirit of heaven and earth is the offspring of the spirit of the universe; thus my body is one with the universe and the gods. Clearly perceiving this truth and acting in accordance with it is obedience to the way.

As for the destruction of self, *kō* is the best means:

Let us take counsel from our original nature, for it is still pure though we be ignorant and wicked. It will teach us that unfilial conduct is the pain of hell and the source of all evil. All we have, body and soul, are derived from our parents. If we injure ourselves we harm what is not our own but theirs.

All the errors of mankind arise from "self" as we think "this is my body," "this is mine," but *kō* slays self.

The above material is interesting because it presents a rather complete "theology" for a "religion of filial piety." Moreover this theology is derived entirely from elements of the general religious system which we have been discussing above. It is, however, a religion with no necessary connection with sect, shrine, or temple. It is indeed a family religion, and it is to the family that we must look for one of the most vigorous foci of religious life in Tokugawa Japan.

The "family religion" of Nakae Tōju cannot, of course, be considered as typical. It represents an extreme of philosophical sophistication and explicitness. Nevertheless it is an expression of the underlying spirit of that religion, only more refined and abstract than most of his contemporaries would have understood. This family religion which was virtually universal in Tokugawa Japan is what is generally called ancestor worship. Every family had a household shrine, usually two, one Shintō and the other Buddhist, in the latter of which tablets or other memorials of the ancestors of the family were kept, as well as statues or symbols of deities. A brief ritual was performed before the shrine each morning and evening, a lamp was lighted and some small offering of food was given. This ancestral cult was a constant reminder of the sacredness of the lineage and of the obligation of all family members to it. Motoori Norinaga (1730-1801) wrote:

Forget not the shielding love shown for ages by your ancestors. My parents for generations are my family Gods, they are the Gods of my house.

From ancestors to parents is but a step, and the step was easily taken. Motoori also wrote:

Father and mother are our family Gods, they are our Gods, child of man take greatest care and worship them.

As we have seen above a "theology" of filial piety showing it as a means of attaining union with the universe, so similarly a theory of filial piety based on the concept of *on* was very widespread. It was often said that one's obligation to one's parents was "higher than heaven and deeper than the sea." Such an obligation could never be repaid. Hirata Atsutane (1776-1843) said:

Should a child support his parents there is no reason for him to talk about his affection. Through whom was it that he was given birth and grew up and who made it possible for him to keep his parent? Was it not through the parent? If this is well considered then no returns of love can repay the parent for rearing the child. The parent never thought of any return in the way of support when rearing the child, out of a truly loving heart he gave his body to nourish the child and his love is ten times more strong than that which expects a return of love or keep.

The family was not only the locus of the ancestral cult. It was the most frequent place of worship for the deities as well. We have noted that most homes had Shintō and Buddhist

shrines. Various Shintō and Buddhist deities
would be worshipped along with the ancestors.
Almost every home had a piece of the shrine of
the Sun Goddess at Ise and thus participated to
some small extent in the worship of the divine
ancestress of the emperor. Visits to shrine or
temple were infrequent and when they were made
it was usually the family head who went as a
representative of the whole, except on festival
occasions when the whole family went. Popular
preaching was widespread and the reading of
sermons and tracts extensive in the Tokugawa
Period. Still we must assume that a considerable
amount of the religious indoctrination took
place within the family.

Just as we can speak of a "religion of filial
piety" so also we can speak of a "religion of
loyalty." Actually this term has been used to
denote *Bushidō*, the status ethic of the *samurai*
class, on which we shall have more to say in the
next chapter. That loyalty had a religious compulsion that could override other religious
commitments is indicated by the following
incident:

When the priests rebelled against Ieyasu at
Mikawa many hesitated to fight against the holy
brotherhood, but Nagayoshi Doi, taking up his
spear, rushed into the enemy's line crying aloud,
"The benefaction of our lord is apparent and at hand,
while the punishment of Buddha is in the dark and
far away. If we were to be burnt in the lurid flames
of hell, how could we help saving our lord from the
hands of the rebels? If we fail to serve our lord in
this emergency, we break the duty of man and
become brutes.—If ye understand me, ye rebels,
surrender and sue for our lord's pardon."

Loyalty was one of the prime tenets of the
family religion. Filial piety did not compete with
loyalty, it reinforced it. Nakae Tōjo, when
questioned as to whether the obligation to
preserve one's body as a gift of one's parents
would prohibit one from going into battle,
replied that the obligation to preserve one's
virtue was higher than to preserve one's body,
and that if need be one should willingly die for
one's lord. This is true filial piety. We may see in
the following quote from Nichiren that filial
piety in the last analysis for the Japanese meant
loyalty:

...when a father opposes the sovereign, dutiful
children desert their parents and follow the sovereign. This is filial piety at its highest.

CONCLUSION

Especially in the last section the close relation
between Japanese religion and the Japanese
value system as outlined in Chapter II has
become apparent. We have seen how the two
types of religious action, one derived primarily
from Buddhism and the other primarily from
Confucianism have come to reinforce the central
values of achievement and particularism. They
establish the particularistic relations to superiors
as sacred and insist on a high level of performance of obligations to them as necessary for
religious justification or salvation. They provide
a metaphysical basis, a view of the nature of
man and deity, which makes these central values
meaningful in some ultimate sense. They
promise some ultimate salvation or enlightenment, the victory of meaning over ultimate
frustration if the values are adhered to, and
misery in the abyss of selfishness if they are not.
It is quite possible that it was on the level of
religious action that these values first received
their clearest and simplest formulation. This
involves a period before that with which we are
dealing. All we can assert here is that in the
Tokugawa Period religious action reinforced the
central values.

In the view of deity which sees it as a benevolent superordinate we may say that the values
of performance and particularism are seen as
defining the religious object. The deity performs
benevolent acts with respect to those who stand
in a particularistic relation to him. This involves
the reciprocal obligations of loyalty and the
return of gratitude. The view of the divine as
"the ground of being" defines the religious
object by the values of particularism and
quality. The religious object does not "act." In
fact it is not really an object because it is beyond
subject and object, it is an identity of self and
other which can be attained by the religious
actor. Performance norms are built into this
process of attainment, but are perhaps so greatly
stressed due in part to the great influence of the
concept of deity of the first type. At any rate the
importance of this second concept of the divine
may indicate that integrative values are very
important in the Japanese value system and that
the need for some form of personal resolution
beyond any demand for performance may be a

compelling result of the strains inherent in the particularistic-performance pattern.

There can be little question that a religion of the type described in this chapter would have the effect of reinforcing a strong motivational commitment to the institutional values of Japanese society. This is another way of saying that it reinforced the values of performance and particularism. What we have seen of the relation of religion to loyalty and filial piety is a concrete example of this. Put in the most formal terms we may say that religion reinforced the input of pattern conformity from the motivational system into the institutional system.

In Chapter II we saw that the various segments of society were subjected to somewhat diverse forms of strain. The problems of the *samurai*, merchants, and famers were all somewhat different. It is therefore not surprising that the reactions to strain of these groups which took on a religious aspect were also different.

Broadly stated, each main class had a status ethic, a form of the central value system especially adapted to its situation. The religious and ethical movements of the Tokugawa Period both codified and formalized these status ethics, and introduced new and dynamic elements into them. Of course certain of the more important new trends cut across class lines. As we have indicated before, the main direction of these new movements was not to introduce new values or weaken the old but to propagate stronger and more intense forms of the old values. Two main areas affected by this intensification of the old values were the political and the economic. The next two chapters will, therefore, be devoted to an analysis of the relation between religion and the political and economic systems in Tokugawa Japan. In carrying out this analysis the main lines of the different status ethics will be sketched in and most of the major new ethical and religious movements will be summarized.

17. FIESTAS IN AN INDIAN COMMUNITY IN PERU

WILLIAM P. MANGIN

Reprinted from Symposium: Patterns of Land Utilization and Other Papers, *edited by Viola E. Garfield. Proceedings of the 1961 Annual Spring Meeting of the American Ethnological Society, pp. 84-92. Copyright 1961, University of Washington Press. William P. Mangin is Professor of Anthropology at Syracuse University; he received his B.A. there in 1948 and his Ph.D. from Yale University in 1954. He began his field work in the Peruvian Andes in 1951 and has returned there many times for research. In 1952-1953, he was field director of the Cornell-Vicos Project in Peru; in 1957-1959, he studied rural migrants to Lima, Peru, and was Visiting Professor at the University of San Marcos, Lima; in 1962-1964, he was Deputy Director of the Peace Corps in Peru. He has conducted a school for high-school dropouts and has been an unsuccessful candidate for political office on three separate occasions. He is currently completing a study of innovations in primary school education in Peru, Venezuela, and Cuba.*

■ Having looked from above at an example of a national religious system, let us lower our eyes and examine agriculturist religion as practiced at the peasant level. Peasants are part of a complex society, and the members of local communities occupy a distinct place in the wider system of which they are acutely aware. Thus, their milieu is made up of complex interpenetrations of local conditions and the surrounding social system. As we will see when we consider peasant values in Selection 22, these values are in part adaptations to local imperatives and in part to the wider political system in which they live. Thus peasant status is political as well as economic, and like all status systems, this one must be dealt with in religious as well as other terms. Specifically religion in peasant societies is both a bridge to the wider national society and a fence holding it at bay.

There is often a wide gap between the institutional organization and ideological tenets of the "high tradition" of a religion (like Buddhism) and its actual practice—the "little tradition"—in the villages. Some observers have maintained that the distinction between "great" and "little" traditions is spurious, but I believe it is useful. The high tradition is usually associated with the dogmatic scripture of a religion or the practices of those who live in and around the major ceremonial centers; these people are generally associated with the ruling classes. The peasants and other local producers, on the other hand, occupy different positions in the national order and as a consequence of this have different interests. Hence it is not surprising that we almost always find that religious practice in the local community and the hinterland differs greatly from that of the ceremonial center, even though both subscribe to the same denomination.

Almost all peasants of Central and South America today refer to themselves as Roman Catholics; this is part of their heritage of conquest and their membership in the larger society. But we should not expect this religious system to be practiced similarly by agriculturists in a Latin American community and the celibate priests of the Vatican. Almost all religious systems are characterized by syncretism—the fusion of elements from different traditions that have come into contact, each local group choosing and rejecting and blending to fit the resulting amalgam to its own sociotechnological imperatives. A peasant—who ekes out a marginal living from a tract of tired soil, hounded and discriminated against by politically and economically more powerful groups—can hardly be expected to subscribe to the same religious beliefs and practices as people who live by tribute and have enormous political power.

An outstanding feature of the religious organization of peasant communities throughout Latin America is a pattern of religious fiestas. In many of these communities, as will be seen later (in Selection 22), poverty and resignation in the face of it are highly valued and there are many techniques by which personally amassed wealth is regularly siphoned off; the greater the community's isolation from the rest of the world, the stronger are the tendencies to equalize wealth and other sources of individual difference. The religious system is one of the strongest mechanisms underlying these tendencies to equalization. As Eric Wolf has noted,

The community possesses a system of power which embraces the male members of the community and makes the achievement of power a community decision rather than a matter of individually achieved status. This system of power is often tied into a religious system or into a series of interlocking religious systems. The *political-religious system* as a whole tends to define the boundaries of the community and acts as a rallying point and symbol of collective unity. Prestige within the community is largely related to rising from religious office to office along a prescribed ladder of achievement. Conspicuous consumption is geared to this communally approved system of power and religion rather than to private individual show. This makes individual conspicuous consumption incidental to communal expenditure. Thus the community at one and the same time levels differences of wealth which might intensify class divisions within the community to the detriment of the corporate structure and symbolically reasserts the strength and integrity of its structure before the eyes of its members (Eric R. Wolf, "Types of Latin American Peasantry: A Preliminary Discussion," *American Anthropologist*, 57 [1955]: 758; reprinted in *The Cultural Present*, p. 367).

In the following selection, based on field research in a Peruvian community, William Mangin provides a detailed example of these processes and traces the complex web of social life of which the fiesta system is a part. As he shows, it is closely intertwined with drinking patterns, land allocation, prestige competition and sexual relationships, in addition to the community's internal political system.

An excellent historical analysis of the origins and dynamics of this political-religious system is provided by Pedro Carrasco in "The Civil-Religious Hierarchy in Mesoamerican Communities: Pre-Spanish Background and Colonial Development" (*American Anthropologist*, 63 [1961]: 483-97); its general setting is described by Fernando Camara in "Religious and Political Organization," *Heritage of Conquest: The Ethology of Middle America*, edited by Sol Tax (Glencoe: Free Press, 1952, pp. 142-64). Along with Eric Wolf's paper on "Types of Latin American Peasantry," cited above, the reader should consult Wolf's "Closed Corporate Peasant Communities in Mesoamerica and Central Java" (*Southwestern Journal of Anthropology*, 13 [1957]: 1-18) for a broader perspective on the relationships of some of these patterns to sociotechnological strategies of adaptation. Closely related is a landmark study of peasant social organization, "An Analysis of Ritual Co-parenthood (Compadrazgo)," by Sidney W. Mintz and Eric R. Wolf (*Southwestern Journal of Anthropology*, 6 [1950] : 341-68). One of the best descriptions of religious syncretism in Mexican Roman Catholicism is provided in *Life in a Mexican Village : Tepoztlan Restudied*, by Oscar Lewis (Urbana : University of Illinois Press, 1951 [paperback 1963] : 253-283). Another, which discusses both the traditional and the changing religious system, is *Tzintzuntzan : Mexican Peasants in a Changing World*, by George M. Foster (Boston : Little, Brown, 1967 : 194-211 and 311-26).

There are many good studies of peasant communities elsewhere in the world. For India, see *Village India : Studies in the Little Community*, McKim Marriott, editor (Chicago : University of Chicago Press, 1955) and *Structure and Change in Indian Society*, Milton Singer and Bernard S. Cohn, editors (Chicago : Aldine, 1970). For Japan, see *A Japanese Village : Suye Mura*, by John F. Embree (Chicago : University of Chicago Press, 1939 : 165-222). There is a very good description of Hungarian peasant religious behavior and its relationship to wider religious systems in *Proper Peasants : Traditional Life in a Hungarian Village*, by Edit Fel and Tamas Hofer (Chicago : Aldine, 1969 : 59-75 and 302-12). ∎

THIS PAPER ATTEMPTS to analyze in part the internal relationships between fiesta behavior and other aspects of culture in an indigenous hacienda community in Peru. A complete analysis would require an interpretation of the interrelationship between the workings of the national culture of Peru, the particular socio-economic system of the hacienda, and the fiesta complex in this community. The roles prescribed by the subculture, the values of the people, and the relationship between cultural goals and individuals' aspirations in the cultural setting, would all be relevant to such an analysis. The present article deals only with the fiestas themselves.

The term "fiesta" encompasses national religious holiday celebrations, patriotic celebrations, local saint-cult festivals, life crisis ceremonies (baptisms, first haircuttings, birthdays, weddings, and so forth), rituals centering on political office, cooperative work group celebrations, plant-curing and harvest ceremonies, and the festive aspects of formal and informal

visiting. Funerals, though not referred to as fiestas, could also be included because they bear an obvious formal similarity to fiestas.

One of the chief aims of cultural analysis is the understanding of the interrelatedness of cultural phenomena. The fiesta complex provides an advantageous point of entry into a study of the social system of Vicos. Fiestas are related to practically all other cultural activities in Vicos, and sooner or later, everyone in the community participates directly in one. In Vicos a number of "complexes" might be taken as points of departure for this type of research. For example, a discussion of the political system, or kinship and *compadre* relationships, or clothes-making, or agriculture, and so forth, would also elucidate the integration of Vicos life. And any of these would involve discussion of the fiesta complex, just as a report on the fiesta complex involves discussion of them. This is not a traditional functional analysis which holds that all elements of a culture are necessarily related to all others. Certain complexes, such as land tenure, ethnobotany, and a few others, could be studied in detail with little reference to fiestas. Vicos does not have a fiesta-dominated culture. But in terms of the positive orientation of the people, the number of people who participate, and the skills, training, and expense involved in fiesta activity, fiestas rank as one of the most desirable and important events in Vicos life. In terms of time spent in an activity, fiestas rank with agriculture and clothes-making as one of the most time-consuming activities. Moreover, a great deal of the time involved in agriculture and clothes-making is directly related to fiestas.

Religious festivals connected with the agricultural cycle and or with various life crises seem to be characteristic of peasant groups the world over. Such festivals generally involve a release from cultural restraints (not "license," but a substitution of new restraints governed by the rules of the festival) and usually are accompanied by ceremonial eating and ceremonial drinking of alcoholic beverages, by music, dancing, processions, and pageants, by some prescribed sexual and social license, and so forth, have a long history.

Attacks by the Catholic church on local festivals, usually ending with the incorporation of the local festival, in a somewhat modified form, into the framework of Catholicism, seemed to accompany the spread of Catholicism at different times, in different areas.

In the countries of Latin America, where the Spanish encountered state civilizations (that is, Mexico, Guatemala, Peru), they also found state religions closely tied to elaborate festival cycles which had been superimposed on local religions. In the development of fiestas in local areas of Peru, at least four important cultural traditions have been operative:

1. Pre-Incaic local traditions
2. Incaic traditions
3. Spanish peasant tradition diffused by haciendados, soldiers, and so forth
4. Ideal Catholic traditions promoted by priests.

These four traditions have been amalgamated to such an extent that any attempt to separate them, even if only to separate "Indian" from "Spanish" is primarily of antiquarian interest. The fiesta pattern, as expressed in individual behavior, is an important functioning reality in most communities of Latin America today.

Vicos is a relatively self-contained community, isolated from the national culture of non-Indian Peru. This does not refer to spatial isolation, so much as to a form of social isolation. Vicosinos, although they do interact with Creoles, mestizos, and Cholos (all culturally non-Indians), do not share with these groups a common universe of discourse. To the extent that Indians such as Vicosinos differ in their social and cultural attributes from these other groups, problems of communication characterize their relationships with members of these different segments. It is difficult for Vicosinos to make comparisons with, or to share in, the value systems of sub-cultures they hardly know. As Moore and Tumin point out, an important social function of ignorance is that it reinforces traditional values. In Vicos the lack of desire to leave the hacienda, the expressed desire to return by many who have left, and the conservatism of the behavior of most of the members of the community, indicate a strong respect for tradition. This is not to say that Vicosinos are all delighted with their way of life. But most of them seem to visualize change *within* the present system rather than *from* it to something else.

In the present discussion, the author finds it convenient to think of four different systems of forces in Vicos life. The four systems of forces referred to are:

1. National influences
2. The economic and social organization of the hacienda
3. The value system of Vicos.
4. The consequences of the fiesta complex.

These four systems are interrelated, and changes in any one would be reflected in all of the others, to a greater or lesser degree. A change in the local fiesta system or in local values, unless it led to some sort of revolutionary activity, would not necessarily have implications for the national culture or for the hacienda organization. In 1954 I said, "A change in the hacienda organization, or in the number or intensity of national influences impinging on Vicos—or a change in the balance between these two forces —would probably have far-reaching effects on the value system and the fiesta system of Vicosinos." I have had occasion to question this statement.

Since my field work of 1951-53, I have returned to Vicos for short visits three times. I saw the fiesta of San Andres in December of 1957 and 1958 and spent a month in Vicos in June of 1960, at which time I witnessed many Vicosinos participating in the fiesta of St. John the Baptist in a neighboring town. The pattern of fiesta activity seemed remarkably stable in spite of a drastic change in the hacienda organization as a consequence of the Cornell-Peru project. It may even be that increased prosperity and the protective atmosphere due to the project have led to an intensification of the traditional fiesta pattern.

One of the most important consequences of the fiesta complex and its associated political system would seem to be the reinforcement of the cultural insularity of the community. This process of reinforcement is to be seen from two points of view: first, the fiesta complex helps to set apart Vicosinos from non-Vicosinos (particularly, non-Indians); and second, the fiesta complex is internally integrative in that it brings Vicosinos into closer relationships with one another. Neither of these interpretative hypotheses holds completely. An analysis which emphasizes integration without consideration of its logical opposite—whether it be called "dysfunction," "nonintegration," or "disorganization"—is likely to give an unrealistic and static quality to the cultural system. In matter of fact, the Vicos community exhibits features of non-integration or dysfunction operating internally, and these must be described. The fiesta complex itself provides some opportunity for the expression of these dysfunctional features, but other aspects of the local culture do so to a greater extent. The contention here is that the fiesta complex is prevailingly integrative in its operation, and that it helps to insulate Vicosinos from the larger society. That this is not wholly the case will become clearer in the following sections.

There are anxiety-producing strains within the community, some of which are handled by the fiesta complex and some of which are not. Rivalry over prestige and esteem is partly expressed within the fiesta complex where it is relatively nondisruptive. One family may try to outdo another in terms of elaborateness of preparation or number of participants, and there are traditional rivalries between families, which are customarily expressed in terms of fiesta preparations and expenses, particularly in such events as weddings, baptisms, first haircuttings, and so forth. A mayor frequently feels that he has to outdo the previous mayor, particularly in the manner in which he organizes the fiestas in which he is involved. Rivalries of this sort engender a certain amount of personal resentment, but their over-all effect seems to be an intensification of the fiesta complex.

Rivalry over land is a more disturbing sort of competition and is in no way handled by the fiesta system. Thievery is also a source of considerable anxiety and one which is not handled within the fiesta system, and there are still others. The following discussion of the functions of the fiesta complex, however, emphasizes the integrative aspects of that particular complex. It does not imply that Vicos is a completely integrated community nor that all the complexes of customs in Vicos have as important integrative functions as the fiesta complex has.

It must also be noted at the outset that the insularity of Vicos, although reinforced by the fiesta system, is not a *product* of that system. The insularity is rather a product of the inter-relationship between the fiesta system, the value system of Vicos, the hacienda social system, and the minimal effects of national institutions on the local community.

A fiesta system is by no means "automatically" integrative. For example, in Marcara, a stratified town, the fiesta system is complicated by differential class participation. Many of the same official statuses and traditional forms are present, for example, sponsors, donors, dance groups, and so forth. Yet in Marcara, each class group has different customs, participates differentially, and emphasizes different aspects of the fiesta. The mestizo and Creole women are concerned with those strictly religious features connected with the role of the priest; Cholo and Cholo-mestizo business men are concerned with attracting Indians to Marcara for business purposes; mestizo and Creole men are concerned with business and sport, and sponsor bullfights and soccer games; school authorities have sales, present plays and recitations, and so forth. The Marcara fiesta, in general, is much more secular and commercial than the Vicos fiesta. It does very little either to reinforce the insularity of the community or to integrate the community as a whole. Rather, the Marcara fiesta tends to set apart each class group, at least in terms of participation. The end result of the heightened activity, within each class group in Marcara, seems to be to reinforce further the divisions within the community. There is also a great deal of intercommunity participation in these fiestas which also manifests a class basis for activity. The mestizo and Creole groups, and, to a lesser extent, the Cholo group, pick up new fads in fiestas from Huaraz and Lima. Certain national holidays such as Carnaval, the 28th of July (Independence Day), Army Day, and the president's birthday are completely secular and often draw people away from their own communities to urban centers where speeches and fireworks are features of these celebrations sponsored by the government. In Marcara, many informants stated that in recent years "los decentes," that is the mestizos and Creoles, have been much more interested in attending fiestas in Carhuas, Huaraz, and Lima than in their own community, and the facts seem to bear this out. This digression is simply to indicate that although fiestas may lead to integration, strengthening of community bonds, and insularity in Vicos, this is not an inevitable consequence of fiestas. It is the relative lack of penetration of Vicos culture by outside influences, the sociocultural uniformity of its inhabitants, and the traditional character of hacienda economic and social organization which permit the Vicos fiesta complex to serve the integrating role it does.

A Vicosino who is "accultured" to the Peruvian national culture, perhaps, would have little motivation to participate in the fiesta system. The presence in Vicos of a large number of such individuals would probably have a negative effect on the present fiesta system. As I have pointed out elsewhere, however, deviant individuals of this type have little motivation for remaining in the hacienda community and, in fact, they are strongly motivated to leave.

Somewhat more descriptive is the individual who is strongly motivated to participate in the political and fiesta systems— that is, not likely to break with the community entirely, yet unwilling to conform entirely to the local code of acceptable behavior. Such an individual's personal behavior may have repercussions not only in the fiesta and political systems but in the hacienda organization as well.

The fiesta system, as has been emphasized, is closely linked to the internal political apparatus of the Vicos community. Indian political officials are subordinate to two other local centers of authority in the exercise of control: the mestizo government (in this case, located at Marcara); and the *patron* of the hacienda. As a consequence, their formal political power is extremely limited, and their ability to secure conformance rests much more on the local conceptions of "right" behavior, than it does on the threat of punishment or the power to mete it out. Accordingly, the major area of activity for these officials, and the area in which their authority can indeed be felt, is that of the fiesta complex. The fiesta offices and the political offices which interdigitate with them are the positions most highly desired by Vicosino adult males, and the positions which Vicosino women want their fathers, brothers, uncles, husbands, and sons to fill.

Outside the fiesta-political hierarchies, the most important posts in Vicos were those of the *mayorales*, or field bosses, who were chosen by the *patron*. Since it was the common policy of the *patron* to choose *mayorales* on the basis of their prestige in the community, for obvious practical reasons, it is interesting to observe the degree of correspondence between *mayorales*

and fiesta and political officialdom. Of the six *mayorales* in Vicos in 1953, all had been fiesta officials and political officials; four had been head of the fiesta and five of the six had served as mayor. A *mayoral* may have used his office to increase his prestige, power, and wealth, but he was usually a man of considerable status already at the time when he was chosen for the post.

The project has introduced a system of elections and of the elected officials in 1960 all had been involved in the traditional politico-religious system of office and several had been fiesta officials.

The only effective nonkinship group in Vicos is an organized group of army veterans. These men speak Spanish and have seen the outside world. In 1952 I suggested that they might change the fiesta pattern by opposing it. In fact, they seem to have entered into it as a group and have sponsored two fiestas in the last four years.

One might justifiably hold that, in Vicos, participation in the fiesta system in itself has become one of the ultimate values. Strong verbal manifestations of local pride are very common during fiestas, and often rivals will drink together and appear friendly because of the occasion. The fiesta is widely recognized in Vicos as an opportunity to see kinsmen who live in other parts of the hacienda or who live outside and are returning.

In addition to the recreational aspects, the sociability, the pleasurable anticipation and preparation the gossip and excitement which precede, accompany, and follow the celebration, the enjoyment of the eating, drinking, dancing, musical, and sexual activity, the feeling of belonging stemming from the joint participation of young and old, powerful and nonpowerful, men and women, all of which contribute to group solidarity, fiestas have more specific integrative functions. Bonds between kinsmen, *compadres*, friends, and neighbors are strengthened by the network of reciprocal obligations and opportunities for mutual aid which are part of the whole system of sponsorship. Debt payments are made through the sponsorship system, and further obligations, to be fulfilled at a later time, are incurred. The fact that this mutual aid takes place in a religious context probably reinforces the strength of these bonds.

The opportunity for courtship and sexual behavior may also be important as an aspect of fiesta integrativeness. There are many opportunities for boys and girls to meet alone and in groups. The fiesta provides a convenient setting for young adults to look over prospects, to arrange meetings, to make love. Many matches are made, and many more are stimulated during fiestas. Fiestas may also help to strengthen the bond between husband and wife: a man cannot give a successful fiesta without the help of at least one woman, in most cases his wife. Contrariwise, a wife cannot give a successful fiesta without the help of her husband. This is plainly recognized, and very often, in reference to a particular sponsor, an individual will say that "so-and-so and his wife" or the "so-and so's" are sponsors of the fiesta. A man cannot occupy a political office without being married, and the importance of a wife in fiesta organization is a corollary of this. The most striking difference between Indian and mestizo fiestas in the Callejon de Huaylas is the active and joint participation of women with men in Indian fiestas, as opposed to the relatively passive and separate participation of mestizo women in fiestas.

Family participation in fiestas is another feature of the complex which reinforces group solidarity and the perpetuation of group values. The identification of the child with the parent is strengthened, particularly when a political or fiesta office is in the family. The very maintenance of the pattern attests to this. The author has considerable direct evidence from young male informants who state that they are proud of their father's activity in a fiesta, proud of the fact that they have assisted, and that they intend to do the same thing when they are adults. The patterns are learned early, and children are encouraged to learn to dance, to play a musical instrument (boys), to drink, and to pray, as well as to enter into mutual aid arrangements with other youngsters. Boys of twelve and thirteen years of age often enter as dancers or are chosen as musicians, and in this way begin early active participation as minor fiesta officials. Generally they do this in association with higher posts held by their father or some close kinsmen, and, in effect, are in a formal mutual aid situation in which they have specific rights and duties in relation to another official. Such a patterning leads to new and different bonds between individuals already closely connected.

Admittedly, each of these aspects of fiesta behavior discussed as integrative has its disintegrative aspects. In addition to kinsmen, an individual meets at a fiesta others whom he would prefer to avoid. Mutual obligations may weigh heavily on some, and may be resented. Courtship rivalries and conflicts between unpopular suitors and parents do occur at fiestas, precisely because of the heightened opportunity the fiesta offers to courting couples. Some wives feel overworked and unrewarded at fiestas. Some husbands are pushed into sponsorships which they would perhaps prefer to avoid. The fact that the whole system persists in strength, however, is evidence that these dysfunctional aspects are balanced by significant forces for integration.

Fiestas also serve a religious function. Religion is essentially a practical matter in Vicos. People perform certain rituals and participate in ceremonies with the expectation of favors in return from the saints honored. These rituals and ceremonies are not rationalized to any great extent. Perhaps, as Sapir has said, there is a certain security implied when a group maintains a custom or a complex without being particularly concerned about its origins or why it is performed. The major fiestas are all accompanied by a mass and procession, and all fiestas, with the exception of the haircutting ceremony, involve some ritual and prayer identifiable as Catholic in origin. Yet even at the high point of the mass of a fiesta (during the procession), mostly those directly concerned with the sponsoring kneel and pray. Many continue drinking and dancing. Many more merely watch or march in the procession without kneeling and praying at the proper moments. The whole fiesta affair is simultaneously religious and recreational, and the specific Catholic rites and prayers are not considered more important religiously than is general participation. They are part of the role activity of the sponsors and the political officials, for others to join in or not, according to strictly personal choice. No one censures those who continue to drink and dance in the plaza during the mass and procession.

For many individuals fiesta activity is a response to tension and anxiety. On a questionnaire concerning reasons for sponsoring a fiesta the most common response was, "To serve the saints." The largest number of specific responses concerned agricultural and health worries. Fiestas are also sponsored to combat witchcraft which is considered by most Vicosinos to be involved in practically all adult deaths. The fiestas of All Saints and All Souls, as well as the festive activity accompanying funerals, are a direct response to the uneasiness and fear about death and spirits of the dead. *Curanderos* and diviners are consulted about sickness and witchcraft but, because of the suspected dual role they play as both curer and bewitcher, the Vicosino frequently does not feel completely secure about leaving the matter entirely in their hands. In addition, there is considerable skepticism regarding the effectiveness of *curanderos*. There is considered to be safety in numbers, and often in case of a serious illness, three *curanderos* will be consulted and then, possibly, a medical doctor in Carhuas or Huaraz. It is the author's impression that the Vicosino places more faith in sponsoring fiestas and asking the saints for aid in curing situations than he does in consulting local specialists. When queried about this, four good informants independently agreed that both methods were effective, and that occasionally *curanderos* would recommend fiesta sponsorship as one of the specific measures for combating illness.

The author was unable to ascertain whether there was any resentment on the part of a Vicosino who sponsored a fiesta in search of a particular "miracle" and got no results. Poor crops or the continued illness or death of a sick person did not seem to interfere with the belief in fiesta sponsorship as an aid in these same situations. It is probably reasonable to assume that the specific ritual acts involved in the sponsorship are, in themselves, of considerable anxiety-reducing value.

There are some data which indicate that anxiety about mestizo relationships is allayed somewhat by fiesta activity. Although most formal relationships between Indians and mestizos tend to be commercially motivated— that is, co-godparenthood relationships, godparenthood relationships, donor relationships at fiestas, and so forth—the fiestas accompanying these relationships nevertheless often seem to be times of pleasant contact between both parties.

Fiestas in Vicos also serve to strengthen intercommunity bonds. This is true mainly in class or subcultural terms; that is, with communities of similar class backgrounds and with Cholos and other Indians in Marcara. The mestizo-Indian fiesta relationships discussed in the previous section tend to be generalized only on a personal level. A mestizo (or, less often, a Vicosino) will say, "Most Indians (or mestizos as the case may be) are brutes, but my *compadre* is different." Viscosino participation in the fiestas of Recuayhuanca, Copa, Collon, and Huapra, and with certain Indian Cholo groups in Macara and Shumay, is characterized by an attitude of good will which is generalized to the whole community. Interestingly enough, reciprocal participation of people from these towns in the fiestas of Vicos seemed to be considerably less during the period of the study. Informants said, however, that usually there was more. The fact that Vicos is so much more heavily populated than these communities may also be a factor.

To avoid distortion, it must again be pointed out that this function has its "dysfunctional" aspects. Some of the most bitter and violent encounters witnessed by the author occurred at fiestas involving intercommunity participation, and took place between members of different communities.

With Indians and Cholos from outside Vicos, the contact is generally on the level of mutual aid, sponsorship, donorship, and so forth, and is often connected with kinship and *compadrazgo*. In other communities more than in Vicos, intermarriage is often inspired by meetings at fiestas. Two Vicosinos married to women from a neighboring hacienda said that they had met their wives while attending a fiesta there.

The marketing and merchandising aspects of fiestas also are important in intercommunity relations. Vicosino often take advantage of fiestas in towns of the valley to buy and sell in the large markets which accompany these fiestas. It has also been noted that mestizo merchants in Marcara are well aware of the importance to them of the Indian fiestas. During the harvest festivals, from August through November, great quanitites of alcohol, coca, wool, textiles, and general food items are sold to Vicosinos. The market also is fairly constant throughout the rest of the year, since the fiesta calendar is a twelve-month affair.

Some mestizos and Creoles, particularly those who have resided for a period in Lima or in some large coastal city, have a feeling, largely tied in with ideas of superiority and paternalism that Indians have many colorful customs which should be preserved, particularly in regard to fiestas. One suspects that closely connected with this mestizo espousal of the preservation of Indian custom is the conscious or unconscious desire of the mestizo not to modify in any way the supply of cheap labor so essential to his way of life.

Fiestas perform the obvious function of marking life crises. Inter- and intrafamilial bonds are strengthened by the small private fiestas which mark baptisms, haircuttings, weddings and funerals; placing the ceremonial recognition of these life crises in religious and recreational settings serves to make them as pleasant and reassuring as is possible. The character of the funeral ceremony is somewhat different from that of the others, but the same function is served. In all private fiestas, the individual or individuals in whose name the fiesta is being held seldom holds the center of the stage for long. The main activity concerns the relationships between the parents and the godparents, the kinsmen, the survivors— in short, all those members of the interacting personnel of the ceremonial.

Fiestas afford an amount of tension release to many individuals. Occasionally, this is disruptive to the community. In such towns as Chichicastenango, Guatemala, and Tajin, Mexico, fiestas often serve as the stage for the acting out of severely aggressive, violent, and socially disruptive scenes involving large numbers of individuals. In a book on the Andean Indian put out by a Protestant missionary organization, several authors refer to scenes of degradation and brutality which they witnessed during Indian fiestas. The author has witnessed several cases of wife-beating and several skirmishes during Indian fiestas in the Callejon de Huaylas. In Vicos, during the field study, only two cases of severe wife-beating were reported, and neither was in connection with a fiesta, although both involved drunkenness. Fighting is not uncommon during Vicos fiestas on the part of a few individuals, but serious injury is rare, and the great majority of the population is reasonably orderly.

Fiestas also serve to provide a formal structure for the release, exhilaration, and pleasure afforded by the drinking of alcoholic beverages, and still to keep drinking in a context where it does not interfere with other important segments of behavior. Drinking is an integral part of the fiesta complex and an important aspect of Vicos life and has been discussed in some detail. The drinking pattern in Vicos is quite similar to the Indian pattern described for a Bolivian group by Heath and different from the Peruvian mestizo pattern described by Simmons.

Fiestas seem to be primarily a conservative and integrative influence at the present time in Vicos culture. They provide a setting for the more or less orderly release of certain tensions and an outlet for what little surplus wealth there is in the community. They provide one of the main opportunities for the circulation of elite in Vicos and channel some potentially disruptive rivalries. The pattern has remained remarkably stable over the last ten years considering the dramatic changes in the hacienda system.

18. RELIGION AND STATUS: AMERICA AND ENGLAND

BRYAN WILSON

From Religion in a Secular Society: A Sociological Comment *by Bryan Wilson, pp. 127-149. Copyright 1969, Bryan Wilson. Reprinted by permission of C. A. Watts & Company Ltd. Bryan Wilson is a Fellow of All Souls and Reader in Sociology at Oxford University. Among the subjects in which he is primarily interested are education, youth culture and the influence of the mass media, and religion. In addition to* Religion in Secular Society, *he is the author of* Sects and Society *and the editor of* Patterns of Sectarianism.

■ Religion serves less of an adaptive role in the technology of modern industrial societies than at any previous stage of development; it is by now a truism that our mastery over the habitat is so great that religion—at least in its conventional forms—has fallen into disuse. It is also significant that whereas until recently in evolutionary history man's relationship with the habitat almost always had religious overtones, the voluminous literature of the last few years dealing with his environment, including all the discussions of pollution, contains almost no references to a deity.

But religion does not seem to have lost its adaptive significance entirely: its role appears now to be confined principally to nontechnological social relations, and especially to symbolizing status differences. It also serves to validate or express national unity, though less than in earlier societies. If, as I have suggested, heterogeneity is one of the important aspects of a nation's social habitat, we should expect to find that it is to this aspect of social relations that religion is devoted in a modern industrial society—and this is the essence of the following selection.

We are increasingly aware of "status politics," of the civil rights of different status groups (including students) and of their conflicts. Wilson observes that although religious affiliation reflects status differences both in England and the United States, there is a difference between the two societies because of the traditionally greater opportunities for social mobility in the latter. When an American rises in the status system, he changes his denominational affiliation. While this happens occasionally in England, the greater tendency there is for denominations themselves to adopt different customs when the status of their members improves as a group. These differences also have to be understood against the background of the declining importance of religion in people's lives and its increasing differentiation from the institutions with which it had previously been commingled. We see here that one of the important and lasting features of religion in industrial societies is that it has been differentiated—to an extent never before known in social and technological development—from economic activities, standards of sexual propriety and other ethical norms, and even from political life.

Wilson also hypothesizes that diversity in status systems has been decreasing and that this is mirrored in a corresponding reduction of denominational differences. There seems to be evidence to support this conclusion, though estates (to use Max Weber's concept) will not disappear entirely; it is instead a matter of degree.

During the mid-1960s there was much talk of the "death of God." Celebrating the values of urban life, many religious spokesmen called for a reformulation of the concept of the deity. If man does, indeed, create the deity in his own image, it is understandable that agricultural and earlier conceptualizations of God—and of human relationships to God—will not be experienced by many industrial people as appropriate. If man's self-image and his relationship to his fellows are part of his strategy of adaptation, then many will also feel that these, too, must be reflected in a new conceptualization of the deity.

A widely known expression of this view is *The Secular City*, by Harvey Cox (New York: Macmillan, 1965). In this book, Cox discusses the sociological, political, and theological dimensions of this changing view of God. In view of the rapidly changing nature of industrial society, it is as yet too early to know what the new view of God will be, but whatever it is, we can expect that God will be seen as wholly uninvolved in the economic sphere of society, reflecting our mastery over our habitat; the extent to which He will be seen as involved in political and social uncertainties remains an open question.

It is impossible even to skim the literature on religion under industrial conditions. Both *Religion in Secular Society*, from which this selection is taken, and Cox's *The Secular City* contain excellent and varied bibliographies that can be consulted by the reader who wishes to explore some of these considerations more fully. An excellent starting point for the reader interested in the relationship between religious sectarianism and social status is the classic and landmark study (in two volumes in the paperback edition), *The Social Teaching of the Christian Churches*, by Ernst Troeltsch (New York: Harper Torchbooks, 1960). Paralleling this is Dietrich Bonhoeffer's *Prisoner for God* (New York: Macmillan, 1959; originally published as *Letters and Papers from Prison*); H. Richard Niebuhr's *Radical Monotheism and Western Culture* (New York: Harper and Row, 1943) and *The Responsible Self* (New York: Harper and Row, 1963); and Paul Tillich's *The Courage to Be* (New Haven: Yale University Press, 1952). Interesting insights into religious change are to be found in "The Birth of a Religion," by Audrey

J. Butt (*Journal of the Royal Anthropological Institute*, 90 [1960] : 66-106). ■

THE ASSIMILATION OF immigrants and the creation of communities were the first social processes to affect the accommodation of European religion to the American context. But in the emergence of a new society, and one with unparalleled opportunities for expansion, other social imperatives follow. Religious movements had to adapt first to the immediate local requirements of their clientele. That clientele had eventually to adapt to the wider social pressures of the new American society. It was evident that religious divisions would either approximate to other more imperative social divisions, or that the Churches would increasingly approximate each other in their general orientation to the wider society. In succession, both processes occurred. The Churches adjusted to the cognizance that their members were becoming Americans in a permanent sense, with a mixture of sentiment for the peasant European past, and realism concerning the increasingly urban and suburban American present and future.

As groups of immigrants settled and strove for economic advancement in American society so the Churches reflected their aspirations for social and economic status. The groups outside the Churches found new, often indigenous religious expressions appropriate to their social situation, and the imported Churches took on characteristics of the level of social status which their clientele attained.

The correlation of religious and social status, which became a marked feature of American religious life, was not, as it had been in England, a religious division of those identified with, and those excluded from, participation in the mainstream of national life in the established and dissenting Churches. There was, precisely because of the wider political tolerance, the reality of economic opportunity, the buoyancy of the American economy and the expansion of the physical and subsequently the technical frontier, no necessary religious bifurcation. All religious groups could claim a prospect of a share in the American future. But here lies another distinction between the denominations in America and those in England. Both had some relation to social status, but the rapidity and normalcy of social mobility in America gave their denomina-

tions an association with particular groups whose status was, especially throughout the nineteenth century, increasing. The appearance in England—although there was some tendency for Nonconformists to rise in the social scale—was of much greater fixity. Such social mobility as occurred was much less recognized, certainly it did not acquire an overt ideology, and members of particular denominations were not constantly faced with adjustment to an improved status position.

It was no accident that, in the later nineteenth-century, post-millennial adventism, and the optimistic mood of movements like Universalism, New Thought and Christian Science, should develop in the longer settled urban areas of the American continent, just as revivalistic and holiness sects had emerged from rather earlier periods—and continued to emerge—in the rural areas and in the newly settled and fast growing towns. Both represented a religious adjustment to a situation of rapid social change. The more established Churches could alter their perspective from the traditional despair for the world and the hope of heaven, to a steady belief that men would bring in their own millennium only after which would all that they had achieved receive the divine imprimatur.

The newer cults were an echo of the same faith in progress among less accommodated populations. The revivalism and the holiness movements were adjustments, in this context of groups not as yet advantaged by the course of the nation's development, and often temporarily dislocated within it.

If the new sects which emerged among the new urban immigrants and the least advantaged members of the society were often remote in emotional tone and liturgical style from the older established bodies in which the wealthy and influential were religiously accommodated, even so there was in this contrast no suggestion that the new sects were politically or socially a threat to the well-to-do. Rather, indeed, the opposite: the opportunity for emotional expression in the religious context might be seen as a deflection of concern from social inequalities. The emphasis on fraternity made possible a certain religious tolerance of extreme outsider groups, including even their economic support by men who were themselves of different religious persuasions. The assumption of the equality of men led to an assumption of the equality in some sense of the differing religious opinions of men. There was less opportunity for the expression of distinctive superiority of particular faiths *per se*, except as reflections of divergent social statuses. The expansionism, freedom and tolerance of the United States in religious matters had profound consequences for the development of religious movements, and were in themselves fundamentally different from conditions in England.

Because America was a society in which status ascription—the fixity of social positions—was never a social assumption as it was in England; because, indeed, social mobility rather than occupational succession was the likelihood for the majority in an expanding society from the very beginning, the believers in a particular movement never needed to define their relation to those in a dominant Church in specific status terms. They, too, had the prospect of "moving up" in their society, and consequently the status connotations of religious affiliation were of much less permanence in the United States than in England. In consequence, even sects which recruited from outsiders and underprivileged groups showed a capacity to change which was never approximated by sectarian movements in Britain. The social mobility of individuals was reflected in the possibility of the social mobility of the movements to which they belonged. The demand for congruence of status—social, religious, cultural, occupational, educational—was most easily expressed, and most quickly effected, in relation to religious affiliation.

The immigrants to America had to adjust to radically different assumptions about social mobility from those which prevailed in Europe: these ideas, often in an exaggerated form, were one of the pull-factors of migration, of course. European societies assumed basic stability and the fixity of status, to a degree which permitted one sociologist writing in the 1890s to describe even great exhibitions as a circumstance which upset men's ideas of the norms of social life, and the appropriate bounds of aspiration. (Today the equivalent consequences on more massive scale follow from tourism.) In such a society as Europe was, part of the function of religion was to vindicate the ascribed and fixed status of society. In the words of the nineteenth-century hymn:

The rich man in his castle, the poor man at his gate,
God made them high and lowly and ordered their estate.

In America, entirely different ideas about mobility necessarily prevailed. It was a society of opportunity, for men to become self-made, for getting on, and even for assuming the life-styles and claiming the status limited, in Europe, to an hereditary elect. Religion necessarily had to adjust to this circumstance, to make itself at least compatible with direct and naked goals of competition, self-seeking and social mobility. Thus religion in America necessarily abandoned some of the functions it had fulfilled in Europe. Even in the mid-nineteenth century, it was already emphasizing love, joy and personal security, rather than the social control functions of hellfire. Universalism and Christian Science were emphatically American products. Religion in Europe has much more slowly adjusted to the idea of high rates of social mobility, and perhaps for this reason has prospered less well in the more affluent society.

Two distinct processes can be observed in American religious development. One was the gradual acquisition of enhanced status by whole movements, and the other was the tendency for individuals who rose in status more rapidly than the generality of their fellows within a religious movement, to shift allegiance to a denomination which more adequately expressed the congruity of religious and social status. Thus the developments of the Disciples, an extreme Baptist denomination in the mid-West, and originally recruited from relatively poor and partly rural groups, illustrate a process of steady enhancement of social status. From simple and undecorated meeting rooms to Gothic-style churches with stained glass windows; from hymns unaccompanied by musical instruments, to the building of large organs; from contempt for education and scholarship, to the eventual endowment of colleges supporting even secular educational aims: this was the process occurring in that denomination as its membership found themselves in greater association with the outside society, sharing increasingly their values and undifferentiated in terms of economic success and economic goals. The history of other groups reflects a similar process—Methodists earlier, and the Church of the Nazarene later. In the latter case the Church of the Nazarene had originally arisen from among groups of Methodists and others who were concerned to find expression for the teaching of holiness which had become rather out of favour with many Methodists, as savouring a type of enthusiasm which they had largely abandoned. The early Nazarenes were undoubtedly people of lower social status and of little education. They recruited many of the lower classes. As their members rose in social status—pushed up from below in some respects by the new tides of immigration—and as the discipline and orderliness of religious commitment led to habits of frugality and responsibility which increased opportunities for economic gain and social respectability, so the Nazarenes ceased to be so dominantly identified with the very lowest sections of society. They gradually came to manifest the concern for status, prestigious buildings and display which characterized other denominations.

The alternative process, of individual mobility and changing religious affiliation is less adequately documented, but the Churches themselves often reported the tendency—and this was something which occurred in some measure in England as well as in the United States. Certainly, it is evident that an individual rising in the world cannot afford to continue in association with religious groups that practice rituals which are strongly associated with lower classes. The man who has been brought up as a Holy Roller is likely, as he advances in the world, to find it less and less attractive for a businessman with a public reputation to roll in the aisles with the least sophisticated members of the locality. So we find, more strongly marked in America than in England, although the point has some application in both societies, a tendency for status discrepancies within a Church to disappear and for a congregation to be drawn dominantly from people who find themselves not simply religiously congenial in terms of belief and ritual practice, but who also find themselves socially and economically compatible. Where the denomination fails to manifest this degree of social and economic conformity, none the less the local church often does so. It is of course a commonplace that Churches have in the past often divided into separate divisions of the same broad religious persuasion largely on economic grounds, and although the relation-

ship does not hold completely, it is often sufficiently approximated to be arresting.

The tendency for denominations to move upwards in social standing does, however, illustrate the extent to which religious movements in America have shared in a system of ultimate values about their society. There is not the same strength of social antagonism expressed between them as was marked by the divisions of Anglicans and Dissenters in Britain, not the same political and social divisions of affiliation which prevailed when the Church of England could be described as the Conservative Party at prayer, or the United and Primitive Methodists be accused (by Wesleyans) of too close an association with the Liberal Party. Social mobility did occur in religious denominations in England, of course, but in a society in which status has been at least partially ascriptive and perhaps is still, the opportunity for mobility has been less obvious—perhaps even less real, in terms of the acquisition of social honour. (This may be suggested despite the conclusions of Lipset and Bendix—whose findings relate only to occupational mobility and this on a crude measure of manual and non-manual professions.)

There appears to be little doubt that those who became Methodists or Salvationists did in fact rise in social status, became respectable by adopting religious beliefs which if themselves heterodox at least led to attitudes which were socially laudable. They provided themselves, in being members of such bodies, with virtual certification of reliability, honesty, self-esteem and self-discipline. They embodied, indeed, the virtues of Victorian society. But the limitations of this social mobility must also be stressed. This was laying a claim to a position in society, it was far from being an assimilation to the standards of social conformity assumed by the ruling classes and the Anglican Church. The Nonconformists of the nineteenth century were always aware that they stood outside and apart from that national institution and its social and political correlates. Such upward mobility of denominations as there was, was very much slower than that which occurred among the denominations of the United States. The assumptions of the social context were different, and the expansionism and optimism of American society were inevitably lacking; the creed of progress had not as yet found its social dimensions in Britain. More important, of course, the very attitude of the Nonconformists was that they did not want to move upwards into a position of parity with, much less association with the Anglican Church, which—particularly in its Anglo-Catholic forms—was to them clearly a betrayal of the principles of Christ.

Where individual mobility occurred, it tended to occur steadily and inter-generationally. Nonconformists who prospered in business sometimes sent their grandchildren to boarding schools, and so, perhaps unwittingly, often exposed them to circumstances in which occasional and nominal conformity were much more laudable than committed Nonconformity, which clearly singled a boy out as an oddity, and as coming from the "wrong" sort of background. There was not in England that American ease of movement—often reflecting the case of geographical mobility—which allowed a man to move up religiously as he moved up socially.

Perhaps the crucial factor in contrast to the upward mobility of American denominations and their increased assimilation to a high status norm of Gothic architecture, decorous services, elaborate liturgies and sacramentalism was the very fact of the Established Church. English Nonconformists knew, from the very institutional position of Anglicanism, what they were against. They had a measuring rod against which to set themselves. They knew what they were not, and they knew the signs of movement towards "churchiness" and how to resist them. Although, in the very broad sweep of two or three centuries there has been an undoubted tendency for English Nonconformity to get "higher" and to espouse customs which were once known only to the Anglicans—and sometimes only to the Church of Rome—none the less the process was, in comparison with the American experience, a very slow process indeed.

It is thus evident that denominationalism represented, and in some measure still represents, albeit in an attenuated form, something very different in the English context from what it means in the United States. The Americans inherited their original denominations. Those which evolved there, grew largely in response to the prevailing social conditions—the rawness of the middle-west, or the depression of the urban slums, the dislocation of immigrants (both in America, and from rural to urban America) or the need for justification and Americanism in the drawing rooms of Boston. They did not stem so emphatically from a circumstance of social protest, from conditions in which men felt themselves excluded from, or too restrictedly admitted to, the presence of God. The absence of an established church, the assumption of the equality of men, and hence the equality of their religious faith, made reasonable the expectation of each sect that it should be regarded as being as fully prestigious and worthy as the next. It meant, then, an implicit willingness to compete, not simply in terms of the religious ideologies which were disseminated, but also in terms of the purely social, architectural and economic style which each sect adopted, and thus denominations vied with each other in their buildings, social standing, patriotism and social acceptability. There was, then, a willingness to be assimilated to the wider society and its values.

However much competition there may have been between denominations in America, their competition was in similar terms, without any one Church being able to claim superiority or advantages in the social and political sphere, and without the relentless antagonism which was implicit in the dichotomization of society into conforming and nonconforming groups. There was, in the American situation, no clear religious group, with its distinctive values, which other movements knew that they were, from their basic charter, against. Hence, it was always possible in the American context that religious movements would increasingly approximate to each other in practice, ideology and organization. And the more fully the movements were exposed to the wider pressures of American society, and the more sensitive they were to these pressures, so increasingly they would tend to respond in similar ways, lacking that vigour of social protest which characterized English Nonconformity.

Given the need in America for the country to assimilate immigrants and to Americanize their home-life and their religious values—those two areas of their experience which were most likely to be least directly affected by life in the new country—it was clear that American denominations were quickly to be exposed to social pressures, and were to reflect the demand that immigrants should become Americans. English denominations were obviously under no such pressure from the wider society—religious divisiveness, indeed religious hostilities constituted no such ultimate threat to social order, and were, on all counts, to be preferred to more explicitly political divisions. In the United States, because there was competition, there was, then, also a certain agreed framework within which competition could take place, and this too promoted that similarity of ultimate orientation, and the accommodation to American values of which Herberg has written so persuasively. As individuals expected to get on so each religious movement absorbed the expectations of growth, progress, enhanced social status and a better place in the sun. These aspirations were, of course, alien in particular to the more sectarian groups in the first place, in America as in England; and in England, much as denominations might have wanted growth, they wanted it not by approximating to the Church of England, and imitating those practices and attributes which made that Church socially preeminent, but rather by the dissemination of their own distinctively divergent ideals and values.

It becomes evident that whereas the secularization process in England was reflected in the diminution of religious attendance, by the emptying churches in the late nineteenth and especially throughout the twentieth century, in the United States secularization occurred in quite different ways. The growth statistics of the American Churches conceal the growing vacuity of American religious belief and practice. Obviously membership comes to mean something quite different in a society in which distinctive religious commitment has in almost all major denominations come to be so purely nominal. Whereas in England secularization has been seen in the abandonment of the Churches —as in other European countries—in America it has been seen in the absorption of the Churches by the society, and their loss of distinctive religious content. Whereas in England religion continues as a compartmentalized marginal item in the society, in America it remains institutionally much more central, but ideationally much more bankrupt. In many ways religion is still, for historical reasons, well represented in Britain, and has more apparent association with government and central authority and with education. In practice, apart from this sphere of institutional influence, however, it is evident that religious practice—worship—is much less prevalent in Britain than in America. The very voluntary element of religion appears to have made Americans more compulsive about Church affiliation, but it is evident that, in a society which is relatively little informed by distinctive religious values, a society which has been described, religious statistics notwithstanding, as the most secular society in the world, Church allegiance is a matter of social respectability.

Church affiliation has different cultural meaning in the United States and in England. We must distrust statistical presentations which suggest that there is direct comparability on the assumption that similar behaviour carries similarity of meaning in different cultural contexts. Clearly it does not. What the difference of statistics does demand, however, is some interpretation of the functions, not of religion, but of institutional affiliation in the two societies. If the religious content of Church practice has declined, then we may assume that the increased attendance in America and its decrease in Britain, reflects differences in the functions of institutional attachment in the two societies. Herberg, has though he is concerned only with the American case, suggested the appropriate explanation here. In America, the Churches act as agencies for the expression of community feeling. Such communities are not natural communities, of those who live in face-to-face contact for generations, rarely moving, and rarely receiving strangers. Such was the condition of traditional societies, and from such a context the European sense of community persisted into modern times. But in America, particularly as immigrants were dispersed, so such stable community life as existed in the early settlements went into eclipse.

The resettlement of the country meant that a steady process of movement became inevitable, and the benefits of stable community life were lost (that such stable communities might also have disadvantages, on a modern assessment, must be clear, but does not affect the present argument). The Church, which had for the immigrants become, as we have seen, the repository of sentiments and practices from the past, was obviously the focus of community life as displaced people knew it, and so the Church became the one agency which appeared to sustain the various functions which communities had once performed. In a context of social and geographical mobility, however, the Church could obviously not forge a community life of the kind which had persisted in traditional societies—that was necessarily abandoned in the development of a modern industrial society. It could, however, maintain the sentiments of community, and so the Churches became the agencies of synthetic community life, drawing people together as neighbours even though many of the natural features of neighbourhoods, as they had existed in Europe, were no longer evident.

This development gave American Churches that distinctly welcoming characteristic on which Europeans so often (and by no means always favourably) comment. People who did not know each other, whose lives, though temporarily lived in physical propinquity, impinged relatively little on each other, except in secondary relationships, could go through the fiction of being a community. It was, after all, a pattern of response to which they were accustomed, and about which they had heard a great deal from their parents and grand-parents, and from literature, even though it now had a very different relevance for their own lives. The search to retain community; the felt need for sociability and association with those around; the persisting desire to "belong"; the need for a context in which to claim status and display status; the persistence of an affective need to be "someone" in terms of the actual direct responses of others, and not simply in terms of abstract consideration of receipt of wages; acknowledgement of identity with the nation or the state—all of these elements were probably involved in the steady growth of the American Churches. The stability of the organized institutional framework could create the illusion of a stable community life, even if the gestures of friendliness and involvement necessarily had to be prostituted by their extension to relatively anonymous people.

In England, where the community has certainly also been in process of attenuation, it can be readily observed that the process has—even after the Second World War—gone less far, and been less obvious. The increasingly fictional quality of assumptions of settled community life, of parishes and local government units in which people have a genuine stake, is a feature of modern life in Britain, but the very steady evolution of the process has had different consequences. There are still in many places, and particularly outside the large metropolitan centres, many neighbourhoods with a continuity of communal life, and there is a continuity of community expression and community institutions, even though they suffer steady attrition. There has never been the need to think consciously of creating community agencies, except in the marginal circumstances of new towns and large new housing estates, and there the experience has been far from an unmixed success.

In the decline of community institutions, the Church itself has suffered. It has not been able to assert itself as the agency of community identity, and the need for that reassertion has been very little expressed in Britain. Those who have felt such a need have been content with the traditional, continuing if declining, agencies. In a country with an uncertain but diminishing place in world affairs, there may also be a loss of nerve, an uncertainty about whether the values and institutions of the past are still worthy of credence. Thus, loyalty, even to immediate personal and local objects, has been thrown into doubt because loyalty seems to be associated with the patriotic and imperial mission of the past, which now has had to be disavowed. Decency is questioned because it, too, belongs to the period of confidence. Religious beliefs become untenable because they took on so much from the matrix of the vigorous, secure, morally righteous society which flourished until a quarter of a century ago. The loss of political and economic dominance has been met with the almost joyful abandonment of large parts of the nation's cultural inheritance which were somehow associated with it.

The rejection of the past has meant not only the open rejection of religion, but also of the institutions and circumstances which supported it. The local community, the home, the school are no longer focal points of allegiance in British society, and the discontinuities of a keenly cultivated mobility make religious traditions difficult to sustain. Thus young people are early bent on getting away from home, from small towns and villages, to college, to work, "and to lead a better life." It becomes apparent, then, that the social meaning of the Church is different in the two cultural contexts and in England is not yet a repository of sentiment concerning the community life of the past—partly because there are still sufficient remnants of community life to make this development unlikely, partly because the past appears suddenly bankrupt, partly because there has been no conscious hankering after a return to community, and that in turn because there has been no such radical break in people's experience as occurred in the uprooting and migration of peoples in the United States.

The Churches in the United States are an expression of status differentiation in some measure, whereas they have had much less importance as a status-confirming agency in Britain. The denominations in Britain expressed rather the basic divisions of social, political and economic orientation, and these divisions in turn had reference to a class stratification of society which needed no further confirmation in religious terms—it was already evident enough. Only in the uncertainty of an increasingly homogenized society, with few elements of ascriptive status (abolished as all the remnants of the pre-immigrant past had to be eliminated) was it necessary for achievement and the struggle for status to find adequate social expression. Thus one circumstance which helped to maintain the denominations in being and to impose additional functions to those of community-identification, namely status-reassurance, existed in America but not in Britain.

But in both countries the significance of denominational differences has diminished, albeit for somewhat different reasons. In America the denominations were, as we have seen, committed to a system of status distribution and engaged, necessarily on increasingly equal assumptions, in the status race of the ordinary American citizen and church-goer. Those assumptions were drawn from the experience of an expanding society, a strong optimism, experience of social growth and increasing affluence. It is a commonplace that in richer nations the differences between rich and poor are less profound than in poorer countries. In America this circumstance is intensified if one excludes the Negro community (legitimate in this argument, since they have separate religious denominations of their own). Consequently among Protestant white Americans, the early differences of socio-economic status between denominations has tended to diminish. Even outsider Churches have, in considerable measure, been able to assume the approved role of offering to their adherents status enhancement.

As the specific teachings of the different denominations have been less emphasized (and Herberg has commented extensively on this) so they have persisted as different but increasingly similar organizations. As the pressure of competition in the field of missioning abroad, evangelization at home, maintaining good community services, fund-raising, welfare work, educational development and the like has developed, so Churches which at one time had little central organization have developed it, and they have done so, necessarily, on increasingly similar lines. The organizational imperatives of large-scale operation in modern society have forced the Churches into the adoption of similar methods and consequently similar structures for all these auxillary operations. Thus even in groups like the various Baptist denominations which subscribe strongly to a theology and an ecclesiology which assert that God's will is revealed directly to individuals and to individual congregations of the saints but not to the denomination, the Church Assembly, the conference or the department within a rational bureaucratic machine, these developments have occurred. The Baptists, theology notwithstanding, have been obliged to develop denominational conferences and to accept the establishment of rational bureaucratic planning with departmental divisions of responsibility for denominational work at a national and international level. Their ecclesiology and their theology sit uneasily under the shadow of the bureaucratic machine which has grown up in spite of these ideological commitments. American denominations, then, have largely come to terms with the wider society in their organization, their value-orientations and their acceptance of the prevailing cultural response.

In Britain the drawing together of the denominations has in large measure proceeded for reasons somewhat different from those which have been influential in America. The pressure of rational bureaucratic organization has played some part even in the less rationally organized and more traditional society which Britain represents. The Nonconformist movements expressed, in the past, the general social and political nonconformity of their members—their dissociation, at the transcendental level, from a religiously constituted society, reflected their sense of dissociation from secular society as well. But inevitably, social divisions change; the class-orientation of the different denominations has weakened. We have already noted that acceptance of religion tended to enable a man to become socially mobile, and we can also note that the disabilities under which the Nonconformist Churches laboured gradually eased, and their dissociation from the wider society lessened. They themselves gradually gave up their distinctive life-styles, their moral peculiarities, and their sense of being distinct outsiders from both Church and state.

As the state became increasingly secularized, so the automatic dissociation from both could be modified. When Nonconformists were increasingly voters they had the prospect of influencing social and political affairs in increasing measure, and this immediately compromised and eventually diminished their social nonconformity. Inevitably, as its social and political base was eroded, religious Nonconformity lost something of its force. Historical differences prevented, within a society which retained strong traditionalism even in nonconformity, a too rapid transformation of Nonconformist attitudes. The separate organizational structure, the reinforcement of allegiances through long segregation, almost into separate community structures, resisted the effect of the disappearance of the social and economic conditions which had made Nonconformists express themselves as a distinct people with a different approach to the transcendental. The old cleavages in society no longer required religious expression, and that diversity of religious expression had now to justify itself in its own terms. And yet, in a context of secularization, it was evident that religious ideology and long persisting communal and organizational separateness were insufficient to preserve Nonconformity in its earlier form. Such new divisions which existed in society no longer required religious expression, having more direct outlet in social or political movements, and these were not drawn from sections of the society in any way coincident with denominational divisions.

If social processes have reduced religious differences between major denominations to merely verbal responses, liturgical patterns and organizational arrangements, has religion then no significant social influence in contemporary society? In the late 1950s an American sociologist attempted to assess the extent to which the Protestant ethic—the commitment to work, free inquiry, and individual initiative among other values—was still influential in the United States. Max Weber himself would not, perhaps, have expected Puritan values to have persisted as a distinctly religious differential in a context so remote in time and place, and in a society so manifestly un-Puritan. From a survey of citizens of Detroit, a city of mixed religious composition, Gerhard Lenski concluded that there was still a significant religious factor at work in affecting the dispositions of Protestants and Catholics. He found that Jews and Protestants had a positive attitude towards work, and Catholics a negative attitude; that Jews and Protestants regarded it as important that a child should learn to think for itself; Catholics that it should learn to obey. He found that Catholics attached more importance to kin-groups, and he believed that Catholic family life might interfere with the development of motivation towards achievement and mobility.

Lenski's findings, however, have been directly challenged in a study of religious adherence and career aspirations by Fr. Andrew Greeley, whose principal stricture on Lenski's work is that it did not take into proper account the differences in ethnic background and degree of assimilation to American society of the Catholics in Detroit. Greeley found little evidence of differences between Catholics and Protestants, that Catholics increasingly accepted general American standards and values, and that once the Catholic has been assimilated the distinctiveness which Lenski noted, entirely disappears. It is only the time-lags in the outworking of this assimilation which create discrepancies between the Catholic and Protestant contributions to the scientific profession for example (in which, hitherto, Protestants have been more than proportionately represented). Greeley found that among his sample of graduates drawn from all over the United States, Catholics in fact made a much more than average choice of business as a career; that Catholics were much more interested in making money than were Protestants; that they were fully as achievement-oriented. Nor did all-Catholic schooling affect Catholic respondents in these various ways. It seemed that American Catholic graduates behaved as fully in accordance with the values of the old Protestant ethic as did American Protestant graduates, and in some respects even more fully.

If Lenski's work was perhaps affected by his failure to isolate ethnic background as an important determinant of attitudes which he took to be specifically Catholic, Greeley's work may have been influenced by the particular age-group and educational-group which he took as his sample for investigation. Young people, and especially those just emerging from universities, are more likely to be achievement-oriented, anxious to get on in the world, than a more representative age-group. They carry with them the values of the institutions—the schools and universities—in which they have spent most of their lives. Both sets of findings have all the limitations of questionnaire procedures, but the conclusion which might be tentatively reached is that whatever the Protestant ethic may have contributed to the general values of western— and particularly American—society of the present day, it appears now to have become effectively disconnected with its point of origin. Catholics appear to be as manifestly imbued with Puritan values in relation to work and achievement as are Protestants in the modern world. Whatever religious diversity prevails in contemporary America, at least as between the two major variants of religion, appears to contribute less and less to social diversity.

It is too simple a thesis to suggest that religious diversity originates in social diversity, and that religious unity will occur as social diversity diminishes. The relation of religion and society is by no means so constant for a thesis of this kind to reveal the really significant changes that have been occurring. Although contemporary society, and this is especially true of American society which was so much more divided in the past, has lost some of its diversity, its regionalism, patterns of stratification and, in some cases, ethnic divisions, none the less the moral unities of European societies of the past have been destroyed rather than restored. The sense of moral rectitude which once extended to almost all social and personal activities even in peasant societies (to dress, forms of speech, eating, courtship, attitudes to strangers, neighbours, kinsmen, etc.) although they were often highly localized moralities were a manifestation of local social unity. Many of these moral orientations were entrenched within a religious view of the world, and both the influence of religious morality and of the religious beliefs which supported them have been largely swept away.

Church unity may be a response to social change, but perhaps not so much to the diminution of social diversity, as to the changed role of religion in society. Mass-media, mass production, rational bureaucratic organization, extensive social and geographic mobility, have been important determinants of the diminution of social diversity. But all of these forces do not produce religious unity. Once religious interpretations of the world have ceased, for the vast majority, to be important (whether organizational affiliation and participation increases, as in America, or not, as in Britain) the barriers to religious unity are lowered, but it is unity at a different level. Even then, it requires perhaps the determined efforts of a profession facing adversity to bring it about, and to promulgate the ideology which will dissolve the hard core of organizational persistence.

IV. VALUES AND IDEOLOGIES

OUR INTIMATE INVOLVEMENT with our own way of life often leads us to overlook that everyone in all societies—and not just in our own—is on a treadmill in perpetual motion. People have always asked themselves in one way or another: "What keeps us going? How can we do the same thing, day in and day out, for all our years?" But societies differ in the energy systems that power their respective treadmills, and the nature of these endless rounds differs greatly from one society to the next and from one group to another within complex societies. As a result, societies differ in the responses with which the individual is equipped to answer these apparently universal questions, in the justifications offered for staying on the treadmill and for getting back on if he should drop off.

The structural frame of a society's treadmill is built out of its adaptive strategy, out of the way people are organized to make effective use of their energy systems. Most of the major activities in which people engage are ideologically legitimated, are provided with "meaning;" these legitimations, sometimes referred to as "values," form an important part of the notion of the "good life" in every society and help to lock the individual into his group's adaptive strategy. The ethnographic and historical records suggest that without such ideas no society—and perhaps no individual—can survive. The development of human self-consciousness obliges man to do things knowingly, to rationalize the order of things and to give himself the feeling that they can be manipulated. Viewed in this way, values and ideologies are an adaptive characteristic of man no less than the implements by which he gains a livelihood. It is a truism that a human society without values is a contradiction in terms.

The point of view adopted here—which is neither original with me nor shared by all social scientists—is that these ideologies cannot, by themselves, give rise to new modes of social organization. Rather, ideologies must be regarded as rationalizations for an existing organization of social relations which is, in turn, an adaptative complex involving particular energy systems and systems of authority. Sometimes new intellectual positions develop that foreshadow the ideological superstructures appropriate to a future adaptation; for example, as we will see, dissenting values in our own habitat may point to a future society based on fully electronic control of productive activities.

Because value systems are inseparable from and dependent on the institutions they legitimate, it is not appropriate to treat them by themselves in an evolutionary framework. To understand their changes, like religious ideas and personality patterns, we must look to the underlying strategies of harnessing energy and organizing social relations. An evolutionary mode of analysis implies sequential development and non-repetitive change, and—at least on the basis of our present knowledge—we cannot analyze the ideological superstructures of human societies in such terms as differentiation or increasing complexity of form.

Ideologies reflect and rationalize the economic and political interests of groups that have different degrees of access to resources. In hunting-gathering and in stateless horticultural and pastoral societies, in which everyone has nearly the same degree of control over resources and in which there is neither individual role differentiation nor fixed group status in relation to the total society, values and ideologies are uniformly shared and are easily identifiable even when there are differences in individual behavior. Once complex societies develop, change occurs more rapidly because (in part) groups compete for power and access to resources, and ideologies are among their most important weapons. The value system—like the religion—that comes to dominance in a complex society belongs to the group that leads that society to a strategy of adaptation which the polity feels, or is made to feel, is more successful than the preceding one. Such groups, whether already in control or foreshadowing the ideological superstructures appropriate to a future adaptation, are always privileged, articulate, and skilled. Even when they are dissident—as currently in the United States—they are part of the ruling group; it is this membership that provides them with access to the resources that they will (or hope to) control in the new adaptation.

Value systems can be regarded as the grammar of social relations; like the grammar of a language, people who use it are not necessarily aware of its rules and structure. Value systems provide definitions of what is desirable and undesirable. They constitute criteria for selecting from available ends and means, for interpreting the world, and for evaluating experiences. Each of these standards must be appropriate to a society's strategy of adaptation and to the conditions by which people live, although, as we will see, there may not be a direct correspondence between values and the realities of social life.

To illustrate, let us consider two sets of values—those dealing with the distribution of resources and the maintenance of group harmony—at successive levels of social and technological development. There are notable exceptions to the generalizations that follow, as to almost any statement about the social behavior of human beings at any level of development. Our purpose here is to paint with broad strokes in describing the experience of the generality of mankind at each level of adaptation, and to do this we must ignore occasional—and frequently inexplicable—deviations from the norm.

Among hunting-gathering people, everyone in a camp is usually entitled to a share of meat when a large animal has been killed, whether he has participated in the hunt or not (Selection 1). This rule reflects the equal access of all to game and the absence of exclusive rights to territory by any group or category of individuals. This is closely tied to the ideological superstructures of hunter-gatherers for maintaining group harmony. Since no individual or group can appropriate or control resources or energy systems, no one can exercise power or impose authority over anyone else. In fact, hunter-gatherers believe that no one has the right to tell anyone else what to do and that everyone should mind his own business; we also saw in Selection 6 that harmony is maintained among hunter-gatherers by allowing the parties to a dispute to split off from a camp. This apparently simple device implies a very different set of values than would a proclivity to remain and either fight things out or suppress one's feelings. We have also seen how this technique meshes with an adaptive need to keep group size small.

In contrast, among horticulturists, the development of exclusive rights to territories and the establishment of solidary and exclusive groups require the adoption of quite different values and ideologies. In such societies, exclusive rights to territory are held by kin groups; this is reflected in the fact that the individual's social gyroscope orients him to his kinsmen above all others. Thus, for example, "the Arapesh view of social relationships is congruent with his conceptions of kinship. He calls by some kinship terms all of those whom he can trust. Similarly, anyone who cannot be classified in some way, through identification with a series of intervening human links, as a blood or affinal connection, is potentially an enemy" ("The Mountain Arapesh. III. Socio-Economic Life," by Margaret Mead, *Anthropological Papers of the American Museum of Natural History*, 40, Part 3 [1940]: 203). The Arapesh solution to the problem of maintaining social harmony is to live neither alone nor among strangers, but with kinsmen among whom one's autonomy may safely be submerged.

The Arapesh live in a habitat of scarcity, in mountainous New Guinea, and they have carried their high valuation of kinship to an extreme in connection with the distribution of resources. "The ideal distribution of food is for each person to eat food grown by another, eat game killed by another, eat pork from pigs that not only are not his own but have been fed by people at such a distance that their very names are unknown. Under the guidance of this ideal, an Arapesh man hunts only to send most of his kill to his mother's brother, his cousin, or his father-in-law. The lowest man in the community, the man who is believed to be so far outside the moral pale that there is no use reasoning with him, is the man who eats his own kill—even though that kill be a tiny bird, hardly a mouthful in all" (*Sex and Temperament in Three Primitive Societies*, by Margaret Mead, in *From the South Seas*, by Margaret Mead [New York: Morrow, 1939], pp. 28-29).

Arapesh patterns with regard to food distribution and kinship cannot be attributed only to the scarcity of resources in their habitat. Similar patterns are found among the Trobriand Islanders, who are culturally and geographically close to the Arapesh but live in a habitat of abundance. In such societies every object and action is defined by its social place and especially its place in the kinship system. In Selection 36, we will see how the demands of raiding and foreign settlement weakened the values appropriate to kinship and local community ties among the Vikings, as reflected in their sagas.

Another major change in ideological superstructures occurs with the evolutionary emergence of agricultural nation-states, where internal divisions become pronounced and formalized as accompaniments of technological specialization and political complexity. These divisions are based on the control that is gained—usually by force— over sources of energy and the allocation of resources by small groups who are thus able to exercise power and impose their authority over the rest of the society. These material factors are reflected in values legitimating the distribution of wealth—which is always unequal in such societies—and the maintenance of harmony. Just as the political rulers of nation-states try to unify their societies by centralizing religious activities, so they seek the same goals in the sphere of secular values. Whatever the nominal policies of the people who speak in the name of the state, it is uniform obedience to their laws and regulations that they seek to gain. The polity must be made to want to do what they are compelled to do, since enforced compliance is fragile and insufficient. Hence states develop their legitimating ideologies, which are taught in their schools, preached from their pulpits, enforced in their courts, communicated in monumental architecture and statuary (and now photographs), and which, it is hoped, all citizens will come to adopt.

Those who are ruled in a nation-state, however, are members of groups that are neither homogeneous nor monolithic; instead, they are divided into occupationally specialized groups and into classes, estates, or castes. Each of these groups has its own vested interests and values which legitimate its social position and economic conditions. Peasants, for example, generally live in what we would regard as painful poverty, but in all national societies they have developed unique ideological systems to legitimate their subservient political status and to make poverty into a virtue. This remarkable achievement is clearly described in George Foster's discussion of the ideology of "limited good" (Selection 22).

These descriptive statements leave many unanswered questions, and some must remain so in our present stage of knowledge. Why do most groups rationalize their situation? Why don't more of them fight back? While there have been peasant and proletarian uprisings in history, they have been remarkably few when their numbers are compared to the extent and intensity of human suffering since the establishment of the first nation-states, and there have been still fewer revolutions. Is it only because of the physical power of national rulers that most people of lower status resign themselves to the apparent inevitability of their fate and adaptively develop ideologies that reflect this acceptance? Most groups do give such an impression, but then how do we account for the fact that revolutions have occurred and that some of them have succeeded against staggering odds? Poverty—absolute and relative—and inferior status do not become painful and demeaning overnight, and these stimuli are always present; usually they are necessary but insufficient to account for revolutionary change. Furthermore, how do we account for the fact that revolutions invariably are led not by the poor but rather by people from privileged groups?

I suggest that revolutionary ideologies can best be understood as the beginnings of a transition to a new stage of adaptation. In those cases where revolutions have succeeded we see that the technology of the new adaptation had already been introduced on a relatively small scale, but the organization of productive, social, and political relations—and the distribution of resources—appropriate to it had not kept pace. Revolutions only gain broad lower class support when the disenfranchised have advanced beyond minimum levels and see the possibility of further improvement. It is this sense of hope—and not a sense of futility or class-conflict alone—that feeds a revolution, and it can only come when the greater success of the new adaptive strategy has been witnessed and remains tempting but inaccessible. Revolutions generally have occurred after the introduction of reforms—for instance, the Russian revolutions of 1905 and 1917 took place after the serfs had been freed—and these reforms can be seen as aspects of a transition to a new strategy—such as the development of industrialization in Russia—but which are partial and inadequate to the needs of a frustrated polity.

Peasants and other lower-class groups have limited knowledge of the skills and of the social and political requirements and potentials of a new adaptive strategy.

Usually they want mostly to be treated materially and socially in accordance with their worth as human beings, which is revolutionary enough from the point of view of ruling groups. Most Russian peasants, for example, had not the faintest idea of the skills and organizations necessary to run an industrial society. But precisely such an awareness is characteristic of the younger members of advantaged groups. They have the education, the taste of power, the articulateness, and the leisure for time-consuming revolutionary activities. They know more about the mechanics of government than most peasants ever dreamed existed. As technological—and therefore ideological—forerunners of a new adaptive strategy, they are inevitably opposed to those whose power lies in the older structure of sociotechnological relationships.

The transition from one adaptive strategy to another creates a sort of ideological vacuum. The sophistication and skills of people in the privileged groups make them aware of this vacuum when it occurs; the lower classes do not have the necessary education and experience. The gulf thereby created between revolutionary élites who hope to control the future society and the lower classes of the old society is reinforced first by the latter's reluctance to join the revolution and later by the brutality with which they are usually controlled in the new world.

There have not yet been any revolutions in any societies that were fully industrialized. This may be due to the fact that industrialization is itself a new strategy of adaptation, and the ideologies (including those of class conflict) appropriate to it have not yet had time to coalesce. It may also be due to the fact that industrial lower classes have advanced beyond minimum levels of subsistence and have embraced ideologies that promise further advances. I do not mean to say that revolution is not possible in an industrial society or that revolutionary ideologies have not already begun to emerge among younger members of the privileged groups; but the necessary ideological vacuum of a transitional period does not yet seem to have occurred in our own or any other industrialized nation.

It must be remembered that the diversity of value systems in agricultural nations continues and proliferates in industrial societies. Just as peasants live by ideologies that enable them to work, produce the surpluses that are essential to an élite-controlled economic system, and give their political support to their governments, so do the workers in factories in the United States and Europe today. Here there is neither the egalitarian sharing principle of hunting-gathering groups nor the communal kinship rules of horticultural societies. Here a man has access to the society's resources only according to the kind of personal labor he can provide. Despite the predominant industrial values of egalitarianism and of an "open" society, there remain groups whose members do not have the necessary skills to exchange for resources and the ruling groups have promulgated ideological systems—both religious and secular—to legitimate the inequality of this distribution. No more remarkable than peasants' acceptance of their plight has been the ideological legitimation of disadvantaged status in industrial societies by the disadvantaged themselves. The alternative is despair and an inability to continue life—and the perpetuation of life is the essence of life and of human adaptation.

The strength of legitimating values and ideologies notwithstanding, peasants and workers do occasionally cease to accept—and in some cases violently reject—established values, even in the absence of élite leadership. This occurs when there is a realistic possibility of improvement within the existing strategy of adaptation or when despair has reached such an extreme (as in slave revolts) that suicidal rebellion promises relief. The distinction between revolutionary ideology and the rejection of established values leading to rebellion is important. One should not equate attempts to gain more human treatment or a larger share of the social pie with attempts to bring about a fundamental change in social structure. Rebellions involving the rejection of established ideologies are confined to the existing adaptive strategy; revolution signals a shift from one strategy to another, with consequent shifts in the locus of political power and in all social institutions and relationships.

If electronically controlled production becomes our predominant strategy of harnessing energy resources, the traditional values and ideologies that have legitimated our distribution of resources—an honest day's wage for an honest day's work and the like—will be inappropriate. Entirely new criteria will have to be found for allocating resources, whether these are expressed in terms of guaranteed annual incomes or other policies. New ideologies will have to develop, to enable people to live and function effectively within the frame of that new way of life.

From an anthropological point of view, it is thus both interesting and explainable that the contemporary rejection of traditional values appears not so much among the economically and politically disenfranchised groups in our society as among the privileged young in our universities. The disenfranchised groups have an ideological commitment to the existing system and its political institutions and are struggling for the improvement of their status within that framework. The younger members of more advantaged groups are trained in the skills of a post-industrial strategy and are committed to new organizations of social relationships and value systems though the nature, consequences, and implications of their nascent ideologies remain to be more sharply defined.

Many of the ideas in this Introduction draw on the work of Karl Marx, especially his *The Eighteenth Brumaire of Louis Bonaparte* (New York: International Publishers, 1957). A recent anthropological study of revolutions is *Peasant Wars of the Twentieth Century*, by Eric R. Wolf (New York and Evanston: Harper and Row, 1969). The best overview of the predominant anthropological approach to the study of values can be found in *People of Rimorock: A Study of Values in Five Cultures*, edited by Evon Z. Vogt and Ethel M. Albert (Cambridge, Mass.: Harvard University Press, 1966); this book contains most of the significant bibliography until about 1965. In addition, the reader may wish to consult *Pluralism in Africa*, edited by Leo Kuper and M. G. Smith (Berkeley: University of California Press, 1968), and "The Study of Values," by Victor F. Ayoub, in *Introduction to Cultural Anthropology: Essays in the Scope and Methods of the Science of Man*, edited by James A. Clifton (Boston: Houghton Mifflin, 1968), pp. 244-72.

19. ESKIMO CULTURAL VALUES

NORMAN A. CHANCE

From The Eskimo of North Alaska *by Norman A. Chance, pp. 70-77. Copyright © 1966 by Holt, Rinehart and Winston, Inc. Reprinted by permission of Holt, Rinehart and Winston, Inc. Norman A. Chance is presently Professor and Head of the Department of Anthropology at the University of Connecticut, Storrs. He was formerly Associate Professor and Director of the Program in the Anthropology of Development at McGill University, Montreal. He studied anthropology at the University of Pennsylvania before receiving his Ph.D. degree from Cornell University in 1957. He has held post-doctoral research fellowships from the Russell Sage Foundation, Harvard University, and the Arctic Institute of North America. He is the author of numerous articles and books on the north including* The Eskimo of North Alaska.

■ Hunter-gatherers, as we have seen, sometimes live precariously. No matter how abundant the resources on which they subsist, they have little mastery over their habitat. As we would expect, their relationship with the habitat is expressed in a set of values that we would call fatalistic. An example is given in Norman Chance's discussion of North Alaskan Eskimo values. In direct contrast to our own values, their orientation to the world does not presuppose an ability to manipulate the elements of their habitat and they do not share our feeling that the individual is master of his own fate.

We have seen how a hunting-gathering strategy prevents the formation of cohesive groups and leads both to group splits and to individualism in legal and religious behavior. These adaptive patterns are also expressed in values that reflect and legitimate individualism. Although this high regard for independence also leads to competitiveness, the Eskimo value system stresses the need to keep rivalry limited : one tries to show that he is at least as good as anyone else, but without putting others down. Such a standard of social relations is an important accommodation to a strategy of adaptation in which no one is empowered to resolve disputes and settle antagonisms. In Section V, we will see how these values mesh with the Eskimos' "basic personality structure."

The reader who wishes to study these value systems further may consult *The North Alaskan Eskimo : A Study in Ecology and Society*, by Robert F. Spencer (Washington, D.C. : Bureau of American Ethnology, Bulletin 171, U.S. Government Printing Office, 1959). *Primitive Pragmatists : The Modoc Indians of Northern California*, by Verne F. Ray (Seattle : University of Washington Press, 1963) is an extensive study of hunter-gatherer values and ideologies. In *The Australian Aborigines*, A. P. Elkin discusses values and ideologies within the framework of religion, mythology, and art (Garden City, N.Y. : Doubleday Anchor Books, 1964). ■

MAN IS NOTED for his ability to adapt to his varied surroundings. This inherent flexibility also has enabled him to select given courses of action from a wide range of alternatives, the extent of choice being largely dependent upon the technological and environmental potential available to him. Within these limits, the range of choice is influenced strongly by the existing social structure and prevailing system of values. Having become familiar with the environment, technology, and social structure of the Eskimo, it is appropriate that we focus attention on the value system.

Values may be viewed as affectively charged ideas influencing alternative courses of action. Through the analysis of values it is possible to learn a great deal about how individuals or groups define their world, express their feelings, and make their judgments. In studying values, we are interested particularly in determining what alternative forms of behaviour are available to the Eskimo and what motivates them to choose one over another. Verbal expressions that connote feelings and emotions also tell us much about values, whether they are directed toward an interest or goal, or are a response to some action that is positively or negatively sanctioned.

Due to the environmental and technological limitations previously discussed, most Eskimo settlements were, until recently, small, relatively isolated, and culturally homogeneous. Since the Eskimo had to devote most of their energies to gaining a living, variations in thought and behavior were largely directed toward experimentation which might better satisfy external demands. In the traditional context, the individuals' desires closely paralleled the cultural definition of the desirable. Because they had little knowledge of Western technology and culture, the Eskimo's ideas of necessity and possibility were closely intertwined.

In spite of the homogeneity of traditional values, adequate description of these values is still difficult because of the Eskimo's culturally prescribed tendency to keep one's thoughts and feelings to oneself. Commenting on this attitude, the anthropologist Spencer has written of the north Alaskan Eskimo: "No one could feel free to indicate to others that he might be out of sorts. This was true in all interpersonal relationships. People talked, and still do so, of the weather, hunting, food. There was no attempt to evaluate situations or to pass judgment on them."

In some contexts this attitude still exists: Eskimo often underplay or conceal their unhappy states of mind. Nor do they appear to pay much overt attention to another's problems, not because they are unaware of them, but because it is tactful not to notice. They are, nevertheless, very sensitive to those feelings of others that are expressed. It is the lack of expression of feelings (but not of sensitivity), coupled with limited choice of alternatives throughout most of the Eskimo's history, that make the task of analyzing values difficult, a fact no doubt contributing to the minimal literature on the topic.

MAN'S RELATION TO NATURE

A missionary trained in linguistics recently spent several years in north Alaska studying the Eskimo language. In the course of his investigations he noted continual use of the word "if" rather than "when" with reference to the future. The Eskimo language does not provide a choice between "if" or "when-in-the-future." With some frustration the missionary regularly heard the phrase "when Jesus comes" translated into Eskimo as "Jesus *kaitpan*," meaning "if Jesus comes."

Given the physical and social conditions in which they live, the Eskimo are quite aware of the tentativeness of life, the constant presence of unforeseen contingencies, and the lack of control over matters pertaining to subsistence and health. It is not surprising that one frequently hears other qualifying expressions such as "maybe", in regard to the future, or "we're all right so far" in response to an inquiry as to the health of a family. Even more explicit reference to life's tentativeness is contained in the common expression, "if I'm still alive," when commenting about some future action.

In each of these instances, the Eskimo reflects in his patterns of speech his fatalistic outlook on the world. It is not the fatalism of resignation, of "giving up" in the face of difficulty, but rather the realization that one has little control over the natural course of events. To a white outsider who sees the forces of nature as something to be controlled, this value can be quite disturbing. Commenting on Eskimo attitudes toward life and death, a public health nurse assigned to Alaska's northern region once said:

I am always surprised to see their easy acceptance of death. On many occasions, I have visited Eskimo villages to find that I arrived too late; that a child had died a day or two before. The usual response to this was, "nurse arrived too late and the child died." There was never any thought, "if only she had come earlier," but a simple acceptance of fate.

We already know that the traditional Eskimo had a very limited knowledge of medicine, and that emphasis was placed on keeping well rather than getting well. Under these conditions, the people had few illusions regarding their ability to cure serious illnesses—other than through the services of a shaman. Even today, many of the village "health teams" are only minimally effective in implementing new sanitation and other health programs, largely because of the lack of support of older, less acculturated residents.

A fatalistic view of the world was given further support through traditional religious beliefs. Although an individual could attempt to exert influence over supernatural spirits by means of magic or ritual, or by following designated taboos, most Eskimo considered themselves to be at the mercy of hostile forces. The power contained in songs, charms, and names gave some feeling of control over the supernatural, particularly when used by a shaman, but even this assumed power often proved incapable of producing the desired result.

Fatalism is still a characteristic mode of response in many situations, but it is not accompanied by lassitude. On the contrary, hard work and industriousness are considered prime virtues. In every village adults are active much of the time, butchering meat, repairing fish nets, mending clothing, painting houses, improving ice cellars. Those adults who regularly rise late or in other ways give the impression of having little to do will be admonished by kin with, "How do you ever get your work done?" Being lazy is actively condemned for children and adults. Every village contains those families that do not like to hunt, are on relief, or cannot keep a job. When kin find that they are giving far more assistance than they receive, they exert informal pressure to equalize the exchange.

Hard work is not thought of as an end in itself, however, as is common among middle-class whites; nor is there any guiding principle that one should "work first and play later." Work and relaxation are both important and a person should not indulge in one too long without the other. The coffee break has become a highly popular part of any work gathering, even where there is pressure to finish a task as in the case of butchering meat. While there are jobs requiring immediate attention, such as storing meat in ice cellars to keep it from spoiling, or following the trail of game, most work is viewed casually, without any feeling that it must be completed at a given time. A girl hanging up laundry may stop half way through and turn to some other activity and perhaps not return until the following day. A young man may paint part of his bedroom wall and then take a nap.

This lack of emphasis on finishing a job for the sake of its immediate completion occasionally presents a problem for Eskimo employed by whites. Both whites and highly acculturated Eskimo have been known to make the generalized statement, "Eskimo have to learn to finish what they start," not taking into account that the Eskimo have a clear sense of job completion. What differs is the work situation in which the concept applies. Eskimo realize that boats need to be secured before a storm, that sufficient driftwood or other fuel must be stored for winter, and that wounded game should be tracked down and killed. But they may see no

need to fill up the gas tank of a jeep at the end of the day, or automatically rewind a movie film or recording tape after using it.

Fatalism also is tempered by the value placed on self-reliance. Given the severity of the arctic environment and the limited food supply, this value always has had an important integrative function—the ability to take care of oneself, serving as a necessary prerequisite for survival. This is seen in the Eskimo's attitude toward physical illness. Only with the greatest reluctance is the individual willing to pass on his daily responsibilities temporarily to another. An Eskimo with an illness considered quite debilitating in Western society is far more likely to continue his or her work without complaint. This acceptance of illness as a normal part of the life cycle has its roots in the traditional culture pattern where attitudes of patience and endurance, as well as fatalism, were basic to the process of survival.

Actually, the man who works steadily at whatever task is before him, keeps his hunting and other equipment in good repair, and maintains an accurate account of the available food and other necessities of life, is not only being self-reliant; he is also exerting greater control over the world around him and thereby leaving less to fate.

MAN'S RELATION WITH MAN

Nobody ever tells an Eskimo what to do. But some people are smarter than others and can give good advice. They are the leaders.

We always try to help each other, that is the best way. Everybody works together, but if you don't do the right things, then people won't help you.

There has always been a strong current of individualism flowing through Eskimo culture, although seldom is it so marked as to lead to open conflict or isolation of the person. It is seen in the permissiveness of child rearing which stresses respect for the thoughts and feelings of the young. The way in which a man provides for his wife and children is largely an individual responsibility. The wife, too, is free to make many decisions such as whether or not she will accompany her husband on a long hunting trip or visit relatives in another village. Prestige is more commonly gained through individual achievements than through association in a particular group.

Aboriginally, man's relation with the supernatural was viewed as a personal struggle, and the shaman gained his power through highly personal experiences rather than in the context of group ritual. Nor did the *umialik* have any clearly defined authority over others, for his role as leader was determined by his own personal qualities and skills. Except within the family, orders and commands were not expected from others and the authoritarian bully met great resentment. Most interpersonal conflicts were settled man to man with little or no outside mediation. Decision making between families was, and still is, undertaken in a spirit of informal consultation. Only rarely did a dominant village leader speak out authoritatively on behalf of those to whom he was not related by kin, and in such instances there was no assurance that his decisions would be carried out.

A recognized sense of competition further highlighted the value placed on individualism, for most rivalry took place between individuals rather than groups. Whaling crews and *karigi* members seldom competed against one another and intervillage rivalry was limited to generous gift-giving exploits at the annual Messenger Feasts. However, the spirit of individual competition always has assumed some importance.

Many Eskimo sports and games continually matched one man against another as in foot, boat, and dog races, tests of strength, song duels, dancing, and storytelling. Ingenuity was tested by one's ability to invent new stories and games. Even kickball, a team effort, featured individual control of the ball. There was betting on which of the good hunters would obtain the largest number of seals in a given season. Competitions were held to determine who could make the best harpoon, kayak, and other material objects. Women competed in skin sewing, making clothing, making baskets, and the like.

This type of competition is common today and as such provides a continuing reminder of the need to perform well. Not only may physical survival someday depend upon it, but feelings of competitiveness in the exhibition of skills motivates others to do even better and often leads to new and improved techniques. This attribute functions equally well in a Western context for one of the qualities highly admired by whites is the Eskimo's ingenuity in using available resources to solve technical problems. Their personal initiative gained from a sense of competition is internally consistent with other Eskimo values of self-reliance, self-confidence, and generosity. In the past the lavish giftgiving of the Messenger Feast gave personal status, but it also served as a reminder of the importance of sharing.

There are several techniques that keep competition from becoming too disruptive socially. Rivalry is expected to be of the good-natured kind, never psychologically injurious to any specific person. Modesty being an important virtue, one should not flaunt one's skills in the face of another or recount one's achievements in a boasting manner. This is not a self-effacing type of modesty, but one that allows people to admit their own merits in a matter-of-fact tone as in "I make good mukluks." Pseudo-self-effacement is occasionally used to draw attention to oneself. A good hunter, who has returned from a trip with an unusually large supply of meat, might remark, "Oh it is nothing, anybody could have done it."

Before the introduction of Christianity, shamans served as a check on the seemingly "too successful" man. The hunter who always got his kill or always appeared able to accomplish any task to which he set himself soon incurred the displeasure of the shaman. If he boasted about his performance or threatened the shaman's own position of leadership, the latter would use his traditional techniques to plot the successful man's downfall. Sanctions such as these had the cultural effect of assuring a certain uniformity of status which paved the way for the expression of another dominant value, that of cooperation and reciprocal exchange.

The idea of cooperation was instilled in the child at a young age. In the earliest years the infant was preoccupied with gratifying his own wants and developing skills to manipulate his surroundings. As he became older, he soon learned that his needs were more likely to be fulfilled when he gave assistance around the house, tended a younger brother or sister, or carried driftwood home to be stored. If he refused to assist or was "lazy," he soon incurred the disfavor of those on whom he was most dependent—his parents, older siblings, and other extended kin. Expectations of cooperation were less apparent among quasi-kin or members of unrelated families.

In addition, the child was encouraged to emulate those older than himself in such a way that they became for him important symbols of identification. Girls learned from older sisters and mothers the performance of skin sewing, meat butchering, making clothes, and numerous household chores. Boys learned how to hunt, prepare skins, make kayaks, and carry out similar masculine endeavors. Children soon learned that family members were highly dependent upon each other for many of their comforts and conveniences in daily life. By the time a child had reached his teens he usually had developed sufficient empathy with close kin to realize that their wishes and needs were important to take into account as well as his own. Achieving manhood, the adult continued to maintain a strong sense of identification with members of his own kin group and as such, was more likely to subordinate his own personal interests to the welfare of the group. To those with whom he identified less, that is, quasi-kin, hunting and joking partners, and other village residents in that order, he was more likely to act in terms of their accommodation to his expectations and needs. Given these conditions, it is easy to understand why the "poorest" Eskimo was defined as the person without kin, the individual who had no one to turn to in time of need. Economic and social security were largely drawn from the extended family, where the giving and receiving of assistance was expected as a matter of course.

If cooperation is still an important ideal in many families, the opportunity for its active expression is becoming more limited due to the increased geographical mobility of many village residents. In those families where traditional economic pursuits are followed, expectations regarding labor exchange, borrowing, and sharing usually are realized. Men hunt together, sharing their catch. Women assist one another with baby tending, carrying water, and similar household responsibilities. Members of related families help each other constructing, repairing, and painting houses, borrow each other's boats, sleds, and dogs, and share the use of generators, washing machines, and other equipment. However, many men, and occasionally women, leave their communities for seasonal or year-round employment elsewhere.

Seasonal migration is very evident at Point Hope. Men leave home for summer jobs as soon as seal hunting is over in early June. They seek jobs as miners in Nome, as construction workers in Fairbanks, Anchorage, and Kotzebue, or at one of the many military sites scattered throughout northern and central Alaska. Most men are hired as wage laborers. A few have become skilled in carpentry, mechanics, and other construction trades. Those belonging to a union may find summer jobs through the employment office in Fairbanks, thus enabling them to leave directly for the work site.

Whatever the position, men soon find that their success on the job depends largely on individual rather than cooperative effort and, as such, conflicts with much of their past experience and cultural outlook. Those who work "outside" are expected to send most of their salary home, an arrangement that is upheld by older married men far more often than by the young single adults.

In Point Hope and other Eskimo villages many men have been able to combine successfully seasonal wage employment in the summer with aboriginal subsistence activities at other times of the year, since their outside employment comes at a time when there is relatively little to do in their villages. Nevertheless, seasonal absence of the male head of the family does weaken family attachments and those with related kin. The younger men gain economic independence working away from home, which limits their ability to learn traditional subsistence techniques, reduces parental authority, and sets them apart socially.

In other villages like Barrow and Kaktovik jobs are available locally, but even here, the nature of the work leaves men little time to engage in traditionally cooperative activities. Working a six-day week, few individuals can give more than minimal assistance to others and therefore can expect little in return. With sufficient cash income to purchase most of their food and other required goods, it would be possible to share these items with the full-time hunter in exchange for fresh meat, fish, and other traditional products. Yet, this modern version of reciprocal exchange is unusual, and the transaction more often occurs through the medium of the native village store.

Many Eskimo express concern over this turn of events, on the one hand wanting the material advantages of a good cash income, but on the other, disliking the penalty they must pay. Those who are uncooperative, without apparent justification, come in for their share of criticism from those who are more tradition oriented. "That family always push for themselves," was said of a couple who remained aloof from their kin. An older man who did little for others was rumored to have made his daughter pay board for her small son when the latter stayed overnight. A coffee-shop owner was criticized for not taking care of her children, "because she was only interested in making money feeding the young people."

As the importance of the extended family continues to decline, we may expect a further reduction of the traditional patterns of cooperation. The question of whether this value can be transplanted to the community at large depends on the root of the Eskimo's cultural identifica- tion and his newly formed goals. The one village institution that consistently has had real meaning for the Eskimo is the Christian church. Here, members contribute freely of their time and energy to repair and maintain the buildings and other facilities. Schools and post offices also are considered vital community institutions. Because of its small size, Kaktovik was without these facilities for many years. After numerous requests to the government had gone unheeded, the local residents obtained sufficient materials from a nearby military site and together con- structed their own school and post office build- ings. Recent United States congressional action now has provided appropriations enabling Eskimo villages to undertake their own "self- help" village projects, and it will be interesting to learn the extent to which the Eskimo of this region make use of these funds. The future of these communities will be determined in part by the members' ability to readapt their coopera- tive patterns to fit the modern context.

20. THE CHEROKEE ETHOS

FRED GEARING

Reproduced by permission of the American Anthropological Association from Memoir 93, *1962. Frederick O. Gearing is Professor of Anthropology at State University of New York at Buffalo. He earned the Ph.D. in anthropology at the University of Chicago in 1957. He previously taught at the University of Washington, 1957-61, and at the University of California, Riverside, 1961– 1969. His research interests have included studies in "action" anthropology, focused on the Fox community in Tama, Iowa, 1952–56; 18th-century Cherokee political organization; village social structure in Kardamili, a rural Greek village, 1960–62; action research on curriculum development and teacher training in a Riverside, California elementary school. Dr. Gearing's latest book is* The Face of the Fox *(Aldine, 1970).*

■ We have seen that man's relationship with the habitat changed with the technological advance to a horticultural strategy of adaptation. An accompaniment of this shift is the development of the notion of exclusive rights to territory claimed by kin groups, to protect investments of time and effort in particular plots. We also saw that solidary kin group organization seems to eclipse the more intense and intimate relationships of family life and that allegiance and loyalty to the wider group is expressed and reinforced religiously.

The human demands made by the social organization of a horticultural society are further reflected in their secular values, which provide measures of appropriate social behavior. In the following selection, Fred Gearing provides an example of these values among the Cherokee Indians. Gearing observes that the maintenance of harmony is the focus of their value system and that it pertains to relationships among men and to man's relationship with nature. Thus, in the interest of group solidarity, a Cherokee is expected to avoid intrusiveness into others' concerns, to avoid con- frontations in pursuing his own interests, and to withdraw from volatile situations. The individual is expected to find these restraints within himself, not in police or troops. Only indirect aggression, as by magic, is permissible in pursuing one's own ends.

A theme that appears repeatedly in ethnographic accounts of horticultural communities is that the demands made in the name of group cohesiveness extend to private thoughts, and Gearing notes this for the Cherokee also. Here we see the ideological superstructure of the underlying conservatism of horticulturists. When we consider the conservative force of religion, which is commingled with almost all other spheres of activity in horticultural societies, it is easy to understand how resistance to change is maintained at this level of development. We will observe a concrete example of such conservatism in Selection 34, when we read about the artist in horticultural society, and in Selection 27 we will consider psychological aspects of the values among the Hopi Indians.

For a good study of the ethical system of a hunting-gathering group, see *Culture and Ethos of Kaska Society*, by John J. Honigmann (Yale University Publications in Anthropology, Number 40, 1949). Once again, Monica Wilson's *Good Company* is relevant (Boston: Beacon Press, 1963). The ethic described in this selection was also predominant among American Puritan communities; although these communities were of course agricultural rather than horticultural, the literature here is relevant and interesting. See, for example, *Wayward Puritans*, by Kai Erikson (New York: Wiley, 1966); *Puritan Village: The Formation of a New England Town*, by Sumner Chilton Powell (Garden City, N.Y.: Doubleday Anchor Books, 1965); and *The Puritan Family: Religion and Domestic Relations in Seventeenth-Century New England*, by Edmund S. Morgan (New York: Harper Torchbooks, 1965). ∎

IN ANY DESCRIPTION of Cherokee social structure, one would mention certain rules about appropriateness and decency in human relations—in other words, Cherokee notions about good men. One would include thus roles recommended of persons. These same rules are the phenomena examined if one inquires as to the nature of the Cherokee ethos. When one inquires as to the ethos, the further question is raised whether all such Cherokee rules taken together might be found to have one focus, or a few foci, giving them a meaningful configuration; that is, all roles might be discovered to have some common quality. Employing the concept of ethos, we are led to ask about the possibility of some overriding moral sensibility among 18th century Cherokees.

Benedict's figurative phrase sends us in the right general direction; she sought some "unconscious canon of [moral] choice." Benedict, however, kept several meanings within the term ethos, two of which must be set aside at the outset. First, she moved too easily between the individual and the group. Persons and roles are group phenomena: enduring public thoughts shared by a people. Nothing reported about Cherokee person and role permits, by itself, assertions about the congeniality of those thoughts to any particular man or to any average or typical Cherokee. A man, deemed by his fellows to be a person, need only be aware that his fellows have this role expectation of him; if this is so, then this role may be put down as a real social fact. Whether that man finds that role expectation congenial, and whether all his fellows or only some of them insist, eagerly or reluctantly, upon their expectation of him, are separate and interesting questions. Ethos might be made to embrace both phenomena, the enduring public thoughts and men's receptivity to those thoughts, but the real presence of public thoughts does not permit assumptions about that congeniality. I narrow the sense of ethos. As here used, ethos includes and orders roles enduring public thoughts about right conduct. This narrowing, I believe, facilitates the very difficult movement, in investigation, from group to individual by helping clearly to distinguish the two.

Second, Benedict spoke of a pattern of thought and action; but one cannot move easily from thought to action. Nothing reported about Cherokee person and role permits, by itself, assertions about actual Cherokee behavior. To any particular man, public thoughts about role are an aspect of his environment; at some moment of action, he knows that his fellows share certain expectations of him, relevant to the matter at hand. How he handles those expectations—his actual behavior—is, again, a separate and interesting question. Ethos could include both expectations and average or usual handling of expectations. As here used, ethos is more narrow; it includes only the role expectations.

This chapter will describe the Cherokee ethos in this narrowed meaning. I pay attention only to role, not to structural niches, and seek the overriding quality of all roles. Later . . . I shall again take up person, particularly that set of persons and roles available to Cherokees for councils, and I shall reexamine the Cherokee ethos in the context of the village council. From that reexamination I shall suggest a still more narrow meaning of the notion of ethos.

The single focus which created pattern in Cherokee moral thought was the value of harmony among men. The good man, in the Cherokee ideal, neither expressed anger nor gave others occasion for expressing anger.

This Cherokee ethos cannot be demonstrated directly by the historical record. Its presence can be suggested by first reviewing facts reported about contemporary Cherokee Conservatives in North Carolina, and by then turning to the historical record in order to seek a measure of support for assuming that the Cherokee ethos then and now is similar in all essential respects.

About contemporary Cherokee Conservatives in North Carolina, Gulick and Thomas tell us that the "basic principle of Conservative values is Harmony." The principle explains for Cherokees much of the phenomena of nature, it defines man's place in nature, and it establishes norms of proper conduct among men. This principle of harmony appears to direct those Cherokees today, cautiously and at virtually any cost, to avoid discord. The emphasis in its application is negative—thou shalt not create disharmony—rather than positive.

The conflict disallowed in Cherokee human relations is of one kind: it is conflict between two men or several, face-to-face, open and direct. Direct, open conflict is injurious to reputation. But we read of "the great amount of malicious gossip and backbiting" and that the "services of conjurers are employed by some." We do not read that gossip is injurious to reputation, and conjuring (in most of its forms) is probably not at all hurtful to repute. Gossip and conjuring, I infer, appear to have an essential place in this harmony ethic: both seem to be means of affecting others at a distance. They are weapons used by clashing wills which yet avoid face-to-face confrontation and the disallowed conflict.

This ethic, disallowing open face-to-face clashes, is operative among contemporary conservative Cherokees defining proper conduct in three contrasting situations.

First, in the usual circumstances of everyday life, one must exercise foresight so as not to intrude. The harmony ethic is maintained by the recommendation that a good Cherokee be a "quiet" man "avoiding disharmonious situations." It is maintained by not giving offense, by "the unwillingness of the individual to thrust his ideas or personality in the limelight, or to make decision for or to speak for others." We read too of a "generalized interpersonal suspiciousness" and that this may or may not be a "general cautiousness and 'feeling out' which is required by the non-interference ethic." In short, the harmony principle, in the usual run of contemporary Cherokee affairs, directs a man constantly to exercise a measure of caution because any of his particular interests may be in unrevealed conflict with the interests of his Cherokee fellows. A man is circumspect.

Second, when contrary interests do become apparent, a good man is expected "quietly [to go] his own way." One does not cease to pursue his own interests. But one takes care not directly to frustrate the actions of others and thereby avoids a confrontation, an overt clash. Primarily, one staves off threatened disharmony by "minding [his] own business."

Third, when direct conflict does inevitably occur, a good Cherokee "withdraws from it— physically if he can, emotionally if he can't." The individuals involved are considered to have acted wrongly. "Aggression of any sort (overtly hostile, competitive or self assertive) is 'giving offense.'" Withdrawal is the punishment seen as proper. A good Cherokee "does not react with counter-aggression. . . . Instead, he simply withdraws." If the offender persists, "the withdrawal develops into ostracism."

One sees, then, a characteristic web of proper relationship recommended to Cherokees: good relations are distant, cautious, quiet so as to avoid potential and apparent conflict of interest. Such moral notions, we read, are part of the cultural equipment carried by these men to their affairs. These are a standard of decency, and by this measure a man gains or fails to gain good repute. We are told this is a "first cosmic principle," pervasively applied by Cherokees, as a measure of propriety in men's behavior, but applied also, beyond that to the universe at large. The portrait, drawn by Gulick and Thomas from observations of the full complexity of ongoing Cherokee life, convinces.

The same standard of moral judgment seems

to have been used by Cherokee villagers in the 18th century. The recorded evidence is much less complete than that available to Gulick and Thomas, but many points in the above portrait are supported, and there is no significant contrary evidence. In the 1700s, Cherokees appear to have recommended with equal singleness of purpose that conflict, open face-to-face clashes among fellow Cherokees, be avoided.

Indirect discord, discord at a distance, was allowed. Magic was prevalent then, more than now. Mooney found reasonable Haywood's earlier report that originally "Cherokees had no conception of anyone dying a natural death." Doctoring was largely a matter of counteracting spells cast by others. The intent of many spells was to compel actions in others, for example, love spells. Probably a practice described as extant just before 1900 by Mooney was not unlike practices of the 18th century.

The root of a plant called *unatlunwe' hitu*, "having spirals," is used in conjurations designed to predispose strangers in favor of the subject. The priest "takes it to water"—that is, says certain prayers over it while standing close to the running stream, then chews a small piece and rubs and blows it upon the body and arms of the patient, who is supposed to start upon a journey, or to take part in a council, with the result that all who meet him or listen to his words are at once pleased with his manner and appearance, and disposed to give every assistance to his projects.

Through this or similar magic, people could be induced, apparently voluntarily, to yield to the wishes of others. Through magic, a man could gain his ends without the loss of repute which would follow repeated, open clashes.

Good Cherokees in the 1700s, as today, seem to have avoided direct conflict in three ways: first, by asserting their interests cautiously; second, by turning away from impending conflict; third, by withdrawing from men who openly clashed with their fellows.

We read that in the usual run of daily affairs, quiet care was exercised to avoid intruding upon others. Timberlake reports:

They seldom turn their eyes on the person they speak of, or address themselves to. . . . They speak so low, except in council, that they are often obliged to repeat what they were saying. . . .

There is a general theme of trickery, running through many Cherokee myths. The animals in the myths incessantly tricked one another. The

rabbit and the deer matched wits: When the rabbit tried to cheat in a race and was caught, the deer won the prize (his antlers). Then the rabbit fooled the deer into letting him file his teeth sharp; instead he blunted them (hence the deer's blunt teeth). Afterwards the deer tricked the rabbit into jumping across a stream; when the rabbit jumped, the deer magically widened the stream so the rabbit could not get back. Similarly, gods were often prone to trickery and counter-trickery.

The Sun was a young woman and lived in the East, while her brother, the Moon, lived in the West. The girl had a lover who used to come over every month in the dark of the moon to court her. He would come at night, and leave before daylight, and although she talked with him she could not see his face in the dark, and he would not tell her his name, until she was wondering all the time who it could be. At last she hit upon a plan to find out, so the next time he came, as they were sitting together in the dark of the *asi*, she slyly dipped her hand into the cinders and ashes of the fireplace and rubbed it over his face, saying, "Your face is cold; you must have suffered from the wind," and pretending to be sorry for him, but he did not know that she had ashes on her hand. After a while he left her and went away again. The next night when the Moon came up in the sky his face was covered with spots, and then his sister knew he was the one who had been coming to see her.

People also, the myths seemed to say, were deceptive.

There was another lazy fellow who courted a pretty girl, but she would have nothing to do with him telling him that her husband must be a good hunter or she would remain single all her life. One morning he went into the woods, and by a lucky accident managed to kill a deer. Lifting it upon his back, he carried it into the settlement, passing right by the door of the house where the girl and her mother lived. As soon as he was out of sight of the house he went by a roundabout course into the woods again and waited until evening, when he appeared with the deer on his shoulder and came down the trail past the girl's house as he had in the morning. He did this the next day, and the next, until the girl began to think he must be killing all the deer in the woods. So her mother—the old women are usually the match-makers—got ready and went to the young man's mother to talk it over. . . .

The recurrent theme of trickery in Cherokee myths suggests a pattern of Cherokee thought— a wariness about the designs of others. Possibly, these myths included symbolic restatement of the general cautiousness required among a noninterfering people.

Thus we can say that, then as now, Cherokees in everyday going and coming were expected to "exercise foresight so as not to intrude."

We find recorded evidence of a mental set to turn away from situations of impending conflict. We read that: "In conversation, they seldom if ever contradict or censure each other. . . ."

Another theme in the myths may be a symbolic reflection of this predisposition to turn away from an unpleasant situation. For example, Mooney reports a myth which explained the origin of a star constellation:

Long ago, when the world was new, there were seven boys who used to spend all their time down by the townhouse playing the gatayu'sti game. . . . Their mothers scolded, but it did no good, so one day they collected gatayu'sti stones and boiled them in the pot with the corn for dinner. When the boys came home hungry their mothers dipped out the stones and said, "Since you like the gatayu'sti better than the cornfield, take the stones now for your dinner." The boys were very angry, and went down to the townhouse, saying, "As our mothers treat us this way, let us go where we shall never trouble them any more."

Later they were lifted into the sky and became the constellation. Again, similarly,

There was a boy who used to go bird hunting every day, and all the birds he brought home he gave to his grandmother, who was very fond of him. This made the rest of the family jealous, and they treated him in such a fashion that at last one day he told his grandmother he would leave them all, but that she must not grieve for him.

Finally, the myth referred to earlier explained the movement of the sun and moon relative to one another. The moon was brother to the sun and had seduced her before she discovered his identity.

He was so much ashamed to have her know it that he kept as far away as he could at the other end of the sky all night. Ever since he tries to keep a long way behind the Sun, and when he does sometimes have to come near her in the west, he makes himself as thin as a ribbon so that he can hardly be seen.

The desirability of avoiding conflict is indicated in the third major ceremony which was devoted to wiping out bad feeling. Bad feeling was a social wrong and was associated with physical disease and pollution.

A Buttrick informant asserts that the word *nuwoli* meant a power that heals disease, and a power that expiates [social] guilt or moral pollution. The same association is seen in a second purpose the above ceremony could serve: at the time of its regular occurrence in the village annual cycle, it celebrated the unity among villagers, but it was also called to combat epidemics. A Buttrick informant reported:

When any town was visited with some fatal disease the people supposed some evil *nanehi* had destroyed the efficacy of the medicine. And other towns, fearing a like calamity celebrated the [ceremony] in order to please God and lead Him to defend them from so great a calamity.

Bad thoughts toward others were treated with the same medicines used for certain physical ills. In 1758 an English trader killed a Cherokee. Relations with South Carolina were then quite uneasy, and both sides feared the event might touch off war. A Cherokee warrior reported to Captain Demere, stationed in Cherokee country, that a priest chief had sent to a cousin of the dead man a "physic" to wash with so "he might be cleansed from all bad thoughts. . . . He accepted the physic and now his thoughts and words are the same."

Perhaps we can say that, then as now, a good Cherokee "quietly [went] his own way."

In the face of most kinds of open, disruptive clashes, good Cherokees in the 1700s probably punished by withdrawing, but in this respect the record is very weak. Later I shall relate an instance where the behavior of a Cherokee was disruptive and his fellow villagers withdrew from him, finally ostracizing him. But the discovery of such dynamics would require the recording of a series of connected events, stretching over weeks or months; such recording rarely occurred. It must also be remembered that withdrawal and even ostracism could be very difficult for an outsider to notice—a matter of unresponsive facial expression, perhaps.

Possibly this predisposition to withdraw also received symbolic expression. Cherokee villagers seem to have characteristically visualized their relations with other villagers in terms of physical distance. That visual image is suggested by phrases habitually used by Cherokees. Repeatedly in the 18th century, when Cherokee relations with South Carolina became strained, the Cherokees would express their fear of further deterioration with the request that King George not "throw them away." In more institutionalized form, warriors on their return from war were considered ritually polluted and were kept apart for some while, as were men generally who were ill or guilty of grevious wrongdoing.

More, unfortunately, cannot be reported. Perhaps the most telling evidence is a silence in the record. There were unruly Cherokee men prone to thrust their ideas and personalities bluntly forward. Yet we read that Cherokees rarely censured one another. The presumption is reasonably strong that the curb, not easily visible to observers and perhaps not easily verbalized by Cherokees, was to withdraw.

If the ethnographic facts be assumed, it seems clear that, in the manner of Benedict, we could describe in Cherokee culture of the 1700s a consistent pattern of moral thought which disallowed face-to-face conflict. We would imagine, following her, Cherokees living through the many prehistoric generations, carrying somewhere deep in their minds an unconscious canon which guided their thoughts so that, as new situations repeatedly arose, they repeatedly made the same kind of moral choice and institutionalized those choices; over the generations, the directive to avoid conflict came finally to pervade the group life and came to be the overriding measure of a good man.

Such a figurative reading of the moral sensibilities in Cherokee culture would not be wholly wrong, but it would lack precision. The imprecision stems not from the neglect of everyday moral imperfections in all real behavior. This study has (so far) dealt not at all with behavior, only with thoughts, But I want to characterize these Cherokee ideals more exactly. I suggest that, when viewed against the several universes of Cherokee persons operative each in its moment, such a reading of culture becomes more nearly exact, ultimately completely precise, but not in these pages. It does not seem necessary to say that there is no such thing as proper behavior except in respect to person. What behavior is regarded as decent or appropriate depends on who one is deemed to be vis-à-vis whom, in the eyes of one's fellows. This is a matter of self-evident truth, in simple societies.

The Cherokee ethos in this first meaning of the term was, then, a single, consistent pattern of thought which provided the measure of a good man. The good man dealt cautiously with his fellows, turned away to avoid threatened face-to-face conflict, and when overt conflict did occur, withdrew from the offenders. The Cherokee ethos disallowed disharmony. . . . I turn now to consider the Cherokee ethos, this time in the context of the set of persons and roles available for councils. The roles during councils were much less uniform than prescribed by the Cherokee ethos. In delineating ethos we employed the words: caution, circumspection. In the description of councils we used those same words but in addition: scolding, duress, censure.

The notion of structural pose sorts Cherokee persons and roles into the four sets in which they were actually made available for work. Those four structural poses were available recurrently through the year to accomplish a series of male tasks. I have used the notion of ethos in an effort to order facts which are pervasive in Cherokee life in such a way as to give understanding of Cherokee culture through calling attention to few, but significant facts. My description of the Cherokee ethos should say something that is true of each structural pose if the characterization it provides is to be useful in the understanding of Cherokee culture.

The Cherokee ethos, seen as a consistent pattern of thought disallowing conflict, has not yet been fully described. We have now before us only one structural pose, that set of persons available for councils, and have yet to look at ethos in the context of other poses. But even within this one pose there is a heterogeneity of role which is not clearly reconciled with the Cherokee ethos as described. It is not enough simply to report that. Benedict tells us that ethos does or does not, in any particular case, penetrate equally all culture (all roles); she reports an interesting fact, but it is not very enlightening. I seek further to discover whether some more narrowed and more useful meaning of ethos does not recommend itself. I examine three meanings of ethos in the light of the heterogeneity of recommended conduct during Cherokee councils. The question is: In what more exact sense can the Cherokee ethos be said to characterize the village council?

The reported Cherokee pattern of moral thought could have the meaning that circumspect caution was more often the recommended conduct than other rules of appropriateness and decency. Guided by that meaning, one would make a check-list of every kind of person a Cherokee man might be vis-à-vis all others; one would weight each of those persons according to the greater or less number of individuals who in fact were expected to be each one. Then one would list the set of corresponding roles. This analysis would only suggest that caution was a feature of the roles most frequently recommended. It is very doubtful that mere frequency was the phenomenon which impressed Benedict or other students of group life, and caused them intuitively to grasp the patterns which they have reported as ethos.

Caution, including minding one's own business, seems to have been the most frequent operating role during councils; this was true, largely because young men were "other clansman" to the members of six of the seven clans, and it was thought to be proper that young men not intrude in the affairs of other clansmen during councils. But that bears only on the fact that the clans arrived severally at corporate decisions, which fact reveals very little about the council and could, in any event, be found out more economically. This meaning of ethos is put aside.

There remain two other meanings suggested by the description of the Cherokee council. One was ethnographically true; the other may or may not have been true; both are significant facts to know about a people.

This next possible meaning cannot be established as true or false from the Cherokee record. This meaning permits us to imagine that, in virtue of the reported consistent pattern of thought, Cherokee roles with all their contrasts had yet a single coloration. We read that Cherokee brothers could morally censure one another; but we do not read whether they were enjoined to leap at every slight opportunity to do so or to do so reluctantly, after exhausting less coercive measures, as a final necessity. Nor do we read how mother's brothers went about demandingly the respect properly due them; whether such demands were made often or rarely, with public bluster or discreetly. So we do not know to what degree these stressful relations depart from others more circumspect.

Consideration of the possibility of a single coloration of roles serves merely to remind that anthropologists put down only the grossest facts about role and have not yet learned to observe important details, even in studies which especially focus on social structure. We virtually never know whether it is recommended that an individual, as some person, speak loud or soft, fast or slow; that he holds his body tense or relaxed; that his eyes be darting about seeking the eyes of his audience, or focused off in space, etc., etc. Such facts about role which need reporting for structural studies are not subtle, though they are assumed to be and are sometimes termed minimal cues. They are public markers, publicly significant behavior speaking loudly to the actors who respond in terms of approval or disapproval. If the actors can see, so can we. We need, in order to describe social structures, to record only those actions which are recognized as publicly meaningful to the actors, but we need all such actions. Now, it seems, though no one states it explicitly, that our curiosity about social structure is satisfied when we have identified persons. We report without apology descriptions of corresponding roles, but these gross reported facts are really by-products of our work—they are the facts, i.e., rights and obligations and other gross markers, which happen to have been recorded by the time we feel secure in the identification of a new person; at that moment we proceed to look elsewhere. Paradoxically, without a much fuller set of role facts, we cannot even discover all the persons used by a group.

A third meaning in the notion of ethos is suggested by the lack of uniformity among Cherokee roles during councils. In this meaning, ethos may be taken to depict that part of a people's pattern of moral thought which recommends the striving to achieve unusual excellence, a moral virtuosity in human relations (according to the group's selected rules), an achievement to be sought and, if reached, rewarded. The good man is an unusual and an honored man. A people may expect moral virtuosity in some class, or clan, or age-group and, within such groups, unevenly among the members. Some notion about moral virtuosity appears to be a human universal. In the Cherokee instance, it seems clear that young men (men younger than about 55) were simply not expected, as a body, to exhibit this quality in a dependably consistent manner. Hence, in the Cherokee case, the goal held up was a lifetime goal, to be achieved in whatever degree possible in one's later years. The record is reasonably clear that events in Cherokee life (for example the major ceremonies) demonstrated and emphasized that being a good elder—and especially a priest—was the highest possible achievement. Being effectively an elder, or becoming a priest, appears to have required some large measure of this moral virtuosity. The capacity for circumspect relations, honor, and influence—these qualities of an elder were to be achieved in a lifetime. Among the old men, achievement was expected to vary, but leaders within that body were expected to come close to the ideal.

Ethos in this meaning is a measure of decent conduct; it is held up as an ideal to all; but conformity to the ideal is not expected within some sections of the society; performance consistent with the ethos is expected of members in other sections but in varying degrees, for moral virtuosity is expected to be rare.

The last two meanings discussed lead to useful inquiries. We ought to know whether diverse roles in one society take on a single coloration different from the colorations of similar roles in another society. We ought to know also a society's notions about moral virtuosity. The two kinds of inquiry deserve distinct names. "Ethos" sems to fit most comfortably the meaning which suggests the last sort of inquiry.

Benedict's phrase, "singleness of purpose," meant many things to her, but it fits well this last meaning. I now say, more narrowly than before, that the Cherokee ethos was a consistent pattern of thought which held up a standard of circumspect, harmonious conduct, and recommended achievement of moral virtuosity under that standard as the overriding moral purpose of a Cherokee lifetime. The essential measure of a good man was the ability to maintain cautious, quiet relations, avoiding clashes of interest; men were expected to honor others who, by that measure, were good, and were expected to hope that they might approximate that goal, as an ultimate achievement in their later years.

So defined, ethos asserts something true and significant about the total set of roles available during councils. Moral virtuosity was a lifetime goal and old men were expected to approximate that conduct. Defined this way, the conception of Cherokee ethos leaves no inscrutable "exceptions" to explain. Harmony was to Cherokees a measure of moral excellence, but Cherokees did not expect young men to achieve that excellence and used forms of decent duress toward and among young men to get necessary

work done. There is no reason to suppose Cherokees felt this incongruous.

So defined, ethos seems to assert important truth about any structural pose. In the Cherokee case, moral excellence was possible only in one's later years, hence old and young were the large contrasting sections of Cherokee society. Among structural poses, the implications vary. In the Cherokee case, the central fact to watch is the combinations of old and young which each pose drew together.

This chapter described the Cherokee council as a set of persons and roles which, if brought effectively into use, caused influence to move in nonrandom ways. Within each clan section kinship roles could force young to yield to old and thereby permit the seven clans to develop corporate sentiments. To the old men as elders fell the task of reconciling the clan sentiments so that the village could arrive at a single sentiment having the appearance of unanimity; the roles among elders were shown to recommend the same conduct seen earlier as the Cherokee ethos.

Elsewhere I presented an approximation of the Cherokee ethos which held up the ability to avoid conflict as the measure of a good man. This chapter reviewed recommended behavior in councils and found these roles less uniform than the ethos as described would indicate. In that light I examined three possible meanings of ethos and chose one—ethos is a measure of moral virtuosity; it is held up as ideal to all; performance by that standard is not expected within some sections of society; performance is expected in other sections but in varying degrees. The good man is expectably a rare man.

In seeking this first characterization of Cherokee ethos I let go of person, as is usually done in ethos studies. If one lets go of person, one must be content with figurative language and approximate meaning. In simple societies, ideas about right conduct vary according to persons. A statement of ethos ought to assert something true about role heterogeneity in each of the actual sets of persons and roles which a people are recommended to be and act.

In the Cherokee instance the narrow meaning of ethos put in focus young and old as contrasting sections of Cherokee society. The Cherokee ethos could be stated as an overriding lifetime moral purpose. This meaning adds to the understanding of all the persons-with-roles which were available during Cherokee village councils. For example, the phrase young man comes now

to mean not-yet-man, and the roles of young men come to be conduct expected of the morally immature.

21. THE INTERNALIZATION OF POLITICAL VALUES IN STATELESS SOCIETIES

ROBERT A. LeVINE

Reproduced by permission of the Society for Applied Anthropology from Human Organization, *Vol. 19, 1960. Robert A. LeVine was born in New York City in 1932. He is Professor of Human Development and of Anthropology at the University of Chicago, where he received his B.A. and M.A. degrees; he earned the Ph.D. at Harvard University in 1958. His field work among the Gusii of Kenya in 1955-57 was part of the Six Culture Study of Socialization. In 1961-62 he did field research on socialization, child development, and personality among the Yoruba of western Nigeria and in 1969 among the Hausa of northern Nigeria. In addition to his anthropological activities, he received training at the Chicago Institute for Psychoanalysis during the period 1962–68. Among his many publications are* Nyansongo: A Gusii Community in Kenya *and* Dreams and Deeds: Achievement Motivation in Nigeria.

■ Most of the case studies in this book illustrate the ways in which particular institutions are aspects of particular strategies of adaptation. The study of cultural adaptation must also include the study of periods of transition; these are much more common in evolutionary history than periods of relative stability. The following selection provides an example of the transition from statelessness to a state society, illustrating the roles played by values and ideologies—and the strains that they reflect. At the same time, this selection sheds light on the values of a horticultural society (the Gusii) and a pastoralist group (the Nuer) in East Africa.

One of the dominant features of the modern world is the creation of nations; these require that people transfer their loyalty to central state institutions. Their habitats are thus transformed, and these changes require adaptive shifts in their social and political values. LeVine compares the Gusii and Nuer with respect to their judicial systems and their reliance on the blood feud to resolve disputes. He notes that Nuer judges are loathe to use their judicial powers, suggesting a resistance to the transfer of loyalties to centralized legal institutions, while Gusii judges are more than eager to do so. The Nuer have tried to retain the custom of the blood feud, suggesting a continued reliance on kinship networks and the loyalties they command, while the Gusii have generally

sought to rely on the courts to resolve disputes.

LeVine traces out Gusii and Nuer values concerning authority in seeking to explain these differences. The Gusii have long recognized and responded to status differences, whereas the Nuer held to egalitarian principles. Such value orientations are learned; they are not acquired automatically and mechanically, and LeVine describes parent-child relations and training with respect to aggression in both groups in order to illustrate their acquisition. In his concern with these processes, LeVine makes clear that it is difficult to distinguish sharply between values and personality processes; this matter will be discussed further in Section V.

Why did the Gusii and Nuer develop different value systems? The Nuer are a pastoralist group in which climate and resources are scarce and more or less unpredictable. Philip C. Salzman has suggested that under such conditions, pastoralists will tend not to develop strong institutions of authority and leadership (Philip C. Salzman, "Political Organization among Nomadic Peoples," *Proceedings of the American Philosophical Society*, 111, No. 2 [April 1967] : 115-31). No one person or group can mobilize and command resources, the members of each household or group going their own ways to seek resources to care for their livestock as best they can; by extension, these appear to be among the conditions that facilitate the development of extreme egalitarianism. Prior to British colonial administration, the Gusii were also predominantly pastoralist, but they seem to have been verging more on a horticultural adaptation than the Nuer, who cultivated very little. After the establishment of British rule, the Gusii became primarily horticultural and are now experimenting with agriculture. Apparently, climatic conditions were more predictable and resources more plentiful among the Gusii, thus allowing the development of a status-hierarchical system, with commensurate values in regard to the exercise of authority.

A very important book dealing with these themes is *Old Societies and New States: The Quest for Modernity in Asia and Africa*, edited by Clifford Geertz (New York: Free Press, 1963); the reader who is interested in exploring further should pay special attention to the papers by Geertz and LeVine. For insight into the relationship between parent-child relationships and adult values and attitudes, see "Relation of Child Training to Subsistence Economy," by Herbert Barry III, Irvin L. Child, and Margaret K. Bacon (*American Anthropologist*, 61 [1959]: 51-63). For a discussion of the concept of the segmentary lineage, referred to in the text, see "The Segmentary Lineage: An Organization of Predatory Expansion," by Marshall D. Sahlins (*American Anthropologist*, 63 [1961]: 322-43; reprinted as Selection 16 in *The Cultural Present*). ■

THE PURPOSE of this paper is to suggest the following proposition: To understand and predict the contemporary political behavior of African peoples who were stateless prior to Western contact, one must take account of the traditional political values involved in their local authority systems, particularly since such values continue to be internalized by new generations after their society has come under the administration of a modern nation-state. Most anthropological students of stateless societies have concentrated their attention on the total-society level, analyzing the structure of inter-group relations in the absence of a central authority. In my opinion, a concept such as "segmentary society," which is at the total-society level of analysis, is an inadequate tool for the investigation of political variation and adaptation in African societies. To illustrate this point, I shall compare political behavior in two East African societies having segmentary lineage systems: the

Gusii of Kenya, among whom I did field work, and the Nuer of the Sudan, on whom four excellent monographs have been published by two independent field workers.

The Nuer and Gusii are similar in many aspects of indigenous socio-political organization. First of all, the two societies resemble each other in size and scale. The Nuer population is about 350,000, that of the Gusii, 260,000. Among the Nuer, there are fifteen so-called tribes, within which compensation for homicide could be collected; the Gusii have seven such units based on the same principle. Both societies lacked superordinate political structures and were, in that sense, "stateless." There were no permanent positions of leadership with substantial decision-making power, and no formal councils. The major social groups within the tribes of both societies were patrilineal descent groups, each of which was associated with a territory and was a segment of a higher-level lineage which contained several such segments. Lineage structure is similar in many details for Nuer and Gusii: a lineage is named after its ancestor; its segments derive from the polygynous composition of the ancestor's family and are named after his several wives or their sons; the growth of lineages from polygynous families and their progressive segmentation are regular features of the system. Although Gusii lineages are more highly localized than Nuer ones, in both societies lineage segments and the territorial units associated with them engaged in armed aggression against segments of the same level. Two segments of equal level within the tribe would combine to fight a different tribe, but would conduct blood feuds against each other at times. This multiple-loyalty situation, plus the effect of mutual military deterrence, resulted in the maintenance of a certain degree of order which Evans-Pritchard has called "the balanced opposition of segments." Thus, in comparing Nuer and Gusii, it is possible to hold constant major structural variables in the precontact political systems.

There are also many similarities in the conditions which the Gusii and Nuer faced in coming under colonial administration. For both peoples, serious administration began in a punitive expedition brought on by an attempt to assassinate the District Commissioner (the Nuer suceeded in killing a D.C., while the Gusii only wounded the first one sent to rule them). British-led forces conducted the punitive expedition in both cases, and the aims of the early administrators were identical: to establish law and order on the pattern of British colonies elsewhere. This meant the abolition of feuding and warfare, and the establishment of chieftainship and native courts for the peaceful settlement of disputes. A major difference in the exposure of the two societies to British administration is chronological. The Gusii came under colonial rule in 1907, while the Nuer were not conquered until 1928. This twenty-year lag must be borne in mind as the analysis proceeds, so that the extent to which it contributes to the sharpness of the contrast may be assessed. With this qualification, it may be said that a comparison of political changes in Nuer and Gusii societies has the advantage of using groups which are matched on pre-existing political structure (in gross aspect) and on the nature of the political institutions introduced.

CONTEMPORARY POLITICAL BEHAVIOR

The contemporary political behavior of the Nuer and Gusii will be compared on two points: the adjustment of individuals to leadership roles in the introduced judicial system and the tendency of the traditional blood feud to persist or die out under British administration. Howell, writing in 1954 of the Nuer courts, states:

. . . there is still everywhere a reluctance to give anything in the nature of a judgement. In many disputes, where the rights of one or another of the disputants are abundantly clear, a rapid and clearcut decision might be expected. This is rarely forthcoming. . . .

He goes on to say with respect to sentencing:

. . . although Nuer chiefs and court members may be aware of the value of punishment, they are still reluctant to inflict it, especially as they are often subjected to recriminations by their fellows when the case is over. A fixed penalty (which they desire) absolves them from this and throws the responsibility on the Government.

It is clear from these statements that Nuer judges do not relish their positions of authority over their fellow men, whose disapproval they fear. They attempt to avoid using the authority

of their offices by making indecisive verdicts and by demanding that the government set fixed penalties for offenses. By contrast, the government in Gusiiland has never had any trouble finding men willing to deliver judgment on their fellows. If anything, Gusii chiefs and judges have, from the early days of administration, tended to err on the side of arbitrariness and severity. Some of them may be charged with favoritism and accepting bribes but not with vacillation. Gusii Tribunal Court presidents complain of the puny sentences they are empowered to inflict. Location chiefs, who act as constables and informal courts of first instance, go far beyond their formal powers, incarcerating young men for insolence to their fathers, threatening legal sanctions against husbands who neglect their wives, punishing their personal enemies with legal means at their disposal. Gusii judicial leaders do not fear the adverse opinions of their fellow men because they know that their judicial authority is respected and even feared by the entire group. Chiefs and Tribunal Court presidents are the most powerful individuals in Gusiiland; immoderate criticism of them to their faces is considered impolite as well as simply unwise.

The second point of comparison concerns the persistence of the blood feud in the face of an established court system for the peaceful settlement of disputes. Howell states of the contemporary Nuer:

Spear-fights between rival factions are not uncommon, and the blood-feud is still a reality among the Nuer despite severe deterrents applied by the Administration. Casualties are sometimes heavy, and most Nuer bear the marks of some armed affray . . . it would be a mistake to believe that the Nuer do not frequently use in earnest the spears and clubs which they keep always at their sides.

Howell also mentions occasional "extensive hostilities" when "the intervention of State police armed with rifles is sometimes necessary." He relates an incident in which he, as District Commissioner, intervened prematurely in a developing feud and

. . . was publicly and most soundly rebuked by the elder statesmen of the area, and was told that such matters should be left to the chiefs themselves.

The Nuer chiefs, though, are sometimes "unwilling or afraid to intervene and restrain their fellows."

The Gusii situation is strikingly different. Despite the persistence of ill feelings between lineage segments, the blood feud was replaced by litigation in the early days of British administration. Nowadays the only occasion on which overt group aggression occurs is at the funeral of a childless married woman whose death is attributed to the witchcraft of her co-wives. People from her natal clan attempt to destroy her belongings so they will not be inherited by her "murderers," and they may even attack her husband for his complicity in the affairs leading to her death. Significantly, however, women are usually the aggressors on such occasions, which are more likely to result in a court case than an all-out brawl. Fights are normally personal and show little tendency to involve groups of individuals. The Gusii, long reputed to be among the most litigious of Africans in Kenya, utilize assault charges in court as an alternative to physical aggression. Soon after one individual insults or threatens another, they are both on their way to chief or court to lodge assault charges. Two-thirds of the vast number of assault cases are dismissed, most of them on the grounds that there is no evidence that assault has taken place. The Gusii are so eager to involve a higher authority in their quarrels that victims of alleged assaults would relate their stories to me and show me their injuries if I happened to meet them on their way to the chief.

To summarize to this point: Nuer judicial leaders are more uneasy about making decisions and inflicting punishments on their fellow men than are their Gusii counterparts. Nuer men continue to practice the blood feud after twenty years of colonial rule, while the Gusii have a strong tendency to resolve their conflicts in court. The hypothesis that these differences are due to the twenty-year head start which Gusii political acculturation had, can be rejected on the grounds that the present tendencies of rulers and ruled in Gusiiland manifested themselves in the early years of British administration.

POLITICAL VALUES

Can these differences in the political behavior of the Nuer and Gusii be related to more general differences in their political values? It is instructive in this connection to examine their values (as expressed in behavior) concerning authority and aggression. Both Evans-Pitchard and Howell use the words "democratic," "egalitarian," and "independent" in characterizing Nuer behavior. Evans-Pritchard also mentions the Nuer possession of "a deep sense of their common equality," and states, "There is no master and no servant in their society, but only equals. . . ." Both investigators give detailed accounts of the Nuer avoidance of using the imperative mode of speech, and the anger with which a Nuer reacts to an order which is not couched in terms of polite request. Nuer men refused to help a sick Evans-Pritchard carry his equipment when he was leaving the field because his way of asking them to do it was not euphemistic enough. They refuse to be ordered about by other Nuer or by Europeans, and they also exhibit little deference to persons in political roles. Referring to the Nuer leopard-skin chiefs, Evans-Pritchard states:

. . . The chiefs I have seen were treated in everyday life like other men and there is no means of telling that a man is a chief by observing people's behavior to him.

Howell says of the contemporary situation:

. . . though the Nuer have a proper respect for the authority of their District Commissioner, no one could argue that this in any way curbs their blunt methods of expressing approval of his decisions, or more often, disapproval. . . . He is addressed by his "bull-name," greeted as an intimate by men and women of all ages, praised, but often severely criticized, by the chiefs.

In characterizing the Gusii attitude toward authority, one finds it necessary to use terms such as "authoritarian" which connote dominance and submission. Command relationships are a part of everyday life and are morally valued by the Gusii. A higher-status person has the right to order about persons of lower status, and this right is not limited to a functionally specific relationship. The contemporary location chief, for example, is surrounded by lackeys ready to do his bidding, and these lackeys have considerable command power over the populace in matters unrelated to the governing of the location. The chief, or someone in his immediate family, can stop anywhere in his location and order a man he does not know to do a personal favor for him, and it will be done. Schoolteachers, by virtue of their prestige; traders, by virtue of their wealth; elders, by virtue of their age; and subheadmen, by virtue of their political position, all have the privilege of telling other people what to do, and they use this privilege to pass onerous tasks on to persons of lower status. Orders are given in imperative terms and often in harsh tones, yet this is considered normal and proper conduct. Europeans are accorded considerable command power, whether or not they are government officials. Deferential behavior to persons of higher status is also pronounced among the Gusii and this was the case in the past as well as today. Traditionally, local community decision-making was dominated by the elders and the wealthiest individuals of the area; the local lineage was an age-hierarchy in terms of deference and dominance. Old men enjoy relating tales of the awe in which people held Bogonko, a nineteenth-century hero and leader of the Getutu tribe. It is said that when he walked out of his home area people fled from their houses until reassured that he would do them no harm. Songs in praise of his wealth, power, and accomplishments were composed. When he attended his grandson's wedding, woven mats were laid down so that he should not have to walk on cow dung. A soft voice and downward glance constitute traditionally proper demeanor for someone talking to an elder, chief, or other figure of importance. It is significant that some of the major political leaders of contemporary Gusiiland started out as servants to the major figures of their day, and that uneducated men with political aspirations often want to be cook or chauffeur to a chief. Gusii leaders are deferential to the District Commissioner and do not often contradict him.

The Gusii, then, appear to have authoritarian values while the Nuer are extremely egalitarian. This difference in values is manifest if one examines community or family relationships in the two societies. Nuer village life is characterized by economic mutuality, and an ethic of sharing surplus goods so intense that it is impossible for a man to keep such goods as tobacco if his supply exceeds that of his neighbors; they simply take it from him. Among the Gusii, who live in scattered homesteads rather than villages, each homestead tends to be an independent economic unit; communal sharing is not considered desirable and the privacy of

property is guarded. Although Gusii men, like Nuer, eat at each other's places, they have a greater tendency to congregate at the homestead of a wealthy man, who can afford to feed them well and who dominates them economically and politically to some extent. Both Nuer and Gusii are formally patriarchal in family organization. The available evidence indicates that the Gusii *paterfamilias* is much more powerful vis-à-vis his wives and sons than his Nuer counterpart. Among the Nuer, men do not beat their wives; sons can go off to live with their maternal uncles; and the eldest sons can curse their parents. Among the Gusii, wives are frequently beaten; sons can find no refuge at their mother's brothers'; and only parents may curse their children. Thus, the contrast between egalitarian and authoritarian values can be found in many spheres of Nuer and Gusii life.

Values concerning aggression are also of interest here. The Nuer have been described as "truculent" and "easily roused to violence."

A Neur will at once fight if he considers that he has been insulted, and they are very sensitive and easily take offense. When a man feels that he has suffered an injury . . . he at once challenges the man who has wronged him to a duel and the challenge must be accepted.

No such code of honor obtains among the Gusii, who consider it preferable to avert aggression whenever possible. Gusii men tend to be quiet and restrained in interaction and, although enemies try to avoid meeting one another, when they are forced into contact they will be civil and even friendly, although they have been backbiting or sorcerizing one another covertly. This is summed up in the proverb, "Two people may be seen together but their hearts do not know one another." Another proverb epitomizes Gusii avoidance behavior toward persons of a quarrelsome disposition: "A biting snake is pushed away with a stick." Serious crimes of violence are committed almost exclusively by intoxicated individuals. Thus the Gusii preference to avoid interpersonal aggression, and to resolve it in the courts when it comes to a head, contrasts sharply with the Nuer tendency to settle quarrels by fighting.

Using the classification of political systems proposed by Fortes and Evans-Pritchard or the revision of it proposed by Southall, the Nuer and

Gusii both fall into the same class, that of stateless segmentary societies. Yet, as has been shown above, they are poles apart in terms of political values which are significantly involved in their contemporary political situation. If authority values were the criteria of classification, the Nuer would probably fall with societies like the Masai, whose political organization is based on age groups, or with the Fox Indians, whose opposition to the concentration of power and authority was expressed in their political, religious, and kinship organization and their resistance to European domination. The Gusii, in terms of authority values, might be classed with African kingdoms or with smaller-scale and less stratified chiefdoms in which inequalities in the allocation of authority were cherished rather than reviled. The corporate lineage is sometimes thought of as an inherently egalitarian institution, but, as the Gusii case indicates, it is also flexible enough to be able to develop in a non-egalitarian direction with an emphasis on generational status differences and a recognition of seniority based on wealth.

Certain aspects of Nuer and Gusii sociopolitical organization which would be considered peripheral under the Fortes-Evans-Pritchard scheme indicate the divergent tendencies of the two societies. The Nuer have an age-set organization which, while it is not an important factor in their political life, nonetheless exhibits some degree of group organization based on relationships of equality. The Gusii have no organized group of peers. In the nineteenth century, Getutu, largest of the seven Gusii tribes, developed a hereditary chieftainship which resulted in some centralization of judicial power in that tribe. The chieftainship later bifurcated along lines of lineage segmentation but the leadership tradition remained strong in Getutu and is so today. This development, although limited to one part of Gusii society, was a movement in a distinctly authoritarian direction, especially when compared to temporary leadership movements among the Nuer. It is probable that, if the Gusii had lived in an area which contained a centralized chiefdom, they would have, as the Uganda-Congo tribes described by Southall did, voluntarily accepted its domination for the authoritarian order it offered. This is speculation and cannot be

verified. But one thing seems certain from the above, and that is that classifying political systems on the basis of their predominant political values, particularly those concerning authority, yields insights into them which cannot be obtained by a scheme based purely on the broad outlines of political structure. The authority structure of cohesive groups within stateless segmentary societies has been neglected by investigators in favor of the structure of lineages and their relation to territorial units. It is time that this situation be remedied by closer attention to problems in the allocation and exercise of authority.

CHILDHOOD EXPERIENCE

The contrasting values of the Nuer and Gusii described above indicate differing means of making decisions and different paths of action concerning the settlement of disputes, in short, basic differences in the political systems of the two groups. In stateless societies with segmentary lineages, decisions are made mostly at the level of the local community and local lineage group, where permanent solidary bonds exist. The extended family as minimal lineage is a unit in the local political system, and its authority structure tends to resemble that of larger units. This resemblance has been made explicit for the Nuer and Gusii. Since the extended family functions both as a political unit and as an institution for the care and training of the young, the individual's induction into the political system actually begins in early childhood. His socialization into the authority structure of the family leaves him with values and role expectations which are adaptive in sociopolitical units above the family level. Because of this connection between the early family environment of the child and the political system, it is reasonable to expect differences in the early learning experiences of typical individuals in Gusii and Nuer societies. Psychological theory and research suggest two aspects of childhood experience as particularly relevant to the learning of values concerning authority and aggression: parent-child relations and aggression training. It should be possible to develop some theoretical expectations about these aspects for the Nuer and Gusii, and the check the available evidence for confirmation or disconfirmation.

PARENT–CHILD RELATIONS

Several investigators in the fields of social and developmental psychology, among them Frenkel-Brunswik, Riesman, and Whiting, have proposed the general hypothesis (based on psychoanalytic theory) that the individual's attitudes toward authority are a function of his early relationships with his parents. The factors often held responsible for the development of such attitudes are: a) the authority structure of the family, that is, the extent to which family authority is concentrated, in hierarchical fashion, or equally distributed among its members. In a family in which authority is concentrated, the child is held to develop authoritarian or rigid absolute values, and where it is equally shared, he internalizes egalitarian, group-oriented, and cooperative values. b) The closeness and warmth of the relationship between the child and the parent with most authority in the household. In particular, Frenkel-Brunswik found that American men scoring high on the F (authoritarianism-ethnocentrism) scale characterized their fathers as "distant," "stern," and "with bad temper," while those scoring low said their fathers had been "warm" and "demonstrative." This finding appears to have had a major influence on thinking in this field of study. c) The degree to which the discipline administered is severe, with physical punishment most important. It is held that the child who has been beaten by a powerful parent will grow up submissive to arbitrary authority and to cherish a non-egalitarian ideal. The comparison of the Nuer and Gusii on these characteristics will be limited to (b) and (c), since (a) has been described above.

The father-son relationship is the appropriate category for studying childhood antecedents of authority values among Nuer and Gusii since both groups are strongly patrilineal, with men occupying all positions of authority in the kinship and political systems. Furthermore, residence at marriage tends to be patrilocal in both societies, so that many men live in close proximity to their fathers until the latter die. For the father, the father-son relationships is

one between lineagemates and is, therefore, likely to reflect the authority values which characterize his relations with other members of his lineage. For the son, the relationship represents his induction into the authority system of the minimal lineage, of which he is likely to remain a member as an adult, and it probably serves also as a prototype for other intralineage authority relationships. Concerning the Nuer, Evans-Pritchard states:

> . . . the father also takes an interest in his infant children, and one often sees a man nursing his child while the mother is engaged in the tasks of the home. Nuer fathers are proud of their children and give much time to them, petting and spoiling them, giving them tidbits, playing with them and teaching them to talk: and the children are often in the byres with the man. I have never seen a man beat his child or lose his temper with him, however aggravating he may be. When a father speaks crossly to his child, as he does if, let us say, the child goes to the edge of a river or among the cattle, where he may be injured, it is evident that the child is not afraid of his loud words and obeys from affection rather than fear.

Among the Gusii, fathers rarely take care of infants, as most mothers have daughters or sisters aged five to eleven who are charged with the responsibility of caretaking in her absence. If there is no such child caretaker (*omoreri*), the mother's co-wife or mother-in-law helps her out in this regard, but the father's role in infant care is minimal. Nor do fathers spend much time with their children, play with them, or act otherwise nurturant. On the contrary, the Gusii father tends to be aloof and severe, being called in by the mother primarily when the child needs to be disciplined. Fathers threaten their sons with punishment, and administer harsh beatings with wooden switches, explicitly intending to make the sons fearful and therefore obedient. The mother and older siblings help to exaggerate the punitive image of the father by warning the child of the dire paternal punishments which await him if he does wrong. At the end of his son's initiation ceremony the father ritually promises not to beat him any more, as an acknowledgement of his maturity. Most Gusii men recall a thrashing by the father for neglect of cattle-herding as one of their outstanding childhood experiences.

The patterns of father-son relations in Nuer and Gusii childhood experiences conform to the expectations generated by psychological hypotheses. The Nuer, who as adults have egalitarian values, grow up with warm, demonstrative fathers who do not beat them physically. The Gusii, who exhibit authoritarian behavior as adults, have experienced, as children, fathers who are remote, frightening, and severely punitive. This indicates the possibility that the difference in values concerning authority between Nuer and Gusii is related to the concomitant difference in early father-son relations.

AGGRESSION TRAINING

Psychologists have done considerable research on childhood antecedents of aggressive behavior. One of the most recent and comprehensive research studies on the topic is that of Sears, Maccoby, and Levin on the child-rearing patterns of 379 American mothers. They found a positive relationship between the mother's permissive attitude toward the aggressive behavior of her child and the degree of his aggressiveness. The more permissive the mother, the more aggressive the child. Although no direct relationship between the aggressive behavior of an individual as a child and his aggression as an adult has been established, it is possible to use the above finding as an hypothetical basis for predicting that the Nuer, who are more aggressive and who set a high value on physical aggression, will be found to permit more aggressive behavior in their children than the Gusii, who tend to disvalue aggression and seek to avoid it. Evans-Pritchard states of the Nuer:

. . . From their earliest years children are encouraged by their elders to settle all disputes by fighting, and they grow up to regard skill in fighting the most necessary accomplishment and courage the highest virtue.

. . . A child soon learns that to maintain his equality with his peers, he must stand up for himself against any encroachment on his person or property. This means that he must always be prepared to fight, and his willingness and ability to do so are the only protection of his integrity as a free and independent person against the avarice and bullying of his kinsmen.

With the Gusii, on the other hand, parents do not encourage their children to fight but rather to report grievances to the parents. Adult disapproval of fighting is so strong that most children learn at an early age not to fight in the presence of parents or other adult relatives. When they are by themselves, herding cattle, however, boys do engage in physical aggression against one another. If a boy is hurt badly or beaten by a boy he does not know well, he will run to a parent, usually the mother, who will question him about it and then angrily cross-examine the other children involved. Mothers describing this procedure said that they "make a case," using the expression for conducting a trial. If the mother concludes that her own child was at fault, she will warn him and tell him he got what he deserved. If she concludes that the fault lay with someone else's child, she will loudly complain to the parents of the aggressor and demand that he be punished and controlled in the future. I have seen this happen and believe it is the normal procedure. When injury to a child is serious or permanent, an actual assault and damages litigation is initiated with the local elders. Older boys are warned against fighting on the grounds that they will involve their parents in lawsuits. Thus, as predicted on grounds of a psychological hypothesis, Nuer parents are permissive toward the aggression of their children and, in fact, actively encourage it, while Gusii parents do not tolerate fighting but promote reliance on adult intervention for the settlement of disputes.

This finding suggests that there may be a relationship between the difference in values concerning aggression on the part of Nuer and Gusii adults, and the concomitant difference in aggression-training of children in the two societies.

DISCUSSION

Since Nuer and Gusii are both segmentary lineage societies, a theory which uses total-societal structures (acephalous segmentary lineages, central state organization, etc.) as the sole means of differentiating one political system from another would be hard put to explain why their contemporary patterns of political behavior under British rule are divergent. I have attempted to explain the divergence in terms of differing values, institutionalized in their political systems and internalized by individuals as they grow up in the family.

The Nuer, whose present-day judicial leaders shrink from passing judgment on and penalizing their fellow men, are seen as having an egalitarian ethic manifested in many aspects of their life, including community and family relations. In their early years, Nuer boys are treated in a nurturant and non-punitive way by their fathers, a pattern which personality theorists have hypothesized as antecedent to the learning of egalitarian values. The persistent feuding of the Nuer is part of a wider value-orientation favoring personal aggressiveness in which honor is easily offended and violence begun on trifling provocation. On the childhood level, Nuer individuals grow up in a mileu of adults who permit and encourage their fighting, and it is suggested here that this promotes the development of aggressive behavior patterns.

The Gusii, whose present-day judicial leaders are only too willing to pass judgment on and to punish members of their own group, are characterized by authoritarian values exhibited in many facets of interpersonal behavior on the local and family levels. Gusii fathers are emotionally distant from and physically punitive toward their young sons, which may be a necessary prerequisite for the internalization of authoritarian values. The tendency of Gusii men to disvalue aggression, attempt to avoid it, and to resolve aggressive conflict in court whenever possible is paralleled by the tendency of parents to express disapproval of childish aggression and to encourage children to report fighting to their elders. This child-training experience probably serves to inhibit overt aggressiveness in the individual and to strengthen litigiousness as an alternative behavior pattern.

By virtue of their greater willingness to submit to hierarchical authority and their greater inhibitions concerning the expression of aggression, the Gusii were able to make a more rapid and "satisfactory" adaptation to a colonial administration which required these very characteristics of them than were the Nuer, whose values concerning authority and aggression were contradictory to the demands of the British government. If and when the Nuer accept the idea of decision-making and peaceful conflict resolution at the level of the total society, they are likely to develop leadership patterns which are less autocratic than those of the contemporary Gusii, but their intergroup antagonisms and preference for local autonomy may block the acceptance of large-scale political integration.

It is not suggested here that child-training variables are independent determinants of political behavior but rather that they are shaped and selected by the functional requirements of local authority systems, just as any social group trains its members to conform to the rules which help maintain it. Thus child training may be *cause* with respect to the behavior of individuals, but is *effect* with respect to the traditional values which aid in the maintenance of social structures. If a pattern of child training is operating effectively, it is producing individuals whose personal values conform to the social values of the groups in which they participate as adults. Furthermore, the analysis presented here does not suggest that value-influenced child rearing practices are the only, or even the most important determinants of political behavior. Since the Gusii and Nuer are matched on two important sets of independent variables, that is, the tradtional structure of group affiliations and the nature of the colonizing power, it has been possible to detect in clearest form the influence of other variables such as child training. My claim is that these latter variables account for some of the cross-cultural variance in political behavior, but not for all of it. While the validity of the analysis presented here is by no means established, it has, at the very least, the advantage of differentiating between two societies whose outward forms of political organization are similar. Furthermore, the aspects of childhood experience in which differences were found were not selected on an impressionistic basis but were investigated because of the indications from psychological theory and research that they are antecedents to personal behavior concerning authority and aggression. The differences in childhood experience conform to the expectations generated by psychological research. Finally, the theoretical approach used here is consistent with the hypothesis of Bruner based on research among American Indians:

That which was traditionally learned and internalized in infancy and early childhood tends to be most resistant to change in contact situations.

This hypothesis lends plausibility to the persistence, under British administration, of those traditional Nuer and Gusii political values which are internalized in the early years of life.

It has not been the purpose of this article to launch an attack on the study of political structure as such, but to add to it a new dimension which, hopefully, will increase its explanatory power by bringing it simultaneously closer to the realities of contemporary politics and to the findings of behavioral sciences other than social anthropology. In line with this aim, it is possible to draw two conclusions from the above study which bear on the comparative analysis of political behavior.

CONCLUSIONS

1) An invariant correspondence between sociopolitical organization at the total-society level and values concerning authority should not be assumed to hold cross-culturally. In the particular case of stateless societies, it is fallacious to assume synonymity between the balanced opposition of equal segments and egalitarian political values, or to assume that corporate lineages are inherently egalitarian. The notion that sociopolitical organization at the total-society level varies concomitantly with authority values should be treated as an hypothesis to be tested empirically. For this purpose, the unit of comparison should be a relatively universal decision-making unit such as the local community. The degree of concentration of authority within local units could

be rated for a large number of societies which would also be classified according to their total-society organizations (see Figure 1). If the hypothesis is valid, then most societies would fall in the cells on the upper-right and lower-left of the chart, that is, stateless societies would prove to have a low concentration of authority within their local units and states would prove to have a high concentration of authority in comparable units. It would also be possible to compare the authority structures of stateless societies having different types of total-society organization, as well as the local authority systems of states of different kinds of central organization. If there were no significant correlations between total society organization and local authority structure, then the influence of other variables on local authority structure would assume high priority for further research.

2) All societies have authority structures and values concerning the allocation of authority. In stateless societies, the proper unit for the analysis of such phenomena is not the total society, where we are likely to mistake lack of a central political hierarchy for egalitarianism, but the maximal decision-making unit (or some cohesive subgrouping within it). Most often this unit corresponds to the village, but it may be a cluster of villages, a hamlet or neighborhood, or even a domestic group such as the polygynous extended family. The local decision-making unit provides adult individuals with a model for behavior toward incipient authority structures in the wider society, and it is simultaneously the model from which the child learns values concerning authority. This dual function is likely

		Total Society Organization					
		Stateless Societies			States		
		Multikin Villages and Bands	Segmentary Lineages	Age and Associational Groups	Segmentary States	Federative States	Centralized States
Degree of Concentration of Authority Within Local Units	Very High						
	High						
	Low						
	Very Low						

FIGURE 1

to continue even after national administration has drastically altered the nature of total-societal political organization by bringing it under state control. For this reason, the analysis of authority and other political values at the local level is most likely to yield valid predictions about contemporary political behavior in newly introduced governmental institutions.

22. PEASANT SOCIETY AND THE IMAGE OF LIMITED GOOD

GEORGE M. FOSTER

Reproduced by permission of the American Anthropological Association from American Anthropologist, *Vol. 67, No. 2, 1965. George M. Foster is Professor of Anthropology at the University of California, Berkeley. He is interested particularly in peasant society, social factors in technological change, public health, and community development. His professional experience includes field work in Mexico and Spain and service as AID adviser in countries such as Zambia, Afghanistan, India, Nepal, Pakistan, and the Philippines. He served as President of the American Anthropological Association in 1970. He is the author of* Culture and Conquest: America's Spanish Heritage, Traditional Cultures and the Impact of Technological Change, *and* Tzintzuntzan: Mexican Peasants in a Changing World.

■ This paper by George Foster introduces us to one of the more interesting and heated debates in anthropology. A major characteristic of national societies is their social and economic diversity based largely on occupational specialization. This heterogeneity is usually manifest in a system of socioeconomic classes paralleling a political continuum from the rich élites to the poor disenfranchised. None of these subgroups is homogeneous; the poorest strata of such a society include both landowning and self-supporting peasants and landless laborers who work for wages. In this selection we will deal with peasants. In Selection 17 we considered the religious aspect of peasant adaptation; in the following selection, by George Foster, we turn to the values by which peasants seek to legitimate and rationalize their way of life, and especially their poverty, as part of their adaptation to the conditions of their social and technological habitat.

The major theme of Foster's essay is the concept of "limited good." Limited good is expressed in many ways in different societies—for example, as in a Jamaican peasant community that I have studied (Selection 29): "One man's rise is another man's fall." The concept is not confined to peasant societies, however; it is widespread throughout the preindustrial world and among many groups in the lower strata of industrialized societies. In the following selection, Foster describes it in terms of its relevance to the peasant way of life. The obverse of this image is the ideology of affluent people in an industrial society, who believe that "there is enough for everyone" and that it is an ethical imperative for each individual to try to improve his socioeconomic position.

In one of the best known critiques of Foster's paper, Chandra Jayawardena ("Ideology and Conflict in Lower Class Communities" in *Comparative Studies in Society and History*, 10 [1968] : 413-46) takes strong issue with Foster's stress on feelings of distrust in peasant communities and the resulting obstacles to the emergence of local leaders and voluntary associations. Jayawardena stresses the solidarity among the workers that he and others observed among Guyanese plantation workers and other proletarians who have rebelled against their employers. Jayawardena, however, appears to proceed on the assumption that since both peasants and hired laborers live at the bottom of the social heap in a complex agricultural nation, and since both are denied social equality with its dominant class, both should be expected to exhibit the same norms with respect to trust and leadership. But status is not a material determinant; it is actually little more than a convenient abstraction. Jayawardena and other of Foster's critics, I believe, overlook the fact that peasants, such as those described by Foster, are landowners or tenants, while plantation workers are landless; the latter are workers in factories in the fields.

This simple fact should lead us to expect important differences between their ideological systems. Proletarian workers are often exhorted that they have nothing to lose but their chains, and when they have little faith in the social order they sometimes do "unchain" themselves. Peasants have a great deal to lose—their land—and this is one of the reasons for their conservatism.

Foster emphasizes that the image of limited good is based on the peasant's reality: "good" is truly limited in the peasants' world. This concept has nonetheless stirred considerable controversy among anthropologists since its original publication. Some of the principal articles it has stimulated are: "Foster's 'Image of Limited Good': An Example of Anthropological Explanation," by David Kaplan and Benson Saler (*American Anthropologist*, 68 [1966]: 202-6), and "Further Remarks on Foster's 'Image of Limited Good,'" by John Bennett (*American Anthropologist*, 68 [1966]: 206-10); Foster's reply to these two papers follows Bennett's paper. Others include "'The Image of Limited Good': Comments on an Exercise in Description and Interpretation," by Steven Piker(*American Anthropologist*, 68 [1966]: 1202-11), and "'Peasant Society and the Image of Limited Good': A Critique," by John G. Kennedy (*American Anthropologist*, 68 [1966]: 1212-25).

Foster has explored this concept in greater detail in his monograph, *Tzintzuntzan: Mexican Peasants in a Changing World* (Boston: Little, Brown, 1967). Three additional monographs that should be consulted for further exploration among these lines are: *Machine Age Maya: The Industrialization of a Guatemalan Community*, by Manning Nash (Chicago: University of Chicago Press, 1967); *Agrarian Revolt in a Mexican Village*, by Paul Friedrich (Englewood Cliffs, N.J.: Prentice-Hall, 1970); and *The Irish Countryman: An Anthropological Study*, by Conrad M. Arensberg (2nd edition, Garden City, N.Y.: Natural History Press, 1968). ∎

Human behavior is always motivated by certain purposes, and these purposes grow out of sets of assumptions which are not usually recognized by those who hold them. The basic premises of a particular culture are unconsciously accepted by the individual through his constant and exclusive participation in that culture. It is these assumptions —the essence of all the culturally conditioned purposes, motives, and principles—which determine the behavior of a people, underlie all the institutions of a community and give them unity.

Human beings in whatever culture are provided with cognitive orientation in a cosmos: there is "order" and "reason" rather than chaos. There are basic premises and principles implied, even if these do not happen to be consciously formulated and articulated by the people themselves. We are confronted with the philosophical implications of their thought, the nature of the world of being as they conceive it. If we pursue the problem deeply enough we soon come face to face with a relatively unexplored territory—ethno-metaphysics. Can we penetrate this realm in other cultures? What kind of evidence is at our disposal?... The problem is a complex and difficult one, but this should not preclude its exploration.

COGNITIVE ORIENTATION

THE MEMBERS of every society share a common cognitive orientation which is, in effect, an unverbalized, implicit expression of their understanding of the "rules of the game" of living imposed upon them by their social, natural, and supernatural universes. A cognitive orientation provides the members of the society it characterizes with basic premises and sets of assumptions normally neither recognized nor questioned which structure and guide behavior in much the same way grammatical rules unrecognized by most people structure and guide their linguistic forms. All normative behavior of the members of a group is a function of their particular way of looking at their total environment, their unconscious acceptance of the "rules of the game" implicit in their cognitive orientation.

A particular cognitive orientation cannot be thought of as world view in a Redfieldian sense, that is, as something existing largely at a conscious level in the minds of the members of the group. The average man of any society cannot describe the underlying premises of which his behavior is a logical function any more than he can outline a phonemic statement which expresses the patterned regularities in his speech. As Kluckhohn has pointed out, cognitive orientations (he speaks of "configurations") are recognized by most members of a society only in the sense that they make choices "with the configurations as unconscious but determinative backgrounds."

In speaking of a cognitive orientation—the terms "cognitive view," "world view," "world view perspective," "basic assumptions," "implicit premises," and perhaps "ethos" may be used as synonyms—I am as an anthropologist concerned with two levels of problems: (1) the nature of the cognitive orientation itself which I see as something "psychologically real," and the ways in which and the degree to which it can be known; and (2) the economical representation of this cognitive orientation by means of models or integrating principles which account for observed behavior, and which permit prediction of behavior yet unnoted or unperformed. Such a model or principle is, as Kluckhohn has often pointed out, an inferential construct or an analytic abstraction derived from observed behavior.

A model or integrating principle is not the cognitive orientation itself, but for purposes of analysis the two cannot be separated. A well-constructed model is, of course, not really descriptive of behavior at all (as is, for example, the term "ethos" as used by Gillin to describe contemporary Latin American culture). A good model is heuristic and explanatory, not descriptive, and it has predictive value. It encourages an analyst to search for behavior patterns, and relationships between patterns, which he may not yet have recognized, simply because logically—if the model is sound—it is reasonable to expect to find them. By the same token, a sound model should make it possible to predict how people are going to behave when faced with certain alternatives. A model therefore has at least two important functions: it is conducive to better field work, and it has practical utility as a guide to policy and action in developmental programs.

A perfect model or integrating principle of a particular world view should subsume *all* behavior of the members of a group. In practice it is unreasonable to expect this. But the best model is the one that subsumes the greatest amount of behavior in such fashion that there are no mutually incompatible parts in the model, that is, forms of behavior cast together in what is obviously a logically inconsistent relationship. Kluckhohn speculated about the possibility of a single model, a dominant "master configuration" characterizing an entire society, for which he suggested the terms "integration" and "ethos," but I believe he never attempted the task of describing a complete ethos. Opler, on the other hand, has described Lipan Apache culture in terms of twenty "themes" which are,

however, to a considerable extent descriptive and which in no way approximate a master model.

How does an anthropologist fathom the cognitive orientation of the group he studies, to find patterns that will permit building a model or stating an integrating principle? Componential analysis and other formal semantic methods have recently been much in vogue, and these techniques unquestionably can tell us a great deal. But the degree of dissension among anthropologists who use these methods suggests that they are not a single royal road to "God's truth." I suspect there will always remain a considerable element of ethnological art in the processes whereby we come to have some understanding of a cognitive orientation. However we organize our thought processes, we are engaging in an exercise in structural analysis in which overt behavior (and the simpler patterns into which this behavior is readily seen to fall) is viewed somewhat as a reflection or representation of a wider reality which our sensory apparatus can never directly perceive. Or, we can view the search for a cognitive view as an exercise in triangulation. Of each trait and pattern the question is asked, "Of what implicit assumption might this behavior be a logical function?" When enough questions have been asked, the answers will be found to point in a common direction. The model emerges from the point where the lines of answers intersect. Obviously, an anthropologist well acquainted with a particular culture cannot merely apply simple rules of analysis and automatically produce a model for, or even a description of, a world view. In effect, we are dealing with a pyramidal structure: low-level regularities and coherences relating overt behavior forms are fitted into high-level patterns which in turn may be found to fall into place at a still higher level of integration. Thus, a model of a social structure, sound in itself, will be found to be simply one expression of a structural regularity which will have analogues in religion and economic activities.

Since all normative behavior of the members of a group is a function of its particular cognitive orientation, both in an abstract philosophical sense and in the view of an individual himself, all behavior is "rational" and sense-making. "Irrational" behavior can be spoken of only in the context of a cognitive view which did not give rise to that behavior. Thus, in a rapidly changing world, in which peasant and primitive peoples are pulled into the social and economic context of whole nations, some of their behavior may appear irrational to others because the social, economic, and natural universe that in fact controls the conditions of their life is other than that revealed to them—however subconsciously—by a traditional world view. That is, a peasant's cognitive view provides moral and other precepts that are guides to—in fact, may be said to produce—behavior that may not be appropriate to the changing conditions of life he has not yet grasped. For this reason when the cognitive orientation of large numbers of a nation's people is out of tune with reality, these people will behave in a way that will appear irrational to those who are more nearly attuned to reality. Such peoples will be seen as constituting a drag (as indeed they may be) on a nation's development, and they will be cutting themselves off from the opportunity to participate in the benefits that economic progress can bring.

In this paper I am concerned with the nature of the cognitive orientation of peasants, and with interpreting and relating peasant behavior as described by anthropologists to this orientation. I am also concerned with the implications of this orientation and related behavior to the problem of the peasant's participation in the economic growth of the country to which he may belong. Specifically, I will outline what I believe to be the dominant theme in the cognitive orientation of classic peasant societies, show how characteristic peasant behavior seems to flow from this orientation, and attempt to show that this behavior—however incompatible with national economic growth—is not only highly rational in the context of the cognition that determines it, but that for the maintenance of peasant society in its classic form, it is indispensable. The kinds of behavior that have been suggested as adversely influencing economic growth are, among many, the "luck" syndrome, a "fatalistic" outlook, inter- and intra-familial quarrels, difficulties in cooperation, extraordinary ritual expenses by poor people and the problems these expenses pose for capital accumulation, and the apparent lack of what the psychologist McClelland has called

"need for Achievement." I will suggest that peasant participation in national development can be hastened not by stimulating a psychological process, the need for achievement, but by creating economic and other opportunities that will encourage the peasant to abandon his traditional and increasingly unrealistic cognitive orientation for a new one that reflects the realities of the modern world.

2. The model of cognitive orientation that seems to me best to account for peasant behavior is the "Image of Limited Good." By "Image of Limited Good" I mean that broad areas of peasant behavior are patterned in such fashion as to suggest that peasants view their social, economic, and natural universes—their total environment—as one in which all of the desired things in life such as land, wealth, health, friendship and love, manliness and honor, respect and status, power and influence, security and safety, *exist in finite quantity* and *are always in short supply*, as far as the peasant is concerned. Not only do these and all other "good things" exist in finite and limited quantities, but in addition *there is no way directly within peasant power to increase the available quantities*. It is as if the obvious fact of land shortage in a densely populated area applied to all other desired things: not enough to go around. "Good," like land, is seen as inherent in nature, there to be divided and redivided, if necessary, but not to be augmented.

For purposes of analysis, and at this stage of the argument, I am considering a peasant community to be a closed system. Except in a special—but extremely important—way, a peasant sees his existence as determined and limited by the natural and social resources of his village and his immediate area. Consequently, there is a primary corollary to The Image of Limited Good: if "Good" exists in limited amounts which cannot be expanded, and if the system is closed, it follows that *an individual or a family can improve a position only at the expense of others*. Hence an apparent relative improvement in someone's position with respect to any "Good" is viewed as a threat to the entire community. Someone is being despoiled, whether he sees it or not. And since there is often uncertainty as to who is losing—obviously it may be ego—*any* significant improvement is perceived, not as a threat to an individual or a family alone, but as a threat to *all* individuals and families.

This model was first worked out on the basis of a wide variety of field data from Tzintzuntzan, Michoacán, Mexico: family behavior, exchange patterns, cooperation, religious activities, court claims, disputes, material culture, folklore, language, and many other bits and pieces. At no point has an informant even remotely suggested that this is his vision of his universe. Yet each Tzintzuntzeno organizes his behavior in a fashion entirely rational when it is viewed as a function of this principle which he cannot enunciate.

The model of Limited Good, when "fed back" to behavior in Tzintzuntzan, proved remarkably productive in revealing hitherto unsuspected structural regularities linking economic behavior with social relations, friendship, love and jealousy patterns, health beliefs, concepts of honor and masculinity, *egoísmo* manifestations—even folklore. Not only were structural regularities revealed in Tzintzuntzan, but much peasant behavior known to me from other field work, and reported in the literature, seemed also to be a function of this cognitive orientation. This has led me to offer the kinds of data I have utilized in formulating this model, and to explain the interpretation that seem to follow from it, as characterizing in considerable degree classic peasant societies, in the hope that the model will be tested against other extensive bodies of data. I believe, obviously, that if the Image of Limited Good is examined as a high-level integrating principle characterizing peasant communities, we will find within our individual societies unsuspected structural regularities and, on a cross-cultural level, basic patterns that will be most helpful in constructing the typology of peasant society. The data I present in support of this thesis are illustrative, and are not based on an exhaustive survey of peasant literature.

2.1. When the peasant views his economic world as one in which Limited Good prevails, and he can progress only at the expense of another, he is usually very near the truth. Peasant economies, as pointed out by many authors, are not productive. In the average village there *is* only a finite amount of wealth produced, and no amount of extra hard work will

significantly change the figure. In most of the peasant world land has been limited for a long, long time, and only in a few places have young farmers in a growing community been able to hive off from the parent village to start on a level of equality with their parents and grandparents. Customarily land is not only limited, but it has become increasingly limited, by population expansion and soil deterioration. Peasant productive techniques have remained largely unchanged for hundreds, and even thousands, of years; at best, in farming, this means the Mediterranean plow drawn by oxen, supplemented by human-powered hand tools. Handicraft techniques in weaving, pottery-making, wood-working and building likewise have changed little over the years.

In fact, it seems accurate to say that the average peasant sees little or no relationship between work and production techniques on the one hand, and the acquisition of wealth on the other. Rather, wealth is seen by villagers in the same light as land: present, circumscribed by absolute limits, and having no relationship to work. One works to eat, but not to create wealth. Wealth, like land, is something that is inherent in nature. It can be divided up and passed around in various ways, but, within the framework of the villagers' traditional world, it does not grow. Time and tradition have determined the shares each family and individual hold; these shares are not static, since obviously they do shift. But the reason for the relative position of each villager is known at any given time, and any significant change calls for explanation.

2.2. The evidence that friendship, love, and affection are seen as strictly limited in peasant society is strong. Every anthropologist in a peasant village soon realizes the narrow path he must walk to avoid showing excessive favor or friendship toward some families, thereby alienating others who will feel deprived, and hence reluctant to help him in his work. Once I brought a close friend from Tzintzuntzan, working as a bracero in a nearby town, to my Berkeley home. When safely away from the camp he told me his brother was also there. Why did he not tell me, so I could have invited him? My friend replied, in effect, that he was experiencing a coveted "good" and he did not want to risk diluting the satisfaction by sharing it with another.

Adams reports how a social worker in a Guatemalan village unwittingly prejudiced her work by making more friends in one barrio than in the other, thereby progressively alienating herself from potential friends whose help she needed. In much of Latin America the institutionalized best friend, particularly among post-adolescents, variously known as the *amigo carnal*, or the *cuello* or *camaradería* (the latter two described by Reina for Guatemala) constitutes both recognition of the fact that true friendship is a scarce commodity, and serves as insurance against being left without any of it. The jealousies and feelings of deprivation felt by one partner when the other leaves or threatens to leave sometimes lead to violence.

Widespread peasant definitions of sibling rivalry suggest that a mother's ability to love her children is viewed as limited by the amount of love she possesses. In Mexico when a mother again becomes pregnant and weans her nursing child, the child often becomes *chípil*. It fusses, cries, clings to her skirt, and is inconsolable. The child is said to be *celoso*, jealous of its unborn sibling whose presence it recognizes and whom it perceives as a threat, already depriving him of maternal love and affection. Chípil is known as *chip* or *chipe* in Guatemala, where it is described in a classic article by Paul, as *sipe* in Honduras, and simply as *celos* ("jealousy") in Costa Rica. *Chucaque* in southern Colombia, described as the jealousy of a child weaned because of its mother's pregnancy, appears to be the same thing.

A similar folk etiology is used among the semi-peasant peoples of Buganda to explain the onset of *kwashiorkor* in a child recently weaned. If the mother is again pregnant, the child is said to have *obwosi*, and shows symptoms of pale hair, sweating of hands and feet, fever, diarrhea, and vomiting. "The importance of pregnancy is such that if a woman takes a sick child to a native doctor the first question he asks is 'Are you pregnant?'." The African logic is the reverse of, but complementary to, that of Latin America: it is the *unborn child* that is jealous of its older sibling, whom it tries to poison through the mother's milk, thereby forcing weaning. In both areas, insufficient quantities of love and affection are seen as precipitating the crisis. In Buganda, "In the local culture it is essential that the mother should devote herself to the unborn child or a child recently born, at the expense of any other children; *there does not seem to be an easy acceptance of the idea that there can be enough love for all*."

Similarly, in an Egyptian village, sibling rivalry is recognized at this period in a child's development. As in Latin America, jealousy is one way; it is always the older who is jealous of the younger. "It is also acknowledged that the youngest child becomes jealous immediately his mother's abdomen becomes enlarged on pregnancy and he is usually told of the forthcoming event." This jealousy, in excess, may have ill effects on the child, causing diarrhea, swellings, lack of appetite, temper tantrums, and sleeplessness.

In parts of Guatemala chipe is a term used to express a husband's jealousy of his pregnant wife, for temporary loss of sexual services and for the attention to be given to the baby. Tepoztlán husbands also suffer from *chipilez*, becoming sleepy and not wanting to work. Oscar Lewis says a husband can be cured by wearing a strip of his wife's skirt around his neck. In Tonalá, Jalisco, Mexico, husbands often are jealous of their adolescent sons and angry with their wives because of the affection the latter show their offspring. A wife's love and affection are seen as limited; to the extent the son receives what appears to be an excessive amount, the husband is deprived. In the Egyptian village described by Ammar a new mother-in-law is very affectionate toward her son-in-law, thereby making her own unmarried sons and daughters jealous. By showing affection to the outsider, the woman obviously is seen as depriving her own offspring of something they wish.

2.3. It is a truism to peasants that health is a "good" that exists in limited quantities. Peasant folk medicine does not provide the protection that scientific medicine gives those who have access to it, and malnutrition frequently aggravates conditions stemming from lack of sanitation, hygiene, and immunization. In peasant societies preoccupation with health and illness is general, and constitutes a major topic of interest, speculation, and discussion. Perhaps the best objective evidence that health is viewed within the framework of Limited Good is the widespread attitude toward blood which is, to use Adams' expression, seen as "non-regenerative." For obvious reasons, blood is equated with life, and good blood, and lots of it, means health. Loss of blood—if it is seen as something that cannot be renewed—is thus seen as a threat to health, a permanent loss resulting in weakness for as long as an individual lives. Although best described for Guatemala, the belief that blood is non-regenerative is widespread in Latin America. This belief, frequently unverbalized, may be one of the reasons it is so difficult to persuade Latin Americans to give blood transfusions: by giving blood so that someone can have more, the donor will have less.

Similar beliefs are found in Nigeria and they are well known in Indian peasant villages. Here the psychological problem is further compounded by the equation of blood with semen: one drop of semen to seven (or forty, depending on area) drops of blood. The exercise of masculine vitality is thus seen as a permanently debilitating act. Only so much sexual pleasure is allotted man, and nothing he can do will increase his measure. Sexual moderation and the avoidance of blood-letting are the course of the prudent man.

In parts of Mexico (for example, the Michoacán villages of Tzintzuntzan and Erongarícuaro) the limits on health are reflected in views about long hair. A woman's long hair is much admired, but the price is high: a woman with long hair is thought always to be thin and wan, and she cannot expect to have vigor and strength. Sources of vitality are insufficient to grow long hair and still leave an individual with energy and a well-fleshed body.

2.4. Oft-noted peasant sensitiveness to real or imagined insults to personal honor, and violent reactions to challenges which cast doubt on a man's masculinity, appear to be a function of the belief that honor and manliness exist in limited quantities, and that consequently not everyone can enjoy a full measure. In rural Mexico, among braceros who have worked in the United States, American ethnologists have often been asked, "In the United States it's the wife who commands, no?" Masculinity and domestic control appear to be viewed much like

other desirable things: there is only so much, and the person who has it deprives another. Mexican men find it difficult to believe that a husband and wife can share domestic responsibilities and decision making, without the husband being deprived of his *machismo*. Many believe a wife, however good, must be beaten from time to time, simply so she will not lose sight of a God-decreed familial hierarchy. They are astonished and shocked to learn that an American wife-beater can be jailed; this seems an incredibly unwarranted intrusion of the State into God's plans for the family.

The essence of machismo is valor, and *un hombre muy valiente*, that is, a *macho*, is one who is strong and tough, generally fair, not a bully, but who never dodges a fight, and who always wins. Above all, a macho inspires *respeto* ("respect"). One achieves machismo, it is clear, by depriving others of access to it.

In Greece *philotimo*, a "love of honor," equates closely with Mexican machismo. A man who is physically sound, lithe, strong, and agile has philotimo. If he can converse well, show wit, and act in other ways that facilitate sociability and establish ascendency, he enhances his philotimo. One attacks another male through his philotimo, by shaming or ridiculing him, by showing how he lacks the necessary attributes for a man. Consequently, avoiding ridicule becomes a major concern, a primary defense mechanism among rural Greek males. In a culture shot through with envy and competitiveness, there is the ever-present danger of attack, so a man must be prepared to respond to a jeer or insult with a swift retort, an angry challenge, or a knife thrust. "Philotimo can be enhanced at the expense of another. It has a see-saw characteristic; one's own goes up as another's declines . . . the Greek, in order to maintain and increase his sense of worth, must be prepared each moment to assert his superiority over friend and foe alike. It is an interpersonal combat fraught with anxiety, uncertainty, and aggressive potentials. As one proverb describes it, 'When one Greek meets another, they immediately despise each other'."

3. If, in fact, peasants see their universe as one in which the good things in life are in limited and unexpandable quantities, and hence personal gain must be at the expense of others,

we must assume that social institutions, personal behavior, values, and personality will all display patterns that can be viewed as functions of this cognitive orientation. Preferred behavior, it may be argued, will be that which is seen by the peasant as maximizing his security, by preserving his relative position in the traditional order of things. People who see themselves in "threatened" circumstances, which the Image of Limited Good implies, react normally in one of two ways: maximum cooperation and sometimes communism, burying individual differences and placing sanctions against individualism; or extreme individualism.

Peasant societies seem always to choose the second alternative. The reasons are not clear, but two factors may bear on the problem. Cooperation requires leadership. This may be delegated democratically by the members of a group itself; it may be assumed by a strong man from within the group; or it may be imposed by forces lying outside the group. Peasant societies—for reasons that should be clear in the following analysis—are unable by their very nature to delegate authority, and assumption of authority by a strong man is, at best, temporary, and not a structural solution to a problem. The truncated political nature of peasant societies, with real power lying outside the community, seems effectively to discourage local assumption and exercise of power, except as an agent of these outside forces. By the very nature of peasant society, seen as a structural part of a larger society, local development of leadership which might make possible cooperation is effectively prevented by the rulers of the political unit of which a particular peasant community is an element, who see such action as a potential threat to themselves.

Again, economic activities in peasant societies require only limited cooperation. Peasant families typically can, as family units, produce most of their food, farm without extra help, build their houses, weave cloth for their clothes, carry their own produce to market and sell it— in short, take care of themselves with a degree of independence impossible in an industrial society, and difficult in hunting-fishing-gathering societies. Peasants, of course, usually do not live with the degree of independence here suggested, but it is more nearly possible than in any other type of society.

Whatever the reasons, peasants are individualistic, and it logically follows from the Image of Limited Good that each minimal social unit (often the nuclear family and, in many situations, a single individual) sees itself in perpetual, unrelenting struggle with its fellows for possession of or control over what it considers to be its share of scarce values. This is a position that calls for extreme caution and reserve, a reluctance to reveal true strength or position. It encourages suspicion and mutual distrust, since things will not necessarily be what they seem to be, and it also encourages a male self image as a valiant person, one who commands respect, since he will be less attractive as a target than a weakling. A great deal of peasant behavior, I believe, is exactly what we would predict from these circumstances. The works of Lewis, Banfield, Simmons, Carstairs, Dube, the Wisers, and Blackman and many others testify to the "mentality of mutual distrust" that is widespread in peasant societies.

Since an individual or family that makes significant economic progress or acquires a disproportionate amount of some other "good" is seen to do so at the expense of others, such a change is viewed as a threat to the stability of the community. Peasant culture is provided with two principal mechanisms with which to maintain the essential stability:

(*a*) an agreed-upon, socially acceptable, preferred norm of behavior for its people, and

(*b*) a "club" and a "carrot," in the form of sanctions and rewards, to ensure that real behavior approximates this norm.

The agreed-upon norm that promotes maximum community stability is behavior that tends to maintain the status quo in relationships. The individual or family that acquires more than its share of a "good," and particularly an economic "good," is, as we have seen, viewed as a threat to the community at large. Individuals and families which are seen to or are thought to progress violate the preferred norm of behavior, thereby stimulating cultural mechanisms that redress the imbalance. Individuals or families that lose something, that fall behind, are seen as a threat in a different fashion; their envy, jealousy, or anger may result in overt or hidden aggression toward more fortunate people.

The self-correcting mechanisms that guard

the community balance operate on three levels:

(1) Individual and family behavior. At this level I am concerned with the steps taken by *individuals* to maintain their positions in the system, and the ways in which they try to avoid both sanctions and exploitation by fellow villagers.

(2) Informal and usually unorganized group behavior. At this level I am concerned with the steps taken by the *community*, the sanctions that are invoked when it is felt someone is violating the agreed-upon norm of behavior. Negative sanctions are the "club."

(3) Institutionalized behavior. At this level I am concerned with the "carrot": major community expressions of cultural forms which neutralize achieved imbalances. Each of these forms will be examined in turn.

3.1. On the individual-family level, two rules give guidance to preferred behavior. These can be stated as:

(*a*) Do not reveal evidence of material or other improvement in your relative position, lest you invite sanctions; should you display improvement, take action necessary to neutralize the consequences.

(*b*) Do not allow yourself to fall behind your rightful place, lest you and your family suffer.

A family deals with the problem of real or suspected improvement in its relative position by a combination of two devices. First, it attempts to conceal evidence that might lead to this conclusion, and it denies the veracity of suggestions to this effect. Second, it meets the charge head on, admits an improvement in relative position, but shows it has no intention of using this position to the detriment of the village by neutralizing it through ritual expenditures, thereby restoring the status quo.

Accounts of peasant communities stress that in traditional villages people do not compete for prestige with material symbols such as dress, housing, or food, nor do they compete for authority by seeking leadership roles. In peasant villages one notes a strong desire to look and act like everyone else, to be inconspicuous in position and behavior. This theme is well summed up in the Wisers' paragraph on the importance of dilapidated walls suggesting poverty as a part of a family's defense.

Also much remarked is the peasant's reluctance to accept leadership roles. He feels—for good reason—that his motives will be suspect and that he will be subject to the criticism of neighbors. By seeking, or even accepting, an authority position, the ideal man ceases to be ideal. A "good" man therefore usually shuns community responsibilities (other than of a ritual nature); by so doing he protects his reputation. Needless to say, this aspect of socially-approved behavior heavily penalizes a peasant community in the modern world by depriving it of the leadership which is now essential to its development.

The mechanism invoked to minimize the danger of loss of relative position appears to center in the machismo-philotimo complex. A tough, strong man whose fearlessness in the face of danger, and whose skill in protecting himself and his family is recognized, does not invite exploitation. A "valiant" individual can command the "respect" so much sought after in many peasant societies, and he can strive toward security with the goal in mind (however illusory) of being able to live—as is said in Tzintzuntzan—*sin compromisos* ("without obligations" to, or dependency on, others). A picture of the ideal peasant begins to emerge: a man who works to feed and clothe his family, who fulfills his community and ceremonial obligations, who minds his own business, who does not seek to be outstanding, but who knows how to protect his rights. Since a macho, a strong man, discourages exploitation, it is clear that this personality characteristic has a basic function in peasant society. Not surprisingly, defense of this valuable self-image may, by the standards of other societies, assume pathological proportions, for it is seen as a basic weapon in the struggle for life.

The ideal man must avoid the appearance of presumption, lest this be interpreted as trying to take something that belongs to another. In tracing the diffusion of new pottery-making techniques in Tzintzuntzan I found that no one would admit he had learned the technique from a neighbor. The inevitable reply to my question was *Me puse a pensar* ("I dreamed it up all by myself"), accompanied by a knowing look and a tapping of the temple with the forefinger. Reluctance to give credit to others, common in

Mexico, is often described as due to *egoísmo*, an egotistical conceited quality. Yet if egoísmo, as exemplified by unwillingness to admit profiting by a neighbor's new pottery knowledge, is seen as a function of an image of Limited Good, it is clear that a potter *must* deny that the idea is other than his own. To confess that he "borrowed" an idea is to confess that he has taken something not rightfully his, that he is consciously upsetting the community balance and the self image he tries so hard to maintain. Similarly, in trying to determine how compadrazgo (godparenthood) ties are initiated, I found no informant who admitted he had asked a friend to serve; he always was asked by another. Informants appear to fear that admission of asking may be interpreted as presuming or imposing on another, trying to get something to which they may not be entitled.

A complementary pattern is manifest in the general absence of compliments in peasant communities; rarely is a person heard to admire the performance of another, and when admiration is expressed by, say, an anthropologist, the person admired probably will try to deny there is any reason to compliment him. Reluctance of villagers to compliment each other again looks, at first glance, like egoísmo. But in the context of the Limited Good model, it is seen that such behavior is proper. The person who compliments is, in fact, guilty of aggression; he is telling someone to his face that he is rising above the dead level that spells security for all, and he is suggesting that he may be confronted with sanctions.

Consider this interpretation as applied to an incident reported in southern Italy: "My attempt, in private, to praise a peasant friend for his large farm and able system of farming brought a prompt and vigorous denial that he did anything special. He said, 'There is no system, you just plant.' This attitude was expressed by others in forced discussions of farming." Dr. Cancian offers this as illustrating the peasant's lack of confidence in his own ability to change his environment. Speaking specifically of agriculture, he writes that "All the examples indicate denial of the hope of progress in agriculture and alienation from the land." I believe the peasant viewed Dr. Cancian's praise as threatening, since it reminded him of his vulnerability because of his superior farming methods. His denial is not of hope of progress, but of cause for anyone to envy him.

3.2. The ideal man strives for moderation and equality in his behavior. Should he attempt to better his comparative standing, thereby threatening village stability, the informal and usually unorganized sanctions appear. This is the "club," and it takes the form of gossip, slander, backbiting, character assassination, witchcraft or the threat of witchcraft, and sometimes actual physical aggression. These negative sanctions usually represent no formal community decision, but they are at least as effective as if authorized by law. Concern with public opinion is one of the most striking characteristics of peasant communities.

Negative sanctions, while usually informal, can be institutionalized. In peasant Spain, especially in the north, the charivari (*cencerrada*) represents such an instance. When an older man marries a much younger woman—usually a second marriage for the groom—marriageable youths serenade the couple with cowbells (*cencerros*) and other noisemakers, parade straw-stuffed manikins representing them through the streets, incense the manikins with foul-smelling substances, and shout obscenities. It seems clear that this symbolizes the resentment of youths, who have not yet had even one wife, against the inequalities represented by an older man who has already enjoyed marriage, who takes a young bride from the available pool, thereby further limiting the supply for the youths. By institutionalizing the sanctions the youths are permitted a degree of freedom and abuse not otherwise possible.

3.3. *Attempted* changes in the balance of a peasant village are discouraged by the methods just described; *achieved* imbalance is neutralized, and the balance restored, on an institutional level. A person who improves his position is encouraged—by use of the carrot—to restore the balance through conspicuous consumption in the form of ritual extravagance. In Latin America he is pressured into sponsoring a costly fiesta by serving as *mayordomo*. His reward is prestige, which is viewed as harmless. Prestige cannot be dangerous since it is traded for dangerous wealth; the mayordomo has, in fact, been "disarmed," shorn of his weapons, and reduced to a state of impotence. There is good reason why peasant fiestas consume so much wealth in fireworks, candles, music, and food; and why, in peasant communities the rites of baptism, marriage, and death may involve relatively huge expenditures. These practices are a redistributive mechanism which permits a person or family that potentially threatens community stability gracefully to restore the status quo, thereby returning itself to a state of acceptability. Wolf, speaking specifically of the "closed" Indian peasant community of Mexico as it emerged after the Conquest, puts it this way: "the system takes from those who have, in order to make all men have-nots. By liquidating the surpluses, it makes all men rich in sacred experience but poor in earthly goods. Since it levels differences of wealth, it also inhibits the growth of class distinctions based on wealth. . . . In engineering parlance, it acts as a feedback, returning a system that is beginning to oscillate to its original course."

4. I have said that in a society ruled by the Image of Limited Good there is no way, save at the expense of others, that an individual can get ahead. This is true in a closed system, which peasant communities approximate. But even a traditional peasant village, in another sense, has access to other systems, and an individual can achieve economic success by tapping sources of wealth that are recognized to exist outside the village system. Such success, though envied, is not seen as a direct threat to community stability, for no one within the community has lost anything. Still, such success must be explained. In today's transitional peasant communities, seasonal emigration for wage labor is the most available way in which one can tap outside wealth. Hundreds of thousands of Mexican peasants have come to the United States as braceros in recent years and many, through their earnings, have pumped significant amounts of capital into their communities. Braceros generally are not criticized or attacked for acquisition of this wealth; it is clear that their good fortune is not at the direct expense of others within the village. Fuller finds a similar realistic appraisal of the wealth situation in a Lebanese community: "they [the peasants] realize . . . that the only method of increasing their incomes on a large scale is to absent themselves from the village for an extended period of time and to find work in more lucrative areas."

These examples, however, are but modern variants of a much older pattern in which luck and fate—points of contact with an open system—are viewed as the only socially acceptable ways in which an individual can acquire more "good" than he previously has had. In traditional (not transitional) peasant communities an otherwise inexplicable increase in wealth is often seen as due to the discovery of treasure which may be the result of fate or of such positive action as making a pact with the Devil. Recently I have analyzed treasure tales in Tzintzuntzan and have found without exception they are attached to named individuals who, within living memory, have suddenly begun to live beyond their means. The usual evidence is that they suddenly opened stores, in spite of their known previous poverty. Erasmus has recorded this interpretation among Sonora villagers, Wagley finds it in an Amazon small town, and Friedmann reports it in southern Italy. Clearly, the role of treasure tales in communities like these is to account for wealth that can be explained in no other manner.

The common peasant concern with finding wealthy and powerful patrons who can help them is also pertinent in this context. Since such patrons usually are outside the village, they are not part of the closed system. Their aid, and material help, like bracero earnings or buried treasure, are seen as coming from beyond the village. Hence, although the lucky villager with a helpful patron may be envied, the advantages he receives from his patron are not seen as depriving other villagers of something rightfully theirs. In Tzintzuntzan a villager who obtains a "good" in this fashion makes it a first order of business to advertise his luck and the source thereof, so there can be no doubt as to his basic morality; this behavior is just the opposite of usual behavior, which is to conceal good fortune.

Treasure tales and concern with patrons, in turn, are but one expression of a wider view: that any kind of success and progress is due to fate, the favor of deities, to luck, but not to hard work, energy, and thrift. Banfield notes in a south Italian community, "In the TAT stories, dramatic success came only as a gift of fortune: a rich gentleman gave a poor boy a violin, a rich gentlewoman adopted an abandoned child, and so on." Continuing, "Great success, then, is obtained by the favor of the saints or by luck, certainly not by thrift, work, and enterprise. These may be important if one is already lucky, but not otherwise, and few would invest large amounts of effort—any more than they would invest large amounts of fertilizer—on the rather remote possibility of good fortune." Friedmann also finds that the south Italian peasant "firmly believes that the few who have succeeded in making a career were able to do so for some mysterious reason: one hit upon a hidden treasure; another was lucky enough to win in the lottery; another was called to America by a successful uncle."

All such illustrations underlie a fundamental truth not always recognized in comparing value systems: in the traditional peasant society hard work and thrift are moral qualities of only the slightest functional value. Given the limitations on land and technology, additional hard work in village productive enterprises simply does not produce a significant increment in income. It is pointless to talk of thrift in a subsistence economy in which most producers are at the economic margin; there is usually nothing to be thrifty about. As Fei and Chang point out, "In a village where the farms are small and wealth is accumulated slowly, there are very few ways for a landless man to become a land-owner, or for a petty owner to become a large landowner. . . . It is not going too far to say that in agriculture there is no way really to get ahead. . . . To become rich one must leave agriculture." And again, "The basic truth is that enrichment through the exploitation of land using the traditional technology, is not a practical method for accumulating wealth." And, as Ammar says about Egypt, "It would be very difficult with the fellah's simple tools and the sweat involved in his work, to convince him that his lot could be improved by more work."

5. It is apparent that a peasant's cognitive orientation, and the forms of behavior that stem therefrom, are intimately related to the problems of economic growth in developing countries. Heavy ritual expenditures, for example, are essential to the maintenance of the equilibrium that spells safety in the minds of traditional villagers. Capital accumulation, which might be stimulated if costly ritual could be simplified, is just what the villager wants to prevent, since he sees it as a community threat rather than a precondition to economic improvement.

In national developmental programs much community-level action in agriculture, health and education is cast in the form of cooperative undertakings. Yet it is abundantly clear that traditional peasant societies are cooperative only in the sense of honoring reciprocal obligations, rather than in the sense of understanding total community welfare, and that mutual suspicion seriously limits cooperative approaches to village problems. The image of the Limited Good model makes clear the peasant logic underlying reluctance to participate in joint ventures. If the "good" in life is seen as finite and nonexpandable, and if apart from luck an individual can progress only at the expense of others, what does one stand to gain from a cooperative project? At best an honorable man lays himself open to the charge—and well-known consequences—of utilizing the venture to exploit friends and neighbors; at worst he risks his own defenses, since someone more skilful or less ethical than he may take advantage of the situation.

The Anglo-Saxon virtues of hard work and thrift seen as leading to economic success are meaningless in peasant society. Horatio Alger not only is not praiseworthy, but he emerges as a positive fool, a clod who not knowing the score labors blindly against hopeless conditions. The gambler, instead, is more properly laudable, worthy of emulation and adulation. If fate is the only way in which success can be obtained, the prudent and thoughtful man is the one who seeks ways in which to maximize his luck-position. He looks for the places in which good fortune is most apt to strike, and tries to be there. This, I think, explains the interest in lotteries in underdeveloped countries. They offer the only way in which the average man can place himself in a luck-position. The man who goes without lunch, and fails to buy shoes for his children in order to buy a weekly ticket, is not a ne'er-do-well; he is the Horatio Alger of his society who is doing what he feels is most likely to advance his position. He is, in modern parlance, buying a "growth stock." The odds are against him, but it is the *only* way he knows in which to work toward success.

Modern lotteries are very much functional equivalents of buried treasure tales in peasant societies, and at least in Tzintzuntzan the correlation is clearly understood. One elderly informant, when asked why no one had found buried treasure in recent years, remarked that this was indeed true but that "Today we Mexicans have the lottery instead." Hence, the "luck" syndrome in underdeveloped countries is not primarily a deterrent to economic progress, as it is sometimes seen from the vantage point of a developed country, but rather it represents a realistic approach to the near-hopeless problem of making significant individual progress.

David C. McClelland has argued persuasively that the presence of a human motivation which he calls "the need for Achievement" (*n* Achievement) is a precursor to economic growth, and that it is probably a *causative* factor, that it is "a change in the minds of men which produces economic growth rather than being produced by it." McClelland further finds that in experimental situations children with high *n* Achievement avoid gambling situations because should they win there would be no sense of personal achievement, while children with low *n* Achievement do not perform in a way suggesting they calculate relative risks and behave accordingly. "They [low *n* Achievement children] thus manifest behavior like that of many people in underdeveloped countries who, while they act very traditionally economically, at the same time love to indulge in lotteries—risking a little to make a great deal on a very long shot." McClelland sees this as showing an absence of a sense of realistic risk calculation.

If the arguments advanced in this paper are sound, it is clear that *n* Achievement is rare in traditional peasant societies, not because of psychological factors, but because display of *n* Achievement is met by sanctions that a traditional villager does not wish to incur. The villager who feels the need for Achievement, and who does something about it, is violating the basic, unverbalized rules of the society of which he is a member. Parents (or government school programs) that attempt to instill *n* Achievement in children are, in effect, training children to be misfits in their society *as long as it remains a relatively static system.*

As indicated above, I would argue in opposition to McClelland that the villager who buys a lottery ticket *is not* behaving in an inconsistent fashion—that is, rationally in traditional economic matters, irrationally in his pursuit of luck—but in the most consistent fashion possible. He *has* calculated the chances and risks, and in a most realistic manner *in the context of the way in which he sees his traditional environment*. The man who buys a lottery ticket in a peasant society, far from displaying lack of *n* Achievement, is in fact showing a maximum degree of it. It simply happens that this is about the only display of initiative that is permitted him by his society, since it is the only form not viewed as a threat to the community by his colleagues.

Banfield, and Fei and Chang, appear to see the economic factors in the presence or absence of initiative in much the same light. The former writes about the Italian peasant, "The idea that one's welfare depends crucially upon conditions beyond one's control—upon luck or the caprice of a saint—and that one can at best only improve upon good fortune, not create it—this idea must certainly be a check on initiative." The latter see, in the Chinese data, evidence that a particular economic attitude is a function of a particular view of life. The traditional economic attitude among Chinese peasants is that of "contentment . . . an acceptance of a low standard of material comfort," which is contrasted to "acquisitiveness" characteristic of "modern industry and commerce in an expanding universe." "Both attitudes—contentment and acquisitiveness—have their own social context. Contentment is adopted in a closed economy; acquisitiveness in an expanding economy. *Without economic opportunities the striving for material gain is a disturbance to the existing order, since it means plunder of wealth from others. . . .* Therefore, to accept and be satisfied with the social role and material rewards given by the society is essential. But when economic opportunity develops through the development of technology and when wealth can be acquired through the exploitation of nature instead of through the exploitation of man, the doctrine of contentment becomes reactionary because it restricts individual initiative." In other words, change the economic rules of the game and change the cognitive orientation of a peasant society, and a fertile field for the propagation of *n* Achievement is created.

For the above reasons, I believe most strongly that the primary task in development is not to attempt to create *n* Achievement at the mother's knee but to try to change the peasants' view of his social and economic universe, away from an Image of Limited Good toward that of expanding opportunity in an open system, *so that he can feel safe* in displaying initiative. The brakes on change are less psychological than social. Show the peasant that initiative is profitable, and that it will not be met by negative sanctions, and he acquires it in short order.

This is, of course, what is happening in the world today. Those who have known peasant villages over a period of years have seen how the old sanctions begin to lose their power. Local entrepreneurs arise in response to the increasing opportunities of expanding national economies, and emulative urges, with the city as the model, appear among these people. The successful small entrepreneurs begin to see that the ideal of equality is inimical to their personal interests, and presently they neither seek to conceal their well being nor to distribute their wealth through traditional patterns of ritual extravagance. *N* Achievement bursts forth in full vitality in a few new leaders, and others see the rewards and try to follow suit. The problem of the new countries is to create economic and social conditions in which this latent energy and talent is not quickly brought up against absolute limits, so that it is nipped in the bud. This is, of course, the danger of new expectations—released latent *n* Achievement—outrunning the creation of opportunities.

Viewed in the light of Limited Good peasant societies are not conservative and backward, brakes on national economic progress, because of economic irrationality nor because of the absence of psychological characteristics in adequate quantities. They are conservative because individual progress is seen as—and in the context of the traditional society in fact is—the supreme threat to community stability, and all cultural forms *must* conspire to discourage changes in the status quo. Only by being conservative can peasant societies continue to exist as peasant societies. But change cognitive orientation through changing access to opportunity, and the peasant will do very well indeed; and his *n* Achievement will take care of itself.

23. AGRICULTURAL ORGANIZATION, SOCIAL STRUCTURE, AND VALUES IN ITALY: AMORAL FAMILISM RECONSIDERED

SYDEL F. SILVERMAN

Reproduced by permission of the American Anthropological Association from American Anthropologist, *Vol. 70, No. 1, 1968. Sydel Silverman was born in Chicago in 1933. She received an M. A. in Human Development from the University of Chicago in 1957 and a Ph.D. in Anthropology from Columbia University in 1963. She joined the Department of Anthropology at Queens College in 1962 and is presently Associate Professor and Chairman of the Department. Mrs. Silverman is primarily interested in peasant society, especially the European Mediterranean. She conducted a community study in the Province of Perugia, Italy in 1960-1961. In 1967 she carried out an exploratory study of a land reform area in Southern Italy. At present she is working on a book on method and the nature of anthropological data.*

■ Ideologies and the social relationships at their base respond to local differences in habitat that are significant within the general strategy of adaptation in which these are imbedded. As Sydel Silverman shows in the following selection, the differing habitats of peasant groups may require somewhat different organizations of productive relations and household and community organization will differ commensurately. Each of these organizations of social relations will call appropriate value systems into play; Silverman shows that these value systems are consequences—rather than determinants—of social relationships, which themselves are accommodations to technological imperatives.

Two areas of Italy are contrasted in this selection; the Center and the Deep South. In the central region, land ownership is concentrated in the hands of a relatively small group. A large proportion of the people are landless participants in a system in which the head of a peasant family enters into a contractual—often antagonistic—relationship with a landowner. This system places a premium on many working hands, leading to the maintenance of three- and four-generation patrilocal extended families. These are in turn accompanied by ramifying interhousehold ties throughout a neighborhood. Correspondingly, this area is characterized by an emphasis on mutual obligations among households, on patron-client relationships, and on formal alliances between families.

In the South, in contrast, the distribution of land ownership is broad and the proportion of landless people is small. Here the productive unit is the nuclear family, or a part of it, and this economic fragmentation of the community is accompanied by less emphasis on inter-household social ties, values of mutual obligation, and formal alliance.

At the end of her article Silverman discusses the implications of her findings for planned social change. She observes that theories of change that give priority to the ideological superstructures of social relations—rather than to their bases in the adaptive strategy—may prevent change from taking place at all. In this light, is it possible that the educational programs in our society that seek to transmit the values of affluent groups to the children of the economically disenfranchised without providing for material change are doomed to failure from their inception?

This article has methodological significance. Silverman's work illustrates the taxonomic method in ethnographic research and shows how materials from different sections of complex societies can be usefully compared and understood.

Robert Redfield's ideas have long been among those dominating anthropological thinking about peasant ways of life; see his books *The Primitive World and its Transformations* (Ithaca: Cornell University Press, 1953), *Peasant Society and Culture : An Anthropological Approach to Civilization* (Chicago : University of Chicago Press, 1956), and *The Little Community : Viewpoints for the Study of A Human Whole* (Chicago: University of Chicago Press, 1955). The Italian Deep South is graphically and memorably portrayed in a novel by Carlo Levi, *Christ Stopped at Eboli* (Baltimore : Penguin Books, 1946). In "Thailand—A Loosely Structured Social System" (*American Anthropologist*, 52 [1950] : 181-93), John F. Embree described a closely related value system. The approach of Edward Banfield in *The Moral Basis of a Backward Society* (Glencoe : The Free Press, 1958), which is criticized by Silverman in this selection, is carried further by Banfield in his latest book, *The Unheavenly City* (Boston : Little, Brown, 1970), in which he discusses the poor in the United States in similar terms. ■

THE PUBLICATION OF Edward C. Banfield's *The Moral Basis of a Backward Society* in 1958 introduced a startling note into the study of Mediterranean societies. The book described a Southern Italian community, with emphasis on political behavior, and it pictured a social system virtually lacking in moral sanctions outside those of the immediate family. The "Montegranesi" were shown as notoriously resistant to cooperation and to any kind of continuing association beyond the nuclear family, unwilling to involve themselves in any public problem or activity in the interest of the community, unable to achieve and maintain formal organizations, and thoroughly self-serving, short-sighted, and fickle in their political acts. To make this behavior intelligible, Banfield suggested that the people behave at all times as if they were following a "rule" that he calls "amoral familism," in his view the dominant ethos of the community: "Maximize the material, short-run advantage of the nuclear family; assume that all others will do likewise."

The concept of "amoral familism" brought forth a rush of justified criticism, and it has continued to be attacked in the years since Banfield proposed it. Yet, now that sufficient time has passed to incorporate the valid criticisms into our thinking, it can be recognized that the concept was an attempt to summarize some salient features of a particular kind of social system, and the fact that it reappears regularly in discussions of Southern Italy suggests that it has a core of validity. It now appears that where Banfield failed was not primarily in his reporting of objective phenomena of this society but in his analytic ordering of those phenomena.

At this writing, Banfield's book remains the best-known treatment of Southern Italian society and the only full-scale account of a Southern community in the published literature. Thus, it may be appropriate to reappraise the work, in the spirit of seeking out its productive aspects. That there are productive aspects to it became evident to me in the course of contrasting the South with the adjacent area of Central Italy. Despite many similarities between the two regions, "amoral familism" seemed wholly alien to the Center. The question of why such an ethos might thrive in one area but not in the other proved helpful in tracing functional interdependencies in the cultural data.

This paper will attempt to answer two questions: (1) in what sense is "amoral familism" a potentially useful concept? and (2) what are the necessary conditions for the existence of an ethos of "amoral familism," that is, the economic and social bases on which it depends? In addition, it may be possible to indicate some of the conditions that need to be changed, if a society of "amoral familists" is to be reformed.

Most of the criticisms that have been levied against Banfield attack his work on two general counts: insufficiencies in his description and weaknesses in his analysis. The objections to Banfield's description emphasize the existence of phenomena that he either minimized or omitted. Thus, it has been pointed out that there is some degree of formal organization in Southern communities (that is, burial societies, recreational clubs, and festival committees), although it is not of great importance in the totality of community life. Extrafamilial ties are not lacking, but those that exist (friendships, patronage relationships, casual groupings, etc.) are shifting, informal, and dyadic. Moreover, political action (as reflected in voting behavior, political machines, and the like) is regular and explicable, though it is flexible and lends itself readily to realignment. These points all supplement Banfield's picture, and they

serve the vital function of turning his description around from an essentially negative statement to a positive one. However, they do not settle the problem he raised. It remains to be explained *why* extrafamilial ties are shifting and dyadic, why political alliances are readily re-formed, and so on. In any case, Banfield's description has not at all been discredited, and anthropologists and others who have worked in Southern Italy generally agree that the behavior he observed in Montegrano is confirmed in essence by the areas they know. At the same time, it should be emphasized that this description was intended only for certain areas of Southern Italy, and there is no basis for applying "amoral familism" to other Mediterranean regions without independent demonstration of its relevance elsewhere.

In general, Banfield was taken to task less for descriptive inadequacies than for his attempt to account for the phenomena described. One critic accepts the premise that ethos shapes behavior, but he offers an alternative ethos; thus, he demonstrates a flaw in Banfield's argument by showing that more than one ethos statement can be derived from and can account for a given set of behavior. This alternative, however, raises more questions than it settles. One is left to wonder why it is that Southern Italians see the world as they do and why it is that they lack certain "conceptual apparatus."

The majority of Banfield's critics (with whom I agree) take the position that an ethos cannot be regarded as a "cause" or satisfactory explanation of behavior. They focus instead on the realistic conditions of Montegranese life, which, to them, easily account for the people's behavior. On the one hand, there are the economic ills of overpopulation, underemployment, land hunger, and an unproductive agriculture. On the other hand, external constraints of the state remove responsibility at the local level, impose restrictive regulations on voluntary organization, and leave limited powers only to officials and those with influence. In these circumstances, the people correctly conclude that political activism is futile. These arguments undoubtedly have validity. Yet "amoral familism" is not the only possible response to the realities of Montegranese existence. Many of the same economic difficulties and governmental constraints have long existed in Central Italy, but there the response has been different. The problem remains, why does one response occur and not another?

At least a partial answer to this problem is in the structure of the rural society of a particular area. In the case of Southern Italy, the basic validity of "amoral familism" may be accepted, but it must be viewed as a reading in moral terms of certain facts of social structure. The position taken here is that "social arrangements make their own values in the process of becoming culture patterns," that social action precedes and gives rise to the norms that symbolize and sanction such action. The ethos of "amoral familism" is a set of ideas that express, evaluate, rationalize, and give meaning to the organization of the Southern Italian rural society. Thus, it is possible to use the "amoral familism" ethos as a summary statement that points up a number of significant features of Southern social organization. These features include:

(1) The nuclear family as the dominant social unit and of overriding functional importance. Each family is an essentially isolated unit.

(2) The absence of corporate groups or informal stable group alliances between the nuclear family and the community. Foster's concept of the "dyadic contract" is relevant to this situation: ties beyond the family are informal, selective, conditional, and hold only between paired individuals.

(3) The temporary and contingent nature of political alignments.

(4) The difficulty of sustaining formal organization ("deliberately concerted action," in Banfield's words) and the absence of leaders in the community (that is, persons who initiate and maintain concerted action on a non-coercive basis).

(5) The weakness of the community as a structural unit. Community-wide activity is slight, and there is no concrete focus for the concept of a public entity.

In sum, Banfield's insight was accurate but his explanation backward: it is not the ethos of "amoral familism" that is the cause of these characteristics of the social system, but they that are the basis of the ethos. For instance, a structural fact is the social isolation of the nuclear family; the idea that "you can't trust outsiders" is merely a statement of how people feel in that situation and how they explain it.

These social structural features, in turn, have their basis in the agricultural system. This causal order is not entirely one-way, for to some extent the organization of agriculture in a given form depends upon certain conditions of social structure. Nevertheless, there are priorities of causation. The agricultural system throws up values directly, and it shapes values indirectly through its effects on social organization; values reinforce agricultural and social patterns but do not create them. These priorities are of crucial importance if one wishes to make statements about change. Thus, although the ethos validates a social system, changing the ideas alone will not alter the social system. Similarly, the social structure (and also the ethos) will respond to changes in the agricultural system, but the latter will not be fundamentally altered merely by manipulating the social structure.

In order to identify those conditions of agricultural organization and social structure that are the basis of "amoral familism," I shall compare the two areas of Southern and Central Italy. They share many of the same problems, including an environment in which agriculture is often difficult, a condition of poverty and ignorance of the masses alongside affluence of the few, and a history of corrupt and restrictive governments. I shall attempt to show how in each area the agricultural organization is directly related to several features of social structure. Furthermore, just as agricultural and social patterns in the two areas contrast, so also do the values that reflect them, including those values that make up the ethos of "amoral familism."

The description of the two areas will outline ideal patterns. It will deal in generalizations; in order to clarify the most predominant patterns, those that appear less frequently will be minimized. The purpose here is not to achieve a comprehensive account of these areas in all their variation, but to point to those characteristic features of agricultural organization which shape distinctive forms of social structure and, in turn, values. The description refers primarily to the time period before World War II. Although the present tense is used throughout, not all statements hold true in the 1960s.

This approach focusses on the local agricultural community in the two areas. This is not to understate the importance of the community's relationship to the larger society; rather, that relationship is viewed as it is played out in the local community. For example, the question of whether major landowners are resident in the agricultural community or absentee depends in large part upon the economic and political history of the state. However, for purposes of the present problem, it is possible to ignore the causes that lie outside and concentrate upon the consequences in the community.

CENTRAL ITALY AND THE DEEP SOUTH

Discussions of Italian culture invariably give lip service to the enormous degree of diversity within that nation, but no framework has yet been offered for defining the boundaries or bases of cultural variation in Italy. In fact, the only significant effort to delimit culture areas of Europe assumes an essential homogeneity of Italy: the "Mediterranean," according to Pitkin's elaboration on Arensberg's scheme, contains all of Italy south of the Po. While any culture-area formulation obviously must encompass considerable variation, in this case the general criteria that define the Mediterranean culture area violate important characteristics of at least one major region, Central Italy. For example, while Central Italy may be considered "essentially urban in its overall orientation," this urban orientation is quite different from that of Southern Italy. Similarly, the peasantry of the Center differ fundamentally from the pecuniary, proletariat-like peasantry of the Mediterranean; stratification patterns in the Central region differ in important ways; and the Mediterranean code of values is to a large extent absent in the Center. Many other differences might be added to this list.

What is needed is a way of demarcating regions similar to the culture area—in that they are based upon a combination of culture traits and focus primarily upon the "folk" traditions —but regions that are less broadly defined than the culture area. For this purpose, it is useful to follow the lead of agricultural economists

who have attempted to mark out agrarian zones of Italy. Agrarian characteristics can provide important clues to identifying units of general cultural significance, because, it is suggested, agricultural organization is highly correlated with other aspects of culture—social structure and value systems. However, while the schemes of the agrarian economist offer a starting point, they are only a starting point. Depending upon the criteria used in drawing up such schemes, it may be appropriate to introduce some changes. Moreover, the hypothesis that there is concordance between agricultural organization, on the one hand, and social structure and values, on the other, must be checked for each area before the zones defined on agrarian criteria can be regarded as cultural zones as well.

For the present problem, the work of the Italian National Institute of Agrarian Economy proved valuable. In their scheme, the area roughly equivalent to Pitkin's "Mediterranean" Italy is divided into three large agrarian-economic zones. (1) "Central Italy" includes the sub-Apennine hills of Emilia and the hills and plains of Tuscany, Umbria, Marche, Lazio, and the Abruzzi provinces of Teramo and Pescara. (2) A broad strip of uplands of the Apennine chain, beginning behind the Ligurian coast and running southeastward through zone (1) along the middle of the peninsula, constitutes the "Northern and Central Apennine Mountains." (3) All of continental Italy south of these two zones is included in "Southern Italy." The term "Central Italy" in this paper refers to the first of these zones, with the exclusion of most of Lazio (an area of very diverse agrarian character) and part of the coastal plain of Tuscany (which is characterized by large estates in extensive cultivation and worked by wage labor). The second zone is not considered in the present discussion. The third zone, "Southern Italy," is very heterogeneous. However, the analysis of Southern agriculture may be simplified by excluding most of Apulia and a number of littoral areas (those that are predominantly in commercially run estates and those in specialized, intensive cultivation); the remainder of the zone is identified as the "Deep South."

Culturally distinctive regions must be delimited in time as well as space. "Central Italy" refers to the period approximately from the early 19th century until World War II. Essentially the same agricultural and social patterns existed for several centuries before, but data on this earlier time are inadequate. On the other hand, since World War II there have been some commercialization of the agricultural economy and a number of significant changes in the social structure of the countryside. The period to which the description of the "Deep South" applies begins in the last decades of the 19th century. Previously, in the years from the Napoleonic regime until after the unification of Italy, the South had been undergoing major changes in land-tenure patterns and other aspects of agricultural organization. The period extends to the postwar years. Since 1950, governmental programs for economic development, particularly land-reform projects, have had some impact on the South.

efforts have contributed to a clarification of some of the dimensions of agricultural systems that can vary independently, and therefore ought to be kept analytically separate, the distribution of roles by no means covers all the essential variables.

For present purposes, agricultural organization is defined as the organization of resources— land, nonlanded capital, and human—for agricultural production. The point of view taken is that of the people involved. The emphasis is upon the organization of people in the manipulation of resources rather than the organization of the ecological system as a whole, and upon the effects of that manipulation on people and their relationships rather than the effects on things (which would involve techniques of cultivation, productivity, and so on).

Each major dimension of the definition involves a number of variables.

AGRICULTURAL ORGANIZATION

If the agricultural system of a region is viewed as the basis of important aspects of its social structure and ethos, it is essential that the concept of agricultural organization be defined comprehensively. No single feature or combination of those features that are commonly the focus of anthropological descriptions —such as agricultural products, land-tenure rules, or the subsistence/market ratio—can suffice.

The complexities of Italian agriculture have stimulated a number of attempts to develop multidimensional approaches to agricultural organization. Thus, Serpieri has achieved a limited typology of Italian agricultural systems by concentrating on the roles of landowner, entrepreneur, and cultivator; the different ways in which these functions are combined in persons identify different agricultural structures. The MacDonalds take this approach a step farther. Pointing out that entrepreneurship actually combines two different functions, decision-making and capitalization, they view agricultural organization in terms of "the structural arrangement of these key economic roles [landownership, operations, management, and investment] and their allocation to various members of the rural population." While these

A. ORGANIZATION OF LAND

A.1. The division of productive land into working units.
A.1.a. The utilization and integration of land units making up an agricultural enterprise.
A.1.b. Size and distribution of land units.
A.2. The stability of the land organization over time.
A.3. The relationship of cultivators to the land.
A.3.a. Rights and obligations of cultivators.
A.3.b. Duration and stability of the relationship over time.
A.3.c. Residence of cultivators with reference to the land they work.

B. ORGANIZATION OF NONLANDED CAPITAL. THE NATURE AND SOURCES OF PERMANENT AND OPERATING CAPITAL

C. ORGANIZATION OF PERSONNEL

C.1 The distribution of functions among persons.
C.2. Relationships among persons performing different functions.

C.3.　The labor unit. The relationship of cultivators to each other, and the organization of the labor unit.

C.4.　The landowners.

C.4.a.　The distribution of land ownership among persons.

C.4.b.　The relationship of land owners to the agricultural enterprise.

C.4.c.　Residence of landowners with reference to their land.

While this outline is not intended as an exhaustive inventory of all traits relevant to the description of agricultural systems, it will provide a basis for comparison of the most striking features of Central and Southern Italian agriculture.

AGRICULTURAL ORGANIZATION AND SOCIAL STRUCTURE IN CENTRAL ITALY

The most typical (or "climax") area of Central Italy, in terms of the following description, is the hills and interior plains of Tuscany and Umbria. The Adriatic zone is similar structurally, but properties and farms tend to be of smaller size there. In general, the region as a whole has a relatively high degree of homogeneity.

A. ORGANIZATION OF LAND

A.1. The division of productive land into working units.

A.1.a. Land is organized into farms dispersed across the countryside. Each farm constitutes a single unified enterprise, and each includes the whole range of crops and livestock in the productive complex. The farm ideally comprises a variety of different resources: arable land (including, if possible, some well-watered plots), olive trees, vines, fruit trees, meadow, pasture land, and woods. The various resources are exploited in a closely integrated manner, in terms of crop rotation, labor expenditures, use of equipment, and so on.

Where a landowner has at least eight or ten farms situated contiguously, they may be further integrated into a *fattoria*, a unit of coordinated production and marketing. The fattoria includes a center containing equipment and services for the common use, such as agricultural machinery, mills, wine cellars, and administrative and sometimes artisan personnel. It is under the direction of the *fattore*, who is usually a trained agricultural technician as well as landlord's agent. (Where a property includes fewer farms or where they are dispersed, a fattore who circulates among several separate farms is frequently employed.)

A.1.b. The size of the farm is limited by two factors: it must be sufficiently large to support a labor unit (a family) of from two to 20 or more individuals, without major dependence upon outside staples, yet within the labor capacity of that unit, given a preindustrial technology. The actual range is from a minimum of two or three hectares (where the land is intensively cultivated) to 30 or more hectares (where cereals predominate and where much land is in pasture or woods). The average size of farms for the whole region is about ten to 15 hectares.

The land of a particular farm is frequently situated within a single bounded entity. However, it may also be divided into a number of nonadjacent plots. In this case, all plots are within easy access of each other and of the farmhouse.

A.2. The integrated farm is maintained as a unit over time, typically for many decades. Each farm has an identity apart from that of the current owner or cultivator. It is valued on the market and transferred to other cultivators and to other proprietors as a unit; alteration of the distribution or the boundaries of land plots is infrequent. Although partible inheritance has been required by law since the early 19th century, the essential integrity of the farm is recognized in the process of inheritance, and breakup of a farm among heirs occurs only under unusual circumstances. This stability of the farm unit is based upon the fact that an effective unit of production requires a combination of the various natural resources, buildings, equipment, etc., that make up a farm; the parts cannot readily be separated and recombined.

A.3. The relationship of cultivators to the land.

A.3.a. Rights and obligations of cultivators are defined by the *mezzadria* contract, an association between a landowner and a peasant family for the cultivation of the farm, on the principle of dividing the investment and the products of the enterprise theoretically half and half. The cultivators' primary obligation is to provide the labor. They receive approximately half of the crops in kind, and half of the cash income from market sales is credited to their account. In addition, they are entitled to cultivate a plot for a kitchen garden and to raise barnyard animals without sharing the profits.

According to a survey based on 1946-1948 data, 59 per cent of the cultivable land area (that is, productive land, exclusive of woods and pasture) of Central Italy is worked under the mezzadria system; 23 per cent is cultivated by peasant proprietors, 6 per cent by cash tenants, 7 per cent by wage laborers, and 5 per cent by sharecroppers working individual plots. Many of the peasant proprietors and tenants, and some of the wage laborers, work self-contained farms similar to those of the mezzadri. For this reason, many of the generalizations made about agricultural organization under the mezzadria system also apply to these other forms of cultivation in Central Italy.

A.3.b. The relationship of cultivators to the land has considerable stability and duration in time. The mezzadria contract is renewed tacitly from year to year, and it is usual for a farm to be occupied by the same family of cultivators for decades, sometimes even for generations. Also contributing to the stability of the mezzadria system are the facts that the terms are made explicit in the contract, contracts are fairly standardized throughout the region, and the whole system is formally controlled by law.

A.3.c. Residence of the cultivators is on the land. Each farm must be provided with a farmhouse, and the peasant family is required to live continually on the farm. Most of the non-mezzadria cultivators also live on farms.

B. ORGANIZATION OF NONLANDED CAPITAL

The capital of the enterprise is provided by both landowner and peasant, according to specific provisions of the mezzadria contract. The farm that the landowner contributes includes—in addition to the farmhouse and cleared land—animal stalls, sheds and other outbuildings, a water supply, and other basic provisions. With the farm, the landowner provides the livestock, whatever inventory (such as hay, feed, and manure) is on the farm, and the most costly equipment. The cultivator is responsible for tools and some of the smaller equipment. Most of the operating expenses are contributed in equal shares by the two parties. The proprietor advances all capital as needed, including the peasant's share, which is debited to his account. Regular reinvestment of capital is also provided for in the contract. Because capital is invested by both landowner and peasant, the risks of the enterprise are shared by both.

C. ORGANIZATION OF PERSONNEL

C.1. The functions of the agricultural enterprise are distributed among several persons: the landowner (*padrone*), the fattore, the *mezzadro* (head of the peasant family), other members of this peasant family. The padrone has effective control of the land, either as outright owner (the usual situation) or as holder of the land by usufruct, rental, or other right. The padrone is the director of the enterprise, a function that he performs either personally or through his representative, the fattore. Decisions are ultimately the padrone's but the mezzadro is consulted on matters directly related to labor; in practice as well as theory, both parties share (albeit unequally) in decision-making. The fattorie sometimes have councils made up of all the family heads, which are used in making and implementing decisions. The fattore's role is as technical advisor and agent to the padrone and as foreman with respect to the cultivators. The mezzadro organizes and directs the labor, which is performed by his family.

C.2. The relationship among persons with functions in the enterprise is hierarchical, with rights to initiation of action following a definite order: landowner—fattore (where present)—mezzadro—others in the peasant family. The padrone-mezzadro relationship is broadly defined and of major importance. They are identified as "partners," in that both are closely involved in the enterprise. However, implicit in the relationship is a clear superordination of the landowner, whose role is ideally one of protection, economic assistance, and general patronage toward the peasant family (a role that is partly spelled out in the formal provisions of the contract and partly an informal expectation). As a result of their mutual participation in the agricultural enterprise, the families of the padrone and the mezzadro interact fairly continuously; this interaction frequently becomes wide-ranging rather than functionally specific. The fattore is generally not involved in any patronage relationship, and his interaction with both landlord and peasant tends to be restricted to the functions of the enterprise.

Despite the complementarity of the landowner-peasant relationship and their mutual concern with the productivity of the enterprise, there is a fundamental opposition of interests between them. While the basic form of the mezzadria association is fixed, there is a continuing push-and-pull over the specific terms, a push-and-pull that is manifested both in attempts on each side to modify the formal contract to their own advantage and in the application of the contract to each case. Furthermore, landowner and peasant are in essentially different positions: the peasant's concern is only with his own farm, while the landowner has several farms and often other economic interests as well; and the peasant's activity is limited to production, while the landowner is involved in marketing, accounting, long-range planning, and sometimes industrial activities related to the agricultural products.

C.3. The labor unit, by requirement of the mezzadria contract, is a peasant family. All members are bound by the contract that the family head enters into, and since family labor cannot ordinarily be diverted to other enterprises, there is a one-to-one relationship between farm and family. The essential minimum mezzadria family includes a male and a female adult. However, the family that is the ideal labor unit is one with a large number of adults and children of both sexes and all ages, upper size limits being set by the possibilities of support of the most productive farms (about 20-30 members). Within these limits, an expanding family has access to larger farms. In a system in which a diversity of crops, combined with animal husbandry, absorbs labor the year round (and, at the same time, increases the yield of the land), a large family group cultivating a

bigger farm means greater unit productivity than the same number of persons working several small farms. Labor can be coordinated for greater efficiency, and less capital investment per person is required. On the other hand, a family with a significantly diminished number of workers may be compelled to move to a smaller farm. In either case, the adjustment between family size and farm size is made primarily by families changing farms.

The labor of the family members is closely coordinated. The mezzadro is the head of the unit, assigning tasks and having sole control of the money. Since most labor is absorbed in the familial organization, there is little place for or availability of hired labor. The primary form in which wage labor is used follows the family model, a hired helper being taken into a mezzadria family with insufficient hands. Labor needs beyond the capacity of the family, which arise at a few crucial times during the agricultural cycle, are met by a system of reciprocal work-exchange among nearby farms.

C.4. The landowners.

C.4.a. The distribution of land ownership tends to a concentration of property within a relatively small group, with a very large proportion of the population, the mezzadri, being landless. Although precise figures are difficult to obtain, data from various sources point to this conclusion. For example, summarizing the results of a comprehensive study of land distribution in Italy in 1946-1948, Medici states: "The data presented demonstrate that it is in Central Italy, particularly in Tuscany, Umbria, and Lazio, where there is the highest degree of concentration of landed property." While there are some peasant proprietors and some noncultivators with small holdings, the development of these types of properties has been impeded in this region. Thus, the general pattern of land ownership is one of a polarization of propertied and landless-peasant classes. The holdings of the landowning group are typically medium- to large-sized, a single landlord owning anywhere from a few family farms to estates of several hundred hectares. It may be noted that the average size of the fattoria (which often includes only part of the landowner's total holdings) is from 150 to 250 hectares, depending upon the particular region.

C.4.b. The relationship of the landowner to

the agricultural enterprise is one of active participation. The landowner, directly or in conjunction with his fattore, is involved in most aspects of production, directing operations, investing and reinvesting, and controlling all major decisions. In many cases, this active role of the proprietors includes a broad interest in agrarian technology.

C.4.c. The landowners reside close to their land, either in the villages or towns around which their farms are dispersed or in nearby urban centers. Absentee owners (whose agricultural concerns are managed by the resident fattori) frequently have part-time residences near their land, where they spend, as a minimum, the summer harvest period.

Given these features of agricultural organization, a number of correlates in the social structuree of Central Italy may be identified.

Community Form

The characteristic community consists of the separated but interdependent town center and dispersed countryside settlement. This plan is directly related to the farm organization, in which each farm corresponds to a separate household, discrete and at some distance from every other household. At the same time, the character of the nucleated center is a consequence of the fact that it is primarily the domain of landowners (living near their land and actively concerned with its management). Even small village centers tend to have an urbane character; a relatively large number of buildings are devoted to commerce, administration, and other services, and a considerable proportion of the residences house prosperous or at least non-rustic families.

Family Organization of Cultivators

As has been seen, there is a premium on households with many working hands. The ideal mezzadria family is the three- or four-generation patrilocal extended family, in which all sons bring their brides into the household. Peripheral unattached relatives, the aged, and small children can all be assets on the farm. Early marriages and high fecundity are desirable, and unrelated orphaned and illegitimate children are readily taken in as extra hands and often adopted.

Relationships within the household are in part concomitants of the agricultural system. The mezzadria contract specifies a formally designated family head, who has both economic and legal authority over and responsibility for the family as a whole. The female head has informal authority over the women, children, and activities around the house. The family is organized hierarchically, with all the children subordinate to the parents until death or formal transference of the headship.

Extrafamilial Relationships

A significant network of social and economic obligations, particularly in the countryside, is formed by the recognition of neighborhoodship. All households within a given radius are considered to be *vicini* (neighbors); the resulting pattern is one of overlapping circles of neighborhoodship. Between vicini there is continuous mutual aid and exchange of services. (In fact, the vicini actually carry out most of the services that ideally are supposed to be performed by kinsmen beyond the household.)

The most important function of the vicini is participation in the traditional system of work exchange, the *aiutarella*. Certain tasks arising regularly throughout the agricultural cycle (the most important of which is the threshing) require that a large number of hands be available on each farm for a short time. The vicini pool their labor to accomplish the task on each farm in turn. The reciprocal exchange is calculated in man-hours; thus, each household gives the same number of man-hours that it receives. This pattern is related to both the dispersion of farms and the scarcity of hands available for temporary hired labor.

Social-class Patterns

The separation of town and country provides the basic distinction in the social-class system: all families associated with the nucleated center are ranked above those identified with the countryside. Within this broad distinction, position in the social-class structure is roughly related to membership in discrete economic groupings. Most families are clearly identified with economic categories, for their occupation or their relationship to the land is full time and long term. The majority of the owners of land fall into two separate groups: the mezzadria padroni (usually with substantial holdings) and the peasant proprietors working their single farm. Similarly, the landless form distinct groups: the artisans and other nonagriculturists, who live inside the town or village; the mezzadri (although they constitute a very large group, there are only minor differences among them); and the few agricultural laborers.

Although landlords and peasants form strongly polarized groups, interaction between them is close and continuing. The mezzadria partnership involves regular contact and close association, and ideally it implies a relationship of personal patronage. This ideal is the traditional model for relationships between the classes as wholes. The proper role of the elite, whether or not they are mezzadria landowners, is one of wide-ranging patronage in relation to members of the lower classes. Such relationships cover a variety of functions, and they tend to be highly personalized.

Political Patterns at the Local Level

The division of the population into discrete groups, with their separate, often opposing interests, has several political implications. Because membership in these groups is relatively permanent, political alignments tend to be stable over time. Political conflicts of local origin turn on their divergent interests, and issues introduced from outside the community readily become translated into them as well. Moreover, the local divisions easily identify themselves with organized class movements of the region and nation. For this reason, Central Italy (particularly the mezzadri) played an important role in the labor organization and agitation that swept parts of the nation in the late 19th and early 20th centuries. This general pattern has continued into the contemporary period. The bids that national political parties make for local support are phrased in terms of the local divisions, and voting behavior in the community follows these lines fairly closely.

Community Organization

Many aspects of community life in the Center are related to the presence in the agricultural community of a landowning class, a class that is prosperous, that is actively involved in their farms and related local concerns, and whose role is defined as one of patronage. Partly in an effort to re-create in the local communities the social activity and elegance of urban life, and partly in the tradition of largesse toward their own clients and toward the community as a whole, the landowners initiate, lead, and support various community associations and activities. Even small centers boast local-level voluntary organizations (bands, dramatic societies, religious confraternities, charity organizations, agricultural cooperatives, etc.). Such associations, as well as other outlets of the landowners' patronage, may add up to a locally originated fulfilment of a number of community functions.

In addition to formal associations of local origin, others are active that are community branches of national organizations. Most conspicuous among these are labor unions, political-party groups, and other organizations focusing around class (or special category) interests.

Community-wide activity is a strong tradition. The ceremonial cycle consists of many events throughout the year, in which the entire community, ideally, participates as a unit. For example, there are series of processions within the community, and to other places, organized Carnival antics, Holy Week enactments, and festivals of special local-significance; often, there is an element of intercommunity rivalry in these occasions. Such activity involves a considerable degree of local initiative and community organization, in which, again, the landowners play a key role.

Summary

Among the social structural features of rural Central Italy that are either consequences of or directly related to agricultural organization, several constitute conditions entirely inconsistent with a society of "amoral familists." The preferred family type is the extended family, a stable and relatively harmonious unit of cooperation, which absorbs the nuclear family. The circles of neighborhoodship are nondiscrete and only informally organized, but they are groups that function for cooperation regularly as a unit. The class structure, based on discrete divisions, each with fairly uniform economic interests, lends support to certain formal organizations. Moreover, this class structure creates stable political alignments, which not only persist over time in the community, but also correspond to regional and national parties and ideologies; this makes political behavior (voting patterns, labor militancy, and so on) quite consistent and predictable, on a regional as well as a community basis. The presence of a local landowning class, who are both prosperous as a group and actively identified with the community, forms the core of a leadership group; most of the locally based formal organizations can be directly attributed to this group. The landowners also account for the existence of a concept of a public entity, in their extension of patronage to the community as a whole (including some acts specifically defined as "for the public benefit"). In addition, the class of local landowners is the catalyst for much of the extensive community-wide activity, among which are ceremonial events that emphasize community solidarity.

AGRICULTURAL ORGANIZATION AND SOCIAL STRUCTURE IN THE DEEP SOUTH

Southern Italy is a patchwork of zones characterized by agricultural arrangements of different types. However, within the region identified here as the "Deep South," agrarian economists recognize two major, discontinuous zones. Most widespread is the zone of "diversified peasant agriculture," in which peasant entrepreneurs raise a number of crops on small, scattered holdings. The second zone is that of the "peasant latifundia," areas of extensive agriculture that are divided up and parceled out to owner-operators and to other cultivators on short-term contracts. Together, these two types cover most of Abruzzi-Molise and Lucania, the interior hills of Campania, scattered parts of Apulia, and most of Calabria behind the Mediterranean coast.

A. ORGANIZATION OF LAND

A.1. The division of productive land into working units.

A.1.a. Throughout the region, land is divided into parcels, each of which is cultivated essentially as an independent unit. (Similarly, land is bought and sold on the market piece by piece rather than in some combination.) A particular cultivator generally works several of these parcels, but there is minimal integration of the several units. Farms, in the sense of unified enterprises with resident cultivators, are virtually absent in the region.

In the "peasant latifundia," most parcels are devoted to wheat and occasionally to other cereals. In the areas of "diversified peasant agriculture," "diversification" has a relative meaning: each cultivator raises wheat (perhaps rotating it with corn or fava), which is combined with one or more additional products (usually grapes, olives, and other shrub and tree crops). Animal husbandry is only slightly developed. Since most cultivators do not have access to a variety of types of land, the full range of subsistence products is rarely provided for in the family enterprise.

A.1.b. The parcels of land are typically small and irregular. The units worked by a given cultivator are generally widely scattered, frequently beyond easy access of each other. There is great variation among cultivators in the number, size, spatial distribution, and quality of the land units worked.

A.2. The division of the land into working units is unstable over time. The land units change hands often, and their dimensions are readily altered. Inheritance practices emphasize the principle of equal shares to all offspring; often this involves not only division of the total property, but also splitting up each plot in order to equalize the quality of land in each share. Through the inheritance process, as well as through dowering in land, parcels tend to be subdivided into fragments of diminishing size, until the limits of practicability are approached.

A.3. The relationship of cultivators to the land.

A.3.a. A variety of different titles and contracts exists, which define the rights and obligations of cultivators. Ownership, rental, share-cropping, and wage labor are all common. Frequently, a particular cultivator works a number of plots on several different bases simultaneously. In order to suggest the relative frequency of the different forms, the results of the 1946-1948 survey may be cited. In Southern Italy as a whole, 41 per cent of the cultivable land area is worked by peasant proprietors, 24 per cent by tenants, 15 per cent by wage laborers, 15 per cent by share-croppers on individual plots, and 5 per cent by mezzadri of the Central Italian type.

The essential features of tenancy (rental) are that the payment is fixed and the cultivator takes full charge of the enterprise, the owner of the land making minimal contribution to costs or operations. Sharecropping is marked by a division of produce in kind between owner and cultivator, but beyond this distinction there is a wide range of variation among the contracts that are prevalent. Most forms of sharecropping in the Deep South leave to the cultivator the main entrepreneurial functions. The contract may apply to a specific plot of land that the sharecropper works independently, to the whole series of operations on a specific crop (with other crops on the same plot worked by other peasants), or only to certain operations related to a specific crop (for example, the sharecropper may perform the labor of the harvest and further handling of certain tree crops, assuming all risks from this point on). Contracts both of tenancy and of sharecropping prevail on holdings of all sizes, and under both kinds of contract the cultivator may utilize his own or his family's labor exclusively or he may use labor which he pays for in wages or in shares. Different types of contracts may coexist on the same plot of land: the ground crops and perhaps also the vines may be cultivated under tenancy, with sharecropping for the tree crops; the ground crops and vines may be sharecropped, while hired laborers are used for the trees; or there may be other combinations. Thus, not only is the cultivator's relationship to the land fragmented in the sense that he works separate, unintegrated plots and that he may work them under different contractual arrangements, but his activity may be limited to only a part of the plot or to only a part of the operations on a crop.

A.3.b. The relationship of the cultivators to the land is unstable. The specific parcels cultivated and the terms under which they are worked change frequently over time. Since land ownership is in flux, peasant proprietors usually do not hold the same plots for a great many years. On the other hand, rental and sharecropping contracts are generally of short duration—for a year or less, rarely longer than

for one cycle of rotation (two to four years). The typical "agricultural enterprise" of the Deep South consists of a cultivator who combines and recombines different pieces of land of his own and other proprietors, changing the combination continually, often from year to year.

The cultivators' relationship to the land is also variable in space. Working arrangements differ from place to place and according to the particular individuals involved; there is little standardization of contracts, and it is common practice for terms to be set competitively on the basis of "what the market will bear."

A.3.c. The residence of cultivators is in fairly large agglomerates, the so-called "agro-towns." Typically, they live at some distance from the land they work. Several hours' traveling time a day is not unusual; even the more enlightened agricultural work contracts of recent years consider three to five kilometers an ordinary distance from residence to fields.

B. ORGANIZATION OF NONLANDED CAPITAL

With a few exceptions, the provision of equipment, animal labor, and working capital is the responsibility of the cultivators, whether they are the owners of the land, tenants, or sharecroppers. Because the peasant must find this capital and sustain the entire risk of the enterprise, capitalization is generally inadequate, limited to the most essential items. Reinvestment in the enterprise is sparse and sporadic, for the preferred forms of investment are fixed savings and nonagricultural property.

C. ORGANIZATION OF PERSONNEL

C.1. The functions of the agricultural enterprise—direction, decision-making, investment, as well as labor—are generally all combined in the person of the cultivator. The differences among the various types of tenure do not substantially modify the general condition of effective isolation of each cultivator (or at most, each family): isolation from sources of capital and technical direction and isolation from other cultivators (for collaboration and reciprocal exchange patterns are absent).

C.2. The relationships among persons connected with the enterprise are correspondingly extremely limited. The noncultivating landowners are mainly rent- or share-collectors. Any ties between a proprietor and the peasant who works his land tend to be brief, unstable, and restricted to the business of the agricultural enterprise. If there is an agent or other middleman, his role is similarly limited to rent-collection.

C.3. The labor unit may consist of an individual, part of a family, or a whole nuclear family, sometimes with the irregular addition of hired day laborers. Access to land is limited by the resources of the family. If they have insufficient land to support themselves (or nothing at all but their labor), they work the scattered parcels of others or combine agriculture with other pursuits. On the other hand, if a family has more land than they can work, they generally contract some or all to other cultivators and become rent-collectors themselves. One reason for this is that the emphasis on wheat (and only a few other crops) minimizes the labor requirement and concentrates it seasonally rather than distributes it the year round. In Southern Italy as a whole, an average of only 56 man-days of labor a year are required per hectare. Since a family's property is not integrated into an entity that can absorb more labor, there would be little advantage to increasing the labor unit itself. Thus, regardless of the size of the holding, there is no basis on which the small family group can be built up into a larger, more complex economic unit.

To the extent that the nuclear family forms a labor unit, its organization tends to be loose. In general, some family members are apt to spend part of their time in pursuits other than the family's land—hiring out for wages on a day-labor basis, working at nonagricultural tasks, and so on. Even when the entire family is fully occupied on their land, the lack of integration of the land units does not encourage a close coordination of family labor.

C.4. The landowners.

C.4.a. The distribution of landownership is broad, and in most areas properties of various sizes occur together. The frequently given picture of Southern Italy as a region of a few large landowners and masses of landless is erroneous. (Moss and Cappannari provide an example of this misconception in their description of the typical situation in the pre-reform South as one in which "the individual peasant rarely owned his own land" and in which estates owned by "large-scale absentee landlords" were the rule.) This view of large properties dominating the South has been contradicted by land-tenure surveys ever since the Italian Parliament investigated the conditions of the Southern peasantry at the beginning of this century. For instance, Serpieri summarizes his comprehensive study of the 1929-1938 period by disputing the belief that Italy as a whole (and the South in particular) suffers from an excessive concentration of land ownership:

> There is little foundation in fact—except for local and particular situations—to the dangers of . . . large properties and landed monopolies in a country in which landed property is widely distributed among a great number of proprietors and the large properties . . . represent only 13 per cent of the total landed income, while the [small properties] represent more than half [56.5 per cent].

This statement is even more true of Southern Italy than of the nation as a whole; in comparison with the national medians, Southern Italy has fewer large properties and more small ones (as measured both by per cent of area and per cent of income). The only regions that have a higher proportion of large properties or a lower proportion of small ones are in the North (Lombardy and Veneto) and Center (Emilia, Tuscany, Umbria, and Lazio). Medici comes to essentially the same conclusions from the results of the INEA study of the immediate postwar years.

The broad distribution of land ownership in Southern Italy is evident from the fact that there are 22.6 private properties per 100 inhabitants (excluding properties of less than $\frac{1}{4}$ hectare). This is the largest proportion of any zone in Italy; Central Italy is near the opposite extreme, with only 5.4, while the national median is 10.7. The average size and value of these properties are, of course, relatively small. However, the most striking characteristics of Southern landholding are (1) the wide range of variation, from landlessness to small holdings to medium-sized and large properties, with all degrees well represented; and (2) the continual circulation of property: landless peasants acquire small plots, smallholders and larger landlords increase their properties, while the reverse processes also occur constantly.

C.4.b. As has already been suggested, noncultivating landlords have a marginal relationship to the agricultural enterprise. They tend to remain detached both from active involvement in their own properties and from agricultural concerns in general.

C.4.c. The smaller noncultivating landowners reside in the agro-towns, along with the agriculturists. Owners of larger properties generally live in the cities, renting their land to middlemen or hiring agents to look after their financial interests in the agricultural community. In any case, absentee ownership is the common goal of landlords.

It is evident that this agricultural system contrasts at many points with that of Central Italy. Similarly, several features of Southern Italian social structure, which can be related to this agricultural organization, present contrasts with the Center.

Community Form

The rural population is clustered into large towns, and the countryside is uninhabited. The character of the agro-town is diverse, since it includes agricultural workers, landowners of small to medium scale, and the nonagricultural provincial elite.

Family Organization of Cultivators

The nuclear family is the rule. In the first place, this agricultural system imposes severe limitations on the size of the family unit. The access of cultivators to land is restricted to what they can acquire or work on a short-term basis, and their control of even such limited land resources is unstable.

However, the difficulty of sustaining extended families involves more than a lack of enough land to support a larger group, because even the more prosperous families retain the nuclear form. On the one hand, the organization of land offers no impetus for large, economically coordinated families. On the other hand, the fragmentation and dispersal of the economic pursuits of family members create a constant pressure toward splits into minimal family units. In the case of families that gain ownership of sizeable properties, the withdrawal from agricultural work, combined with the practice of partible inheritance, militates against the formation of extended families.

Extrafamilial Relationships

Because of the fragmentation of economic activity there is no basis for stable cooperative associations between households. Each small family group makes its own way by combining and improvising a variety of different sources of sustenance. Neighborhoodship, which is of such fundamental importance in Central Italy, is insignificant here. First of all, the close clustering of the whole population in towns diminishes the dependence of neighbors upon each other. At the same time, the random arrangement of residences in the towns does not place persons of common interests in exclusive, close proximity. Moreover, there is no functional necessity for work exchange among cultivators; temporary wage workers are available in abundance to fulfill occasional labor needs in excess of a family's capacity.

Corresponding to the individual nature of economic pursuits, ties beyond the household, both horizontal (friends, friendly kinsmen, etc.) and vertical (patrons and clients), take the form of informal contracts between paired individuals. The next nondyadic social unit beyond the nuclear family is the community itself, for there is no functional basis for any division into stable groups smaller than the town.

Social-class Patterns

The social-class system of Southern Italy is generally described as disjunctive, with division into an upper and a lower class. However, within the larger lower class, the broad distribution of landholding, together with the variety and overlapping of different arrangements for working the land, creates a situation in which persons are ranked along a continuous range. Status is not determined by membership in discrete categories: a "landlord" might be just a slightly better-off peasant, a "peasant" is often a part-time nonagricultural worker, agriculturalists are also townsmen, and so on. In this situation, there can be no sharp boundaries between economic and social groupings. An individual's rank is decided by his own particular combination of arrangements at any given time —the quantity of land owned, the occupations practiced, and other attributes.

Vertical relationships between the elite and the lower class are sporadic. The agricultural system does not offer any model for such relationships. Patronage ties are formed on bases other than agricultural roles, but they tend to be less stable and more impersonal than the padrone-mezzadro relationship of Central Italy. In contrast to the mezzadria pattern, there is neither the reinforcement by the necessity for close and continuous contact nor the historical tradition of a landowner's *noblesse oblige* toward his "own" peasants.

Political Patterns at the Local Level

The political characteristics of the Southern community are to a large extent accounted for by the absence of discrete groups with economic interests distinctive to themselves and opposed to those of other groups. Political alignments are shifting. Rather than follow distinct categorical lines, they are formed about particular issues or particular powerful persons, and when new issues arise or other powers are involved, realignments readily occur. Furthermore, political affiliations form locally, on local issues, and they are not easily extended to regional or national divisions. It is this fluidity over time and this priority of local terms that have made voting behavior in the Southern communities often appear erratic.

Since few persons have full-time and non-conflicting membership in a particular category, it is difficult for identification to be made with organized class movements. The MacDonalds have made the point that in the South the traditional reaction to economic difficulty has never been class-based militancy, but rather individual and familistic strategies—notably migration. Typically, the aim of such migration has also been familistic rather than class-oriented—to return and raise the nuclear-family group a few notches on the local rank scale.

Community Organization

The scarcity of formal organizations in the community can be related to two factors: the lack of stable group interests and associations larger than the nuclear family, and the absence of a leadership group. Recreational clubs may be introduced by political-party and other initiative from the outside with varying degrees of success, but formal associations of local origin are lacking. The elite members of the rural community dissociate themselves from agricultural interests and other local affairs and look outward to the cities, with which they identify themselves and to which they aspire. In addition, since patronage is limited to temporary ties with individual clients only, the community as a whole does not benefit either materially or organizationally.

Community-wide activity is infrequent, usually limited to one festival a year. Church sponsorship generally plays a more important role in it than local initiative.

Summary

In this description there appear those social-structural characteristics of which "amoral familism" is the expression: the prevalence and isolation of the nuclear family, the absence of functioning groups beyond the family, the instability of political alignments, the rarity of local formal associations, and the weakness of the community entity. These features have been seen to be based on the agricultural organization of the Deep South—in particular, the nonintegration and instability of land units, the fragmentation of economic activity, the isolation of the cultivator in the conduct of the agricultural enterprise, the broad range and fluctuation in the distribution of land ownership, and the absence of locally based major landowners.

VALUES

The ethos of "amoral familism" may be viewed as emerging out of Southern Italian social patterns. To the extent that moral sanctions are lacking in relation to persons outside the nuclear family, this is a reflection of the scarcity of lasting extrafamilial ties. The contrast provided by Central Italy is instructive, for in this region the value system recognizes important mutual obligations (that is, "morality") between neighbors, patrons and clients, co-members of formal associations, those who share certain socioeconomic conditions, and even members of the same community. As has been seen, all of these relationships constitute relatively stable alliances.

Other aspects of the "amoral familism" ethos are also expressions of Southern social organization: the mistrust of persons outside the immediate family, the skeptical attitude toward cooperation, the absence of a concept of "common good," the unwillingness to identify oneself with either a "public interest" or a special-group interest. Closely related to this ethos is a general apprehensiveness toward the world and the future and a feeling of helplessness about one's ability to control the environment. This view of the world is at least in part a statement about (1) the noncontinuity of the relationship to the land, and (2) the impermanence of alliance relationships both with social equals and with protectors.

In a number of other ways, the dominant values of the typically Mediterranean areas of Italy contrast with those of Central Italy, along lines corresponding to differences in agricultural and social organization. In general, the literature on Southern Italy has been more concerned with values than with their structural origins. Much of the interest in Southern Italian values was stimulated by Redfield's "excursion into problems of peasantry as a human type," in which he proposed a complex of recurrent "peasant attitudes and values." This complex included: an intimate and reverent attitude to the land, the idea that agricultural work is good and commerce not so good, an emphasis on productive industry as a prime virtue, a sober attitude toward sex and marriage, a tendency to minimize sexual experience as a good in itself, and a distaste for violence. However, students of Southern Italy had contradictory evidence. They offered a picture of cultivators who are not reverent toward the land but feel themselves enslaved by it, who value and are sophisticated in matters of money and commerce, who regard manual labor as degrading, who prize leisure above work of any kind, who emphasize sexual exploit, and who engage in violence for the demonstration of masculinity.

Insofar as these values concern attitudes toward the land and the economic world in general, they can be related directly to the dispersal of the Southern cultivators' activity and their unstable relationship to the land they work. Central Italy provides a marked contrast. Although (perhaps partly because) the mezzadri are not peasant proprietors, there is a semipermanent association of families with particular farms, and on the farm is concentrated all the family's activity and effort. Since the farm unit itself has great stability over time and since the peasant family tends to occupy the same farm for many years, there is a strong identification with the land they work. While this does not necessarily imply love for the soil or a reverent attitude, the farm tends to be the center of interest, the focus of the traditional way of life.

Moreover, where there is continuity of occupation of the land and where resources are managed in an integrated manner—as is the case in the Center—productive industry may have its rewards. The Southern pattern of cultivating plots for short spans of time encourages the peasant to aim for short-term exploitation of the land, rather than patiently to invest his labor in work that pays off only in the long run. The Southern value on leisure (as opposed to industriousness) may be merely a reflection of organizational inadequacies of the agricultural system. In Central Italy, leisure is valued in another sense: it represents primarily the landowners' freedom to indulge themselves in the "civilized" activities appropriate to their role.

The lack of self-sufficiency of the Southern agricultural family, and the fact that most families either hire some of their labor out for wages or hire laborers themselves, imply involvement in the market. In this situation, there is a premium on skill in manipulating money and commerce. The mezzadri, in contrast, are in effect in a subsistence economy: their share of the produce is mainly consumed for their own subsistence, and most money dealings are handled by the landowner. Thus, pecuniary sophistication is lacking. Commercial values have positive connotations because of their association with the prestigious landowning and nonagricultural classes, but they are not part of mezzadro life.

The values related to manual labor also differ in the two regions. Among the diverse population of the Southern agro-town, whether or not one works with his hands is an important status distinction. In Central Italy this distinction exists, but it is submerged by more critical lines of differentiation. Above all, there is the contrast between townsman and country-man. The town (or village) group is further subdivided, essentially into *signori* and common-folk. While manual workers (artisans) are placed in the lower group, so are most white-collar workers, merchants, policemen, and agricultural foremen. The class structure breaks up along different lines in the two regions. In the South, the agricultural worker is likely to be simul-taneously or in close succession also a non-agricultural laborer; a separation between manual and nonmanual worker is more easily made. In the Center, agriculturists and non-agriculturists form distinct groups, and their difference is underlined by the separateness of the spheres of town and country; in the presence of these distinctions, the mark of working with the hands recedes into the back-ground.

In a sense, the values related to sex have some basis in the agricultural system. Family honor in Southern Italy, as in other Mediterranean areas, is largely vested in the virginity of the girls. Masculinity is asserted (sometimes vio-lently) by the protection of one's own virgins, the vindication of one's violated girls, and the conquest of other families' virgins. In Central Italy, these themes of virginity and the contest over it are much softened. Girls have consider-able freedom of movement, loss of virginity is not taken seriously, violence is almost unheard of, and the whole subject is injected with humor. Insofar as the mezzadri are concerned, the reason is clear: because of the value of extra hands on the farm, the prime quality of a potential wife (in addition to her skill in farmwork) is fecundity. Pregnancy in an engaged girl merely hastens the marriage date and is often welcomed by all concerned. In fact, in some areas "trial marriage" is practiced, to avoid the conclusion of an infertile marriage; a successful trial is, of course, one that results in pregnancy, and a marriage in church follows quickly.

In both Central and Southern Italy, urbanity is a central value: the city is ultimately the source of all that is most highly prized by the society as a whole. In both regions, "civiliza-tion" (*civiltà*) is of fundamental importance, and it implies urbanity: the best of all persons, things, behaviors, etc., are "civilized," which requires, as a minimum, being urbanized.

Furthermore, in both regions, town and village in many ways replicate in miniature the culture patterns of the city. At the same time, urban values have quite different form and meaning in the two areas.

All members of the Southern community—elite, petty landowner, and landless cultivator alike—play out the major part of their lives in an urban-like agglomerate. The piazza, the marketplace, the café are their natural habitat. Even the lowest strata are directly involved in town life, though their participation in some areas of it may be limited. In Central Italy, in contrast, a significant part of the population—the cultivators—are marginal to the life of the nucleated center. Their participation in it is restricted to special occasions, and they are regarded by all (including themselves) as out-siders in village or town. The major portion of their activity and interest is on the farm and in the circle of farms surrounding their own. Nevertheless, they know of urban life indirectly, through close contact with the landowners.

Southern Italy lacks a soil-bound tradition. Agricultural and "country" interests are incon-sistent with the values of the Southern elite, and these values are shared by the whole society. Here, values flow in only one direction, the sources being exclusively urban. In Central Italy, on the other hand, there is a two-way flow. Although urban values have priority, there are others that originate in the countryside. The agriculturalists of the Center are peasants in the sense of carrying on "a common and traditional way of life into which their agri-culture intimately enters." The land is the focus of a distinctive folk tradition. Furthermore, the landowning class has its own traditions, in which their land, their peasants, and their sojourns in the country have an important place, although they are themselves urbanites in every sense of the word.

Urban values have a different significance in the two regions in still another way. In the South, each individual or small family aspires to emulate ever more closely the "civilized," urbane ideals of the society. This is the motive for the petty peasant proprietor so readily becoming an inactive rentier. Within the limited possibilities open to the cultivator (and emi-gration has long offered the best opportunities), these values become personal goals. In Central

Italy, with the sharp demarcation between town and country and between landlord and peasant, civiltà is the hallmark of the landowning class. While the cultivators recognize the same values, they do not adopt them as personal aspirations, for it is virtually impossible to bridge the gap separating them from the "civilized" group.

In the Center, civiltà and other urban values are most readily attained by the peasants indirectly, through the identity of the community as a whole. To a large extent *campanilismo* in Central Italy takes the form of pride (touched with cynicism) in the greater "civilization" of one's own community in comparison with others of similar size. It is, of course, the landowners—in their own style of living and in their leadership of and material contributions to community activity—who establish the community's "civilization." This content appears to be lacking in the campanilismo of Southern Italy, which is generally expressed merely as a defensive deprecation of other communities.

IMPLICATIONS FOR CHANGE

Southern Italy has long been regarded as a "problem" area—by the Italian government, by the Southerners themselves, and by social scientists and other observers. Since World War II, it has been the target of several programs for agricultural reform, industrial development, and various other aspects of social change. In the continuing dialogue over what ought to be done for and to the South, a prominent place is given to the need for reforming elements of the ethos of "amoral familism" and the social-structural conditions they reflect. There is unanimous agreement on the necessity for change but serious disagreement on the strategy for change.

In Banfield's view, the problem centers around the ethos itself:

That the Montegranesi are prisoners of their family-centered ethos—that because of it they cannot act concertedly or in the common good—is the fundamental impediment to their economic and other progress.

The present discussion has emphasized that the Southern Italians are "prisoners" not of their ethos but of their agricultural system. Therefore,

agriculture organization must be central to any program for reform. I have argued that changes in social patterns and in ethos will follow from modifications in the agricultural system, and I have attempted to indicate the specific features of agricultural organization that underlie "amoral familism." However, this is not to suggest that desired social and attitudinal changes occur entirely automatically and with appropriate speed. Training must also be provided in those skills that are necessary in the altered social and moral order, such as literacy, the means of functioning in a national-scale political system, techniques for implementing cooperative alliances, and so on.

If the priorities in the causal order argued here are accepted only as an hypothesis, it is one that can readily be tested. In various areas of Southern Italy, agricultural changes have already been enacted. In general, land reform has meant a redistribution of large estates in dispersed fragments to peasants of the area; this has increased the proportion of land in peasant proprietorship, but it has not significantly altered agricultural organization. However, in certain reclamation zones, land has been reorganized into farms on which families have been settled, technical assistance and credit facilities have been made available, and cultivators' cooperatives have been fostered. A locally based holistic study of what happens after these changes are instituted would make it possible to determine whether different social patterns are formed, whether changes in values follow, whether "amoral familism" loses its foothold. It would be especially useful to have these findings in conjunction with an adequate and comparable study of a traditional, still "amorally familistic" community in the same area. Such a project is now in the planning stages.

Central Italy no less than the South is today in need of agricultural reform and development. The situation described in this paper has been significantly modified in recent years. An agricultural system that was relatively effective—in the context of a traditional society and in comparison with less fortunate areas during the same period—now is in crisis. The form of the system has been retained, but its functioning has changed. Technological advances and an increasing orientation to outside markets have altered the distribution of roles and have made the mezzadria arrangement steadily less rewarding. In addition, there has been a depolarization of landowning and peasant classes, and the major landlords have become detached from the agricultural enterprise and from the rural community; these changes, too, have undermined the agricultural system. Moreover, there is little doubt that the agricultural organization of traditional Central Italy is poorly adapted to a modernized national society and to full integration into a European economy.

A theory of change that gives priority to ethos can have unfortunate consequences. It may lead to programs for change that concentrate on values, with inadequate treatment of the agricultural base. Worse, it may lead to minimizing efforts at change because people are believed to be hopelessly enmeshed in an ethos. If it is misleading for the social scientist to regard values as the foundation of a society, it can be tragic for the planner to do so.

24. AMERICAN CULTURAL VALUES

CONRAD M. ARENSBERG AND ARTHUR H. NIEHOFF

Reprinted from Conrad M. Arensberg and Arthur H. Niehoff, Introducing Social Change *(second edition) (Chicago: Aldine · Atherton, 1971). Copyright © 1971 by Conrad M. Arensberg and Arthur H. Niehoff. Conrad M. Arensberg is Professor of Anthropology at Columbia University, where he has taught for many years. He has studied the cultures of a variety of peoples throughout the world, including American Indians, the people of the Middle East, Japanese Americans, Detroit factory workers, and peasants in India and Ireland. He is the author of* The Irish Countryman: An Anthropological Study *and co-author (with Solon T. Kimball) of* Family and Community in Ireland. *Arthur H. Niehoff received his Ph.D. in anthropology at Columbia University. He has served as a curator at the Milwaukee Public Museum, community development adviser for AID in Laos, research scientist at the George Washington University, and teacher in several universities. He is now chairman of the Department of Anthropology at California State College, Los Angeles. His professional experience includes field work in South and Southeast Asia, Africa, and Latin America.*

■ We have considered the value systems of peasants in Mexico and Italy. The adaptive roles of these systems have been observed, especially as an aspect of the heterogeneity of their societies. We are all familiar with the ideological oppositions that reflect the heterogeneity of society in the United States today. We will consider these oppositions in the next two selections; this Introduction will serve for both of them.

Both selections represent value systems that begin with the same premises. An industrial strategy of adaptation has led to a degree of material abundance never before known in human history, a domination of the landscape by industrial urban centers, and an unparalleled mastery over the habitat. This social and technological order produces values by which people respond to the habitat and enable them to sustain it: "Man is the master of his milieu; he is perfectible by improving his material conditions and by controlling his habitat." These statements mirror the optimism that is often spoken of as American but that is actually the standard of an industrial strategy of adaptation. The habitat consists of a series of challenges to be overcome and conquered; the rectification of undesirable conditions is inseparable from attempts to establish a just and compassionate social order. It is said that these are the true human uses of an industrial technology in which each person is (ideally) judged on his own merit—an open-class system in which status is achieved, not inherited.

In the first selection that follows we consider an account of the values to which most American adults subscribe today. Arensberg and Niehoff assert that our values reflect our industrial organization: a man is judged by his work, people should be paid only for time spent in sustained effort, and effort is rewarded by success. Most Americans over forty would agree with this formulation and the conclusion that ours is a society in which comfort and affluence are the rewards of hard work, and poverty results from indolence and failure to improve oneself. Furthermore, since no one has a right to the entire pie, everyone must yield when disputes arise, so that a high value is placed on compromise. A further conclusion consistent with this ideology is that violence is unnecessary as long as everyone behaves according to these standards.

Richard Sennett, the author of the second selection, starts from the same values of optimism and human perfectibility as aspects of an industrial strategy; in fact, he speaks explicitly of industrial technology as having a "true and human use." Like Arensberg and Niehoff—and in contrast to the peasant's value of "limited good"—he believes that there are enough resources to improve the quality of everyone's life. But here the similarity between his picture and that of Arensberg and Niehoff ends.

It must be remembered that Sennett represents the university-trained generation that grew up after World War II; this is the generation that, as I have suggested, is ideologically committed to a post-industrial strategy of adaptation in which human labor will be replaced by electronically controlled production. There is here not a rejection of the grammar of social relations but rather of its currently predominant style.

At the core of the value system that Sennett reflects is a belief that material abundance will lead to permanent disorder and, in turn, to an enhancement of human communication (rather than to mere abundance) in a new strategy of survival. Elsewhere in the book from which this selection is taken, he says, "The great promise of city life is a new kind of confusion possible within its borders, an anarchy that will not destroy men, but make them richer and more mature." Sennett maintains that the American city has been reduced to a set of warring enclaves, none of which contains the resources to sustain a decent life, for which the city as a whole has the necessary wealth. The duplication of facilities among neighborhoods reduces the opportunities for interaction among different groups. If urban life is to become richer, he suggests, zoning restrictions and territorial barriers will have to be broken down, and when these are abandoned, people with different styles and values will be forced to live together and confront each other. They will no longer be able to "close their eyes to what they cannot abide in each other." The resulting clashes will force them to cope with each other, and they will thus emerge with a mutual respect for each other's humanity.

Sennett thus sees disorder—the open display of aggression—as a means of using wealth and abundance in this future strategy because, as an outlet for what people fear, aggression is a serious human experience. This variety of the optimism of traditional industrial values—the potential uses of industrially produced wealth in the service of human perfectibility—is superimposed on his vision of the city in this new society. The new city will be based on the experience of aggression; in providing freedom for expressing conflict, it will embody a new organization of social relations leading to a new set of ethical standards and, as a consequence, a more just and compassionate social order. Sennett is clear that his view of aggression—unlike its rejection by traditional values—excludes the result of mutual destruction. It is a dimension of human communication stemming from the refusal of the young (and a few older people too, as he notes) to accept the simplicities of the past—which, he suggests, are outgrowths of the complacency and boredom induced by affluence-laden suburbia.

Every social system and its values are designed to solve the recurrent problems created by a particular strategy of adaptation, but each also creates its own strains and contradictions. Different readers will be struck by different aspects of these two selections; I would like to note a few that struck me and that may serve as a basis for discussion. In the selection by Arensberg and Niehoff, there is only passing reference to the inequality suffered by blacks, Puerto Ricans, Mexicans, and poor whites—to say nothing of our genocidal destruction of American Indians. The violence and lack of compromise manifested in Mississippi and Watts stand in contradiction to the values of the affluent on whom this description of American values is based. Note also the implicitly colonial context in which the authors phrase their statement; they say little about the place of imperialism in this value system nor do they try to reconcile it with American values of human worth and dignity. And historical events do not quite bear out the notion that, in the American value system, bad conditions need only to be recognized in order to be rectified. Activism, which they say is celebrated in our values, has become an epithet in some sectors of the population subscribing wholly to this value system.

A comparable problem in Sennett's chapter is his high valuation of aggression. Without gainsaying that a good fight clears the air better than most commercial deodorants (as every well-married couple knows), it seems to me that Sennett uses aggression in much the same way that people misused Freud's ideas about sex. That is, many people tended to regard untrammeled sexuality as the base on which decent human relations should rest, to the relative exclusion of everything else; Sennett uses the notion of aggression in a similar way. Also: Sennett believes (as stated explicitly elsewhere in his book) that "we can learn to put the material wealth in city life to use as an agent of freedom, rather than voluntary slavery," and this is refreshing. But what about the mindless, routinized work that people must perform to produce material wealth? What of the future when little work will be needed to manufacture what we need? Though this question was outside the scope of Sennett's critique of the affluent city, I believe that it is of overriding importance to the future society's organization of social relations and its ethical standards.

Contemporary American values are in such rapid change that it is not possible to provide a representative list of readings for further exploration along these lines. The standard sociological view is presented in *American Society*, by Robin M. Williams, Jr. (New York: Knopf, 1963). An interesting set of primary documents paralleling the selection by Arensberg and Niehoff is a collection of speeches, *Frankly Speaking*, by Spiro T. Agnew (Washington, D.C.: Public Affairs Press, 1970). Taken as ethnographic data, this can be compared with such books as *Soul on Ice*, by Eldridge Cleaver (New York: Dell Publishing Company, 1968), and *Revolution for the Hell of It*, by Abbie Hoffman (New York: The Dial Press, 1968). ■

IN THE AGE of cultural pluralism what is meant by "American culture?" Is not the United States several streams of culture flowing side by side? . . . There is probably more acceptance of this idea today than at any time since the founding of the country. And yet, there is still a national core, usually characterized as that of the middle class, having its origins in Western European culture. The language is English, the legal system derives from English common law, the political system of democratic elections comes from France and England, the technology is solidly from Europe, and even more subtle social values such as egalitarianism, though modified, seem to be European derived. Thus, it seems justified to characterize the middle class value system of the United States, derived originally from Europe but modified to suit local conditions, as the core of American culture.

All people born and raised in this country will have been conditioned by this national culture, though obviously the middle class will be most strongly marked. And though it is not implied here that there are no differences in other sub-cultural streams, it does mean that irrespective of region, national origin, race, class, and sex, there are points of likeness that will occur more frequently than among groups of people in other countries. . . .

Where does this American character come from? As mentioned above, it seems to come from a European base that has been subsequently modified to meet local conditions. The values derived from life on the frontier, the great open spaces, the virgin wealth, and the once seemingly limitless resources of a "new world" appear to have affected ideas of freedom. Individualism seems to have been fostered by a commitment to "progress" which in turn was derived from expansion over 300 years. Much of the religious and ethical tradition is believed to have come from Calvinist (Puritan) doctrine, particularly an emphasis on individual responsibility and the positive work ethic. Anglo-Saxon civil rights, the rule of law, and representative institutions were inherited from the English background; ideas of egalitarian democracy and a secular spirit spring from the French and American Revolutions. The period of slavery and its aftermath, and the European immigration of three centuries, have affected the American character strongly.

AMERICAN CULTURE

Is it possible to provide a thumbnail sketch of the most obvious characteristics of this value system? Most social scientists would probably agree to the following.

The number of people in America is considerable compared to other countries, and they are located primarily in the cities and towns of a large area of diverse natural environments, still with considerable mineral and soil wealth and still not intensively exploited. There is an exceedingly elaborate technology and a wealth of manufactured goods that is now the greatest in the world.

Although the country has a strong agrarian tradition in which farming is still regarded as a family occupation, and though farming produces an extraordinary yield of foodstuffs and fibers, the nation has become urbanized and dominated by the cities. The farming population consists of less than ten per cent of the total, and agriculture has become so mechanized it can now be considered as merely another form of industry. Daily living is characteristically urban, regulated by the clock and calendar rather than by the seasons or degree of daylight. The great majority of individuals are employees, living on salaries paid by large, complex, impersonal institutions. Money is the denominator of exchange, even property having a value only in terms of its monetary worth. The necessities of life are purchased rather than produced for subsistence.

Because of the high standard of living and high level of technology, people have long lives. The birth rate is low but the death rate is among the lowest in the world. Thus, although there is a continuing expansion of population, it is much less rapid than in most of the agrarian nations.

Americans exhibit a wide range of wealth, property, education, manners, and tastes. However, despite diversities of origin, tradition, and economic level, there is a surprising conformity in language, diet, hygiene, dress, basic skills, land use, community settlement, recreation, and other activities. The people share a rather small range of moral, political, economic, and social attitudes, being divided in opinion chiefly by their denominational and occupational interests. Within the past decade there seems also to have been a separation of opinion based on age. There are some regional variations, but these are far less than the tribal or ethnic pluralisms found in the new nations of South Asia and Africa. The narrow opinion range throughout the country seems to be primarily a product of the relatively efficient mass education system which blankets the country and the wide spread of mass communication, from which all people get the same messages.

There are status differences, of course, based mainly on occupation, education, and financial worth. Achievement is valued more than inheritance in determining an individual's position. Although in theory all persons have equal opportunities, certain limitations exist, particularly those based on ethnic background and sex. A Negro may be appointed a member of the Cabinet, but it is improbable that he would be elected President at the present time; that there are now Negro mayors, but there are still no Negro governors. Women also are prevented from serving in certain positions or occupations. Despite these limitations, most people move about freely; they change jobs and move up and down in status with considerable frequency.

The basic American kinship unit, though evidently weakening, is still the nuclear family of husband, wife, and children. Newly married couples set up their own small households and move several times in a lifespan. The family rarely has continuing geographical roots. Most couples have few children. Marital relationships are fluid and not particularly stable, with divorce quite common. Old people and unmarried adults usually live apart from their kin. Instead of strong kinship ties, people tend to rely on an enormous number of voluntary associations of common interest — parent-teachers' association, women's clubs, social fraternities, church clubs, recreational teams, political clubs, and many others.

The general level of education is high, with literacy normal but not universal. From the age of five to eighteen the child is usually in an academic institution, learning the culturally approved goals of good health, character and, citizenship. Also, he learns basic and standard skills rather than specialized skills based on his hereditary—reading, writing, arithmetic, typing, liberal arts, driving cars, basic mechanics, housekeeping. Specialization comes later, in the professional training that ordinarily takes place in college. More and more young people are extending their education through four years in college, though this is not yet required as the normal social course.

The moral tone of the country is heavily Calvinist Protestant but there are many other sects of Christianity, besides other religions and cults. Religious beliefs and practices are concerned almost as much with general morality as with man's search for the afterlife or his worship of deities. Family relations, sexual customs, man's relationship to other men, and civic responsibility are all concerns of religion. A puritanic morality has become generalized and secularized, part of the total culture rather than that of any single religious sect. Formal religion is compartmentalized, as are many other aspects of American life. A high percentage of the Protestants who form the bulk of the population attend church infrequently, and religious ideas are seldom consciously mixed with secular ones. The church serves a strong social function, being the center of many clubs and groups. Religion can hardly be considered a particularly unifying institution of American life. The spirit of the country is secular and rationalistic. Most people are not anti-religious but merely indifferent. . . .

MATERIAL WELL-BEING

The rich resources of America, along with the extraordinary growth of its industrial economy, have brought a widespread wealth of material goods such as the world has not seen before. There has been a wholesale development and diffusion of the marvels of modern comfort—swift, pleasant transportation, central heating, air conditioning, instant hot and cold water, electricity, and labor saving devices of endless variety. The high value placed on such comforts has brought into being new industries to produce always greater quantities and ever improved versions. Americans seem to feel that they have a "right" to such amenities.

Associated with this attitude toward comfort, which has itself resulted in elaborate facilities of waste disposal and an advanced state of medical knowledge, Americans have come to regard cleanliness as an absolute virtue. A most familiar slogan is "Cleanliness is next to Godliness," and though this is not heard as often as it once was, the word "dirty" is still one of the chief epithets in the language, as in "dirty old man," "dirty hippie," "dirty business," "dirty deal," etc.

Achievement and success are measured primarily by the quantity of material goods one possesses, both because these are abundant and because they indicate how much money an individual earns. This material evidence of personal worth is modified by the credit system, but still, credit purchases will carry an individual only so far after which credit agencies will refuse to advance more without evidence of fundamental wealth.

Since there is little display value in the size of one's paycheck or bank account, the average individual buys prestige articles that others can see: expensive clothing or furniture, a fine car, a swimming pool, a fancy house, or any of the endless variety of devices that may have other functions but can also readily be seen by visitors —power mowers, barbecue paraphernalia, television and hi-fi sets. A person's status is affected to a secondary degree by his level of education, type of occupation, and social behavior; but even these qualities seem to be significant only in terms of how much income they help him obtain. Thus, a college professor who has earned his Ph.D. will have less status in the general community than a business executive or film actor who has no college education but commands a much larger salary.

People other than middle class Americans also value comfort and the saving of human labor, and one of the motivations to change everywhere is to perform traditional tasks more easily. However, many peoples of the world have found themselves unable to acquire labor-saving devices and have concentrated on the satisfaction of other needs; and it should be recognized that many of the spiritual or esthetic goals they pursue will outlast most of the machine-made we treasure. But their choices have been limited by their comparative poverty. Comfort in such circumstances has not been so highly valued, and in fact, Americans have been accused by this token of being excessively materialistic. . . .

TWOFOLD JUDGMENTS

A special characteristic of Western thinking, fully reflected in American ways, is that of making twofold judgments based on principle. The structure of the Indo-European languages seem to foster this kind of thinking and the action that follows. A situation or action is assigned to a category held high, thus providing a justification for positive action, or to one held low, with justification for rejection, avoidance, or other negative action. Twofold judgments seem to be the rule in Western and American life: moral-immoral, legal-illegal, right-wrong, sin-virtue, success-failure, clean-dirty, civilized-primitive, practical-impractical, introvert-extrovert, secular-religious, Christian-pagan. This kind of polarized thinking tends to put the world of values into absolutes, and its arbitrary nature is indicated by the fact that modern science itself no longer uses opposite categories, in almost all instances preferring to use the concept of a range with degrees of difference separating the poles.

Judgment in terms of principle is very old and pervasive as a means of organizing thought in Western and American life. It may derive from Judeo-Christian roots. In any event, it is deeply rooted in the religions that have come from this base as well as in the philosophy of the West. Its special quality should be recognized. More is involved than merely thinking in opposites. Other peoples have invented dual ways of thinking: the Chinese Yin-and-Yang, the Zoroastrian dual (though equal) forces of good and evil, male and female principles, and the Hindu concept of the forces of destruction and regeneration as different aspects of the same power. However, other peoples do not usually rank either pole as superior and thus to be embraced on principle as a guide to conduct.

This kind of thinking seems to force Americans into positions of exclusiveness. If one position is accepted, the other must be rejected. There is little possibility of keeping opposite or even parallel ideas in one's thinking pattern. This is not the case in other cultures. In Buddhism and Hinduism, disparate local beliefs exist alongside beliefs that are derived from the main theology. No one questions the fact that in Japan people may worship in a Buddhist temple as well as in a Shintō shrine, or that in the southern form of Buddhism, in Laos and Thailand, people propitiate the local spirits ("phi") as well as observe the ritual forms of Buddhism. This is quite different from the Christian attitude in which all that is believed to be supernatural but is not Christian is classified as superstition or paganism.

The average Westerner, and especially the American, bases his personal life and community affairs on principles of right and wrong rather than on sanctions of shame, dishonor, ridicule, or horror of impropriety. The whole legal system is established on the assumption that rational people can decide if things have been "wrong." The American is forced by his culture to categorize his conduct in universal, impersonal terms. "The law is the law" and "right is right," regardless of other considerations.

MORALIZING

One of the most basic of the twofold decisions Americans make is to classify actions as good or bad. Whether in the conduct of foreign affairs or bringing up children or dealing in the marketplace, Americans tend to moralize. Judging people and actions as absolutely right or wrong may have been a source of considerable strength in American history but it has also created pitfalls, particularly in the way it has influenced Americans in their relationship with other peoples. The attitude has frequently led Americans to indignation and even to warfare about the behavior of other peoples, Vietnam providing the most obvious recent example.

Every people has its own code of proper conduct. This is such an important part of any culture that some effort to understand it must be made. But ... this aspect of a cultural system is probably the most difficult to learn. And the greatest difficulties will occur if the outsider assumes that other people's basis of judgment is the same as his, or even that proper conduct will be based on moral rather than other kinds of principles.

In many other cultures, rank or esteem, the dignity of a person, the honor of an individual, compassion for an unfortunate, or loyalty to a kinsman or co-religionist, may be the basis for judgment as to proper conduct. Most forms of sexual behavior may not be considered subject to moral considerations. The American, as an heir to the Western tradition, is familiar and comfortable with a code of conduct derived from absolute principles (mostly religious) and supported by a code of law enforced by central authorities. This entire code is supposed to be impersonal, and to a considerable extent it is. The morality tale of the honest, law-abiding policeman or judge who punishes his own law-breaking son probably does occur more frequently in America than in societies where kinship considerations are given more weight.

One other feature of this kind of thinking that can lead to considerable personal and public problems ... [is that] the American tends to over-react to the discovery that the ideal behavior he was taught to expect from parents, public servants, spouses, and other adults is not always present in real life. Some individuals react by becoming "tough" and "cynical" and "wise" to the corruption of the world. Others, particularly exemplified by the youth of the 1960s, may organize to eliminate by whatever means are available the "failures" of the older generation. This kind of thinking encourages the individual to believe that whatever differs from the ideal version of high moral excellence is of the utmost depravity. It tends to direct the individual to see corruption and evil everywhere. And while such moralistic indignation may serve the culture well in some instances (as in the fight against pollution), it can also have negative consequences, particularly when the moralizer is trying to work with people of another culture. . . .

WORK AND PLAY

Another kind of twofold judgment that Americans tend to maintain is based on a qualitative distinction between work and play. To most persons brought up in the present-day American environment of farming, business, or industry, work is what they do regularly, purposefully, and even grimly, whether they enjoy it or not. It is a necessity, and for the middle aged, a duty. A man is judged by his work. When strangers meet and attempt to establish cordial relationships, one of the first topics of discussion is the kind of work each does. It is a primary role classifier. Work is a serious, adult business, and a man is supposed to "get ahead" or "make a contribution" to community or mankind through his work.

Play is different. It is fun, an outlet from work, without serious purpose except possibly to make subsequent work more efficient. It is a lesser category, a later topic of conversation after one's occupation is identified. And though some persons may "enjoy their work," this is a matter of luck and by no means something that everyone can count on, since all jobs contain some "dirty work," tedium, and tasks that one completes just by pushing on. Work and play are considered to be different worlds; there is a time and place for each, but when it is time for work, then lighter pursuits should be put aside. There is a newer emphasis in contemporary America on pleasure-seeking as a primary goal in life, but so far this seems to be an attitude es-

poused by a minority only, the young who have rejected the former goals of society and the old who have already completed their years of work.

The American habit of associating work with high or necessary purpose and grim effort and play with frivolity or pleasure seems to have a positive function in the American cultural context, but it may be quite out of place in another culture. For many peoples the times of most important work may also be times of festivity or ceremony. Work and play may be interwoven. A threshing floor may be a dancing arena, building a new house or netting a school of fish may provide the occasion for a whole community to sing and joke together. Preparing the proper songs or dishes will be as "practical" an activity as cutting thatch or caring for nets.

The combination of work and play is not completely foreign to Americans, although urban industrial society does not seem favorable for it. The American frontier, and even Midwest farming communities until thirty or forty years ago, combined the two in their husking bees, house-raising, and threshing parties. In the early decades of this century, before wheat combines and farms of large acreage dominated agriculture in the Midwest, farmers made the social and work rounds for several weeks in midsummer. Not only did they work together, but they also feasted, socialized, and even managed a considerable amount of courting. It was a point of pride for each farmer's wife to have the large and elaborate quantities of food available for the men when they came in from the fields. The unmarried girls made a particular effort to be there to search out the bachelors. It was a gay time as well as a time of hard work. It should also be pointed out that song and work has been well represented in the American past in the vast repertory of work songs that were once sung by occupational groups.

Basically, the non-industrial societies have patterns of work and play that are closer to those known to pre-industrial Americans; work and play are intermixed rather than distinct forms of activity.

TIME AND MONEY

Closely related to the American distinction between work and play is a special attitude toward time. Whenever Americans interact with people in non-industrial countries, both quickly become aware that their outlook in regard to time is different. In many such countries the local people actually make a distinction in the spoken language, referring to *hora Americana* versus *hora Mexicana* or *mong Amelikan* versus *mong Lao*. When referring to the American version, they mean that it is exact, that people are punctual, activities are scheduled, time is apportioned for separate activities, and the measure is the mechanical clock; their own time lacks this precision.

Probably misunderstandings with people of other cultures occur most frequently in relation to work. For Americans, "time is money." Work is paid for in money and one should balance his work against time or through regular periods for a fixed salary. A person works for $4 or $6 per hour and eight or ten hours per day for 40 or 48 hours per week. Work beyond the normal is "overtime." Play or leisure time is before or after work time. An employer literally buys the time of his workers along with their skills and schedules and assigns work to be balanced against the gain he will obtain. In this way of thinking, time can be turned into money, both for the employer and employee, and work turned out faster than planned can release extra time for more work and more gain.

Equating work with time, using the least amount of time to produce the largest amount of work, expecting that time paid for will be marked by sustained effort, budgeting of man hours in relation to the cost of the end product —these are all central features of the American industrial economy that have contributed a great deal to its productiveness. And although Americans may complain about the necessity of routine and the tyranny of the clock during working hours, they are thoroughly accustomed to such strictures. The activities of leisure— eating, sleeping, playing, courting—must take place during "time off." No wonder time to them is scarce and worth saving.

Such a precise concept of time is usually foreign to peoples of non-industrial cultures. In most agrarian societies, especially in the villages, time is geared to seasonal requirements and the amount of daylight available. Many routines reflect, not hourly or daily repetitions

based on wage labor, but the needs of individual and social life, the cycles of crops, fluctuations in daily temperature, and the round of ceremonial observances. The cities of these countries have all adopted the Western concept of time to some degree, although it is frequently noted that the rural pattern is still maintained in modified form in the urban context. Individuals simply do not keep hours or appointments precisely and are surprised when they learn that an American is irritated by a missed appointment. . . .

EFFORT AND OPTIMISM

Americans are an active people. Problems should be identified and effort should be expended to solve them. Effort is good in itself, and with proper effort one can be optimistic about success. The fact that some problems may be insoluble is very difficult for an American to accept. The high value connected with effort often causes Americans to cite the principle that "It is better to do something than to just stand around." This thinking is based on the concept that the universe is mechanistic (it can be understood in terms of causes and effects), man is his own master, and he is perfectible almost without limit. Thus, with enough effort, man can improve himself and manipulate the part of the universe that is around him.

This national confidence in effort and activity, with an optimism that trying to do something about a problem will almost invariably bring success in solving it, seems to be specifically American. Such an attitude is probably a product of the continual expansion of American culture during the past 300 years, first along America's frontiers and later in its industrial growth. Obstacles existed only to be overcome, and bad conditions needed only be recognized to be rectified.

Effort and optimism permeate the life of the individual because of his cultural upbringing. Coming from an "open class system," where status is usually achieved rather than inherited, both privilege and authority should be deserved and won.

Effort, achievement, and success are woven through the fabric of American life and culture. Activist, pragmatist values rather than contemplative or mystical values are the basis of the American character. Serious effort to achieve success is both a personal goal and an ethical imperative. The worthwhile man is the one who "gets results" and "gets ahead." A failure "gets nowhere" or "gets no results," for success is measured by results, though there is a little "credit for trying." The successful man "tackles a problem," "does something about it," and "succeeds" in the process. A failure is unsuccessful through his own fault. Even if he had "bad breaks" he should have tried again. A failure in life "didn't have the guts" to "make a go of it" and "put himself ahead."

This is a very severe code. No one is certain how widespread it is among Americans but it is probably recognizable to most. It indicates a culture in which effort is rewarded, competition enforced, and individual achievement paramount. Unfortunately, the code raises serious problems. One of the most important is that it calls all those in high positions "successes" and all those in low ones "failures" even though everyone knows the majority must be in lower positions. A code of this sort by its very nature creates much frustration, in all those who have not been able to achieve high positions.

This traditional optimism of the American personality has been tempered to a certain degree in recent years, though primarily in the kind of goals sought rather than in goal-seeking as the ultimate objective. A concentration on pragmatic effort seems unchanged, and even those Americans who are most disillusioned with the current state of affairs seem convinced that enough effort will produce success—though for new goals rather than old ones.

But it has become clear to everyone that whatever effort is expended, some situations are beyond the American's ability to control. Problems once thought to be simple are now seen to have a complexity not previously recognized. A weaker enemy cannot simply be bombed into submission with more and more explosives. Industrial production cannot be guided by the profit motive alone if one wants to breathe clean air and to swim in clean water. The inner city of an industrial nation cannot survive if it is abandoned by the well-to-do who move to the suburbs. These are some of the problems that have arisen because of a

simplistic view of manipulation of the environment, both human and natural. Some pundits now feel they are beyond human correction, but although the optimism of the average man has probably been tempered in recent decades, his method of overcoming these obstacles is unchanged—simply put in greater effort.

The American overseas is prone to evaluate people and situations according to this code. When he observes that those in authority have achieved their position by means other than their own effort, he may become bewildered, angered, or cynical. He may quickly make an activist judgment and try to remedy the situation, using his own code. Or he may shift (usually unconsciously) from the notion of work as task oriented, which many peoples share in their own fashion, to an emphasis on busy work, on hurrying and pressuring, on encouraging activity for its own sake.

To peoples in other parts of the world a history of failure in recent times has been as compelling as our technological and economic achievements are to Americans. Their experiences may have taught them to value passivity, acceptance, and evasion rather than effort and optimism. This will not be because they have no interest in getting things done but because of their history of reversals. They lack the confidence of the American.

Before taking action, other peoples may therefore make many preparations which the American, so concerned with technical efficiency, will consider unnecessary. These may consist in extensive consultation with others to build up a consensus, giving favors to win personal loyalties, trying to adjust proposed plans to religious and other traditional beliefs, and considering all alternatives, including the real possibility of not risking action at all. American demands for bustle and effort, for getting down to business, may not only be interpreted as nagging, pushing, and ill-mannered, but sometimes as downright frightening, especially when a wrong judgment could lead to personal disaster. After an initial failure, the American determination to "try again" or "try harder the next time" may seem particularly foolhardy. Merely to intensify one's effort and to try again on a bigger scale when resources are limited may appear as the most reckless compounding of original folly.

And as is not unusual, other peoples frequently do judge American behavior correctly. The American passion to exert greater effort in the face of continuing difficulties has not always produced the hoped-for success. In Vietnam, for example, although an admittedly much weaker enemy clearly and early indicated they would fight differently than in previous wars in which we have engaged, the military heads of the United States went ahead with conventional bombing and ground maneuvers for almost ten years without ever altering their procedures significantly except to intensify them. At the end of this decade, the enemy seemed hardly any weaker than at the beginning. And it must be admitted that such a procedure is only possible for America because it has unprecedented wealth and industrial production.

The effort to which Americans normally commit themselves is expected to be direct and efficient. Americans want to "get down to business" and confine themselves to the problem or proposal specified. Misunderstandings have consequently occurred because other peoples, particularly Latins, tend to be less direct. They indulge more in rhetorical speech during conferences and discussions, refusing to confine themselves rigidly to the agenda at hand. All this indicates more concern with social values than is usual in the American manner of conducting affairs. Perhaps the impersonal, technological approach leads to more production but the social verities have their place also, and they are still significant in many parts of the world.

American assumptions about effort and optimism include a faith in progress and a constant view toward the future. Practically all life is arranged to fulfill the needs of children and of the generations to follow. There is a pervasive accent on youthfulness; the values exemplified in commercial advertising and entertainment almost always emphasize the young and the old are not commonly sought out for their experience. Adults attempt to hold back middle and old age. In general, elderly people are bypassed, either left in old folks' homes or living in isolated retirement, in both cases removed from practical affairs. An ironic aspect of the situation in the 1960s has been the rejection by a considerable part of American youth of this idealized "youth culture." "You cannot trust anyone over twenty-nine," they say.

An accent on youthfulness is particularly American, though it seems to be shared to a lesser degree by other achievement-oriented industrial societies. In the agrarian nations, or wherever tradition is important, people tend to equate age with experience. The old are treated with deference and the oldest male is usually the chief decision-maker of the basic kin unit.

Other cultures have had their periods of progress, but it appears rare for progress to be a central value throughout the entire existence of a culture. It is only since World War II that American faith in the future has been modified significantly, with the realization that there are many undesirable consequences if technological progress is allowed to take place with few controls. But despite recent reversals, the general American attitude is still that the future should contain bigger and better successes, if not on this planet, then on others. This attitude also implies that the new and modern are better than the old and traditional. Technological and economic life must progress. No one—not even the strongest dissidents of the left or the right—expects to keep America as it is today or to return it to what it was yesterday. . . .

MAN AND NATURE

The greater effort that normally marks the American's response to obstacles may sometimes seem shallow, irreverent, or premature to people in other cultures. Some obstacles deserve respect and there are limitations to what man can do, even if he is the cleverest manipulator of the environment to have appeared so far. The new ecological approach is an indication that the American is becoming aware of some limitations on his capacities, but whether this will deflect his value system in a basic way remains to be seen. Up to now, American man has attempted to conquer nature. It has been something to overcome, to improve, to tear down and rebuild in a better way. He has tried to "break the soil," to "harness" the natural resources, in other words, to treat the natural environment like a domestic animal. He has divided the plants and animals into categories of useful and harmful. Harmful plants are weeds and harmful animals are "varmints"— the first to be uprooted or poisoned and the second to be trapped, shot, or poisoned. American farmers and ranchers have been notorious for killing predators. The only kind of hawks they knew until recently were "chicken hawks" which were shot any time they appeared and their carcasses hung in long festoons on wire fences. Coyotes and bobcats are still trapped and hunted without compunction by Westerners, who can get bounties of a few dollars for the feet and ears of one of these animals. And though on occasion hawks and coyotes may kill a few chickens or sheep, they primarily live on mice, rats, rabbits, and other small animals whose population must be kept in balance by such predators. Even a weed is merely a "plant growing out of place" from man's point of view.

It must be admitted that many of the achievements of Americans are due to this conquering attitude toward nature. Our enormous agricultural productivity is one such achievement, although credit must also go to the fact that there were large expanses of very fertile land available. But it must also be admitted that the American has paid and is continuing to pay high prices for these agricultural successes. Natural resources, particularly forests, water, and the air, have been squandered and despoiled over large areas. Nature's balance has often been upset. Such "wonder" insecticides as DDT are now under strong attack by conservationists as destroying as many "useful" insects and birds, as well as for their effect on human health.

This conquering attitude toward nature appears to rest on at least three assumptions: that the universe is mechanistic, that man is its master, and that man is qualitatively different from all other forms of life. Specifically, American and Western man credits himself with a special inner consciousness, a soul, for which he does not give other creatures credit. In most of the non-Western world man is merely considered as one form of life, different only in degree from the others. Of course, the Western biologist also shares this view, which is the primary reason that traditional Western culture came into conflict with biological views in the 19th and 20th centuries. In the so-called animistic religions, all living creatures are believed to have something corresponding to a

soul, with no sharp dividing line between man and the other animals. Spirits are even attributed to plants and inanimate objects such as soil, rocks, mountains, and rivers. In the Hindu and Buddhist world the belief in a cycle of rebirths strongly affirms man's kinship to non-human forms. In the cycle of existences man can become an insect, a mammal, another type of man, or even a form of deity. The validity of such beliefs is far less important than the fact man's attitude toward nature is influenced by them (and after all, there is no more empirical basis for Christian beliefs than for Buddhism or Hinduism). Basically, most people except for Westerners, consider man and nature as one and these other peoples more often work with nature than they simply attempt to conquer it.

During long periods of trial and error, peoples of all cultures have worked out adaptations to their natural environments. These adaptations may lack much by Western standards but they do enable the inhabitants to survive, sometimes in quite difficult circumstances. Such peoples have evolved through experience systems of conservation, methods of stretching and restoring their slim resources, and elaborate accommodations to climate, vegetation, and terrain. Some such adaptations now embedded in tradition and religion are the Middle Eastern desert-derived pattern of Islamic ritual hygiene, austerity, and almsgiving; pre-industrial Japanese frugalities in house structure, farming, and woodworking; and Southeast Asian village economies in the measured use of rice, bamboo, and fish. These and similar adaptations to natural environments are high developments in the balanced utilization of limited resources.

When, with a facile confidence that nature can be tamed by ever-costlier mechanical devices, Americans and other Westerners attempt to brush aside the experience of centuries, it is perhaps temporarily exciting to the local people. However, they are not apt to be reassured if they have information about the realities of the environment that is ignored by the rushing, pushing, self-assured newcomers, particularly since the local solutions sometimes outlast the glamorous innovations of the specialists. . . . [For example, a] well-drilling project in Laos was based on a system that had been worked out in Florida where the water table is high all year round. The specialist drilled wells in one large area of Laos during the rainy season and found water almost every time, at a relatively high level. However, all these wells went dry during the dry season, since the water level drops markedly during this period in Southeast Asia. Most Lao probably knew this and would have revealed it if asked.

In environments that seem adverse, such as the rainy tropics, the arctic, or the desert, experience has shown that Western man's goods and machines rot, rust, freeze, or grit up all too quickly, requiring huge and costly effort merely to keep them going. This is not surprising, since this machinery was developed primarily for use in a temperate zone where precipitation is spread more or less evenly throughout the year.

A graphic example of the lack of adaptability of Western machines has been observed during the military struggles in Southeast Asia in recent years. Tanks and other mechanized equipment were developed with the solid land forms of America and Europe in mind. However, their use has been drastically curtailed in the rice paddies of Vietnam and Laos. The mobile foot soldier, unencumbered with heavy gear, can slip through the soggy fields and marshes in constant readiness to fight while the tank or halftrack is bogged down in mud. The insurgent forces in Laos and Vietnam have made their greatest drives just before the heavy rains set in, knowing that the mechanized forces with American equipment will be mostly immobilized until the land dries again.

EQUALITY OF MEN

The tendency to moralize has been operative in supporting another important trait of American culture—egalitarianism. Americans believe all people should have equal opportunities for achievement. This is more of a moral imperative than an actual fact of American life and has always been so. From the earliest times there have been some groups of people who were treated as inferior, and great differences of wealth, education, influence, opportunity, and privilege exist in the United States. Nevertheless, the experiences that Americans underwent along the frontiers and through the process of immigration did represent a huge

historical experiment in social leveling. Our legal and institutional heritage prescribes equal rights, condemns special privileges, and demands fair representation for every citizen. The latest efforts to obtain equal treatment for minority groups has been spear-headed by legal resolutions (Supreme Court decisions) and renewed emphasis on the egalitarian nature of the society. Inequality, unless a product of achievement or lack of it, is considered to be wrong, bad, or "unfair."

There are, of course, ethnic minorities which have not been assimilated into the major society and which are treated unequally. The main disadvantaged groups are now of African, Mexican, and Amerindian ancestry. And although it is currently fashionable to regard this difference of treatment as based on race, other explanations are just as plausible. None of these groups really constitute a race and people with basically very similar appearances and genetic background (such as those of Italian, Spanish, Chinese, or Japanese ancestry) face much less discrimination. But these latter groups have attempted to adopt the Euro-American cultural pattern while Mexican-American and Amerindians have tended to maintain certain distinctive cultural patterns. The case of the Afro-American is probably unique, in that these people constitute the only group whose ancestors were held in slavery by the majority.

It is probable that the American attitude toward equality of treatment really means "within the major value system"; that is, people are, or should be, treated equally if they accept the basic beliefs and behaviors of the social majority. In this sense, the American idea is similar to that of the Muslims, who have always taught that all men are equal under Allah; discrimination by race or any other criterion has been rare so long as one was dealing with acceptors of the faith, and within the ranks of believers the only significant feelings of superiority have been based on supposed relationships with the Prophet. People on a direct line of descent from Mohammed are considered higher than those on a more remote line.

There has been one other form of unequal treatment in American society, that between males and females. Although female liberation movements are fashionable now, the plain fact is that the American female is already in a position of more nearly equal treatment than in most other nations, and certainly those outside the West. In practice, women are barred from the highest positions and are discriminated against in certain professions. But there are few educational limitations and they can enter freely into economic affairs. Even marriage is considered to be a kind of partnership, an unusual arrangement among the vast range of cultures of the world.

Despite the remaining evidence of unequal treatment toward the unassimilated ethnic minorities and women, the basic American value judgment of equality among men (and women) has not changed. Open patterns of subordination, deference, and acceptance of underprivilege call forth sympathies for the "underdog," and American activist values call for efforts to do something about these matters. This impulse tempts Americans overseas to interfere directly in the life ways of other peoples. The American does not have the patience to deal with persons whose authority seems neither justified nor deserved, or to wait for the ordinary man who will act only when he has received the go-ahead from the figures of prestige or respect in his culture. . . .

Another consequence of American egalitarianism is a preference for simple manners and direct, informal treatment of other persons. This can work to the American's advantage if kept within limits, but where people differ in rank and prestige, offense can be given if all are treated in a breezy, "kidding," impersonal manner. It is much better to try to acquire some of the local usages of long titles, elaborate forms of address and language, and manners of courtesy and deference, than to try to accustom other peoples to American ways. American "kidding" and humor are very special products of an egalitarian culture and generally work best at home.

Since all Americans are supposed to be equal in rights, and since "success" is a primary goal that can only be measured by achievement, a high value must be assigned to individuality. This accent on individual worth seems to be largely a heritage of frontier days and later economic expansion, when there were plenty of opportunities for the individual to achieve according to his abilities However, with population expansion and the filling up of the country, individuality has had to be limited to

some extent. It is now known that the ravages of the natural environment are largely due to unchecked drives by industrialists toward individual achievement.

Though individual equality has been stressed throughout American history, the goals and ways of achieving success have been limited. The successful man was one who was better than everyone else but in a way similar to theirs; one might have more and better things than another, but they should be the same kind of things. And with the full development of urban, corporate life, this similarity of goals seems to have evolved into personal conformity. The organization man has superseded the rugged individualist. Thus, individual self-sufficiency has steadily decreased. One indication of this development is a growing demand for security. And since Americans have abandoned the kinship system for this purpose, they now try to protect themselves with impersonal group insurance, which they hope cover all contingencies. In their efforts to attract new employees, corporations now advertise insurance benefits as much as the challenge of the work and the salary, and these "fringe benefits" are just as often the main concern of prospective employees. Americans buy insurance for the smallest items in their lives, even insuring household appliances against breakdown. Government too becomes more and more a giant insurance corporation, to its direct employees and to the citizenry in general.

HUMANITARIANISM

The American trait of coming to the aid of unfortunates is widespread and well known. It expresses itself in impersonal generosity which is activated by calls for help when unpredicted events of unfortunate or disastrous effect occur. Earthquakes, floods, famines, and epidemics are only a few of the kinds of events that strike a responsive chord in American society. At the end of both world wars, American generosity was primarily responsible for getting European nations back on their feet. Not only are they generous, but Americans also show a tremendous amount of efficiency at such times, often more than in "normal" times.

A dramatic illustration of this competence

was witnessed in the aftermath of a battle in Vientiane, Laos, at which time the capitol was badly damaged. American diplomatic and assistance efforts in the preceding years had not been particularly impressive. In fact, the battle occurred principally because American diplomatic and military bureaus had come to the point of backing two opposing ideological factions of Laotians, supplying both groups with weapons. U.S. assistance efforts had been bogged down by a lack of cultural understanding of the Lao and by administrative problems in the aid mission itself. But after the capitol had been heavily damaged by shelling, the American International Cooperation Administration, as well as other American groups in the city, went into action in a manner that was truly impressive. Although many areas had been flattened and an unknown number of people killed, within two to three weeks the city was on its feet again. Besides providing needed goods, the American officials thought nothing of working day and night, and their organizational ability was much more clearly demonstrated than in their inept efforts at military diplomacy which led to the battle. In three to four months, there was hardly a sign that the battle had taken place.

American humanitarianism is a characteristic that can hardly be criticized. It is of a special type, however, and contains one possible basis of misunderstanding in that it is usually highly organized and impersonal. For many other peoples, humanitarianism is personal. They consequently do not share with everyone; they cannot. But through personal and kinship obligations, by religious almsgiving and in other traditional ways, they give what they can. The American must not blind himself to the existence of these other patterns and also must perceive that other peoples are just not as rich as he is. The American tendency can hardly be praised if it is merely converted into a standard of negative judgment against other peoples' ways.

An American tends to condemn begging and the systems that support it, presumably because it involves personalized asking and giving. But it is worthwhile to look into the realities of such a system, like for instance *baksheesh*, the Middle Eastern begging tradition. The halt, lame, and blind line up with outstretched palms at the mosque or church door. The American is likely to condemn the cruelty of such a system, but in fact these people are being taken care of by their community according to traditional rules. Every member of the Islamic faithful is expected to give ten per cent of his income (*zaka*) in direct alms to the unfortunates who personally ask for it. This particular pattern of generosity is one that has been worked into the communal life of the society, in keeping with its meager resources. The difference between this system and the Community Chest is mainly one of organization and personalization.

25. THE CITY AS AN ANARCHIC SYSTEM

RICHARD SENNETT

From The Uses of Disorder: Personal Identity and City Life, *by Richard Sennett. Copyright* © *1970 by Richard Sennett. Reprinted by permission of Alfred A. Knopf, Inc. Richard Sennett was born in Chicago in 1943 and took his B.A. at the University of Chicago in 1964 and his Ph.D. at Harvard in 1969. He teaches sociology at Brandeis University and is director of the Urban Family Study Center and a co-director of the Cambridge Institute. Mr. Sennett began his career as a musician and still plays the cello in chamber music groups. In addition to* The Uses of Disorder, *from which this selection is taken, he is the author of* Families Against the City: Middle-Class Homes of Industrial Chicago.

TOWARD THE END of the nineteenth century a small band of men instituted a wave of assassinations, bombings, and other terrorist acts in the name of what they called anarchism. As a consequence anarchism in many countries became a proscribed doctrine, and anarchists criminals in the eyes of the law. Anarchism literally means "without government" or "without control" (an-archy). The term became overlaid with violent and terrorist associations in the late nineteenth century for peculiar reasons.

E. H. Carr has said that anarchism in the last century was a critique of society, not a plan for social reconstruction. The virtues of being without government were conceived as correctives to the emerging industrial order, and it was difficult for anarchists to think about an anarchic society as having an ongoing life of its own. Therefore, although the rigidities and injustice of the industrial order gave the anarchists a powerful rationale for what they were against, the terms of their own thinking never told them what they were really fighting for. The Marxian terms, on the other hand, did.

Originally, anarchists and Marxians were part of the same fledgling movement. Proudhon, taken by many to be the first anarchist, thought of himself as a disciple of socialism; his ideas for "federalism" in the conduct of just social affairs were hardly plans for life without government. But as the anarchist idea ripened, as the fact of disorder seemed to become in itself a challenge to the manufacturers, anarchists moved away from the discipline and the search for internal structure that characterized the First International of the Marxian socialists. It was the Russian Bakunin who personified this movement away from organized socialism; he was an intense, childlike rebel who made his sense of outrage at the cruelties around him a self-sufficing state of mind rather than a springboard for trying to change society.

I believe this limitation of the anarchists' vision, this static quality of their rejection, is what led them to violence and terrorism at the century's end. For, lacking a notion of what should be instituted when injustice was overthrown, these men were naturally drawn to look at the act of rejection as a moral region of its own. The more powerful the process of rejecting, the more complete, the more purging an event it would be. If, unlike the Marxians, all they

had was the fact of saying no, their statement had to be cataclysmic, had to be everything. This was the path by which Georges Sorel, the great anarchist-syndicalist writer, was led to see violence as a great purging, cleansing act in society. The violent catharsis was so great that what happened after seemed petty and anti-climactic.

The ideas about anarchy in cities advanced so far in this essay are inherently hostile to the enshrinement of violence to which the anarchist movement of the nineteenth century was finally led. For I have tried to look at what society should be like once it is freed of economic injustice and becomes affluent. Now, I believe, disorder is an enduring way to use the wealth and abundance of modern times; the result of this anarchy in abundant city life will be to decrease the need for violence rather than idealize the desire for it.

Such statements as there are on postrevolutionary social structure by nineteenth-century anarchists lean to a society antithetical to the dense, diverse city. Among the greatest virtues of the Paris commune, to men like Proudhon, was its small-group character and tightness. Carr has pointed to the same desire for little, intimate communities in Bakunin's beliefs and in those of his fellow countryman Kropotkin, who looked back to the village community of the late medieval period. After the purging cataclysm of violent overthrow, the tight little band of believers—this is today Fanon's dream as well. It is a millennial vision bound to decay, for such little communities permit the flourishing of desires for solidarity, and these desires in turn repress creative, disruptive innovations in life style and belief.

Unlike the anarchists of his time, Marx envisioned the shape of postrevolutionary society, and discussed mechanisms that would make disorder, constant change, and expanding diversity its hallmarks. But he assumed these things would come to pass of themselves, once economic injustices were routed. Marx refused to explore the possibility that rigid order, a fear of change, and a desire for sameness were innate to human beings, were generated by the very processes of human maturation. Seen in a different light, his refusal was an article of belief in the basic dignity of men. His hopes for a natural liberation, in light of the psychological researches that followed him and the experiences of "liberated nations" who have become affluent, seem now no longer possible to entertain. In an affluent world, be it pre- or post-revolutionary, the real problem is for men to be encouraged to abandon their deep-down natural desire for a comfortable slavery to the routine. This encouragement is what purposely dense, purposely decentralized, purposely disordered cities could provide.

But the question arises as to how such cities could endure as social systems. Isn't it a contradiction in terms to talk of an anarchic environment as enduring, and therefore somehow stable? Furthermore, wouldn't men, faced with the disorder, gradually give it up and return to the more comfortable slaveries of the past?

SOME SOCIAL POSSIBILITIES OF AFFLUENCE

The modern social use of technology has been to provide men with a coherent image of order—consisting of actions that are performed by passive agents. A machine in which one part or operation deviates from its preconceived use makes the whole go out of order, and stop functioning. The usual modes of urban planning are executed in such metropolitan, "system" terms, derived from the model of machine productivity.

This image of technology ignores its true and humane social use, a use that makes practicable the system of social disorganization men need in order to become adults. For the productive capacities of modern industry, technologically in excess of what is needed for a society's bare survival, permit a greater range and complexity of conflict than under scarcity conditions. Labor union strikes are a good example of this. In prosperous sectors of the economy where strike funds and personal income are developed, the occurrence of a strike does not mean that the conflict becomes a question of whether the workers are brought to the starving point or the company to bankruptcy; the affluence provides a certain floor to the conflict. The material base of the economy is such that social conflicts need not escalate to life or death struggles between the parties involved.

Sociologists have usually looked at such a flooring to the economic disaster caused by group conflict as a sign of the emergence of social solidarity and sameness in a culture. Supposedly, the less cataclysmic a conflict, the less the desire or need for it. This entirely misses the point. This economic floor, which is the result of technological affluence, can actually permit *greater* regions of conflict than in scarcity societies, because the stakes of group conflict need not escalate to the point where one of the parties must obliterate the other.

One of the most ridiculed and most feared innovations of American social planning in the last decade was the federal government's establishment of funds for local groups to use in pressing their demands against city hall and state agencies. This program could have had an enormously creative impact had it been adequately funded, for the government revenues were used by decentralized groups to fight only for the programs they wanted. With such a flooring they did not have to fight city hall for their economic existence as well; the existence of the groups were not dependent on the success or failure they had in funding particular programs. The local organizations did not need to tie themselves to a fixed ideology or function in order to stay alive, but were permitted an independent existence. Thus they were free to grow and change direction. The point about an affluent society is that there is enough money around for this kind of economic "flooring" of conflict groups to be created. The amounts of money needed are not really large compared to the massive outlays made for nonproductive military activities. When such "flooring" exists, so that conflict over particular issues need not escalate to the level of whether one or the other of the parties must be destroyed, the organizations can attain a great deal more internal flexibility in their goals and programs.

The proper uses of technological abundance, then, permit a social conception of survival *different* from that obtaining in the scarcity economies of the past. Survival comes to be defined in terms of concrete actions taken to change behavior of individuals or groups in opposition: the slavery of a material reference point of existence, as Marx called it, does not interfere with this experiential interaction. In this way, Marx's idea of a postrevolutionary anarchy would touch on the city anarchy envisioned here.

Putting abundance to such social ends, as has occurred in both American and European labor unions and intermittently for local community organizations, is one way that disordered relationships and conflict grouping could practicably have an ongoing life. Unlike the conflicts in times of scarcity, survival is framed in terms of whether people will be able to communicate with each other, not whether they will be able to stay alive. Again I am forced to refer to Marx: he believed that in an abundant society permanent disorder is possible because survival depends on social acts and experiences rather than the brute possession of material goods.

But there is another reason why the disordered city can have an ongoing, viable existence, a reason not referable to such theories as those of Marx.

STABILITY THROUGH DIRECT AGGRESSION

Aggressive feelings are inherent in people's lives, but aggression itself is a little-understood phenomenon. Psychologists and anthropologists have bitterly debated the question of why aggression exists to a much greater degree in men than in other animals. Some researchers claim aggression is the result of frustration and therefore developed in the course of a life in individual ways and through personal experiences; others claim aggression to be an instinctual response, existing in the psychic make-up of men in advance of any of their particular experiences. Whatever the origin of aggression, the fact of its importance in men's social activities cannot be denied.

The structures modern affluent communities are built on are such that basic aggression is denied outlets other than violence. Because the images of social order are functional images of preset roles to be played so that the social whole will function, aggressive behavior among the players seems at best to be a diversion from the proper workings of the community, and at worst a threat to the very idea of achievement and accomplishment. "Aggression resolution" is regarded as necessary for further group action to occur.

But if aggression is so deeply engraved in the life of men, then a society that regards aggressive outbreaks as a hindrance rather than as a serious human experience is hiding from itself. Indeed, one school of social thought now considers modern ideas for sublimating aggression, such as directing attacks away from their original targets into more socially manageable forms, as actually conducive to the kind of emotional buildup that can suddenly burst forth in acts of unprovoked violence.

The clearest example of the way this violence occurs is found in the pressures on police in modern cities. Police are expected to be bureaucrats of hostility resolution, unresponsive to taunts and attacks on them, passive in the performance of enforcing set rules on an unruly or violent clientele. Apart from all the theories about ethnic hatreds, "working-class authoritarianism," and the like now invoked to explain police riots, is it any wonder, in simple human terms, that the imperative to respond passively has a terrible effect on these men? The need to work aggression out of their systems builds up to the point where they have to brutalize indiscriminately when unleashed on their own. A society that visualizes the lawful response to disorder as an impersonal, passive coercion only invites such terrifying outbreaks of police rioting. I am convinced, therefore, that no officer of "law and order" can preserve his decency under these conditions, where he is supposed to be a passive "instrument" of justice, a justice machine.

But in a dense city where power has been changed so that people are forced to deal directly with each other as men, not as parts of a planned order, aggressive hostilities involved in conflict could be directed to the objects of provocation. We are so enslaved to cowardly ideas of safety that we imagine direct expression of hostilities can only lead to brutal outbreaks. But such experiments in direct confrontation as the psychiatric "attack" sessions of Synanon games, where people are encouraged to express their hostile feelings about each other, almost never lead to blows, for the simple reason that there is no need for it. Hostility is actively expressed when felt, not left to fester and grow provoking.

It is said that American and western European cities are growing more violent. Some writers, like Oscar Handlin, doubt the historical validity of the assertion, and perhaps they are right to think that violent crime is no greater now than in the past. But the potential for "irrational crime," for violence without object or provocation, is very great now. The reason it exists is that society has come to expect too much order, too much coherence in its communal life, thus bottling up the hostile aggressiveness men cannot help but feeling.

These new anarchic cities promise to provide an outlet for what men now fear to show directly. In so doing, the structure of the city community will take on a kind of stability, a mode of ongoing expression, that will be sustaining to men because it offers them expressive outlets. Anarchy in cities, pushing men to say what they think about each other in order to forge some mutual patterns of compatability, is· thus not a compromise between order and violence; it is a wholly different way of living, meaning that people will no longer be caught between these two polarities.

WHY MEN WILL WANT THE NEW CITIES

We have examined, thus far, why it would be good for the health of society if the cities of our times were changed, and why such good cities might be viable over time. But there remains an unanswered question in such a change: why should men *want* to make over their lives and inhabit these difficult cities? It is a question of convincing men who have succeeded quite well in isolating themselves in warm and comforting shelters in the suburbs, or in ethnic, racial, or class isolation, that these refuges are worth abndoning for the terrors of the struggle to survive together.

In exploring such personal desires, an urban study like this is invading what was once the domain of moral philosophers and theologians. Indeed, social studies are now attempting definitions of the good and bad goals of a life, the desirable forms of identity. Society has passed beyond the stage where it sought from divine authority firm and immutable answers to such questions, but the questions remain, in all their messiness and refusal to submit to the scalpel of numbers and quantitative answers: why should men want to lead a better communal life than the comfortable one they now lead?

The immediate answer to this problem might seem that these new cities would make a more just, compassionate social order, and so in the end men would come to desire them. This has been a great motive for belief in the Christian sects—that one can come to desire a good end one has not yet experienced—but this belief is, I believe, a great illusion as well. If men were saintly enough to respond to such a plea, then the problems of untruthfulness and selfishness would never have arisen in the first place. Indeed, these complex, overwhelming cities would not really lead to a *self-conscious* awareness of being a good person.

An anarchic survival community would not produce in each man a knowledge that he is caring or learning to care: he learns to care in order to survive, not in order to be good. Such a break constitutes one divide between the ethics of our own time and the religious ethics of the past. Instead of advocating the practice of goodness for its own sake, which has, as Weber believed, come to such selfrighteous and intolerant ends, a modern system of ethics must make an ethical condition emerge from social situations that are not consciously understood by the actors to be a search for a "better" ethical state. Looking for ethical situations in the structure of society is more honest, to my mind, than making pleas for a change of heart, more genuine than a conversion experience in which each man resolves to be good for ever after. People are too frail, and acts of mercy too easily perverted.

In his later novels, Dostoevsky gave another reason for looking at ethical desires in this way. He went so far as to believe a man could not be a good person if he were conscious of performing good acts; Dostoevsky felt that generosity and spontaneous giving become, when they reach a level of self-conscious, a smug form of self-denial. Yet all the truly good figures in his later novels—Prince Mishkin, Alyosha, Maria—fail to survive; they are torn apart by their own goodness, because they have no other force animating their lives. These truly good men are beings without a consciousness of themselves, and with a total consciousness of others, so that they are destroyed by the very complexities of the people around them, into which they become enmeshed.

But the fate of such figures could be changed

in the real world we could create in cities. In these cities, men will need to have some consciousness of themselves, they will continually be asking what it is in them that fails to be adequate for the social world they live in, what parts of their own lives are reconcilable or irreconcilable with the lives of the people around them. They cannot be unconscious of themselves if they are to survive; yet, like the good figures Dostoevsky pictured, they will be not conscious that what they do is good. For men struggling to understand each other in order to survive, the question of goodness would be irrelevant.

For example, we could imagine the everyday situation in which a man refuses to face the fact that a store he is building in a certain place in a neighborhood will eliminate a vacant lot children have needed to play in. The businessman is obdurate, and thus the neighbors, who are the only force to curb him in the absence of any central control, must begin a long process of threatening, cajoling, and harrassing so that they finally make him relent and look for a more socially acceptable site for his store. But applying this pressure—organizing boycotts and picket lines, etc.—is hardly a nourishing, satisfying task for most of the men involved in this new city role; the fact that they do something good for the community doesn't mean they like the substantive business of arguing with someone who regressed by willfully ignoring the people around him. It is the essence of a good act, as Dostoevsky said, that it does not bring a person pleasure to have been good.

How then can men become willing to endure the painful processes of a more civilized order? The force driving men into this new situation is, I believe, a specifically modern kind of boredom.

The people who in the last decade have searched in their minds or activities for a new sense of "community" were products of the affluent suburbs for the most part. Their attitude toward these places where they grew up was strong and simple: the suburbs were boring, they were empty of life or surprise, and so on. The complaints are familiar to the point of becoming clichés. What is important about them is that a large segment of the present generation means to act according to their disenchantment with a boring past, and try to find

something better. A sense of resignation is absent in these young people; they want actively to bring something new into being.

Part of this search for a new community is seen in the areas where young people are living and want to live. It has been known for some time that some of their parents, suburbanites whose children have grown up and left home, have been moving in increasing numbers back into the center of cities, when the housing is available. But an equally significant movement of young people into the center of cities is occurring. A growing minority of young adults, as they acquire family responsibilities and children, are refusing to make the trek out to the suburbs, and are searching instead for ways to remain in the center of town. The reason for this is that they hope for something "richer" in social life than what the suburb offers. It is true that a majority of the young married adults of this generation are moving into suburban homes of their own, just as the previous generation did. Yet among the more active, vital minority, a minority much greater than that to be found in the past, the old pattern is being rejected. These young people are refusing to be bored, refusing to accept the dead security in which they grew up.

It is my hope that this active refusal to accept the simplicities of the past will make it feasible for complex, disordered settlements to be desired and accepted by this generation nurtured in affluence. What someone has called the "great refusal" of the present generation to accept the secure cocoons the parents have woven can be the reason men now would be willing to endure the disorder and possible dislocation of an anarchic city environment.

This boredom is, however, rather strange. Most animals live by instinctual routines quite well; few men in agricultural, pre-industrial walks of life suffered from boredom, although their lives were hard and the rhythms of life fixed. The peculiar character of a secure, affluent routine is that it does not arise from the needs of adaptive survival with the environment or with other members of the race. It arises instead out of the fact that affluence permits men, through coherent routines, to hide from dealing with each other. Rather than face the full range of social experience possible to men, the communities of safe coherence cut off the amount of human material permitted into a man's life, in order that no questions of discord, no issues of survival be raised at all.

It is this "escape from freedom," in Erich Fromm's words, that ultimately makes a man quite consciously bored, aware that he is suffocating, although he may refuse to face the reasons for his suffocation. The boredom that rises out of this hiding is quite natural, for it is, as Nietzsche said, the voice of the creature in each man trying to make itself heard.

If social situations can be moved, step by step, toward a social environment in which human diversity is permitted to express itself, I believe this "creature in the man" will take hold and become involved, driven by the boredom with what men do unnecessarily to keep themselves secure. The feeling of boredom in the new middle-class generation is the hidden, and, as yet, undeveloped expression of a desire for diversity. Once this hidden desire has a field in which to express itself, once cities become responsive to human needs, the tiredness with routine that men now experience will be the conscious force moving people step by step into encountering social diversity. Inevitably the question of how differences between men can coexist will then arise, and the men involved will be caught up in the process of urban growth such as I envision it.

The refusal of the young who have grown up in affluence to accept its routines as reality is a distinct emotional break with the traditional acceptance of routine under conditions of scarcity or deprivation. For the routinizing act has a real dignity when times are hard, and a refusal to accept routine seems to be the expression of a spoiled child. But that temper does not fit well the processes of a large segment of modern-day society. The routines of affluence seem, and are, *unnecessary*; there is no need for them when people have an adequate economic base. If there is any truth to the journalistic cries about the generation gap, it is that the old do not understand youth's perception of present reality and that they forget that the young have never known the corrosive power of scarcity, scarcity that drove their elders to see comfort and security as humanly dignified ends in a life.

Because of the great freedom for expressing conflict that affluence could bring, because of the possibility for satisfying men's desires to aggress against each other without the result of mutual destruction, because the routines of hiding produced by the present communal uses of affluence are proving so distasteful to those nurtured in them, I have dared to hope that the anarchic city might be more than a utopian dream, that it might be a viable alternative for what now passes as social life. Our affluence in its present form is becoming an intolerable weight to those who supposedly enjoy it. That is to say—beyond the fact that in much of western Europe and America affluence is so inequitably distributed—that even those who have it have not learned to use it for humane ends. Unlike Marcuse, I am convinced that affluence can be put to good ends, in a viable, enduring, anarchic society. I believe that the disgust and anxiety affluent communities presently cause in their young will make the people of this generation ready to explore the human unknown, and perhaps permit themselves to be hurt for the sake of preserving their vitality.

V. THE INDIVIDUAL IN ADAPTATION

IN EVERY SOCIETY there is a complex of subjective experiences shared by members of the group with regard to the institutions by which they live. These are distinct from the personal and idiosyncratic ways in which individuals evaluate the objects of their perceptions, including their institutions. It is the former with which we are concerned in the anthropological study of adaptation. We seek to understand how the individual fits into the institutions of his society and how he acts for their perpetuation, change, or replacement.

Each individual born enters a world he did not make but with which he must come—or be brought—to terms. He must learn to use the established means of coping with the natural habitat, to live among the particular organizations of people designed to exploit these means, and to share in the prevalent value systems, if he is to succeed socially and biologically. But a newly born individual is a mass of relatively unorganized impulses, potential feelings and perceptions; these must be shaped and directed in ways that will enable him to participate in his society. The shaping of man's mind takes place by means of the selection of particular goals from among a wide range of alternatives in order to maintain the group's strategy of adaptation.

A hunter hunts not only with bow and arrow or rifle; he must also organize his social relations with his fellow hunters so that he can effectively find, stalk, and kill his prey. Before he can do this, he must learn not only how to use his weapons and the techniques of the chase but also how to behave with respect to his fellow hunters. For example, his kill must be prepared and divided among his dependents and the other members of the camp, and this requires that he learn appropriate attitudes toward sharing. Similarly, a factory worker's job includes more than his machine; his productive activities are organized in networks of people who make certain that tools and raw materials are available when they are needed, who pay him wages, and who produce and distribute food and other goods into which he can convert his wages. All of this involves a particular type of family organization, a complex merchandising system, and also the acquisition of attitudes, feelings, and techniques of behaving with others so that he can participate in the system effectively.

The human mind is shaped in a variety of learning situations, and every society provides institutions and procedures through which its growing members will learn

351

how to participate in the prevalent strategy of adaptation. In some societies, almost all learning takes place in the context of kinship, but one of the themes of the evolutionary record is that the shaping of young minds is progressively removed from kinship in successive levels of social and technological development. The most recent educational form is that of contemporary industrial nations, where the individual attends schools—which are distinctively nonkin institutions—from a very early age through late adolescence and often well into adulthood.

Here, as in the case of religion, it is only organizations of social relations and not ideas as such that can be analyzed in an evolutionary framework. We can show that affective life and shared subjective experiences must "fit" the institutions in a society, but we can apply an evolutionary frame of reference only to organized modes of teaching and to learning the attitudes that are appropriate to each strategy of adaptation. In addition, however, it is clear that the members of any single society have a common stamp; a society-wide set of shared experiences overlap all the differences of caste and class and locality that may exist among them. Such commonalities in affective experience are often grouped into what is referred to as the "basic personality structure" of a group or of its members. A cognate concept, "modal personality," refers to the personality elements that appear most frequently in a population; it is a composite statistical description to which no individual in the group may correspond. "Basic personality" is a more general (and less precise) concept, denoting the personality characteristics shared by most of the members of a group in their responses to hunger and sex, dependency and independence, aggression, love, self-confidence, authority, and the like. Just as values represent the grammar of organized social relations, basic personality can be thought of as the grammar of emotions and impulses.

The concept of basic personality is descriptive, not explanatory, and it is not a new concept, having been used effectively by Plutarch and Thucydides. As a matter of fact, it is a descriptive tool that has generally been put to its best use by novelists, chroniclers, and others who make no claim to scientific rigor. The concept of "national character" is akin to that of basic personality, and was introduced into the anthropological study of personality, largely as a result of the research of Margaret Mead, to describe the many basic personality structures that seem to distinguish complex national societies.

There is considerable disagreement among anthropologists about the sources and nature (and even the existence) of basic personality or national character. Some, following psychoanalytic hypotheses, tend to view it as largely an outgrowth of shared experiences of infancy and childhood; others tend to regard it as the commonly learned or acquired characteristics which—individual differences notwithstanding—enable people to fit into the social relationships characterizing their society's adaptive strategy. In this latter sense, basic personality denotes the accommodation of individuals to their society's adaptations, and the psychosocial techniques required are learned throughout the life cycle, not only during infancy and childhood. Here I am going to focus on childhood learning, since there are few data regarding later learning.

Let us begin with hunter-gatherers. It will be recalled that population density among such groups is low, rarely exceeding one person per square mile, and that the groups themselves move around a great deal. We can summarize what we have learned about such groups in terms of five major characteristics, specifying the adaptive strategy into which the shared subjective experiences of hunter-gatherers must "fit" so that the individual can function effectively.

(1) As a result of geographical mobility, the number of owned items is small. This helps to equalize economic status and underlies social and political egalitarianism. (2) Groups larger than 50 members may exhaust available resources; hence there is a constant division of groups and exchange of people among camps to keep group size at an effective level. (3) Generally, local groups do not have exclusive rights to resources. The fluid composition of groups allows people to move from one area to another, and the hosts of one season may be guests in the next. (4) There is little margin between what is needed for consumption and what is hunted and gathered, and since everyone knows where food can be found and all movements are public, there is no apprehension that a few people will appropriate the food resources of the group. Correspondingly, productive effort is constant throughout the year but varies considerably over shorter periods; when enough meat is available for three or four days, there is no need to hunt until it has been consumed. (5) Frequent visiting and interchange among groups prevents people from becoming attached to any one area, and when groups split up—for example, because of disputes—people move without a sense of loss of land and objects. (This profile is based on "Problems in the Study of Hunters and Gatherers," by Richard B. Lee and Irven De Vore, in *Man the Hunter*, edited by Lee and De Vore [Chicago: Aldine, 1968], pp. 3-12).

How do hunter-gatherers perceive these conditions? How do they subjectively experience their habitats and the organizations by which they adapt to them? There are no comparative studies of this problem, and I will rely on two independent investigations for describing the features that seem to be characteristic of most hunter-gatherers. The profile drawn by A. Irving Hallowell in his essay on "Some Psychological Characteristics of the Northeastern Indians" (in *Culture and Experience*, by A. Irving Hallowell [Philadelphia: University of Pennsylvania Press, 1955], pp. 125-50) is based on accounts by 17th- and 18th-century traders and missionaries, psychological projective tests administered by 20th-century anthropologists, and ethnological field studies. "One thing which seems to have impressed all Europeans alike," writes Hallowell, "is what may be characterized as a multifaceted pattern of emotional restraint or inhibition." This is evident not only in psychological tests but also in a variety of observed behaviors, notably in stoicism and patience in the face of vicissitudes and in the "fact that any overt expression of anger was characteristically inhibited." This is characteristic of small groups (Selection 6) in which interpersonal relations are intense; the tendency of groups to split as a consequence of conflict appears to be an aspect of the inhibition of aggression. Similarly, as Hallowell and other students of hunter-gatherers have observed, they rarely refuse a favor outright; apparently, such an act would not only contravene expectations of cooperation but also would be too forthright an expression of emotion and might provoke too strong a response in others.

But people in every society are confronted daily by events that elicit strong feelings; how do hunter-gatherers cope with such situations in the light of their characteristic inhibition and self-restraint? "One procedure," Hallowell observes, "would be to maintain a certain emotional indifference to things, to avoid investing too much emotion in anything, and when deep feelings were aroused to put them consciously aside as quickly as possible. . . . Perhaps it was a factor in the so-called haughtiness of the Indian. It represents an extension of the idea of fortitude to all aspects of the affective life. . . . If emotion could not be successfully handled by a stern indifference, and, particularly in cases of anger, face-to-face encounters were precluded, the individual had to discharge his affect in some less direct fashion." This does not mean that aggression is never expressed directly, or even homicidally (see Selection 6); but if it cannot be suppressed, it is expected that it will be expressed in covert form, as in sorcery or witchcraft or by leaving the group.

Richard K. Nelson, in his book on *Hunters of the Northern Ice* (Chicago: University of Chicago Press, 1969), confirms Hallowell's observations that hunter-gatherers are expected never to tell others what to do or to criticize them; instead, their inclination is (to use our own idiom) to mind one's own business. "Eskimos have learned not to disagree with one another openly or to issue orders to one another, qualities which are helpful in the avoidance of conflict," Nelson writes. This, in turn, appears closely related to the social and political egalitarianism of these groups and to the sense of independence and individualism—or "atomism"—that is often noted among their characteristics.

Nelson describes several additional qualities of mind that round out our picture of the perceptual apparatus of hunter-gatherers. They have a vast amount of knowledge about their habitat, which they seek constantly to extend; this is why they spend so much time in "shop talk," so that they may teach and learn from each other. Nelson notes that an Eskimo seldom doubts what he has been told by others, especially if they are his elders and are more experienced than he. Closely related is another highly adaptive quality: their perseverance at each task until it is completed. An excellent example is seen in the ethnographic film, *The Hunters*, in which four Bushmen (and their intrepid ethnographer-cameraman, John Marshall) stalked a wounded giraffe for several days until it died of a poisoned arrow wound. Part of a hunter's adaptive apparatus is a quick alertness—for game and all other unexpected situations—and a flexibility that enables him to improvise. This is necessary because no two situations in his experience are alike, and his material resources—especially his repertory of implements—are very limited.

The upbringing of children in hunting-gathering societies is commingled in the family and the camp. Not only parents and kinsmen but also other members of the small group participate in teaching and there is almost nothing in the camp's daily life to which youngsters are not exposed. Little boys are given miniature bows and arrows or other hunting implements with which to practice in groups that replicate those of their seniors; little girls learn the physical and social procedures of gathering by accompanying their mothers during foraging expeditions, and they are introduced early to the care of the infants who are carried along. As Hallowell notes, corporal punishment is rarely employed as a means of discipline; ridicule, praise, and other social pressures train people early in such societies to be sensitive to the opinions and sentiments of others, in the family and in the larger group.

We have seen that the social and technological changes required for horticulture make human demands that are met by adaptive responses in family and kinship organization, religion, law, and value systems. Similarly, horticulturists exhibit distinctive personality patterns that enable them to maintain and live within the sedentary and often intense kin groups that are important in their adaptive strategy. These kin groups also require the suppression of aggression, but with the important difference from hunter-gatherers that horticulturists cannot simply pack up and leave the group when the emotional going gets rough. Sedentary villagers have too great a physical investment in their land to do this, and they must develop different techniques for coping with their feelings.

There is more variability among horticulturists than among hunter-gatherers, but several manifestations of shared subjective experience are common to most. An outstanding example is their extreme circumspection in pursuing their own interests and their expectation that one will yield to majority opinions and feelings when dissenting points of view threaten to upset consensus and unanimity. As Gearing observes of the Cherokee in Selection 21, and as we will see in Dorothy Eggan's analysis of Hopi life (Selection 27), these pressures extend to people's private thoughts, especially those that are considered "bad." Life in such kinship groups is so intense and the urgency of peaceful sedentary existence is so strong that surface compliance alone is insufficient. The distance between feelings and action is a hair's breadth, so that feelings and thoughts must be subjected to the same control as overt behavior. This underlies a behavior pattern that can be described as "the man in the gray flannel loincloth."

Contributing strongly to this pattern is the lack of privacy—as we understand the term—in advanced horticultural societies. In such societies one is expected to find his satisfactions in others and through association with them, a particular kind of selection among alternative styles of affective life that is highly adaptive to the imperatives of sedentary, corporate, and intense social relations. The person who regularly wishes to be alone and seeks primary satisfaction within himself is thought to be practicing sorcery, engaging in illicit sexual liaisons, or both.

A closely related characteristic of corporate kin groups is that each member is expected to assume responsibility for the other members and they for him. In all societies, the sense of responsibility that characterizes people is an important feature of their personalities and their shared subjective experiences, and it is generally expressed in their legal systems. I will illustrate this with a pattern that is sometimes found in hunting-gathering societies and in a few agricultural groups, but is most frequently found in horticultural and pastoralist societies.

The predominant institutional expression of mutual responsibility in tribal societies is the principle of "joint legal liability." This means that if the perpetrator of an unlawful act cannot be apprehended or cannot meet his legal liability, then—and only then—his liability falls on members of his kin group. Thus, if a murder automatically sets penalties into motion—a retaliatory murder, let us say—one of the culprit's kinsmen will have to assume the onus if the actual culprit escapes. If the legal system stipulates that a woman's adultery must be compensated in money and if she cannot be made personally liable for her behavior, specified members of her descent group must make the payments to her husband. Legal concepts of responsibility of this kind cannot exist in contradiction to the feelings of responsibility people hold, and these must be regarded as adaptations to the imperatives of social and technological organization. Such feelings are extensions of the sense of "self" that is held by the members of a group, involving not only the formal positions in which they stand relative to each other but also the ways in which they see themselves in relation to each other.

People acquire such a sense of responsibility in a variety of ways; I will describe one. We saw (in the Introduction to the section on "Marriage and the Family") that there is an incompatibility between the strength of kin group relationships and those of the family and that primary anchorage in one leads to a weakening of the other. In societies with joint legal liability, family solidarity is weakened by the customs of "extrusion" and pubertal initiation ceremonies. These customs often occur in the same society, but the first is apparently more important in this regard than the second.

"Extrusion" occurs when boys or girls (and sometimes both sexes) are dislodged from the parental household at an early age, usually between eight and ten. In societies where this practice occurs, the child usually spends the day with his family but must go to sleep elsewhere at night. In a few societies, such as the hunting-gathering Andamanese and the horticultural Tikopia, the child is informally adopted at this stage of the life cycle by friends or distant kinsmen and goes to live in their households, returning to the parental home for periodic visits. Where this does not take place, extruded children may sleep at night in a hut built for this purpose, in a men's house or bachelor's dormitory, on the roof of the house (as among the Hopi described in Selection 27), in the open around a fire that burns all night for warmth and protection from wild animals or, as among the Nyakyusa of Tanganyika and Nyasaland, in whole villages of their own that carry the practice to its most extreme form.

Pubertal initiation rites are characterized as follows: (1) The rite is presided over by elders who are usually senior members of the child's descent group and were involved in the child's upbringing; parents are usually excluded from participation. (2) It involves a process of indoctrination into the customary practices of the group. (3) It involves physical ordeals, such as circumcision or some other form of genital mutilation, or scarification. (4) It must be universal for members of the sex for which it is prescribed. (5) It must be conducted in a group, not focused on a single individual. (6) The opposite sex is usually excluded from witnessing the rite.

Note that both these customs are group experiences; those with whom a boy or girl is initiated in a pubertal rite are generally those with whom he is going to spend the rest of his life, and those with whom an extruded child goes to sleep at night similarly constitute the group on which he will rely as his first line of social and economic defense; these socializing techniques must also be regarded as adaptations to the imperatives of sedentary, corporate kin groups. It seems that a major goal of customs like extrusion and pubertal initiation is to weaken the child's tendency to identify emotionally with his family and to direct these energies toward the wider kin group. Children identify with those who bring them up; significantly, where extrusion and pubertal initiation are practiced, the responsibility for children's upbringing is lodged with kinsmen in addition to parents, thus, it would seem, establishing a base for their identification outside the household.

In summary, then, we can describe the relationships among horticultural technology, socialization practices, group relations, and personality as follows: Horticultural technology leads to the formation of corporate kin groups in which land ownership is vested; such groups require that the individual partly submerge his identity in this larger group; one of the ways in which this is expressed is in the custom of joint legal liability which, in turn, requires an emotional identification with his wider group of kinsmen; this requires a deflection of emotional energies away from household and family toward the kin group; this is accomplished by the customs of extrusion, pubertal initiation rites, and child rearing by kinsmen in addition to parents.

Such customs as extrusion and pubertal initiation rites disappear after corporate kin groups are weakened by the technological and political changes leading to complex agricultural and industrial societies. But in pastoralism, the demands made by the herds that have to be tended lead to still other kinds of institutional, ideological, and affective systems. In Walter Goldschmidt's paper on "Theory and Strategy in the Study of Cultural Adaptability" (*American Anthropologist*, 67 [1965]: 402-407;

reprinted as Selection 19 in *The Cultural Present*), he points to the basic personality structure of pastoralists, which can be regarded as adaptive to their social and technological system. He notes that because pastoralists spend much of their time alone or in small groups, they have to learn early in their lives to make decisions independently and to follow through on them; this is especially important in assessing grass and water conditions for their herds. At the same time, pastoralists have to learn to operate within the framework of larger groups and to accept authority when they come together seasonally and when they engage in military operations. Thus, they display what he calls an "aggressive militarism," a willingness to take risks, and such characteristics as "bravery, fortitude, and the ability to withstand pain and hardship." Their similarity with hunting-gathering people suggests that these features may be in part adaptive to a way of life in groups that often have to split up and in which the individual is often on his own in his exploitation of the habitat. Many of these features of pastoralist life are discussed in Thomas Gladwin's description of the Plains Indians in Selection 28.

It appears that people in stateless agricultural societies more closely resemble horticulturists than those in agricultural nation-states; and as to the latter, it is extremely difficult to generalize about personality structure because of inter- and intrasocietal diversity. Each of the specialized ways of life in such a society makes different demands on the individual, in addition to the imperatives of particular family and kinship systems, modes of dispute resolution and social control, religious experience, and ideological superstructures. But although there are few data about the personality structure of village people, it is possible to infer some of their expectations from the shared experiences in such societies.

One of the first institutions to be weakened by national rulers, in their efforts to undermine local groups, is the traditional system of joint legal liability. This results in an adaptive change in the sense of responsibility to a response that is compatible with the "long arm of the law" reaching out for the individual. For example, there is not a single provision in the Code of Hammurabi for joint legal liability in the event that a culprit cannot be apprehended, nor are there any such provisions in the English common law during that country's agricultural stage of development. Thus, we can assume that the sense of "self" an individual is expected to maintain is very different from that observed in a horticultural society, in which his major social relationships are organized by corporate kin groups.

Another inference that can be made from the legal systems of agricultural societies arises from the frequent occurrence of a law that prescribes capital punishment for adultery. Not all agricultural states had such a law, but those that did were generally national systems that developed from within—for example, ancient Babylonia (Selection 10) and Tokugawa, Japan (Selection 16). Such a law promotes sexual exclusiveness and promotes (and reflects) stronger bonds between husband and wife. As William J. Goode has shown (in "The Theoretical Importance of Love," *American Sociological Review*, 24 [1959]: 38-47), marital solidarity and exclusivity subvert wider kin ties, thus supporting the rulers of new nations who must weaken the solidarity of local corporate groups that are potential competitors for authority and the command of loyalty.

It is in complex agricultural societies that we find the first anticipations of the personality structure that is generally associated with the "Protestant Ethic"—sexual puritanism, emotional restraint, the motivation to amass wealth as an end in itself and (closely related) the deferment of gratification. This complex of controls underlying a motivational system of affective austerity is an accommodation to the discipline connoted in such state policies as military service and annual taxation. It is in agricultural societies that people are first directed to produce surpluses for the economic benefit of the ruling classes and to save their earnings for their own and their children's advancement. This requires a different sense of responsibility from that found in horticultural kin groups; the affective austerity associated with nation-states is necessary for the effective functioning of the economic enterprises usually found in such societies.

These controls may be relaxed when the establishment of centralized political authority nears completion, when the autonomy of local groups has been largely eroded. I think this is an important part of what we are observing today in many industrial societies that are beginning a transition to a postindustrial stage of development. Many younger people feel that it is senseless to adhere to an ethic that stresses individual motivations to work when there will be few jobs available and little work will be required to sustain life. The younger generations in the United States and other industrial societies already seem to sense that the psychological consequences of the Protestant Ethic may no longer be adaptive, and they are anticipating this new level of social and technological organization.

It is, of course, difficult to generalize about the basic personality structure (or national character) of people in industrial societies. This is not only due to the diversity in each of these societies but also to the apparent lack of the same close "fits" between role and personality that we find in preindustrial societies. We do not have the data that would indicate whether this is due to factors inherent in the strategy of adaptation, to complexity, or to the beginning of a transition to a postindustrial stage of development. In any event, it does not seem that we can pose the same questions about the relationship between personality and the strategy of adaptation in our society as in preindustrial society. For example, it is not unusual to read of a Japanese man in his late 20s who has gone through a succession of roles, like docile son and pupil, extremist nationalist-revivalist, political activist in Maoist causes, and impeccably attired executive in a new electronics corporation specializing in computers. Similar sequences of roles can be observed in the younger generations in West Germany and the United States, and they raise many questions about the concept of basic personality structure (or national character) that cannot be answered in our present stage of knowledge. But it is not so much answers that are needed as fresh questions that are not simple transplants from the models of preindustrial or even early industrial societies.

The materials in the preceeding text on joint legal liability, extrusion, and pubertal initiation rites are based on my book, *The Transition from Childhood to Adolescence: Cross-Cultural Studies of Initiation Ceremonies, Legal Systems, and Incest Taboos* (Chicago: Aldine, 1964). The materials on capital punishment for adultery and affective austerity are based on my article, "Ends and Means in Political Control: State Organization and the Punishment of Adultery, Incest, and Violation of Celibacy" (*American Anthropologist*, 71 [1969]: 658-87). One of the most interesting documents dealing with recent changes in the ideologies of sexual behavior is *Sex and Morality: A Report Presented to the British Council of Churches* (Philadelphia: Fortress Press, 1966).

A psychoanalytically based book which has appealed to many social scientists who are concerned with shared subjective experiences is *Childhood and Society*, by Erik H. Erikson (second edition, New York: Norton, 1963). A significant book that represents a major methodological advance is *Dreams and Deeds: Achievement Motivation in Nigeria*, by Robert A. LeVine (Chicago: University of Chicago Press, 1966). An important and provocative book by a leading anthropologist who perhaps more than anyone else has been responsible for the study of the individual in culture is *Culture and Commitment: A Study of the Generation Gap*, by Margaret Mead (Garden City, N.Y.: Natural History Press, 1970). Among the following are represented most of the basic points of view taken by anthropologists who are concerned with this aspect of social life: *Personality in Culture*, by John J. Honigmann (New York and Evanston: Harper and Row, 1967); *Culture and Personality*, by Anthony F. C. Wallace (New York: Random House, 1961); *Studying Personality Cross-Culturally*, edited by Bert Kaplan (Evanston: Row, Peterson, 1961); *Social Structure and Personality: A Casebook*, by Yehudi A. Cohen (New York: Holt, Rinehart and Winston, 1961); *Personality and Social Systems*, edited by Neil J. Smelser and William T. Smelser (New York and London: Wiley, 1963); *Personalities and Cultures: Readings in Psychological Anthropology*, edited by Robert Hunt (Garden City, N.Y.: Natural History Press, 1967); and *Psychological Anthropology: Approaches to Culture and Personality*, edited by Francis L. K. Hsu (Homewood, Illinois: Dorsey Press, 1961).

26. ESKIMO VALUES AND PERSONALITY

NORMAN A. CHANCE

Reprinted from The Eskimo of North Alaska *by Norman A. Chance, pp. 77-79. Copyright 1966, Holt, Rinehart and Winston.* (For biographical information, see p. 277.)

■ In its original publication, the following selection is the concluding part of the chapter from which Selection 19 was taken. This brief selection shows that the separation between values and personality is difficult and, in fact, arbitrary at the least complex levels of sociotechnological development. The establishment of criteria for such distinctions remains an important task for anthropologists.

Here Chance points to many of the psychological characteristics of hunter-gatherers that I discussed in the Introduction to this section, especially the repression of aggression. It is on this that Chance focusses, and he notes that the trait is a source of strain for the individual. On the one hand, we have seen that the conditions of hunter-gatherer life demand that hostile feelings be suppressed, especially in view of people's need to rely on each other. On the other hand, as Chance observes, Eskimos are occasionally forced into cooperative relationships with those whom they dislike, and he notes that the results in the past were sometimes extreme. But aggression cannot be bottled up permanently and, as in the case of the Cherokee (Selection 20), there are permissible ways of expressing aggression indirectly or symbolically.

There is a very good and detailed account of socialization practices among Alaskan Eskimo groups in Robert Spencer's *The North Alaskan Eskimo* (cited in the Introduction to Selection 19). A good comparative study of socialization among North American Indians is *Primitive Education in North America*, by George A. Pettitt (University of California Publications in American Archaeology and Ethnology, 43, 1946, No. 1). A. Irving Hallowell discusses many different features of personality among North American hunter-gatherers in *Culture and Experience* (Philadelphia: University of Pennsylvania Press, 1955). ■

WHEN A PERSON is motivated to do what is culturally defined as desirable, when his own values are similar to those of the culture of which he is a part, then cultural values and personality traits are as identical as they ever can be.

However, when individuals are unable to fulfill culturally approved goals, or are inclined to fulfill culturally unapproved goals, conflicts arise which often develop into characteristic reactions. Attempts at accommodation to these internal stresses may be culturally approved or disapproved, healthy or neurotic, but in either instance, they frequently become a subconscious part of the personality.

A good illustration of this process is seen in the Eskimo's repression of aggression. From an early age, the child is encouraged to be friendly, open, genial, warm, and outgoing. White visitors to the arctic generally comment upon the frequent smile on the face of the Eskimo child. Although the child occasionally masks hostile feelings, he learns early that a friendly approach to others brings high rewards in the way of affection and praise. "That boy is even tempered, he never gets mad at anybody" is a common statement of praise. Warm personal attachments give a kind of social and psychological security that further adds to the desire to be friendly.

The aggressive child, on the other hand, is condemned as being "unfriendly." The Alaskan Indian is pointed out as an example: "They not friendly. They walk with fists (doubled up) all the time." Young bullies with strong tempers are characteristically subjects for gossip.

This type of upbringing is little preparation for facing the many conflicts and frustrations of adult life. The Eskimo youth is expected to be self-reliant in a physical and supernatural world over which he has little control. He must be friendly even with those people he may dislike. He should maintain a sense of pride but remain modest, be prepared for action but have patience. We may assume that these long-continued frustrations build up impulses toward

360

aggression in the individual. Since others strongly condemn any overt expression of these feelings, the individual simply suppresses them (that is, they seldom come to his conscious awareness) except during sudden seemingly unexplainable outburts of temper during which a mother shouts at her children, or a man beats his wife or destroys someone's property. On rare occasions today, but more frequently in the past, these severe outbursts resulted in murder—or when turned inward, suicide.

Though physical aggression is disapproved of, there are a number of other outlets into which these feelings may be channeled. Verbal aggression takes the form of gossip. When the object of aggression is a white man or group, hostility may be expressed more openly in "hate" talk and fantasies of vengeance. Another way of expressing hostility toward non-Eskimo is to talk about them in their presence, in the Eskimo language. This is one of the major uses that Eskimo teen-agers see in their language today, although the practice is not limited to them. People seem to fear even a suggestion of verbal hostility, so that individuals are never left to determine for themselves whether a personal remark is a joke or not. The speaker invariably makes his harmless intention explicit by saying, "I jokes." This pattern, too, is true of all age groups.

Another acceptable way of expressing hostility is by not speaking to the offender. If people become sufficiently angry they may not speak to one another for several weeks or even months. When sharply criticized, an Eskimo may simply leave the room or area without saying a word and not return until he feels that the critic has calmed down. If one cannot avoid a hostile situation, then it is best to leave. In the past whole communities have moved in order to avoid a conflict of major proportions; the most recent example occurred in Greenland, when the Thule Eskimo relocated themselves following a conflict with a recently established United States Air Force base.

The image the Eskimo presents to others is one of sociability and resourcefulness. Not infrequently, however, his private image of himself contains feelings of loneliness and/or inadequacy. An Eskimo usually tries to surround himself with familiar, friendly people. Rarely does a youth or adult entertain himself alone, preferring the company of others. Under the conditions of high individual and family mobility described previously, people often complain of feeling lonely. Darkness is "lonely." "Loneliness' is a synonym for boredom. A person living in a house alone must be lonely. Attachment to one's home is strong and when teen-agers go away to boarding schools, they often become extremely lonely and homesick. A person who likes to be alone is viewed with suspicion and distrust. Individuals seen alone in an open boat or on the tundra are rumored to be Indians or spies.

Feelings of inadequacy, too, are becoming more evident in recent years, particularly in those villages undergoing rapid Westernization. In Kaktovik, for example, many middle-aged women indicated strong feelings of inadequacy in response to a psychological questionnaire administeered by the author. These women had had less contact with the Western world than either their husbands, many of whom work steadily at a nearby radar site, or their children, who attend school locally or farther south. As a consequence, the women felt socially isolated from many of the changes going on around them. Furthermore, some of their traditional mechanisms for gaining prestige and contributing to family support, such as skin sewing, had diminished without adequate replacement. Under these changing conditions, many middle-aged women felt insecure and inadequate, yet these feelings did not lead to the expressions of anxiety that we would expect to find in Western society. The Eskimo repress feelings of anxiety because they conflict with the high value placed on self-reliance and resourcefulness in much the same way that aggression conflicts with the values of friendliness and cooperation. Instead, the questionnaire results suggested that feelings of anxiety were inverted and appeared as symptoms of inner tension. . . .

27. INSTRUCTION AND AFFECT IN HOPI CULTURAL CONTINUITY

DOROTHY EGGAN

Reprinted from the Southwestern Journal of Anthropology, *Vol. 12, pp. 347-370, 1956. Dorothy Eggan lived from 1901 to 1965. The central focus of her anthropological work was the study of Hopi personality through the medium of dreams, and the importance of this approach began to be recognized during the last decade of her life. A high point in her life was her adoption by the women of the Fire Clan at Old Oraibi and her very close relationships with them for many years.*

■ In previous selections, we observed several characteristics of horticultural strategies of adaptation : corporate kin groups and extended family systems, customary law and localized political controls, the reinforcement of group solidarity by religious and magical practices and beliefs, and value systems that channel the individual into conformity. For instance, we saw in Selection 20 that in horticultural groups a high valuation is placed on the maintenance of harmony, and this extends even to the internal thought processes of the individual.

In the next selection we turn to the psychological side of these processes. Here we see in detail some aspects of the strong emotional controls in the lives of the Hopi Indians, and the relationship of these controls to Hopi social relationships. There is an elaborate system among the Hopi for the continuous manipulation of such emotions as guilt and dependency, which serves to maintain group solidarity especially in the absence of formal institutions and roles of authority. People in tightly knit kin groups, like those found among the Hopi, are often preoccupied with the danger of splits, and group solidarity is protected by religious ritual, among other things ; a major theme of this article is the way in which religion is used to manipulate emotions to maintain conformity and group solidarity. It is thus shown how the individual is motivated to sustain exclusive social (clan) relationships. The pressures pointing him in this direction are not only economic, religious, and ideological but also, as this selection shows, psychological.

An important article related to this selection is "The Interpretation of Pueblo Culture : A Question of Values," by John W. Bennett (*Southwestern Journal of Anthropology*, 2 [1946] : 361-74). Among the best descriptions of Hopi culture are *Old Oraibi : A Study of the Hopi Indians of Third Mesa*, by Mischa Titiev (Papers of the Peabody Museum of American Archaeology and Ethnology, Harvard University, 22, 1944 [1]), and *Social Organization of the Western Pueblos*, by Fred Eggan (Chicago : University of Chicago Press, 1950, pp. 17-138). Many of the themes in this paper are portrayed more fully in *Sun Chief : The Autobiography of a Hopi Indian*, edited by Leo W Simmons (New Haven : Yale University Press, 1942). Also significant is *The Tewa World : Space, Time, Being, and Becoming in a Pueblo Society*, by Alfonzo Ortiz (Chicago and London : University of Chicago Press, 1969). ■

EDUCATION AND ANTHROPOLOGY have proved in recent years that each has much of interest to say to the other for both are concerned with the transmission of cultural heritage from one generation to another—and with the means by which that transmission is accomplished. And although anthropology has tended to be preoccupied with the processes of cultural *change*, and the conditions under which it takes place, rather than with cultural continuity, it would seem, as Herskovits has said, that cultural change can be best understood when considered in relation to cultural stability.

Both education and anthropology are concerned with learned behavior, and the opinion that early learning is of vital significance for the later development of personality, and that emotional factors are important in the learning process, while sometimes implicit rather than explicit, is often found in anthropological literature, particularly in that dealing with "socialization," "ethos," and "values." From Mead's consistent work, for instance, has come a clearer picture of the socialization process in a wide variety of cultures, including our own, and she examines early "identification" as one of the problems central to all of them. Hallowell, too, speaking of the learning situation in which an individual must acquire a personality pattern, points out that "there are important affective components involved," and elsewhere he emphasizes a "need for further investigation of relations between learning process and affective experience." Kluckhohn, writing on values and value-orientation, says that "one of the severest limitations of the classical theory of learning is its neglect of attachments and attitudes in favor of reward and punishment." And DuBois states explicitly that, "Institutions which may be invested with high emotional value because of patterns in child training are not ones which can be lightly legislated out of existence."

In fact, increasing interaction between anthropology and psychiatry (which has long held as established the connection between emotion, learning, and resistance to change in individuals) has in the last decade introduced a theme into anthropology which reminds one of Sapir's statement that "the more fully one tries to understand a culture, the more it takes on the characteristics of a personality organization."

Psychologists, while perhaps more cautious in their approach to these problems, since human emotional commitments—particularly as regards permanency—are difficult if not impossible to examine in the laboratory, emphasize their importance in the learning situation, and frequently express dissatisfaction with many existing methods and formulations in the psychology of personality. The shaping factors of emotion—learned as well as innate—are stressed by Asch in his *Social Psychology*, and focus particularly on man's "need to belong." He feels that the "psychology of man needs basic research and a fresh theoretical approach." Allport speaks of past "addiction to machines, rats, or infants" in experimental psychology, and hopes for a "design for personality and social psychology" which will become "better tempered to our subject matter" as we "cease borrowing false notes—whether squeaks, squeals, or squalls . . ." and "read the score of human personality more accurately." And Murphy, starting with the biological foundations of human learning, particularly the individual form this "energy system" immedi-

ately assumes, examines man as psychologically structured by early canalizations in which personality is rooted, to which are added an organized symbol system and deeply ingrained habits of perception, and suggests that the structure thus built is highly resistant to change. He says that, "The task of the psychology of personality today is to apply ruthlessly, and to the limit, every promising suggestion of today, but always with the spice of healthy skepticism," while recognizing "the fundamental limitations of the whole present system of conceptions . . ." as a preparation for "rebirth of knowledge."

Anthropologists as well as psychologists are aware that any hypotheses in an area so complex must be regarded as tenuous, but since the situations cannot be taken into the laboratory, there is some value in taking the laboratory to the situation. Progress in these amorphous areas can only come about, as Redfield has said, by the mental instrument which he has called a "controlled conversation"—this discussion, then, must be considered a conversation between the writer and others who have brought varied interests and techniques to the problem of resistance to cultural change. It begins logically with a recent paper on "Cultural Transmission and Cultural Change" in which Bruner discusses two surveys of the literature on acculturation and adds to the hypotheses presented in them another which he finds relevant to the situation among the Mandan-Hidatsa Indians. As stated in his summary paragraph we find the proposition: "That which is learned and internalized in infancy and early childhood is most resistant to contact situations. The hypothesis directs our attention to the age in the individual life career at which each aspect of culture is transmitted, as well as to the full context of the learning situation and the position of the agents of socialization in the larger social system."

This proposition will be further extended by a consideration of the *emotional* commitment involved in the socialization process among the Hopi Indians; here the "conversation" will be directed to emotion in both teaching and learning, and will center around resistance to cultural change which has been remarkably consistent in Hopi society throughout recorded history *until the Second World War brought enforced and drastic changes.* At that time the young men, although legitimately conscientious objectors, were drafted into the army. Leaving the isolation of their reservation, where physical violence between adults was rare, they were rapidly introduced to the stark brutality of modern warfare. In army camps alcoholic intoxication, an experience which was the antithesis of the quiet, controlled behavior normally demanded of adult Hopi on their reservation, frequently brought relief from tension and a sense of comradeship with fellow soldiers. Deprived of the young men's work in the fields, many older people and young women were in turn forced to earn a living in railroad and munition centers off the reservation. Thus the gaps in the Hopi "communal walls" were, for the first time, large enough in numbers and long enough in time— and the experiences to which individuals had to adapt were revolutionary enough in character —so that the sturdy structure was damaged. It is emphasized, therefore, that in this discussion *Hopi* refers to those members of the tribe who had reached *adulthood* and were thoroughly committed to their own world view before 1941. Much of it would not apply as forcefully to the children of these people, and would be even less applicable to their grandchildren.

The major hypotheses suggested here, then, are:

(1) That the Hopi, as contrasted with ourselves, were experts in the use of *affect* in their educational system, and that this element continued to operate throughout the entire life span of each individual as a *reconditioning* factor; and

(2) That this exercise of emotion in teaching and learning was an efficient means of social control which functioned in the absence of other forms of policing and restraint, and also in the maintenance of stability both in the personality structure of the individual and the structure of the society.

These hypotheses may be explored through a consideration of (a) the early and continued conditioning of the individual in the Hopi maternal extended family, which was on every level, an inculcation of *interdependence* as contrasted with out training for *independence*; and (b) an early and continuing emphasis on religious observances and beliefs (also emphasizing interdependence), the most important facet

of which—for the purposes of this paper—was the central concept of the Hopi "good heart."

If we examine the educational system by which a Hopi acquired the personal entity which made him so consistently and determinedly Hopi, we find that it was deliberate and systematic. Students of Hopi are unanimous on this point but perhaps it can be best illustrated by quoting one of my informants who had spent much time away from the reservation, including many years in a boarding school, and who was considered by herself and other Hopi to be an extremely "acculturated" individual. In 1938 when she made this statement she was about thirty years old and had brought her children back to the reservation of be "educated." Said she,

It is very hard to know what to do. In the old days I might have had more babies for I should have married early. Probably some of them would have died. But my comfort would have been both in numbers and in knowing that all women lost babies. Now when I let my little son live on top [a conservative village on top of the mesa] with my mothers, I worry all the time. If he dies with dysentery I will feel like I killed him. Yet he *must* stay on top so the old people can teach him the *important* things. It is his only chance of becoming Hopi, for he would never be a *bahana* (White).

The education which she considered so vital included careful, deliberate instruction in kinship and community obligations, and in Hopi history as it is seen in mythology and as remembered by the old people during their own lifetimes. The Hopi taught youngsters fear as a means of personal and social control and for the purposes of personal and group protection; and they were taught techniques for the displacement of anxiety, as well as procedures which the adults believed would prolong life. Children were instructed in religious lore, in how to work and play, in sexual matters, even in how to deal with a *bahana*. Good manners were emphasized, for they were a part of the controlled, orderly conduct necessary to a Hopi good heart.

Constantly one heard during work or play, running through all activity like a connecting thread: "Listen to the old people—they are wise"; or, "Our old uncles taught us that way— it is the *right* way." Around the communal bowl, in the kiva, everywhere this instruction went on; stories, dream adventures, and actual experiences such as journeys away from the reservation were told and retold. And children, in the warmth and security of this intimate extended family and clan group, with no intruding outside experiences to modify the impact until they were forced to go to an alien school, learned what it meant to be a good Hopi from a wide variety of determined teachers who had very definite—and *mutually consistent*—ideas of what a good Hopi is. And they learned all of this in the Hopi language, which, as Whorf has made so clear, has no words with which to express many of our concepts, but which, working together with "a different set of cultural and environmental influences . . . interacted with Hopi linguistic patterns to mould them, to be moulded again by them, and so little by little to shape the world outlook."

Eventually these children disappeared into government schools for a time, and in the youth of most of these older Hopi it was a boarding school off the reservation where Indian children from various reservations were sent, often against their own and their parents' wishes. Here White teachers were given the task of "civilizing" and "Christianizing" these wards of the government, but by that time a Hopi child's view of the world and his place in it was very strong. Moreover, trying to transpose our concepts into their language was often very nearly impossible for them, since only Hopi had been spoken at home. Examining Hopi memory of such a method of education we quote a male informant who said:

> I went to school about four years. . . . We worked like slaves for our meals and keep. . . . We didn't learn much. . . . I didn't understand and it was hard to learn. . . . At that time you do what you are told or you get punished. . . . You just wait till you can go home.

And a woman said:

> Policemen gathered us up like sheep. I was scared to death. My mother tried to hide me. I tried to stay away but the police always won. . . . Then we were sent to Sherman [in California]. . . . It was far away; we were afraid on the train. . . . I didn't like it when I couldn't learn and neither did the teachers. . . . They never punished me, I always got 100 in Deportment. . . . I was there three years. . . . I was so glad to get home that I cried and cried . . ., glad to have Hopi food again, and fun again.

As children, the Hopi usually solved this dilemma of enforced education by means of a surface accommodation to the situation until such time as they were able to return to their own meaningful world. For, as Park has said, man can "make his manners a cloak and his face a mask, behind which he is able to preserve . . . inner freedom . . . and independence of thought, even when unable to maintain independence of action." In other words, because the inner core of Hopi identification was already so strong, these children were able to *stay* in a White world, while still *living* in the Hopi world within themselves. And while for some there was a measure of temptation in many of the things learned in White schools so that they "became friendly with whites and accepted their gifts," the majority of these older Hopi acquired a White education simply as a "necessary accessory"; they incorporated parts of our material culture, and learned to deal with Whites astutely, but their values were largely unaffected.

If we now examine more closely the pattern of integration through which the Hopi erected a communal wall around their children, we find in their kinship system the framework of the wall, but interwoven through it and contributing greatly to its strength was a never-ending composition which gave color and form, their religious ceremonies and beliefs.

Let us first contrast briefly the affect implicit in the way a Hopi born into this kinship system experienced relationships and the way in which Western children experience them. In the old days it was rare for a growing primary family to live outside the maternal residence. Normally each lived within it until the birth of several children crowded them out. And in this household each child was eagerly welcomed, for infant mortality was high and the clan was always in need of reinforcement. Thus, in spite of the physical burden on the biological mother, which she sometimes resented, the first strong *clan* sanction which we see in contrast to our own, was the absolute need for and desire for many children. From birth the young of the household were attended, pampered, and disciplined, although very mildly for the first several years, by a wide variety of relatives in addition to the mother. These attentions came both from the household members and from visitors in it. In no way was a baby ever as dependent upon his physical mother as are children in our culture. He was even given the breast of a mother's mother or sister if he cried for food in his mother's absence. True a Hopi saying states that a baby is made "sad" if another baby steals his milk, but it has been my experience that these women may risk making their own babies sad temporarily if another child needs food.

Weaning, of course, when discussed in personality contexts means more than a transition from milk to solid food. It is also a gradual process of achieving independence from the comfort of the mother's body and care, of transferring affections to other persons, and of finding satisfactions within oneself and in the outside world. Most people learn to eat solid food; many of us are never weaned, which has unfortunate consequences in a society where *individual* effort and independence are stressed. The Hopi child, on the other hand, from the day of his birth was being weaned from his biological mother. Many arms gave him comfort, many faces smiled at him, and from a very early age he was given bits of food which were chewed by various members of the family and placed in his mouth. So, for a Hopi, the outside world in which he needed to find satisfaction was never far away. He was not put in a room by himself and told to go to sleep; every room was crowded by sleepers of all ages. He was in no way *forced to find satisfactions within himself*; rather these were provided for him, if possible, by his household and clan group. His weaning, then, was from the breast only, and as he was being weaned from the biological mother, he was at the same time in a situation which *increased* his emotional orientation toward the intimate in-group of the extended family—which was consistent with the interests of Hopi social structure. Thus, considering weaning in its wider implications, a Hopi was never "weaned"; it was not intended that he should be. For these numerous caretakers contributed greatly to a small Hopi's faith in his intimate world—and conversely without question to a feeling of strangeness and *emotional insecurity* as adults in any world outside of this emotional sphere. The Hopi were often successful outside of the reservation, but they have shown a strong tendency to return frequently to the maternal household. Few ever left it permanently.

In addition to his extended family, while a Hopi belonged to one clan only, the clan into which he was born, he was a "child" of his father's clan, and this group took a lively interest in him. There were also numerous ceremonial and adoptive relationships which were close and warm, so that most of the persons in his familiar world had definite reciprocal relations with the child. Since all of these "relatives" lived in his own small village, or in villages nearby, his emotional and physical "boundaries" coincided, were quite definitely delimited, and were explored and perceived at the same time. It cannot be too strongly emphasized that the kinship terms which a Hopi child learned in this intimate atmosphere were not mere verbalizations—as, for instance, where the term "cousin" among ourselves is sometimes applied to someone we have never seen and never will see. On the contrary, each term carried with it definite mutual responsibilities and patterns of behavior, and, through these, definite emotional interaction as well. These affects were taught as proper responses, together with the terms which applied to each individual, as he entered the child's life. This process was deliberately and patiently, but unceasingly, worked at by every older individual in the child's surroundings, so by the time a Hopi was grown kinship reaction patterns were so deeply ingrained in his thinking and feeling, and in his workaday life, that they were as much a part of him as sleeping and eating. He was not merely told that Hopi rules of behavior were right or wise; he lived them as he grew and *in his total environment* (as contrasted to our separation of teaching at home, in school, and in Sunday school) until he was simply not conscious that there was any other way to react. Note that I say *conscious*! The unconscious level of feeling, as seen in dreams and life-history materials, and in indirect behavior manifestations (jealousy and gossip), often presents quite a different picture. But while ambivalence toward specific persons among the Hopi—as with mankind everywhere—is a personal burden, the long reinforced conditioned reaction of *interdependence* on both the emotional and overt behavior level was highly uniform and persistent. Perhaps the strength of kinship conditioning toward interdependence which was conveyed in a large but intimate group, living in close physical contact, can be best illustrated by quoting from an informant:

My younger sister —— was born when I was about four or five, I guess. I used to watch my father's and mother's relatives fuss over her. She didn't look like much to me. I couldn't see why people wanted to go to so much trouble over a wrinkled little thing like that baby. I guess I didn't like babies as well as most girls did. . . . But I had to care for her pretty soon anyway. She got fat and was hard to carry around on my back, for I was pretty little myself. First I had to watch her and joggle the cradle board when she cried. She got too big and wiggled too much and then my mother said to me, "She is *your sister*—take her out in the plaza in your shawl."

She made my back ache. Once I left her and ran off to play with the others for a while. I intended to go right back, but I didn't go so soon, I guess. Someone found her. I got punished for this. My mother's brother said: "You should not have a sister to help you out when you get older. What can a woman do without her sisters? You are not one of us to leave your sister alone to die. If harm had come to her you would never have a clan, no relatives at all. No one would ever help you out or take care of you. Now you have another chance. You owe her more from now on. This is the worst thing that any of my sisters' children has ever done. You are going to eat by yourself until you are fit to be one of us." That is what he said. That is the way he talked on and on and on. When meal time came they put a plate of food beside me and said, "Here is your food; eat your food." It was a long time they did this way. It seemed a long time before they looked at me. They were all sad and quiet. They put a pan beside me at meal time and said nothing—nothing at all, not even to scold me.

My older sister carried —— now. I didn't try to go near her. But I looked at my sisters and thought, "I need you—I will help you if you will help me." I would rather have been beaten or smoked. I was so ashamed all the time. Wherever I went people got sad [that is, quiet]. After a while [in about ten days as her mother remembered it] they seemed to forget it and I ate with people again. During those awful days Tuvaye [a mother's sister] sometimes touched my head sadly, while I was being punished, I mean. Once or twice she gave me something to eat. But she didn't say much to me. Even she and my grandfather were ashamed and in sorrow over this awful thing I had done.

Sometimes now I dream I leave my children alone in the fields and I wake up in a cold sweat. Sometimes I dream I am alone in a desert place with no water and no one to help me. Then I think of this punishment when I dream this way. It was the worst thing I ever did. It was the worst thing that ever happened to me. No one ever mentioned it to me afterwards but —— [older male sibling], the mean one. I would hang my head with shame. Finally my father told him sharply that he would be punished if he ever mentioned this to me again. I was about six when this happened, I think.

This informant was about forty when she related this incident, but she cried, even then, as she talked.

Nor was withdrawal of support the only means of punishment. There were bogey Kachinas who "might kidnap" bad children, and who visited the mesas sometimes when children were uncooperative; thus the "stranger" *joined effectively* with the clan in inducing the "ideal" Hopi behavior. But children *shared* this fear, as they also frequently shared other punishments. Dennis has called attention to the fact that a whole group of children often shared the punishment for the wrongdoing of one. This method may not endear an individual to his agemates, but it does reinforce the central theme of Hopi belief that each person in the group is responsible for what happens to all, however angry or jealous one may feel toward siblings.

Before we examine the religious composition of the Hopi "communal walls," we might contrast more explicitly the emotional implications of early Hopi conditioning to those experienced in our society. From the day of *our* birth the training toward *independence*—as contrasted to *interdependence*—starts. We sleep alone; we are immediately and increasingly in a world of comparative strangers. A variety of nurses, doctors, relatives, sitters, and teachers march through our lives in a never-ending procession. A few become friends, but *compared with a Hopi childs' experiences*, the impersonality and lack of emotional relatedness to so many kinds of people with such widely different backgrounds is startling. Indeed the disparity of the relationships as such is so great that a continuity of emotional response is impossible, and so we learn to look for emotional satisfaction in change, which in itself becomes a value. In addition, we grow up aware that there are many ways of life within the American class system; we know that there are many choices which we must make as to profession, behavior, moral code, even religion; and we know that the values of our parents' generation are not necessarily ours. If the permissive intimacy in the primary family in our society—from which both nature and circumstance demand a break in adulthood—is too strong, the individual cannot mature so that he can function efficiently in response to the always changing personalities in his life, and the always changing demands of the society. He becomes a dependent neurotic "tentative between extreme polarities." But precisely because the permissive intimacy, as well as the punishing agencies, in a Hopi child's life were so far and so effectively extended in his formative years he became *interdependent* with a larger but still definitely delimited group, and tended always to be more comfortable and effective within it. His self-value quickly identified itself with the larger Hopi value, and to the extent that he could continue throughout his life to identify with his group and function within it, he was secure in his place in the universe.

We have now sketched the situation which surrounded the young Hopi child in his first learning situations, and contrasted these with our own. For descriptive convenience this has been separated from religious instruction, but in the reality experience of the children—with the exception of formal initiation rites—no one facet of learning to be Hopi was separated from others. To understand the meaning his religion had for a Hopi one must first understand the harsh physical environment into which he was born. While it is agreed that it would not be possible to predict the character or the social structure of the Hopi from the circumstances of this physical environment, it is self-evident that their organized social and ritual activities are largely a response to it. And such activities are at once a reflection of man's need to *be*, and his need to justify his existence to himself and others. If those who doubt that the forces of nature are powerful in shaping personality and culture were confined for one year on the Hopi reservation—even though their own economic dependence on "nature" would be negligible— they would still know by personal experience more convincing than scientific experiment the relentless pressure of the environment on their own reaction patterns. They would, for instance, stand, as all Hopis have forever stood, with aching eyes fastened on a blazing sky where thunderheads piled high in promise and were snatched away by "evil winds," and thus return to their homes knowing the tension, the acute bodily need for the "feel" of moisture. When rains do fall, there is the likelihood of a cloudburst which will ruin the fields. And there is a possibility of early frost which will destroy

their crops, as well as the absolute certainty of sandstorms, rodents, and worms which will ruin many plants. These things on a less abstract level than "feeling" resolved themselves into a positive threat of famine and thirst which every Hopi knew had repeatedly ravaged his tribe. Is it possible that the effects of this silent battle between man and the elements left no mark on successive generations of individuals? It certainly was the reinforced concrete of Hopi social structure, since strongly conditioned interdependence was the only hope of survival.

Thus, the paramount problem for the Hopi was uncertain rain, and the outward expression of their deep need for divine aid was arranged in a cycle of ceremonies, the most impressive of which, at least among the exoteric rituals, were Kachina dances. These were, for the observer, colorful pageants in which meticulously trained dancers performed from sunrise until sunset, with short intermissions for food and rest. Their bodies were ceremonially painted; brilliant costumes were worn, along with beautifully carved and painted masks which represented the particular gods who were taking part in the ceremony. The color, the singing and the drums which accompanied the dance, the graceful rhythm and intense concentration of the dancers, all combine into superb artistry which is an hypnotic and impressive form of prayer. Ideally, the Hopi preceded every important act with prayer, and with these older Hopi the ideal was apt to be fact. A bag of sacred cornmeal was part of their daily equipment.

In the religious context also, we must remember the intimate atmosphere which surrounded a Hopi child in the learning situation. Here children were taught that if *all* Hopi behaved properly—that is, kept good hearts—the Kachinas would send rain. It was easy for the children to believe this because from earliest babyhood these beautiful creatures had danced before them as they lolled comfortably in convenient laps. There was a happy, holiday atmosphere throughout a village on dance days, but while each dance was being performed, the quiet of profound reverence. Lying in the mother's lap, a baby's hands were often struck together in the rhythm of the dance; as soon as he would walk his feet were likewise directed in such rhythm, and everybody praised a child and laughed affectionately and encouragingly as it tried to dance. As the children grew older, carved likenesses of these gods, as well as other presents, were given to them by the gods themselves. And as he grew in understanding, a child could not fail to realize that these dancers were part of a religious ceremony which was of utmost importance in his world—that the dancers were rain-bringing and thus life-giving gods.

When first initiation revealed that the gods were in reality men who danced in their stead, a *reorganization* of the emotions which had been directed toward them began, and there is much evidence in autobiographical materials of resentment, if not actual trauma, at this point. For some of them the initiation was a physical ordeal, but for those who entered this phase of their education by way of Powamu there was no whipping, although all initiates witnessed the whipping of those who were initiated into the Kachina cult. However, the physical ordeal seems to be less fixed in adult memories than disillusion.

In Don Talyesva's account of initiation into Kachina we find:

I had a great surprise. They were not spirits, but human beings. I recognized nearly every one of them and felt very unhappy because I had been told all my life that the Kachinas were Gods. I was especially shocked and angry when I saw my uncles, fathers, and own clanbrothers dancing as Kachinas. . . . [But] my fathers and uncles showed me ancestral masks and explained that long ago the Kachinas had come regularly to Oraibi and danced in the plaza. They explained that since the people had become so wicked . . . the Kachinas had stopped coming and sent their spirits to enter the masks on dance days. . . . I thought of the flogging and the initiation as a turning point in my life, and I felt ready at last to listen to my elders and live right.

One of our informants said in part:

I cried and cried into my sheepskin that night, feeling I had been made a fool of. How could I ever watch the Kachinas dance again? I hated my parents and thought I could never believe the old folks again, wondering if gods had ever danced for the Hopi as they now said and if people really lived after death. I hated to see the other children fooled and felt mad when they said I was a big girl now and should act like one. But I was afraid to tell the others the truth for they might whip me to death. I know now it was best and the *only way to teach* children, but it took me a long time to know that. I hope my children won't feel like that.

This informant was initiated into Powamu and not whipped. She was about thirty when she made this statement to the writer.

Another woman, from a different mesa, speaking of her initiation into the Kachina society, said to me:

The Kachinas brought us children presents. I was very little when I remember getting my first Kachina doll. I sat in my mother's lap and was "ashamed" [these people often use ashamed for shy or somewhat fearful], but she held out my hand for the doll. I grabbed it and hid in her lap for a long time because the Kachina looked too big to me and I was partly scared. But my mother told me to say "asqualie" [thank you] and I did. The music put me to sleep. I would wake up. The Kachinas would still be there. . . . I dreamed sometimes that the Kachinas were dancing and brought me lots of presents. . . .

When I was initiated into Kachina society I was scared. I heard people whisper about it. . . . Children shook their heads and said it was hard to keep from crying. . . . My mother alway put her shawl over my head when the Kachinas left the plaza. When she took it off they would be gone. So I knew they were gods and had gone back to the San Francisco mountains. . . . My ceremonial mother came for me when it was time to go to the kiva [for initiation] and she looked sad [that is, serious]. She took most of the whipping on her own legs [a custom widely practiced among the Hopi]. But then I saw my father and my relatives were Kachinas. When they took their masks off this is what I saw. I was all mixed up. I was mad. I began to cry. I wondered how my father became a Kachina and if they [these men, including her father] would all go away when the Kachinas went back to the San Francisco mountains where the dead people live. Then when my father came home I cried again. I was mad at my parents and my ceremonial mother. "These people have made me silly," I said to myself, "and I thought they were supposed to like me so good." I said that to myself. But I was still crying, and the old people told me that only babies cry. They kept saying I would understand better when I got bigger. They said again that the Kachinas had to go away because the Hopi got bad hearts, and they [the Kachinas] couldn't stand quarreling, but they left their heads behind for the Hopis. I said why didn't they rot then like those skulls we found under that house? They said I was being bad and that I should have been whipped more. . . .

When children asked me what happened in the kiva I was afraid to tell them because something would happen to me. Anyway I felt smart because I knew more than those *little* children. It took me a long time to get over this sadness, though. Later I saw that the Kachinas were the most *important thing in my life* and that children can't understand these things. . . . It takes a while to see how wise the old people really are. You learn they are always right in the end.

Before we try to find our way with the Hopi to an "understanding of these things" we must examine their concept of the good heart which functions both in their kinship system and religion to maintain the effectiveness of the "wall of Hopiness." Of greatest significance in all activities among these people, and particularly their religious ceremonies, is the fact that everything of importance is done communally. Thus each individual who has reached maturity is responsible *to* and *for* the whole community. The Hopi speak of this process as "uniting our hearts," which in itself is a form of prayer. A slight mistake in a ceremony can ruin it and thus defeat the community prayer for rain; so too can a trace of "badness" in one's heart, although it may not be visible to the observer. Thus their religion teaches that *all* distress— from illness to crop failure—is the result of bad hearts, or possibly of witchcraft (here the simple "bad heart" must not be confused with a "Two-heart," *powaka*, witch), an extreme form of personal wickedness in which an individual sacrifices others, particularly his own relatives, to save himself.

This concept of a good heart in *conscious contradistinction* to a bad heart is of greatest importance not only in understanding Hopi philosophy but also in understanding their deep sense of cultural continuity and their resistance to fundamental change. A good heart is a positive thing, something which is never out of a Hopi's mind. It means a heart at peace with itself and one's fellows. There is no worry, unhappiness, envy, malice, nor any other disturbing emotion in a good heart. In this state, cooperation, whether in the extended household or in the fields and ceremonies, was selfless and easy. Unfortunately, such a conception of a good heart is also impossible of attainment. Yet if a Hopi did not keep a good heart he might fall ill and die, or the ceremonies—and thus the vital crops—might fail, for, as has been said, only those with good hearts were effective in prayer. Thus we see that the Hopi concept of a good heart included conformity to all rules of Hopi good conduct, both external and internal. To the extent that it was internalized— and all Hopi biographical material known to the writer suggests strongly that it was effectively internalized—it might reasonably be called a quite universal culturally patterned and cultur-

ally consistent Hopi "super-ego."

There was, therefore, a constant probing of one's own heart, well illustrated by the anguished cry of a Hopi friend, "Dorothy, *did* my son die as the old folks said because my heart was not right? Do *you* believe this way, that if parents do not keep good hearts children will die?" And there was a constant examination of one's neighbors' hearts: "Movensie, it is those —— clan people who ruined this ceremony! They have bad hearts and they quarrel too much. That bad wind came up and now we will get no rain." Conversation among the Hopi is rarely censored, and the children heard both of these women's remarks, *feeling*, you may be sure, the *absolute belief* which these "teachers" had in the *danger* which a bad heart carries for everyone in the group.

In such situations, since human beings can bear only a certain amount of guilt, there is a great game of blame-shifting among the Hopi, and this in turn adds a further burden of unconscious guilt, for it is difficult to love properly a neighbor or even a sister who has a bad heart. However, in the absence of political organization, civil and criminal laws, and a formal method of punishment for adults, this consistent "tribal super-ego" has maintained, throughout known history, a record almost devoid of crime and violence within the group, and it has conditioned and ever *reconditioned* a Hopi to feel secure only in being a Hopi.

For through the great strength of the emotional orientations conveyed within the kinship framework and the interwoven religious beliefs, young Hopi learned their world from dedicated teachers whose emotions were involved in teaching what they believed intensely, and this in turn engaged the children's emotions in learning. These experiences early and increasingly made explicit in a very personal way the values implicit in the distinction between a good heart and a bad heart. For public opinion, if intensely felt and openly expressed in a closely knit and mutually dependent group—as in the case of the child who left her baby sister alone—can be more effective potential punishment than the electric chair. It is perhaps easier to die quickly than to live in loneliness in a small community in the face of contempt from one's fellows, and particularly from one's clan from whence, as we have seen, comes most of one's physical and emotional security. Small wonder that the children who experience this constant pressure to conform to clan dictates and needs, and at the same time this constant reinforcement of clan solidarity against outsiders, are reluctant as adults to stray too far from the clan's protective familiarity or to defy its wishes.

There was much bickering and tension within the clan and village, of course, and it was a source of constant uneasiness and ambivalence among the Hopi. But tension and bickering, as I have indicated elsewhere, "are not exclusively Hopi"; the Hopi see it constantly among the Whites on and off the reservation. What they do *not* find elsewhere is the *emotional satisfaction* of belonging intensely, to which they have been conditioned and reconditioned. For, as Murphy says, "It is not only the 'desire to be accepted' . . . that presses the ego into line. The basic psychology of perception is involved; the individual has learned to see himself as a member of the group, and the self has true 'membership character,' structurally integrated with the perception of group life." Actually the Hopi clan, even with its in-group tensions and strife, but with all of the advantages emotional and physical it affords the individual, is one of the most successful and meaningful "boarding schools" ever devised for citizenship training.

In this situation, where belonging was so important, and a good heart so vital to the feeling of belonging, gossip is the potential and actual "social cancer" of the Hopi tribe. It is devastating to individual security and is often senselessly false and cruel, but in a country where cooperation was the only hope of survival, it was the *servant* as well as the policeman of the tribe. Not lightly would any Hopi voluntarily acquire the title Kahopi— "*not* Hopi," and therefore not good. Throughout the Hopi life span the word kahopi, *kahopi*, KAHOPI was heard, until it penetrated to the very core of one's mind. It was said softly and gently at first to tiny offenders, through "Kahopi tiyo" or "Kahopi mana" to older children, still quietly but with stern intent, until the word sometimes assumed a crescendo of feeling as a whole clan or even a whole community might condemn an individual as *Kahopi*.

It is true that we, too, are told we should keep good hearts and love our neighbors as ourselves. But we are not told that, if we do not, our babies will die, *now*, *this year*! Some children are told that if they do not obey the various "commandments" they learn in different churches they will eventually burn in a lake of hell fire, but they usually know that many of their world doubt this. In contrast, Hopi children constantly *saw* babies die because a parents' heart was not right; they *saw* evil winds come up and crops fail for the same reason; they *saw* adults sicken and die because of bad thoughts or witchcraft (to which bad thoughts rendered a person more vulnerable). Thus they learned to *fear* the results of a bad heart whether it belonged to themselves or to others. There were witches, bogey Kachinas, and in objective reality famine and thirst to fear. Along with these fears were taught mechanisms for the displacement of anxiety, including the services of medicine men, confession and exorcism to get rid of bad thoughts, and cooperative nonaggression with one's fellows, even those who were known to be witches. But the best technique was that which included all the values in the positive process of keeping a good heart, and of "uniting our hearts" in family, clan, and fraternal society—in short, the best protection was to be *Hopi* rather than *Kahopi*.

It is clear throughout the literature on the Hopi, as well as from the quotations given in this discussion, that in finding their way toward the goal of "belonging" Hopi children at first initiation had to deal with religious disenchantment, resentment, and with ever increasing demands made by their elders for more mature behavior. These factors were undoubtedly important catalyzing agents in Hopi personality formation and should be examined from the standpoint of Benedict's formulations on discontinuity. Here we must remember that shock can operate either to destroy or to mobilize an organism's dormant potentialities. And if a child has been *consistently* conditioned to feel a part of his intimate world, and providing he still lives on in this same world, it seems reasonable to suppose that shock (unless it were so great as to completely disorganize personality, in which case the custom could not have persisted) would reinforce the individual's *need* to belong and thus would tend to reassemble many of his personality resources around this need.

If the world surrounding the Hopi child had changed from warmth to coldness, from all pleasure to all hardship, the discontinuity would have indeed been insupportable. But the new demands made on him, while more insistent, were not unfamiliar in *kind*; all adults, as well as his newly initiated age-mates, faced the same ones. He had shared the shock as he had long since learned to share all else; and he now shared the rewards of "feeling big." He had the satisfaction of increased status along with the burden of increasing responsibility, as the adults continued to teach him "the important things," and conformity gradually became a value in itself—even as we value nonconformity and change. It was both the means *and* the goal. Conformity surrounded the Hopi—child or adult—with everything he could hope to have or to be; outside it there was only the feeling tone of rejection. Since there were no bewildering choices presented (as is the case in our socialization process), the "maturation drive" could only function to produce an ego-ideal in accord with the cultural ideal, however wide the discrepancy between ideal and reality on both levels.

And since the Kachinas played such a vital role in Hopi society throughout, we must consider specifically the way in which the altered faith expressed by informants gradually came about after the first initiation. First, of course, was the need to find it, since in any environment one must have faith and hope. They also wanted to continue to believe in and to enjoy that which from earliest memory had induced a feeling of pleasure, excitement, and of solidarity within the group. A beginning was undoubtedly made in modifying resentment when the Kachinas whipped each other after first initiation; first, it was again sharing punishment, but this time not only with children but *with adults*. They had long known that suffering came from bad hearts; they also knew, as indicated above, that something must be done about bad hearts. The Kachinas whipped to cleanse the bad hearts implied by disobedience to the rules of Hopi good conduct and then whipped each other for the same reason; thus there was logic in an initiation which was actually an extension of an already

established conception of masked gods who rewarded good behavior with presents but withheld rain if hearts were not right, and who sometimes threatened bad children.

Another reorganizing factor explicitly stated in the quotations was "feeling big." They had shared pain with adults, had learned secrets which forever separated them from the world of children, and they were now included in situations from which they had previously been excluded, as their elders continued to teach intensely what they believed intensely: that for them there was only one alternative—Hopi as against Kahopi.

Consistent repetition is a powerful conditioning agent and, as the youngsters watched each initiation, they relived their own, and by again sharing the experience gradually worked out much of the bitter residue from their own memories of it, while also rationalizing and weaving the group emotions ever stronger into their own emotional core—"It takes a while to see how wise the old people really are." An initiated boy, in participating in the Kachina dances, learned to identify again with the Kachinas whom he now impersonated. To put on a mask is to "become a Kachina," and to cooperate actively in bringing about the major goals of Hopi life. And a girl came to know more fully the importance of her clan in its supportive role. These experiences were even more sharply conditioned and directed toward adult life in the tribal initiation ceremonies, of which we have as yet only fragmentary knowledge. Of this one man said to me: "I will not discuss this thing with you only to say that no one can forget it. It is the most wonderful thing any man can have to remember. You know then that you are Hopi. It is one thing Whites cannot have, cannot take from us. It is our way of life given to us when the world began."

And since children are, for all mankind, a restatement of one's hopes to be, when these Hopi in turn became teachers (and in a sense they had always been teachers of the younger children in the household from an early age), they continued the process of reliving and rationalizing, or "working out" their experiences with an intensity which is rarely known in our society except, perhaps, on the psychoanalytic couch. But the Hopi had no psychiatrists to guide them—no books which, as Riesman says, "like an invisible monitor, helps liberate the reader from his group and its emotions, and allows the contemplation of alternative responses and the trying on of new emotions." They had only the internalized "feeling measure" and "group measure" explicit in the concepts of Hopi versus Kahopi.

On the material level, the obvious advantages of, for instance, wagons versus backs were a temptation. And to the extent to which White influences at first penetrated to these older Hopi it was through this form of temptation. But outside experiences usually included some variation of hostility, scorn, or aggression, as well as a radically different moral code, and these were all viewed and reinterpreted through the Hopi-eye view of the world and in the Hopi language, so that a return to the familiarity of the Hopi world with its solidarity of world view and behavior patterns *was experienced as relief*, and increased the need to feel Hopi *however great a burden "being Hopi" implied.*

In summary, the hypothesis here developed, that strong emotional conditioning during the learning process was an instrument in cultural continuity among the Hopi, is suggested as supplementary to that of early learning as being resistant to change. It further suggests that this conditioning was *constantly* as well as *consistently* instilled during the entire lifetime of an individual by a circular pattern of integration. For an individual was surrounded by a series of invisible, but none the less solid, barriers between himself and the outside world.

To change him, influences had to breach the concentric walls of social process—as conveyed through the human entities which surrounded him and which were strengthened by his obligation to teach others—and then to recondition his early and ever increasing emotional involvement in Hopi religion, morals, and mutually dependent lineage and clan groups, as well as those attitudes toward White aggression which he shared with all Indians.

In 1938 one old Hopi, who in his youth had been taken away from his wife and children and kept in a boarding school for several years, said to me:

I am full of curiosity; a great *bahana* [White] education would tell me many things I've wondered about like the stars and how a man's insides work. But I am afraid of it because I've seen what it does to folks. . . . If I raise a family, clothe and feed them well, do my ceremonial duties faithfully, I have succeeded—what do you call success? . . . [And again, while discussing fear in connection with a dream, his comment was] Well, yes, we are afraid of *powakas* [witches] but our medicine men can handle them. Neither your doctors nor your gods can control your governments so you have more to fear. Now you are dragging us into your quarrels. I pity you and I don't envy you. You have more goods than we have, but you don't have peace ever; *it is better to die in famine than in war.*

As the old man anticipated, enforced participation in modern warfare soon replaced instruction for Hopi citizenship, and the concentric walls were finally seriously breached. But for these older Hopi the walls still enclose "our way of life given to us when the world began."

28. PERSONALITY STRUCTURE IN THE PLAINS

THOMAS GLADWIN

Reprinted from the Anthropological Quarterly, *Vol. 30: 4, pp. 111-124, 1957, by permission of the author and the* Anthropological Quarterly. *Most of Thomas Gladwin's professional work to date was at the National Institute of Mental Health, where his interests moved from personality to cognition and he became increasingly concerned with problems of poverty and race. His two most recent books,* Poverty, U.S.A. *and* East is a Big Bird: Navigation and Logic on Puluwat Atoll, *reflect these interests, the latter offering perspective from Micronesia on thinking processes in undereducated Americans. He is currently working on a comparative study of postrevolutionary development in several countries.*

■ Pastoralism is a strategy of adaptation in which there is a significant cross-cut of forces. On the one hand, the animal herds require seasonal divisions and regroupings of the society determined by climatic factors. On the other hand (as we saw in Selection 3), there is a strong kinship orientation in pastoral social organization. This cross-cut is paralleled in the psychological makeup of pastoralists. As Walter Goldschmidt observes, pastoralists "must be able to operate within a larger context and even to accept the authority of others either when groups congregate or when military action is called for," but their way of life seems to elicit "aggressive militarism . . . a high degree of independence of action, a willingness to take chances; a readiness to act, and a capacity for action; self-containment and control, especially in the face of danger; bravery, fortitude, and the ability to withstand pain and hardship; arrogance, sexuality, and a realistic appraisal of the world" ("Theory and Strategy in the Study of Cultural Adaptability," by Walter Goldschmidt, *American Anthropologist*, 67 [1965] : 402-407; reprinted as Selection 19 in *The Cultural Present*).

In this paper we are provided with an example of the Indians of the North American Plains, whose pastoralist strategy was based on the use of horses for hunting. Gladwin's paper focuses on socialization, masculinity, and sexuality. As Goldschmidt points out, sexuality was among the standards of behavior that pastoralist men set for themselves; as Gladwin makes clear, Plains Indian men were not as sexually active as they may have wished to appear.

There are no good first-hand studies of the subjective side of life among any of the Plains Indian societies. The analysis of Comanche personality on which Gladwin draws heavily is in *The Psychological Frontiers of Society*, by Abram Kardiner (New York: Columbia University Press, 1945, pp. 81-100). An important description of Plains Indian social patterns is in *Rank and Warfare among the Plains Indians*, by Bernard Mishkin (Monographs of the American Ethnologic Society, Number 3, 1940). *The Cheyenne Indians: Their History and Ways of Life* (two volumes), by George B. Grinnell (New Haven: Yale University Press, 1923) and *The Fighting Cheyennes*, also by Grinnell (Norman: University of Oklahoma Press, 1956), are excellent studies. A very good study of the impact of Euroamerican civilization on a group of Plains Indians is *The Changing Culture of an Indian Tribe*, by Margaret Mead (New York: Columbia University Press, 1932). *The Nuer*, by E. E. Evans-Pritchard (New York: Oxford University Press, 1951) is one of the most illuminating accounts of pastoralist life in East Africa. In *Fields on the Hoof : Nexus of Tibetan Nomadic Pastoralism* (New York: Holt, Rinehart and Winston, 1968), Robert B. Ekvall devotes a chapter (pp. 84-93) to an impressionistic account of Tibetan nomads' basic personality. ■

THE INDIANS of the High Plains of North America have always been a favorite topic of anthropological discussion. Theirs is a unique record of cultural unity achieved from diversity. The Plains form one of the most clearly delimited and the most homogeneous of the culture areas of North America, yet most of the tribes we associate with the flowering of this area entered it within a very short period of time and stemmed from a wide variety of cultural and linguistic backgrounds.

Until the horse spread through this area, often in advance of the white men who had introduced it on this continent, the High Plains were only sparsely populated outside of the few river valleys. Although game, and particularly buffalo, was abundant, hunters could not subsist in any numbers in most of the area because of the great distances which separated the sources of water. Hunters wandering in search of a herd could well die of thirst before they made contact with it. There were seasonal hunts carried out into the Plains by those who lived on their peripheries and a few tribes, such as the Querecho described by Coronado's expedition, apparently did live all year in some sections of the area. But the difficulties of traversing the Plains on foot were enough to discourage most of the surrounding tribes from capitalizing on the resources of food represented by the vast herds of buffalo.

The horse removed these limitations. Now it was possible to camp near a stream, range widely each day, probably bring down a few buffalo or antelope, and carry the meat back packed on the horse. The lure of an assured food supply in a free and open country was irresistible. Almost overnight, during the 17th and early 18th Centuries, thousands of people flowed in from all sides to fill the vacuum. As each tribe emerged into this swirling, shifting potpourri of peoples, they repeatedly made contact with others they had never seen before, many of them groups of very different origin from themselves. Occasionally they made peace and an alliance, however informal, with another tribe, though this was rare; the Cheyenne and the Arapaho are an example. More commonly they fought. The horse provided not only the means but a major incentive for highly mobile warfare. This was characterized by hit and run raids, whose principal goals were acquiring honor and stealing horses. All the tribes of the Plains participated in this warfare; it was the most striking common feature of their various cultures, and provided the basic orientation of all of these societies. Whatever may have been their prestige structure before their emergence onto the Plains, in every tribe the people now centered their attention upon the young men of fighting age.

The most significant fact for the social scientist, however, is that few of these peoples were culturally equipped for dealing with the problems of horse nomadism before they left their home territories. As a result, they borrowed these skills from their neighbors; despite the state of almost constant hostility which characterized practically all intertribal relations, each new technique which was developed by one group spread rapidly to all the others. Thus in a short time a whole new way of life was evolved and as rapidly taken up by all the Plains tribes. Not only were the technical aspects of warfare and hunting methods so diffused, but also many associated beliefs and attitudes and values, as well as their characteristic social organization in bands, and even ceremonies, of which the Sun Dance is the most familiar.

They apparently acquired the habit of borrowing and could not stop. By the beginning of the 19th century, when the Plains peoples entered their Golden Age of thirty or forty years of untrammelled freedom, all these tribes of so diverse origin shared what was almost a common culture, whose principal values centered on warfare and whose subsistence was based almost exclusively on the vast herds of buffalo (bison) which roamed the prairie.

Mooney, in writing of the Cheyenne, summarizes graphically the degree of transformation undergone by the culture of one of the tribes usually considered to be among the most typical of the Plains societies. He describes the Cheyenne as:

A sedentary and agricultural people cut off from the main body of their kindred and transformed by

pressure of circumstance within the historic period into a race of nomad and predatory hunters, with such entire change of habit and ceremony that the old life is remembered only in sacred tradition and would seem impossible of belief but for the connected documentary proof of fact. The Cheyenne chasing buffalo on the Staked plain were a stumbling block in [the historical study of] Algonquian philology. The Cheyenne planting corn in Minnesota, in friendly neighborhood to the Ojibwa, are a perfectly feasible Algonquian proposition. Practically all that they have to day of tribal life and ceremony, excepting the Medicine Arrow rite, has been acquired in the course of this migration, and the oldest things date back not more than two centuries.

With their cultures so uniform and yet so new to each, the question naturally arises whether this new life had the same meaning for all of the Plains peoples. In other words, did they shed their old personalities at the same time that they abandoned their old ways of life?

In order to explore this question, I have selected two of the better known of the typical Plains tribes for examination, the Comanche and the Cheyenne. The Comanche have already been analyzed from the psychological standpoint by Abram Kardiner on the basis of Ralph Linton's notes. No such analysis has been attempted for the Cheyenne, but Grinnell's highly sympathetic two volume work on these people is a rich source of relevant information, supplemented by a number of more specialized accounts. Using this material, plus the three fragmentary biographies of Cheyennes which have been published, I have sought comparisons with Kardiner's Comanche analysis.

It is obviously beyond the scope of this paper to summarize the cultures of these two peoples; a few contrasts will be sufficient to set the stage, remembering that in spite of these differences each bore a much closer cultural resemblance to the other than either did to the erstwhile neighbors which they left in order to take up the romantic life of the Plains.

The Comanche were originally one of the western Plateau Shoshonean tribes, whose home was in southern Wyoming, and whose former humble way of life is still followed by many of the Shoshoni and Paiute, who until recently eked out a bare and rude existence by simple hunting and the gathering of wild berries and roots and seeds. The people wandered in very small economically self-sufficient groups throughout the year, coming together with other bands very briefly in the summer; the need for social organization and social controls was at a minimum. The Comanche carried with them into the Plains this extremely fluid, unstructured and informal way of life.

The Cheyenne, on the other hand, were an Algonkin people, previously sharing the general Woodland culture of the western Great Lakes area. During the 18th century they had moved down to the Missouri River; before they took up the nomad's life they had been for some time in close association with the Mandan, a well-organized agricultural village people like themselves. They brought with them a more structured social and political organization, and a far greater emphasis on ritual and etiquette.

After their establishment among the nomadic horsemen of the Plains, with the revolutionary adaptation to the new cultural patterns and way of life this entailed, it is not surprising to find that the Comanche and Cheyenne also came to share in common a number of new cultural determinants of personality, which we would expect to have had a strong influence in shaping their personalities toward a common pattern. In both we find, as might be expected from their major orientation toward warfare, an emphasis on masculine vitality and courage, which found its ultimate vindication in the terrifying and uncertain moments of the attack. Although in the Cheyenne a very few men could take up the homosexual role of the *berdache*, neither society offered to the majority of youths any approved means of avoiding this test, nor to the adult any permanent respite from the hazardous trials of warfare without shame and loss of status.

In both Comanche and Cheyenne, the major burden of the upbringing of small children devolved upon their grandparents and their older siblings, real or classificatory, especially sisters. These were the people primarily responsible for imposing disciplines and restraints, though in this respect the Cheyenne leaned rather more heavily than did the Comanche on the grandparents, the older siblings being responsible primarily for only the physical care of Cheyenne infants and children. It might be concluded from the fact that in the Cheyenne siblings had less disciplinary functions than

among the Comanche, sibling hostility would be less pronounced in the former than in the latter. However, in keeping with the generally more restrictive nature of Cheyenne social controls, a severe taboo was placed on all relations between adult brothers and sisters in this society, amounting to a ban on even speaking to each other in ordinary circumstances. Consequently, neither hostility nor its opposite could be expected to find overt expression in this relationship.

In keeping with the shifting of the disciplinary functions to siblings and grandparents, the Cheyenne and Comanche parents treated their children not as a different order of beings, but simply as smaller and not yet fully competent adults. The first animal a boy killed in either society was the occasion for great acclaim and compliments from his parents and other adults, as great as if he had brought down a buffalo bull. This pattern was retained for all childhood accomplishments, so that the parents were consistently rewarding agents, while others did the punishing. Not only did this reduce ambivalence in the child's attitude toward those upon whom he was most dependent, his parents, but it also made the transition into adult life extremely easy: there was, to use Benedict's concept, no discontinuity of role between childhood, adolescence, and adulthood. There were no puberty ceremonies for boys in either tribe, though adult status was considered achieved only after the first war party. The psychological effects of this experience were undoubtedly more severe, however, for the Cheyenne boy than the Comanche, for in the former he went out when he was fourteen or fifteen, as against seventeen or eighteen in the latter, and sex experience was denied him until this time, a restriction not imposed upon the Comanche youth.

Despite these several important parallels in childhood development, there was one crucial respect in which they differed fundamentally. Kardiner found that probably the most striking single characteristic of Comanche childhood, adolescence, and adulthood was the almost complete freedom of expression granted to the individual, aggressively, sexually, or otherwise. Sexual conquests provided a major source of adolescent diversion, and even adults found a number of possible channels for such activity.

Fights within the group, leading even to killings, were the concern only of the principals and perhaps their close friends and relatives. In the Cheyenne, on the other hand, repression and moderation of all overt emotional expression within the group was the rule, enforced from earliest childhood. These differing points of view found their expression in every aspect of daily life, and it is in consequence of these that we would expect to, and actually do, find the greatest differences between these peoples at the personality level.

The Cheyenne child though enthusiastically rewarded for any achievements reflecting technical skills was severely condemned for any aggression or even undue affection shown in interpersonal relations; at the same time a constant stream of advice and admonitions, particularly from the grandparents but echoed by the parents, served to build up the anxieties associated with such behavior. Though information on childhood sexuality is lacking, it seems almost certain that this too was repressed; we do know that the grandparents began early to warn the child of the calamity for the family if the child, and particularly the daughter, did not marry in the formal and respectable manner through family gift exchange. Such a marriage was made impossible not only if the girl chose to elope, but even if she were unchaste. To be unchaste a girl did not have to have intercourse with a boy; she was defiled if he touched her genitals, or even her breasts. For this reason, a Cheyenne girl after her first menstruation donned a rope and rawhide cover which acted quite effectively as a chastity belt. The woman whose account Michelson published remarked:

My mother would always tell me that the main purpose of her teaching me, as well as the object of my owning my own bed, was to keep me at home, and to keep me from being away to spend my nights with my girl chum [and hence away from parental supervision]. This was done so that there would be no chance for gossip by other people. . . .

After I was married I thought I would have more freedom in going around with my girl friends, but my mother watched me more closely and kept me near my husband, day and night. This was done to prevent any gossip from my husband's people.

We may contrast this with Linton's comment on the Comanche:

Sexual play between children began at an early age, and was carried on quite freely as long as the two children were not brother and sister. The Comanche paid no attention to virginity; they took these childhood relations more or less for granted.

The Cheyenne repression of self-expression was particularly emphasized in dealing with parents and other adults. The child was, to use our phrase, to be seen but not heard; he had always to speak quietly, respectfully, and politely in the presence of adults. A breach of this rule brought down the wrath not only of the people involved, but also of the supernatural; loud and boisterous activity was irritating to a man's "power," which hung in a little bag in his tipi, and dire consequences of this annoyance were conjured up to warn the child to restraint. Practically the only outlet the society provided the children was in play groups, which during later childhood included both sexes, whose principal activities were elaborate imitations of adult activities, including home life, warfare, and hunting. These play groups were similarly organized in both Comanche and Cheyenne, but we may be fairly sure that the anxieties inculcated by the adults carried over into the play situations of the Cheyenne children; we are told that any wide deviations from acceptable behavior might be made the subject of adult gossip and hence reprimand. Despite these reservations, it seems doubtful that a Cheyenne child could have grown to adulthood with even the limited capacity for self-expression he did show without the warmth of these playmate relationships and the opportunities for ego development they provided.

The differential expectations of these peoples in regard to interpersonal relations are perhaps most clearly shown in their attitudes and beliefs regarding the guardian spirit. The concept of the guardian spirit, the personal supernatural helper, was known to both, as it was to all Plains tribes, but their interpretations were totally different. The guardian spirit came to a Cheyenne through suffering: he fasted and prayed, often alone, and frequently inflicted tortures on himself. Even then the vision of the helper, usually an animal, bird or reptile, did not always come; and even when it did come, more often than not it gave advice or foretold the outcome of a projected activity, and left, never to return. Only rarely could a Cheyenne rely upon a guardian spirit of his own to help him in a succession of difficulties. On the other hand, practically every Comanche had his own guardian or "power," upon whom he could call at will; this helper was his for life. And he did not have to suffer to get it. Though a few who wished to obtain the power of a great man already dead spent a night by his grave waiting for the power to come, enduring nothing worse than fright, the usual practice was to ask a man who had the desired power to share it, giving a present in return; occasionally it came uninvited in a dream. Thus the Comanche asked for what he wanted and got it, and could rely upon his power thenceforward; the Cheyenne suffered desperately for the same thing, and was often not rewarded. While a Comanche's power came almost exclusively from his guardian spirit, much of a Cheyenne's power was of a more mechanical nature, from the little bag of amulets he carried or hung in his tipi, and from the careful observance of endless rituals.

Moving into the early adult level of the Cheyenne, we see these childhood and adolescent anxieties concerning interpersonal relationships and particularly sex expressed again in courtship and marriage. Courting techniques were extremely tentative, and even then frightening. The hero of Grinnell's biography stood by the trail covered with a blanket for days just to catch a glimpse of his sweetheart as she went out with the other women to get water. Finally one day she lagged behind and he dared reveal himself. "She stopped and we stood there and talked for a little while. We were both of us afraid, we did not know of what, and had not much to say, but it was pleasant to be there talking to her, and looking at her face. . . . After that, I think she knew me whenever I stood by the trail, and sometimes she was late in coming for water, and I had a chance to speak to her alone." At this time he had already been out on a war party, penetrating to the middle of an enemy camp alone, and was in the society's eyes a man. He went through several more years of indecision before finally marrying her. Again, we may compare Linton's account of the Comanche:

Boys often talked under the tipi edge to a favorite girl, then pulled out a tipi stake and crawled in to spend a large part of the night in her bed, getting away before dawn if he did not want to marry her. These contacts ended variously. If the couple suspected the opposition of the parents, or if some man had a previous claim, the couple would elope and return after a short time. Generally the marriage would then be accepted. If no opposition was expected, the boy simply slept late in bed with the girl, and the proper behavior for the father when he found them was to make the boy a brief and friendly speech—that is, that he was glad his daughter had found a husband—and invite him to breakfast.

Even after marriage, it was not unusual for a Cheyenne girl to continue to wear her chastity ropes for several weeks. The woman of Michelson's account said, "We had our first child after we had been married a year. It was at this time that I really began to love my husband." The ideal couple did not have a second child for ten years or so, meanwhile remaining continent.

For a Cheyenne girl, the prospect of marriage was often made doubly forbidding by her parents' attempts to marry her off to a man she found personally distasteful. While she could refuse, there was great pressure upon her to avoid the shame for her family which would result from such a refusal, or, even worse, an elopement. The admonitions and veiled threats of years had led up to this moment; most girls gave in, but some, feeling that they would be outcasts from their own family anyway, eloped with someone else, while many were forced into suicide.

An additional fear also colored a Cheyenne boy's attitude toward courtship and marriage: these were only possible after he had been subjected to the terrifying ordeal of going on his first war party; the association between the two was inescapable. The Comanche placed no restrictions on a boy's relations with girls as we have seen, so that the first war party, while perhaps no less frightening, carried no identification with women as threatening creatures.

The anxieties of the Cheyenne were inevitably expressed in unconscious hostility between the sexes, and found clear symbolic expression in a mock fight. This took place when the women returned to the camp laden with roots after a day's digging; the phallic identification of the roots is obvious. When the women neared the camp they stopped, and, laying the roots out on the ground before them, uttered a war cry. The men charged out on old scrawny horses and staged a mock attack, the bravest dashing in to steal some roots.

More direct was the custom, described by Llewellyn and Hoebel whereby a man punished an unfaithful wife. Inviting his entire soldier society to a "feast" on the prairie, he brought out the offending girl, and "gave" her to them. All the men who were not related to her raped her in succession; though there are no cases of a death resulting, the girl apparently seldom fully recovered, physically or socially. The authors conclude that "as a gang of individuals reinforcing each other in some off-the-line activity, also possibly, as a release of sex antagonisms by which men could make a woman suffer for her defiance of male authority, it was possible for men to do collectively that which they did not individually hold to be honorable."

The Comanche, both men and women, could express what aggression they felt toward other members of the group as directly as they wished, and often did; in-group murders were not infrequent, and were not regarded very seriously. On the other hand, this continued to be repressed throughout the life of a Cheyenne. Ideally, this suppression was complete; the chiefs and other men of high prestige who formed the ego-ideals for the tribe were expected to ignore completely the inroads of other men, even when they stole the chief's wife. Most men, however, could and did claim damages to sooth their tarnished egos.

Some outlets for aggression were socially sanctioned for the Cheyenne, the most obvious of these being the outward expression of aggression in warfare. But even here there is a contrast with Comanche, for Cheyenne warfare was surrounded with ritual and etiquette, and the highest achievement was not in killing an enemy, but in touching him on the field of battle—counting coup—irrespective of who killed him or even of whether he was dead. Comanche warfare was on a much more free-for-all basis, and most Comanche bands did not count coup at all, striving only to kill the enemy and steal his horses.

Another outlet lay in competitive games; such games are characteristic of all Plains societies, but the Cheyenne apparently far exceeded the Comanche in the number of games and the amount they were played. The Cheyenne were also enthusiastic gossips, but even this was a double-edged sword, for as we have seen

it formed one of the strongest sanctions in favor of restraint and conformity.

In contrast again to the Comanche, if in-group aggression ever became so severe among the Cheyenne that a murder within the tribe resulted, the whole tribe was affected. The sacred medicine arrows were sullied, and a special ceremony had to be performed to renew them before any hazardous undertakings could be made by anyone. The murderer was an outcast within his group, and often fled to the Arapaho until things cooled off. Even on his return he remained in the lowest possible status for the rest of his life; such degradation applied even to war chiefs. These extreme sanctions not only represent another repressive mechanism, but bear witness to the implicit recognition by the Cheyenne of the chaos and carnage which would result if their suppressed hatreds were ever given an opportunity for free expression.

Sorcery is frequently interpreted as symptomatic of aggressive anxieties in a society, and the contrast between these tribes in their attitudes toward sorcery and sorcerors is revealing. While there were sorcerors recognized by the Comanche, they were little feared; if they became too troublesome, an excuse was found and they were simply killed. On the other hand, only a few very powerful medicine men dared practice sorcery among the Cheyenne; but the people greatly feared those who did, and were powerless against them.

It is characteristic of strong hostility at an unconscious level that when its outward expression is blocked, it often turns inward upon the individual in the form of masochism. It is no accident that the Cheyenne reached a peak for the Plains in self-mutilation and torture. The extreme forms consisted in attaching ropes to skewers passed through holes cut in the flesh. These ropes usually ran from a pole to skewers on the chest, and the man would swing about the pole for hours, leaning against the rope and trying to pull out the skewers by breaking the loop of flesh. Or they might be attached to his back, and used to drag a collection of heavy buffalo skulls about. These ordeals were reserved for times of greatest anxiety: for a young man before he led his first war party, or in response to a vow made in requesting supernatural aid during the serious illness of a close relative. They were often performed during the Sun Dance, when power was running high; but they might also be done on a lonely hill, with a vision as a possible reward. For occasions of somewhat lesser anxiety, the cutting of strips of skin from the arms with accompanying ritual sufficed; the typical Cheyenne male had both arms covered with scars from such offerings. In either case the correlation of masochism with increased anxiety and its attendant rise in hostility is clear.

Thus with aggression, as with sex and interpersonal relations in general, we see the Cheyenne deeply inhibited and frustrated, while the Comanche gave full reign to their feelings. Why then, when each took on the common culture, did they interpret it in such diametrically opposite ways?

As we have already seen, the Comanche came onto the Plains with an extremely loose social organization and an almost complete lack of social controls, made possible by the very small social groups typical of Plateau life. When they fell heir to the potentially highly destructive attitudes and techniques of the Plains, most of the aggression which might have been disastrous for their now somewhat larger groupings was directed outside, and their free system permitted what was left to dissipate itself without major damage within the community, as Kardiner has pointed out. The freedom in sexual expression, while not so pronounced for adults as for adolescents, was still sufficient to make marriages highly unstable; however, the organization into still fairly small shifting bands on the Plateau pattern, with an option for families to live alone, was sufficiently fluid to prevent disastrous disruption.

The Cheyenne, on the other hand, emerged from a tightly knit agricultural village culture with well structured social controls and an integrated social organization. Faced with the increased potentialities for aggression of warrior life, they channellized and circumscribed their hostilities now just as they had before channellized those which arose from the lesser frictions of sedentary village life, and rigid repression of in-group aggression resulted. Much the same processes were operative in regard to sex, for the informal and unregulated nature of nomadic life made the disruptive potentialities of casual sex relations far greater, and the society had to fortify the superego to compensate for the decreased effectiveness of external sanctions. It is clear from material upon the Algonkin tribes of the western Great Lakes, neighbors of the Cheyenne in their erstwhile habitat, that this process of internalizing the sex mores and thus creating anxieties in regard to sex was already well started before the Cheyenne became nomads. But the training in these eastern tribes is not nearly as strict nor as absolute as among the Cheyenne, and applies almost exclusively to girls; the fact that boys are expected and tacitly encouraged to have affairs and attempt the seduction of virtuous girls demonstrates that these peoples are far less concerned with the possible effects of such activities upon the society than were the Cheyenne.

These two cultures, though representative, are not all of the Plains; nor have we explored all the ramifications of Kardiner's analysis of the Comanche with which comparisons could be made. But it is clear that the Plains people, for all their cultural homogeneity, were anything but identical in their basic personality structures, and that the opportunity to siphon aggression out of the group in warfare is not by itself enough to keep tensions within the group at a low level.

The other Plains tribes came from yet different cultural and historical backgrounds. A review from this standpoint of others of these peoples should prove highly instructive.

29. CHARACTER FORMATION AND SOCIAL STRUCTURE IN A JAMAICAN COMMUNITY

YEHUDI A. COHEN

Reprinted from Psychiatry, *Vol. 18, pp. 275-296, 1955. Copyright* © *1955, the William Alanson White Psychiatric Foundation. Yehudi A. Cohen is Professor of Anthropology, Living-ston College, Rutgers. He has conducted field work in Jamaica, Okinawa, and Israel. His principal interests are political anthropology, cultural evolution, culture and personality, religion, and cross-cultural research. He is the author of* The Transition from Childhood to Adolescence *and* Social Structure and Personality: A Casebook. *He was the 1955 recipient of the Socio-Psychological Award of the American Association for the Advancement of Science.*

■ We saw in Foster's discussion of the image of limited good (Selection 22) that among the characteristics of peasants are their distrust of leadership and their inability to form voluntary associations. These characteristics, which must be understood in terms cf the position of peasants in a complex society, are consistent with a number of different personality systems, all of which may nonetheless be adaptive to the general needs of life in the peasant world. In the next selection, which describes a small community in the central highlands of Jamaica, we see one personality profile accompanying this peasant adaptation.

The basic personality of these people is unusual in the world of peasants. Their monetary greed and miserliness is exceptional. For example, the patterns of hospitality and festivals that in other peasant groups help to equalize economic status are nowhere to be found here. Amassing personal wealth is an end in itself among these Jamaicans. In common with other peasants, they clearly exhibit their sense of limited good, their fear of the outside world and deep distrust of each other, their inability to organize—but the means by which these personality patterns are elicited in the course of child rearing are unusual, to say the least. One of my reasons for including this paper is to show that there is no one-to-one correspondence between a particular set of values—or any other feature of social life—and any single personality pattern and socialization experience.

To illustrate Foster's contention that the image of limited good is based on the peasant's reality, I want to note a change in the community described in this selection. During 1950-1951, the period of work on which this paper is based, these people repeatedly told me, "Look how poor we are." To a large extent, that was true, especially by American standards. I restudied this community in 1957; by then, as a result of a large influx of wealth from the development of the international bauxite industry in Jamaica, these suddenly affluent peasants had begun to send their children abroad to study and acquire professions. Another significant change was in parent-child relations, both parents behaving more warmly and less punishingly to their children. Interestingly, in 1957, no one said, "Look how poor we are." Instead, the constant plaint was, "Look how hard we work"; that was also very true.

A similar pattern of socialization in the peasant world is described by Oscar Lewis in *Life in a Mexican Village: Tepoztlan Restudied* (Urbana: University of Illinois Press, 1951, 1963). The reader who wishes to explore West Indian patterns further should consult *My Mother who Fathered Me: A Study of the Family in Three Selected Communities in Jamaica*, by Edith Clarke (London: Allen and Unwin, 1957); *The Negro Family in British Guiana: Family Structure and Social Status in the Villages*, by Raymond T. Smith (London: Routledge and Kegan Paul, 1956); *West Indian Family Structure*, by M. G. Smith (Seattle: University of Washington Press, 1962); *Caribbean Studies: A Symposium*, edited by Vera Rubin (Seattle: University of Washington Press, 1960); and *Family and Colour in Jamaica*, by Fernando Henriques (2nd edition, New York: Humanities Press, 1968). ■

SYSTEMATIC FORMULATIONS of character structures derive almost entirely from observations made in Western cultures, and have been subjected to little comparative verification or analysis. Apart from controversies over the justification of speaking of paranoia in alien societies, little attention has been paid to characterological paranoid manifestations in social systems observed by anthropologists. The purpose of this paper is to present data from Rocky Roads, Jamaica, British West Indies, bearing on the structuralization of interpersonal relationships and, in particular, on the dynamics of the paranoid character of the members of that community in relation to the social system.

In a general way, Rocky Roads represents a rare phenomenon in the annals of ethnography. It is a community in which a sense of collective unity—a sense of community—is lacking not only in actual behavior, but even on the purely verbal or ideal level. The problems and pressures which objectively affect the entire community are not perceived and designated by the Rocky Roaders as community problems, but rather as problems of the individual. Within the structure of the community there is an absence of both leadership and ties of mutual obligation, either to kin or to other people. The members of the community are characterized by deep-seated hostilities which rarely are expressed directly. They fear one another, and each is convinced that there are secret conspiracies which aim to destroy him economically. These conspiracies are usually supposed to attain their pernicious ends by such means as sorcery, called "obeah" or "jealousy," and only occasionally by more overt means. Despite the tremendous anxieties pervading interpersonal relationships in the community, the author knows of only two persons who might be described as grossly aberrant; both were widows past the menopause. One was probably prepsychotic, or "half-mad" as the Rocky Roaders called her. The second one, referred to as "maddy maddy," was a deluded, hallucinated woman who would probably be diagnosed as paranoid schizophrenic.

Rocky Roads is between one and one-half and two square miles in diameter; it is situated in the central mountains of Jamaica, and is occupied by 277 people who make up 57 households. The Rocky Roaders are English-speaking Negroes, descendants of former slaves brought to Jamaica from the Gold Coast and Sierra Leone of Africa. Today they are independent, relatively well-to-do farmers raising varied crops which they sell for cash in weekly urban markets. The community is accessible by a secondary motor road which runs through it.

The material presented in this paper was gathered through observation, interviews, and participation in the daily life of the community. The number of subjects observed and informants interviewed varied, depending primarily on the nature of the information gathered. In all, close to sixty Rocky Roaders contributed, directly and indirectly, to the data. In those areas of activity in which the Rocky Roaders were self-conscious and reticent—as in the sphere of sorcery—direct questions were avoided as much as possible. Questionnaires and projective tests were not administered.

INFANCY, CHILDHOOD, AND ADOLESCENCE

One of the first things a Rocky Roads infant learns is the meaning of hunger, although there is no real shortage of food in Rocky Roads. For the first two or three months an infant is fed on the average of four times daily. A scheduled feeding usually consists of nursing at one breast for about five minutes—one-fourth the amount of food the mothers admittedly feel their children need. During the third month of infancy a child begins to be nursed three times daily, again only five minutes at one breast. After a few more months of breast feeding, the child is offered the breast only twice a day, the third scheduled feeding consisting of a cup of tea. Infants are never fed at night, and even when they awake and lustily demand food, their pleas are completely ignored. Weaning usually occurs at twelve months and is imposed on the infant arbitrarily and suddenly; some mothers apply a bitter substance to the nipple, while others simply cease offering the breast. The diet does not improve after the first year; it consists of sweetened black tea for breakfast, black tea at noon, some sort of porridge or mash during the afternoon, and black tea for the evening meal. Roasted yams or ears of corn, dried or roasted, are added when the child becomes capable of nibbling at them, but green vegetables are never eaten by the child and only occasionally by the adult. After the age of three or four, children, like adults, eat meat once a week. As far as my wife and I were able to determine, the quality and quantity of food given to children did not differ in terms of the economic condition of the family. . . .

Rocky Road infants engage in frequent emotional outbursts, which rarely elicit parental response. These outbursts almost always seem to be motivated by hunger. The mothers rationalize their almost total lack of response by claiming an inability to alleviate the situation, saying that all they can do is to let the children "cry it out." An infant will often cry for as much as an hour before the mother or mother-surrogate will show the slightest attention. She may then change the infant's diaper or merely change his position. Only in the youngest of infants will a temper tantrum receive the attention of the mother to the extent that she will pick him up, lightly hold him in her lap for a moment or two, and then return him to his former position, where he will go back to his vocalizations and thrashings. Infants are not responded to when they cry at night. . . .

Mothers in an exceptionally good humor occasionally tease their infants with food. When a baby reaches for a morsel of food which his mother holds out to him, she may keep moving it out of his reach, urging him to come and get it. Or if she is in a less playful mood, she will simply place the food in a high spot where it is almost physically impossible for him to reach it. Usually the infant, after a number of frustrating attempts, begins to cry and then throws a temper tantrum. Again depending on the mother's mood, she may give him the food or may tell him, "You rude pickney [pickaninny]," and refuse to give it to him. Another technique of teasing which mothers sometimes use is to demand part of the food which the child is eating. Rather than be punished for refusing a parental request, the child sheepishly hands over what has been asked of him, and then receives it back after shedding a few plaintive tears. However, to be certain that the child does not become unduly accustomed to parental generosity, the mother will sometimes eat the food herself. This pattern, too, is carried on only when the mother has nothing in particular to do and is in high spirits.

Although neither of the investigators was ever able to observe any gratifying aspects of the mother-child relationship other than the fact that the food is received from the mother, we have assumed that there must be additional re-warding or pleasurable aspects of this relationship, for both children and adults prefer their mothers to their fathers. The Rocky Roaders express their ideas of their fathers as wholly punishing, while they do not feel their mothers to be so punishing.

During the first three or four years of a Rocky Roader's life, the father is a source of neither gratification nor punishment. After this, the father begins to administer punishment at the instigation of the mother. It is not until the child is ten, however, that the father establishes any sort of stable relationship with any of his children, and then only with his sons. While the father spends most of his time in the fields, he is often at home. He devotes some days to the repair of the home; he often remains at home during the rainy season; and he is at home on Sundays. But even on these occasions, when he is relatively relaxed, he avoids the younger members of the household and keeps them at a distance.

Paralleling the deprivation in the area of food experienced by the young Rocky Roader is the severe corporal punishment he receives throughout the years of his socialization, beginning with the not-too-soft slaps which he receives at five or six months for biting the nipple while nursing. It is probably not coincidental that this first direct punishment is associated with food; in fact, all through childhood the most severe corporal punishment is for behavior in connection with food.

There are two kinds of flogging. One is with a strap; the other is with a switch, a small but strong and flexible branch of a tree, which produces a shrill whistle when swung. The Rocky Roads mother flogs her infant with a switch, holding on to the little one with one hand and administering the flogging to his bottom with the other. Floggings are very effective since little girls wear short dresses and little boys wear only shirts. "If you don't hit your child when he is young," say the people of Rocky Roads, "he gets hard, and you cannot bend him as you would like to bend him."

An infant who cries for more food after he has just been fed is ignored; but a child of five or six years who cries for more food after he has been served a meal is flogged. By this time, say the parents, a child should have enough "sense" to know that he receives whatever food there is for him.

The mother has definite ideas as to which food belongs to a particular member of the family, and which to another; but she does not always communicate this clearly to the child. The child is doled out his ration, which is rarely enough, and he is not supposed to eat what is not given him. Of itself, this should be a rather simple thing to learn. But ears of corn do not have this restriction placed on them; they may be within easy reach of the child, since they are often put out to dry in front of the dwellings. And if the child helps himself to an ear of corn, this is acceptable. Although this rule is unique for corn, the child is apparently never told of its uniqueness. As a result, the child sometimes fails to discriminate between corn and some other food which the mother in her mind has designated for another member of the family. As a result of the child's inability to discriminate he may receive many terribly severe floggings on this score alone before he understands the difference between corn and another food.

Any act which may be interpreted by a parent as aggressive brings on a severe flogging. The ideal Rocky Roads child is the docile one who remains seated in one spot without attracting any attention and without making any demands, especially for food. The thwarting of independent behavior begins in infancy and increases in intensity during childhood. Thus Rocky Roads socialization is extremely restrictive.

At about the same time that children begin to be flogged for asking for more food and for taking food which was not meant for them— that is, at about five years—they begin manifesting what might be termed food-hoarding behavior. The investigators assumed that these bits of food were saved to supplement future inadequate meals. Even more significant is the distrust of people as sources of food, which is being learned at about this time. When a three-year-old would begin hoarding the sweets we distributed, we would tell the child to eat them, for there were more where they came from; and he would follow our advice. But slightly older children were not as trusting. They would mumble that they were not hungry or wanted to save the food for some future occasion; no amount of cajoling would get them to eat it— unless, of course, they had already gone four or five hours without anything to eat.

Up to the age of five years, there are no differences in the manner in which boys and girls are raised, with the possible exception that boys may get slightly more food. But at five years changes occur in the socialization process; role training begins, and the similarities in the upbringing of boys and girls end. It is generally contended by the parents of Rocky Roads that girls are more obedient than boys but are more difficult to teach. At the age of five, girls begin to learn domestic tasks. They begin with simple housework, such as weeping and washing floors, and are then elevated to the washing of dishes and utensils. After they have mastered these domestic skills, they are taught to cook and prepare foods. Most mothers state that they wish their sons would learn these skills, but that the boys refuse to do so. The only tasks which boys will do is to tend the chickens and hogs and run errands. What the parents fail to report, and only observation discloses, is that the girls are just as reluctant as the boys to do this sort of work—but work they must. When a boy refuses to wash floors, his refusal is accepted, and he is not troubled further. A girl may also begin by refusing to do such things, but she is flogged for her refusal. This accounts for the fact that girls are reported to be more obedient and a greater help in the home than are the boys. But even more important, this accounts in part for the fact that *the girls of Rocky Roads receive more than twice as many floggings as their brothers.* This is also the age at which parents become noticeably more strict with their daughters than with their sons. By the time a girl is seven she is extremely adept in the performance of almost every household task.

There are other sources of more severe and more frequent corporal punishment for the girls of Rocky Roads. At about the age of five or six years both boys and girls begin to go on errands for their parents. This marks the emergence of the child from the confines of the home, for Rocky Roads children are not allowed to play with "strange" children. But the running of errands is not a complete liberation, for the mother knows how long it should take the child to buy something at the store or to carry food to the men in the fields, and if he overstays the necessary amount of time, he receives a rather severe flogging. Parents are much more strict with their daughters on this score than with their sons. The temptations involved in exploring the grandeurs of the world outside the home are so great that almost all adult Rocky Roaders remember such floggings as some of the worst and most frequent of their childhood careers. The running of errands marks the first time that children handle money; and yielding to the temptation to steal a few pence here and there brings them additional floggings. Girls, both observation and parental reports indicate, seem to steal more than boys, and here too is a source of greater punishment for them.

At about the age of four the children learn that they can avoid some of the frequent floggings by literal flight and avoidance. To avoid a flogging, a child runs and hides the moment he is told "You rude"—the usual warning that a flogging is on the way—and waits for the parental temper to subside. But there are some acts, such as taking food meant for someone else, which never go unpunished. If the child is sufficiently skilled in eluding the mother's arm, she will not exert herself in chasing him; the flogging is administered by the father when he comes home from the fields. In some families the act of taking food meant for someone else always goes unpunished by the mother; she knows that the father can mete out a more severe beating, and will therefore make no attempt to punish the child herself.

Toilet training is usually begun at the age of three years and is almost never accompanied by punishment. There is never any parental interference with erotic or genital play during infancy, childhood, or adolescence, save for the imposition of the incest taboo during late infancy. Infants and children, both boys and girls, masturbate frequently and openly and without any evidence of shame or guilt. At no time in their lives are they punished, teased, or praised by their parents for their autoerotism; the parents are aware of the erotic play of their children, but never comment on it.

The children were seen by the investigators to masturbate most frequently when they were hungry, when they were threatened with whippings or had just been whipped, when they were threatened with loss of fingers for sucking their fingers, and when they were threatened with the loss of some inanimate object of which they were fond. Masturbation ceases completely, according to observation and the reports of

parents, at about the age of four years and is rarely resumed in adolescence or adulthood.

For the first seven years a Rocky Roads child does not play with anyone except his own siblings. The reason most frequently cited for this by the parents is that if children "mix" and play with "strangers" they may be "spoiled" and influenced by them. Organized play among siblings is infrequent—Rocky Roads children do not seem to know any games—and the children do not have any toys. For the most part, they just sit or wander about quite aimlessly. The mutual play which does take place among the children is usually aggressive and is immediately stopped by floggings by the mother. The most typical household scene is one in which the children are spread out over the yard, one or two soliloquizing in flat monotones, another sitting against the kitchen wall gazing at the sky, one wandering to one end of the yard and back again, and still another standing and staring at his feet. Most wear rather mournful expressions, and it is quite an event to see one smile.

Children are never praised or rewarded, for "it will make them bad." When a child completes a task, no matter how well he did it, he is usually told that it was performed improperly and that a better job must be done next time. As a result, say the parents, the child will always strive for improvement. Thus, a parent might tell a girl who has just washed a shirt brilliantly clean and ironed it perfectly that the garment is filthy and the only reason it will be worn is that there is no other shirt available. When a child does a particular household task improperly while learning it, he is not punished for it; but if the child continues to do a bad job—a rare occurrence—he will be flogged.

Rocky Roads children never strike their parents or overtly exhibit any hostility toward them. Only once did we see a child, a three-year-old girl, make a move to hit her mother. The slap she directed at her mother seemed more like an automatic response after a flogging than a deliberately contemplated act. The little girl was so terrified at her own behavior that no sooner had she realized what she was doing than she froze with her hand in mid-air. The three-year-old carefully and studiously avoided her mother for several days.

While it is extremely rare for a Rocky Roads child of any age to admit to any consciousness of aggression toward either parent, there is a traditional method by which the child covertly expresses his hostility against his parents. Beginning at about the age of six or seven, children begin to take things which belong to their parents and either throw them away or give them to anyone they may meet. Invariably, the children select those items most highly valued by their parents—rings, watches, jewelry, and the like. No adult Rocky Roader ever denies having done this as a child, but none of them will ever admit that the intent was aggressive. The children are severely flogged for such activities when they are caught. As a result of a mechanism inherent in Rocky Roads property relationships, the items stolen and given away can always be reclaimed by the parent without any financial liability; this is in contrast to the fact that when, for instance, a child injures another, the parent is liable. The child does not continue this type of theft for very long, demonstrating the efficacy of floggings.

Rocky Roads children start attending school at the age of seven years. Most children enjoy going to school, and many adults remember their school days as the most pleasant times of their lives. School marks the first occasion on which the children are freed from the completely restrictive environment of the home and the first situation which allows any degree of freedom not bought at the price of floggings. While children are flogged by their teachers for misbehavior or for slowness in learning, most of them are able to get by with no more than one flogging a day in school, considerably fewer than are received at home on an average day. But some children are extremely slow in learning, do not enjoy school, and seek out every opportunity for missing school. Parents do not object to teachers hitting the children, feeling that unless a child is punished he will never learn properly. They make no attempts to encourage their children to outdo others in their schoolwork, and while they sometimes frankly admit before their offspring that the latter are "thickheaded," such a remark is never meant or taken as a remonstrance. Only on rare occasions do children receive homework, and they are never helped in this task by their parents.

In school, Rocky Roads children have their first opportunity to make friends and explore the regions of the world beyond their homes.

They now have playmates upon whom they may vent their aggression without interference by adults, and the play in the school-yard, aside from cricket, is usually aggressive, with a good deal of horseplay and fisticuffs—in short, the sort of play which, at home, would surely bring on severe floggings. But even this greater freedom of movement is somewhat restricted by the parents. Children may not linger after school but must hurry home, and they are flogged if they are late. Again, this rule is more strictly enforced for the girls than for the boys. Children never bring their friends home with them, nor are they ever permitted to meet for play after they return home.

A new phase of socialization begins for the boys at the age of ten years, when a radical change occurs in the parent-child relationship. The relationship between girls and their parents remains unchanged, however. From this time on, equal control and domination is exercised over the boys by both parents. Rocky Roads fathers, it should be noted, do not attempt to alienate their sons from their mothers, nor is any attempt made by the mothers to foster either affection or hostility between the fathers and sons.

The boys now begin to spend more time with their fathers. They go with their fathers to the fields, at first being taught rather simple tasks, and then proceeding to more advanced skills. The boys stand by and watch their fathers cultivate and harvest, and when the father lays down his machete, hoe, or fork, the boy will pick up the tools for a while and begin doing what he saw his father doing. The father will watch the youngster, and will correct anything which he feels is wrong. As the boys gain in proficiency, they take on small agricultural tasks, always under the supervision of their fathers.

While learning these tasks, the boys are never flogged for anything that they may do wrong, just as the girls, at an earlier age, are not punished while being taught household tasks. The only difference between the role learning of boys and girls is that the girls at first refuse to do the work which is demanded of them, and hence are flogged before they submit, whereas the boys are only too happy to work in the fields because they have learned early in their lives that the father will rarely punish except at the instigation of the mother. It is for this reason that both boys and girls attempt at an early age to go with their fathers to the fields; the boy's wishes are granted after the age of ten, but the girl hardly ever gets to go to the fields.

Adolescence, according to Rocky Roads culture, begins for both boys and girls when the child leaves school, usually at fourteen years. It is characterized by the assumption of a larger share of adult activities, preparatory to full-fledged adulthood. There is also a gradual weaning from dependence upon the parents—a process which is never really completed, however. The Rocky Roader now begins to devote full time to the activities at which he will spend the rest of his life.

The boy now spends all of his time doing farm work. He is given a portion of his father's land to cultivate as his own, and he may also hire himself out for wage labor. While he does not have to seek his father's permission to do the latter, he must inform his father of his intentions, and should his father forbid him to work for someone else, he must obey. He must also work for his father, without remuneration, whenever the father needs help in the fields.

On the portion of land given the boy by his father, he is more or less free to raise whatever crops he wishes. He does not pay rent for the land, and, technically, he enjoys absolute ownership of all that the land yields. But since Rocky Roads parents, theoretically, are not obligated to support their sons after they have reached adolescence, the son must contribute anywhere from one-third to half his earnings to his father to pay for his room and board. Thus one of the incentives for the adolescent son to keep working is that the parent will not house and feed him unless he contributes to the family coffers. The remainder of the money that a boy earns is his to do with as he pleases. But while this is true in theory, it is somewhat qualified in practice, for the money may be spent only for clothes—which his parents no longer provide— and for occasional entertainment *of which the parents approve.* A boy who spends his money indiscriminately and in violation of parental direction will receive a flogging.

There are two aims to the labors of the Rocky Roads adolescent, in addition to paying his parents for his room and board. The first is to accumulate enough money so that he can purchase land—or rent land if purchasable land is not attainable—and become economically self-sufficient. But this wish to acquire land is never stated by the adolescents as a desire to be completely free of their fathers. In fact, no matter how much land a boy can purchase or rent, he still holds on to the land his father allows him to use; relinquishing a parcel of land is tantamount to giving up part of one's income, something no Rocky Roader will ever do. Every man strives to buy and rent more and more land; no one ever feels that he has enough.

The second goal is directly connected with the first. The constant and prepotent aim of life in Rocky Roads is the maintenance of economic "independence"—that is, wealth or self-sufficiency. Around the time of adolescence this motivation becomes fully crystallized and assumes the proportions that it will have throughout life. More accurately, this is the time that the Rocky Roader first becomes capable of verbalizing these strivings. Whenever a boy of thirteen or younger was asked why he saved whatever pennies he earned, he put his motivation in terms of parental encouragement in this direction. At fourteen years and older his motivation is in terms of himself: "Me want to be rich, man! Me want to be rich." Earlier he would have said: "My daddy flog me if me no save."

While the degree of discipline for boys decreases during adolescence, it never completely disappears. Floggings still continue, but their administration depends on several factors. First, if the boy is so big and strong that his father cannot hold on to him, the father must content himself with boxing the boy's ears or administering a clout to his head. The second factor is the young man's earning capacity. The greater his earning capacity, the less right does his father have to flog him. This is a crucial fact, for until now the Rocky Roader has resorted to flight to escape punishment from others. Now he learns an even stronger defense—economic independence.

While a boy at this age may receive a flogging for gross disobedience of parental orders of any sort, the main point of contention between parent and son is generally of an economic nature—usually parental disapproval of the manner in which the boy spends his money. Other actions which will bring on a flogging are staying away from the house for too long a time or beginning to smoke before the age at which this is permitted—usually seventeen or eighteen. The boy's choice of friends, both male and female, is also strictly subject to the approval of his parents.

The strongest disciplinary measure which is held over the heads of the boys is the threat of expulsion from home. A young man who persists in laziness, and who does not take advantage of every opportunity to better himself economically, is told that he will find himself without a roof over his head and without domestic conveniences unless his behavior alters immediately. The motivation is not parental interest in the advancement of the son but in his financial contribution to the home. A man whose son tarries along the path of financial advancement feels deprived of an additional source of revenue; he never takes such a prospect lightly and is both sure and swift in the manner in which he reacts. Thus the Rocky Roads boy learns to fear failure in seeking economic independence.

It is not until adulthood that a Rocky Roads man can come and go as he pleases. Unmarried adult men spend as little time as possible at home, usually coming home only to eat and sleep and never consulting their parents about anything. The parents rarely question their son's activities so that they rarely know, for example, when he leaves the house to go into the fields or when he has returned. After marriage, sons visit neither parent.

For the girls the pattern is a somewhat different one. The first important variation shows up in the cultural rule that, while boys must be supported only until they are fourteen, girls must be supported as long as they live at home. Furthermore, girls do not have to contribute toward their maintenance while living at home. Another important distinction is that girls must seek permission for everything they want to do.

When a girl leaves school, her first wish is to find employment as a household worker—the only thing for which she has been trained. Since there are only a few such jobs in and around Rocky Roads, many of the girls must leave the community and seek work in the urban areas of the island. As a result, there are few adolescent or young adult girls living in Rocky Roads.

A girl must receive her mother's permission to accept a position away from home; even while away from home she is subject to her mother's discipline and must return home whenever called. Whatever a girl earns is hers, and as long as her parents are not aware of how she spends it, she may do with it as she pleases. Girls of this age return home very rarely, usually only because of pregnancy or serious illness. Most of them do, however, return to Rocky Roads to marry, although some find their husbands in the town or in the capital.

If an adolescent girl is living at home, she remains under the same parental control and discipline which characterized her childhood, since she contributes neither food nor money to the household. The slightest infraction of the rules of family life—disobedience, absence from home without permission, and the like—brings on a flogging either by the mother or, at her instigation, by the father. An unmarried adult woman living at home makes some attempt to maintain the same sort of independence of the parents that her brother does; yet she must still seek permission to accept employment and must usually keep her parents informed of her whereabouts. The very fact that she is at home much of the time makes her subject to greater parental scrutiny. She does not stay out late at night, for a woman in Rocky Roads when alone is very afraid of the dark. Women have no culturally approved places of congregation; loafing along the road is considered a shameful thing to do. Hence, when they are not actively engaged in some sort of activity outside the home they must return to the "yard" where they are put to work by their mothers, who are always able to find something for them to do and are frequently critical of what they do.

The dependency of women continues after they are married. Specifically, this dependence is on the mother, not the father. The women of the community are vaguely aware of their dependence, and on rare occasions will rebel against it. This rebellion is never overt, never constitutes a severance of ties with the parent, and is not manifest in any attempt to establish independence. Instead, it is on the verbal level; the woman may wish out loud to herself—but never to the parent—that "the whole of them go to hell." Criticism by the mother is always more apt to bring a daughter into line than a son. Girls react with much greater intensity than do their brothers to the post-flogging type of punishment—silence. Even grown women, with families of their own, are more certain of their opinions and their actions when they have concrete and visible evidence that these are approved of by their mothers. Daughters respond to the death of a mother with greater sorrow and grief than do sons. Finally, when women visit their parents' homes after having married, the express purpose is to visit their mothers, rather than their fathers.

Premarital sexual intercourse begins at puberty for boys and girls. There seem to be few indications of anxiety or guilt surrounding sexual behavior in Rocky Roads. Nor do there seem to be any differences in the degree of satisfaction and enjoyment of sexual behavior between males and females in the community. During the first two or three years of adolescence, unions are struck up wherever and whenever convenient. At about the age of seventeen, semi-permanent heterosexual unions are formed, although these hardly ever terminate in marriage. In the relationship the boy "owns" his "girl friend" and the girl "owns" her "boy friend." Aside from sexual gratification, there appear to be no positive emotional bonds in these friendships; no particular affection is either required or exhibited between premarital sexual partners. In fact, it is culturally permissible to have an affair with a person for whom one nurtures a not too superficial dislike.

ADULTHOOD

The chief and uncompromising end of every Rocky Roads adult is the amassment of money and the maintenance of an adequate food supply; he is constantly motivated by the drive to be economically "independent"—that is, wealthy. The dependent adult is frowned upon, shunned even by his own siblings and offspring, and relegated to the lowest social stratum of the community; and if he finally loses the struggle and becomes completely dependent upon an outside agent for his physical survival, he perceives himself as impotent before the demands of his organism, and worthless before the world. He lives in a state of perpetual anxiety which renders him completely immobilized. He sinks into abject apathy, despondency, and utter helplessness. The incessant complaint of the dependent adult is that "No one knows me anymore."

But while the Rocky Roader's perception of self as wealthy is often an absolute value, more often than not it stands in competitive relationship with other selves—his acquaintances, relatives, and neighbors. When a Rocky Roader beholds another's economic misfortune, his first response is a gleeful "One man's fall is another man's rise." Yet when the tables are turned and he must watch another attaining greater economic success than his own, he sinks into an extended fit of morbid depression.

The Rocky Roader often equates money with food. A favorite saying is "If the tummy is all right, everything else is all right"—which clearly defines the predominant area of interest if one bears in mind that the welfare of the Rocky Roader's "tummy" also refers to the state of his pile of money, and that both measure his happiness and well-being. Almost all anxieties, fantasies, conflicts, inhibitions, and feelings of guilt among the folks of Rocky Roads center about food and money. Thematically, food and money constitute the basic motivating factors in religious ideas and practices, interpersonal and intrapunitive aggression, marriage, the formation of nonsexual friendships, and political behavior. Significantly, most dreams are interpreted by the Rocky Roaders as omens of economic success or failure.

The people of Rocky Roads live in a perpetual state of anxiety over their economic welfare. The Rocky Roader expresses this anxiety in the belief that he never has enough money, that he is poor, and that everyone else is undermining his opportunity for earning a satisfactory livelihood. Actually, eighty per cent of the people in the community live above the subsistence level, and no more than three per cent of the adults can be classed as dependent upon others for their physical survival. Thus these economic anxieties are completely out of proportion to objective reality.

No matter how "independent" a person may be, he always believes that everyone else, no matter how obviously poor, is better off and has accumulated more money. This is not to say that the people are ignorant of each other's financial state of affairs; on the contrary, although a Rocky Roader will never divulge the amount of money in his possession, others in the community are able to render a fairly accurate account of his financial affairs. The belief that everyone is more "independent" than oneself contributes strongly to this high level of anxiety.

One's own state of perceived poverty is almost always the fault of some wealthier person who will not lease land, because he "doesn't want other people to make a living." It is true that there are wealthy Rocky Roaders who own a considerable number of acres of land which are not under cultivation. One of the claims of these landowners is that they eventually reap greater profits if they allow the land to lie fallow until they can cultivate it themselves. Crop failures are often admittedly the result of droughts and hurricanes, but these in turn are frequently attributed to the machinations of the sorcerer working at a neighbor's behest.

"Jealousy"

Rocky Roaders use "jealousy" instead of the "evil eye"—a term which they are familiar with but do not use. Jealousy is morbidly feared, and great pains are taken to avoid arousing it in others, for once it is aroused, one's fortunes are sure to disintegrate. Most well-to-do people in Rocky Roads are firmly convinced that they are universally disliked because they "try to be independent." Most people, when seeing a successful crop which is not theirs, wish that something would happen to it, and occasionally admit this. When the jealous wish itself is incapable of doing the task, they may resort to the sorcerer.

On the score of meticulously avoiding the arousal of jealousy, the Rocky Roader is confronted with a rather delicate conflict. On the one hand, custom dictates that one should always be well dressed when walking along the main road, unless one is at the same time indulging in some heavy manual activity; on the other hand, habitual adornment in clean, untattered garments may convey to one's fellow villagers the impression of independence, and this impression is certain to arouse the feared jealousy. Most persons are conscious of the conflict, but only few have solved it in any consistent fashion. Most women have adopted the solution of alternating neatness and sheer unkemptness— by Rocky Roads standards, not the writer's.

Some women, however, are consistently neat and others habitually unkempt. Among men, the fear of jealousy appears to be less intense, and the conflict not so severe. Since they work in the fields most of the time, custom tolerates tattered garments for them every day except Sunday. The most bitter and frequent complaint which the folks of Rocky Roads made during conversation with the investigators was that their neighbors would not agree that they were poor. Yet the frequency and intensity of such complaints were markedly higher among those in whom the values for neatness were most rigidly implanted and who most disliked unkemptness in themselves.

Money—pence, shillings, pounds—is the mainspring of the Rocky Roader's personal stability. The most typical attitude towards money was well expressed by one male informant who said, "You have to take in more than you give out," and by another who said, "Man ha' to save every penny." A woman informant working in the fields, said, when asked what she was doing, that she was "looking for money." All Rocky Roaders agree that money is to be saved, not spent. The chief incentive to save money is the anticipation of sickness, which, to them, is synonymous with economic dependency. Every anticipation of the future, which is always in economic terms, includes the frightening prospect of sickness without financial security. In addition to this long-range savings plan, the close of the Christmas season marks the commencement of saving for Easter, and Easter is the time to begin saving for Christmas. These savings are supposed to be used for holiday gifts. But since the money saved is never spent on these designated occasions, it is added to the ever-growing fund of savings for illness. The women of the community exhibit these traits with greater intensity than do the men; they are more reluctant to part with money, they are much more difficult to move during bargaining sessions, and so on.

The striving for independence, despite its intensity and importance to emotional stability appears to be fraught with guilt. Every Rocky Roader who was asked to define the word "sin" said that "It is wanting too much." In fact, all earthly desires are considered sinful. But compromises must be made, for people must have food and money and adequate shelter. It is for this reason that sin is equated with excess and temptations to excess. When the people of the community say that all people are born in sin, they mean that every person enters this world with material and aggressive strivings and must make every attempt to purge themselves of these desires. Generally, this expurgation takes place through the medium of confessions during religious services.

Dependency

While the Rocky Roader strives to be the wealthiest member of his community—or the most "independent," to use his term—he also manifests strong dependency strivings in these very same areas. These dependency longings, together with the conflicts surrounding them, appear, for instance, in the areas of marriage, begging behavior, and religious and political ideas.

A man rarely, if ever, marries before his mother's death. This is not because of any cultural rationalization that he must care for his mother; nor does the mother show any desire to keep her son out of the clutches of some other woman. Rather, a man rarely thinks of marrying so long as he has someone to look after his meals, mend his clothes, and care for his living quarters. Moreover, the culture directs that a man not marry until he is able to support a family. "Foolish ones get married even if they can't support a family," say the people of the community. Ideally, a man is first considered able to support a family when he is about thirty-five. Thus the motives which impel a man to seek a spouse are material or economic. Likewise, the chief things which a man expects of a wife are of an economic nature. He expects her to cook for him, wash and mend his clothes, and care for his living quarters. When his mother is no longer alive to perform these functions for him, he will seek to marry a woman capable of doing these things, and one who has money so that she "can help him out." In the absence of such a desirable person, he will marry a girl who can do something to "help herself," for should he cease to earn money, he will then be sure of some source of income for the family. In short, a Rocky Roads man seeks the woman with the most money or greatest earning capacity.

Almost every young woman wishes to marry as early as possible and spends many of her hours day-dreaming and longing for marriage, which signifies emancipation from the domination of her parents. But, more important, it represents full material care by someone else and freedom from financial obligations. Such obligations arise from the fact that almost every Rocky Roads woman has at least one illegitimate child before she marries; and while an illegitimate child is assigned to the care of the maternal grandparents, most grandparents demand that the daughter assume part of the responsibility of providing for the child. Thus marriage is looked forward to by the women as a resolution of conflicts arising from economic pressures, needs, and aspirations.

When a man proposes marriage to a woman, she will first estimate his wealth by the number and types of crops he plants and the probable income from them. As the women themselves put it, they want to know how much the man "will be able to buy" for them. Most women overestimate the economic powers of the men they eventually marry. Many of the women say that their disappointment in their husbands' earning powers is the cause of much of the strife characterizing family life in Rocky Roads.

The insistence on receiving food from others is a frequent source of friction in marital relationships. For instance, a man will fly into a rage if his meal is not ready on time. He will also be enraged if his clothes are not properly washed and mended. A woman will often direct temper tantrums against her husband, bitterly complaining that he does not provide adequately for her. A woman's refusal to help her husband in the fields is a frequent source of quarreling. Food and money are used by spouses to accentuate their dependency needs, as well as to express their hostilities. A woman may be late in preparing her husband's meals, or may make them unappetizing. Her greatest expression of hostility is refusing to prepare his meals at all. A man may refuse to eat food which his wife has raised, confining himself to food which he has raised himself. His greatest anger is expressed in his refusal to eat any food which she has prepared. No act on his part could constitute a more deadly insult, for to refuse an offer of food by another Rocky Roader is tantamount to an open declaration of contempt.

Dependency is also expressed in begging. While the most usual greeting in Rocky Roads, at any time of the day, is "Good evening," the second most popular greeting is "And what are you carrying for me today?" The latter symbolizes precisely the attitude in which the people of Rocky Roads regard everyone else—that every person is a potential source of revenue or material goods which must be tapped and exploited. Indiscriminate begging is predominantly the province of the women. A man will "beg you a bread"—bread symbolizing literally anything—only after a protracted and fairly friendly relationship with the person whom he is begging from. Often he will beg for something definite—a cigarette, rum, or something of the sort. The women, on the other hand, do not abide by these amenities; the presence of another person is sufficient provocation for them to beg, and their usual request is for "anything." Furthermore, their begging is completely out of proportion to their objective need. There are, of course, a few who are genuinely needy.

The people of the community are well aware of the differences in behavior between the sexes on this score. Men explain the begging of the women as an indication of their laziness and refusal to work for a "pay day." This, however, does not explain the equally prevalent begging among very young girls. The women explain that they are forced to beg because of the ungenerosity of the men who, they say, do not support and provide for their families adequately.

Rocky Roaders presumably hope that their begging will be successful—although it rarely is; yet the receipt of a begged object arouses tremendous anxieties in the recipient. Begging is a competitive affair, and when two Rocky Roaders are competing for the same thing, the aggression which the situation automatically arouses is directed not at the prospective donor of the item but rather at the other competitor. Hence when one receives something for which he has begged, he is certain that someone else has also begged for that item and that he is going to receive the brunt of the unlucky competitor's hostility. But a source of even greater anxiety is that it may become known to the community at large that he has begged and *received* something from someone, and that he is, by implication, a person dependent upon the donor for his survival. He fears that the community will make this inference because of the

generally held notion that a person does not receive something for nothing unless he is in great need.

Another source of conflict over dependency strivings is indicated in the "sin" which surrounds this behavior. It is considered unquestionably wrong to ask for and take something which one does not need and for which one has no use; moreover, many Rocky Roaders will admit, however reluctantly, that it is wrong to beg at all. Thus while economic dependency behavior is an expression of a deep conflict, the gratification of dependency strivings is itself fraught with conflict.

Religious and political ideas also indicate the presence of dependency longings. Hurricanes and droughts are caused by God, but His reasons for sending them are unknown and unquestioned, and there is no doubt in anyone's mind that when the resulting famines appear He will provide for the people of Rocky Roads. The Good Lord is seen as an ultimate provider when all other sources fail. The emotions concerned in religious feelings are often expressed in the same terms used about food. For instance, when asked to describe his personal feelings about experiencing Christ, a Rocky Roader might say, "I'm no longer hungry."

Heaven is a place where all the pains and unpleasantries of this life are totally absent. In Heaven one works but one does not feel it because one is truly rich; no one suffers, and no one knows privation. "You enter this world empty handed," say many Rocky Roaders, "but in Heaven you have all you need." This world has nothing to give a person, and one can expect nothing from it. Only in Heaven can one expect something. That is why they want to go to Heaven. Incidentally, none of our informants knew of any suicide in the history of the community.

Finally, in this connection, it is interesting to consider briefly their attitudes toward the government. Most people are bitterly condemning of the Jamaican government and its political machinations, not on ideological principle, but mainly on the grounds that the government is not a source of revenue for the people. That, the Rocky Roaders believe, should be the main function of government, but the politicians are interested only in "making themselves comfortable."

Hostility and aggression

Interpersonal relationships in Rocky Roads are characterized by the inhibition of direct aggressiveness. A Rocky Roader operates at an extremely high level of latent hostility, but is he at the same time incapable of meeting a situation which requires the overt expression of hostility. He is often well aware of the necessity of responding aggressively, yet he is also aware of his inability to do so, and he will occasionally become conscious of his fear of the impulse. As a result, a Rocky Roader gives an impression of docility, an impression reinforced by his denial of aggressive impulses and by his withdrawal in the face of all aggression—both of his own and that of others.

This broad picture is particularly true for the women of Rocky Roads and must be qualified in slight degree for the men. Almost all adult Rocky Roaders are subject to severe headaches, but the more effective internalization of aggression among the women is amply demonstrated by the fact that the women suffer from this malady on the average of two or three times a week. The severity of these headaches is sometimes incapacitating, and they may last for several days; they rarely respond to conventional analgesics. The average man gets by with one or two of these headaches a month, and they are less severe.

The behavior for expressing anger most frequently cited by informants as the most desirable is to talk loudly and, by shouting, to provoke a quarrel. While this is sometimes resorted to, in reality the very opposite is the predominating pattern, for Rocky Roaders usually express their anger, especially in family situations, by a wall of complete silence. The refusal to talk on the part of the vexed person is first and foremost a function of his or her inability to respond aggressively, and only secondarily is it an act of aggression, however indirect. From the point of view of the person at whom it is directed, such silence is the most severe form of rebuke, for, like all Rocky Roaders, he suffers an exaggerated fear of criticism, but he does not in this instance know precisely what is being criticized. He therefore has no grounds for entering into a quarrel. But the silence is a rebuke, and hence arouses reciprocal aggression which must also remain unexpressed. The result is a headache,

usually for both parties. Silence as an instrument of hostility is more frequently used by the women of the community, and is more sharply responded to by them than by the men.

The second method of expressing anger—"quarreling with oneself"—is a favorite pastime of many Rocky Roaders. This consists of talking heatedly to oneself out loud proclaiming rather volubly all the things one would say to the object of one's aggression. This undoubtedly represents a compromise between directing aggression at the intended object of the anger and completely internalizing it. A favorite manipulation of this compromise is to employ it within earshot of the person for whom it is intended, although not to his face. The latter can never respond to this quarreling, for he will always be told, "Is not you me talk to," and this cannot be disproved. "Quarreling with oneself" is much more frequent among women than men.

Almost all of these "quarrels" which we were able to overhear, understand, and record followed a single pattern. The aggrieved person would first recite his own affection for the person whom he was talking about, citing all the things he had done for that person and how self-sacrificing he had been for him. After this plaintive prologue, the speaker would cite the cause of the recitation. Invariably, it would emerge that he had asked for something material and had been refused. This would be the core and the longest part of the recitation. The refusal would be pointed to as proof that the reciter was really disliked by the one who had denied the request. It does not pay to be nice to people, the argument would usually run, for they never wish to alleviate the plight of one who is kind and providing. The refuser would be pointed to as a person who attempted to convey the impression of liking the speaker; this affection was now proved to be a guise for hostility and dishonesty.

In addition to the internalized proscription against culturally defined acts of aggression, any action committed in the face of *threatened* aggression or retaliation of any sort is itself perceived as an aggressive act. Hence adult Rocky Roaders are extremely law-abiding. On occasion, for example, a woman will consider suing the father of her illegitimate child for the child's support, but she will refrain from doing so if the man threatens "to kill her in court."

This is not a literal threat of murder, but one of sorcery. Even though the effects of sorcery can be easily combatted and nullified, it is not provoked because it represents aggressive retaliation.

It is also interesting to note that Rocky Roaders do not like to be touched physically by other persons. A greeting which includes a light pat on the back or on the arm would be considered distinctly unfriendly. Rocky Roaders are not in the habit of shaking hands with strangers; characteristically, they acknowledge an introduction with a mere nod of the head. Furthermore, premarital sexual partners engage in no physical contact, holding of hands, embracing, and the like, outside of the immediate situation of sexual intimacy.

The frequency of gossip can be accounted for in terms of its malicious and indirectly aggressive function. Its effectiveness can be accounted for by the dread of being talked about and is equated with criticism. The rationalization of the aggressive component of gossip is provided by the cultural differentiation of two types of gossip. The first, gossip per se, is permissible, for there is "nothing wrong in telling the truth about someone." The second type, "back biting," or saying false things about another person, is prohibited. All Rocky Roaders deny ever indulging in this form of conversation, although they constantly accuse one another of it. In reality, Rocky Roads gossip is contrived of systematic distortion manipulated to fill the needs of the moment.

Needless to say, murder, larceny, destruction, and arson are absent in the life of Rocky Roads. We knew of only one instance of physical assault within the last two generations—an incident involving two men.

PERCEPTION OF THE SOCIAL ENVIRONMENT

"Me never vex; everybody else him always vex, but me never vex"—thus does a Rocky Roader describe his perception of his social world and his position within that environment. Basically, the Rocky Roader fears other persons, for to him most everyone is a source of potential punishment and aggression with which he cannot cope. The Rocky Roader considers aggressive impulses unacceptable and denies their existence in himself; but he sees lurking in every other person an unfathomable mass of hostility awaiting its discharge in his direction. So intense is this fear that the Rocky Roader does not make the discrimination of fearing only specific acts of aggression directed at him; he perceives almost every person as wholly made up of aggressive impulses. And so his avoidance of aggression in others necessarily leads him to the avoidance of other people.

For the Rocky Roader the world is a dangerous place fraught with conspiracies which are aimed at his economic downfall. People are unfriendly and are never to be trusted. A person is rarely thought of as committing an aggressive act of his own volition; he behaves as he does because of a conspiratorial group which is goading him on and which is using him as a "front." The Rocky Roader is convinced that people are always meeting in secret to hatch their evil plots, although no one knows how, when, and where. But at the same time, each claims innocence of ever having participated in such monstrous evils.

Along with the principle that one man's fall is another man's rise goes the conviction that one's fall is almost always the result of malicious behavior on the part of some conspirator. This is so extreme that a Rocky Roader may even refuse to accept the responsibility of his own actions if their consequences are disadvantageous to him. Perhaps he has decided against planting corn one season because the government price is too low to warrant the risk involved in the crop; if the government raises its purchasing price just before the harvest of the corn crop, he is sure to blame someone else in the community for his misfortune. If he resigns a lucrative job in a moment of rash anger at his employer, he will often, after a few days, deny that he quit the job; he will insist that some other Rocky Roader who was jealous had gossiped against him to his employer, causing his dismissal.

As in the case of the inhibitions of aggressiveness, these systematized ideas of social reality are more pronounced among the women than among the men. These ideas are present in most men of the community, in varying degrees of intensity, but they have to be prodded before they will express them. The women of the community, on the other hand, are always prepared to offer such explanations without encouragement, for they are constantly preoccupied with them. The following extract from our data illustrates this:

The Scott family had been having a hard time of it these past few years. Their land was insufficient and the number of mouths to be fed was increasing. We knew Mr. and Mrs. Scott equally well, and there was little reticence among us. They were actively attempting to purchase some land, and at times Mrs. Scott would spend the entire two hours of an interview complaining to the ethnographer of the maliciousness of the people who had land but would not sell it because they did not want other people to make a living. In other words, she did not have to be asked why it was difficult to buy land. Mr. Scott, on the other hand, would admit that he was having a difficult time purchasing land, but would not add the explanations his wife always had at hand. Isn't there any land around here, he would be asked, which someone isn't using? Yes, he would answer, there was quite a bit of such land. Had he tried to get some of that land? Yes, he had, on innumerable occasions. Do these people ever plan to sell their fallow land? No, he thought they did not. What would these people do with it if they did not cultivate it? He had not the faintest idea. Then why don't they sell it, he would be asked. Probably, he would say, because they didn't want anyone else to make a living.

What element of truth is there in this idea? It is true that no Rocky Roader wishes to see another succeed, but it is equally true that no Rocky Roader would forgo the opportunity to make a profit through the sale of parcels of land. Most people want to buy land, and it is possible to sell it in sufficiently small parcels to keep any one owner from extracting too large a profit from it—a line of reasoning which is not alien to the Rocky Roaders. The owners of idle land cite one of three reasons for holding on to it: (1) they are very old, know that they are going to die shortly, and want to leave it to their children to do with as they please; (2) it will later yield more profit if they allow it to lie fallow; and (3) they are waiting for the price of land to rise. One large parcel of land was bought several years ago at five shillings an acre; at the time we were in Rocky Roads the highest bidding price was five pounds sterling (one hundred shillings) per acre. And the price is still rising.

The ideas of reference, and the like, which preoccupy practically every Rocky Roader are always consistent and systematic and are often quite complicated. Never are they randomly or promiscuously conceived and constructed. There is always some connection with objective reality. The people who compose the core of the ever-present conspiratorial persecutions are real people, neighboring Rocky Roaders, who are always named, and whose real actions and statements are the seeds of the elaborate systems of ideas subsequently constructed. The Rocky Roader's conviction that he is being criticized is an excellent illustration of this point. Criticism is never felt where it does not actually exist. But once any indication of criticism, however insignificant, is given, it is used as the reality basis of a consistent, systematic, and complicated set of persecutory ideas. The object of these persecutions, every Rocky Roader knows, is the destruction of one's economic independence.

A Rocky Roader cannot accept either criticism or praise. Criticism of any sort is always felt as a rebuke for a deliberate action and always results in a feeling of depression or a headache. When, for example, we would offer our cook some suggestions for improving a dish which she had served, she would indignantly demand to know why we had accused her of deliberately spoiling it. When a Rocky Roader is praised for something he has done, he may simply reply, "Oh, you only say so; you no mean it." He also cannot accept defeat in a game without feeling that the other has won by cheating and foul means. Games, such as dominoes, cards, and cricket, are played to be won, and anger and depression seethe in the losers. While almost every Rocky Roader feels that he is universally disliked, he frequently states his wish to be liked, and constantly seeks reassurance that he is liked. But when it is demonstrated to him that he is liked, he will express his disbelief.

Patterns of Friendship

Friendships are rare in Rocky Roads. Sometimes a man will form what is apparently a friendship with another man, but this is, in reality, an economic arrangement in which labor is exchanged. Such friends spend considerable time together, but their relationship is subject to the same anxieties which pervade the interpersonal relationships of the community. Each member of the pair believes that he is a better friend than his partner, that he is the more loving of the two, and that the other is participating in the relationship for purely selfish reasons and will never grant a favor which he is not forced to. Characteristically, these accusations are not made *to* one another but rather *about* each other. These friendships occur mainly among unmarried adults, and are discontinued, for some reason, after the marriage of one of the partners. Such friendships are less frequent among the women. For one thing, the women have no cause for such economic unions, since they do not habitually work in the fields.

Friendships among men gave no indications of overt homosexuality. When close friendships among young adult women do exist, they are usually homosexual unions to fall back upon in the absence of heterosexual outlets. These friendships, too, completely dissolve upon the marriage of either of the partners. All evidence suggests that whatever homosexual impulses exist among the women of the community are conscious and are not subject to repressing factors or mechanisms.

Neither heterosexual nor homosexual ideas are ever expressed or indicated in persecutory systems.

There is no pattern of visiting, and the culture makes no provision for hospitality or for the treatment of guests. Rocky Roaders do not like other people to "come on" their yards, and only on the rarest of occasions is one invited into the home of a Rocky Roader.

30. MALE AND FEMALE ADAPTATIONS IN CULTURE CHANGE

LOUISE AND GEORGE SPINDLER

Reproduced by permission of the American Anthropological Association from American Anthropologist, *Vol. 60, No. 1, 1958. George Spindler is Professor of Anthropology, Stanford University. With Louise Spindler, he has done field work among the Menomini Indians of Wisconsin, the Blood Indians of Alberta, Canada, the Mistassini Cree of Quebec, and in Germany. He has also worked with school teachers and administrators in California schools. He is the author of* Sociocultural and Psychological Processes in Menomini Acculturation, Transmission of American Culture, *co-author (with Alan Beals and Louise Spindler) of* Culture in Process *and (with Louise Spindler) of* Dreamers without Power, *and editor of* Education and Anthropology, Education and Culture, *and* Being an Anthropologist. *From 1963 to 1967, he was editor (with the assistance of Louise Spindler) of the* American Anthropologist. *Louise Spindler teaches anthropology at Stanford University. Before turning to anthropology, her major interests were in romantic poetry and drama. She has been particularly interested in women's roles, and witchcraft and culture change. She is the author of* Menomini Women and Culture Change. *She is co-editor, with George Spindler, of the series* Case Studies in Cultural Anthropology, Studies in Anthropological Method, *and* Case Studies in Education and Culture.

■ Like Selection 21, the following paper focuses on a transitional period, in this case a forced change from hunting-gathering to an industrial society. Whenever one group is conquered by another or emigrates to a host society, it must, to survive, undergo change in every sphere of life, moving toward the norms of the dominant group. (There may be reciprocal influences on the dominant group, but that is a phenomenon we will not discuss here.) Anthropologists refer to this particular process of change as "acculturation," by which is meant the transformation of one culture as a result of the dominance of another. In this study we consider the psychological accompaniments of acculturation among the Menomini Indians of northern Wisconsin.

The particular problem the Spindlers set for themselves was to learn whether Menomini men and women had to make different personality accommodations in the acculturation process. They found that the impact of acculturation was much greater for men than for women, the former exhibiting more anxiety and less control than the women, who emerge as more conservative. They then tie these personality differences to male and female roles in the traditional and the new cultural systems, showing that women were able to retain many of their traditional roles—with their corresponding psychological features—while the men were forced into new roles in conflict with their personality patterns, which themselves had largely been instilled by conservative mothers.

The Spindlers also emphasize the methodological problems in studying such questions. They rely not only on ethnological observations and the direct study of group differences, but also on materials from the Rorschach ink-blot test, which they administered to a group of Menomini. The blots on the ten Rorschach cards are standardized stimuli, and there are standardized techniques for analyzing the responses to them. The Rorschach test was originally designed to make psychological diagnoses of brain-damaged people, but in its anthropological use the test can be thought of as an unchanging conventionalized stimulus presented to people who share a common background. In seeking to learn how they respond to this stimulus, the researcher tries to learn how and why they respond similarly and how and why—that is, under what conditions—they respond differently. As we will see, the groups among the Menomini into which these responses fall parallel the groups that can be observed directly. The value of the Rorschach test is that it enables us to infer psychological patterns that are not directly observable.

George Spindler has presented many of the data from this research project in his monograph, *Sociocultural and Psychological Processes in Menomini Acculturation* (University of California Publications in Culture and Society, Vol. 5, University of California Press, 1955). A good introductory survey of acculturation and other types of change can be found in "Culture Change," by Nancy O. Lurie (in *Introduction to Cultural Anthropology*, edited by James A. Clifton (Boston : Houghton Mifflin, 1968, pp. 274-303). The reader first being introduced to the study of acculturation can get a good picture of the concepts involved from two methodological papers: "A Picture Technique for the Study of Values," by Walter

Goldschmidt and Robert B. Edgerton (*American Anthropologist*, 63 [1961] : 26-47) and "The Instrumental Activities Inventory : A Technique for the Study of the Psychology of Acculturation," by George and Louise Spindler (*Southwestern Journal of Anthropology*, 21 [1965] : 1-23). A study of acculturation from the point of view of adaptation is "Tappers and Trappers : Parallel Process in Acculturation," by Robert F. Murphy and Julian H. Steward (*Economic Development and Culture Change*, 4 [1956] : 335-53 ; reprinted as Selection 18 in *The Cultural Present*). In my estimation, one of the most important papers in connection with this aspect of change is "Social Change and Acculturation," by Robert F. Murphy (*Transactions of the New York Academy of Sciences*, Ser. 2, 26 [7] [May 1964] : 845-54). ■

THE PROBLEM

THIS PAPER has a dual purpose: to compare the psychological adaptations of adult males and females to the exigencies of sociocultural change in an historically primitive but rapidly acculturating population—the Menomini Indians of Wisconsin—and to present the methodology that makes it possible to describe these differences accurately. In so doing, we hope to help to fill a lacuna in anthropological literature on the differential adjustment of the two sexes in culture change situations, and to illustrate a method of analysis for such situations that may prove useful as a model for comparisons in other situations.

Although an awareness of the problem has long existed, few anthropologists have explicitly dealt with differences between the adaptations of males and females in their adjustment to a new environment created by the impact of an alien culture. Among those writing on American Indians, Mead was one of the first to recognize that acculturating females in one Plains Indian group undergo fewer abrupt changes in role playing than do the males. Joffe was impressed with the conservatism displayed by Fox Indian women in acculturation, as were the Hanks in their study of the Blackfoot, Vogt in his study of the Navaho, Elkin with the Arapaho, and Caudill with the Ojibwa. In studies where psychological tests such as the Rorschach were used, male-female differences in adjustment were again noted by Hallowell, who found that Saulteaux women were in general making a better adjustment to white culture than were the males. Caudill likewise found acculturating Ojibwa women less anxious than the men. While these studies are suggestive, they were not mainly concerned with male-female differences, and make little or no attempt to analyze these observed differences systematically.

In a general way, the Menomini data fit the model of male-female differences in culture change suggested by these studies. Menomini males appear to be more anxious and less controlled than do the women. And the women are psychologically more conservative. This suggests that for some reason the disruptions created in rapid culture change hit the men more directly, leaving the women less changed and less anxious. We will first demonstrate that these psychological differences are present, and in so doing apply some new techniques of analysis to Rorschach data that will permit accurate location of the sources of these differences on the Menomini acculturative continuum. Then we will turn to the sociocultural context, and particularly to differences in male and female roles, to seek explanation of the psychological observations.

Particular attention is given in this paper to methodology and its derivation. This is done in part because the Rorschach technique is used in this study and we wish to illustrate a method of analyzing Rorschach data that is not dependent upon acceptance of the usual interpretations of the meanings of scores developed by Western psychologists, since the validity of many of them has been questioned. Further, we wish to show how the technique used in this manner can provide essential information on modalities and distribution of psychological adaptations in culture change that would be difficult to gather or treat without a tool that provides quantitative data. And finally, we hope to show that when the subjects from whom protocols are taken are accurately located with respect to group identifications, acculturative and social status, and degree of social deviancy, meaningful relationships may be inferred between the psychological and the sociocultural processes in culture change.

The data and sample used in this study consist of 68 Rorschachs from males, and 61 from females, all over 21 years of age, one-half Menomini or more, and in the same acculturative categories (70 per cent of the females are married to Menomini males in the sample), a schedule of 23 sociocultural indices for each subject (house type, language, religious identification, etc.) which afforded data for placing subjects on an acculturative continuum and defining explicit values associated with the native or American culture; and short autobiographies expressly structured in terms of culture change process (15 from women, 8 from men) collected from individuals in each acculturative category and selected for their representation of both modal and deviant characteristics. Interviews of each individual in the sample (and many others), participant observation over seven summers of field work, and ethnohistorical data, provide context for the sample data listed above.

INITIAL TREATMENT OF THE DATA

So that new procedures developed in this paper will be clear, it is necessary to summarize the methodological steps taken up to this point and described in detail elsewhere.

For purposes of study, the Menomini sample was divided into four acculturative categories, ranging from a native-oriented group, through transitional levels, to a fully acculturated category. Religious identification and participation were used as initial criteria for tentative placement of individuals (first men, later women). The categories thus constituted were then validated for both sexes separately by application of a measure of association (tetrachoric r) to each sociocultural index from the schedule of indices referred to previously, in relationship to the posited placement of individuals in the acculturative categories, and by statistical tests of differences between categories with respect to these same items (using chi square). The fully acculturated category was then subdivided into two socioeconomic status groups on the basis of group memberships, residence, income, and occupation.

The five categories thus distinguished for both males and females are:

1. *Native-oriented*—all members of the Medicine Lodge and/or Dream Dance group where the patterns of traditional culture survive to the greatest extent.

2. *Peyote Cult*—composed of participating

members of the Cult and constitutes a unique variation of culture conflict resolution within the transitional position.

3. *Transitional*—consisting of persons in cultural transition who have participated in native-oriented religious activities and groups but have moved towards Catholicism and Western culture during their lifetimes, and are at present

acculturative categories. The differences revealed for the males were numerous, highly significant statistically, and "made sense" with respect to convergences between psychological and sociocultural process. There is no space here for discussion of the psychological content of these differences. In summary, this application of standard statistical techniques revealed

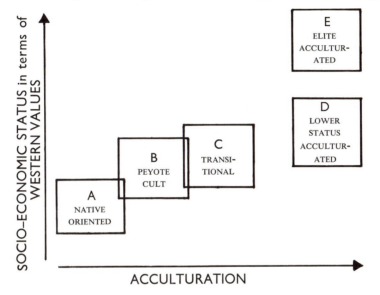

FIGURE 1.
Sociocultural categories in Menomini acculturation

not clearly identified with either Western or native-oriented groups and values.

4. *Lower status acculturated*—persons who were born Catholic and maintained this identification, know little or nothing of native traditions, but who have acculturated to a laboring class standard.

5. *Elite acculturated*—composed of persons who participate regularly in Catholic services, are members of the prestigeful Catholic Mother's and Holy Name Societies, and, if male, occupy managerial or semiprofessional positions in the reservation lumber industry or agency.

Figure 1 expresses the relationship between these categories in graphic form.

Standard statistical techniques (chi square and "exact probability") were applied first to the Rorschach data for the male sample to discover what statistically significant differences existed in the distributions of various Rorschach scores and combinations of scores among the

that there was a homogeneous psychological structure characterizing the native-oriented males which was like that of Hallowell's least acculturated Ojibwa and which apparently represented psychological as well as cultural continuity with the past. This structure tended to persist among the ungrouped transitionals but exhibited clear signs of corrosion in anxiety and breakdown of emotional control. The Peyotists exhibited high homogeneity of psychological structure marked by the same signs of anxiety and loss of control that appeared among the ungrouped transitionals, but exhibited special and deviant (within the Menomini sample) forms of introspective fantasy and self-concern that seemed to be a direct function of identification with cult ideology and experience in cult ritual. The lower-status acculturated were not clearly differentiated from either the transitionals or elite acculturated. The latter exhibited a dramatic psychological reformulation, in the setting of the Menomini continuum, that is apparently appropriate to their comparatively full participation in the structure of behaviors and rewards associated with middle class American culture.

GROSS MALE-FEMALE DIFFERENCES

We anticipated that the same order of differences would be exhibited by the females. Consequently, the same statistical procedures were initially applied to the Rorschach data from females. The laborious process of applying exact probability and chi square tests (where size of sample permitted) to all possible comparisons of acculturative categories among the women, and between comparable categories of men versus women, revealed very little by way of either statistically significant or logically consistent differences. Apparently the females were a sample of a universe that was not responding to the same forces as the males. Or they were responding to the same forces, but differently.

In an attempt to discover statistically the differences in Rorschach responses between the two sexes that we hypothesized as existing on the basis of participant observation, autobiographies, and interviews, we applied chi square tests to the Rorschach data of all females compared to all males, in a massive test of difference without respect to acculturative categories. Significant differences were revealed by this technique.

1. Women as a whole respond to the Rorschach ink blots with quicker reaction time than do the males (significant at .005).
2. Women exhibit less loss of emotional control (.05), in spite of the fact that they tend to express their emotions more openly (marginally significant at .06).
3. Women use more animal content than do men, to the greater exclusion of other types of content, indicating a less wide range of interests and experience (.001).
4. Protocols of the women contain more animal movement than do those of the men. There is thus the possibility that women are more involved with biologically oriented drives (eating, sex, reproduction) and exhibit less compulsion to produce abstract concepts (.05).
5. Women exhibit fewer tension and anxiety indicators than do the men: less anxiety of a free floating type (.05); less tension and conflict awareness (.005); and less attempt at introspection as a possible resolution of personal problems (.02).
6. Women as a whole show a higher degree of reality control than do the men (.05).

While we do not wish to make a case for these differences at this point, it is apparent that they are psychologically consistent within themselves. Women appear to be more controlled both intellectually and emotionally and yet retain enough open affect to be flexible. They appear to ruminate less about problems of conflict and are more involved with the problems of everyday life. There is apparently some significant tendency for females to adapt with less difficulty to the exigencies of culture change than do the males. All of the separate signs listed above, and they are all the signs isolated by this technique, are consistent in this respect.

But this information is not a very sizeable advance over what we already had hypothesized on the basis of other data, and does not go very significantly beyond what other studies have revealed. Furthermore, this technique affords no way of discovering the contribution of the various separate acculturative categories to the overall differences exhibited by the two sexes. Nor is it possible to isolate the contribution of what might be quite unlike personality types to the fractionated differences in specific indices that were revealed. In short, the differences in psychological adaptations for males and females thus revealed are too abstract and too gross, and do not permit the positing of relationships between psychological and sociocultural adaptations in discriminating terms.

THE APPLICATION OF A MODAL PERSONALITY TECHNIQUE

With the knowledge that these gross overall differences did exist between males and females in the adaptive processes, the problem became one of finding a technique that would make it possible to refine and exploit the meaning of these differences and explicate the contributions to them of personality type and acculturative position. After much exploration it was decided that the modal personality technique applied to Tuscarora Rorschachs by Wallace would serve best. In contrast to the application of the technique in Wallace's study, however, the modal personality is related to the acculturative groups delineated for the Menomini. The technique was first applied to the data from the Menomini women in a separate study by Louise Spindler, then to the males and in terms of relationship to the females in the present study.

A brief description of the technique will be necessary in order to make its application intelligible. One of the most crucial values in the technique is that the personality structure (as revealed by the Rorschach) is not fractionated—it permits expression of a holistic configuration of interrelated psychological characteristics. This configuration is most directly expressed by the Rorschach psychogram, a bar graph of the thirteen most important determinants of perception (see Fig. 2) such as human movement (M), animal movement (FM), form in outline (F), form-controlled shading (Fc), form-controlled color (FC), color predominant (CF), and so on, in usages standardized in the Klopfer system of scoring responses. A psychogram of this kind, summarizing the total number of responses given in each determinant category, can be constructed for any individual protocol or for a group of protocols in some expression of central tendency such as the mean.

The difficulty with using the mean of a group of protocols as a measure of central tendency is that the distribution of most scores in Rorschach usage are highly skewed (most people give 1 or 2 "M" for example, but some give a few, or many more), and the extreme scores bias the mean out of proportion to their significance. Other objections of this kind apply also to the raw mode and the median. In addition, what is wanted is an expression of range around the measures of central tendency that will include the Rorschach records of all those individuals who are enough alike to be psychologically indistinguishable, so that this "class" of individuals can be located wherever they may be in the acculturative continuum.

The following is the procedure of construction of modal personality types, in the form of modal Rorschach psychograms, with expressions of acceptable range. First, the crude mode was found for each score (of which there are 21) for all males and all females separately. Then a function of the standard error of measurement for Rorschach scores, based on an estimated

reliability for the Rorschach test of 0.800, was used to set limits on either side of these crude modes. This operation defined the "modal range" for each score. All scores falling in the modal range are considered indistinguishable from each other. Therefore, all individuals whose Rorschach protocol scores fall within the modal ranges for all 21 scores were regarded as belonging to a "modal class." One such modal class was found for the males, and one for the females. The scores of all the individual protocols in each modal class were then averaged, so that a modal psychogram could be drawn for the men and for the women. The results are expressed in Figure 2, and will be discussed later.

It will be noted that the use of twenty-one Rorschach indices (thirteen of which are expressed in the modal psychograms) provides rigorous selective criteria for what is modal or most representative. In most populations, even homogeneous ones, the selective criteria will eliminate more from the modal class than are included. But the fact that the number of indices used as criteria is large, and that the indices are organized in the form of a personality type, means that selection is dependent upon a configuration of indices rather than upon single criteria.

With a modal psychogram established for the Menomini women, and another for the men, it became possible to answer certain questions that could not be asked until now. What are the salient features of difference in these psychograms, as complex expressions of psychological adaptation, between males and females in the Menomini sample? Do these modal characteristics account for the differences between the sexes in psychological adaptation which were uncovered in the statistical test of fractionated factors? Or are the latter the result of fortuitous, non-representative convergences? What is the distribution of the modal psychological type throughout the continuum of acculturation for the two sexes? What is the location of what we have chosen to call "the psychocultural center of gravity" for the men and women in the acculturative continuum, and how is it different for the two sexes? The remaining pages will be devoted to analysis of data relevant to these questions and to discussion of the corollary sociocultural processes.

MODAL MENOMINI: MALE AND FEMALE

The modal psychograms for Menomini males and females are presented in Figure 2.

We will try to avoid the technical language of standard Rorschach interpretation and confine the following discussion to application of "middle range" interpretive hypotheses that

that there is less control by form perception (F) over color perception (C) than is the case with the modal women. These determinants together, as usually interpreted, combine to produce a picture of disturbance, tension, and diffuse anxiety, and decrease in emotional controls among the modal males that is not represented among the females. While the presence or absence of one or two of these indices would be insufficient evidence, and while specific inter-

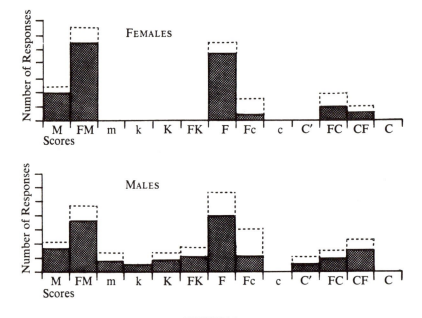

FIGURE 2

Modal Menomini Rorschach profiles

make extremes of non-operational assumptions about the meaning of scores unnecessary. Later we will demonstrate a technique that makes even these modest assumptions unnecessary. Upon examination of the modal psychograms, it is apparent that the one for the males is quite different from that for the females. The "m," "k," "Fk," and "C'," determinants are represented in the former and absent in the latter, and the "FC"/"CF" ratios are reversed. These determinants express inanimate movement in tension or conflict (m), "squeezed down" two-dimensional percepts of what are ordinarily three-dimensional concepts (k), diffuse, vague percepts (K), vista (introspective) percepts (FK), and use of achromatic color (C'). The CF dominance over FC in the male psychogram indicates

pretive hypotheses for any one of them may be only tentatively acceptable, the presence of a complex of factors pointing to an internally consistent picture in one case, and the total absence of this same complex in the other, is highly convincing.

It is interesting that all of the differences uncovered by the gross test of male-female difference described previously are represented by the differences between the two modal psychograms (with the exception of the difference in reaction time, which cannot be represented in a psychogram). These factors are all congruent in contributing to a complex of less anxiety and disturbance for females in adaptation. And apparently it is the modal type in the sample of each sex, and from all acculturative categories, that is contributing to this differential relationship, and not fortuitous convergence of fractionated psychological factors drawn from diverse psychological types.

THE PSYCHOCULTURAL CENTER OF GRAVITY

With the modal psychological structures established and compared, the next problem in the analysis of male-female adaptations in culture change is to locate them for males and females separately on the acculturative continuum. The points on the continuum where these structures are concentrated, as located by three convergent techniques to be described below, we have chosen to call "psychocultural centers of gravity." We are not strongly committed to the label but wish to use it as a matter of convenience. The ramifications of the concept will become clear as we locate the p.c.g.'s (as they will henceforth be called) for men and women, compare them, and compare the departures from them in the acculturative continuum. This application of the Rorschach, combined with data on acculturative position, requires minimal acceptance of conventional interpretive hypotheses about the meaning of scores. While the other usages developed in this paper have been as operational as possible, given the purposes of the analysis, this application depends primarily upon the concentration and dispersion of a complex of behavioral indices of psychological process and not upon the formal psychological meaning ascribed to Rorschach scores. The only assumption we must grant is that the Rorschach reliably samples psychological, perceptual process. We do not have to grant the validity of the conventional meanings of the sampling in order for the results to have significance for the study of psychological adaptation in culture change.

The p.c.g. can be located through several convergent procedures. The first is to compare the modal psychogram for each sex to the typical psychograms of each acculturative category. The construction of typical psychograms for each category requires a separate operation not described in this paper, but presented elsewhere by G. Spindler. When this is done for the male sample of Menomini it is clear that the modal

male psychogram for the whole sample is most like that of the transitional acculturative category, and that for the females is most like that of the native-oriented group. This location of the p.c.g. by inspection is a simple but forthright procedure which suggests that Menomini females tend typically to be psychologically more conservative than do males. It also suggests that the males typically tend to be neither acculturated nor native-oriented, psychologically speaking, but suspended between the two more culturally coherent stages of acculturation.

The second procedure for locating the p.c.g. is to find the proportion of each acculturative category which is composed of members of the modal class for males and for females, on which the modal psychograms for each sex are based. Figure 3 presents this information in graphic form; Table 1 details the basis for the chart. The percentages of each acculturative category composed of modal class representatives are denoted. Of course, the percentages do not total 100 per cent, since they are proportions of different total numbers. For example, the native-oriented female category "A" numbers 8 women, 4 of whom are in the modal class; "C" numbers 12 women, 4 of whom are in the modal class; and "D" totals 26 women, 6 of whom are in the modal class.

This procedure produces additional information concerning the p.c.g., and affords new data on the distribution of typical psychological adaptation for each sex. The p.c.g. for the

TABLE 1

DISTRIBUTION OF MODAL PERSONALITY TYPE IN ACCULTURATIVE CATEGORIES

Category	No. Protocols	No. Modal Cases	Modal as Per Cent of Category
Males			
A	17	2	12
B	13	1	8
C	15	1	7
D	10	3	30
E	13	1	7
Totals	68	8	
Females			
A	8	4	50
B	7	1	14
C	12	4	33.3
D	26	6	23
E	8	0	0
Totals	61	15	

women is still clearly the native-oriented group. The picture of psychological conservatism is strengthened. It is also important that all acculturative categories excepting that of the elite acculturated contributes significant to the female modal class. The prototype is the native-oriented psychological structure and cultural position but apparently this prototype, in both

least acculturated status. The distributional chart also conveys the information that each acculturative category contributes in some degree to the male modal class. Apparently there is continuity here also, but in lesser degree, and the continuity is in terms of transitional psychological characteristics and cultural position rather than native.

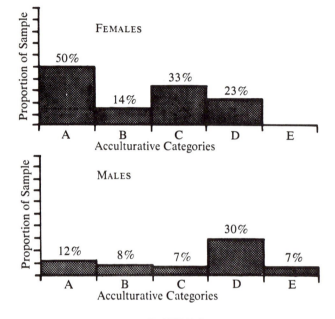

FIGURE 3

Distribution of modal personality type in acculturative categories

of its dimensions (as indicated by data to be analyzed shortly), exhibits continuity throughout the acculturative continuum for the women until the elite acculturated position is reached. At this point there is a "cutoff." Elite Menomini women are clearly deviant in terms of central tendency in the Menomini acculturative continuum.

The distributional chart for males both confirms and modifies the interpretation of the results of location of the p.c.g. by inspection. The p.c.g. is even further along the acculturative continuum than the inspection procedure indicated—in the lower status acculturated category. The psychocultural position of the males is therefore practically the reverse of that for the females. The central tendency in psychological adaptation for Menomini males is far toward full acculturation. For females it is toward a

The third procedure for locating the p.c.g. is to turn to the actual people composing the modal class for each sex and ask what characteristics, in both psychological and sociocultural dimensions, they exhibit with respect to the norms of their groups. Such an analysis could quickly reach proportions that would be unfeasible for presentation in this paper, so only a summary of salient features will be included.

The native-oriented women in the female modal class are typical members of their group. They all exhibit a full complement of nativistic cultural retentions, and self-consciously try to raise their children as Indians. The one modal class woman in the Peyote Cult group was born a Peyotist, not driven to it by the experience of culture conflict as were most others, and retains social and cultural ties with the native-oriented group. She is thus deviant in the context of the cult. The nature of the Peyote group as a "systematic deviation" within the Menomini continuum must be taken into account here. The transitional women in the modal class lack any clear-cut group identifications but express traditional Menomini values in their behaviors. They are not psychologically deviant within their group in the sense that 75 per cent of the women in this acculturative category either fall within the modal class or exhibit all but one scoring criterion of this class—a fact that dramatically bespeaks the psychological conservatism of this group. With one exception, the modal class lower status acculturated women self-consciously chose to interact and identify with older relatives who had experience with the traditional Menomini culture, even though these modal women themselves have had no direct experience in groups or patterns representative of it. They are deviant in their group, since the majority of lower status acculturated women are second or third generation Catholics who, at the verbal level at least, exhibit values not unlike those of middle class white women. There are no modal class women in the elite acculturated group. This category is composed of women striving for acceptance on middle class white terms, but they represent a marked deviant minority in the acculturative continuum for women, together with others from the lower status acculturated category, though these two status groups are separated by rather impermeable social barriers.

The analysis of individual cases in the modal class of Menomini males does not require so full a treatment. The males in this class all express in varying degrees, in both their Rorschach records and in other behaviors, the psychological features of disorganization in emotional control, presence of anxiety and tension, and worrisome introspection that are aspects of what may be called a transitional syndrome in the Menomini acculturative continuum. There are three partial exceptions to this statement. They are men who exhibit highly constricted personality structures that presumably represent the result of social withdrawal and psychological defense against threat. This latter structure may be considered a permutation of the first.

These modal class males represent the central tendency of psychological adaptation in the male acculturative continuum. However, they are all deviant in some degree within their particular acculturative categories. This is necessarily the case because the male categories are so sharply differentiated from each other, as the statistical treatment of the male Rorschach data indicated. Each represents an ingroup homogeneity of psychological adaptation which differentiates it from each other category—with the exception of the transitionals. This group is psychologically more heterogeneous than the others. The process of adaptation for the male is apparently more disjunctive than for the females.

The picture of disjunctive psychological adaptation for the males and continuous adaptation for the females is strengthened by the fact that only 12 per cent of the males in the whole sample are in the modal class, and 25 per cent of the females. This means that there is a greater tendency for the latter to exhibit psychological homogeneity in adaptation; it also helps to account for the fact that no important differences were found between the various acculturative categories for women, and conversely, for the fact that acculturative categories for males were highly differentiated, in the initial statistical tests applied to the sample.

The information revealed by individual case analysis confirms and amplifies conclusions concerning the p.c.g. for each sex in the acculturative process existing at present among the Menomini. The p.c.g. for women is the native-oriented type, which is retained in surprising degree all the way through the acculturative continuum (disregarding the Peyote group as a special case) until the acculturated departure, which represents a small minority, takes place. Other forms of adaptation constitute deviations from the p.c.g. For males, the information again conveys a quite different picture. The male p.c.g. in terms of individual cases is transitional-disturbed. The acculturative process is sharply disjunctive for males, but permits the maintenance of psychological continuity for women in conservative terms.

CONTRIBUTING SOCIOCULTURAL FACTORS

Having observed covariance in psychological and sociocultural process, and having compared this covariance for Menomini males and females, we are obliged to attempt an explanation of the observed processes. Our attempt to explain rests at the level of plausibility, and with reference to role expectations and life experience in the social environment patterned by the influence of traditional Menomini culture, the impact of Western culture, and the conditions of contemporary reservation life. We can only draw selectively from this complex of factors and summarize briefly what appear to be factors of possible significance.

Important social factors which serve to generate and support female psychological differences are found in the dynamics of the Menomini reservation social system. For example, it is pertinent that the mobility pattern for the males differs markedly from that for the females. Women may change groups readily and easily, by marriage and by adoption of the accessory behaviors, among the native-oriented, Peyote Cult, and Transitional categories. By definition, only those males and females who are born Catholic and have no religious identification with native groups comprise the acculturated categories. However, unlike the situation found for the males, comparatively impermeable class barriers exist for the acculturating females between the lower status acculturated group and the elite. Lower status acculturated females are rarely accepted in the elite group, where status is almost hereditary. The males, on the other hand, through gaining occupational and economic success and the proper symbols of middle class culture, do move from lower status to elite status within the reservation community. Having achieved elite status, the males select wives who are less than one-half Indian or entirely white, since middle class values are associated with white skin color, in Menomini perception.

Many lower status acculturated women, realizing that the status and goals of white middle class culture are unavailable to them, either choose to identify with relatives raised in Menomini traditions, join the drinking crowd of women, or attempt to achieve the material symbols of middle class culture, disregarding the appropriate means for attainment. The female modal psychological structure was exhibited by all those women in the lower status acculturated category who chose to identify

with Menomini relatives, and by no others. But none of these kinds of adjustments facilitate the radical psychological reorganization necessary for a change from a Menomini cultural position to that of a middle class white.

Another explanation lies in the relationship between traditional and contemporary role expectations, values, and their psychological corollaries. Historically speaking, Menomini culture was male oriented, with most public activities such as hunting, warfare, ceremony and ritual, centering on the male. The men, who took these important public "instrumental" roles, operated within rigidly defined role prescriptions. On the other hand, women's roles, almost by default, were loosely defined and were interpreted in a flexible manner. Women had the choice of either assuming traditional female roles or they could gain respect without censure if they chose also to engage in male activities such as fishing, hunting, dancing in a male fashion, or foot racing. They could even become practitioners of native medicine. During the acculturative process, women continue to adapt in this flexible fashion. Except in the most acculturated categories, Menomini women continue to play the affective, supportive, "expressive" roles of wife, mother, and social participant in a more or less traditional Menomini fashion, unhampered by rigid role prescriptions stemming from either the traditional culture or from Western culture. It is hypothesized that because of this role continuity, they do not find the flux and conflict of rapid culture change as disturbing as do the males.

In contrast to the females, the acculturating Menomini males continue to take instrumental roles of public leadership and gaining of livelihood in the acculturation situation, as they did in the pattern of native culture, but roles in which the prescriptions for behavior have changed drastically. The male wage earner, for example, is forced into making immediate accommodations to role expectations patterned into the socioeconomic structure in which he must make his own and his family's living, and from which he must in part derive his self-concept. And these expectations are often discontinuous or in direct conflict with those of his traditional Menomini culture, even the attenuated part that is "built into" his personality under contemporary conditions. He must learn to be punctual in his arrivals and departures, and run his daily and weekly cycle by the clock and calendar. He has to learn that accumulation of property and money is the way "to get ahead." And he has to learn that getting ahead in this fashion is the most important thing a man can do. There are no precedents for these and many other expectations in the traditional pattern of instrumental roles for males in Menomini culture. Not only does the male have to learn new behavior patterns and accept new goals that are in conflict with the traditional ones, but in so doing he meets with prejudicial attitudes of whites toward Indians, even in the relatively favorable situation of the Menomini, that women encounter more infrequently in their habitual roles. So in his very striving toward acculturated values he experiences rejection, and this must in many instances engender anxieties and self-doubt. In short, the crucial respects in which contemporary American culture conflicts with native culture and maintains barriers against full acceptance, are encountered most directly and dramatically by the males in their exercise of instrumental roles. Furthermore, the wives of these men, in continuing to play their expressive roles in more or less traditional fashion, make it more difficult for their husbands to play the contemporary male instrumental roles appropriately, since the men are encountering problems of adjustment which their wives do not fully understand, at least at the emotional level. Therefore, the women cannot play the supportive aspect of their expressive roles adequately, and this probably

helps to account for the insecurity of males in the instrumental roles.

A dimension of behavior lending support to this interpretation is furnished by the comparatively high degree of retention of traditional Menomini values exhibited by the women. These values apparently are not directly contested during the acculturative process and the only drastic changes that take place in value retention are at the elite acculturated level where women have had little or no contact with the old culture.

Table 2 presents a few explicit indices from which the differential rate of value change between males and females may be inferred.

The data are self-explanatory. These indices of specific value retentions begin to drop sharply in the Peyote Cult category for the males, while females retain them in much greater proportion through the lower status acculturated category.

CONCLUSION

Menomini women do not encounter the sharply disjunctive role expectations in acculturation that the men do, as long as they continue to play the feminine, expressive roles. Even when they move into the arena of instrumental roles in acculturation, as a minority of women do, the traditional flexibility of the feminine position probably helps make it possible for them to adapt to new expectations without much disturbance and without deep psychological reformulation. Furthermore, these movements into the instrumental roles are

TABLE 2

COMPARISON OF THE RETENTION OF NATIVE VALUES BETWEEN MALES AND FEMALES

Acculturative Category	Sex	No.	Know Some Native Lore	Use Indian Medicines	Full Knowledge of Menomini	Display of Native Objects
A	F	8	100%	100%	100%	100%
	M	17	100	100	88	88
B	F	7	100	100	86	100
	M	13	84	92	54	15
C	F	12	100	100	67	100
	M	15	67	86	40	6
D	F	26	73	61	50	12
	M	10	10	10	30	0
E	F	8	25	12	25	0
	M	13	30	7	30	0

usually tentative or partial, and rarely dominate the woman's purposes or energies. But for the males, the new roles that they must necessarily appropriate in acculturation and that dominate their lives, are in sharp conflict with what they have had "built into" their personality systems by their usually less acculturated parents, and particularly by their mothers, who, being women, maintain in greatest degree the traditional cultural patterns and their psychological concomitants and must pass them on to their children. The struggle of psychocultural forces— values, attitudes, and role expectations internalized during early socialization, versus their contemporary complements in the role expectations which men must adopt in getting a living and acting in the context of public affairs—is mirrored in the anxiety, tension, constriction, and breakdown of emotional controls characterizing the modal Menomini male in acculturation. This role conflict, the preconditions for which are laid down in socialization, is maintained and heightened by the acculturative lag between husbands and wives. The discontinuity of roles for males is concomitant with the psychological discontinuity they exhibit. And the impelling nature of the new instrumental roles they must adopt is projected in the location of their psychocultural center of gravity further along the continuum of acculturation than is the case with the women. The psychological differences between Menomini males and females may therefore be seen as the result of a complex of interlocking factors that appear to assume the form of a self-sustaining cycle, the key factor of which may be the psychocultural position of the women.

31. SOCIAL CHANGE AND SOCIAL CHARACTER: THE ROLE OF PARENTAL MEDIATION

ALEX INKELES

Reprinted by permission of the publisher from Journal of Social Issues, *Vol. 11, pp. 12-23, 1955. Alex Inkeles is Professor of Sociology at Harvard University and Director of Studies on Social and Cultural Aspects of Development at Harvard's Center for International Affairs. He combines an interest and expertise in the sociology of Soviet society as well as in the developing areas. He holds a B.A. and M.A. from Cornell University and a Ph.D. from Columbia University. As an outgrowth of an intensive program of interviewing refugees from the Soviet Union, Professor Inkeles published several studies:* Public Opinion in Soviet Russia, Soviet Citizen, *and* Soviet Society. *Professor Inkeles is currently directing a six-nation study of the sociocultural aspects of economic development. His international interests are combined with a concern for the inter-relations of personality and social structure, and the integration of psychological and sociological theory.*

■ What kind of person does a modern industrial nation require and create? I suggested at the conclusion of the Introduction to this section that it is difficult to generalize about basic personality structure in industrial societies because of their internal diversity and because there do not seem to be the same close "fits" between role and personality as in preindustrial societies. Nonetheless, it is possible to discern a compatibility between the imperatives of such a system and some of the ways in which the mind is shaped. The two main shaping elements in the human demands of an industrial society are political and technological, and we will briefly consider them in turn.

Beginning with technological demands: in industrial society the machine sets the standards not only for the organization of factories but for almost all other productive activities as well. The individual is expected to function as efficiently as a machine and, to do so, he must learn to see himself as mechanized: reporting for work on schedule, continuing to work except during regularly scheduled rest periods, obedient to the commands of his supervisors, and orienting himself toward the economic and material rewards of the occupational world and away from traditional considerations.

Politically, the individual in a national society must orient himself to the "long arm of the law" rather than to the particularistic standards of his local group. Even more than agricultural nation-states, industrial societies require him to renounce traditional patterns of interpersonal reliance and learn to live as a responsible individual rather than as a unit in and responsible to a tightly-knit group. But dominating all these imperatives is the requirement of obedience to distant and impersonal authority. Obedience on the job is related to political obedience, and just as one must learn to "play it safe" on the job so must he avoid politically dangerous activities.

The central point in the following selection is that the partial success of the Russian leaders in creating this "new industrial man" has been accomplished through the socialization process affecting basic personality patterns. Soviet parents consciously or unconsciously recognized the new demands the system would make on succeeding generations and brought up their children to meet those demands. Thus there has been a marked decrease in traditional religious upbringing and in the maintenance of strong family ties and traditions. There has developed an increasing emphasis on "getting along," on staying out of trouble, on keeping a sharp eye on one's own security and safety. This individualistic way of looking at the world is also to be seen in the inculcation of highly personalized moral values as ends in themselves. In Inkeles' emphasis on techniques for dealing with the established government, we see a reflection of the modern emphasis on "adjustment" as a personal and individualized process.

Unfortunately, there are few studies of this kind; we need more of them, but at the same time we must realize that many of them may contain a serious trap of which we must be aware. Research like this may be used as a rationalization for trite and inhuman dogma which asserts that those who do not "make it" in an industrial society have "failed to measure up" to the demands of the social and technological order. Inkeles did not design his study to learn why some succeed and others fail; his purpose was only to learn how different facets of a social system respond to the imperatives of others. Of course there are psychological reasons for success and failure, but success in an industrial nation—whether the Soviet Union or the United States—is a social and political privilege denied to members of some groups regardless of their personality characteristics. This is a political problem, not a psychological one.

A comparable study for the United States is *The Changing American Parent: A Study in the Detroit Area*, by Daniel R. Miller and Guy E. Swanson (New York: Wiley, 1958). There is a wonderful collection of 40 personal accounts in *Work*, edited by Ronald Fraser, in two volumes (Harmondsworth, Middlesex, England: Penguin Books, 1968, 1969) which should be consulted by the reader interested in the subjective experiences of people at this level of adaptation. Also relevant are *Male and Female: A Study of the Sexes in a Changing World*, by Margaret Mead (New York: Morrow, 1949); *The Psychological Frontiers of Society*, by Abram Kardiner (New York: Columbia University Press, 1945); *Childhood and Society*, by Erik Erikson (New York: Norton, 1963, second edition); and *Psychological Needs and Cultural Systems: A Case Study*, by Joel Aronoff (Princeton, N.J.: Van Nostrand, 1967). ∎

IN HIS GENERAL essay on national character Gorer provides a clear and succinct formulation of one of the major premises underlying most of the related literature. Gorer indicated that we can deal with the simple but imposing fact that "societies continue, though their personnel changes" only because we can assume that "the present generation of adults will be replaced in due course by the present generation of children *who, as adults, will have habits very similar to their parents.*" Implicit in this general pattern, of course, is the further assumption "that the childhood learning of the contemporary adults was at least very similar to the learning which contemporary children are undergoing."

Gorer recognizes, and indeed states explicitly, that this model is probably not applicable to "societies which are in the process of drastic change." As Margaret Mead points out, however, so few individuals may now hope to grow up under conditions of sociocultural stability that we may regard this situation as almost unusual, and its products as in a sense "deviants." Gorer's model, therefore, requires elaboration, extension, and adjustment to enable it to deal adequately with national character as it develops and emerges under conditions of social change. The question is essentially this:

Insofar as rapid social change interrupts the simple recapitulation of child training practices and produces new modal personality patterns, by what means are such changes mediated or effected?

The literature on national character contains several important and interesting efforts to answer this question. Margaret Mead, for example, has explored the significance for personality development of growing up in a culture that is no longer homogeneous, and posits the development under those circumstances of what she calls a "tentative" personality syndrome. Riesman, developing in full detail a point also made by Mead, has discussed the significance for social character of growing up under the strong influence of peer group pressures and standards. Erikson has stated the implications for personality development that arise from the absence of adequate and valued role models with which to identify, and from the associated lack of roles through which the individual can find socially sanctioned and culturally meaningful outlets for the discharge of his emotions.

Despite the diversity of these studies they seem to have one element in common in their approach to the role of the parent as "child rearer" under conditions of social change. Implicitly, if not explicitly, the parent is conceived as having available a relatively fixed repertory of child training procedures provided by his culture and learned by him in the period of his own childhood. Two main alternatives as to his utilization of those techniques are then generally considered. On the one hand, the parent is seen as acting as the passive agent of his culture, raising his children according to the procedures he had learned earlier in his own childhood, even though these techniques may have lost their appropriateness. It is assumed in that case, that as his children grow up the gulf between parent and child will rapidly grow great, and relations will become strained as the child meets and learns the conflicting behavior patterns and underlying values of his "own" new culture. On the other hand, the parent may know enough not to try to apply the training procedures under which he was raised, and in that case he either surrenders to other cultural surrogates such as peer group, teachers, mass media, etc., or borrows, and of course generally ineptly

applies, some prefabricated set of rules. In the lower classes the borrowing might be from the local baby clinic, and in the upper classes from books and lectures on child rearing. In short the parents will manifest what Mead terms "disturbed and inconsistent images of their children's future."

Without doubt these descriptions are faithful to the facts in many situations. Nevertheless, they seem to have made inadequate allowance for the positive adjustive capacity of human beings and for the process of continuous interaction that goes on between them and their sociocultural environment. Very often the global impact of Western contacts on a nonliterate people may be almost totally disorienting, but parents need not be either unimaginative and passive agents of their culture, raising their children by rote, nor so disorganized and disoriented as is suggested by Mead's discussion. Although parents are adults, they may nevertheless still *learn*, and learn what they feel to be major "lessons," from their experiences under conditions of social change. This learning, furthermore, may influence the parents to seek purposefully to bring their children up in a way different from that in which they were raised, and in a manner intended better to suit the children for life in the changed social situation This has been clearly recognized by Aberle and Naegele, who in a passage not easily duplicated elsewhere in the literature affirm that:

All in all child rearing is future oriented to an important extent. The picture of the desired end product is importantly influenced by the parents' experiences in the adult world, as well as by their childhood experiences. When adult experience changes under the impact of major social change, there is reason to believe that there will ultimately although not necessarily immediately, be shifts in the socialization pattern as well.

Of course, if either the parental experience of change or the response to it were purely idiosyncratic, then even where such experiences were widely distributed their effect on the character of the next generation would be essentially randomized. But it is in the nature of social structure, particularly in modern industrial society, that large groups of the population will be exposed to and perceive on-going change in similar fashion. Furthermore, it follows both from the existence of modal personality patterns and the shared cultural heritage of those in the subgroups of any population that they are very likely to react to this experience in systematically patterned ways. One very probable reaction to the experience of social change is to adjust the training of children to better prepare them for life in the future as the parent now anticipates that life in the light of his own experience. There is reason to assume, therefore, that the influence of large-scale social change occurring at any one time may be reflected in the character of the *next* generation because of mediation by parents living under and experiencing the change.

To test these assumptions one would ideally want a research design permitting the exploration of two distinct although intimately related questions. The first involves the hypothesis that parents who have experienced extreme social change seek to raise their children differently from the way in which they were brought up, purposefully adapting their child rearing practices to train children better suited to meet life in the changed world as the parent now sees it. To test this hypothesis we would need detailed information about the child rearing practices utilized by two consecutive generations of parents in the same culture, the first of which lived and raised its children in a period of relative stability, whereas the second lived and brought up its children under conditions of fairly extreme social change. A different requirement is posed by the question of how effective the parents in the second generation are in developing new traits or combinations of traits in their children. The extension of the ideal research design in this direction would require that we secure data on the modal personality patterns prevalent in the third generation. We would anticipate that as a result of their different socialization experience those in the third generation would manifest modal personality patterns different in important respects from those of their parents in the second generation.

Clearly such a design is extremely difficult to execute. Fortunately, however, we can approximate the ideal, although admittedly very imperfectly, through the utilization of some of the materials collected by the Harvard Project on the Soviet Social System. In that research program detailed life history interviews were conducted with about 330 former Soviet citizens, yielding a well-balanced sample in regard to such factors as age, sex, and occupation. The interview extensively explored the life of the respondent in both his family of orientation and procreation. Particular attention was paid to the values in regard to character development and occupational goals that dominated in child rearing as practiced by the respondent's parents and by the respondent himself in the role of parent. Through an exploration of these data we may hope to see some of the effects of social change in the Soviet Union as the parents who "lived" the change adjusted their child rearing practices in response to their own adult experiences, and thus acted as intermediaries in transmitting the effects of their current change to a future generation.

We may begin by testing the first assumption, namely that a generation experiencing extreme social change in adulthood will adapt the methods whereby it raises its children, and that as a result its children will be reared differently than it had been and yet more in keeping with the changed social realities. For our first generation, which we shall call the "Tsarist" generation, we need a group that raised its children during a period of relative social stability. The most recent period of that sort in Russia unfortunately falls as far back as the time immediately preceding the First World War, roughly from 1890 to 1915. Since we are interested in child rearing practices, and particularly of people who raised their children to adulthood (taken here as age 15) in those years, then eligible respondents would have been at least 33 by 1915 and at least 68 by the time of our interview in 1950. Indeed, most of those who could qualify as parents in our first generation were probably dead by 1950, and in any event only three of those living appear in our sample. We can learn about the child rearing practices utilized by that generation, therefore, only by relying on what their children report to have been true of the parents. The children of the Tsarist generation do, of course, appear in our sample. In this group we include all respondents over 45 in 1950, and we call it the "Revolutionary" generation because its members, born in 1905 or before, were young adults at the time of the Revolution and lived as mature individuals through the subsequent Civil War and the later periods of momentous social change represented by the forced collectivization and industrialization programs. It was this second generation that was raising its children to adulthood during the main period of Soviet development.

It will be recognized, therefore, that, although dealing with the child rearing practices of two different generations of parents, we draw our information from but a single set of respondents, namely those in our sample over 45 years of age in 1950. In telling us how their parents brought them up they provide us with data about the child rearing practices of the Tsarist generation, whereas in describing the training of their own children, they provide our materials on the child rearing practices of the Revolutionary generation. Although limits of space do not permit presentation of the evidence, we have data that indicate that this procedure of ascertaining the child rearing values of an earlier generation by accepting the description given by those who had been the children of the group being studied, is methodologically less suspect than might appear to be the case. The description by the youngest generation in our sample of the manner in which it was reared agrees so closely with the report of how the training was done as related by the middle generation, which actually reared the children, as to yield correlations of .89 and .95 on the two available comparisons.

Relative to the child rearing materials we have a detailed summary code of the dominant values governing child rearing, both as to character and occupational goals, characteristic for each generation acting as parents. In no case, however, is the rating of the parent based on his observed behavior, but only on the values deduced by us to have been operative on the basis of the interview. Furthermore, as already noted, the respondents from the prerevolutionary Tsarist generation could not speak for themselves and we had to rely on the retrospective report of their children.

In the following analysis a larger number of code categories had been grouped into a set of six major dimensions that were prominent value orientations in the child rearing efforts of those in our sample. The value of "tradition" was coded mainly for emphasis on religious upbringing, but it included as well references to maintenance of strong family ties and traditions; "adjustment" reflects emphasis on "getting along," staying out of trouble, keeping an eye on your security and safety, etc.; "achievement"

was coded when parents stressed attainment, industriousness, mobility, material rewards, and similar goals; "personalistic" was checked when the parent was concerned with such personal qualities as honesty, sincerity, justice, and mercy; "intellectuality," where the emphasis was on learning and knowledge as ends in themselves; and "political" when the focus was on attitudes, values, and beliefs dealing with government and particularly with *the* government of the land.

When we consider the profound differences, during their years of child rearing, in the life experience of the Revolutionary generation as contrasted with that of its parents in the Tsarist generation, what differences may we expect in their values with regard to child rearing? The revolutionary upheaval of 1917 and the subsequent programs of forced social change struck a great blow at the traditional structure of Russian society and profoundly altered it. Massive programs of expansion were undertaken in industrialization, in urbanization, in formal organization and administration. The pattern of rural life, in which the bulk of the population was involved, was drastically revised through the forced collectivization of agriculture. Centralized political control and political terror were ruthlessly imposed. Opportunities for mobility increased greatly. Under these circumstances we might well expect the traditional values to suffer the greatest loss of emphasis, with a consequent shift to stress on either simple successful adjustment or the more secularized morality represented by the personalistic values and the pursuit of knowledge as an end in itself. In addition, our knowledge of the growing opportunities for advancement, associated with the generally expanded development of the formal occupational structure, leads us to anticipate that greatly increased weight would be given to achievement. Finally the central role played by the state in Soviet affairs, the existence of the political terror, and the additional fact that our respondents were disaffected from the political system, lead us to anticipate heightened concern with political considerations in child rearing.

In Table 1 we have indicated the distribution of emphasis among the dimensions in our set of dominant value orientations. The relative stability of the gross rank order is testimony to the fact that both generations of parents represented a common cultural tradition which they

TABLE 1

Child Rearing Values of Parents in Russian Prerevolutionary and Postrevolutionary Times

Areas	Distribution* of Emphasis in: Tsarist Period	Post-Revolutionary Period†
Tradition	75%	44%
Achievement	60	52
"Personalistic"	32	44
Adjustment	16	21
Intellectuality	12	22
Politics	12	20
Number of Respondents	77	78

* These per cents total more than 100, since respondents were scored for as many themes as cited, but percentaging is on the basis of total respondents.

† The percentages in this column have been adjusted to equalize for the effect created by the larger number of responses given by our informants in describing their own activity as parents, as against the manner in which they had been raised by the Tsarist generation.

carried forward through time. Nevertheless, it is clear that there have been very substantial shifts in the relative weight of several value orientations, and they go largely in the expected direction. Perhaps the most striking finding is the sharp decrease in emphasis on the traditional values, accounted for overwhelmingly by the decreased emphasis on religious training and belief. Under the impact of industrialization and urbanization, perhaps abetted by the anti-religious and "proscientific" propaganda conducted by the regime, parents in the Revolutionary generation clearly shifted toward an emphasis on more secular values. This shift is reflected in the increased emphasis on learning (intellectuality) and positive personal qualities *as ends in themselves* rather than as *means* to the attainment of the good life lived, as it were, "in the sight of God." Thus, secular morality replaced traditional and religiously based morality.

Perhaps most directly and explicitly related to the intervening experience of the parents under conditions of social change is the increased attention paid to political considerations in the education of one's children. The greater emphasis on political problems arises from the fact that the Soviet regime has progressively "politi-cized" more and more areas of human activity that in most Western societies fall outside the political realm. A person at all alert to his situation and surroundings could therefore hardly fail to realize that if he wished to prepare his child adequately for life under Soviet conditions he must train him to an awareness concerning the political realities of the system, even though such training had not been important in his own childhood. This interpretation is borne out by the statements made by our interviewers.

Finally, it is necessary to comment on the major instance in which the data fail to confirm expectation, namely in regard to emphasis on achievement values. This failure is, of course, only relative, since achievement was the most emphasized value in the rearing of children by those in the Revolutionary generation. Nevertheless, in absolute weight it declined in importance even though it had been expected to increase. It might be that since our respondents were refugees from the system, and since many of them looked upon too active pursuit of a career as suggesting involvement with the regime, they did not admit fully the importance they actually attributed to inculcating achievement strivings in their children. On the other hand, it may be that the expectation was unrealistic quite apart from specific Soviet conditions. There is some evidence that values such as security, adjustment, and personal attractiveness are becoming ever more important foci in child rearing in the United States and that stress on achievement *as an end in itself*, although still prevalent, has become somewhat old-fashioned. This pattern may be associated with the combination of mass industry, education and communication, and the consumer culture of which the Soviet Union is but one example.

All told, however, the data certainly seem strongly to support the assumption that the experience of extreme social change that the Revolutionary generation underwent did have a marked effect on that generation's approach to the rearing of its children. As compared with the way their parents raised them, they can hardly be assumed to have merely "recapitulated" the earlier pattern of child rearing. On the contrary, having experienced marked social change, they adjusted their child rearing practices, the better to prepare their children for the life they expected those children to lead.

To test the effectiveness of the changed general child rearing orientations of the Revolutionary generation, we would need data on the personality patterns prevalent among their children in the third generation, which we unfortunately do not have. Nevertheless, we can make a very approximate approach to our second question concerning the effectiveness of the changed child rearing emphases if we shift our attention to the realm of occupational choices. In that area we have data not only on the values stressed by parents, but we also have information on the values which the individual held in regard to himself. In treating value orientations relative to the occupational world we are, of course, dealing not with personality

to assume that economic and material rewards would have come to be much more stressed among the goals set before the child, as would the necessity of finding work that permitted an appropriate accommodation to the highly politicized occupational structure in Soviet society.

As a comparison of the first and second columns of Table 2 indicates, three of these four expectations are rather strongly supported by the responses of our interviewees. We see, to begin, a sharp decline in the importance of family tradition as a criterion in shaping the child's occupational orientation, along with a marked increase in the role played by self-expression or free job choice. In addition, we

TABLE 2

CHANGING VALUES CONCERNING THE OCCUPATIONAL REALM

| | Distribution of Emphasis Among Values Stressed | | |
| | In Child Rearing by: | | In Hypothetical |
Value Areas	"Tsarist" Generation	"Revolutionary" Generation	Choice by "Soviet" Generation
Rewards	41%	25%	14%
Tradition	35	14	11
Self-expression	21	38	62
Politics	3	23	13
Number of Responses (equal to 100%)	58	63	931

patterns in a psychodynamic sense, but rather with something more closely akin to "social character" as it has been defined by Riesman and Inkeles.

The influence of their experience with social change on the child training practices adopted by the Revolutionary generation is perhaps even more strikingly evident in the area of occupational choices. In addition to asking about the specific occupations for which parents wished to prepare their children, we asked the reasons for the selection. The reasons cited provide us with a guide to the values that were dominant in the home atmosphere created by the parent for the child. Considering the nature of the social change experienced by the Revolutionary generation and described above, we might again well expect that as part of the general weakening of the traditional way of life there would have been a decline in the importance of family tradition, as against self-expression or free choice, as values emphasized in orienting the child toward the occupational world. In addition it is reasonable

may note the much greater emphasis on guiding the child toward a job that is politically desirable, which for our respondents generally meant one safe from danger of political arrest and not too directly involved in the regime's political objectives. Finally, it should be observed that here again the data fail to support our expectation that the material and psychic rewards on the job—roughly equivalent to earlier discussed achievement value—would be more emphasized by the Revolutionary generation than by the Tsarist generation. Indeed, the relative weight of such rewards as values to be emphasized in orienting children toward the occupational world declined markedly from the one generation to the next.

Now to return to our original research design, do we have any evidence that the different child rearing patterns utilized by the middle generation as a response to their experience of social change actually were effective? Or did the parents in that second generation, despite their apparent intention, act in fact as passive agents of the culture and, *nolens volens*, raise their children in their own image and much as the first generation would have done the job? For a proper answer to this question we should have access to the children of the Revolutionary generation, and to data on their job choices coded by the same categories used to describe the child training values of their parents. Unfortunately we can only approximate each requirement. Respondents on both our written questionnaire and oral interview remained anonymous, and we therefore have no way of identifying the actual children of the Revolutionary generation. But we can secure a reasonable equivalent of that third group, which we call the "Soviet" generation, by taking all respondents under 35 in 1950. Most of them were raised and reached adulthood in the same period in which the Revolutionary generation was acting in the parental role and could well have been their children. As for the values that governed their job choices, we are obliged to draw on our written questionnaire, which presented the respondents with a choice of precoded categories not strictly comparable with those used in assessing child training values. For example the check list included the omnibus category "I feel suited to it," which we have equated here with "self-expression," but which obviously could have meant many more things to the respondents.

Quite apart from such methdological difficulties, it would be naive to expect a near-perfect correlation between the values that the parents in the Revolutionary generation stressed while they reared the Soviet generation and the ones which that generation emphasized in its own job choices. Such training always produces only an approximation of the parents' desire. More important, those in the Soviet generation have had their values shaped by many influences other than those exerted by their parents. Nevertheless, our expectation is that on the whole the pattern of value orientations of the Soviet generation will be quite close to those that were stressed in child training by their parents in the Revolutionary generation as contrasted with those inculcated in an earlier era by the Tsarist generation. The relative degree of fit between the two sets of orientations may be taken as a rough measure of how successful the Revolutionary generation was in training the Soviet generation to orient in new directions.

The appropriate comparison may be obtained by examining the third column of Table 2—which contains the distribution of emphasis in the operative values guiding the job choices of the younger generation—in relation to the first and second columns. The over-all comparison strongly suggests that those in the Revolutionary generation were highly successful in their purposive effort to shape the values their children would carry into adulthood. This is most evident in the marked emphasis that the Soviet generation places on self-expression rather than family tradition as a criterion for its job choices, much in keeping with the lesser emphasis that its parents had put on tradition in orienting their children's thoughts about the world of jobs and work. Even if we make allowance for the strong pull of the actual code category, "I feel suited for it," this interpretation would clearly not be materially affected.

It will be noticed, further, that in raising children those in the Tsarist generation gave extremely slight attention to political considerations, whereas those in the Revolutionary generation stressed it very heavily, indeed more heavily than tradition. In their own job choices, those in the Soviet generation again show the apparent influence of their parents' concern for this dimension, although in their own value scheme it does not loom quite so large as it did in their parents' efforts at socialization. Finally, we may note that material and psychic rewards such as income and prestige had roughly similar relative weight, as compared to politics and tradition, in the child rearing practices of the Revolutionary generation and in the actual job choices of the Soviet generation.

It seems reasonable to conclude again, therefore, that the Revolutionary generation did not merely act passively as the agent of the old culture, recapitulating in its own parental activities the socialization practices that had earlier been used by *its* parents. On the contrary, it may be said that the middle generation, responding to its experience of social change under the Soviet regime, in large measure turned away from the pattern of child rearing under which it had been raised earlier and in its approach to the new Soviet generation stressed goals and values of a different sort. It appears, furthermore, that this training of the youth in new value orientations was relatively successful.

Because the numbers are small and the sample unusual, the material presented here is perhaps little more than suggestive of the results that might be yielded by research specifically designed to increase our knowledge in this area. Indeed, a stronger case could have been made with the material at hand had not rigorous limits of space precluded the presentation of quotations from our interviews that show graphically the way in which conditions of social change experienced by the parents influenced their approach to raising their children. Nevertheless, the material presented should serve to alert us to the role that the parent plays, through both purposive and unconscious adjustments in his child rearing practices, in mediating the influency of social change to his children and consequentle in better adapting them for the changed social conditions they may meet as adults. Furthermore, although the demonstration presented above dealt only with the more surface level of attitudes and value orientations, there is reason to believe that similar processes operate with regard to the development of personality at deeper levels.

VI. THE ARTS

CAN THE ARTS be regarded as aspects of human adaptation? Are they among the means by which people maintain viable relationships with the habitat in order to assure their survival? For the present, the answer must remain moot. We do not know enough about the principles that govern the organization and functioning of societies and the mechanics of their strategies of adaptation to trace out the specific connections between creative activity and the efficient use of energy systems. Anthropologists are not alone in facing such puzzles; although biologists have learned a great deal about the adaptations of existing species that have assured their survival in particular habitats, they have not been able to decipher the adaptive functions of each physiological and behavioral system in every species studied. These unknown relationships between observed phenomena and their sources are the great challenges in the study of life, physical and social, and whether these unknown processes are knowable at all is itself a matter for future research.

I am concluding this book with a brief consideration of some of the arts for several reasons. First, I want to show that although anthropologists have learned a great deal about the evolution of human society and the adaptive purposes of many of its institutions, there remains much to be learned; the task of a scientist and teacher is to present a balanced picture of what is and is not known about a particular problem. Second, I want to show that one must be prepared to find answers, or hints to them, in what appear at first to be unlikely places. The arts may appear nonessential because they do not enter directly into man's relationship with his habitat, into the energy systems that he harnesses or the social relationships in which he uses his energy systems to gain a livelihood. Paintings, stories, songs, and dances never built a house, made a yam or a wheat field to grow, made water to flow along directed courses, or kept a person alive so that he could reproduce and transmit his genes to future generations. Moreover, in most societies it is only a very small proportion of people who are responsible for the group's artistic output. Nevertheless, there are correlations to be observed between the forms of art and the major social and technological activities in which people engage, and these correlations suggest that there is a direct relationship between the arts—or at least some of them—and the strategies by which people adapt to their habitat.

Third: even if the arts were wholly unrelated to strategies of adaptation, they provide an important means of appreciating the experience of being human in different societies. People everywhere have criteria for beauty which they try to represent in one way or another, and these representations are an important aspect of their affective and intellectual experience. But what is beautiful or stimulating to people in one society may be quite ordinary or an aspect of an entirely different dimension of experience to people in another. For example, people in contemporary industrial societies may acquire carvings from tribal societies for reasons that are purely aesthetic; but these objects were made for entirely different reasons, as tools in a religious ritual or for ceremonial or political purposes. This is not to say that there were no aesthetic standards in their production; horticulturists often distinguish between aesthetically pleasing and displeasing hoes, just as we have our fashions in the clothing that is at base intended to cover our bodies. But the purposes served by what we consider exotic art to be placed on a living room table are entirely unintended—and may even be alien—to its producers, who meant their work as representations of ancestors or other spirits for a religious ceremonial, with "true" significance only for the group with which those ancestors or spirits are associated.

Nor is this a purely abstract exercise; there are many aspects of social and political life that cannot be fully appreciated without reference to the arts. In the United States today, for example, it is necessary to consider music, painting, and literature if we are to understand the ethnic revitalization movements currently under way among urban blacks. We cannot grasp the relationship between generations in this society without an appreciation of the sounds of rock music, nor can we distinguish the international aspects of student protest without reference to jazz and other musical forms. In the mid-1950s, when both President Dwight D. Eisenhower and the Soviet Premier, Nikita Khrushchev, expressed strong distaste for abstract expressionist art, they unwittingly reflected a basic concept about society: Art is as much an aspect of the organization of social relations and the maintenance of order and conformity as are the norms of marriage and the standards of law and religion.

Because our knowledge is so limited concerning the relationship of the arts to different stages of social and technological development, I am going to alter my procedure in this section: instead of proceeding from the least to the most complex stage of development, I am going to focus on three specific areas of artistic activity. First, I will review some of the salient anthropological notions about the relationship between music and the organization of social relations; these are among the data which suggest most directly that the arts may be integral to a society's strategy of adaptation. Then I will turn to the evolution of sculpture; these data also point to a way of evaluating the possible adaptive components of arts, by considering a negative criterion: the absence of sculpture at certain sociotechnological levels. We will then briefly consider some aspects of myth and folklore.

In a volume reporting the results of one of the most breathtaking collaborative research projects in the history of anthropology, Alan Lomax and his co-workers have analyzed the musical styles of societies at all stages of development and have shown that there is an intimate relationship between musical style and life style more generally (*Folk Song Styles and Culture* [Washington, D.C.: American Association for the Advancement of Science, Publication No. 88], 1968). Their results can be summarized in the generalization that as people live and work, so do they sing and play. Among their more specific conclusions is the observation that "diffuse and individualized song performance seems to represent three types of work situations: the voluntary and temporary teams of simple, band-organized societies; and the individual or small family teams of much of plow agriculture. Both stable work teams and good vocal blend are found among mid-level producers, such as Zuni, Kraho, Samoa, and Bemba, with low to moderate super-structure. 'Groupiness' in communication style, then, seems to rest on non-compulsory, community performance of common tasks." This conclusion is further exemplified in their finding that "two or three varieties of social settings exist in which a feeling of solidarity and an ability to act or sing together with empathy or cohesiveness develop at the same time. The first is the large, permanent, community work team, with sufficient organizational spine to carry it through the years, but without the excess of authority or caste division that would lend a coercive or non-egalitarian, patronal, condescension to its usual festive gatherings. The second situation is the group of clan brothers dwelling within a small stable community. The third is the lineal kin group functioning within a nonnomadic and nonstratified social web. Age grades, extended families, and various combinations of the institutions already cited may sometimes contribute to the institutional framework of the cohesiveness we find in singing organizations."

These findings conform to some of our own observed correspondences between levels of adaptation and forms of social relations. It will be recalled that hunting and gathering, for example, are characterized by individualism in legal relations and religious practice, and this is paralleled in musical style by what Lomax calls "diffuse and individualized song performance." The solidarity and cohesiveness of horticultural kin groups is reflected in the "groupiness" of their music. But these musical and life styles are diluted by the social and technological developments in agricultural nationstates; here the solidarity and cohesiveness of autonomous kin groups are broken up, and this is reflected in the evolutionary reappearance of "diffuse and individualized song performance" paralleling, it would seem, the situation in which each individual and household stands alone "facing" the state.

We have seen that as societies increase in their complexity, their internal diversity is reflected in every sphere of activity, and this is also the case for the arts. Just as it becomes impossible to speak of *the* family organization or values or national character of any modern nation, so we cannot speak of *the* national music, art, or literature. Critical essays dealing with modern writing in the United States increasingly seem inadequate if they do not distinguish among Jewish, WASP, black, and southern literature; such distinctions are also becoming fashionable in the social sciences. Similar differences are becoming a matter of conscious concern in connection with painting and sculpture, music, and drama as well. And even within the different musical traditions in our society there is further variation; Selection 37 provides an excellent description of the diverse aspects of Afro-American music.

These differences are often couched in political and ideological rhetoric, but I think they are best understood in terms of the increasing diversity of industrial societies, especially the specializations of different social and economic groups which, in turn, display different life styles. These styles are reflected, legitimated, and reinforced in the arts as well as in value systems and religious experience. An example of this diversity is that while "individualized song performance" is characteristic of our musical style there are also to be found examples of "grouping" or the "ability to . . . sing together with empathy or cohesiveness," as in glee clubs and the regular and popular performance of oratorios like Handel's "Messiah." These cannot be said to reflect the styles of the entire society, but rather the tastes of socially distinct and specialized groups within it.

It is often said that the art of tribal societies has a religious basis or, more accurately, that art and religion are inseparable in these societies. But religion and art were also commingled in Europe, and it was not until about the second half of the 14th century and possibly in ancient Greece that secular themes began to make their appearance in Western art. The commingling of art with religion and other spheres of activity is an aspect of traditional societies; the differentiation of art from religion is an aspect of the overall process of specialization in agricultural nations, which includes the first separation of religious and political institutions as well. But it must be remembered that the differentiation of the religious and political spheres in Europe did not accelerate until the 18th century, and this more or less coincided with the final separation of art from religion in the European tradition.

When we look at art in an evolutionary framework to learn whether it can be regarded as an aspect of adaptation, we have to focus on its quantifiable elements and disregard the question of artistic quality. And of course the field of art is very broad and difficult to encompass as a whole; it is more feasible to consider only one aspect at a time. This is why I propose to focus on sculpture: unlike graphic or decorative art, sculpture is not found in all societies, and this makes it possible to apply primitive measures, such as presence and absence. In what follows, I draw on some of my own unpublished cross-cultural research.

By sculpture I mean the transformation of an object in nature, such as a piece of wood, stone, metal, or bone, into the representation of another object in nature, such as a person, animal, fish, or bird. The elements of sculpture that concern us here are the degree to which one object is used to represent an entirely different object, the degree to which a sculptural representation realistically portrays an object in nature, freedom from stylization, and the extent to which the texture of sculptural materials is included in the design or form.

(1) The more advanced the strategy of adaptation, the greater is the degree to which one object is used to represent an entirely different object. Consider, for example, the use of a decorated skull to represent a person, as among the Eskimo of Point Hope, Alaska; here a significant part of an object is used to represent the object (person) itself. The people of Point Hope were relatively sedentary foragers, and they represent the earliest stage of development to possess sculpture.

Now consider the transformation of a piece of wood or ivory or stone into a mask or figure. Disregarding the artist's metaphor about releasing the figure from its container, the process of changing one object into another is qualitatively distinct from using a skull to represent a human being. The use of a piece of wood, ivory, or stone may be regarded as more complex, more sophisticated, and as an evolutionary advance over the former mode of representation. By this token, a still greater sculptural advance is seen in a medieval Japanese representation of a samurai warrior by the arrangement of his clothing and armor but without the direct representation of any bodily parts. Such representation is qualitatively different from the use of a painted skull to represent a human being because an illusion is provided by the use of symbolic materials such as armor and insignia, rather than a literal part of the body that cannot be associated with another form (unless a deliberate attempt were made to provide such an illusion). The most advanced type of sculptural portrayal by this criterion is (for example) Pablo Picasso's "Goat," in which the face of the goat is represented by a toy jeep; here found objects are used to provide an illusion of another reality which has no necessary connection with the objects used. Possibly even more advanced, according to this criterion, is the evocation of an attenuated reality out of empty space and metal without content, as in the sculpture of Henry Moore.

It must be remembered that this criterion and those that follow do not apply to the total range of a society's artistic productions at advanced levels of social and technological development. As noted, it is not possible to speak of *the* art of a modern nation. An industrial society has several artistic traditions, with variability in each. I am not suggesting that all modern sculpture exhibits the principles that are reflected in the works of Picasso and Moore, but only that they are found in the sculpture of industrial nations and not in societies at simpler levels of adaptation.

(2) The more advanced the strategy of adaptation, the greater the freedom from stylization. This criterion refers to the artist's freedom from conformity to a traditional style of expression and from conventionalization, as measured by the variety and lack of predictability in the total range of the group's sculptural representations. The totem poles, figures, and masks of the Northwest Coast of North America; the *katchina* dolls and masks of the Hopi Indians; the sculpture of Benin; Chinese sculpture of the Ming Dynasty; and the sculpture of contemporary Western Europe and United States represent in this sense successive steps in sculptural development. Significantly, each of these societies also represents a successive level of social and technological development.

Let me give some illustrations of sculptural stylization, some of which are not readily discernible. In the wood carvings of the Sepik River people of New Guinea (Selection 34), there is systematically an inverse ratio between the size of the nose and the size of the penis. In female carvings of the Senufo of West Africa, there is a nearly perfect plumb from the tip of the nose to the tip of the breast; there are comparable proportions in their male figures. Benin bronze busts manifest a stylized repetitiousness like the decorative art of Melanesia and of North American Indians. At the other extreme, consider an exhibition of contemporary "funk art," in which no two pieces are remotely alike, even when they are by the same artist.

Of all the elements of sculpture, this is the one most amenable to analysis in terms of adaptation. Stylization is an aspect of the strong pressures to conformity that are generally found in horticultural societies and in agricultural nation-states during their early stages of development. Leaving aside the question why people produce art in the first place—not because it is unimportant but because we have no answers—stylization in art expresses the selfconscious traditionalism that is required to maintain their social organization. This is reinforced by the commingling of art and religion in many preindustrial societies, and the other side of this coin is seen in the enormous variety of styles used by the secular artists of our time.

(3) The more advanced the strategy of adaptation, the greater is the use of the texture of the sculptural material as part of the design or form—for example, the use of the grain in wood to represent lines, clothing, movement, or even tears running from an eye, or the use of the original texture of metal surfaces when they are retained as elements in the content and form of the representation. This retention of texture seems to be associated with advanced technologies in which there is greater control of the habitat and also greater sophistication about the nature of materials amenable to sculptural treatment. It can thus be considered as a degree of mastery over the limitations of the materials themselves.

Sculpture first appears in the European evolutionary record in the caves of the Upper Paleolithic period (Selection 32), and in North America in the archeological sites at Point Hope. It is abundant among the sedentary fishermen and gatherers on the Northwest Coast and it is present among North American horticulturists. But not all hunter-gatherers and horticulturists sculpt. Among the former, sculpture is present only among those groups that are relatively sedentary; it is absent among nomadic groups. At the horticultural level, sculpture is present except among the loosely organized New Guinea highlanders, such as the Tsembaga Marin (Selection 15).

Sculpture is generally absent among pastoralists; the rare instances of its appearance are distinctly inferior in almost all respects to the sculpture of horticultural societies. This may seem anomalous, because the level of technological development in pastoral societies is at least equal to that of horticulturists and much greater than that of sedentary hunting-gathering groups. Transportation is no barrier, since pastoralists normally carry hundreds of pounds of necessary and unnecessary baggage with them anyway, and we should not assume that they would be reluctant to abandon sculpture once made; this would apply our own standards of possessiveness to others who may not hold to such values. At any rate, sculpture reappears on the evolutionary scene with the development of agricultural nation-states; these societies not only produced considerable surpluses but also some of the finest sculpture known to us.

The absence of sculpture in a particular society surely does not mean that a people are unfamiliar with or incapable of producing it. Although the Hottentot of South Africa—like most other nomadic hunter-gatherers—do not produce sculpture, their children often model toys out of clay—but as Isaac Schapera observes, "the talent here shown is not carried over into later years, and no modeling or carving of any description analogous to this is done by adults." Among the Tuareg, pastoral nomads of North Africa, children sculpt animals and people in clay but adults do not. Among the Pomo Indians, nomadic hunter-gatherers of western North America, "we must look to basketry for the chief and almost only expression of the art sense of the people. . . . The Pomo, like the Central California Indian in general, knew practically nothing about plastic art or painting. A single example of plastic art might be found in the dolls which were used by the women for the purpose of becoming pregnant, and by the poisoners. These were, in both cases, rude images made out of clay" (E. M. Loeb, "Pomo Folkways," University of California Publications in *American Archaeology and Ethnology*, 19 [1926]: 191).

To what extent can the absence of sculpture in Islamic and traditional Judaic cultures be attributed to religious proscription? I think that cases like these have to be regarded as examples of the religious rationalization of processes already existing in the cultures: Islamic and Biblical prohibitions of sculptural representations are aspects of the ideologies of pastoral societies. Most pastoralist societies are without sculpture, but not all proscribe it; the factors in societies at this stage of social and technological development which inhibit the production of sculpture may or may not be legitimated religiously.

It is precisely the presence (or absence) of sculpture at particular stages of development which suggests that art, or at least some aspects of art, is as much part of the adaptive process as marriage, religion, and other aspects of human social behavior. If the presence of sculpture is neither random nor fortuitous, what is the reason for this regularity? When the empirical record shows that its appearance corresponds with particular levels of social and technological development, the reasons for its occurrence have to be sought within strategies of adaptation and the relationship of sculpture to them.

The precise relationships between creative activities and different strategies of adaptation are matters for subsequent research. I have merely tried to point to one direction these explorations can take. But the regularities observable in the relation between ways of life and their music and sculpture suggest that the arts do enter into man's relationship with his habitat. It may be that their role is confined to reflecting and reinforcing—and sometimes helping to change—the prevalent values and ideologies. This is suggested by Lomax's findings concerning music and my own about the use of materials in sculpture and the conformity of artistic expression in conformist societies. But there may be more to the matter than this.

What is the significance of the absence of sculpture among nomadic hunter-gatherers and pastoralists (and the loosely organized horticulturists of highland New Guinea)? This raises another question (or the same one looked at from a different point of view): The absence of sculpture means also that there are no sculptors; what prevents this role from developing in these societies?

It is evident that sculptors' roles are commingled with religious and political roles in stateless societies and that they are differentiated in agricultural nation-states, as in Europe during the Renaissance. To what degree is the artist's role tied to conflict in the society, and to what extent to stability? Does this have any bearing on the failure of societies at some stages of evolution to develop the sculptor's role? Why, even when sculpture is absent, are pictorial and decorative arts present? Taking creative activity as a whole, we find that the arts not only reflect and legitimate existing norms and ideologies but also mirror the conflicts in society (as does the mythology described in Selection 36). Thus some of our most revealing clues to the problems posed by the evolution of sculpture may be provided by the study of literary forms; together they may shed light on the nature of adaptation and evolution.

I deliberately conclude with questions that are at present unanswerable to emphasize that the study of adaptation—though it has a long and established history—is still in its earliest stages of development in the science of man. Like our species itself, it has a very long way to go.

Several works can be consulted by the reader who wishes to explore further along these lines, and others will be cited in connection with the case studies that follow. See, for example, *Psychoanalytic Explorations in Art*, by Ernst Kris (New York: International Universities Press, 1952; New York: Schocken paperback, 1966); *Feeling and Form* (New York: Scribner's, 1955) and *Reflections on Art* (Baltimore: The Johns Hopkins Press, 1958) by Susanne Langer; *Structural Anthropology*, by Claude Lévi-Strauss (New York: Basic Books, 1963); *Centuries of Childhood*, by Philippe Ariès (New York: Vintage Books, 1966); *Literacy in Traditional Societies*, edited by Jack Goody (New York and Cambridge: Cambridge University Press, 1968); and *The Social History of Art*, by Arnold Hauser (in four volumes, New York: Vintage Books, 1958).

32. PREHISTORIC ART AND IDEOLOGY

MORTON LEVINE

Reproduced by permission of the American Anthropological Association from American Anthropologist, *Vol. 59, No. 6, 1957. Morton H. Levine is Professor of Anthropology, City University of New York. He received his Ph.D. from Harvard University in 1962. In addition to his professorial position, he is a Research Associate at the American Museum of Natural History and Science Advisor to the Pyrrenean Institute of Anthropological Study (Toulouse). He has done field work among French Basques since 1962. Among his research interests are general anthropological theory, the anthropological study of art and culture, and Basque culture and ethnography.*

■ In the following selection, Morton Levine begins his analysis of the art of hunter-gatherers by asking what can art tel' us about the rest of a group's culture—what they think and believe, how they perceive reality, what they value. His underlying assumption is that a group's values and world view are outgrowths of their relationship to the habitat and that they are expressed in art, and he gives us examples of two overlapping sets of relationships: first ecological conditions and beliefs and then beliefs and artistic productions. He shows in his analysis of Australian aboriginal art that a complex system of beliefs and practices associated with fertility stems directly from the exigencies of the habitat, especially in connection with the relationship of life and rain. At the same time, art-making among these people is a principal element in ritual and ceremonial action intended to promote fertility. Many design elements used by Australian groups are sacred, and Levine explores the interrelationships of art and religious belief and practice.

This paper is broader in scope than its title indicates; it discusses the art of Australian aborigines as well as the work of cave dwellers during the Upper Paleolithic (Ice Age) period. In comparing these two artistic traditions, Levine illustrates one of the focal methods of modern archeology: the interpretation of prehistoric cultures by comparing their remains with the products of living societies. The inert remains of societies that have long been extinct are difficult to interpret because modern man has only his own conceptual lenses through which to view them. However, by examining similar phenomena among groups now living by a similar strategy of adaptation, one may see these remains from the point of view of a different stage of development. Thus, this paper is methodologically as well as substantively illuminating.

Toward the end of his paper, Levine takes up the question of whether there can be diverse artistic traditions among people like the Australian aborigines and shows that there cannot. If we view art as an expression of a world view, Levine's conclusion adds support to the hypothesis that hunter-gatherer groups are very homogeneous. His analysis also lends considerable support to the point of view which asserts that art, no less than any other sphere of activity, has to be regarded as an aspect of a group's adaptation to its habitat.

For a very good introduction to some of the new techniques in archeology just referred to, see *New Perspectives in Archeology*, edited by Sally R. Binford and Lewis R. Binford (Chicago: Aldine, 1969). For a review of the art of hunter-gatherers of the North American Northwest Coast and other tribal groups, see "Art in the Life of Primitive People," by Erna Gunther, in *Introduction to Cultural Anthropology*, edited by James A. Clifton (Boston: Houghton Mifflin, 1968, pp. 76-115). A major methodological advance in the study of prehistoric art—the use of the microscope —which seems to add a great deal to our knowledge of the thinking and behavior of Upper Paleolithic people is reported in "The Baton of Montgaudier," by Alexander Marschack (*Natural History*, 79, No. 3 [March 1970] : 67-63). ■

"The material remains of past civilizations are like shells beached by the retreating sea. The functioning organisms and the milieu in which they lived have vanished, leaving the dead and empty forms behind . . . understanding . . . of ancient societies must be based upon these static molds which bear only the imprint of life."
                                                GORDON R. WILLEY

THE MATERIAL REMAINS of past civilizations sometimes include art. Where this is so, as in the spectacular case of Upper Paleolithic art in

Western Europe, we may be able to add an ideological dimension to our understanding of the ancient people.

Traditional anthropological interest in art treated the subject as an isolated ethnographic category, focussed almost exclusively on the technique of art-making, on the iconography, and on the uses to which art is put. But attention has turned increasingly to questions about the ties between art and other aspects of culture. For example, monographs by Mills and McAllester, produced under the aegis of the Harvard Values Study project, have looked for relationships between aesthetic values in Navaho art and music and Navaho value culture as a whole. Malraux's *Voices of Silence* exhibits a convergent trend in art history. These and similar studies are laying the foundation on which efforts to interpret prehistoric art must rest.

Translating into achievement the prospect of reconstituting prehistoric "idea culture" through the study of prehistoric art depends upon finding ways and means for archeologists to ask, however indirectly, the same questions which ethnologists increasingly pursue among recent and living art-makers. If relationships between art and other parts of culture can be discerned and described in individual cultures and compared across cultures so as to yield generalizations, if we can make a reasonable case for the idea that a people's art is patterned by the point of view of their culture, if we can suggest the ways in which art exhibits this patterning, we might hope to put the lessons learned to work in behalf of a plausible reconstruction of the attitudes and outlook of a prehistoric people. We might gain a means of narrowing the gap between that span of time for which we know something of man as an economic animal and that much shorter period for which we are acquainted with him as a thinking, believing, feeling creature.

The concern of this paper is two-fold: What kind of controls on interpretation can we derive from the study of ethnographic materials? And, what problems can we approach fruitfully through the analysis of art style? The crucial general issues about the "nature of artistic behavior" and the character of the "relationship between Art and Culture" are not confronted directly.

The present discussion moves beyond ground already taken by anthropological field forces.

This has its obvious advantages and disadvantages. The attempt was stimulated by studies in the art of the Upper Paleolithic and in aboriginal Australian art. In pursuing the concerns of this paper, we will have recourse to the former to exemplify problems in reconstruction of ideology, and to the latter for examples of what ethnographic materials can provide by way of suggestions for and limitations on interpretation. Further, we will deal solely with painting and sculpture, the only arts common to the ethnographic and archeological record.

THE ARCHEOLOGICAL RECORD AND ETHNOGRAPHIC COMPARISON

Drawing on material survivals and on the data of paleo-studies in geology, geography, and zoology, archeology develops a picture of the life of Upper Paleolithic man in broad terms of habitat-economy-society:

He was a cold climate big game hunter. His environment was at once bountiful and threatening. Animal and plant resources abounded; but bringing down game, even with the refined and varied arsenal then at hand, was extremely difficult if not dangerous. The natural setting which enveloped the Ice Age hunter was uncommonly labile and must have seemed brutally capricious: the weather in Würm times was fairly drastic, and the landscape was tortured by tectonic upheavals. But life appears to have been relatively sedentary. Small local societies may have migrated with the change of season; but evidence for a plentiful food supply and the elaborate art in the caves refute any suggestion of incessant wandering. The existence of art of such a high level of achievement points to specialization of some sort within the groups; but we can only wonder whether the artistic function was or was not combined with religious or chiefly roles. Stylized, intentional burials appear in the record to suggest not only some sort of funeral exercise, but an explicit recognition of life and death as opposed and remarkable states.

These people or peoples left for posterity one of the great art collections of all time. It was a refined and varied art, produced over many millennia. Taken as a whole, the artistic universe of the Upper Paleolithic offers large animal "portraits," animal figures bearing geometric designs, other beasts studded with darts, sculptured women in the round and in relief—the famous "Venuses"—anthropomorphs of which the best known is the "Sorcerer" at Les Trois Frères, profusely superposed engravings on the walls of caves and on pebbles, handprints on the cave walls, some of which betray mutilation of the fingers, geometric figures and dots and club-shaped forms, and the vivacious meanders dug into the then soft clay with the fingers or with hafted animal teeth—the so-called "macaroni."

Archeology gives us a sense of the character of existence and the realistic problems which confronted these ancient hunters. We are presented, too, with a rich corpus of art. The "missing link" is what these early men thought and believed—how they perceived reality, what they valued and what they took as problematic. This is precisely what we hope to recover to some extent from a sensitive, systematic study of the art. But we cannot do this by unaided recourse to the art itself. Granting the assumption that values and world view reach expression in art, this general confidence is of no help in the enterprise of specific interpretation. If we want to eschew impressionistic insights and reconstitute the "missing link" in a way which is communicable and subject to restudy and confirmation or revision by others, then we will have to base our work quite explicitly on the clues and limits afforded by researches among living peoples. To illustrate the potential advantages of exploiting ethnographic materials, let us begin with a brief summary of elements in the life situation, thought and belief, and art of the aboriginal Australians. But not without first entering a caveat:

The material here is a compilation, a summary of and selection from diverse researches pursued among various regions and cultures of Australia. The data on art tend to emphasize that which is characteristic of the Oenpelli district of Arnhem Land in particular and north central and northwest Australia in general. The items on ecology and general culture are more widely eclectic. An effort has been made to avoid gross mismatch in coupling material about various aspects of aboriginal life and art; but error or simplistic generalization is built into this kind of summary. This "lumping" is justified, if at all, from the standpoint of our illustrative purpose and does not pretend to be a satisfactory review of the Australian situation as such. Such a summing up must await many more studies like the recent Mountford volume, *Art, Myth and Symbolism*, in which we are provided with a specific account of aboriginal art and belief in Arnhem Land which discriminates three artistic subcultures (Groote Eylandt, Oenpelli, and Yirrkalla) and details the corresponding ideology. Pending the availability of such material from many regions of Australia, the generalizations which are offered below must be regarded as at least highly tentative.

The ungenerous character of the Australian ecology, the utter dependence of the aborigine upon the environment, and the intensity and intimacy of his relationship with it form a classical syndrome in the literature. It is vividly and systematically described by Birdsell, and Tindale and other writers going back to Spencer and Gillen have given witness to the picture of a people who live in groups of less than 50, wander constantly within their tribal territory, and sustain themselves on a diet which reads virtually like a biological inventory of their locality.

The life situation of the Australian aborigine is not merely reflected in but rather imprinted on his belief and behavior. Basic is the perception of a profound connection between human life and that of plants and animals—and between all life and the rain. Mythology extends this to the notion of a common origin of men and other natural species. Anxiety, induced by dependence upon the environment and its parsimony, is expressed in various ways: there is a whole complex of belief and action associated with fertility and increase, a theme which pervades mythology and forms one of the main bases for ritual and underlies the exuberant ramification of sexual symbolism. The unpredictability of the environment echoes in the belief in benign and malevolent spirits, as well as sorcery, as causal agents. And there are rituals of atonement and propitiation which function to redress the feeling of being vulnerable to retribution for the killing of animals. Marrett describes such ritual as a "composition in the matter of blood revenge."

Some of the themes in art and artistic behavior among the Australians are:

1. Art-making as one of the principal forms of ritual and ceremonial action. The Australians hold many designs sacred and, further, believe that a design *is* what it represents. For example,

the painted actor in ceremonial *becomes* the mythological personage whose role he enacts by virtue of the ritualistic applicaton ("singing on") of the design.

2. Several other forms of ritual art-making include the palimpsest, or repetitive superposition of engraved and painted forms at certain places; the periodic ritual retouching of the *Wondjina* in the Kimberley caves to "reactivate" their power; ground painting as part of the ceremonial and the remaking or at least repainting of ceremonial objects for each use.

3. The affiliation between men and other living things is a frequent theme in Australian art, especially exemplified in anthropomorphic figures.

4. "X-ray" art is a popular motif, often showing pregnancy or the inner "works" of men and animals, all of this explicitly reflecting an intense concern with life and, more to the point, with fertility and increase. The emphasis on sexual motifs and the outsize portrayal of genitalia in both X-ray and non-X-ray art is another manifestation of this emphasis.

5. The Australian landscape is familiar to the inhabitants on the most intimate level; and features of the landscape are often invested with sacred meaning. The Australians leave their handprints at sacred places as a ritual of personal identification. Elsewhere in this paper we shall have occasion to discuss footprints in the caves and the animal track motif in art as a reflection of elements of the life situation in style.

How much of Australian belief (and its manifestation in art) refers to the particulars of the Australian situation and what may be referred to aspects in which the Australian and Upper Paleolithic situations are comparable? This important stage of analysis requires recourse to material from other living peoples. As an example, let us consider the question of whether the importance of the food quest to the Australian modes of belief is related to the sheer fact of scarcity.

The Chukchee, Gilyak, Lapps, Eskimo, and other hunting peoples of the world live in ecological circumstances which are by no means as adverse as those faced by the Australians; some of the environments may even be described as relatively bountiful. Yet, in one way or another, these people exhibit anxiety in the face of nature, perceive the world in animistic terms, and take vari-

ous steps to propitiate the spirits and to compensate nature for what has been taken in the hunt.

Sverdrup offers this revealing account of the Chukchee world view:

The Chukchi concept of nature is fundamentally based on the fear of unexpected and unavoidable events. To them the regularly repeated natural phenomena . . . represent no problem. . . . The hostile nature manifests itself in the unexpected event, in the catastrophes, the storms, the heavy snowfalls . . . disease.

. . . the Chukchi . . . have formed a system of their own which explains nature to their satisfaction, and which they think protects them against the catastrophes. They have populated nature with spirits and consider every unforeseen happening as evidence of the direct action of evil spirits, but . . . they can approach them and negotiate with them— they can hope that their sacrifices will be accepted by the spirits and that the spirits will show mercy or become reconciled if they have been offended.

The belief in good and evil spirits is also found among the Gilyak, according to Seeland, who notes further that evil spirits predominate and must be propitiated. Hawes reports that the Gilyak have a two-cycle year, marked by the seal and sable hunting seasons respectively. The hunters dedicate their first land-hunting catch to the "lord of the forest" at a special place; and the seal bones are tossed back into the sea. Similar restitution is found among the Lapps, who set aside certain parts of the slain elk for later burial; among the Minnetaree Indians, who believe the skeleton of the bison will again take on flesh if the bones are undestroyed; among the Baffinland and Hudson's Bay Eskimo, where a boy's first seal is stripped of its skin and flesh and the bones are thrown by his mother into a deep hole so that they may rise again as live seals for the boy to catch in later life.

The fertility-increase complex encountered among the Australians is conspicuous by its absence among these people; and this must be regarded as specific to the Australian situation. But it is noteworthy that an animistic view of nature, anxiety about continuity of the food supply, and propitiation and restitution ritual are manifest nevertheless. This persistent syndrome of thought and ritual action, apparently independent of the relative bounty of the environment, seems then to be a function of the dependence upon and intimate relationship with the natural setting. In this case, such characteristics would appear potentially attributable to prehistoric hunters like those of the Upper Paleolithic.

The Gilyak data relating belief and art offer a few details suggesting the extension of certain features in Australia beyond the local situation. We might consider them briefly. The Gilyak make art ritually and impute mana-like power to the art product. Seeland refers to "idols" which are both symbols for and dwelling places of the spirits. Small carved figures are worn as magical charms, recalling the Australian *tjurunga*. Hawes reports crude murals in the village houses: some representations of bears, and a rough design like a chessboard. (Without implying that this has any resemblance of which one could make interpretive use, the reference to a mural chessboard pattern recalls two interesting similarities: a like design occurs at Lascaux; and Birdsell has shown the writer a map drawn for him by an Australian informant which looks like a multicolored chessboard.) Kreinovich reports this interesting art ritual among the Gilyak; on the sea-going hunt, an indispensable part of the preparation is the making of a carved figure to be placed on the prow or stern of the boat. The ritual is called *ln,aj*, which also means "image" or "picture" or "figure." It affords protection on the hunt.

Now, with respect to connections between art and belief, some extension of the Australian material beyond the specifically local situation may be suggested: The ritual production of art. The equation of a work of art with that which, from our point of view, it merely represents. The investment of pictures or carvings with mana-like power.

Before proceeding to examine similarities and differences in Australian and Upper Paleolithic art, it might be useful to take stock of the procedure thus far. We began with a brief summary of the picture which archeology provides of the life situation of Upper Paleolithic man, and followed this with a very broad inventory of the art. Alongside this account was offered an overview of the conditions of life in Australia, their imprint on belief and behavior, and the expression in art of aspects of Australian world view and values. It then became evident that any extension of the Australian data to Upper Paleolithic man would require further ethnographic comparison to filter out elements specific to the Australians. Examples were offered relevant to two overlapping sets of relationships: (1) the life situation and belief, and (2) belief and the practice of art. Certain very broad positive and negative suggestions were developed in these illustrative comparisons. To narrow the interpretive possibilities further requires that we turn to the art itself, to its content and, above all, to its style. The analysis of style offers two potential contributions. Before exemplifying the more detailed kind of interpretation which can be made when the sort of study outlined above is followed by scrutiny of the art itself, the concept of style and its potential value to our undertaking deserves consideration.

POTENTIAL CONTRIBUTIONS TO THE INTERPRETATION OF PREHISTORIC ART IN STYLISTIC ANALYSIS

STYLE AND MEANING

"By style is meant the constant form—and sometimes the constant elements, quality and expression—in the art of an individual or a group." In this compact statement by Schapiro are two implications of potential importance for the study of prehistoric art. One is that style, as well as subject matter, yields "meanings." The other is that an art style refers to a specific group. Our discussion of style will be devoted to developing these two implications.

Style is not, as is sometimes assumed, an aspect of art independent of subject matter or "content." This distinction merely refers to different lines of sight on the same phenomena. When we talk about subject matter, the objective is principally to identify the items of experience to which the painter has turned for his models, or to characterize the anecdotal situation which has served him for a metaphor. When we talk about style, we may be said to be concerned with identifying the principle or principles of selection which distinguish the artistic utterance.

Selection occurs on three levels. First, it affects the choice of subject matter. The universe of Upper Paleolithic art is predominantly a carnival of the animals—and the big game animals at that. The art of Australia offers a much more representative sample of the plant and animal life of the region, and humans are frequent subjects. This is a gross contrast, but it will serve to illustrate the point: If we were to approach the matter from a primary interest in "content," our problem would be solved with an inventory of the creatures who inhabit the artistic universe. The stylistic approach, however, aims at detecting the bias which such a census might reveal and then trying to interpret its significance.

Even when the subject matter is merely identified, there is usually some attempt to describe the manner of depiction, the second level on which selection occurs. The suggestion here is that the manner of depiction is properly and usefully regarded as an object of analysis in its own right. The same subject matter is sometimes found in two quite distinct bodies of art—for example, the fish paintings in Arnhem Land and at the Gorge d'Enfer in France. Discriminating the piscine species is hardly sufficient to account for the contrast in point of view expressed by the art. More to the point is the X-ray treatment of the fish in Australia as against the full-fleshed presentation of the Upper Paleolithic fish. The difference in this case is stylistic, a difference in the selection of relevant elements from the model encountered in real life. This is what distinguishes an Altamira bison from the buffalo on a nickel. On this level, selection is defined by such questions as: What aspects of the model are retained? What aspects are stressed, by disproportion or color or other means? What aspects are attenuated or ignored?

Many Australian paintings present a tableau, built either on some situation encountered in daily life or on a fantastic recombination of various individual elements of ordinary experience. In such a work, the artist creates and populates a milieu. This expresses the third level of selection, that which involves patterns of arrangement of the subject matter in the total composition. In the *Mimi* paintings in Arnhem Land, we may see inordinately tall human figures hurling spears at kangaroo. Some of the bark paintings from the same region offer a synthetic situation: A man dominates the center of the picture. He is ringed by fish, two of which are converging on his huge, extended penis. In the former work, the milieu is modeled on a mundane event, whereas the latter presents a microcosmos whose overall arrangement or gestalt is synthetic, a product of fantasy. In both, however, the elements of subject matter have been selected; the depiction of the subjects shows selection; and, in the frame of reference of the total composition, the "environment" is established through selective principles expressed in juxtaposition, relative size of the elements, the character of the *lebensraum*, and suggestions about time through treatment of sequence, and so forth.

In contrast with Australian art, one of the most striking features of Upper Paleolithic art is the rarity of "scenes." Where they do occur, as in the famous one at Lascaux, the style is markedly different from the rest of the art. They are generally very economical delineations, almost stick figures in some cases, rather than opulent paintings; and their "sketchy" quality suggests a kind of reportage, perhaps the illustration of a verbal narrative. Most of the art, however, is "portraiture" of one kind or another, that is, the presentation of an animal which is not placed in a context but rather preempts the "milieu" of the painting. Not only does the analysis of compositional selection become much more refined, but we are faced with interpreting the significance of the absence of any kind of *mise en scène*.

Thus far, we have described style as the expression of principles of selection on three levels and have sought to specify them. In order to suggest the "meanings" which style may yield, we must turn to a more general canvass of the idea of selection per se.

Boas derives selection from the limitations of the artistic media. The materials of the painter and sculptor do not permit truly literal imitation, but constrain them to select. This is self-evident, but it doesn't explain why the selection should not turn out to be random. The fact is that the selection is not random, or else we could never talk about "Gothic" art or "Cubism" and so on; so that we must work toward some idea of the source of the patterns of selection.

Tylor said that the purpose of art "is not imitation, but what the artist strives to bring out is the idea that strikes the beholder". In relating selection to creative intent, rather than to the constraints imposed by the media, Tylor puts us on the path to a useful conception of meaning in style. Malraux develops this theme:

> Whatever the artist himself may say on the matter, never does he let himself be mastered by the outside world; always he subdues it to something he puts in its stead. . . . For the visible world is not only a profusion of forms, it is a profusion of significances; yet as a whole it signifies nothing, for its signifies everything. . . . Thus, styles are *significations*, they impose a *meaning* on visual experience . . . always we see them replacing the uncharted scheme of things by the coherence they enforce on all they "represent." Every style, in fact, creates its own universe by selecting and incorporating such elements of reality as enable the artist to focus the shape of things on some essential part of man.

This will recall the parallel statement by Whorf in quite a different context, worth quoting here because it refers in a more general way to the source of selection as a function of symbolic behavior in man's organization of reality:

> The categories and types that we isolate from the world of phenomena we do not find there because they stare every observer in the face; on the contrary, the world is presented to us in a kaleidoscopic flux of impressions which has to be organized by our minds. . . . We cut nature up, organize it into concepts, ascribe significances as we do, largely because we are parties to an agreement to do it in this way.

A few years earlier, in *Patterns of Culture*, Benedict defined the ethos of a culture as a selection from the great arc of human possibilities. Her analogic reference to the configuration of culture and art style in the same work is not merely heuristic; the conception of art style was as much a model as a metaphor.

An art style is a particular set of selective principles. Taken as a whole, the style of a particular work of art expresses the perceptive bias of the individual artist, as conditioned by (1) his peculiar life history and (2) the context in which his life unfolds, that context being the human group to which he belongs and its culture. But there is also a style attributable to a corpus of art by many artists, as the synoptic collections of any historically organized museum will confirm. Sapir's distinction between individual and social behavior can be projected to reconcile the individual and social dimensions in art style: those aspects of "individual style" which may be referred to shared patterns of selection represent the art style of the group or culture. The "cultural meaning" of an art style,

then, is the organization of reality, the conceptual modes, the various levels of value—in short, the collective representations—of the culture which produced it.

STYLISTIC UNITS AND CULTURAL UNITS

Up to now, we have been concerned with interpreting art—with the use of ethnographic materials and with the meanings which may be derived from the analysis of style. Along with Schapiro, we have assumed that a particular art style is the product of a particular historical sociocultural entity. The concept of style outlined above would seem to warrant this assumption. And, although taxonomic arrangements of non-artistic archeological materials in "industries" and "assemblages" have not been equatable with cultures, archeology has used art styles to achieve culture historical integration. On the premise that art styles refer to historic cultural entities, archeologists have plotted their distribution geographically and chronologically and have been able to order their assemblages in a space-time matrix. Bennett's reconstruction of a Central Andean area cotradition summed up historical and methodological contributions by Kroeber and Willey, among others, and remains today a prime example of the effective use of art styles in plotting culture history.

But to say that an art style belongs to an historic sociocultural entity doesn't quite do away with the problem of coincidence between an artistic unit and a group unit. We must consider Schapiro's point that a culture may foster two art styles contemporaneously. If this were true, we could not be sure whether our ideological reconstruction referred to part of the outlook of a group, or to the whole of it; and out unit of reference would slip from our grasp.

From the standpoint of the present concern with cultures on the hunting and gathering level, that is cultures which are likely to be homogeneous, the problem does not appear formidable. An apparent instance of diverse art styles maintained by a single culture in Arnhem Land disappears upon closer inspection. The Mimi paintings in the caves are, in most stylistic respects, markedly different from the bark paintings and other art produced today and in the recorded past. We cannot assume, because the Mimi paintings figure in contemporary belief and ritual, that they represent another art style of the aborigines of today, who do not make them, do not know or have forgotten who did make them, and regard this art as both representative of and produced by spirits. The fact that present-day aborigines project an explanation on the art does not put them in possession of two art styles.

Turning more directly to Schapiro's point that, "The variation of styles in a culture or group is often considerable within the same period", we are led to inquire into the unit characterized as "a culture or group." Considering the range of examples adduced throughout the article, it is fair to assume that he refers to contemporaneous variety within something like "Western culture." The tremendous diversity within this frame of reference is a plain fact, but are we justified in referring to it as "a culture"? To the extent that we are justified in taking Western culture as a unit, it is vis-à-vis non-Western cultures; and then it is the similarities within our unit, not the differences, that are being stressed. If, however, we are going to focus on variation within this huge geographical, historical, sociocultural framework, then we have to recognize subcultures in space, time, and the organization of society and social thought. And the question becomes one of co-incidence between a single art style and a single subculture.

The recent history of modern art gives vivid testimony to the overlapping and side-by-side existence of diverse artistic styles; it is fruitless to seek a common denominator for Expressionism and Cubism or for Norman Rockwell and Picasso. There is parallel diversity in views of reality and values. The artistic subcultures can be characterized by different orientations in belief and behavior. However, in no case can a variety of styles be attributed to one artistic "school." The problem which Schapiro raises is not, in the end, a problem of reconciling cultural homogeneity with stylistic diversity, but one of establishing meaningful coincidences between art styles and sociocultural entities.

This problem is yet to be solved with respect to the Upper Paleolithic. Breuil has organized the art into two great cycles, the Aurignacian-Périgordian and the Solutréo-Magdalenian, on the basis of archeological evidence, stylistic criteria (which assume a progression toward accomplished naturalistic rendering and increasing elaborateness in technique), and similarities in certain broad features of execution. This grouping of the material, granting its validity, is nevertheless unsuited to the purposes outlined in this paper. The units are chronological and lump obviously disparate art styles. The Altamira polychrome bison are placed in Magdalenian VI. So are the bison at Font-de-Gaume. Yet they are remarkably different in style. The former are thickly outlined, presented in a variety of poses, very detailed, adorned with a stylized, fringe-like treatment of the hair. The latter have more generalized forms, are rather delicately outlined, are mostly standing erect, with emphatic development of the hump and other rounded parts of the body. The refinement of delineation in the French bison contrasts with the Spanish cave paintings as Japanese art might contrast with Rouault or Picasso.

In order to obtain units against which the analysis of style can be projected, it will be necessary to cross-cut Breuil's chronological classification with groupings based on spatial distribution. Despite their apparent contemporaneity, and whatever similarities in outlook they may have shared, there were differences in the principles of selection between the people at Altamira and those at Font-de-Gaume. We have to assume, provisionally at least, that these were variant local cultures. What might, for convenience, be called the "Font-de-Gaume Style" and the "Altamira Style" must be plotted geographically. Once the distribution is known, the archeology of the area which corresponds with the art style must also be treated as a unit distinct from the remainder of the larger region. In short, a stylistic-cultural region must be plotted and dealt with as an entity.

The outcome of such "style-mapping" will be individual units with which we can begin to do interpretive work. It will not result in a sequence of Upper Paleolithic art history, for the present state of our knowledge of art styles and the logic of their progression is totally inadequate to allow us to convert several different art styles into an historical series on internal evidence. For sequences of styles, we will have to continue to depend for a long time on the data of dirt archeology.

SOME TRIAL INTERPRETATIONS OF UPPER PALEOLITHIC ART

Let us proceed now to some attempts at interpretation of some features of Upper Paleolithic art, using the guides developed above. The following suggestions were developed in ethnographic comparisons, taking off from a review of the Australian data:

Dependence upon nature is one of the crucial features of a hunting and gathering subsistence, regardless of the relative bounty of the environment.

The relationship with the natural setting is intimate and intense.

Hunting is difficult with the inadequate arsenal possessed by these peoples; and cornering and killing big game animals is not only problematic but often dangerous.

The unexpected and irregular manifestations of nature produce major crises in the lives of such dependent people.

These situational factors are reflected in several themes in the outlook and behavior:

Nature is perceived as active and purposive and personal, sometimes in animistic terms and sometimes in outright anthropomorphic terms; and there is some tendency to identify to greater or lesser degree with nonhuman living things.

Even when the food supply is abundant, dependence, unpredictability in the total situation, and the resistance of big game to the hunter's purpose invoke anxiety which is expressed by peopling the universe with spirits or gods which (a) account for the character of the situation, and (b) provide the possibility of appropriate action to control or at least salvage the situation.

Nature, thus regarded, is approached from two directions: It is perceived as accessible to propitiation; and compensation for what man must take from it in order to survive is regarded as possible and necessary.

In turn, these themes are reflected in certain attitudes and patterns of behavior with respect to art:

The main belief in this connection is that a work of art is the same thing as that which it represents.

From this stems the idea that art objects have mana-like power.

In the realm of behavior, we have seen that hunting and gathering people who engage in art-making do so ritually.

This represents the range of possibilities filtered from a description of Australian life, belief, and art by virtue of comparisons with other hunting and gathering peoples designed to distinguish between what is specific to the Australian situation and what might remain for use in interpreting Upper Paleolithic art. In approaching the prehistoric material, the art itself guides us to a still closer range of potential explanation. The selection reflected in the subject matter, depictive treatment, and compositional arrangement of the art is the clue to the selection which characterizes the outlook of the ancient people. In view of what has been said about the need for well articulated art styles for the Upper Paleolithic, it is only possible to deal here with discrete features which cannot be added up and offered as the values and outlook upon reality of a true sociocultural entity.

The handprints in the caves are the remains of a ritual of identification ("Kilroy was here"), the mark of the pilgrim's visit to a sacred place. The very way of life, as we have seen, develops an intimate sense of locality and the imputation of sacred character to features of the landscape. This is elaborately expressed in Australia, where there are also handprints and where the natives are able to identify the owners who have placed them there in a ritual act.

The profusely superposed drawings are the traces of a restitution ritual: whenever an animal was killed, his essence was restored to Nature by ritual rendering of his image at a sacred spot. Basic to this interpretation are the following beliefs: an image is what it represents; restitution can and must be made to the spirits or gods who stand for Nature. These express anxiety over the continuity of the food supply, born of dependence upon nature, and the notion that taking life is dangerous not only vis-à-vis the powerful beast but also the powerful spirits who inspire and protect all life.

The superposed drawings occur at selected places, often surrounded by available areas for drawing. On occasion, as at Les Trois Frères, they are placed in juxtaposition with other art—in this case the "Sorcerer"—in a manner which suggests sacrifice to a spirit or god. Above all, the palimpsests of this kind suggest a compulsive superposition rather than mere overpainting or overdrawing; and this compulsiveness inspires the notion of ritual. Similar artistic phenomena are reported from Australia by Basedow, who cites rock carvings at Yunta in the Flinders mountains where "one design has been carved over the top of another, time after time, until eventually the ground appeared as though it were covered by an elaborate carpet." Speaking of the "impression of profuseness" in the cave galleries of rock painting in Arnhem Land, Elkin says: "The drawings overlay one another. This suggests that satisfaction lies not so much in admiring the finished picture, as in the act of painting it or in some practical desire it expresses and in some result it will effect . . . he believes that this 'ritual' act will bring about the desired result."

The anthropomorphic figures, as a general class of art, express the affiliation between men and other living creatures and, as well, the personification of nature. This is a very vague generalization; but it does suggest the direction of productive analysis. Assuming the significance of anthropomorphic figures suggested here, the most informative path would seem to require a close study of the factors of selection—human and animal elements used—and composition of these elements into a synthetic figure. This is not an easy task for the Upper Paleolithic, where anthropomorphic figures are not a strongly expressed artistic theme and where they tend to occur as one-of-a-kind examples.

The animals which occur with darts or spears sticking in them have been popularly interpreted as imitative magic; and although this kind of interpretation is again very general, it does gain support from other evidence discussed above. This involves the same kind of equation of the artistic depiction with that which is depicted as do the superposed drawings of the palimpsests, although the intent here is clearly not restitution but rather to gain power over the animal. Thus, we have an expression tending to confirm the perception of the game animals as dangerous in a literal sense. In the more specific treatment of *perspective tordue* below, there seems ample

justification to impute this sense of problem to Upper Paleolithic man.

Perspective tordue in Upper Paleolithic art is not a manifestation of inept perspective rendering but evidence for the intense concern of the hunter, with his inadequate armament, over the danger he faced from the horned wild beasts. "Twisted perspective" is Breuil's name for an artistic practice encountered in the Upper Paleolithic in which the horns of animals otherwise shown in profile are turned around full face to the viewer. The accepted interpretation of this phenomenon has been that it represents less accomplished naturalism than later art. To put it another way, this style has been designated as earlier and assigned to the Périgordian, largely on the assumption that there is a progression in Upper Paleolithic art as a whole toward the Renaissance ideal of perspective.

This assumes a kind of progressive learning which took place over many thousands of years. It also ignores the possibility that perspective tordue expresses a principle of style, a kind of compositional selection which is designed to stress the significance to the artist of the horns of the animal. However, recourse to the Australian material yields evidence that such twisting of usual appearances is purposeful and refers to aspects of the life experience of the artists.

In Australia there are many pictures in which the figure of a man or an animal is presented in profile, standing or running, but with the soles of the feet turned up to face the viewer. We know why the Australians do this. From early childhood, boys are taught to identify human and animal tracks with extreme subtlety. Their lives depend on the success of the hunt and game is scarce, and no means of detecting the opportunity for a kill can be neglected. Animal tracks themselves are a prominent motif in Australian art; in the pictures described above they merely become an element—albeit an important one—of a larger composition. It should also be noted that footprints of humans, as well as handprints, are found in the caves and are part of the syndrome of identification. Tracks are the mark of men and animals in Australia.

In this light, it is evident that the presentation of the soles of the feet in the Arnhem Land bark paintings and other art represents a selective principle, a violation of literal truth in behalf of a more profound reality, reflecting the intense concern with identifying animals and men and even spirits.

In the Upper Paleolithic, we cannot overlook the possibility of an analogous situation in the art, which takes its shape from the particular situation that obtained then and there. We have referred to the inefficiency of the weapons of Upper Paleolithic man in dealing with large animals; and he doubtless used traps and pit-falls and other means to bring them down. It is also quite likely that one of the perils of wandering around the countryside to hunt or to collect vegetable food was the possibility of attack by these beasts. This was a real problem for him; and the notion that his art features the selective principle which gives prominence to the horns on these grounds seems more plausible than inept rendering—an idea which applies esthetic values limited to a particular period of Western art history. Further, in the famous "wall-scene" at Lascaux, which appears as noted earlier to be illustrating an actual event, we get a depiction of an event in which the disem-boweled beast looms over the fallen hunter, horns pointing to the fallen man and to the viewer.

The above are some examples of interpretations of Upper Paleolithic art, offered to illustrate how artistic selection may be projected on a range of possible explanations to narrow that range considerably. This paper has been designed to suggest procedures whereby ethnographic materials, the data about ecology and the life situation and art afforded by archeology, a concept of style as selective perception, can contribute to a systematic, verifiable sequence of analysis and reconstruction. The essence of the procedure is a progressive narrowing down of the variety of explanation for which plausibility can be asserted. The objective is a limitation on plausible explanation; patent demonstration is out of the question. Even so, with much work on a more modest scale than indicated here, on many fronts which demand study, there is some prospect of narrowing the span between that period for which we know something of man as a highly evolved animal and that brief epoch for which his attitudes and outlook are known to us in specific detail.

33. MASKS AS AGENTS OF SOCIAL CONTROL

ROY SIEBER

Reprinted from African Studies Bulletin, *Vol. 5, May 1962, no. 11, pp. 8-13. Roy Sieber is Professor and Chairman of Fine Arts Department at Indiana University. He has conducted three research trips to Africa; the first, in 1958, resulted in the monograph, "The Sculpture of Northern Nigeria" (Museum of Primitive Art, New York, University Publishers, December, 1961). It was during that research tour that the data concerning the Igala mask were discerned. Two later trips to Ghana centered on the study of the history of leadership arts among the Akan.*

■ We saw in the previous selection that art and religion are commingled among hunter-gatherers and that both are aspects of their adaptation. In the next selection we turn to an example of this admixture in horticultural societies. We have also seen that in these societies religion is not only involved in productive activities but also contributes to the maintenance of order and conformity. Hence, the commingling of art and religion points to the hypothesis that art also has political implications in these societies. Since the maintenance of conformity is of special concern in kin-based horticultural groups, we can feel a little more certain about attributing adaptive functions to creative work if we can show that art is part of this process.

In the following selection we have an example of the integration of art with social and political life in northeast Liberia. Sieber focuses on masks, objects that we regard as art and that indeed are products of creative activities. But in their original settings, these masks are specialized tools that serve as instruments in the integration of a social, economic, and political order.

Masks in northeastern Liberia occupy a central position as embodiments of the authority of local chiefs, and these objects command as much respect as the chiefs themselves. A chief is always masked when he appears in public and his regalia not only symbolizes his status but also the corporate identity of the group he represents. The chief's political position and the group's solidarity not only have a strong economic base but are also religiously validated; thus corporate identity, political power, art, and religion are commingled. The masks worn by the chiefs are felt to carry supernatural power within them. Sieber describes four types of masks, each of which is believed to contain particular spiritual forces that symbolize and legitimate controls over particular human actions: the "god spirit" masks that represent the authority of the council of elders; lesser masks that validate decision-making in inter-group disputes; masks that serve as sacred objects (analogous to altar pieces) in cult houses; and masks that are associated with particular sub-groups.

An excellent summary of social and political organization in northeast Libera is presented by James L. Gibbs, Jr., in "The Kpelle of Liberia," in *Peoples of Africa*, edited by James L. Gibbs, Jr. (New York: Holt, Rinehart and Winston, 1965). Sieber notes that the possession of masks gave power to their owners, and this is a familiar theme in many tribal societies, perhaps best exemplified by the Yir Yoront; see "Steel Axes for Stone Age Australians," by Lauriston Sharp, in *Human Problems in Technological Change: A Casebook*, edited by Edward H. Spicer (New York: Russell Sage Foundation, 1952; reprinted as Selection 6 in *The Cultural Present*). Clothing as an aspect of social relations often plays a role similar to that of art; in this connection see "The Amish Use of Symbols and their Function in Bounding the Community," by John A. Hostetler (*Journal of the Royal Anthropological Institute of Great Britain and Ireland*, 95 [1963]: 11-21). A fuller account with photographs of the masks described here can be found in *Masks as Agents of Social Control in Northeast Liberia*, by George W. Harley (Papers of the Peabody Museum of American Archaeology and Ethnology, Harvard University, Vol. 32, Number 2, 1950). ◼

TRADITIONAL AFRICAN ART for the most part was more closely integrated with other aspects of life than those which might be described as purely aesthetic. Art for art's sake—as a *governing* aesthetic concept—seems not to have existed in Africa. Indeed, the more closely an art form is related to a major non-aesthetic aspect of culture such as religion, the more distant it is from such separatist philosophical concepts.

In fact traditional African sculpture might best be described as based on a concept of art-for-life's sake. It was, in most cases, closely allied to those cultural mechanisms dedicated to the maintenance of order and well being. In short, sculpture was oriented to those social values upon which depended the sense of individual and tribal security.

These values were often formalized in exceedingly practical and common sense terms, as is demonstrated in this Bambara prayer addressed to the ancestors:

I sacrifice this hen to you in the name of my children and myself. Protect us from all evil. Give us rain at the time the rains begin; give us a good harvest, a happy old age, women, children, and the health to cultivate our fields. Do not be angry with us. We love you, we honor you. Be happy during your sojourn in Lehara, the realm of the invisible.

In these circumstances it is necessary for the art historian to realize that his responsibility extends beyond stylistic, biographical, and iconographic studies into the realm of social values, if he is to lay claim to an understanding of these arts, or, for that matter, if his findings are to have interdisciplinary relevance.

Thus I should like, for the purposes of this paper, to lay aside this traditional triumvirate of the art historian in a brief discussion of certain masks which were used as agents of social control.

First, however, it is necessary to note that, in general, masks may be described as symbols or foci for the spiritual forces that loaned their authority to the edicts and acts that emanated from the masks.

Further, the masks *were* recognized as symbols by the initiated, that is, by those possessed of the secret or semi-secret knowledge that these were, after all, objects of wood, carved for a price by known artisans and which, between appearances, had to be stored and protected from the effects of climate and insects. Yet, even the initiated believed that these objects carried with them, or within them, a very real spiritual power, which in a sense invested the wearer and the costume as well as the mask during its ritual appearances. I should like to add, parenthetically, that so much is this the case that the presentation of an isolated mask in a museum constitutes a gross misrepresentation, not only of the social values inherent in the complex comprised of mask, costume, dance, music and other related traits, but of the aesthetic component of the mask in its original context.

Four mask types, each from a different tribe, will be described in order to show that each is believed to be the embodiment of spirit forces that authorize specific controls over particular human actions.

The functions of the "god spirit" (*Go ge*) masks of the tribes of north-eastern Liberia have been described by George W. Harley. In order to comprehend the functions of this mask type it is necessary to note that the

old, indigenous government functioned on two (overlapping) levels. . . . The first, which might be termed the civil phase, was concerned with the everyday management of the town and its citizens, common laws governing conduct, etc. On the second level, which may be thought of as religious, were the mechanisms for handling the crises and emergencies of life. It was in this second level of government, calculated to deal with the powerful, hidden, spiritual forces, that the masks found their special place.

Harley describes this system as

a socio-democratic government by chiefs whose authority was reinforced by a council of elders. That council sought to follow the customs and traditions of the clan. When a problem threatened to cause disagreement or a feeling of resentment on the part of the loser or his surviving friends and relatives, the elders sought to obtain a decree (and even the act of execution) from the spirit world itself, through the medium of the mask and the ordeal. This system had the effect of keeping the ancestors near by, and not only vitally interested in the affairs of men but able to do something about them! In the last analysis it was government by tradition, enforced by the fear of disapproval of the ancestors. Decisions were reached with the approval of the clan fathers both living and dead. The living merely used a technique, placing both the responsibility for these decisions and the blame for the administration of justice on the ancestral spirits.

This description sets the stage for the functioning of the "god spirit" mask which represented the final spiritual authority investing the decisions and edicts of the council of elders.

This sytem functioned in secret through a high council of elders meeting at night in a sacred place, called together and presided over by the *gonola* or "owner" of the land. The *gonola* was also a high priest in that he was the keeper of the great mask referred to as *Go ge*, "god spirit." When there was to be a meeting of the elders he carried this mask to the secret place, laid it on a mat on the ground, and covered it with a white cloth. Around it the elders sat and discussed the special palaver for which they had been called together by the *gonola*, who acted as chairman. When they had discussed the case fully the chairman guided their opinion into a judgment, which was tentative until approved by the mask, *Go ge*. In arriving at this decision the owner exercised the function of judge or chief justice.

The functions of *Go ge* included that of lawmaker, since the session of elders hearing a case and rendering judgment would often decide that a decree was necessary to proscribe similar offenses. Such a decree, announced by the crier, had the effect of law.

In describing a particular Mano mask "owned" by Zawolo, Harley adds that:

After the old men had talked the case through and reached their decision Zawalo would uncover the mask, call it by name, and review the case, telling the mask:
"We have decided so and so. We want to know if you agree with our decision. If you agree let the cowrie shells fall up. If you disagree let them fall down."
Then he would take the shells and throw them like dice on the mat in front of the mask. The decision was supposed to be the decision of the ancestral spirits and it was final.

In his description of the "god spirit" mask of another village, Harley notes:

Sometimes the council would be called to consider the making of laws or decrees considered necessary under the circumstances. Perhaps a town was not prosperous, or people were running away to other sections. Perhaps the young men were refusing to take responsibility in public affairs. Sometimes the chief was not receiving due respect, or the older men needed to be impressed with their responsibility to the younger people.

And

In the old days this mask and its keeper had discussed *Poro* and *ge* palavers. It had seen men tried and condemned to death. It had been smeared with the blood of any person executed because he had broken sacred laws. Almost one hundred years ago it had been made and consecrated by human sacrifice. During the first years of its existence it had been "kept alive" by similar sacrifice every year in the middle of the dry season. Later a sheep had been substituted for the human sacrifice.

The "owner" by means of the authority of the mask held command over all the lesser masks of the clan. Further, "he had the power to stop war and fighting and could severely punish any breach of peace in the clan. . . . He could plan . . . [and] he sanctioned and assisted in the creation of a new Zo (priest)."

Harley notes that the power and prestige of the "owners" was considerable.

Each was a big man in ordinary life, but a bigger man because of the secret power conferred on him through the ancestral mask of which he was the keeper. To help him in his work of judging and ruling his people, each had a number of associates who were of some importance in daily life; but they also were of more importance when they functioned as wearers of masks.

The lesser masks

. . . presided at various public functions, and those associated with the crises of life of the individual, such as birth, puberty rites . . . calamity and death. . . .

They appeared also at the erection of important buildings and bridges, on the election of a new chief, on town holidays and feasts, at celebrations of victory in battle, at rain rites in time of drought, and at public witch trials—where a person suspected of witchcraft was tried, judged guilty or innocent, and executed if guilty, all by the simple procedure of forcing him to drink an infusion of sasswood (*Erythrophleum guineense*).

The various functions of the lesser masks acting under the authority of the "god spirit" mask indicate that they exercised controls over activities as diverse as the arbitration of arguments between clans, villages or lesser masks, buying on credit, the collection of debts, irregular sexual activity, and the cutting of the chief's farm.

Admittedly, the degree of power exercised through the "god spirit" mask is exceptionally broad. More usually, rather less authority emanates from a mask; its range of controls is more circumscribed.

For example, the *Egu Orumamu* or "chief of the masks" among the eastern Igala acts in a judicial capacity. Its power apparently is derived from the ancestors and it oversees the general well-being of the village. Certain of its appearances, for instance, are related to agriculture. More pertinent here, however, is its judicial role in cases of murder and petty civil offenses. (But not, curiously, in cases of theft.)

Orumamu does not discover a murderer by divination or ordeal in the way, for example, that Harley reports the latter method was used among the Mano. Rather, he called upon the family or village of the murderer to give up the criminal. If necessary he could quarantine a compound or village until the murderer was found simply by placing his staff across the entrance. No food or water could enter the restricted area. No person could enter or leave. Fields were left untended. Women could not go to market and this could be disastrous, for the economy of the Igala depended on the women's market activities. In short, all normal activity halted until the criminal was apprehended.

Execution was performed by a member of the victim's family and rather rigorous purification rites were necessary to free the executioner of the danger of retribution by both the dead criminal's spirit and the living members of his family. This seems to have been a form of almost remote control exercised by the mask which served more to oversee that retribution was confined to a proscribed, "legal" form.

On the other hand *Orumamu* was more directly involved in certain lesser cases of a civil nature. At reasonably fixed times *Orumamu* (hidden in a hut) arbitrated complaints and arguments of the women. These were usually of a financial nature, relating to market transactions, credit and debt failures, and the like. In these instances *Orumamu* pronounced judgment and ordered lesser masks to carry out sentences, at times to administer punishment, such as whippings, at times to oversee the payment of debts. Finally, *Orumamu* could send his minions to punish children who had gotten in trouble or to supervise the water supply in times of shortage. Thus it seems evident that this mask exerted controls that parallel certain of those of the "god spirit" mask, but that its range of total activities was far smaller.

The third example is one of still more limited power. The masks of a number of Bambara cults were used both in public appearances and as sacred objects—analogous to altar pieces— in the cult house. Each, in addition to its role as the spiritual authority for the cult, was instrumental as the agent of quite specific social controls. The Komo society, for example, had as its responsibility the seeking out and punishing of thieves and unfaithful wives. The duty of the Kono society was to ferret out poisoners; the Nama society, cannibals and the practitioners of witchcraft.

In the three examples given, the controls exercised through the masks are public; that is, they relate to all strata within a cultural unit (the tribe or village). The fourth and last example is really only a note to indicate that the controls of a mask may be limited to a society or other subgroup (for example, only men or only women). This example is from the Idoma tribe which until recently supported a group of head-hunting societies. Each of these had a mask which, among its other attributes, acted to control the behavior of the members of the society, imposing restrictions, especially with references to secret knowledge, and punishing members who transgressed those laws.

This list of examples could be extended considerably, for nearly every African mask functioned within a value context relating in some degree to the direction or control of human actions.

These examples might seem to be primarily of historic or academic interest. However, I feel constrained to point out that little or no cognizance has been taken of the role of masks in the establishment of political, economic, judicial, or police structures in the recent past. Whereas certain elements of native law or custom are quite carefully retained, the symbols of spiritual validification of those traditions have been ignored, ridiculed, and even outlawed. It would seem that both Christian and Moslem rejection of the masks because of the religious element present in them has clouded the consideration of other aspects of their functions.

Thus, I would suggest that a full understanding and assessment of the current economic, legal, and political attitudes of those tribes once committed to the Poro society is possible only if due consideration is given the conflicts and adjustments resulting from the loss of power—real and symbolic—once centered upon the masks.

Also, it seems to me inescapable that Igala, Bambara, and Idoma concepts of judicial power, crime, and punishment can be analyzed only if the shift of focus from the masks to a mixture of European, Koranic, and native law is taken into consideration. (Further, in this shift the traditional Igala chief who controlled the mask has been supplanted by an appointed magistrate; thus the concept of political succession, status, and power is seriously altered.)

In summary, the point I wish to make is that masks were used as agents of social control within a wide range of human activities and in a variety of combinations. Further, in many instances the character of the legal, economic, or political developments in contemporary Africa might be more fully understood if the role of the masks were taken into consideration.

34. THE ABELAM ARTIST

ANTHONY FORGE

Reprinted from Maurice Freedman, editor, Social Organization: Essays Presented to Raymond Firth *(Chicago: Aldine Publishing Company, 1967); copyright © 1967 by Maurice Freedman. Anthony Forge is Senior Lecturer in Social Anthropology at the London School of Economics. His formal training in anthropology was received at Cambridge. His research interests and field study include primitive art in New Guinea and kinship in London, and he has also been involved in a cooperative study of kinship in a middle-class sector of London. He has several publications resulting from these ventures. During the fall term of 1969 he was Visiting Professor of Anthropology at Yale University.*

■ What about the artist himself? Is he always a free agent, working in isolation, concerned only with his own creativity? Anthony Forge suggests in the following selection—which deals with artists among the Abelam, a horticultural people of lowland New Guinea—that the artist in all societies makes use as best he can of the styles and techniques provided by his group's tradition within the limits and potentials afforded by his group's adaptation. Similarly, the role of the fortuitous event in breaching the wall of traditionalism for an artistic innovator is much the same in Abelam as in many other societies: its effects are limited by the constraints inherent in the culture. Forge describes a few situations in which artistic innovations were made; not all of them were adopted. Unsurprisingly, it is the older men who emerge as the pillars of traditionalism, innovation coming from the ranks of the younger members of society.

This is not a study of a particular artist but, rather, an analysis in depth of a status and a role in the classic anthropological sense. Here we see the artist—all artists—as a member of a particular society, and we see the relationship of his role to other spheres of activity. In the previous selection we examined the relationship of art to religious practices and belief focusing on the mask, the art object itself; in this selection we examine that relationship from the point of view of its creator.

A well known report which should be consulted in the present connection is "Artist and Critic in an African Society," by Paul J. Bohannan, in *The Artist in Tribal Society*, edited by Marian W. Smith (New York: The Free Press, 1961, pp. 85-94). A good comparative study is "Personality and Technique of African Sculptors," by Hans Himmelheber, in *Technique and Personality*, by Margaret Mead, Junius B. Bird, and Hans Himmelheber (New York: Museum of Primitive Art, 1963). A significant collection of papers is *Tradition and Creativity in Tribal Art*, edited by Daniel Biebuyck (Berkeley: University of California Press, 1969). Anthropological analyses of the role of the artist owe a great deal to Raymond Firth, whose views are clearly spelled out in Chapter 5 ("The Social Framework of Primitive Art") of his book, *Elements of Social Organization* (New York: Philosophical Library, 1951; Boston: Beacon Press, 1963). ■

ONE OF RAYMOND FIRTH's earliest articles, "The Maori Carver", published in 1925, testifies to the early formation of that interest in art which has remained with him ever since. It is an enthusiastic piece, establishing the right of the Maori artist to be judged by his own standards and not merely as a primitive whose attempts to reach the style and vision of the Greek artist are vitiated by his dull and brutish nature. That such arguments do not have to be repeated today is due to the change in attitude which

Raymond Firth has had a part in shaping. Although he would hardly have called himself a social anthropologist in those days, his approach to the problem of the artist in society was basically sociological, and that it was also ahead of its time is amply demonstrated by the several officious and carping footnotes inserted by the editors of *The Journal of the Polynesian Society*. A quotation shows his approach well and might be taken as a text for the present essay in his honour. "It is important to know what kind of a person the carver was, what position he and his work occupied in the social scheme, and the seriousness with which both he and his labour were regarded." This attitude, which was elaborated and refined in his later publications, has always distinguished him from his contemporaries and immediate successors in social anthropology. He has always made it clear that to him art is not only a fit subject of study by social anthropologists but also a field of human activity which they ignore at their peril. Always opposed as he has been to any narrowing of the field of social anthropology, this attitude stems both from his interest in and appreciation of art, and from his view that it is in such highly regarded and deeply felt activities as art that human societies and their members express their values.

This essay is rather heavily ethnographic. I wish it could be more analytical, but despite Firth's advocacy we have still not developed the necessary concepts to be able to handle the relation of art and its creators to their society at anything above the descriptive level. However, it is at least now realized that such concepts are necessary, not only for plastic art, but for music, dance, architecture, and poetry as well as ritual and myth.

The truism of art history, that art reflects the society that produced it, is usually expounded with reference to some period of history in which known artists expressed their view of their culture and times in terms of the acceptance or rejection, and subsequent modification, of the art of the period immediately before their own. The artist is envisaged, as is the poet or musician, as expressing himself and his times in two main ways; first, by developing and perfecting forms and techniques used by his predecessors; second, by expressing in his art different conceptions and values, either by modification of the available styles and forms, or by the introduction of new ones. In short, the artist is seen as an individual receptive to his social environment and capable of mirroring his view of it in his art. The artist also codifies change; he starts with the conception of beauty common to the society of his childhood, and if he is great, he leaves the society with a modified conception of beauty, with new standards — a changed aesthetic. This view of the artist in his social setting presupposes change both in the society and the art; not just actual change, but also a conception of change, frequently, but not always, of progress. What the artist really expresses is not the values of his culture in any direct way, but the change in those values. A study of the art can therefore tell us nothing about the artist or even his values unless we also know something of the society and culture in which he operated, as the reflections of aestheticians on prehistoric and ethnographic art have frequently demonstrated. Just as it is impossible to have history without some concept of change, so art history and its techniques, being concerned primarily with change, cannot be used in any simple way on the sort of material presented by New Guinea societies. These societies have no concept of history or indeed of change, although since the advent of various European administrations they have become aware of the effects of change. In the view of members of these societies, they had always been the same since they came into existence and should ideally remain the same for ever. Similarly, the art of these societies had magico-religious value for them precisely because it re-created the art of the ancestors; its whole social function consisted in being unchanging. What then becomes of the artist as the super-sensitive receiver and distiller of the essence of his culture and times? Does he become merely a craftsman skilfully reproducing traditional objects in the traditional style to satisfy social demands whose springs are in concepts of magico-religious efficiency rather than any ideal of beauty? Someone must have created the art, and to judge from the favour many, though by no means all, of the highly prized objects have found with European artists and critics, the creator or creators were artists rather than craftsmen.

I shall not be able to give final answers to the problems outlined above, but hope at least to clarify some of them. In this essay I shall be examining the artist in his society with reference to the Abelam tribe of New Guinea. The Abelam number about 30,000 and live in the southern foothills of the Prince Alexander mountains to the north of the Sepik River. They live in large villages from 300 to 800 in population, and have a vigorous art. They are also distinguished for a cult of long yams; single yams of up to twelve feet long have been recorded.

THE CONTEXT OF ABELAM ART

As in most New Guinea societies, all art among the Abelam is basically cult art and can only be displayed in the context of the ceremonials of the tambaran cult. Decorative art, of course, exists, but its *motifs* are entirely drawn from the art of the tambaran cult; and it carries with it overtones of status from that cult. Half coconut shells, polished black and beautifully engraved with designs filled with white, are among the finest small objects produced by the Abelam; they are used for drinking soup, but may be carried only by big-men or men fully initiated in the tambaran cult and successful in the yam cult; young men can and do inherit them but cannot use them until they have the full ceremonial status of organizers of ceremonies. Similarly the engraved pottery bowls, holding anything from one to four gallons of white soup, made by women but decorated by men, can be used for serving soup only when ceremonial exchanges are taking place. Such examples could be multiplied to cover the whole field of decorative art, showing that not only is it stylistically derived from the cult art, but that the use and display of decorated objects are limited, by virtue of their decoration, to prescribed contexts and statuses also stemming from the cult. There are therefore no artists who produce decorated objects who are not also cult artists, and it is in the context of the cult that they acquire and perfect their skills. There is one exception to this statement: the women who make netted string bags (*wut*) using red, yellow, white, and a sort of dark purple string, in various excellent designs. The use of the bags by the men is determined by their ceremonial status, one design being reserved for fully initiated men, another for those who have only one ceremony to go, and so on. The small bags used by young men gradually increase in size with the age and status of their users. The production of the bags, however, is regarded simply as a skill which a woman learns from her mother or mother's or father's sister, and the ability to produce any design, although highly prized, is no indicator of status.

The tambaran cult shares its basic features with such cults throughout New Guinea. In essence it is a series of ceremonies at each of which the initiates are shown art objects of one sort or another and are told that these are the sacred spirits, tambaran. At the next ceremony they are told that the last one was just pretence but that this time they are going to see the real tambaran, and so on until the last of the ceremonies when they are in fact shown the most sacred objects; and as fully initiated men they may go through the cycle again, this time as stagers of the ceremonies and themselves initiators. Each ceremony is performed by one half of a dual organization, called *ara*, who initiate the sons of their exchange partners in the other *ara*; the initiators are fed by their partners while they prepare the ceremony, and after the initiation are presented with pigs. *Ara* perform ceremonies alternately: one will perform ceremonies 1, 3, 5, and 7, the other 2, 4, 6, and 8, going on then to 1, 3, 5, and 7, so that two full cycles have to be performed before an individual has been initiated into all the eight ceremonies.

All ceremonial activity is regarded as balanced exchange between *ara* and the individual partners who compose them. There is three-way reciprocity with increasing exactness of return at each level. First the food and the live pig are regarded as a return for ceremonial services in preparing the ceremony, acting as initiators, and providing decorations for the initiate (the son of the donor). A man will reproach his partner if the decorations are not up to standard, asking whether he has been eating all the food provided just to produce this. Second, the next ceremony of the cycle will be performed by the other *ara* and the donor will now be recipient. Rough equivalence is expected in size of pig between each pair of ceremonies, 1 and 2, 3 and 4, etc.; the scale increases until 7 and 8, which may require three months each to prepare, a very large

drain on the resources of the *ara* responsible for feeding the initiators, and demanding the most enormous pigs for presentation at the end. The third and final form of reciprocity, at which exact equivalence in the girth of the pig presented is essential, comes with the next cycle, when the *ara* who initiated at ceremony 1 last time are now paying for their sons to be initiated into the same ceremony. The lapse of time involved in the completion of a cycle can never have been less than ten years, and is nowadays, and probably always was, considerably longer. Although this is not the place for an analysis of the social structure, it is worth noting that these inescapable reciprocal obligations, stretching over the decades covered by two full cycles, are a potent factor in maintaining the stability of the component groups of the ceremonial organization, since to default imperils the ceremony and exposes the culprit to sanctions from the whole village and not just from his own clan or ceremonial partner.

The preparation of tambaran ceremonies provides the context in which all Abelam artists work, and the ceremonies themselves the only opportunity for them to display their work to any large group of people. It is also during the preparations that the training, if it can be called that, of future artists takes place. All the ceremonies have as central features the display of some series of objects which stand for the *nggwalndu*, that is, the major clan spirits. The earliest of the sequence are said to be very simple, but I have never seen either of the first two in any part of the Abelam area, and it would seem that they have been dropped from the repertoire, at least since the war. To go by the descriptions of older informants, the tambaran consisted of patterns on the floor of the ceremonial house made with the four earth paints (red, yellow, white, and black) with the addition of flowers, particularly the scarlet single hibiscus, and certain leaves, those with a silvery grey back being present in all tambaran ceremonies. While these patterns are the focus of the initiation and the representation of the *nggwalndu*, and give little scope for artistic expression, they are surrounded by painted panels of sago spathe which line and provide the ceiling for the initiation chamber constructed inside the ceremonial house—the painting and arrangement of which provide ample opportunity for the artists to display their skill, and which are the basis on which visitors from other villages evaluate the success of the ceremony. These paintings on the flat are sacred in that they are associated with the *nggwalndu* and the ceremonial house, whose façade is decorated with similar paintings, but the designs are not tambarans, being open and visible on the façade to women and uninitiated males. When used inside the house the designs and the panels on which they are painted are called *wut*, and referred to as the beautiful string bags of the *nggwalndu*. *Wut* has, however, many other meanings and is one of the most emotionally loaded words in Abelam. In this instance the most obvious symbolic referent is *nyan wut*—womb (*nyan* meaning child)—the initiation chamber being a small dark room built inside the large female house with its low entrance through which the initiates crawl when entering and leaving. The women are not supposed to know that *wut* is used for the painted panels which they, of course, never see in place, and I have heard artists, as they paint, laughing at the women's illusion that only they can make beautiful *wut*.[1]

Wut panels are to be found at all eight stages of initiation into the tambaran cult, but in later ceremonies the tambaran itself has a larger and more elaborate structure. There is a great deal of variation within the Abelam area in what is displayed at each stage, although there is far less variation in the names of the ceremonies, the same name being used for very different displays in different parts of the area. Much more is involved than simple wood-carving and painting on the flat in all parts of the area. For example, there is the setting up of 50 ft. poles with great masses of dry and thorny yam vines, and leaves of the spiny lawyer cane fastened on them to represent *nggwalndu*; bamboo roots are made into bird heads; and larger than life-size seated figures with extended arms and legs, covered with brightly painted patterned matting and stuffed with fibre, have to be constructed on armatures of wood and palm, themselves difficult to construct, with only split cane lashings to fasten the pieces together. Of such a

figure all that is saved after the break-up of the display is the carved wooden head. The fact that much of the work of the artist for such ceremonies is ephemeral does not mean that the demands of the public are less, or that a high degree of both technical skill and aesthetic sense is not essential in the artist.

Each ceremony of the tambaran cycle has as its core a specified tambaran with a definite name and a prescribed form. The form is traditional and highly valued because it is believed to be that used by the ancestors and therefore the most powerful in a supernatural sense. Abelam tambaran ceremonies appear to the casual attender to be secular occasions; the emphasis is all on the magnificence of the decorations, both of the objects and of the initiators, and the desire to create an impression on the visitors. The fathers of the initiates are watchful that all should be correct, but when they do complain it is on the grounds of value for the food and pigs they are providing rather than out of concern for the proper instruction of their children. In general, the initiates, the ostensible purpose of the ceremony, get scant attention, the parts of the ceremony that concern them are often rushed, and they are hustled off and told to wait until wanted again. In most ceremonies a few initiates get lost at some stage, either because they have run away or have simply wandered off; their fathers may protest, but the rituals continue without them and they are considered fully initiated, whether they were there or not, as long as the father has fulfilled his exchange obligations. Nor is there any sort of instruction of the initiates; they are told what to do but never why to do it. There are puberty initiations which involve seclusion and a certain amount of instruction of youths, but these are usually separate from the tambaran ceremonies and the instruction is not about these ceremonies.

The initiates have to observe some minor food taboos and a period of sexual abstinence before and after the ceremony, but it is on the initiators that the burden of the ritual restrictions falls. It is only during the preparations for a ceremony that the observer becomes aware of the magico-religious elements of the whole: elements that are represented during the ceremony by a brief invocation almost drowned by the noise of the

---

1. In view of the anomalous position of *wut* as an artistic production of both sexes, it is worth noting that for a man to use the words *nyan wut* in the presence of a woman is a formidable insult, certain to result in a quarrel, and possibly leading to a hostile exchange relationship with her protector, or even to a complex village-wide ceremony of cross-sex hostility.

audience, or the fumbling of the bewildered initiates as they try to perform some ritual actions of which they understand nothing. The supernatural benefit of the ceremony to the community, the other communities that assist, and the individuals concerned, accrues during the long and careful preparations, and the observance of a whole series of taboos and ritual performances by the initiators, some continuing for three months before and six months after the ceremony. All the artistic and other work of preparation is performed in the name of the *nggwalndu*, and their benevolence is assured, first by the performance of ritual and the observance of taboos, and second by the skill of the artists in creating the objects to which the *nggwalndu* names are given, and the magnificence of the ancillary *wut* and other decorations both of humans and objects. The magico-religious benefits of the ceremony may be released during the noisy and crowded public climax, but they are created by artists and organizers working in small groups during the preceding months behind sago palm frond fences which may not be passed by women, uninitiated men, or even initiated men of the other *ara*.

There is a clear necessity for artists in Abelam society. Every ritual group has to be able to draw on artists with the varied skills necessary to produce displays adequate to please the *nggwalndu* and other spirits, maintain the prestige of the groups vis-à-vis other ritual groups and villages, and keep up the ceremonial exchange system within the group. The *ara* dual organization and the exchanges between partners which provide the social framework for ceremony also act to restrict the availability of artists from within the group. Each ceremony is prepared by one *ara* for the other, and members of the initiates' *ara*, whether fully initiated or not, may not take any part in the preparations, or even see the raw materials used, until all is ready and displayed at the ceremony itself. Thus any artist, no matter how skilled, may only work on alternate ceremonies within his own ritual group. It is very rare for one *ara* of any ritual group to be able to supply all the necessary talent from its own ranks, and recruitment from outside is the rule.

Peace is anyhow necessary for the performance of a ceremony, but neutrality is not enough; active cooperation is necessary between enemy villages for any of the more elaborate ceremonies. Peace ceremonies involve the exchange of men of equal age and social status between villages; each pair so exchanged become *waunindu* and call each other brother, and it is through these relationships that help is mobilized. Usually the work is sub-contracted, that is, so many painted panels of specified sizes and so much patterned matting are prepared in the enemy village and ceremonially carried in when the whole job has been done. The party bringing such contributions appears as a war party in full war paint, preceded by a screen of spearmen. They cut down young trees and lop branches off bigger ones, destroy banana plants, and generally leave a trail of licensed destruction in their wake. As they approach the ceremonial ground the spearmen advance and throw spears at warriors from the recipient group. These warriors are especially selected for their ability to dodge; no reciprocation is allowed and casualties are said to occur—certainly on the occasions when I have been present, great skill in dodging was very necessary. The rest of the party throw armfuls of rubbish and the remains of the ruined breadfruit and banana trees into the doorways of the dwelling houses. The demands of hostility are then superseded by the demands of hospitality, and the visitors are stuffed with the finest soup and yams, and laden with yams and pork to take away with them; but uneasiness prevails on both sides until the visitors are safely on the way home, having promised to attend the final ceremony and a further and major food distribution after it.

Aid from friendly and allied villages is obtained in more informal ways, but again only by the activation of specific pre-existing interpersonal relationships. Help, whether for general labour or from a specific artist, can only be solicited through established relationships, and for a big ceremony every possible link, through kinship, clanship, and the various forms of quasi-brotherhood and exchange relationship, is utilized. From the point of view of the artist, the *ara* system means that although he may be debarred from half the ceremonies of his own ritual group, if he has any sort of reputation he will be in demand for the ceremonies of others, and his rewards are not only in the immediate return for his work in food, honour, and prestige, but in the activation of remote and otherwise dormant ties with men in other villages. Wide-spreading ties are of benefit to him in everyday life and enhance his prestige within his group. In short, a successful artist is sought after both within his ritual group and outside it, and if he can speak well in debate and grow reasonably long yams for presentation to his partner, he is assured of high prestige. An artist of considerable experience will often be called a big-man, but very rarely are artists big-men in the aggressive entrepreneurial sense —they are not leaders in secular affairs and manipulators of public opinion as are the real big-men. Although I am neither competent nor possessed of adequate systematic material to make any generalizations about the temperament of Abelam artists and big-men, my entirely subjective impression from acquaintance or friendship with several dozens of each is that the artists are nearly always comparatively modest men (no Abelam could be called modest *tout court!*), not given to violent expressions of emotion; their debating style tends to be quiet and authoritative but not excessively contro-versial, and they can usually expect a respectful and attentive hearing; the practice of their skills gives them general prestige and particu-larly a reputation for understanding and knowledge of the supernatural which invests their opinions with something of wisdom. These differences have some social concomitants; successful carving and painting are believed to be incompatible with the practice of sorcery, whereas the entrepreneur big-man is usually believed to be an adept at sorcery. Furthermore, the artist's reputation may be expected to grow until he is literally too weak to hold an adze or a paint brush, while the big-man is in con-stant danger of being displaced by more energetic rivals from the moment he achieves his position, and is virtually certain to have lost his position by late middle age. Whether it is due to an increased sense of security or a mani-festation of the artistic genius, artists, in my experience, claim fewer homicides, their adul-teries are more discreet, and they quarrel less flamboyantly with their wives and clansmen. In fact, the Abelam expect their artists to be good men (*yigen ndu*), and by and large the artists conform to those expectations.

THE MATERIALS AND TECHNIQUES OF ABELAM ART

Although the tambaran cult demands the use of many materials for its ceremonies, an artist's reputation is based primarily on his ability as a wood-carver and painter; skill in engraving on coconut shell, bone, and pottery is also highly valued, but is considered to go with ability as a carver, while the making of basketry masks, and shell decorated mannikins from string by a sort of crochet technique, are important, but much more widely distributed, skills. The traditional equipment for carving was thoroughly neolithic: polished stone adzes, pig, dog, and flying fox teeth mounted as awls, gravers, and chisels, certain lizard skins and even a rough-surfaced leaf for smoothing. Fire was used for hollowing out drums or the backs of large figures. Softwoods were used green and the splits that tended to occur were de-plored but disregarded unless they seriously distorted the figure. Current tools, although vastly improved by the use of steel, have hardly changed; the steel plane blades are mounted in exactly the same way, with the same angle between blade and handle as before. Indeed, some of the handles, beautifully carved, were originally made for stone blades and have been inherited from the preceding generation of artists. Cheap trade knives or large nails replace the teeth, but the method of mounting and use is traditional; sides of tins full of nail holes make a sort of rasp, but finishing work, now less necessary because of the superior edge of steel tools, is often done with the old materials. European adzes may be used for roughing out, but never for carving. The adze is always used with short rapid strokes towards the carver, removing only very small amounts of wood at each stroke. Modern carvers using four or five graded adzes often carve so finely that no further smoothing is needed. The backs of figures and masks are usually left rough, or hol-lowed out to reduce the weight, but in the case of pierced plaques and wood headdresses both sides are carved and engraved with equal care.

All Abelam carvings are painted in poly-chrome and engraving is often added round the eyes, penis, and navel so that the effect of the paint is enhanced by low relief.

Paint itself is highly valued by the Abelam, and almost all magic involves some form of coloured mineral substance that is classified as paint; a form of paint is also the active principle of sorcery and long yam magic. The paint used for tambaran ceremonies is not, unlike the other types, inherently powerful; it is obtained locally or in open trade, and large quantities are assembled, whereas the powerful paints are always obtained in small quantities in secrecy from distant villages. Red and yellow ochres and white and black are the only colors used, the first three being stored in the form of powders; the black, however, has to be made as required by chewing scrapings from the bottoms of cooking pots, sap from a species of shrub, and leaves from a tree, and spitting the result into a paintpot as needed. This rather unpleasant task is delegated to young assistants, and forms a part of the apprenticeship of the would-be artist.

Although the paint itself is not intrinsically powerful, painting is a sacred activity, and after the paint has been used on tambaran carvings, or *wut*, or on the initiators themselves, it becomes the principal vehicle by which the benefit of the ceremony is transmitted to the participants. Carving, although carried on in seclusion either in the bush or in an enclosure near the ceremonial house, is hardly a ritual activity; some artists have their own spells to stop the unseasoned wood splitting, but carving has no communal ritual connected with it. It is only when the artist has finished the carving and put in the eyes and pubic hair with a piece of charcoal that the figure becomes an object of concern to the whole ritual group. If the charcoaling is done in the village, the log gongs are beaten to announce the arrival of the tambaran. This call also serves to warn everybody that the final phase of preparations is about to begin. Stocks of paint are checked and augmented, and the final food distribution before the ceremony takes place. The work of painting is carried out under taboos similar to and almost as stringent as those of the long yam cult; men who are going to participate in the painting bleed their penes and must abstain from all sexual contact until after the ceremony; meat and certain vegetable foods are forbidden, but they can and do eat large quantities of the yam soup and finest steamed

yams provided by their exchange partners. Painting is done at great speed—usually all the workers sleep within the ceremonial enclosure and work from dawn till dusk with frequent but short breaks for food and betel nut. To begin with, any old figures that are being re-used have to be washed, and this is done in running water, the standard Abelam way of disposing of potentially dangerous material. Then both wood and the sago spathe *wut* have to be coated with the mud base on which the painting is done. A good deal of technical expertise is needed to get just the right sort of mud mixed to the right consistency, so that it will provide a smooth absorbent surface and adhere to the material. Sago spathe, which has a very shiny surface, is particularly difficult and is usually rubbed down before the mud is applied with stinging nettles and the bulb of a species of wild ginger (?), both substances which, in the Abelam view, bite and therefore improve the adhesion. The mud base used is black throughout the southern and eastern Abelam but grey in the north. On the grey mud, black has to be applied as a separate color, but with the black mud those portions of the design calling for black are usually left unpainted, simply being glazed with tree sap when the painting is finished

Abelam painting technique is extraordinary because it combines great speed with firm control by the artist. All the preparers of the ceremony join in the painting and all are found employment regardless of their lack of talent. The artist outlines the design to be painted in thin white lines. He may use lengths of split cane to help him work out the proportions of the design relative to the panel, or cane tied in rings to give him a guide for a smooth curve or circle; but he usually just starts from one edge and builds up the design as a series of elements as he works across the panel. With carved figures, artists usually start with the head, which is the most intricate part; the proportions are of course given by the form of the carving, but otherwise the techniques for figures and panels are identical. As soon as the artist has painted a few white lines for one part of the design, he instructs an assistant to paint a red or yellow line just beside it. Abelam art rarely uses a single line—multiple lines of varied colour, often further emphasized by white dots on one of the colours, are the rule. The artist now moves on to the next part of the design but keeps an eye on his first assistant. When the white lines have been satisfactorily doubled or trebled by the assistant or assistants, a second grade of assistant is employed to fill in solid areas of a single color: subordinate grades of assistant are employed to put on the lines of white dots and glaze the black mud with tree sap or chew up black paint if the painting is on grey. Other men will be employed powdering and mixing paints and coating objects and panels with mud. An artist at work on painting usually keeps from eight to ten men more or less busy while still maintaining complete control over the design and its execution.

The paints are mixed with water in which certain very bitter species of wild lime have been steeped; again the idea of bite is produced as an explanation. The containers are usually half coconut shells, but they must be lined with a portion of wild taro leaf; wild taro is an important plant in all Abelam ceremonial—intimately connected with the ancestors, it is also a symbol of the *ara* and their rivalry, and is much used in tambaran ceremonies. Brushes are made from fibres tied to the end of a splinter of wood; small feathers or the chewed end of a fibrous twig are similarly used. For the drawing of white lines a long narrow single chicken feather, made pliable by bending, is drawn along with about two inches of the feather flat on the surface. This technique, which properly used produces a narrow line but manages to keep a reasonable charge of paint on the brush, is employed with great boldness by experienced artists and enables them to draw the sweeping curves characteristic of Abelam design with speed and accuracy.[2]

Although supplies of mud base are kept handy

2. In the Wosera area, S.W. Abelam, a further type of brush is used, made of a single short feather, found between the tail plumes of the lesser bird of paradise, mounted in a grass stem. This will produce exceptionally fine lines, which are used mainly in polychrome cross-hatching. Bands of such cross-hatching are typically used to replace the polychrome multiple lines of the northern Abelam, and as an embellishment to certain other patterns otherwise common to both styles. The technique is laborious but aesthetically effective. Painting with these brushes cannot be delegated to the less skilled, and the number and size of the *wut* panels so painted were a sure index of prestige. Although painting with the fine line technique was visible on the façades of Wosera ceremonial houses, the means by which these results were produced was secret, the brushes themselves being regarded as a tambaran and very carefully concealed; they were called *vi* (spear) and were integrated into the spear/penis symbolic complex. Brushes elsewhere in the Abelam area are not specially regarded and are abandoned without concern.

in case of mistakes, artists rarely need it; they refer to no model or sketch and appear to lay out the whole design in their heads. When several artists are painting together, as happens during the painting of a ceremonial house façade, they share out the available width between them and each paints his own section of the bands of identical motifs that stretch across the façade. In such a case they agree in advance on the proportions and number each is going to paint; while working they watch one another's progress to ensure that the styles are reasonably matched and that the meeting of their respective zones will be harmonious, but there is nothing like copying involved; no artist who is not known to be capable of producing the required designs in isolation would be employed on a façade.

At the conclusion of the painting stage, when the display has been completed, the log gongs are beaten to announce the fact to the entire area, and the artists are honoured by having the log gong calls of their totems beaten immediately after the announcement. The initiation chamber is now sealed and final arrangements are made about facepaint, feathers, headdresses, and other decorations by the initiators, and about pigs by their exchange partners. The ceremony follows in three or four days.

THE ARTIST IN SOCIETY

Every initiated Abelam man aspires to be an artist in some way or other. All, in the context of the tambaran ceremonies, have a place in the process of artistic production. The amount of time they spend helping with the actual painting and carving, as opposed to the many other activities necessary in the preparation of ceremony, is largely a matter of choice. A rebuff to a middle-aged man for bad work from one of the directing artists can be expected to disillusion him with artistic activity for the rest of that ceremony, but younger men are less conscious of their dignity and stay and learn.[3] The training and selection of artists are completely informal. A youth who shows aptitude

3. Since the only two essential qualifications for initiation into a ceremony are that the initiate be alive and that the father or guardian be prepared to pay, babies are frequently initiated; it follows that youths of fifteen or so appear among the initiators.

will be encouraged and allowed to perform increasingly difficult tasks under supervision until he is allowed to try the painting of a minor figure and later a small *wut* panel for himself. The artist will correct and guide him, taking over now and then when difficulties occur. A young man will have to do all stages of the painting himself, unless a friend will help him, since the various grades of assistant are attracted only to artists of established prestige. A young man with interest in becoming an artist is not restricted to his own village for tuition, nor does he attach himself to one artist as an apprentice; he can of course attend all the ceremonial preparations in his own village for which he is qualified as an initiator, and assist and learn from all the artists who are at work there. He can also, through ties of kinship or clanship, help in ceremonies at allied villages or with contracted-out work which his own or allied villages are performing for enemy villages, always provided he has been initiated into the ceremony concerned. In this way a young man may well be able to work every year on some preparations or other, and come into contact with artists from villages five or more miles apart. Since considerable variation in style and type of production is to be found even in such short distances among the densely packed Abelam, a would-be artist will acquire a wider range and understanding of tambarans and their production than would be possible if he were confined to the set traditional to his natal village.

What has been said about training applies to the painting and constructional phases of ceremonial preparation; to obtain instruction in carving is more difficult, while a reputation as a carver is essential if an artist is to have prestige. Every Abelam male claims to be able to paint, and painting is a semi-sacred activity, the responsibility of personnel laid down by the social structure (particularly the system of initiation grades and the dual organization), performed at a prescribed time during the ceremonial preparations, preceded and closed by essential ritual, and governed by a series of taboos which apply to all the initiators whether in fact they paint or not. Carving, on the other hand, is a much more personal activity and not subject to the formal prescriptions of painting. All carving is undertaken either for the clan of the carver or as a commission from another clan or village, and except for the head board that goes across the base of the painted façade of a ceremonial house, a carving is the responsibility of a single artist. "Commission" does not imply a contract with a stated reward. Carvings are occasionally produced in return for a stipulated payment in shell rings and pigs, but usually only under exceptional circumstances for a major undertaking such as the carving of new *nggwalndu* when the village and its immediate allies lack sufficient talent, or in the introduction of new types of figure or tambaran where what is being bought is not just the carvings but also the right to display them and to reproduce them in the future. In general, however, carvers are recruited with the promise of no more than good food, as much betel and tobacco as they need, and, of course, the prestige that will accrue to them. All the work of preparation is divided up among the initiators according to their clans and sub-clans; each sub-clan owns its own figures and assumes responsibility for them as well as its share of the *wut* panels and other decorations. Large clans have one *nggwalndu* and are split into sub-clans divided between the *ara* so that there is always a group among the initiators to care for the *nggwalndu*; clans too small to have sub-clans have to form pairs, one in each *ara*, and look after two *nggwalndu* at any ceremony. It is the responsibility of the clan to provide the necessary artistic talent, and it is through the social relationships of individual clan members that the artists are recruited. In addition to the panels or figures necessary for the particular ceremony, each clan has minor figures, often unnamed, which it also includes in the display. Their number and beauty reflect the prestige of the clan, although in many cases they are so numerous that they have to be placed on top of one another and sometimes even obscure the tambarans that are the focus of the ceremony. A big-man would usually commission at least one minor figure at an important ceremony as a mark of his prestige. Such a new carving would become the property of his exchange partner at the end of the ceremony and exchanges; the exchange partner of course would provide all the food for the artist, and reciprocation would be expected at the next suitable opportunity.

A carver selects his timber on the land of the commissioning clan, and they cut it and drag it to his studio, also doing the cutting to size and other unskilled tasks. The studio may be on the ceremonial ground. If so, it will be away from other activities; more frequently it is in a secluded patch of bush near the artist's house; it will always be in the shade to minimize the risks of splitting. The artist does not welcome company or conversation, and spends a good deal of time sitting in silence and looking at his work—this is in great contrast to normal Abelam activity, and especially to painting, where speed, movement, and noise are predominant. An assistant is usually present, but some artists carve entirely alone; anyone else, such as the curious ethnographer, is regarded as a pest. Young men who cheerfully help in the painting do not always care to spend days in silence and inactivity doing occasional minor tasks, and it is only the minority who persist and start to acquire carving skills. These gradually undertake more and more skilled parts of the work until they try some small simple object themselves, showing it to the artist at each stage and relying on him to give the finishing touches. When such a piece is accepted for inclusion in a display the apprenticeship phase is coming to an end. It is here, in the carving and the acceptance of their work for display, that the relationship between the artist and his society can be seen most clearly.

From the view of the Abelam as a whole the tambaran cult and the art associated with the long yam cult are means of creating and releasing magico-religious power and benefit; the art is essential for the performance of ceremonial, and the artist is a technician whose chief virtue is his power to reproduce exactly the powerful patterns and designs used by the ancestors. The tambarans and their benefit are traditional; to be effective they must be re-creations of the original tambarans, and, furthermore, the fathers of the initiates are anxious to ensure that the ceremony they are paying for is full and correct. These are both forces opposed to innovation, but at the same time the ceremonies are opportunities for display and the acquisition of prestige by the village, ritual group, *ara*, clan, and individuals concerned; magnificence is consciously sought; magical bundles are fastened to the newly painted figures and carvings, not connected with the ritual but solely so that the eyes of the beholders shall be dazzled by the brightness of the paint and the beauty of the workmanship. Obviously this aspect of the ceremonial allows an element of fashion into the art, but since the benefits of the ceremony extend beyond the village, innovation that has not some good magico-religious justification or precedent will be subject to wide disapproval.

The Abelam artist works within fairly narrow stylistic limits sanctioned by the total society in which he lives; any work he produces cannot be shown outside the tambaran cult, and will only be accepted for that if it satisfies the criteria of magico-religious effectiveness. A young man of Malmba village who had found a growth on a tree that resembled in general shape the human head, had taken it home and carved on it eyes, nose, and mouth and painted it in the traditional style. When he produced it during the preparations for a ceremony at which he was an initiator, the organizers refused to display it or allow it in the ceremonial house; although the painting was in correct style, the shape of the head was nothing like any of the head shapes of tambaran figures. His plea that it was the shape of a human head carried no weight and he was forced to wrap it up and hide it in his hut until he sold it to me in 1959. In 1962, at Yanuko village a mile or so to the south, two artists painting the façade of a new ceremonial house introduced a very narrow band of stylized leaf decoration similar to a traditional form but with important differences. There was some doubt about it, and some of the older men were against it; the two artists and their helpers were adamant—they were both of high reputation and no alternative artists were available; in the event this innovation was much admired in the surrounding villages. The artists were courted by people from other villages who wished to be able to call on them for houses in the future, while the ritual group whose house it was, won more prestige than the other ritual group of Yanuko village whose new house, without any innovation, opened at much the same time.

A much more important example of innovation occurred at Wingei village in 1959. While a new house was under construction the organizers and the six artists involved decided to abandon the traditional style of façade-painting in favour of one that was used around Kalabu, a village about ten miles to the west; the reason for the change was the superior length of long yam grown in Kalabu. The experiment was not a great success—the bottom row of huge *nggwalndu* heads, which was the principal innovation, was badly painted, mainly because of the unaccustomed style. That Wingei changed the style of their ceremonial house façade to get longer yams, rather than change the planting season which is three months earlier in Kalabu, indicates the confidence the Abelam have in the power of art, and brings into focus the position of the artist who, if not exactly a mediator between man and the supernatural, is in contact with it and able to influence it through his skill as a carver and painter. The latter point is reinforced by the explanation offered for the bad painting: one of the artists died a week after the painting had been completed; the sorcery that killed him had obviously been working in him and prevented him and his fellows from correctly releasing the supernatural energy inherent in the design. Since this explanation was accepted even among traditional enemies of Wingei it was presumably sincerely believed and representative of Abelam thought on these matters.

The Abelam language has no vocabulary of aesthetics; there are two words of approbation used about art; one means "good" and can be used about almost anything; the other appears to mean primarily "correct", that is, traditional, powerful. Neither has any necessary connotations of beauty and I know of no word that has. The social demand for art is concerned with its magico-religious power. This is said to depend on the correct placing of the elements of any design with no prescription of a harmonious relation between them. Criticism of art is always in terms of correctness and effectiveness. Artists, particularly when carving, discuss among themselves such things as the shape and size of a limb and its relation to other parts of the figure, but these things are not appreciated by the non-artist. I have heard carvers reproached for holding up the beginning of the painting by fiddling about, taking a piece off here and there, when the figure already had all the necessary attributes, legs, penis, navel,

arms, and head. The artists, although they lack any specific terms, do talk about such things as form and proportion, and derive considerable pleasure from carving and painting things satisfying to their aesthetic sense. They carefully examine and discuss works by other artists and rate one another as more or less talented by criteria that are primarily aesthetic. Although not capable of, or not interested in, discussing art in the same terms, most non-artists asked to rate a group of figures or paintings in order of effectiveness, both in ritual power and secular prestige, rank them in the same order as do the artists and the ethnographer. Since, with Raymond Firth, I believe in a universal human aesthetic, this is not surprising; what is important, I think, is that the skilful artist who satisfies his aesthetic sense and produces beauty is rewarded not for the beauty itself but because the beauty, although not recognized as such, is regarded by the rest as power.

Apart from conscious innovation seen as such by the whole community, there also occurs a gradual change in style which is much more difficult to document. Several villages possess very old *nggwalndu*, and at least two villages have a series of *nggwalndu* obviously made at various dates. How far back these specimens go it is difficult to say, but genealogical information about their carvers suggests that the oldest might be eighty to a hundred years old. These old figures invariably show a different style from that of the present; those in series show a consistent change in style, the development of the recent style from the antecedent one. The differences are much greater than could be attributable to a change from stone tools to steel—there are definitely changes in the way the human form has been conceived over the period. This situation leads to some difficulties, since the present style is the correct style, that is the ancestral style, yet it is different from the style in which the old *nggwalndu* were actually carved by the ancestors. When such *nggwalndu* are washed and repainted, as they are for the final ceremony of each tambaran cycle, the current style of painting does not fit happily on the old style of carving; the surfaces and their relationship to each other are different and the painted designs sit uncomfortably on forms intended for different designs. While the painting is going on such difficulties are recognized. Normally, however, the stylistic difference does not worry anyone; it is simply ignored; only when the impertinent ethnographer holding an artist firmly by the wrist has pointed out all the differences, will he admit their existence; otherwise, the insistence is firm on all sides that the present style is the ancestral style. In discussion with me, artists have speculated on the change in style, wondering whether their style or the old style is the right one, ending by saying that anyhow they know how to carve only in their present style and could not recreate the old style if they wanted to. It is interesting to note in passing that the older figures invariably have much more definite sculptural form—the features are boldly carved and in general they do not seem to be merely pleasant surfaces for painting as much of the present Abelam carving is. Their forms, though varied, are often more reminiscent of the Iatmül styles of the Middle Sepik to the south. It seems possible that the very high development of polychrome painting so much admired among the Abelam may have resulted in the declining interest in sculptural form evident in the figure sequences. With its conscious desire for ostentation and display it has to be confessed that some Abelam sculpture tends to be rather vulgar by European standards.

This gradual stylistic change makes it obvious that whatever they believe, Abelam artists do not slavishly reproduce the work of their predecessors. It would be surprising if they did since, as already mentioned, they never copy one another or any model. A famous artist of Kalabu, asked by a village across a dialect boundary to produce a type of figure that was used in their ceremonies but not at Kalabu, was given a 2-foot-high carving to work from. This he studied but kept in his house, never taking it to his bush studio until the 10-foot carving was finished, when he satisfied himself that he had done it correctly. As everything an artist produces comes from his picture of what the object required should look like, every artist must to some extent impose his own vision of a "good" piece on the work in hand.

The artist is free to express himself within the stylistic limits prevailing at the time, and by so doing may marginally change those limits. There is of course a feedback here; the society may impose stylistic limits on what is acceptable for a tambaran ceremony and so control the artist, but the artist creates all the art and therefore forms the society's conceptions of what is acceptable. In such a situation gradual change is probably inevitable. It offers the artist self-expression, and keeps the art vital and capable of expressing the changing values of the society, while at the same time ensuring that it can continue to fulfil its main function of being the traditional and powerful mode of access to the supernatural. I have argued elsewhere that Abelam art is intimately connected with the values of Abelam society, and that it makes statements about Abelam society that are not made by other means. If this is so the artist must be the essential link. Up till now the contact with the Australian administration and the missions has not affected the art in style or content. The war and its aftermath virtually stopped artistic activity, but it has been taken up again, at least in the north, with great vigour. This revival has coincided with, and been a symbol of, a withdrawal from excessive contact with European values and a reaffirmation of traditional values. In fact up to now, the art, far from changing, has been reinforced in its conservatism by taking on the additional value of acting as a symbol of Abelam culture in the face of colonial culture.

35. THE REVOLUTION IN PAINTING

DIEGO RIVERA

From Creative Art, *IV, pp. 28-30, 1929, published by Albert and Charles Boni Company. Reprinted with permission of the American Federation of Arts. Diego Rivera studied in Spain, France, and Italy from 1910 to 1921. Though he worked for a time in the cubist tradition, his later fresco style, taking Mexican revolutionary history as its subject matter, came to be regarded as characteristic of Mexico. Throughout his life, Rivera's involvement in Mexican and world politics has been expressed in his art.*

■ A corollary of the commingling of art with religion and social and political relationships is its public nature; whether the art object is regarded as a tool or in purely aesthetic terms—neither of which, as we have seen, is valid without the other— it is not confined to a particular group in hunter-gatherers and horticultural societies; it is shared by all. The association of art with wealth and social and political privilege seems to have begun in the middle of the 13th century in Germany (an agricultural society) and accelerated in Renaissance Italy, where, embedded in patron-client relationships, it took on even more the patina of political and economic elitism.

The elite nature of the "high" artistic tradition has continued to the present day, and it cannot be understood outside the framework of group differences and social stratification in a complex society —but art cannot be viewed only as a force for the objectification of tradition and the status quo. Looked at in an evolutionary and historical framework, it is noteworthy that every major change in Western art coincided with far-reaching changes in the economic and political order of society. Adaptative institutional changes in complex societies are generally brought about by—or first established among—their advantaged groups. An important aspect of this, as we have seen, is that revolutionary ideologies first develop among such groups early in the transitions to new stages of adaptation. At the same time, it is the advantaged groups who support artists, whether by direct patronage or by purchase of their creative work.

By virtue of its association with privileged status, art is an instrument of change in the ideological armamentarium of a modern complex society, and we see an example of this in the following selection. This is a short statement by Diego Rivera, one of the great artists of Mexico, who regarded his painting in terms of his revolutionary ideology. Though in part a recitation of trite Marxist dogma and a serving of stale Stalinist omelet, it is nonetheless an excellent exposition of the role of art in a changing social order. Incidentally, although Rivera did not have to depend on wealthy purchasers and patrons for his livelihood, the Mexican revolutionary groups that subsidized his work were themselves financed by members of the Mexican elite. This statement was made by Rivera in 1929.

The debate between the proponents of "pure art" and "revolutionary art" was heated in the 1920s and 1930s, and most of the statements— like this one—are encrusted with dogma that makes them difficult to read today. But the issues involved are interesting and important and deserve the reader's further attention. Perhaps the best general statements of the Marxist view of the relation of art and society are to be found in G. V. Plekhanov's *Essays on the History of Materialism* (New York: Fertig, 1967) and Christopher Candwell's *Illusion and Reality: A Study of the Sources of Poetry* (London: Macmillan, 1937). Opposing points of view are perhaps best represented by the work of F. R. Leavis; see especially his *The Common Pursuit* (London: Chatto, 1952); *The Great Tradition* (Garden City, N.Y.: Doubleday, 1954); *Mass Civilization and Minority Culture* (Cambridge, England: Minority Press, 1930); and *Two Cultures? The Significance of C. P. Snow* (New York: Pantheon Books, 1963). ■

ART AND THE PROLETARIAT

January, 1929

A FEW YEARS AGO before the Great War, I often discussed the role which art would assume once the power of the State was in the hands of the working class. After the Mexican Revolution, my revolutionary confrères—then living in Paris—thought that if they gave modern art

451

of the highest quality to the masses this art would immediately become popular through its instant acceptance by the proletariat. I was never able to share this point of view, because I always knew that the physical senses are susceptible not only to education and development, but to atrophy and desuetude; and also that the "aesthetic sense" can only be reached through the physical senses themselves. I had also observed the indubitable fact that among the proletariat—exploited and oppressed by the bourgeoisie—the workman, ever burdened with his daily labor, could cultivate his taste only in contact with the worst and the vilest portion of bourgeois art which reached him in cheap chromos and the illustrated papers. And this bad taste in turn stamps all of the industrial production which his salary commands—public expositions being difficult of access for him because he is at work day in and day out.

Popular art produced by the people for the people has been almost wiped out by this kind of industrial production of the worst aesthetic quality throughout the world. And I also believed that a popular peasant art could not achieve an effective substitute in modern industrial production of fabrics, utensils, illustrated books, and so forth.

ART AS A SOCIAL INSTRUMENT

Only the work of art itself can raise the standard of taste. Art has always been employed by the different social classes who hold the balance of power as one instrument of domination—hence, as a political instrument. One can analyze epoch after epoch—from the stone age to our own day—and see that there is no form of art which does not also play an essential political role. For that reason, whenever a people have revolted in search of their fundamental rights, they have always produced revolutionary artists: Giotto and his pupils, Gruenewald, Bosch, Breughel the elder, Michelangelo, Rembrandt, Tintoretto, Callot, Chardin, Goya, Courbet, Daumier, the Mexican engraver Posadas, and numerous other masters.

What is it then that we really need? An art extremely pure, precise, profoundly human and clarified as to its purpose.

An art with revolution as its subject: because the principal interest in the worker's life has to be touched first. It is necessary that he find aesthetic satisfaction and the highest pleasure appareled in the essential interest of his life.

REVOLUTIONARY ART

I have therefore arrived at the clearest and firmest conviction that it is necessary to create that kind of art. Is it necessary therefore to discard all our ultra-modern technical means, necessary to deny the classic tradition of our métier? Not at all. It would have been as foolish to believe that in order to construct a grain elevator, a bridge, or to install a communal cooperative, one should not use the materials and methods of construction achieved by the industrial technique of the bourgeoisie. It is on the contrary the duty of the revolutionary artist to employ his ultra-modern technique and to allow his classic education (if he had one) to affect him subconsciously. And there is absolutely no reason to be frightened because the subject is so essential. On the contrary, precisely because the subject is admitted as a prime necessity, the artist is absolutely free to create a thoroughly plastic form of art. The subject is to the painter what the rails are to a locomotive. He cannot do without it. In fact, when he refuses to seek or accept a subject, his own plastic methods and his own aesthetic theories become his subject instead. And even if he escapes them, he himself becomes the subject of his work. He becomes nothing but an illustrator of his own state of mind, and in trying to liberate himself he falls into the worst form of slavery. That is the cause of all the boredom which emanates from so many of the large expositions of modern art, a fact testified to again and again by the most different temperaments. That is the deception practiced under the name of "Pure Art", two new resounding words which attest to nothing more in the work of talented men.

36. THE PROCESS OF DISENCHANTMENT: MAGICAL AND DISENCHANTED MORAL LOGIC

ROSALIE H. WAX

Reprinted by permission of the publisher from Rosalie H. Wax, Magic, Fate and History: The Changing Ethos of the Vikings, *pp. 127-143. Copyright 1969, Coronado Press. Rosalie H. Wax has a continuing interest in cultural history and the transformation of cultural patterns. She has especially devoted herself to studies of ethos and worldview and in addition to the book from which this excerpt has been selected, she has published a number of essays in this field with her husband (Murray L. Wax). Her field researches were conducted in the Japanese-American Relocation Centers and among American Indian communities; these furnish much of the materials for her book on field methods to be published by the University of Chicago Press in 1971.*

■ We have seen that people's images of themselves are colored and shaped by the kind of relationship they maintain with their habitat. Built into each man's self-image is his group's systematized way of thinking of the cosmos, and these are as inevitably reflected in the group's artistic productions as in their religious and secular values. Sometimes this reflection is tenuous, in what to outsiders may seem to be arbitrarily defined categories; sometimes—as in myths and folk tales—views of the cosmos are quite explicit. Such reflections help us to understand people's perceptions of themselves and the imperatives of their social systems, especially during periods of change. In the following selection we consider an example of such a set of ideas in the sagas of the Vikings.

Myths and tales are among the symbolic means by which the members of a group express their shared participation in a way of life, whether it is that of an isolated, preliterate community or of a socioeconomic class in a complex society. Myths simultaneously reflect and reinforce the deepest assumptions about how the world is and should be ordered and about the rewards and punishments that stem from appropriate and inappropriate behavior. Inevitably, there are close links between a group's level of development and its world view. Among preagricultural people, all objects in the universe exist interdependently, not separately and side-by-side as among us. All objects, including man, are part of a single design, each influencing the others, and often the force governing this design—what Wax calls the Vital Power—is placed in the realm of the deities. In some pre-

agricultural societies, the universe is seen as in such delicate balance that the individual is enjoined not to disturb its wholeness, and there are many taboos against interfering with nature; such concepts are especially useful in explaining people's relationship to their strategies of adaptation. Myths and folklore are thus important vehicles for the study of sociotechnological systems.

Viking society was a gusty system in which many people alternated between farming and raiding or trading expeditions; for some, raiding and long distance exploration were full-time occupations, and at times they made our own frontiersmen look sedate. Viking raids covered all of Europe, and they appear to have taken place within well-developed political systems; Sweden, for instance, had a well-established monarchy before long-distance raids began in earnest in the 10th and 11th centuries.

The imperatives of Viking agriculture and raiding are clearly mirrored in their sagas, as Wax shows. One of their major themes is self-reliance; another, which we have seen to be general among agricultural societies, is a strong reliance on the deities and the fatalism which this reliance engenders. Their literature also reflects the transition from an agricultural society to one based on distant war, trade, and foreign settlement. Here we see a world view that is in between the social order associated with an agricultural system—including obligations of community and kin—and the individualistic amoralism of armed raids and territorial aggrandizement. As Wax observes elsewhere in the book from which this selection is taken, Viking literature "reflects a hard-headed materialistic individualism—a self interest that is shrewd, down-to-earth, and pragmatic. The gods are often depicted as masters of expediential trickery. The law is stated so that its enforcement rests on man's inclination to guard his own interests" (p. 89).

A good introduction to these exciting people is *The Vikings*, by Johannes Brøndsted (Harmondsworth, Middlesex, England : Penguin Books, 1965). The reader who wants to get a broader introduction to the anthropology of myth and folklore can find a variety of approaches in *The Study of Folklore*, edited by Alan Dundes (Englewood Cliffs, N.J. : Prentice-Hall, 1965) ; *The Anthropologist Looks at Myth*, compiled by Melville Jacobs and edited by John Greenway (Austin : University of Texas Press, 1966). *Studies on Mythology*, edited by Robert A. Georges (Homewood, Ill. : The Dorsey Press, 1968) and *Myth : Its Meaning and Functions in Ancient and Other Cultures*, by G. S. Kirk (Berkeley : University of California Press, 1970). For an approach to the analysis of literature based on concepts of class-conflict, see *The Concept of Freedom* (London : Lawrence and Wishart, 1965), by Christopher Caudwell (Christopher St. John Sprigg). For a fusion of several of these approaches to folklore in a contemporary setting, see *Deep Down in the Jungle : Negro Narrative Folklore from the Streets of Philadelphia*, by Roger D. Abrahams (Chicago : Aldine, 1970). ■

THE PROBLEM

IN THE MAGICAL world, the man who accomplishes deeds of worth and grandeur is able to do so because of his Vital Power. Thus, in ancient Scandinavian society, if a man's family were hale, his trading or raiding ventures successful, and his party triumphant and unscathed amid storms and battles, then surely he possessed Power. Such Power might issue either through his fortunate relationship with a potent Being—as when Víga-Glúm's good fortune depended on keeping the cloak, sword, and spear given him by his grandfather—or it might issue from his own innate nature—as when the saga writer traces Egil Skallagrímsson's more than human talent, strength, and ferocity to his giant or etin ancestors. In any event, he had *gipta*, *gaefa*, or *hamingja*. Conversely, if nothing of his turned out particularly

well, then he had no such relationship and no such Power; while if he were really unlucky, then wittingly or unwittingly, he had done some dangerous or ill advised deed—he had offended some being who was paying him back by withdrawing his favor or using sorcery against him.

Life, health, and well-being in the magical world are inextricably related to virtuous or correct behavior. The wise person does not even uproot a flower without taking proper moral (or social) precautions.

In the hole from which the root was withdrawn a pinch of tobacco was left. Often a knife or some money was left there also, and the taker of the root uttered a brief prayer, "I have taken what you have given, and I am leaving this here for you. I want to lead a long life and to have no harm strike me or my family."

If we translate this philosophy into terms more familiar to us, we may say that in the magical world, every grave mishap is perceived as having a specific cause, which very often is proved to have been an ill intentioned or careless deed. The man who is switten with woe may have offended someone, intentionally or unintentionally. Perhaps, if nothing else, his prior prosperity and health aroused the enmity or greed of others. Contrariwise, the man who is blessed above all others has offended no one. He has done all the "right" things and none of the "wrong". Or again, an individual who suffers mishap, illness, or death may have been exposed to the malevolence of an innately destructive or dangerous being, just as the extremely fortunate or lucky man may have been exposed to the health and power infusing influences of an innately benevolent being. Because of this causal emphasis, the tales told by peoples who live by the precepts of the magical world tend to be etiological, which is to say that, primarily, they explain why good or evil things happen to particular persons or peoples.

This magical perspective, as outlined above, dominates a good part of the early Old Scandinavian literature. Appearing in the myths and in some of the Eddic poems, it shows itself later, in occasional incidents, in the sagas. For example, in *The Lay of Grotti*, King Fródi meets a terrible fate because he mistreated his giant thralls; in *The Lay of Völund* King Níðoð loses his sons because he enslaved and abused the magically gifted hero. Similarly, in *Ynglinga saga*, King Vanlandi dies because he was not permitted to return to his witch-wife and King Vísbur because he refused to give his sons their inheritance. Kormák the skald, who lived in the tenth century, refused to compensate a witch for the death of her sons; thereupon she laid a spell upon him so that he was never able to possess his beloved.

By the thirteenth century, a distinctly different perspective and moral philosophy was being manifested in the literature of the classic sagas. These seem to exhibit what may be termed an eschatological point of view in that the sagas focus not on a cause or explanation of misfortune but on the long and intricately linked series of events which lead to a predetermined apocalyptic resolution, usually the death of the hero. He is portrayed as a man of excellence and honor, and his death confronts the audience with a moral paradox, namely that the reward of virtue may be misfortune and defeat. The Norse hero is no Job, and his demise is usually an act of vengeance which he himself had helped to provoke, but the moral issue is as clear as the Book of Job:

One of the most disturbing experiences of the old saga writers appears to have been the recognition that worthy men, too, must endure suffering and defeat—merely because they lack a sufficient measure of "good fortune."
Great gifts and ill fortune go hand in hand . . . everything is constantly shifting. . . . And in the midst of the general dissolution we still find individual men of remarkable integrity and blamelessness. And—lest the drama should point too simple a moral—these men fare not a whit better than the others—but not a whit worse either.

The difference between the magical point of view and the saga writers is profound; within the former view all of the crucial phenomena of man's experience are morally and socially explicable, while within the latter the coherence is troubled by rationalistic disenchantment. In this chapter it will be my task to describe some aspects of the change from one to the other. So far as I have been able to determine, the first literary manifestation of the change appears in some of the early heroic lays (*c.* 600–800). Here, and in the subsequent literature, it is associated both with a change in the conceptions of fate and of the nature of man—or of the "self." The point of view of Snorri

Sturluson or others of the sophisticated saga writers probably represents an extreme or ultimate aspect of the process, as it was reflected in the writings of an elite class of men who were acutely aware that their way of life had undergone marked changes and that their values were increasingly out of tune with each other.

THE CONFLICTING MORAL IMPERATIVE OF THE HEROIC LITERATURE

Some of the oldest poems in the Old Scandinavian literature are based on situations which rarely, if ever, appear in mythological or magical stories: the hero is placed by fate in a situation where he must choose between defending his personal honor or slaying someone near to him, either his blood kin or his beloved. Thus, in an ancient Gothic lay, Hiltibrant is obliged to slay his son, while in a later Scandinavian variant, he must go into battle and be slain by his half-brother. Brynhild must kill the hero Sigurð, whom she loves, because Sigurð pledged her his love and then married another woman. Guðrún is obliged to kill her children and her husband because her husband slew her brothers. Starkaðr is "fated to kill the chief and friend who has trusted him."

In some of the heroic lays the hero (or heroine) laments his (or her) woes and tells us, either at the beginning or end of his discourse, that his sad lot was brought about by fate or by evil norns. In other poems, like *The Lay of Atli*, we are shown by the narrative and by the words of the characters how fate has made inevitable the series of disasters.

So that the reader may gain some notion of these lays, here is a synopsis of one based on a legend which is very old—perhaps fifth century. As recorded in the Edda, *The Lay of Atli* may itself date from the ninth century.

Gunnar, King of the Gjúkungs, and his brother Högni possess the great gold hoard of the Niflungs. Atli, King of the Huns, invites Gunnar and his court to visit him. Atli and Gunnar are brothers-in-law, Atli being wedded to Gunnar's sister, Guðrún. When the invitation is presented, Gunnar turns to his brother for advice. Högni advises against the journey, pointing out that Guðrún, their sister, has sent them a warning token by the Hunnish messengers, a ring wound with wolf's hair. For reasons not made clear (experts think certain stanzas are lost), Gunnar ignores Högni's advice and the brothers set out for Atli's court. When they arrive, Gudrún begs them to flee, but Gunnar says that it is too late. Thereupon, Gunnar and

The Saga of Gísli:

Gísli Sursson, an uncle of Snorri godi, lived in the third quarter of the tenth century. The earlier of the two sagas about him may have been written in the latter part of the twelfth century.

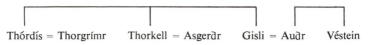

Thórdís = Thorgrímr   Thorkell = Asgerdr   Gisli = Audr   Véstein

Högni are captured, though Högni defends his brother most valiantly, slaying seven men with the sword and throwing another into the hearth fire. Atli now demands that Gunnar give him the Niflung hoard or die. Gunnar says that he will reveal the hiding place of the treasure only if his brother Högni's heart is laid in his hand. The Huns first cut out the heart of a thrall, but Gunnar is not deceived, because, he says, only a thrall's heart would beat so much. The Huns then cut out Högni's heart, whereupon Gunnar tells Atli that now only he knows the secret of the hoard and he will not tell. Atli then has Gunnar thrown into a serpent pit, where he holds off the serpents for a time by playing the harp. When Atli returns to his hall he is met by his wife, Gudrún, who offers him young game to eat. After the Huns have eaten, Gudrún announces that to avenge her brothers she has slain her two sons by Atli and that this is the meat they have eaten. That night she kills Atli in their bed and, after warning the housecarls and freeing the dogs so that they may escape, she sets fire to the hall, burning up the dead Atli and his sleeping men.

Like the lays, some of the sagas show how fate relentlessly pursues its ends by placing individuals in situations where honor demands that they do something dreadful to their relatives or neighbors. The deeds committed in the name of honor are usually not so extreme in the sagas as in the lays: no mother kills and cooks her own children, no wife slays her husband with her own hand (though Hallgerdr stands by and lets her husband be killed because he had once slapped her). The sagas also differ from the lays in the painstaking and explicit manner in which they reveal the influence of fate in every chronological step of the action.

The saga begins in Norway and introduces us to three siblings: Thórdís, the handsome and wilfull sister, who takes her fun where she can find it; Thorkell, the elder brother, who is easy-going and inclined to make friends outside of the family; and Gísli, who is ruthless and zealous in defending family honor. Before the family leaves Norway for Iceland, Gísli has killed three of Thórdís' suitors and two of Thorkell's friends, always for reasons compatible with his code of honor.

In Iceland the three siblings and their spouses settle in the same district and are joined by Véstein, the brother of Audr, Gísli's wife. Gísli hears that a man has predicted that this powerful family group will be at odds within three years. Thereupon he suggests that he, Véstein, Thorkell, and Thorgrímr, swear an oath of blood brotherhood. But the men qualify their oaths so that Thorgrímr is not bound by an oath to Véstein and Gísli is not bound by oath to Thorgrímr. Gísli remarks that he thinks that fate will have its way in this matter.

Subsequently, Audr (Gísli's wife) makes an unguarded remark which reveals that Asgerdr (Thorkell's wife) is having an affair with Véstein. This remark is overheard by Thorkell. Thorkell now asks for a division of property, leaves Gísli's homestead, and goes to live with Thórdís and Thorgrímr. Audr tells Gísli about her unlucky words and asks him not to be angry with her. But he does not blame her, saying: "Fate's words will be spoken by someone."

Véstein having gone abroad, Gísli does all that he can to keep him from returning to the district. But fate thwarts Gísli's efforts: Véstein returns and is slain by Thorgrímr (egged on by his brother-in-law, Thorkell). Audr tells a thrall to take the weapon out of her brother's corpse, but the thrall is afraid. Then Gísli comes in and removes the weapon which (so the saga writer asserts) obligates him to take vengeance.

Subsequently Thorgrímr reveals to Gísli that he is the slayer. Now it is Thorkell who tries to stop the progress of fate by counseling peacefulness, but his friend Thorgrímr will not listen to him and once again insults Gísli by demanding that Gísli send him some tapestries that belonged to Véstein. Gísli sends the tapestries but asks the carrier to slide back the bolts of Thorgrímr's house on that night. Then Gísli takes the spear which slew Véstein and, in the dark of night, he kills Thorgrímr, even though he is lying in bed with his wife, Gísli's sister. Gísli also leaves the weapon in the wound.

Gísli's sister, Thórdís, now marries her slain husband's brother and proceeds to egg him on to vengeance. The matter is taken to the Thing and Gísli is declared an outlaw. Gísli tries several times to get his relatives and other chieftains to arrange a settlement, but matters always turn out badly for him. This, the saga ascribes to witchcraft, for Gísli had killed a sorcerer who had laid a curse on him—so that no man on the main island would help him. An isolated, hunted man, he flees from hiding place to hiding place. His dreams are haunted by two supernatural women, one gentle and the other bloodthirsty, but neither of these dream creatures helps him. And when his dream women tell him that his time has come, he proceeds to his doom without hesitation, defending himself against fifteen adversaries. Even when his entrails fall out, he ties them up in his kirtle and kills a man with his last blow. So valiant is his defense that the characteristically restrained Icelandic saga writer goes so far as to remark: "And it is everywhere agreed that never in this country has one man put up a more famous defense, so far as such things can be known for certain."

Gísli's wife, who is portrayed as a loyal and honorable woman, does not urge her husband to avenge her slain brother, though by ancient custom a woman's primary loyalties were to her blood kin. After Gísli's death she goes to Rome to end her days. Thórdís, Gísli's sister, first encourages her second husband to kill Gísli; then, when Gísli has been slain, she tries to kill her husband's cousin, the man who led the party that slew her brother. Véstein's young sons kill Thorkell.

Njál's Saga:

The events on which this saga is based occurred shortly after the turn of the eleventh century. The saga about Njál is relatively late—around 1300.

Njál's saga is even more complicated than Gísli's. First it tells, step by step, how Gunnar, an honorable but not very astute man and a loyal friend to Njál, is brought to his doom because of his own impulsive acts and because he follows the well-intentioned and just advice of Njál. Next it tells how the Christian Njál—wise, restrained, and respectful of the law—pursues a path that inexorably brings about his death and the death of most of his kin. Then it tells how Kári, the blood-brother of Skarpedin, one of Njál's sons, takes vengeance.

Njál's sons are contentious and jealous of their honor and they make many enemies. When the relatives of the men they have slain approach Njál's homestead, the sons wish to stand outside and fight—and the saga makes it clear that, had they done so, their adversaries might not have attacked. But Njál tells them to go into the buildings, pointing out how well Gunnar defended himself against a great number of men. Skarpedin retorts that the men who attacked Gunnar were of "noble mind" whereas the men they are facing are likely to set the house on fire. But Njál has his way. The avengers fire the house and their leader, who does not want to kill Njál, offers the old man permission to leave. But Njál answers in the words of a man of honor, saying, "I will not come out, for I am an old man and little fit to avenge my sons, and I do not want to live in shame." The avengers then ask his wife to come out, but she says, "As a young woman I was married to Njál and vowed that one fate should befall us both." She then notices her little grandson and tells him that he is to go out of the house. But the boy says, "You promised me grandmother, that we two should never part, and that's the way I want it to be." The grandmother says not a word; she picks the boy up and carries him to the bed to die with herself and her husband.

THE EMERGENCE OF MAN AS INDIVIDUAL

In magical or mythological literatures man, as an individual or character, often plays a petty role; sometimes he does not appear at all. Most of the important actors are Beings who demonstrate their nature and Power by doing wonderful deeds. When humans are introduced they are usually featureless young men who cannot be distinguished from each other by any of the aesthetic criteria of a sophisticated society. Judged aesthetically, the heroes of most American Indian "hero tales" are monotonously alike, the narrators rarely mention whether the hero is brave or cowardly, tall or short, clever or stupid—since, from their point of view, these individualistic aspects of personality or character are not worthy of comment. What is important is that the young hero establish a proper and advantageous relationship with some Being, thereby gaining Vital Power which he will use to help himself and his relatives.

Old Scandinavian mythology retains some of this magical indifference to individuality or personality. The gods are Beings with idiosyncratic Powers rather than strong, resolute, or peculiar characters. Specifically human beings or individuals rarely appear and the gods are not always anthropomorphic: Óðin, for example, is not so much a "human" character or personality as a Great Being who may assume the shape of a serpent or eagle as easily as that of a man. Similarly, the warriors in *The First Lay of Helgi the Hunding-Slayer* are not individual characters, but men who are acting so much like proper warriors that without labels one cannot be told from the other.

An entirely different phenomenon appears in *The Lay of Völund, The Second Lay of Helgi the Hunding-Slayer, The Lay of Atli,* and even more dramatically, in the sagas. Here, as Hollander remarks, there are true characters "limned with a few bold strokes" who "stand before us indelibly." Völund, Sigurð, Gunnar, Guðrún, and Brynhild are distinct personalities, not by reason of their particular magical Power or their particular position in a society, but because they feel and behave differently in the face of similar crises or dilemmas. It is the intense interest of the poet in the particular pattern of response of his hero (or heroine)—a pattern expressing the personal sense of honor of a distinct individual—that sharply distinguishes these lays and sagas from the Power-oriented myths, the ritual dramas, and the deed-encrusted eulogies of the skalds. An obvious but fine example is the account of the burning of Njál. Every person who dies, warrior, old man, woman, or child, meets death bravely. But each meets it in his own way.

It is probably no accident that the literary works in which these genuine and unforgettable human characters appear pay scant attention to gods, giants, dragons, and other remarkable Beings. They may be referred to by the human actors, but they no longer show their faces or speak lines.

SELF-RELIANCE AND RESOLUTION

Another peculiarly sophisticated aspect of the "character structure" of the heroes is their self-reliance and their unfaltering resolution. In a thoroughly magical literature, a hero almost never does any remarkable or virtuous act by himself. Indeed, the more remarkable the deed, the more certain would be its observers that it had been accomplished through the aid of Powerful Beings. While the *Iliad* is by no means a simple tribal tale, it has retained this particular aspect of the magical world view, for the poet is always careful to point out that any noteworthy deed was accomplished through divine possession or coaching.

In marked and even striking contrast, the heroes of the dilemma-oriented lays and sagas of Old Scandinavia tend to keep their own counsel, act for themselves, and take the consequences. Gísli is an outstanding example. He makes all of his decisions for himself. No one shelters him but his wife, a bondmaid, and an impoverished cotter. When he asks his brother for aid he is told, "A man is his own company for most of the way." At the end of the saga he stands and dies "bereft and robbed of everything but his innate worth and ability." This type of hero would not make sense to persons thoroughly immersed in the enchanted world view.

It is the singular self-reliance and resolution

of these human beings that makes many of the death scenes described in the sagas so moving. When they know that they are to die, they look for support to no one but themselves. Having made a resolve, they see it through to the end; or, if, as warriors, they have taken a stand, they fight with all their might and main. There was no higher praise than this: "His attackers said that he never gave ground, and they could not see that his last blow was weaker than his first."

FATE IN THE MAGICAL WORLD

In that part of the ancient heathen literature which does not emphasize moral dilemmas, a man's fate, doom, or lot is usually bound up with or determined by one or more remarkable Beings. There are the birth-norns or *dísir* (female beings of Power) who may appear at the birth of a child and "spin out his fate," granting him gifts both useful and otherwise. There is a story in Saxo Grammaticus about a Danish king who took his three-year-old son "to pray to three maidens in the temple," whereupon the first two gave him charm and generosity but the last decreed that he should be niggardly in giving gifts. We are told that the heathen held feasts in the winter to honor the dísir, but whether these particular female beings were honored because they controlled men's fate or for other reasons, we do not know.

There are beings called *fulgjur* (sing. *fylgja*— "guardian spirit, attendant"), who attach themselves to certain individuals or families and are intimately related with their fate. Sometimes a man's fylgja may warn him of danger and save his life. But when he sees his fylgja leaving him he knows that his luck is gone or that he is about to die. There are also female beings who control the fate and fortune of warriors in battle; these are called Valkyries (corpse-choosers), or again, not very helpfully, dísir or battle-norns. Moreover, like the birth-norns, these choosers weave the spells that protect their favorites and doom those who are to be slain. One of the most fearful of the Eddic poems pictures the battle maidens as weaving a web of men's entrails with blood-spattered spears as treadles and men's heads as weights. By this spell they doom certain brave warriors to death and protect their favorite. Then there

are three grand maidens of the *Völuspá* who water the world tree, Yggdrasil, and are said to control the fate of men and gods alike. Occasionally we find poems in which the gods (like the divinities in the *Iliad*) favor a human being or doom him to commit dastardly deeds. The unfortunate man can only say, "I was fated fell things to do." When Óðin covets a warrior's services in Valholl, and causes him to fall in battle, this too is likely to be called his "fate." And finally, when a sorceress lays a curse upon a warrior, he may retort defiantly, "My fate does not lie on your tongue."

Fate in this magical or relatively "unheroic" literature is rarely envisaged as truly inexorable or final, for it lies in the hands of Beings who, like human relations or friends, may give welcome or unwelcome gifts, may be bribed or propitiated, or may be thwarted by the power of another Being. In like manner, fate in the magical literature is rarely seen as an amoral, impersonal force, generating moral dilemmas for unsuspecting human beings. Instead, it is referred to as if it were a kind of immanent justice. For example, when Kormák kills a witch's son she curses him so that he is "fated" never to possess his beloved. When King Fróði abuses his giant thralls, they grind out his terrible fate between the millstones. When Hamðir and Sorli kill their half-brother, they "doom" themselves to disaster. Men who swear an oath bring their fate on themselves. If they keep to the oath they will prosper. If they break the oath, the gods, before whom they swore, will destroy them.

In some of the early lays the idea of fate may be used in a somewhat different and less magical sense—as the ultimate explanation of an event which cannot be blamed on sorcery or attributed to the gods. Fate is described by the characters themselves as the force against which there is no remedy. A good example is the incident in which Helgi tells his beloved, Sigrún, that he has killed her brothers and asks her not to grieve because it "avails not to fight against fate." Again, when Helgi himself is slain, his grieving friends remark that his enemy was able to slay him because "the hour was evil."

It is possible that fate, defined as the ultimate explanation of misfortune, may fulfill a useful and necessary function in communities which otherwise see the world in magical fashion. When all magical or supernatural devices fail to alleviate suffering or avert calamity, the unfortunate event may be blamed on the mysterious power "against which it avails not to fight."

FATE IN THE WORLD OF MORAL DILEMMAS

The kind of fate pictured in the classic sagas and some of the heroic lays is an entirely different phenomenon. It is an impersonal, amoral force, pursuing its own fathomless ends, and lacking the attributes commonly associated with beings. Unlike the temperamental and fallible gods, it can be neither placated nor bribed; it does not punish the evil or the ignoble, nor does it reward the good, the noble, or the brave; it does not assist the pious nor afflict the impious; and from its decrees there is no escape. For the saga writer, this idea of fate becomes a marvelously effective device for the organization of material. Every event in a long and intricate story is put into its proper chronological place and portrayed as having contributed its bit to an ordained and inevitable end. It is here, perhaps, that we see the genesis of the Northern writers' emphasis on causality and linear progression. On the other hand, fate is simultaneously seen as a "personal" attribute of the individual human being, an attribute that develops with him as inevitably as a child within the womb. Each character, great or petty, has "his fate" which he is somehow going to act out as part of the great comprehensive, chronological pattern of the saga. In the parlance of psychoanalysis, one might say that in some of the lays and sagas man is seen as having internalized his fate.

The chief dramatic interest of the fate-oriented lays and sagas lies in the fact that their heroes or heroines never surrender or meekly submit to the power that determines their doom. They are, so to speak, the very opposite of the common conception of "fatalists." If their fate forces them into a situation where honor demands that they commit an excruciating and even inhuman deed, they do not flinch, but act and commit the deed. If they realize that their time has come, they proceed to die honorably and with steadfast courage. Even the most unsympathetic of readers cannot help but conclude that in these Old Scandinavian characters, the

notion of fate or determinism has met as close a match as it is ever likely to meet. For though fate may drive these heroes to commit dreadful deeds, it is never portrayed as having the power to turn them into dastards or cowards. Fate may force a man into a dishonorable or hopeless situation, but it cannot determine how he will feel or how he will act in this situation. His emotions and his deeds are his private responsibility.

COMMENT AND COMPARISON

This "heroic" literature shows us what no enchanted or magical literature hints at, namely, that a man may be blessed with all manner of excellent gifts and qualities and nevertheless commit a deed which law and custom define as evil. At the same time, however, it shows us that it was fate that put the individual into the position where he was obliged to commit the deed and that, moreover, the deed was demanded by the individual's personal sense of honor. Second, this literature shows us that men and women may suffer extreme misfortune and pain through no fault of their own and through no deficiency in their conduct toward the deities and Beings of Power. It is fate that determines what they are and what they must do. Third, the literature shows that in spite of the abysses into which the ruthless dictates of fate may plunge them, human beings may still behave honorably and keep to the code of excellence. Somewhat less explicitly, it demonstrates that doing right can be painful in and of itself and may yield no reward but the expectation that men will remember the deed. The literature also provides an exaltation of the man or woman who keeps to the ideal of excellence under the most demanding of circumstances—the individual who is put to the ultimate test and does not falter or fail.

Both the heroic tradition of the lays and sagas and the magical world view attempt to answer the question, How is it that the virtuous man, the man filled with Vital Power, has been brought low? The enchanted view offers a number of answers: he may have been bewitched; he may have offended a deity, or his time may have come. In any event, he has lost his Vital Power, and unless he can regain it, he is as good as dead. In the heroic tradition it is fate that brings the great man lower and he retains his manly power until his last breath. In the enchanted view, well-being and happiness are synonymous with virtue and Power. It is doing "good" that has brought happiness; it is doing "bad" that has brought suffering. The idea that being moral or virtuous is a painful process—that doing what is right may hurt not only the doer but his closest kin or the people he loves and admires—does not appear at all. As Lee says of the Trobrianders, "To be Trobriand [to follow the Trobriand pattern] is to be good." In marked contrast, a crucial implication of the fate-oriented lays and sagas is that great virtue and great suffering are inseparable.

If a concern with the meaning of existence is philosophical, the "ethic of manly excellence" is probably the Northman's closest approach to a philosophy. Consciously or unconsciously, the poets and some of the saga writers synthesized two mutually inconsistent ideas: the idea that everything was determined by an amoral, impersonal destiny, and the idea that the excellent man could not be *compelled* to do anything he did not wish to do. With this synthesis, they seem to have produced a kind of naive existentialism, a belief that nothing in life had lasting value except the deeds or actions which brought man fame or good repute:

> Cattle die and kinsmen die,
> thyself eke soon wilt die;
> but fair fame will fade never,
> I ween, for him who wins it.

In this chapter I have tried to show that the Old Scandinavian literature reflects a significant change in world view. At one extreme we have the enchanted view (as reflected in mythology and folk tales) where we are shown that the universe is a morally responsible realm, in which life, health, and well-being are inextricably related to virtuous or correct social behavior. At the other extreme we have the disenchanted view of the sceptical and reflective Icelandic saga writers, who painstakingly show us that there is no such moral relationship between man, his deeds, and his fate. Between these extremes, we have the heroic poems which exalt and idealize the men and women who conform to the demands of honor—as they see it—and do what they are fated to do, even if this means that they kill their own flesh and blood.

In so far as dates may be ascribed to these views, the magical view seems to be the oldest and the most persistent. The heroic view was already well developed in the poetry of the ninth century. The disenchanged view of men like Snorri Sturluson reached its peak in the thirteenth and early fourteenth centuries.

I do not suggest that the heroic literature caused the disenchantment it reflects, nor do I try to explain its genesis. My guess is that the idea of the heroic dilemma, inexorably brought about by fate, had its roots in the barbarian migrations of the fifth century and is connected with the rise of chieftains and kings who drew their followers from different lineages and communities. Warriors of this type would almost inevitably develop a moral code differing from that of the folk who stayed at home. The court poets of the "Germanic invasions" and the Viking Age were themselves likely to be warriors from families of rank. How much this relatively sophisticated ethic, which exalted the heroic virtues over and above the powers of magic and the gods, influenced the ordinary man of the Viking Age, I cannot say. If he was in any way a fighter it certainly had the power to move him, for we know that the Christian King, Saint Oláf, asked his skald to intone the Old Lay of Bjarki (which tells how an ancient heathen Danish king's warriors died for him) before the decisive battle of Stiklarstaðir (1030). On the other hand, the Old Scandinavian literature also suggests that there were at all times different levels of "sophistication" among different classes and in different regions. Warriors of the ninth century, listening to poets exalt the heroic ethic, might themselves be devotees of the warrior-sorcerer Óðin, or friends of Thór, just as, in the eleventh century, they were professing Christians. By the late tenth and early eleventh century there were individual warriors who did not put much trust in any Being of Power. By the twelfth century there were literate men who could compose a work like Kormák's saga, in which an enchanted and a disenchanted interpretation are set side by side. And by the thirteenth century, there had developed an elite class of men who were able to conceive of an entirely disenchanted and impersonalized universe. Meanwhile, the unlettered folk continued to see the world through the spectacles of the more or less enchanted little traditions, trimmed and frosted with selected aspects of Christianity.

Be all this as it may, I think it likely that the already well developed and prestigeful heroic tradition, which grappled so courageously with the fact that fate may doom a blameless and talented individual to a terrible end, provided an attractive ideological framework for the disillusioned, sceptical, and reflective saga writers. Living in an age during which the enchanted heathen tradition could no longer be taken seriously by a learned man, and the Christian tradition seemed to bring only increased confusion and disorder, they created works which demonstrate with a relentless consistency that the universe is an amoral and impersonal establishment and that there is no meaningful relationship between a man's virtues and his victories.

OTHER INTERPRETATIONS OF THE HEROIC ETHIC AND FATE

Phillpotts suggests that the Northmen's emphasis on lasting fame

is an assertion that there is something greater than Fate; the strength of will and the courage of human beings, and the memory which could preserve their deeds. Fame and human character: these were the two things against which Fate could not prevail.

Ker also sees the heroic ethic as an assertion of the power of man's "free will." Perhaps I am splitting hairs, but I feel that our contemporary notions of "free will" or "freedom of the individual" are more formal, self-conscious, and more defensive than the ethic of the Northmen. It is my impression that the Northmen took a free man's right to act without compulsion so much for granted that they did not need to assert it. When the heroes stand and fight their hopeless battles they are most clearly and obviously demonstrating that they are *men*, and that they cannot be moved, broken, or turned aside from the state of manliness by any force whatsoever.

Gehl states emphatically that the major Old Scandinavian (and Old Germanic) literature was not concerned with free will or with a tension between man and his fate. He asserts that fate is not seen as a mysterious, hostile power, alien and external to man, but as a "personal" phenomenon, the fate of a particular hero. Since fate is an essential part of a hero's being, from

his birth to his death, there cannot (for Gehl) be any conflict. The fact that the characters in the sagas often try to avoid or forestall the events which bring their fate upon them might be cited as evidence for conflict. But for this Gehl has an ingenious explanation. The heroes only try to avoid their fate before it is made clear to them. Once they perceive what they must do in order to maintain their honor, they are united with their fate and accept it courageously and joyfully. *Wollen und Müssen* (personal wish and inner obligation) become one, and it is this mystical union which explains the almost incredible courage, resolution—and even the laughter—with which the Northern hero meets his death.

While I find much of Gehl's analysis very perceptive and would agree that the authors of the Old Scandinavian literature often speak of fate as if it were "personal" (though the heroes themselves often speak of fate as if it were something pushed upon them from the outside), I do not feel comfortable with Gehl's psychological explanation of heroic courage. It seems to me that the Old Scandinavians and their poets and writers took it for granted that an excellent man or woman would die bravely and would, invariably, prefer death to dishonor. There was no other path open to them, for to die bravely was the final assertion of personal and familial worth, the ultimate act of honor.

Gehl further suggests that the Northern hero's belief in fate was fundamentally devout in character and speaks of his *Schicksalsfrommigkeit*. He further suggests that the great hero saw his personal fate as an integral part of the all encompassing fate of the cosmos. On this point I think Gehl may have been led astray by his intense interest in integration. For me the disposition to see the fate of the individual as meaningfully related to the fate of the cosmos is much more characteristic of the Old Scandinavian mythology and of the more homely episodes of the family sagas than of the heroic literature. Perhaps the most striking example of a pious or devout life-close, in which individual and "organic" fate are beautifully integrated, is the story of the death of Unn, a Christian lady, as described in the Laxdoela Saga. Unn, full of years, realizes that her time has come. She puts her house in order, arranges a wedding feast for her grandson, bids the guests enjoy themselves, and then walks "with a firm step" along the hall to her bed. The next morning she is found dead. In contrast, the hero Bjarki, dying on the battle-field, asserts that he will kill Óðin, the god of battle, because Óðin aided the enemy.

Gehl's depiction of the Old Germanic view of fate as pious and integrated also does not take into account that the essence of the fate-oriented literature is the presentation of a moral dilemma: if the individual man is to be the primary source of "right" or "law," he himself must stand ready to be both the executed and the executioner. Nor does it take into account

the poems which depict the god Thór quarreling with the god Óðin. Thór, who along with Frey was a favored god of hereditary land-owners and farmers, accuses Óðin, the god of warriors, skalds, and landless men, of oath-breaking and contempt for the bonds of kindred. Needless to say, respect for the bonds of kindred and the oath were the very backbone of the law and moral order of the little community. And, significantly, in the heroic literature, the most noble of the heroes and heroines are depicted as conforming to the demands of honor, even though this means breaking an oath or slaying their kin.

37. MUSICAL ADAPTATION AMONG AFRO-AMERICANS

JOHN F. SZWED

Reprinted from the Journal of American Folklore, *Vol. 82, No. 324, pp. 112-21, 1969. John F. Szwed is Director of the Center for Urban Ethnography at the University of Pennsylvania. His research experience has included field work among Anglo-French peasants in Newfoundland and Afro-Americans in Trinidad and North America. His publications include* Black America *(1970) and* Afro-American Anthropology: Contemporary Perspectives *(1970, co-edited with Norman E. Whitten, Jr.).*

■ Just as a mask or a carving of an ancestral figure cannot be understood only in aesthetic terms and outside the social uses for which it was originally intended, so music must be understood in terms of the specific contexts that give rise to it. We saw in the Introduction to this section that as people work, so do they sing, and we consider an example of this in the next selection. John Szwed's major point in this examination of the evolution of Afro-American music is that musical forms and styles reflect alternative adaptive strategies and that—mirroring the diversity of a complex society—different musical styles coexist in the same group or subgroups.

Szwed begins his discussion by pointing directly to the interplay between the African background of Negro music, American slavery, and the dominant white culture. As he notes at the outset of his paper, "Africanisms" have not exerted a single influence on American Negro music; instead, their intensity varies with time and different social and economic conditions. We see here the emergence and differentiation of secular music—the blues—from sacred music and the ways in

which these musical styles are opposed: blues rest on solo singing, which characterizes individualized work patterns and is directed by an individual performer to a collective group, whereas the sacred music out of which blues emerged symbolized and reinforced church participation and the cooperative work team. As Szwed shows, blues were among the instruments that eased the transition from an agricultural society to an urban way of life; in his words, "blues suggest that men are being presented as musical models in a shifting social order."

One of the best recent books in the anthropology of music and social relations is *The Urban Blues*, by Charles Keil (Chicago: University of Chicago Press, 1966), in which it is shown that urban blues are a unifying group ceremony. In addition to Alan Lomax's book cited by Szwed, the basic works introducing the reader to this aspect of anthropological research are *The Anthropology of Music*, by Alan P. Merriam (Evanston: North-western University Press, 1964); *Enemy Way Music*, by David McAllister (Cambridge, Mass.:

Harvard University Press, 1954) ; and *Theory and Method in Ethnomusicology*, by Bruno Nettl (New York : The Free Press, 1964). ■

THE EARLIEST AFRO-AMERICAN STUDIES were devoted to the music of African slaves. Nothing about the Negro seemed more fascinating than the mystery of the origins of his music. Was it an African product, reshaped to fit the New World? Or was it Anglo-American music, refashioned by African sensibilities? As basic questions these were appropriate, but instead of leading to deeper understanding the passion to illuminate origins resulted in explanations that frequently were short-sighted and territorially limited. Melville J. Herskovits was interested in origins, but he clearly warned that research suffered from a severe lack of knowledge about both African music and the secular music of the Negro. Part of the problem has been poor observation and selective neglect. If students of Afro-America had been more interested in the Negro in the United States, they would have noted that in some areas of expressive culture—notably music, dance, and oral narrative—"Africanisms" have varied in intensity over time, rising and falling with specific conditions. It is still heard, for example, that African musical influences persist most strongly in sacred contexts, a point belied even by a casual acquaintance with Negro popular music today.

The rest is simply a matter of inadequate conceptualization. Since anthropologists and folklorists have chosen to reject biological-instinctual explanations of musical behavior in favor of cultural explanations, they must offer statements in social-cultural terms that realistically explain long-persisting patterns of musical behavior. Once we move beyond questions of origin to problems of persistence and change, we need answers to questions such as the following. What is the relation between normative musical traditions and those that challenge them? How do individual learning experiences relate to the normative patterns? Is there some direction or drift in the change of musical models? Do the models rise and fall in popularity? What variability from normative models is permitted? In general these are questions that remain unanswered in our understanding of music.

Recently several significant contributions to the study of Afro-American music seem to point the way towards broader understanding. Alan Lomax's cantometric analysis, for example, has richly illuminated the cultural dimensions of music and raised the essential issue of the adaptational nature of song style. Norman Whitten's recent work on Colombian and Ecuadorian Negroes reveals suggestive directions for the study of social change through symbolic musical behavior. What is needed now is a conceptual framework in which changes and retentions of musical style and context can be understood within a synthesis of social and cultural change. Such a framework would not only take into account the social and cultural facts of a musical society, but it would also integrate a people's musical forms and their associated performance roles and styles. It is to this central point that this paper is directed: song forms and performances are themselves models of social behavior reflecting strategies of adaptation to human and natural environments. For Afro-America, then, the problem becomes one of defining the situations within which blacks have found themselves and of relating their musical conceptions to their experience.

The distinction between sacred and secular music—the most significant native musical categories of the Negroes of the United States—was possibly set by the middle 1800s, and certainly before 1900. Jeanette Murphy spoke of the opposition between church songs and "fiddle" songs in 1899. Although Calvinist notions contributed to the dichotomy, reformulated African religions were also important in defining the differences between sacred texts and the "devil's music." Alan Lomax has remarked on the widespread belief that skill on the fiddle required a pact with the devil, in a churchyard or at a crossroads. Later, a similar pact was required of the blues singer:

As part of his initiation into the vaudou cult, the Negro novice must learn to play the guitar. He goes to the cross-roads at midnight armed with a black cat bone, and as he sits in the dark playing the blues, the Devil approaches, cuts the player's nails to the quick, and swaps guitars. Thus the vaudouist sells his soul to the Devil and in return receives the gift of invisibility and the mastery of his instrument. These practices may explain why the religious often call an expert Negro folk musician "a child of the Devil" or "the Devil's son-in-law."

The significance of the sacred-secular distinction lies not only in perceived differences between the two categories as music, but also in their mutual exclusiveness in defining the social character of the individual performer. The literature of American Negro music abounds with this musical distinction and its implications as to the nature of the singer and the motivations that underlie the songs. For example, in an interview with the Rev. Robert Wilkins (a former blues singer), Peter Welding summarizes Wilkins' comments on the two musical forms:

Distinguishing between spirituals and blues, Rev. Wilkins remarked that he performs only the former currently because of his conviction that the "body is the temple of the spirit of God" and that only one spirit can dwell in that body at any time. Blues, he feels, are songs associated with the devil spirit, that the feeling blues expresses is not spiritual but sorrowful. It is true that blues help to relieve the "natural soul" of the singer but they fail to provide the sufferer any real spiritual solace; this can come only of praising the Lord and giving Him thanks for all things, good and bad alike. . . . The blues, he said, describe and relieve emotional troubles one might experience during life. The blues singer composes his songs primarily for himself but always is conscious of other potential listeners who might "be happy and enjoy it as I sing it."

It is common even today for religious leaders to exhort their followers "to give up blues singing and join the church." Zora Neale Hurston quotes a sermon in *Jonah's Gourd Vine*, "The blues we play in our homes is a club to beat up Jesus." Even the practicing bluesman may hold this view. Harriet J. Ottenheimer comments on New Orleans blues singer Babe Stovall: "He calls his talent a God-given gift and explains that because talent comes from God, it should be used for the playing of spirituals only, as a way of thanks for the gift. He styles himself as a sinner, however, and so plays other music, especially blues, besides spirituals. He plans to repent someday, and cease playing blues altogether, sinful music, in his opinion." And the mother of infamous Mississippi bluesman Robert Johnson claimed that on his deathbed her son hung up his guitar and renounced his blues life, thus dying in glory.

As these examples reveal, the sacred-secular dichotomy is not as clear as it might first appear to be. Secular function and text are not enough to place a form of music in opposition to church songs. The literature of Afro-American folksong shows that work songs and field hollers, for example, are not objected to by committed church members and religious leaders. Rather, it is the blues and bluesmen that represent the essence of the profane. The basic issue, as American blacks have seen it, is one of a sacred-blues dichotomy.

The importance of this dichotomy has not gone unnoticed. Roger Abrahams in his rhetorical analysis of urban Negro folklore, sees this as another example of the distinction between two types of "men-of-words" or "good-talkers" in the Negro community: the street corner bard and the preacher. Abrahams conceives of this as a contest for verbal power, the street talker addressing himself to the "homosexual, anti-feminine world of the early adolescent," the preacher directing his words "to women as well as men." However, in *Urban Blues*, Charles Keil devotes himself to an intensive discussion of the sociological similarities underlying the two performance roles, commenting on the fact that many blues singers have become preachers (though, as he suggests, the process is not reversible). Common role characteristics, apparently, are the reason why perceived differences in behavior become so necessary, for, as Keil notes, "Bluesman and preacher may be considered Negro prototypes of the no-good and good man respectively."

Abrahams and Keil point out a very real opposition in the nature of the roles of bluesman and preacher, but the same opposition exists in the structure, style, and function of their performance. The church songs and spirituals of the Negroes in the southern United States closely resemble West African song style, particularly in their strong call-and-response pattern. An 1867 description of this pattern still remains one of the most succinct:

There is no singing in parts, as we understand it, and yet no two appear to be singing the same thing— the leading singer starts the words of each verse, often improvising, and the others who "base" him, as it is called, strike in with the refrain, or even join in the solo, when the words are familiar.

When the "base" begins, the leader often stops, leaving the rest of his words to be guessed at, or it may be that they are taken up by one of the other singers. And the "basers" themselves seem to follow their own whims, beginning when they please and leaving off when they please, striking an octave above or below (in case they have pitched the tune too low or too high), or hitting some other note that chords, so as to produce the effect of a marvelous complication and variety, and yet with the most perfect time, and rarely with any discord . . . they seem not infrequently to strike sounds that cannot be precisely represented . . . slices from one note to another, and turns and cadences not in articulated notes.

This early description accurately notes the tightly woven interplay between members of the singing group, where a leader sets the pattern for the song but the group shapes its response independently. The nature of the group song-response was such that the song was participatory in nature; it invited the participation of all church members by leaving melodic and harmonic "holes" in the song that could be filled or left empty as the choice was made. At the same time, it was redundant enough to allow easy entrance into the message at any point. The church-song was a group phenomenon, hinged loosely on a leadership pattern, and in this sense the traditional spiritual (or, for that matter, the shout and other religious forms) perfectly paralleled the organizational structure of the American Negro church and the cooperative work team.

The blues, on the other hand, are almost unique among traditional American Negro folksong forms. First, they are sung solo, without the typical vocal call-and-response pattern so well known in other song forms. Of course, other songs than blues are sung solo—for example, the field holler and the lullaby—but these are forms that imply physical or social distance. In the case of the holler, the singers are separated from each other on the work field; the lullaby is addressed to an infant, itself not able to participate in song. Since the blues are solo, the form itself implies authority as much as does the classic Western European ballad; although the audience or the guitar may comment supportively, there is no song space for group participation. But because the blues are completely personalized (an example of what Abrahams calls the "intrusive 'I'"), there is an absence of the "objectivity" so widely commented upon in the ballad form. The blues are the least redundant of all American Negro forms. There is greater concern for textual message and meaning; they are information-oriented.

On the first look, of course, the blues appear wholly distinct from Western European song forms, and commentators have always pointed to the "blues scale" and the improvisatory character of the song as marks of its African character. This is deceptive. The blues performance is in many ways closer to white American folk music than to most other Afro-American song forms. When compared to Lomax's white American and African cantometric song profiles—particularly in the parameters of vocal group organization, wordiness of text, embellishment, melisma, and raspy voice—the blues fall between these two musical orientations. Lomax's analysis is also helpful in suggesting the kinds of "normative messages" carried by the blues. Being solo, rather than in the more familiar style of the interlocked leader-group song, they suggest a tendency towards authoritarian leadership patterns. The lesser use of nonsense words and redundancy present in the blues is another shift towards complexity typical of the music of complex societies. By the same token, solo singing characterizes individualized work patterns, as opposed to the more highly organized work groups of West Africa and American slavery. Since blues were usually sung by men (in the rural setting) as opposed to the mixed female-male singing of the churches, blues suggest that men are being presented as musical models in a shifting social order.

Blues, like religious behavior, are highly ritualized, apparently with the intention of easing or blocking "transformations of state in human beings or nature," rather than merely "entertaining." That is to say, ritual events attempt to restore social equilibrium, change organizational structures, or ease personal conditions of stress. Thus, singers speak of the blues as "relaxing the nerves," "giving relief," and "kinda helpin' somehow." Gospel singer Mahalia Jackson makes the point: "'But he (the Negro) created his songs to lift his burden . . . so those that did not believe in God, they created the blues in the same vein that almost they wrote their spirituals.'" The blues allows some things to be sung that could not otherwise be expressed. Henry Townsend of St. Louis says,

In other words there's several types of blues—there's blues that connects you with personal life—I mean you can tell it to the public as a song, in a song. But I mean, they don't take it seriously which you are tellin' the truth about. They don't always think seriously that it's exactly you that you talkin' about. At the same time it could be you, more or less it would be you for you to have the feelin'. You express yourself in a song like that. Now this particular thing reach others because they have experienced the same condition in life so naturally they feel what you are sayin' because it happened to them. It's a sort of thing that you kinda like to hold to yourself, yet you want somebody to know it. Now I've had the feelin' which I have disposed it in a song, but there's some things that have happened to me that I wouldn't dare tell, not to tell—but I would sing about them. Because people in general they takes the song as an explanation for themselves —they believe this song is expressing their feelings instead of the one that singin' it.

The blues singer is by no means a shaman, but he performs in many of the shaman's capacities. He presents difficult experiences for the group, and the effectiveness of his performance depends upon a mutual sharing of experience. Another former blues singer, now turned religious singer, L'il Son Jackson, makes the point this way:

You see it's two different things—the blues and church songs is two different things. If a man feel hurt within side and he sing a church song then he's askin' God for help. It's a horse of a different color, but I think if a man sing the blues it's more or less out of himself. . . . He's not askin' no one for help. . . . But he's expressin' how he feel. He's expressin' it to someone and that fact makes it a sin, you know, because it make another man sin . . . you're tryin' to get your feelin's over to the next person through the blues, and that's what makes it sin.

The essential difference between the two means of psychological release focuses on the "direction" of the song: church music is directed collectively to God; blues are directed individually to the collective. Both perform similar cathartic functions but within different frameworks. There is a potential in song for individual and group expiation, as the singers themselves testify. At the same time, there is a means by which the personal conditions of both singers and listeners may be socialized, even under large-scale pressures that threaten individual or group identity.

I have briefly described the structure of these opposed musical forms in order to arrive at my central point: that musical forms and their associated performance roles and styles reflect alternative adaptational strategies, and that styles and counter styles can and usually do coexist in a single society.

Blues arose as a popular music form in the early 1900s, the period of the first great Negro migrations north to the cities. The blues were a form of secularized ritual—a breakaway from sacred forms, the spiritual or the gospel song, but performing parallel functions. As such, the formal and stylistic elements of the blues seem to symbolize newly emerging social patterns during the crisis period of urbanization. Unlike the group-conservative orientation of the sacred songs, the blues were authoritarian and aggressive, offering a secular-personalized view of the world; they were a "tough-minded" solution to social problems. Lomax quotes an anonymous informant: "The blues is just *revenge*. Like you'll be mad at the boss and you can't say anything. You out behind the wagon and you pretend that a mule stepped on your foot and you say, 'Get offa my foot, god-dam sonafabitch!' You won't be talkin' to the mule, you'll be referin' to the white boss . . . That's the way with the blues: you sing those things in a song when you can't speak out." By replacing the functions served by sacred music, the blues eased a transition from a land-based agrarian society to one based on mobile, wage-labor urbanism. This is made all the more apparent by the characteristics of the blues singer's role. Unlike the stable, other-worldly, community-based image of the preacher (approved by Negro and white communities alike), the bluesman appears as a shadowy, sinful, aggressive, footloose wanderer, free to move between sexual partners and to pull up stakes as conditions call for it. Keil makes this point: "The bluesman is in a sense every man: the country bluesman is an archetype of the migrant laborer; the city bluesman, a stereotype of the stud, the hustler; the urban blues artist, something of an ideal man or prototype for his generation as well." The bluesman, for example, formalizes weak familial ties by making them appear culturally normative rather than just a problem for the individual. To paraphrase a gospel song, although I am inverting its meaning, he "lives the life he sings about in his song." Finally, as a stylistic mode, the blues mediate between the African and North American white musical sensibilities and thus provide an aesthetically satisfying musical statement of social reality, one most adaptive in aiding the transition from African slave to Afro-American.

These stylistic models are more than just descriptive manipulations. In the fullest sense, they have power in symbolizing and reinforcing social behavior. When Martin Luther King and the southern leaders of the Civil Rights Movement sought to collectivize group action, they returned to the older and more stable group orientation of the spiritual to coordinate activity. But when northern leaders of Black Power such as Stokely Carmichael operate, they surround themselves with jazzmen (the instrumental analogue of the blues singer) and singers of up-dated secular folksongs. In the last few years, however, there has been a conscious rejection of both spirituals and blues by urban Negroes. Spirituals and their traditional performance styles have almost disappeared, replaced by the more complicated, professionally oriented "gospel music," which Arna Bontemps calls a compound of "elements found in the old tabernacle songs, the Negro Spirituals and the blues." A strong rhythmic structure with hand-clapping, shouting, and aggressive interplay characterizes this new type of church song. Gospel music frequently is not performed by the church members themselves but by trained choirs. Since they think of themselves as professionals, they often perform outside the church at quite secular functions. E. Franklin Frazier saw this change in musical style as a change in Negro religious life-style: "The Gospel Singers . . . do not represent a complete break with the religious traditions of the Negro. They represent or symbolize the attempt of the Negro to utilize his religious heritage in order to come to terms with changes in his own institutions as well as the problems of the world of which he is a part."

Blues today—even of the electrified, city variety—are characterized by many urban Negroes as "dirty," "down-home," and "old-time." What has risen to replace both the blues and the spiritual is the broad category of music known as "soul," a popular, secular music, markedly similar to gospel music in everything but its verbal content. Soul music is so very close to gospel music that it often draws criticism from older followers of the sacred-secular distinction. Bluesman Big Bill Broonzy criticized

Ray Charles thus: "He's got the blues he's cryin' sanctified. He's mixin' the blues with the spirituals. I know that's wrong." Soul-singing—typified by such as Sam Cooke, Aretha Franklin, and Otis Redding (all of them former church singers)—is a polished, arranged blending of European bel canto and African call-and-response allowing for formalized group interplay with highly developed solo passages. Although it may be premature to see it as such, it appears that soul music draws from the older models of spirituals and the blues and, by unifying the sacred-secular dichotomy, has produced a stylistic mode adaptive to the urban Negro situation—a trend toward stability within self-contained ghetto subcultures based on mutual aid and individualism, best captured in the concept of "Black Power."

Soul music embodies a revival of "Africanisms," really older Afro-American style features, particularly in its rhythmic characteristics and call-and-response features. This borrowing of older musical patterns has been possible because some members of the community have continued to operate with former musical-social models. Although the older patterns have not been popular in the mass media, they have remained operative in some influential and slow-changing social institutions of the Negro community: the store-front church and the neighborhood bar, as well as grandmother's rocking chair and children's schoolyard games. Previous musical forms have been retained by older members of the community, who act as repositories of past traditions and of outdated adaptational features. In short, though at any given time in a society there are a normative performance style and performance role, there are also counter styles and roles, surviving from the past and available for reworking into new styles.

It remains to be seen whether the same model of musical adaptation will hold for other parts of Afro-America. At first glance, it would appear that areas of slavery lacking a strong Protestant reinforcement would not conform to the sacred-secular musical dichotomy found in the United States. Tentatively, however, it appears to have application at least in the West Indies, Colombia, and Ecuador, areas under varying degrees of Catholic and Protestant influence. In Trinidad, calypso—a form often compared with the blues—holds a parallel position in relation to the songs of the cults and organized churches. Like the blues, calypso developed after slavery, during the period of urbanization on the island, and seems to have a similar behavioral and stylistic base. Calypso is sung solo, is minimally redundant, and is highly personalized. Certainly calypso is authoritarian in performance pattern and text, and the combative nature of calypsonians during (and out of) performance is widely noted. It is also clear that the exponents of calypso are drawn from the most independent, "rootless," and aggressive strata of Trinidad society.

Unlike the blues, calypso continues to dominate the urban musical landscape long after its nineteenth-century origins, functioning with immense popular support. The difference seems to lie in the fact that the middle class, regardless of color, has chosen to adopt calypso as a musical-social model for emerging Trinidadian-Tobagonian nationalism, making it the focus of its most important public ritual, the Carnival, and one of its most successful aesthetic exports. To be sure, calypso song is a veritable statement of national character for Trinidadian residents and for those of the other islands in the West Indies as well, where Trinidad is identified as the epitome of urbanization and aggressive independence.

In Colombia and Ecuador there is again a dichotomous conception of music, but Norman Whitten's analysis suggests that Euro-American, sacred-secular distinctions are absent or irrelevant. Instead, musical forms and roles are pure statements of alternative behavioral strategies. Here, the marimba dance (*currulao*) and the saloon dance (popular "national" music) are in contrast. In the marimba song male and female singers and musicians are divided both in terms of repertory and performance. A call-and-response style expresses the views about household and sexual realignment of the two sexes, and in so doing provides stability to existing structures. In saloon dances, on the other hand,

bands or phonographs provide the musical setting for token exchanges of drinks and dancing partners between males, leading to solidification of cooperative men's groups during times of economic gain and to new sexual partnerships. In both musical events dancers symbolically express contrasting notions of sexual alignment. In urbanized areas these musical oppositions are more intense, and they are staged on the same nights so that a choice of attending one or the other must be made. In fact, individuals attend one and then the other on different occasions. Yet, in doing so, they deny their participation in the other events, and even their existence.

Whitten's observation that individuals do participate in different musical events, even though they see them as mutually exclusive, leads us to believe that our understanding of Afro-American musical categories may be incomplete and even superficial. Further inquiry may reveal that alternative musical forms not only exist simultaneously but may be more available to individual option than we have so far been led to believe. This may indeed be part of what Lerone Bennett, Jr., means when he warns against Euro-American interpretations of the Negro tradition: "The essence of the tradition is the extraordinary tension between the poles of pain and joy, agony and ecstasy, good and bad, Sunday and Saturday. One can, for convenience, separate the tradition into Saturdays (blues) and Sundays (spirituals). But it is necessary to remember that the blues and the spirituals are not two different things. They are two sides of the same coin, two banks, as it were, defining the same stream." But whether or not a dichotomous model of musical social reality is fully applicable to Afro-America, a unified musical form and performance role analysis appears necessary. An awareness of styles and counter styles in all aspects of expressive culture should offer us a richer and more realistic picture of the New World Negro experience.

INDEX